I0159935

Presumably Ladies

A COLLECTION OF 19TH-CENTURY WOMEN'S ETIQUETTE LITERATURE

Presumably Ladies

A COLLECTION OF 19TH-CENTURY WOMEN'S ETIQUETTE LITERATURE

Edited with an Introduction
by Monica Nowik

WHITLOCK PUBLISHING
Alfred, NY

Original publication dates:

How to Get Married, Although a Woman; Or, The Art of Pleasing Men by Irene Hartt, 1892

The Ladies' Book of Etiquette and Manual of Politeness by Florence Hartley, 1860

True Politeness, a Hand-book of Etiquette for Ladies by an American Lady, 1847

The Ladies' Guide to True Politeness and Perfect Manners; or Miss Leslie's Behaviour Book by Eliza Leslie, 1834

The Ladies' Vase; or Polite Manual for Young Ladies by an American Lady, 1843

First Whitlock Publishing edition 2023
Whitlock Publishing
Alfred, New York

Editorial matter @ Monica Nowik

ISBN: 978-1-943115-52-5

Cover art courtesy of Wikimedia Commons
Image: *Godey's Ladies Book 1855; Godey's unrivalled colored fashions*

Table of Contents

Introduction

SELF-HELP BOOKS, YOUTUBE CHANNELS GUARANTEED to enhance your productivity, and magazines in the checkout line touting "10 Ways You (Yes, YOU!) Can Be Better Today!"—come one, come all to the altar of self-improvement. Sound familiar? Try logging onto any website without at least two or three pop-up ads that claim *you are not good enough,* and have fun finding a highway devoid of billboards that advertise ways to make you…well, not you anymore. You're lacking in everything except mediocrity, but don't worry—you're fixable. You're improvable.

This collection of 19th-century American etiquette books might remind the reader of modern-day counterparts; some pieces of advice, written well over a century ago, are peddled around today almost word for word. We view etiquette literature, perhaps, as antiquated and irrelevant, but self-improvement and class markers remain at the forefront of Western society. To understand how we came to run on behavior currency, we must dive into the past. Although the medium has evolved into a global industry worth billions of dollars and distribution has expanded to instantly available online content, self-improvement guides have been inherent to cultures around the world for millennia.

History of Etiquette

Around 2375–2350 BC in Egypt, the Vizier Ptahhotep wrote the literary and instructional text *The Maxims of Ptahhotep* to his son. The composition contained wisdom the Vizier felt he had gained in his old age like humility, good table manners, and self-control. Egyptian customs passed down through word of mouth most likely inspired the Vizier's writings, but unlike the text of *Ptahhotep,* many other texts have been lost to time. Later in history, Ancient Greek philosophers like Epicurus, Plato, Aristotle, and the Stoics would contribute significantly to the well of self-improvement philosophy, which scholars and students still study today when discussing light topics such as "What is the meaning of life?"

Religious texts shaped the ethical and moral backbone of countries worldwide, building a strong foundation for civilization. The Jewish Tanakh contains mitzvah, or commandments, from God, which depict the Hebrew people's relationship with the Abrahamic God as well as instructions for daily life. The Christian Bible expands on these commandments, adding the teachings of Jesus of Nazareth in the New Testament. Both taught about nonphysical improvements of the soul, but they also spoke about how to treat your neighbor, what to eat and what not to eat, appropriate conduct surrounding money, and more—these are expectations and behaviors rooted in concrete, everyday life. They provided (and continue to provide) structure to many different cultures. Similarly, Chinese Confucianism, founded by Confucius sometime around 500 BC, built a code of ethics and behavior revolving around social structures and domestic hierarchies.

The Book of the Civilized Man marks a turning point as the first English conduct book. Daniel of Beccles wrote the poem in Latin verse most likely towards the end of the 12th or beginning of the 13th century. The poem tells readers how to conduct themselves in society. The advice, "…while food is hidden in your mouth, let your tongue not minister to words," belongs more staunchly in the "manners" category than the "morals" one, although the book begins by reminding the reader of their duty to God and the Church. Some parts of the text promote patriarchal ideology, such as the tidbit: "When there is something you do not want people to know, do not let your wife know it."

As the Western world changed and behavior became an indicator of class, Baldassare Castiglione wrote *The Book of the Courtier*, beginning in 1508 and finishing in 1528, to give advice on how to navigate the social world of the Italian royal court. In 1761 England, John Gregory wrote *A Father's Legacy to His Daughters,* which supposedly he based on the opinions of his late wife about education, marriage, and behavior. Gregory's son James published the book in 1774, following his father's death, though Gregory had probably never meant for *A Father's Legacy* to go further than his own family. The book instantly resonated with English and American readers, going through several editions within the first thirty years; readers praised the book for the caring, fatherly figure that generously endowed not only his daughters but new generations of readers with what was thought to be sound instruction. Also in 1774, *Lord Chesterfield's Letters to His Son* by Philip Dormer Stanhope, 4th Earl of Chesterfield was published, a collection of letters containing lessons of both academic and social nature. Chesterfield was one of the first English writers to use the term "etiquette," from the French *"une petite ethique,"* or, as he called it, "a little ethics"—an extension of morality and ethics that carried less moral weight and was distinct from virtue.

As their popularity grew, these step-by-step instruction manuals for how to eat, sleep, talk and even think reached audiences of all genders, but men continued to dominate the industry, even when advice veered into women's behavior. *The Lady's Pocket Library* (1792), a compendium published by Mathew Carey, included some works by women, such as *Lady Pennington's Unfortunate Mother's Advice to Her Daughters* and *Mrs. Chapone's Letter on the Government of the Temper*. However, it also contained Gregory's *A Father's Legacy* as well as Jonathan Swift's *Letter to A Very Young Lady on Her Marriage*, both of which propagate little respect for the female voice.

Women On Etiquette

Etiquette serves as both a social and a power structure that defines clear lines between standard and unacceptable behavior. In a patriarchal society, women must fulfill their traditionally established roles as women or face exclusion. Rules for how a woman *should* act set boundaries for how she should *not* act. Mary Wollstonecraft—18th-century British philosopher, writer, and women's rights advocate—criticized male writings on female behavior (especially Gregory's *A Father's Legacy*). In her book *A Vindication of the Rights of Woman: with Strictures on Political and Moral Subjects* (1792), she claims that male-authored etiquette books treat women "…as a kind of subordinate beings, and not as a part of the human species…" This kind of "othering" dictated appropriate conduct for women and further controlled the female narrative.

While Wollstonecraft may have been one of the few women voicing her frustrations, many others supported the demand for female-centric literature. A major catalyst for change came in the form of the American magazine *Godey's Lady's Book* in 1830. Although headed by Louis A. Godey, editor Sarah Hale greatly influenced what went into the magazine. She promoted works written by women and increased the subscriber count by over 100%, staying on as editor until 1877 when John Hill Seyes Haulenbeek bought the magazine and changed the title to "Godey's Magazine." Works included in the magazine under Hale contained recipes, fashion advice, literature, and sheet music, much of it marketed towards women. *Godey's* provided a safe haven for women to submit their own thoughts and feel heard.

19th-century etiquette literature intertwined virtue and (Christian) morality with manners and conduct but took care to specify the difference. In Eliza Farrar's *The Young Ladies' Friend* (1836), the author notes this divide: "…those lesser graces of character and manners…which, though of little value unless they spring from that love to God and man, which is the root of Christian virtue, are not always growing by its side." Farrar seems like she's treading on eggshells here, not devaluing the Christian beliefs that many of her readers and critics would have held but maintaining that her book is not a Sunday school lesson. A review of *The Young Ladies' Friend*, published in the 1838 Volume 16 issue of *Godey's*, praised Farrar's work for bringing attention to the specific needs of young women in a world that rarely does so: "The destiny of women! How much it embraces—how little it is studied and understood!"

When women claimed their right to author their own etiquette, they gave female readers a more nuanced version of what a woman could be. Women authors set expectations for their gender that went beyond appearances and serving men. In *How to Get Married, Although a Woman, or, The Art of Pleasing Men* (included in this collection), Irene Hartt writes to young women, "It is well to have a good opinion of yourself: it will give you an ease in society and a confidence to go ahead and win." At least in this respect, Hartt completely differs from Gregory, who gives opposing advice to his daughters: "I should be glad that you had an easy dignity in your behaviour at public places, but not that confident ease, that unabashed countenance, which seems to set the company at defiance."

Themes of Etiquette Literature

Two of the works published in this anthology have anonymous authors: *True Politeness, a Hand-book of Etiquette for Ladies* and *The Ladies' Vase; or Polite Manual for Young Ladies* both credit "An American Lady" as their respective authors. Since many people in the 19th century believed that writing was far too public a career for women, anonymous authorship became a popular choice for women who wanted to write but didn't feel comfortable publicizing it. "A Young Widow" originally appeared as the author of *How to Get Married, Although a Woman; Or, The Art of Pleasing Men,* but research since has shown the author to be Irene Hartt, writing under a pen name. Eliza Leslie of *The Ladies' Guide to True Politeness and Perfect Manners; or Miss Leslie's Behaviour Book* and Florence Hartley of *The Ladies' Book of Etiquette and Manual of Politeness* have more extensive biographies, as both wrote many other books. All of these women appear to have well-rounded educations and be of similar middleclass or upper-middleclass backgrounds.

Behavior towards men takes up a good portion of each book in this collection. *How to Get Married* obviously deals primarily with the subject of marriage; Hartt believes that more often than not (with some exceptions), unmarried women are unhappy, and that this sorry state of being is entirely one's own fault. She recommends that women use their "arts" to secure a man, and that the successful practice of these arts will lead to marriage. The anonymous author of *The Ladies' Vase,* though, disagrees with Hartt on how to go about getting a husband: "Never condescend to use any little arts or manœuvres to secure a pleasant beau at a party, or during an excursion…"

Some of the works included in this volume, like *The Ladies' Book of Etiquette*, contain fashion and beauty tips; within, you can find (questionable) recipes for anti-freckle lotions, tooth powders, and one "very excellent lip-salve." In regard to hygiene, *True Politeness* reminds young ladies to keep their "finger-nails scrupulously clean, and avoid the disagreeable habit of allowing them to grow to an unnatural length." *Miss Leslie's Behavior Book* devotes a section to table manners, many of which resemble contemporary ones; Miss Leslie advises against talking of "sicknesses, sores, surgical operations, dreadful accidents, shocking cruelties, or horrible punishments" while eating dinner (sound advice!), and more succinctly, "Abstain from picking your teeth at table."

Christianity regularly makes an appearance in four of the books here with *Miss Leslie's Behavior Book* and *The Ladies' Vase* dedicating entire chapters to the subject. Irene Hartt thinks women should strive to be "Christian wives," while Florence Hartley opens *The Ladies' Book of Etiquette* with the golden rule of the New Testament, "Do unto others as you would others should do to you." To Hartley, the fine print of etiquette doesn't matter as much as Christian virtue, which grants an inherent politeness to the beholder: "...though you may err in the ceremonious points of etiquette, you will never be impolite." *True Politeness* makes no mention of Christianity, being a book that concerns itself more with manners than religion.

The books published here also attempt to separate from British etiquette literature and establish themselves as distinctly American. Hartley prepares her readers to encounter American stereotypes: "The universal remark of travelers visiting America, as well as the universal complaint of Americans themselves, relates to the ill health of the fairer portion of the community." To combat this assumption, she offers "a few words" on maintaining health. Miss Leslie assumes the universality of her views on American superiority, often contrasting the behavior of rude Europeans to polite Americans or simply naming faults that Americans just don't possess: "To laugh deridingly, or to whisper unfavourable remarks during the performance of a concert or a play, is a rudeness of which few American ladies are guilty."

Oppression or Empowerment?

Although the increase in women authors allowed female voices into the mainstream of etiquette literature and provided another way for women to make their own money, the vast majority of advice found in this collection is also deeply problematic by contemporary standards. The contents of these books enforce complete deference to men; they push stereotypes of feminine weakness and sensitivity to an extreme. They may encourage women to be smart and well-educated but oppose them showing it. "Be not obtrusively positive in the assertion of your opinions—modesty of speech, as well as manner, is highly ornamental in a woman," we read in *The Ladies' Vase,* and "A man likes a smart girl. Your smartness or your brilliancy must, however, be kept in the background" in *How to Get Married.*

This complicated and multi-faceted issue of internalized misogyny allows women to not only put on blinders against their own oppression, but actively encourage oppression (not perceived to be oppression) for other women. Many of the works published here explicitly reject the idea of "women's rights," which is expressed in this passage from *The Ladies' Vase*: "Instead of seeking hopelessly, and in direct opposition to the delicacy of her sex, to obtain for her political privileges; instead of bringing her forward as the competitor of man in the public arena; we would mark out for her a sphere of duty that is widely different." Modern political figures like Phyllis Schlafly in the 1970's believed the Equal Rights Amendment would make traditional gender roles socially obsolete and take away "women's privileges"; Schlafly herself was a working woman who utilized her right to free speech. Over a century earlier than Schlafly, Miss Leslie showed her disregard for the same issue: "…none make poorer livings than those who waste their time, and bore their friends, by writing and lecturing upon the equality of the sexes, and what they call 'Women's Rights.'"

As women broke into the etiquette literature scene, they represented other women as well as themselves; etiquette imposed the values of the authors (and of their specific socioeconomic class) on *all* women. Women who didn't conform to the standard became the "other"; they experienced a kind of female-on-female oppression for refusing to or not being able to conform to the norm. Even though all women endured gendered discrimination in solidarity, class intersected with gender to further separate women. "There can be no conversation that is mutually agreeable, between a real lady of true delicacy and refinement, and a so-called lady whose behaviour and talk are coarse and vulgar," says Miss Leslie. A "lady" fits into the societal mold and a "so-called lady" does not; a "lady" sees no value in engaging with women below her own class. Women could and still can be guilty of enforcing their own and other women's oppression, whether through perpetuating classism and racism or overlooking their own patriarchal ideology.

In the article "The Feminization of Etiquette Literature: Foucault, Mechanisms of Social Change, and the Paradoxes of Empowerment," Jorge Arditi addresses the "one step forward, two steps back" conundrum of female empowerment and internalized misogyny:

The paradox also forces us to contextualize and problematize the very concepts of empowerment and disempowerment. As is the case with the private/public dichotomy, the effects of the feminization of the etiquette literature suggest a more complex process than the one captured by a clear distinction between empowerment and disempowerment. For despite its conservative, disempowering side, the anchoring of a concept of behavior in a discursive space that 19th-century women claimed as their own helped create the conditions for women's empowerment in general….In this sense, the discursive transformation helped change the very condition of womanhood among middle-class American women from one that was primarily the product of forces outside their control into one that, *in part because of women like Hale and Farrar,* would increasingly become the product of forces powered by women themselves.

If we share Arditi's point of view, we might say that women writers of etiquette took a step in the right direction. Despite the issues we find in 19th-century women's conduct literature and the contradictions posed therein, women's etiquette played a role far different from that of male-authored etiquette. Female authors opened up a space, small but present, for women to speak plainly and express their own views. Though we may strongly disagree with *what* those writers said, the fact that they could say it *at all* gives other opinions an opportunity to be heard as well. On the other hand, if one group drowns out the voices of everyone else and fails to recognize its privilege, that space loses its potential for inclusion.

* * *

Connecting the works in this collection back to modern conversations allows us to explore ideas like class and power in more depth. Etiquette still exists as an underlying influence in Western cultures even if hiding beneath the labels of self-help and self-improvement. Stephen Covey's highly influential book *The 7 Habits of Highly Effective People* (1989) asserts the "interdependence" approach to life which not only allows the individual to effectively meet their personal goals, but to become a better member of society—exactly what the books collected here attempted to do a century earlier. Household names like Martha Stewart and Oprah Winfrey came into prominence towards the end of the 20th century and remain symbols today for female independence and entrepreneurship, offering their (largely female) audiences new ways of organizing their homes or careers. YouTube and Instagram influencers constantly generate content that lets consumers know what they should eat, read or watch, who to follow, vote for, or cancel, and so on. We revise the specific rules for behavior, but society's insistence on having rules never changes.

By examining the authorship of etiquette, invisible power structures become clearer. Who gets to speak? Who's writing the behavior canon? And who gets no voice—who is being repressed? If we can determine the dominant voice and patterns in a society at any given time, we can understand not only cultures past and present, but whatever new culture arises out of our current behavior trends.

MONICA NOWIK, APRIL 2023
ALFRED, NY

Etiquette Timeline

2375–2350 BC	Egypt. The Vizier Ptahhotep, *The Maxims of Ptahhotep.*
551–479 BC	China. Writings of Confucius.
12th/13th cent.	England. Daniel of Beccles, *Book of the Civilized Man.*
13th cent.	Syria. Gregory Bar, *Hebraeus Kethabha dhe-Ithiqon*, "Book of Ethics", and *Kethabha dhe-Yauna*, "Book of the Dove."
1290	Italy. Bonvesin della Riva, *Concerning Fifty Gentilities for the Table.*
1528	Italy. Baldassare Castiglione, *The Book of the Courtier.*
1687	England. John Shirley, *The Accomplished Ladies Rich Closet of Rarities, aka, The Ingenious Gentle Woman and Servant Maids' Delightful Companion.*
1774	England. Philip Stanhope 4th Earl of Chesterfield, *Lord Chesterfield's Letters to His Son.*
	England. John Gregory *A Father's Legacy to His Daughters.*

AMERICA

1792	Mathew Carey, *The Lady's Pocket Library.*
1830	*Godey's Lady's Book* magazine first published.
1834	Eliza Leslie, *The Ladies' Guide to True Politeness and Perfect Manners; or Miss Leslie's Behaviour Book.*

Bibliography

Arditi, Jorge. "The Feminization of Etiquette Literature: Foucault, Mechanisms of Social Change, and the Paradoxes of Empowerment." *Sociological Perspectives*, Vol. 39, No. 3, 1996, pp. 417-434.

Beccles, Daniel. *Book of the Civilised Man.* Translated by James Hannam et al, 2009.

Carey, Mathew. *The Lady's Pocket Library.* 1792. Ulan Press, 2012.

Castiglione, Baldassare. *The Book of the Courtier.* Translated by Leonard Eckstein Opdycke, Charles Scribner's Sons, 1902.

Covey, Stephen. *The 7 Habits of Highly Effective People.* Free Press, 1989.

"The Earliest Books Written of Etiquette and Table Manners." *Etiquipedia, Etiquette Encyclopedia*, 13th March, 2014. https://etiquipedia.blog spot.com/2014/03/the-earliest-books-written-of-etiquette.html.

Farrar, Eliza. *The Young Ladies' Friend.* Boston, American Stationers' Company, 1836.

Gregory, John. *A Father's Legacy to His Daughters.* Boston, James B. Dow, 1834.

Godey's Lady's Book. Accessible Archives, 2023. https://www.accessible-archives. com/collections/godeys-ladys-book/.

"Review of the Young Ladies' Friend." *Godey's Lady's Book,* Vol. 16, 1838, pp. 167-169.

Stanhope, Philip. *Lord Chesterfield's Letters to His Son.* 1774. Oxford World Classics, 1998.

Wollstonecraft, Mary. *A Vindication of the Rights of Woman: with Strictures on Political and Moral Subjects.* J. Johnson, 1792.

Note on the Text

The texts in this anthology contain the archaic spellings as first published, such as "visiter," and the original punctuation. The authors' footnotes have been included. Original editorial typos have been corrected. Racial slurs have been censored.

The text of *How to Get Married, Although a Woman; Or, The Art of Pleasing Men* in this anthology includes only the content by Irene Hartt and not the poetry and ads published in the original edition.

The 1864 edition of *The Ladies' Guide to True Politeness and Perfect Manners; or Miss Leslie's Behaviour Book* by Eliza Leslie has been included here.

Acknowledgements

Thank you to Dr. Allen Grove for his guidance throughout the many classes I've taken with him and for his continued interest in my learning. Thank you to my advisors, Dr. Susan Mayberry, Dr. Melissa Ryan, Dr. Nick Schlegel, and Dr. Emrys Westacott for believing in me and giving me the confidence to keep working towards my goals. Thank you to English Division faculty Dr. Juliana Gray, Dr. Susan Morehouse, Dr. Rob Reginio, and the numerous faculty members at Alfred University who have been a part of my journey.

I would like to thank my parents, John and Martha Nowik, for always encouraging me, providing me with the means to keep reading and writing, and supporting my ongoing education. Thank you to my siblings for their help in developing my critical thinking and argumentative skills.

Endless gratitude to my friends Ashton Julian and Sabre Sumner for their unending support, patience, and ideas.

HOW TO GET MARRIED, ALTHOUGH A WOMAN;

OR,

THE ART OF PLEASING MEN

BY A YOUNG WIDOW

CHAPTER I.
GIRLS AND MATRIMONY.

IT IS NATURAL FOR GIRLS TO wish to marry. The desire to do so is not to be condemned, but rather applauded, for it is Heaven-born. The Creator implanted it in the human heart, man and woman alike. God made man for woman and woman for man. He did not intend that they should live apart from each other. When He said, "It is not good for man to be alone," He included woman in the man. It is not good for woman to live alone. He put a longing in the heart of man and woman alike which is only satisfied by the love of the other. He made a void in the heart which can only be filled by the companionship and love of one of the opposite sex. Man and woman are alike in this. It is as natural to her as to him: she can no more help it than he can. The unnatural part is that a woman must keep still about it, and if no one comes to woo, try to stifle the longing.

There are plenty who hold up their hands in holy horror when it is said that a certain girl wishes to marry. It is nothing at all out of the way when Mr. Jones says he has determined to marry. If his sister Mollie gave voice to such a sentiment, it would be shocking, however. It would be shocking for her to give expression to the longing the all-wise Father has implanted in her heart. It is a heart, too, that will never be satisfied with yearning only, with fame, with any vocation, with dumb animals, with other people's children; and it is a wise thing it will not. It is not a wise thing, however, that Mollie will be condemned because she cannot be satisfied without having a fireside and home of her own, because she wants a big loving fellow to care for her and to protect her, and whom she can love and make happy, because she wants her own home, no matter how small it is, to adorn and make pretty, her own housekeeping to look after, her own and his children to care for; because she wants her own wifehood, just as her brother wants a wife and home of his own and will not be satisfied to be a bachelor.

Let him make up his mind to marry. The world will approve of his decision. Let Mollie do the same thing. I want to see girls marry. I am always glad when I hear that one is engaged to do so. To help some to do so, I write these few chapters. There are too many old maids. There are more than there need to be.

I feel particularly sorry for the girl who has passed the line of youth and who has no admirers. Her brothers are all married, and most of her girlhood friends are absorbed in a husband and a baby. She has none, when doubtless she has it within her to make a good wife and mother. She is often restless, unsatisfied, disappointed. If she is at all weak-minded, she becomes sour as she grows older. She grows envious of all happily married women, and has a secret grudge toward men because she feels that she has been slighted by the sex generally. Many a girl who would make a good wife is soured by her failure to become one, and turns out an unpleasant member of society. All old maids are not by any means like this, however. There are many unmarried women in the world that will take up cheerfully any fate, turning their disappointment into a blessing for others.

But I fear that, after all, they go through life with a heart unsatisfied. Alone, when they look into the secret chambers of that uncomplaining heart, they see there the old longings for love.

There are unmarried women who do a great deal of good in the world. They accept their solitary lot as the will of the Heavenly Father. But is it His will? Does He give the heart longings which He will not satisfy? No. A thousand times, No. That would be tantalizing us. Too often we make mistakes in life, and then declare the consequences to be His will. It is so in failing to marry. Girls make mistakes in their conduct and remain spinsters. The fault is their own. They do not know how to attract, and so are passed by.

Plenty of girls do so well understand the art of attracting men, that they have numberless offers of marriage. I know women who could not count up on their ten fingers the men who have been in love with them: among them men who for their sakes have remained unmarried through life. I have had personal acquaintance with women who have been married three times, and could, some of them, be married again. I know other women who have never had one admirer.

I know girls who can attract men to them, and almost as soon as they are attracted, repel them. That sort of a girl never marries. She wants to do so, and acts through ignorance. I have sometimes felt like giving a girl a good shaking when I have seen her spoil her own chances. I have been dying to whisper a word of advice at times, but was too wise to do so, knowing it would not be well received. Girls know so fearfully much! The experiences of a mature woman count for nothing beside the wonderful knowledge some girls in their teens have! In the hope that some of these maidens will be willing to read what they would not hear, when it was too personal, I determined to write down what I know about being attractive to the other sex, what I know about girls' failures, and why they fail.

Not long ago there appeared in "The Woman's Department" of one of our daily papers a letter from a young girl, in which she confessed that she loved a young man who did not return her affection. She asked what she should do to win him. The editor could not tell her, advising her to give him up, very much as if it were a pleasure excursion the poor girl was writing about. There are times when it is necessary to give up all hope of winning a man. This, however, did not appear to have been one of them. The girl should have been told just how she could attract, then win him. Perhaps the editor did not herself know.

If a girl is thrown much in the society of a young man whose affections are not previously engaged, and if she knows how to do it, she is quite sure to make him love her. If, however, he cares for some one else, who cares for him, no true woman will in any way try to come between the two: she will rather avoid doing so. If the girl has become interested before she knows of his engagement, it is a case of misplaced affections. There I must advise giving him up. Get interested in another man, and win that one. It might be well always for a girl to find out first whether or not a man is interested in some one else. That would often save a world of trouble. A misplaced affection, when foolishly adhered to, will stand in the way of a happy marriage. It is not always the man you love. Not unfrequently it is your ideal which you make a certain man fill. Often, if you are not blinded, you will see that instead of filling it, he "wobbles" around in the large space you have given him. That ideal can easily be transferred to another man. Very few hearts are so true that they love but once. They may do so in stories, but in real life we change. We rarely marry our first love, and almost always forget all about him.

After marriage it is a different thing. Then it is no ideal: it is real. The man you love is real. The love is real, and continues even after "death do you part."

So, let no misplaced affection stand between you and marriage. Return a love if it is offered you and the man is desirable, or set yourself to win one. Do not go about sighing for a man who belongs to another girl. He never gives you a thought—they are hers. Have too much self-respect, and too high an opinion of your charms to think about him. In a few years, impossible as it may seem now, when you meet him middle-aged and a family man, you will wonder what you ever saw in him to care about. This sounds heartless, but it is true. It goes to prove that in early life before marriage it is the ideal and not the man a girl often loves. If I am mistaken in that, I am not mistaken in saying that a girl is happier married to a man for whom she cares less than she did for this ideal, than in remaining a spinster because some other girl bore off the heart she craved. To my mind a woman is happier married under almost any circumstances than single. That I know is against the teachings of to-day, and does not savor the least of woman's rights. I believe her "rights" is to be married.

Sometimes a girl who is attractive enough to win any man is kept from marriage by the selfish attentions of one man who either cannot or will not say anything to her about marrying him. This is not an unfrequent occurrence. A man who, on account of his circumstances, cannot marry, or who, because he prefers his freedom, will not marry, will pay attention to a girl for years. He wins her affections, and keeps away others who would be glad to marry her. Meantime she hopes that every day she will hear the words he has given her a right to expect to hear. In the end, if she allows this thing to continue, she will be an old maid.

No matter how much you care for a man, give him up if, after a certain length of time, he says nothing to you about marriage. You will lose nothing in the end by doing so, and may gain him. If he really cares for you, the danger of losing you will make him more anxious to possess you. Then, if ever, he will find means to ask you to marry him. If he does not then, he never would. If giving him up hurts you, heal the wound by remembering that his intentions could not have been serious, and that he has allowed himself to lose you. Remember, too, that the hurt will come some time, anyway, and most likely when you are beyond the age to attract any one else. So giving him up while you are yet young means a marriage with some other man. Clinging weakly to him means, without doubt, that he will, when you are no longer young and attractive, cast you away for a fairer face.

Never so far forget your self-respect as to ask a dilatory lover his intentions. Never allow your father or brother so to demean you. If a man has intentions, no matter how bashful he is, he will declare them. If he does not do so, he has none, and you had better give up all hope in that direction. There are always plenty more men about who will care for you, and who will let you know it too.

Three such cases have come to my knowledge. The girl acted differently in each one. The first clung to her dilatory lover till he finally left her when she was too old to attract any one else. Now, alone in the world, she supports herself by keeping a boarding-house. The second one had her father ask the lover his intentions, and in that way roped him in. It was not a happy marriage. A third gave up the man who would not propose, and shortly afterwards married another man for whom she grew to care a great deal more.

Some attractive girls live in small towns where they can meet no one whom they could or would marry. Consequently they have to remain single. In such a case a man would go out and seek a wife. A girl cannot exactly do that. She can, however, sometimes change her place of residence for that purpose. When it makes little difference, as far as business is concerned, where a family live, I believe a father owes this duty to his unmarried daughters. He can take her where she will be likely to meet an eligible man. I once knew a father with two young daughters who left his country home for their sakes. He took a nice house in Philadelphia, and remained there till they were both married, then returned home. A widow with three daughters left her farm and rented a large furnished house in New York City. As a means of support she took first-class boarders. The eldest was considerably over thirty, but they were all three attractive. Being so placed where they met gentlemen, none of them were long in marrying. A maiden lady of forty-one, very jolly, bright, and good-natured, interesting but not pretty, and so fleshy she was a sight, had never in the east met a man whom she could marry. She went to California to visit a sister, and in less than a year was married to a wealthy widower.

Change of residence will often change the lonely spinster, young or advanced, into a happy wife.

CHAPTER II.
THE GIRL WHOM MEN LIKE.

Leaving matrimony out of the question, it is desirable for a girl to aim to be a favorite with men generally. She should be a girl whom all men like, whether or not that liking ripens into a feeling more tender. Then she always stands the chance of its so ripening. Many a man goes through life till he has made a success of his business without giving a thought to marriage. When he is ready to marry, he looks about him without any sentiment often to see whom of his lady friends he would like for a wife. Ten to one he hits upon a girl whose character has called forth his friendly admiration. This once settled he straightway falls in love with something to build upon. Widowers will frequently marry a girl of whom they thought well when the wife was yet living.

Mere beauty counts for less in the long run than is generally supposed. It has less power in determining matrimonial choice than you would think. Its first effects are too strong in proportion to its other effects. It is seen at once, and instead of growing upon the beholder, its power rather lessens as it becomes familiar. The two most beautiful girls I ever met are now old maids. The most winning girl I ever knew had absolutely a plain face. There was a charm about her which attracted all men, and which made them swear, after they knew her, that she was a most beautiful creature. Even after she had refused a man, he loved and admired her.

You all want to look as pretty as you can, but you must not place any dependence upon beauty to settle you in life. Many men prefer stylish girls to pretty ones. Look about you at the married women of your acquaintance. How few of them are pretty now, or were in their youth. Two of the worst wives I have ever known are pretty women. Their husbands made the mistake of marrying for beauty. A vain girl is generally selfish, and men do like an unselfish girl. A man wants an unselfish wife.

If you wish men to admire you, you must first be a true woman with a noble character. Look to your home-life. Men catch glimpses of that when you least think it. They know well that an industrious, sweet-tempered, unselfish daughter makes an industrious, sweet-tempered, unselfish wife. A girl of whom her brother is very fond, and whose special friend she is, goes into the society of men, where it is known, with a wonderful recommendation. As a general thing you can tell how a girl will treat her husband by the way she treats her brother. I once knew a young man who asked a girl to marry him because he saw her tender, loving solicitude for her brother.

Men like bright girls. Even the most sober prefer a jolly, laughing girl. As I once heard a man say about a very merry one, "Think of having such a creature always in your home! You wouldn't have much chance for blues." I knew a wonderfully homely girl who was so jolly that men surrounded her wherever she went. Men like a good time, and a lively girl will give it to them. If you cannot all be jolly, you can be bright, talkative, and interested. Jolly girls are never sentimental. A man hates a sentimental girl. Sentimental looks, long faces, teary expressions are only attractive in novels. Men, out of books, do not like to wipe away tears—they prefer to walk away from them. Never forget that a man is a selfish being. Keep that little fact in view continually; and if you want to please him, pander to it. If anything will disgust a man with a girl, it is to see her make a fuss. Even if you have real heart-sorrow, the more you control yourself, the more you will be admired. Remember you look your very worst when you cry. The tears do not "well up," and "overflow," "chasing each other down your alabaster cheeks like so many pearly drops," as they do in novels. No: your face squints up, while your eyes and nose get red. Instead of being attractive, unless the man for whose benefit you have gotten up this scene loves you, he will walk away. It is manlike to walk off at the first sign of a storm, and to avoid everything uncomfortable. Bear that in mind. When you treat a man to a scene on any subject, you lose your hold upon him. Ten to one he will leave you to seek the society of some lively girl who is wise enough to hide her tears.

A man likes a sensible girl. He likes real good common sense. Nothing is more trying than an unreasonable woman, and a man will not have anything to do with her when he does not have to do so. He may be politely pleasant to her, but he does not care to have her for his wife. To be sure plenty of unreasonable, trying women are wives. (I would they were not!) They had the faculty of hiding their real character before the binding vows were spoken. It is better to have nothing to hide. Be your honest true self always. If you are naturally endowed with common sense, try to cultivate it. Learn to be reasonable, and try not to be governed by your feelings. A man never cares for a girl whose feelings and not duty are her guide. Bear in mind that I am not talking about the man who is in love with you, but the one who views you calmly but may sometime love you.

Men like good-natured girls. I know two sisters, the eldest of whom is quick-tempered, resentful, ill-spoken, and is over thirty without a gentleman friend. She never had one. The younger, not yet nineteen, is good-natured and lively. All the men who know her like her. One man, in fear of her being carried off by some one else, has secured her promise to marry him.

A man likes to feel that the wife he takes to his home is going to brighten that home. He does not want a high temper to contend with. A girl never shows off to a worse advantage than when she is angry. Men are attracted by sweetness of disposition. No greater compliment could be paid to any woman than is paid to the Princess of Wales when she is called Her Royal Sweetness. Directly we hear that, we are drawn to her.

Sweetness of mind and manner is woman's greatest charm. A sweet woman is beloved by every one. It is woman's province to be sweet. Gail Hamilton says, "It is the first duty of woman to be a lady." I say, it is her first duty, after being a Christian (which is certainly first of everything), to be sweet. She says to be a lady is more than to be a prince. Let me add that to be Her Royal Sweetness is more than to be Her Royal Highness. We all are won by a sweet manner. A sweet smile will even draw us to a stranger. It can be yours if you will cultivate it. Begin at home. Lay the foundation there. Be sweet at heart. Do not put on gracious smiles and winning ways for the outside world only. If they are not natural, you will be caught tripping sometimes. Circumstances may arise when you will show the man whom you are the most anxious to win what you truly are. Although that will be a good thing for him, it will be bad for you. Be genuine. Counterfeit is detected in the long run. I know a woman who outside is the very ideal of sweetness, but who is a perfect demon at home. She won her husband, whom she now drives almost to madness, by that assumed sweetness. In spite of smiles and graciousness, she is the most friendless woman I know. The world demands genuine coin, and will detect counterfeit. So begin at home to be sweet, and unconsciously it will become your natural manner. You will not have to assume it: it will be your own.

A girl may be more than plain, even homely, but if her manners are gentle, her voice sweet and low, her bearing womanly, her power is wonderful. A charming smile unlocks many a door which is barred to a stiff, ungracious manner. A charming smile warms every one it greets. It is particularly winning to a man. It has in it a welcome which fascinates him, and brings him to you again. A gracious, sweet manner is of more account in winning your way with the sterner sex than millions. More girls are married for their sweetness than for their money. A charming, bright greeting will sometimes engage a man's interest or attention on the spot.

"Be courteous" at all times. "Be courteous" under all circumstances even the most trying, in your family, among friends, and with strangers. I remember it was said of a sweet girl at school, "She would be polite to Satan himself if he came to her room." I almost believe it. I once heard a truly sweet girl say, "I was so provoked;" when another girl broke in, "I don't believe that. Any one knows that you cannot get provoked."

Sensible men like an economical girl. A man does not want to feel that after marriage all his money, especially if he does not have much of it, is going to be wasted.

Men like healthy girls. A man hates to hear a woman complain. He is not sympathetic. Men rarely are; but then you must take them as you find them, not as you would have them. Just there lies the secret of some girls' failure to attract; they have no patience with a man's imperfections, and are unwise enough to allow him to see that they have discovered them.

Men like girls who are hearty and who have a hearty interest in things. A real live girl is always a favorite. A man avoids a sentimental girl. Do not quote poetry. Do not look languishing. Do not model your conduct after the heroines of novels. Study real life, and be real. Do not expect anything to occur to you as it does to girls in novels: it never will.

Do not exact too much attention. A man hates to give it where it is exacted, even when it is your right. It is their way to pay it only when they feel like doing so. A man never wants to be controlled. Before he is in love, he is particularly alive to any effort to do so. When he is in love, he is more blind to it; but even then it is not well to press it.

To be thoroughly attractive you must have a great deal of tact. Tact has been called the supremest weapon in a woman's hands. Without it, she is helpless. With it, she is powerful. Tact will enable you to see just what to do, how to do it, what to say, and how to say it. Men are not all alike. What will please one may not please another. They are all built on the same general plan, however, and if you know one well, you know pretty much all there is to be known about the whole sex. Yet different lines of conduct are to be pursued with different men. A girl with tact grasps this in a moment. Indeed, she grasps the situation every time and pleases every time. You must understand man-nature. You can learn a great deal of it from your brother. Let me tell you too that if girls would more frequently advise with their brothers, they would get along a hundred-fold better. A brother can give you an insight into other men, and at the same time look after your interests. You will rarely fail to go right, and to do right, if you will make him your confidant. Find out what he likes, and you will know what other men like.

If you would be attractive, you must hide your feelings. I know of no time at home or abroad when it is well to show your real feelings if they are disagreeable. Bear in mind that I do not lay down a code of laws to be practised only abroad regardless of your home-life. Let the first man upon whom you try your winning arts be your father. Make him sure that you are the most perfect of girls. Then try your brothers. As the most lovely of daughters and sisters, you will be real when you are attracting other men by your winning manners.

A man likes a girl who is read up—at least in the news of the day. He does not want to be instructed, and he never likes a girl who knows better than he does about things. If even you are sure he is wrong, do not correct him. That would be a wound to his vanity, which is itself a fatal thing to do. If you are better educated than he is, do not let him know it. Appear to receive instruction, and let your knowledge be a sort of cushion for his. Be interested in what he talks about, and willing to learn. Give him your full attention when he talks to you. It is a lack of tact that makes a girl show a want of interest. It is a lack of tact too that makes a girl let a man see what a good opinion she has of herself, when she ought to be showing him what a good opinion she has of him. It is very well to have it settled in your own mind just what you are, and what your attractions are, but do not let any know of that opinion. It is well to have a good opinion of yourself: it will give you an ease in society and a confidence to go ahead and win. Be sure, however, that you are worthy of that opinion. Be sure that you are not deceiving even yourself.

Never allow a man to sacrifice his comfort for you. If he is rude enough even to ask to smoke in your presence, with your sweetest smile give him permission to do so. Promote his comfort in every possible way. They notice these things and like such attentions. Do not feel it your right always to have the best of everything and he the worst. Decline to accept the sacrifices that he as a gentleman will insist upon making. Some girls will heedlessly accept anything with a sort of blind gross selfishness. The girl who is unselfish at home, and who looks out for the comfort of her family before she does her own, will unconsciously carry the same winning spirit with her wherever she goes. The girl who is selfish at home, and who puts on her sweetness with company dress, will often forget all about it, especially under any excitement.

Do not allow a man to spend much money upon you. He rarely cares to do so, but does it because it is customary among a certain class, and thinks that you expect it of him. Give him a pleasant surprise when he invites you into a restaurant or elsewhere, by declining. You do not want to be indebted to him in a monetary point of view—it lessens your dignity. It would not be a pleasant thing to hear him count up how much he has spent upon you. A man will do it, and make remarks about it to other men too. They have it all done to a fine point, and know just which girl is expensive in her tastes, and which one it costs the most to take out. I have heard them talk when I have been behind the scenes. Some girls, I am sorry to say, will even go so far as to hint that they would like to be taken to a certain entertainment or out for refreshments. There is much bitter truth in the jokes we read about the ice-cream girl. The writer of them, I always think, has smarted under the custom.

No matter what a man is himself, he likes a modest girl. True modesty has a great charm. A girl without it is like a faded flower. As a general thing, her end is sad. Beauty is fleeting, but modesty gives a charm which outlasts youth. A retiring, gentle girl is something to seek after; and a man rather seek. A bold girl may receive more attentions from a certain class of men, but less love in the long run. That "certain class of men" you want to avoid instead of seeking to attract them. The real gentleman, the kind for whose attentions you care, never wants anything to do with a bold, loud girl. The loud girl is never a lady. Cultivate a low, sweet voice at all times. Abjure slang and chewing gum. Of the two evils I do not know which is the worst; but I do know that no true lady is addicted to either.

Men like large-minded, large-hearted girls. They like girls who have no envy in their nature, who can be fair and just even to a rival, who will see good in every one, and speak of that instead of the evil.

If you meet a girl whom you feel is your superior, emulate her; try to become all she is. At the same time, be large enough to acknowledge her excellence. Your very humility and sweet praise of her will be a winning grace. Ten to one the man will think how sweet you are instead of seeing the excellent traits you point out in her. Bitter, narrow-minded girls have an idea they can bring a superior girl down to their level by casting mud at her. It is a species of mud that always flies back, with a sort of a double back-action arrangement, and does all the harm to the thrower. In the first place, it is not Christ-like to speak unkindly of any one; in the second, men hate to hear it. It is only a weak one who will join in with you. In the third place, it is so small, and tells so plainly that you are narrow, envious, inferior. Instead of trying to pull a girl down, always try to climb up beyond her heights. Be large enough to discern and acknowledge whatever good you see in any one. Be charitable to the wrong-doings of your friends. Never mention the plainly seen faults of another girl. In this evil world, be as though you saw no evil. Be pure. "To the pure all things are pure." Let all things and all people be pure in your sight.

Make yourself worth having, and men will want to have you. Strive to cultivate a true womanliness and to become an efficient person. Be a girl who can help herself, who is not ignorant of work or too lazy to do it. Do not be a mere toy whom men will flirt with and then drop when they want to marry a woman who will be a helpmeet. Sensible men do not want to marry a bundle of nothing for a wife. When they are cheated into doing so, they repent it all their lives. You do not want to think that the man whom you will marry is going to repent the act. I know I would rather die on my wedding-day. I think that if a man to whom I was married should hint by word or deed of such a repentance, I would feel that my life was a complete failure, and should want to go out of it then and there.

Be accomplished and brilliant if possible, but above all things prepare yourself to be a helpmeet for a man. Men like talents in a girl, especially music; but a man likes to have his wife know how to keep house. Learn that. Learn to make all sorts of garments and to cook, even if you are wealthy.

CHAPTER III.
THE GIRL WHO WINS.

Being an attractive girl whom all men like is not exactly the same thing as setting about deliberately to win some one man's heart. It has been said that the girl thinks of matrimony before the man does. He goes on blindly and thoughtlessly until he is so deep in love that he cannot retreat; while from the very start she thinks whether or not she would like to wed him.

It may be that you know some young man whom in a womanly way you would like to win. Let us suppose that in the secret recesses of your heart you have decided that you would like to marry him.

In the first place, you must not fall deeply in love with him. If you fail, you do not want to be broken-hearted; and too, when a girl is really up and down in love, she loses control of herself. She is no longer sure of herself and of her conduct. You must keep cool and calculating. You must admire the man, and feel that at that time he is the only one you could love. Lose just enough of your heart so that, when he is won and asks for your love, you can give it to him.

You must be able to arrange your mode of warfare, and always have perfect possession of yourself. There must be no silly excitement when he is present, and downcast face when he is away. Such a course would surely provoke comment; and your conduct must not be commented upon. No one must be allowed to suspect that you are interested in him. It is not your province in any way to go a-wooing; but you can work wonders in the way of winning the man you want. I have read that a woman may marry whom she will. I almost believe she can. You cannot, however, go about in an open way as a man can. With him the battle is sometimes half won when he makes it known that he wishes marriage. With you it would be all lost.

You must never run after a man. Make yourself so attractive that he will seek you. Then it is all in your own hands. You can keep him beside you. You may have to wait some time for him to come. Be patient. Nothing is ever accomplished without patience. An impatient, nervous anxiety on your part will be likely to spoil everything. Never go where you know he will be and where he does not expect you, if you can avoid doing so. Better, by far, let him miss you where he anticipates seeing you than to see too much of you. His disappointment will show him how much he is interested in you.

Do not hesitate to let him see that you have a modest, maidenly interest in him. Men like that. It must be done in a retiring way as if you did not intend to have him see it, but could not help yourself. While a man will boast of a girl running after him, this little secret of yours, which by his acuteness(!) he has discovered, he will keep sacredly to himself. The very modesty with which you try to veil it will heighten its value in his eyes.

Do not hesitate to let him see by your greeting that he is welcome. I do not mean that you are to be effusive. It is done by your smile, your look, more than by words. Girls make the mistake of greeting a man coolly in fear of appearing forward or of showing a regard. Never be cool to the man you want to win. Ward McAllister says in his "Society as I Have Found It": "The value of a pleasant manner is impossible to estimate. It is like sunshine; it gladdens. You feel it, and are at once attracted to the person without knowing why."

Young girls are rarely mistress of these sweet, little, but telling arts. The knowing just how comes later in life. Balzac has said that a woman of thirty is at her most fascinating and dangerous period. The women who have been the most famous for their power over hearts have all been nearer forty than twenty. This seems incredible to you yet in your teens. You now look upon twenty-five as a species of old age. At thirty, you think, as far as men are concerned, a woman is in the sere and yellow leaf; while at forty they are little less than in their dotage. Look out, that while you are counting on your youth to marry you, some of these females in the sere and yellow leaf, or even in their dotage, will carry off the prize, because she knows how and you do not. The fact is, the woman of thirty is still young now-a-days, whatever she was in our grandmothers' time.

She can win men's love too. She knows the world so well that she takes men as she finds them, while the girl in her teens does not. The girl aspires too often to make them fit in her narrow mould. Girls are too often narrow in their ideas. In the secret acceptance of a man's faults, or taking him as you find him, lies a great deal the secret of power over them. You girls are too sure of yourselves, too fixed in your opinions, too certain that you are right and that others are wrong. You are too anxious to set a man right. They have a way of their own of not wanting to be set right. They never want to be corrected. If they are wrong, their ignorance is bliss to them.

Girls have little charity. They are generally hard in their judgments of everything and of everybody. They take delight in showing off what they know, and making a man feel like a fool. A man never allows the same girl to make him feel like a fool twice. Once is enough for any man. He seeks the society of another straightway. Girls are given to display a superiority, and make a man feel small. Again he walks off. A man never falls in love with a girl who makes him feel small. Now the charming girl hides her own opinions—her superiority, and brings out what is best in the man. This is what you must do every time. When you seek to win a man, make him pleased with himself. The better he is pleased with himself the better he will like you. This is not done by bold, outspoken flattery (although a man will swallow larger doses of that than you suppose), but by adroitly showing him his own best side. If you have to touch his tender places, do it with a soft hand that will soothe instead of wound.

A man likes a smart girl. Your smartness or your brilliancy must, however, be kept in the background. You must not use it to dazzle him, but to make him feel that he is brilliant. If he is witty, never try to be more so than he is. If he is highly educated and you are more so, still be willing to be instructed by him. Never aspire to teach him. A man does not want to be set right by a woman.

If he is a talker, so manage that he will do all the talking, if he wishes to, while you are the interested listener. I do not mean that you are to be mum: you are to be so interested that you cannot help sometimes breaking in. All your remarks should be to the point, and so worded that he will be led on until he is even surprised at his own powers of conversation and brilliancy. There is no surer way than this to keep him at your side. If he looks at his watch it will be to see how much longer he can remain with you, not because he wishes to hurry away. When he finally must leave you, he will have so much better an opinion of himself that he will be quite a new man. His thoughts of you will be most flattering. He will not know why. Men rarely analyze their emotions. If they did, it would be worse for us and our little arts. In a certain way they go about blindly.

A man is self-centred. He loves to talk about himself. His vanity is his weak point. If he is no talker, and all other topics fail, lead him to talk about himself. Only one man in a hundred will fail to respond to this bait. He does not know that he is engrossing the conversation in this way: he only knows that you are delightful.

The wonderful charm some girls have for men lies in the interest she shows in him, and the tact with which she makes him think well of himself.

A man will not be snubbed. In novels, especially of the Duchess kind, the abject small creature whom she calls the hero thrives upon it. His love feeds upon snubbing, and grows more intense. He falls in love at first sight, and the worse his charmer treats him the more he loves her. This is not true to life. These books are full of false ideas, and do much harm to the girl who reads them.

It seems almost coarse to advise flattery. Flattery is coarse. You can, however, discover a man's good qualities, talents, etc., and praise them without limit. Men will swallow large doses of praise without so much as a wink. They do not even know you are praising them; they are only conscious of being pleased. You must be discreet, however, in giving your doses, and above all things avoid getting the name of being a flatterer. You can sometimes give praise with an unsparing hand, but you must be sure of the right occasion. A public man may be praised ad libitum. In fact, a man who sings, acts, speaks in public needs it.

The private man wants it too. He gets less of it from the world in general, and your good opinion, delicately expressed, will be all the more acceptable. When you have a field all to yourself, be sure and improve the occasion.

The girl who is affectionate wins. I do not mean to imply that you are to embrace every man you meet or to allow anything of the kind from them. You are to show a certain warmth of feeling. No man likes a cold girl. Ice repels. A friend of mine, whose great attraction was her warmth of manner, mowed down hearts like ten-pins. Her greeting always was more than cordial. She gave almost an affectionate grasp of the hand, allowing her hand to lie there a mere shadow of time, while her beaming smile showed her delight at the meeting. There was life and warm blood in the touch of her slender fingers which made many a man's heart beat quickly for her. She made a man feel that in winning her he would be winning a loving wife, and that is what a man always wants.

Another equally successful girl made the man with whom she was talking feel that he was the only man of much importance in the world; all her interest was in him—just in him. Every look was flattery of the worst kind.

We sometimes say that a girl has an indescribable charm and a way with her that no man can withstand. I think her power is simply that she makes a man think better of himself. She gives him a confidence in himself. She makes him pleased with himself. She shows an interest in his greatest interest, himself. Instead of wounding his vanity, which is almost greater than his heart, she flatters it. Men rarely overlook an insult to the former. A girl who has made a man think less of himself may give that man up on the spot. She is crossed off of his books forever.

There are occasions when you must exercise a good deal of forbearance with a man if you wish to win him. A man is prone to wander. He may be paying attention to some other girl when you most want him. Although it is very annoying, there must be nothing cold in your greeting when he comes to you again. You must not reproach him. You must simply make yourself a great deal more fascinating than she is. You must be more sweet and winning if possible than you were before. Take pains never to speak ill of this possible rival. It is neither Christian-like or lady-like to do so. It is bad taste. The man knows you are jealous. He hates to hear bitter words. It looks very much as if you could and would make bitter remarks to your husband. If you reproach him now for wandering, he may judge truly that your husband will have little liberty. If you are jealous and inclined to make a fuss before there is even any engagement, what will you be like after marriage?

If you would win, cultivate a sweet, gentle, forbearing spirit. Be always gracious. Cultivate a kindly manner. "Be free from arrogance, self-assertion, self-consciousness, considerate of the feelings of others." Be courteous and kind in manners to every one.

CHAPTER IV.
THE GIRL WHO FAILS.

"The young man fights shy of the girl who makes a dead set after him," was the inelegant, but o'er-true paragraph I read in the paper not long since. The paragraphist was evidently a man and knew his sex.

The girl who runs after a man fails. She more likely disgusts him than flatters him. He does not want her or her attentions when he can have them without the seeking. It is man's province to woo, and his whole nature seems to revolt against a turning of the tables. I call to mind a schoolmate who on this account was a complete failure. She was pretty, bright, even witty, well educated, moved in good society, and had money, but no man wanted her. Her boldness disgusted all of them. When she saw one she fancied, she paid such open court to him that he avoided her. Some time afterwards, when she saw the uselessness of pursuit there, she turned her attentions elsewhere, running after another man. Although naturally attractive, I never knew a man who wanted her.

I have known of other girls who have never married for this same reason. It seems to be a common fault. It is a serious one. If you are at all inclined to be forward with men, stop it. You will not only fail to marry, you will lose respect. You gain nothing and lose all. You cheapen yourself and your charms when you "throw yourself at a man's head." As it has been decreed from the beginning of the world that man is the head of the woman, so it is decreed that as he shall protect her, he is the one to woo and she the one to be won. You will meet coarse men who will respond to all your advances. They will pay you attention just for the fun of the thing. They will never marry you, and it would be a good lesson to you if you could hear them talk of you among themselves. A man never spares a girl who has no respect for herself. A man whom you run after may even say many tender things to you. He may lead you up to the point where, if you had not begun it, you would have a right to expect him to ask you to marry him. He doesn't. He stops just there.

A girl's great charm is a sweet, womanly modesty, which appears to hide a love she cannot help feeling.

It is a great mistake to let your male friends see you with any blemishes upon you. If you have a breaking-out on the face, a swollen cheek, a red nose, or anything which disfigures you, hide yourself till it is over. Men like to idealize a girl whom they admire, and they cannot idealize a swollen face or a red nose. I knew a girl who continually had styes on her eyes. She was not wise enough to hide herself at the time, but continued to go out where she would meet her male friends. She has never married, and I have always thought that this is the reason. Another girl had her front teeth drawn, and went about toothless for a while. Other girls do not hesitate to let men see them with their bangs in curl-papers. A man will never let you see him with his hair not combed or with his face lathered for shaving.

Be tidy always. Have your hair combed, your dress neat, even if it is old. Patches are to be respected, while holes mark the sloven. Always, even if you are scrubbing the floor, be ready to see any one who comes. The very one in whose eyes you most desire to appear well may come then. Some men have a way of dropping in at such unexpected times. Many a man has been disillusionized by a dirty dress or a frowsy head. Men like a nice appearance. They never want to marry a sloven if they know it. A bright and interesting writer has never married for this reason. Her head is never combed, and there is always a rip somewhere in her dress. Her hands are generally touched off with ink.

The independent, self-reliant girl is rarely a favorite with men. A man loves to protect. He does not like a masterful, bossy girl. He does not want to follow as if he were a spaniel. It is a poor specimen of a man who does not want to lead. Three sisters were left with a very little money at the death of their father. They were self-reliant and thorough business women. They invested their money to such good advantage in real estate that in a few years they became wealthy women. They were never married. It would have been impossible for any man with any self-respect to have loved either of them: they were so mannish, independent, and self-reliant.

Do not be of the so-called woman's rights order. Men hate strong-minded women who are forever harping on the wrongs of women and of the rights they are going to have. That kind of girl generally does have a wrong—the wrong of being neglected by the sterner sex. A woman's right is a husband, a home, and children. It is her right to have something to love and to make happy. When she wants to usurp a man's place, she is going out of her sphere and makes a failure of her life. If you have a leaning towards "woman's rights," erect yourself and lean the other way. If you do not, you are doomed to unattractive spinsterhood, dress reform, and the lecture platform, and to feed on husks. That sweet little wife yonder, who hardly knows who is being voted for, and whose horizon is bounded by her husband, is feeding on corn. She believes that her rights are wifehood and motherhood, and she has them.

A self-assertive girl fails. A self-assertive, selfish, self-centred girl is no man's ideal. It is unwomanish as well as unwomanly. A girl who can push ahead and take her own part is generally allowed to do so. It is a mistake to be anything that is unfeminine. Men never admire girls who have masculine characteristics. Only a fool will marry her. Do not ape men in dress or manner. Strive to be womanish and womanly at all times in every way. The attractive woman is womanly sweetness personified.

The girl who insists upon attentions gets none. The girl who looks upon her escort as her slave pro tem. loses him. You must never treat a man as if he were your servant. He will not stand it from you, although you may be attractive in other ways. His manhood will assert itself, and no matter how much he has loved you, that love will be killed. It is a poor outlook for married happiness. He does not care to wed where he knows he will be henpecked.

A poor girl will marry before a wealthy one will. The latter has it written upon her that it costs a mint to keep her. She may be much admired, but she is an expensive luxury. Unless a young man has exceptional means, he must give her up. You will find numbers of unmarried women in the highest society everywhere. Men are afraid to marry the daughters of millionnaires, unless a large dowry is going to be among the wedding presents. Extravagant habits, they know, have been her rule. She has never been taught to economize in anything. She must have an establishment as elegant as her father's. She could not think of beginning as humbly as her parents likely did. So she either fails to marry at all, or marries late in life, when the death of her parents has given her an independent fortune.

A girl who shows her anxiety to marry generally fails to do so. A man feels that it is marriage and not himself that she wants. That wounds his vanity. She is never self-possessed in the society of men. She is so anxious to please that she plans beforehand what she will say. When she says it, it comes out wrong and does not fit in. She is trembling and eager even if she does not run after him. Like vaulting ambition, she o'erleaps herself. Every time you meet her, she has new and fresh hopes. She is waiting always anxiously for a proposal, and would accept any man who offered himself regardless of creed (almost color), circumstances, character, and condition.

The sharp, snubby girl never succeeds. A man will not stay where he is snubbed or where his vanity is wounded. Some girls, especially very young ones, have an idea that they are saying smart things where they are only saying sharp things. You hardly realize what a great mistake you are making when you try to be witty at a man's expense. You only make a greater one when you are cutting in your remarks. Girls have an idea that it does a young man good to have, as they express it, "the conceit taken out of him." I doubt if it does, and even so, you are not the one to do it. Let him have a good opinion of himself in his youth. Help him to it, rather than to try to take it away from him. The outside world will give him knocks enough as he battles his way up in it, to take any amount of conceit out of him. Maybe he comes to you sometimes just smarting from one. Let him find for his wounds a balm. Learn to soothe and sympathize instead of hurting. Your tongue is sometimes so unwittingly cruel. Your laugh is so heartless that you make a man with a rhinoceros skin shrink. It all flies back upon your own head, however. You will suffer for it afterwards. It will only drive him from you. Girls often can attract who cannot keep a beau. Notice them. See if they have not sharp tongues and do not love to take the conceit out of a man. "He has too good an opinion of himself, but I let him know what I thought of him," I have heard girls say. One thing is certain—if you have done that, you will never hear from him that he thinks much of you.

So round off your sharp corners. Remember that the young man with a good opinion of himself is the more easy to win, because you can play upon his vanity.

Do not speak your mind plainly. Certain persons pride themselves on plain speaking, as if there were a virtue in hurting some one else's feelings. When you hear any one say, "I always speak my mind," you may know she says disagreeable things. She thinks when she has said that that she can go ahead, cutting right and left with her tongue. They are never people who praise. It appears that those who say "just what they think" generally think unkind things.

Avoid doing so, especially to a man. It is unkind. It makes more enemies the world over than anything else. Men will swallow praise ad nauseum, but they will not take censure.

The eccentric girl had better never have been born, as far as men are concerned. They will have nothing to do with her. If you are eccentric and have prided yourself upon it, the sooner you become like folks the better for you. A man will not pay attention to an oddity. An outlandish hat that causes comment will sometimes drive him away. He may not know what is the matter with it, but he knows he will not ask you out while there is any danger of your wearing it. It is a mistake to be odd in your conduct or language. Eccentricity grows upon one. If you are given to it in your youth, what will you be in your old age? A man would know that if he were rash enough to marry you, every day you would make him ashamed.

The girl who has too many gentlemen friends hardly ever marries. There is something in every man's heart which subscribes to

> "The rose that all are praising,
> Is not the rose for me."

There are cases where jealousy of another's man's attentions will hasten a proposal. But two are in the case there, however, and both are in love. Avoid many gentlemen callers. Do not allow your house to become a meeting-place. A man will not fall in love where he sees you smile as sweetly on another man as you do upon him. He will reign alone. He never goes on shares where a heart is concerned. A man may call often, where he knows he will meet other men, but it is only as a friend. He does not fall in love with his hostess. When he marries it will likely be some little modest girl who hardly knows any man but himself.

When I was very young I remember hoping that when I grew older I would have as many gentlemen callers as a certain young lady who lived near us. Every night her parlors were thronged. It seemed to be a general meeting-place for young men. Her sister and herself lavished their smiles upon them. She never married. Her sister married a man whom she met in another place, and who hardly ever came to the house. Another girl had quite as many callers. She must have seen her danger, for she ceased to receive them. Some time later she married.

It is flattering to your vanity to have a great many gentlemen friends who call, and who take you out, but it will certainly stand in the way of marriage. It is fun, doubtless, to count up a long list of escorts, but the girl who can do so rarely counts up a long list of offers. A girl who was so retiring that she was rarely invited out by a gentleman, was loved by almost every man who got well-acquainted with her. She could have counted up a long list of offers but a short list of escorts. At a party she was a wall-flower. She had few gentlemen callers, yet it seems as though all men longed to possess her. She passed most of her evenings alone with her family, and married well. So it shows that knowing many men would rather indicate no marriage than a surety of one.

The cold girl never succeeds. A man would as soon make love to an icicle. A man prefers fire. He likes a warm, living heart. He wants to see that a girl has that heart. A pretty, stylish young girl whom I want to see settled in life is failing to do so on just that account. She is not naturally cold, but when she is at all interested in a man, she becomes almost frigid in his presence. She is too afraid of showing her interest in him to allow him to see that she responds to his. A man wants an affectionate, warm-hearted wife. So he will marry what seems to him to be an affectionate girl. There is a certain warmth of manner that will show this disposition.

A girl fails who will not let the man who is beginning to love her see that she can return love. It must be shown modestly, however. You must be sympathetic. Man has his success and his failures in life. As he comes to you, he is thinking of them more than he is of you. He wants to talk of them. If you do not show a sympathetic interest, he will go where he can get it. Draw him out on his favorite topic, no matter if it is himself. I remember once walking two squares with a gentleman who talked of nothing else but a slight injury on his hand.

An interesting, intellectual lady is going through life unmarried for no other reason, I believe, than her lack of sympathy. You are conscious of this lack whenever you converse with her. If you mention yourself, your humble aim and ambitions, a dead silence falls. You feel as if you were undone and wish you could hide your head. A woman will hasten to change the subject and to make amends. A man leaves and never returns.

A man likes to look, as it were, in a mirror. He likes to see himself reflected in the eyes that meet his. He wants to feel that the girl has so much interest in him that she is interested in every word he says about himself.

The girl who talks about herself usurps his prerogative. He does not relish that, and her society is stupid to him. I is a man's pronoun. You is a woman's. Very young girls who are filled with themselves and their own affairs are very much given to this. As they grow older, they see it does not do. Bear in mind that no matter how pretty you are or how sweet, if you will talk about yourself to a man, you become "as tedious as a twice-told tale vexing the dull ears of a drowsy man." There is an old witticism which tells the truth in a nutshell: "What is a bore? A man who talks about himself when you want to talk about yourself."

The high-tempered girl fails. A man bent upon matrimony avoids her if he is aware of it. If you have such an infirmity, try to get rid of it as you would a facial blemish. Try harder; for it is indeed far worse than any bodily disfigurement. Our Lord, whose strength is sufficient for you always, will help you to do so. Some girls falsely call it a high spirit. It is anything but that. It is a weak spirit. A girl who gives way to temper has no control over herself. She is weak instead of high and strong. Her doors are always open, and whoever will may come in and upset her. Instead of being proud of it, be ashamed of it. While possessing it, your life is a failure everywhere.

A sweet, interesting, lively conversationalist is one thing, and a girl with a long tongue is another. Avoid gossip and meddling.

It is a mistake to entertain a gentleman with an account of your neighbor's failings and backslidings. His interests are broader. He rarely stoops to such little things, and they weary him. Men never care for girls who have the reputation for being gossips. Fill your mind with better things. Read and enlarge your powers of conversation.

It is a mistake to be inquisitive. While a man likes a girl to be interested in him and in his doings, he does not want to be questioned about them. A walking interrogation point is never a pleasant companion. When you draw him out it must be with tact.

A precise, prim, what we call an old maidish girl is a failure. She is born to a lonely life of spinsterhood. Unless she changes she cannot escape her fate. At heart she may be all that is true and good, but no man will ever find that out. As a rule men judge of us by outward appearances. They take women more for what they seem to be than for what they are. The good qualities of the prim girl are all lost upon him.

With gentlemen a loud girl never succeeds. She can always attract the attentions of coarse men, but a well-bred man avoids her. He loves modesty. He does not want the girl whom he escorts to be conspicuous by boisterous talking and laughing. He does not want her to be hail-fellow-well-met with every man they meet. It shows she has no modesty. He cannot respect her and will not marry her. It is never nice to be "gay" or "fast." The men whom you attract about you by it are not the men you want to marry. They are the kind who do not want to marry you or any one else.

Loud, conspicuous dressing is never an attraction. Men like stylish, well-dressed girls, but they never like anything that is flashy or that attracts attention.

The girl who imagines every man she meets is in love with her rarely is loved by one. This is a common fault with young girls. It comes either from innate silliness or from the reading of too many novels. The worst of it is, she is not even cured of her folly when the men do not propose to her, but do to some other girl. She imagines some insurmountable difficulty was in his way, and that he has only married the other girl out of pique. That is the way it was in the last novel she read. Girls, be sensible. Every man you meet will not fall in love with you. When one does, he will let you know it. Men are not given to sighing in secret over one girl, then marrying another without love. A man who loves you will be open about it. He will not avoid you. He acts on the spot: sometimes without much thought. So when a man does not pay attention to you, rest assured, unless you have offended him, that he does not want to do so. He is not in love with you. He is more likely to pay attention without loving, than to love without paying attentions.

A vain girl fails. The pretty girl who depends altogether upon her looks and is proud of her beauty, rarely marries. I have spoken of this before. It has been thought that in matrimony, as in other fields, the plain-featured girl has the greatest success. A pretty girl starts out with false notions of her charms. She thinks that she has only to be seen to be loved. She overestimates her one gift, and does not try to cultivate others. Youths who easily fall in love and as easily out again are caught by a merely pretty face. Men want something more.

Let me quote from an article on this subject which I read the other day: "Look about you and count the number of faded, thwarted beauties you know, who are embittered dependents, or else late in life have picked up a broken stick in the shape of a partner to help disguise their crippled vanity. In fact, so frequently is this the case that between the ages of sixteen and twenty-six only extraordinary virtue and talent ever saves a belle from grievous folly in her aspirations." So if you are a beauty and wish to marry, I advise you strongly to put aside all vanity, and to cultivate the superior charms of your plainer sisters.

Never allow your mother to do the courting. There are times when a girl can win a man against his will, and he will never know that it was she who did it. A mother never can do this. A man knows it every time. When he sees her efforts, he is forewarned and on his guard. It is all done in cold blood and deliberately by the mother. The daughter has less deliberation and a great deal of warm blood when she attempts it. He is likely to think: "What an interesting girl! I believe I could get her if I tried," and may try. Of the mother's efforts, he thinks: "That old woman wants me to marry her daughter. I can see through her. I won't do it."

A mother may make herself so attractive that, if she were a girl, she would win him. Notwithstanding that, he hardens his heart against the daughter. A lady who, even as a grandmother, is attractive to men, tried in her early married days to win a young man for her sister. He responded quickly to her overtures, and seemed glad to come to the house. She thought she was succeeding, when one day he said to her: "I know what you are about. You might as well give it up, you won't accomplish it. If you were not married, however, I would propose to you to-day."

She did give it up.

A girl makes a mistake who brags of her conquests. She should never speak of them to any one. If a man whom you cannot accept offers you his hand, forget that he did so. By your manner to him when you meet afterwards, endeavor to make him forget it. The girl who tells about the hearts she has won, wins no more. Men grow afraid of her. She is not to be trusted, they think. If she will lead other men on to propose only to reject them, then tell of it, she will do the same to them.

A girl who fears that the man to whom she only is pleasant will think she is in love with him, is not likely to accomplish much matrimonially. She grows too self-conscious and stiff in her manner. You must forget yourself, or remember only that a man is won by a pleasant manner. If he did think you were a bit interested in him, he would be flattered by it, and might return it shortly.

By a pleasant manner I do not mean a continual giggling. While you must be animated and lively, you cannot laugh continually. A sensible girl can be grave as well as gay. There are times, and plenty of them, when laughter jars. There is certainly a time to laugh and a time to cry; but there is never a time to giggle. Solomon gives a list of almost everything for which we have time, but he never says a word about giggling. A bright, animated manner and continual giggling are two different things. A bright girl is everywhere a success. A giggler is generally considered half-witted. A giggler has no depth of feeling. A bright, lively girl generally has a great deal of feeling; she is not slow to show it, either.

Do not laugh when you talk. Do not laugh the moment a man speaks to you, keeping it up all the time he is with you. It looks as if you were delighted out of your senses. Do not laugh every time he looks at you till he begins to wonder if there is a black spot on his nose. Some men may prefer a grave girl any way. You might study the man and the place before you are too lively.

It may be that some of you who read these chapters have failed so far to win any man's love. Examine yourself and your peculiarities to see wherein the trouble lies. When you have found it, strive to overcome the difficulty. You cannot do it in your own strength. The Lord will help you. He will give you grace to overcome every evil temper, every disagreeable habit, every unlovely manner. If you ask Him, He will make you sweet and lovely. Rest assured that He is interested in your success; for He did not intend woman to live alone.

CHAPTER V.
SOME UNFAILING METHODS.

It is universally known that when a man and woman have a mutual interest, they get interested in each other. When they are in any way drawn together, they soon find that they cannot live apart. When a man grows accustomed to a woman with whom he is pleased, he desires to keep her with him. So we may consider that a companionship with a man is an unfailing way to win him. This companionship unfortunately is not always easy to arrange.

It is often difficult to get up a mutual interest. When you can, be sure to do so. It must come naturally however. A forced arrangement, plainly seen, would defeat itself.

Marriages frequently take place between parties who board in the same house. Seeing each other daily, getting well acquainted, and the mutual interest, even of the table, will draw them together. A young lady boarded, with her brother, in a house where there were no other young ladies, but a number of gentlemen. All admired her, several were smitten with her, and two asked her hand in marriage. A third began to think more of her than of the girl to whom he was engaged.

A widow, with a nice home of her own, took two clergymen to board. It was not long before both wanted to marry her. She did not want either of them, but took the one who was the most persistent.

Singing together is another mutual interest. It is the means of many a marriage. In a quartette, the soprano and tenor marry, the bass and alto. The singer may marry his accompanist. Jennie Lind married her unknown pianist, Goldschmidt, who was younger than herself. Actors, who are always thrown much together, marry and unmarry ad libitum in a disgraceful way.

The marriage of the type-writer and her employer is so frequent that it has passed into a joke. They grow interested in each other from mere companionship.

A student falls in love with the sister of his friend where he visits during vacation. The late Henry Ward Beecher met his wife at her father's home whither he had gone with a college chum, her brother. I had an aunt who had offers from two students brought home by her brothers. This is such a common occurrence that enterprising mothers sometimes urge sons to bring home desirable students to introduce to her daughters.

A lawyer will marry a fair client. I might add that he is the more likely to do so if he is settling up a large estate for her.

A physician rarely marries a patient. If your heart is set upon a certain physician do not play the rôle of an invalid. When you are sick you should have a married physician. A young lady was taken ill with pneumonia. Her family were strangers in the place, and, without knowing it, called in an unmarried physician. He was interested in the case, but not in the least in her. A year later he met her, when in perfect health, at the house of a mutual friend and fell in love with her.

Living next door to each other will often make young people interested in each other. Church-work which brings young men and maidens together is fruitful of many marriages. A young man was put on a fair-table with a number of ladies. He fell in love with the only unmarried one on it. A young clergyman comes in contact with so many girls, and is so run after, that going to his church and entering into the work for his sake is but lost labor. If you want to work in a Church, do it for the Lord, without a thought of who has charge of that body of worshippers.

We learn from Abelard and Heloise what the pupil will become to the teacher. Almost always, when neither are married, free lessons in love accompany another kind of a lesson—that is, if the lessons are private. Men fall in love with a lady who teaches them anything. A young lady was taught Hebrew by an unmarried clergyman. They married about a year after the lessons begun.

A man and woman who are in business together almost always marry. An author has been known to marry her publisher. A Mr. Maxwell published Miss Braddon's novels, and now she is Mrs. Maxwell . Margaret Sydney is the nom de plume of a writer who married her publisher, Daniel Lothrop, of Lothrop and Co.

An almost certain way to win a man's love is to win his confidence. When a man talks to a woman about his greatest interest, he becomes interested in her. When he opens his whole heart to her, he gives her that heart. I never knew this to fail. How to win this confidence is the puzzle. The very man you want may be the one who knows the most about keeping his affairs to himself. You will have to use tact and patience in drawing him out. Get him to talk about his business, or make him talk of his books, his pleasures, his family: always about himself. Persist in this gently. Show him you can keep a secret. Encourage him to talk about himself until he touches upon something that is nearest his heart. Some men will do this sooner than others. The man who readily confides in you, readily falls in love—and almost as readily falls out. It is said that the heart which is easily won is hard to keep; and that the heart which is hard to win you never lose. When you have drawn any man to tell you his heart unreservedly, he is yours.

A young man was in love with a girl of whom his mother did not approve. He was much distressed by the fuss she made. He did not want to give up the girl or to pain his mother. He must talk of his trouble to some one, and he selected a young girl who was visiting the family. He told her all his troubles. She encouraged him with infinite tact until he spoke unreservedly. Whenever he could find her alone he talked of that and of nothing else. Then he planned to be alone with her. Before three months he loved her better than he did the first one.

CHAPTER VI.
A WORD OF WARNING.

The greatest mistake a girl can make is to allow familiarities from men. A girl must be circumspect in her conduct. She must be self-respecting. Having a proper self-respect and being a prude are two different things. A man never likes a prude. He never, in his heart, cares for one who has no self-respect. A man, of a certain class, will pay her attention and take advantage of the liberties she allows, but he never marries her.

You are not safe if you allow the least digression from the right path. A slip once made can never be recalled, and the second follows very easily on the first. Then comes the third, and so on, till ruin is the end for you—not for him.

It is a girl's own fault if she fall. It is her place to guard her honor.

You will meet many a man who is lover-like and fascinating, but if he says nothing about marriage, leave him alone. You do not want to hear of love, if that is all he has to say. Never mind if you do love him. If he loves you and finds he cannot possess you otherwise, he will want to marry you.

Beware of the beginning. Be careful of your conversation. Never smile at a joke with a double meaning. Meet it with silence. Do not pretend you do not understand if you do: there are men who would take pleasure in enlightening you. There are times when it is well to show that you do not approve of it; you may even have to rebuke it. Thereafter avoid that man. If he cares to continue your friendship, he will know how he must behave himself.

Never let a young man repeat a story to you that he would not repeat if your mother were present. A man who would do that, means no good to you. An old and excellent rule is, never talk about anything to a man you would not talk about before a third party; and never talk to a girl as you would not talk if a man were present. Never say anything to either which you would not repeat to your mother. A well-known writer has lately said: "It is always a mistake for a young girl to talk to a man as if she were blasé and widely experienced in all human emotions, frailties, and faults. Many inexperienced, innocent girls adopt this manner, thinking it will render them fascinating in the eyes of men. Men take us for what we seem, not for what we are. The most hardened mondaine who wears a mask of frank innocence fares better with them than the good, sweet-hearted girl who puts on blasé airs and pretends to be a little wicked."

Let your heart be pure. Keep your lips pure. God can make and keep them so. He can take away all interest in sin.

Never make an appointment with a young man of which you cannot tell your mother. When a young man urges you to deceive your mother, he means to deceive you. Your mother is your best friend; make her your confidante in all things, then you will never go astray. On the first approach of familiarities, consult her and be guided by her advice.

Men do not have to be told: they know what girl they may approach familiarly and what one they must treat with respect. You may be sure there is something wrong in your conduct if you are approached as you do not wish to be.

Be careful not to call a man by his first name unless he is a relative. A well-bred lady will not even address a man thus whom she has known in her childhood. Do not allow a man to call you by your first name. You can easily show by your manner that it is distasteful to you. Check even the liberty of your Christian name with the prefix Miss. Although you may have an older sister, you have a right to your father's name. If you cannot be Miss Jones, you can be Miss Mary Jones.

When you are out walking with a gentleman, do not allow him to grasp your elbow. Some men do this instead of offering the arm. He is ill-bred if he attempts it. It is too familiar altogether, and is becoming too common. A polished gentleman will not do it. He will offer his arm.

Beware of allowing a caress from a man to whom you are not engaged. Stifle in the beginning any attempt to do so. Do not so much as allow him to hold your hand. No matter if you do like him, and if his warm grasp does send the happy blood to your heart, it is a happiness you have no right to—neither has he, until he has spoken. Sometimes these things, small as they seem, are but the first step on the broad path that leads to destruction. Perhaps you like as much to feel that strong arm about you as he does to put it there. It is in his power to make it right to do so; it is not in yours, so refuse it. Believe me, you will gain nothing by it, and may lose all. If a man finds he cannot embrace you unengaged, he will take steps to be engaged to you if he loves you.

Poor child! You allow it because you love him. It may be anything but love for you and your good that prompts his action. A man rarely binds himself to a girl who allows his caresses without it. Another thing, while you are treasuring up this caress as a closely-guarded secret, he is doubtless telling his comrades what liberties he can take with you. That is too true. The indiscretions which a girl will hide, he will boast of—it is a man's nature. He judges you by himself, too. He knows that he kisses other girls when he can get a chance, and he supposes that you allow other men's caresses. A man cares more for the caress than for the girl. When he is not genuinely in love, one girl will do almost as well as another. He supposes it is the same with you. He argues that if you are cheap to him, you will be cheap to other men.

"Never speak of love till your lover speaks of marriage," is a good old rule. Men do not talk much about marriage to a girl who will profess her love before he asks her to be his wife.

Be careful to whom you give your photograph. Like figures, they cannot lie. If you have given it, you cannot deny doing so: it is there, a fact, in the young man's possession—he may show it to whom he pleases. He generally pleases to show it to all his male friends. It is another thing which cheapens you. Your picture is one of a collection he has of girls. Maybe for a while, when exhibiting his gallery of beauties, he may call you his best girl. He does it all lightly, and as the young men look over the collection, they will make remarks about you all which, if you heard them, would make you blush. If a girl has no more respect for herself than to give a picture to every man who asks for it, you must not expect men to respect her. It is no sign a man loves you because he asks for your picture. If he does, let him ask for you first. He more likely wants to enlarge his collection of photographs. If you went into his room, you would see it stuck up in his mirror with a dozen or so of others.

It is a mistake to imagine that an engagement breaks down all barriers. Engagements are so frequently broken. Instead of being almost as sacred as marriage, they are held lightly. You must continue after your engagement to be careful of your conduct and not to allow any undue liberties. Do not let your lover's caresses be too frequent or passionate. Some young people act as if they only become engaged so they might kiss each other—they spend all their time at it when they are alone. Some of these things are sweeter if they are waited for. Couples who are parted during their engagement generally are the most happy when they are married. They have not exhausted their affection; instead of its being an old story, it is fresh.

If it were worth the while, I would advise you not to sit on a man's lap till you were his wife. It is quite customary with lovers, I know; but it seems to me to be letting down bars which should be left up. Engagements are so easily broken that there should be stricter lines drawn. Surely no true woman who has entered upon her second engagement wants to remember how she sat on the lap of the first betrothed. While there is no harm in so doing, you will be on the safe side not to.

It is wrong to take money from your betrothed. If you live on dry crusts and work till you drop, refuse it. Be married in calico rather than have his money buy your wedding-dress. Sometimes girls will urge a speedy wedding-day. You have no more right to do that than you have to ask him to marry you—the two go together. If he is too slow and you know of no reason why he should be, he does not care much for you; you had better break the engagement. However, if your heart would break with the engagement, try to make him more anxious to have you all to himself. It is not a girl's place to be eager for the marriage. If you are self-supporting and want to marry him because you are tired of working, you wrong him. No matter what reason you may have for wishing an early marriage, it is never your right to propose it.

Attentions from a married man are blasting to a girl's reputation. No matter how fascinating he is, how much you admire him, how much you like his attentions, refuse to accept them. He is desecrating the most sacred ordinance, marriage. He is insulting you and wronging his wife. Eventually he will return to her, leaving you with a tarnished name. His wife will forgive him, and society will forget he went astray; but his wife will never forgive you, and society will never forget it. You will always be spoken of as the girl that was "crazy after him." It will stand in the way of a marriage for you. Men do not care to marry a girl who has been talked about, or whose name was coupled with a married man's. You lose everything by it, almost your character. There is no such food for gossip as the attentions of a married man to a girl. They suspect you are not all you ought to be, they have good reason to do so. They may think if you will encourage a man to trample on his marriage vows, you would trample on your own. You are condemned by every one.

Your vanity may lead you to feel a degree of triumph in winning a husband from a wife. It is no triumph, however, to do so. The man who will be so won is in most cases extremely weak and decidedly untrue. It is not that your attractions are superior to hers, it is that he is fickle, and you were the first girl who accepts his unlawful love. Instead of being a triumph, it is a sin. Instead of being a subject for boasting, it is something to be ashamed of. Instead of encouraging him for one moment, flee from him. Instead of looking upon him as your lover, consider him your worst enemy: an enemy who for the selfish indulgence of the time would ruin your whole life. In this world of sin and sorrowful consequences of sin, you cannot be too careful of yourself, your conduct, and your associates. If a man is known by the company he keeps, much more is a girl. Much misery will come from one imprudent, maybe innocent, act. A trifle may sometimes be what starts you on the road to destruction. That road is broad, and very enticing to some; but the end is death. Never drink with a man. The pity of it that this should have to be written down! There is a class of girls who aim to be a little fast. They think they make themselves attractive to men by keeping pace with all their sins. They think men will like them if they have a "good time" with them. They call this a "good time." It is an unmitigated bad time; a time that will make you and him bad too. You will fail in your object, for you will not attract him. It is a low man who will care for a girl who cares so little for herself.

Instead of drinking with a man, keep him from doing so. Your power over men is very great, girls; it is much greater than you think. You can make him good or bad, if he loves you. If he is only your friend, you can help him withstand temptation and turn him from wrong. Try to exhibit the ideal woman always. Let your character be so elevated that you will raise the man who walks beside you. Be a pure, true girl, and he will be a better, purer man. The very thought of you, as he goes out into a sinful world and meets temptations of which you are ignorant, will be a shield to him. Next to the strength God can give him, will be the remembrance of your goodness and purity. He will, for your sake, abhor things which before had a fascination for him.

Always be wrapt in a cloak of sweet maidenly reserve and dignity. Then no tongue can assail you, no man will dare to offer you any familiarity; the conversation and conduct of men will take a better tone in your society.

Try to make every man you meet, even a passing acquaintance, better. Resolve that you will know no man whom you will not influence decidedly for good. So act that when you look back in after years you can honestly say that you tried to make every man whom you knew well, a Christian. So strive to lead young men to Christ that you will see the fruits of your efforts dotted all along your path of life. Let every man whom you know be able to say, as he looks back, "I have been a better man for knowing her."

In all your intercourse with men, do everything to ennoble and nothing to lower his character. "Let him see that you are a true woman and a Christian: one whose life is beautiful in its maidenly dignity and attractive loveliness."

CHAPTER VII.
THE SECRET OF THE WIDOW'S POWER.

There is no doubt that a widow can, if she choose, attract a man where a girl is powerless to do so. She has a charm which is irresistible when she pleases to exercise it. This power lies greatly in her knowledge of man-nature. It lies also in her taking a man just as he is. Instead of wounding his vanity by trying to make him conform to her ideas, she makes him pleased with himself as he is. Girls have sharp corners which hurt a man if he runs against them; widows never have. Girls are unkind; widows never are. Girls like to tease and ridicule a man; a widow is too wise to do so. Girls will wound even a man who is not sensitive; a widow sooths. Girls never remember a man's feelings; a widow never forgets them.

She has studied one man thoroughly. She knows his peculiarities, his weaknesses, his strong points, his likes and dislikes. In knowing one man well, she knows his sex. She has learned well what will please one man. In learning that she knows what will please all men. She has learned to sink her own individuality. She has learned to follow, and has no desire to lead. She knows that men like to be obeyed. She knows they like their ease. She knows they would rather be amused, entertained, than to dance attendance. She knows that the best way to entertain a man is to make him talk of himself or his hobby. She never minds how much he rides this hobby when he is with her. A girl would forbid its entrance. A widow may even get up and ride with him. When a girl would show a man she has no interest in his affairs, a widow would make him believe she was even more interested than he was. A girl would say, "I get so sick of hearing that man talk on that subject that I won't listen to him." The widow draws him out. Where a girl would cut him short, she encourages him to go on at length. He begins to connect her with his hobby. He learns to come eagerly to her with every new development, sure of sympathy. When he is downcast about it, he comes to her as quickly for the encouragement he is sure to get. He begins to feel that there is no one in the world who understands and appreciates him as she does. The rest soon follows.

A widow is sympathetic—she is sincere in that sympathy. She has suffered and feels for all who suffer. She can understand a heartache, because she knows what it is to have her dearest earthly hopes shattered. Her life is a disappointment, and she can weep with those who have been disappointed. She has found out that life is not a bed of roses only, but has many thorns. She will help sooth the wounds that thorns have made in other hearts. She knows that men have troubles, little or great; and she knows too much to give him any more. She has stood by one man as he has fought with the world, and knows that it is woman's province to strengthen him by her sympathy and helpful word for the battle. She knows that when a man seeks a woman's society he wants peace. She knows his vanity is wounded every day in his contact with men, and that when he comes to her he wants it flattered.

So a widow tries to make a man happy and comfortable. She rarely alludes to her own grief. It is more interesting because she does not. She mutely appeals for sympathy, while she gives that same sympathy. Few young girls know anything about sorrow; they cannot understand what it is. They are generally so full of themselves they cannot sympathize. Herein lies their weakness, and herein lies a widow's strength. Sympathy is a woman's greatest power. Girls are self-centred; a widow never is. A girl is absorbed in her own pleasure; a widow has learned to make the pleasures of another hers. A girl puts herself forward prominently; a widow sinks her personality. She has learned to do so. She knows the man with whom she is talking is more interested in himself than he is in her. She knows that no man cares as much for her interests, plans, hopes, as he does for his own; and she talks of his only. She lets him take the lead in the conversation, she follows.

A young girl has moods; a widow has none. She is always the same. A man is sure of her. He knows when he leaves her, she will be the same when he meets her again. I have known girls to lose an admirer by a cool greeting or change of demeanor. A widow never would. It is said that Madame Recamier's great charm was her gracious sweetness, which was under all circumstances the same.

A girl fancies that a man thinks of her all the time, as she does of him. She likely thinks of him all day and dreams of him by night. A man, out in the world, is engrossed in business—that is his first consideration. It is only his leisure he can give to her. He goes to her for his pleasure. A widow knows this. She has other things to occupy her mind, and comes as fresh to him as he does to her. She knows that he has not lived over and over her last remarks, and she has not dwelt upon his. She makes no mistakes in estimating his affection for her.

She never puts his affection to a test. Girls love to do so. A widow knows that it will have to be a pretty strong one that will stand it. She never makes any experiments. She knows him in and out. She knows what will please him and what will not please him. She knows what flatters his vanity and what will drive him away. Her lessons have been too thorough to allow any mistake.

Experience has taught her that the best way to win a man is to make him think more of himself. Experience has taught her that she can have her own way easily by proper management. A girl fights openly for her own way. She is unsuccessful as her plans are open.

A widow knows that the royal road to a man's heart lies through his stomach. Her little dinners and tempting lunches are a part of her mode of warfare. A man will always go where he can get a good dinner. He does not wait for a second invitation, and hardly a first. A man is always pleased with himself (unless he is a bad case of dyspepsia) when he has a good dinner. When he is pleased with himself, he is pleased with those about him.

When a man knows that an evening call means a pretty little lunch, he is quite sure to come again. He goes first for the sake of his stomach, and later for the sake of his heart.

A widow never forgets that the better friends she and the man become, the more likely he is to love her. With a man and woman there is but a short step from friendship to love. It has been said that there is no such thing as Platonic friendships between the two sexes. A widow knows that friendship ripens more quickly over the well-laden table than under any other circumstances. A girl trusts to romantic surroundings. A widow never does. She has found out that her hero was fleshly, and she knows that all men are. She knows that only a boy, wildly in love, prefers moonlight to a substantial meal.

If a girl takes a meal with a man it is always at his expense. A widow never allows a man to spend much, if any, money upon her. She knows just how little he cares about doing so. She has heard the opinion of one man strongly expressed on that subject. She will not put one stumbling-block in a man's way.

A widow knows how to dress. She knows just the kind of dresses a man likes. She rarely is given to display. She chooses quiet tones or continues to wear black. Costly apparel she is well aware will frighten away a man of limited means. She studies herself, and how to dress, so as to make the best of both. Her art is so perfect that it is hidden.

A widow is in no haste to wed. Many do not wish to do so at any time. She does not have to marry for a home: she either has inherited one or is able to support herself. She has no fear before her eyes of being an old maid. Years do not lessen her chances, as they do a girl's. She does not pretend to be young. Youth is not her attraction. In these respects she is as independent as a man. It is not matrimony alone she cares for, if she marries, but a congenial companion. If she does not meet the right one this year, she may the next. She can afford to wait.

A widow is conscious of her power. That gives her a good command of herself. She knows, from one man at least, if not from more, the full value of her charms. She knows her power to retain one man's love even until the end. She knows how to make a man happy. She has done so. She knows that what once won love will do so again. She knows a man's weak points: she knows his strong ones. She knows her own weak points: she may have been told of them very plainly. These she takes pains to strengthen.

Old bachelors are proverbially hard to win. When one does marry it is almost always a widow. She only seems to know how to attract him. She knows what a hard fight it will be, and sets deliberately about doing it. She knows he is selfish. Only a selfish man tries to avoid family ties and troubles. Your warm-hearted, unselfish men always marry. A widow is not shocked at his selfishness. She has not looked for perfection. She helps him be selfish. She makes him look upon her as one who will encourage his pet foibles. She shows him that she will help him with them; instead of having to give up for her "my dog and my cat," she will pet "my dog and my cat."

Yet a widow has a great drawback. There are some men at whom she can never get a chance. A man who does not wish to marry avoids a widow. He will pay attention to a young girl, perfectly sure he can withstand her charms; but the young widow is a different person. He knows that if he allows himself to begin there, he cannot break off. Dickens gave the key-note to the whole situation when he said, "Samivel, beware of the widders." For ages Samivels who do not wish to marry have obeyed that injunction.

CHAPTER VIII.
"LADY BEAUTY."

The following is quoted, verbatim, from an English novel entitled, "Lady Beauty; or, Charming to Her Latest Day." As it bears upon this subject, and many may not have read the book, I copy some parts.

"You will find that your own enjoyment is heightened by the consciousness of power to please others.... Let this ever be in your mind: 'I am a creature formed to give pleasure.' Be courteous, be gentle, be refined, be sweet in all your dealings. Never lose your temper: it ruins the face; and it always leaves a disagreeable impression which nothing rubs out. Depend upon it, men may respect those creatures who are called women of character, which generally means women who perform awkwardly duties which with a little thought they might perform in a charming way: men may respect them, but when they want enjoyment they turn to women who study the art of pleasing. Now, what I want to teach you is, to be solid and pleasing too. Believe me a woman is seldom called upon to do anything which she may not do in an agreeable style if she will only take pains.... Never disarrange for an instant the drapery of pleasantness which a woman ought always to wear: keep it on you even for your husbands.... Be agreeable even when you are alone with your look-ing-glass. Please everybody as far as you can. Study morning, noon, and night to be agreeable.

"Don't expect too much of men and women, and you will learn to be good-humored over their selfishness and hypocrisy.

"Learned talk is very affected. Be as well-educated as you please, but don't seem so.

"She had a frank, spontaneous sympathy with life all around and in every part, such as I never met in any one beside herself. By reason of this virtue she was always interested in what was going on, and the very quality which subdued her individuality in one way made her character fresh and delightful in another. She resolved to charm others with happiness and goodness in view, not mere society conquests.... She used worldly methods for most unworldly means. The polish, the graces, the social attractions, the accomplishments, literature, and wit, which some despise, she used as the very material out of which her noble purpose must be woven... In the secret interior of her intentions she was truly devoted, trying by the spell of a beautiful womanhood to make those with whom she lived better and happier.

"'Tell me about it,' she whispers, oh so low, so deliciously. She meant, 'Any-thing you say will be sweet to hear.'

"Too womanly for coquetry or coyness, she gave her answer at once.

"Warmth, purity, tenderness, principle, all the finer parts of character were hers... Her face was beautiful because it was the image of the soul.

"It is a good maxim: 'Never really be angry.'

"To the opposite, her sister relied on her beauty for a place among her sex, and was at no pains to cultivate conversation, letters, or any branch of the art of pleasing except the setting forth of her personal charms. Had her manner and her talk been what she might easily have made them, she would have shone out as a beauty in the prime of her womanhood. She had no lack of sense nor of education, either; but proudly reposing on her incontestable loveliness, she rather withdrew than put forward her attractions.

"I wish to convince women that it is a great mistake on their part to suppose that their power to please departs with youth. At all times I have noticed that men of sense seldom admire—or grow enamored of—women for beauty alone, but for character, manner, taste, and conversation. Now, while beauty, we must admit, lessens with time, character, manner, taste, and conversation may each be refined and enriched... Mere beauty is but one bright unchanging beam: it will even grow wearisome; but wit, sense, courtesy, and humanity are forever casting forth new and unexpected rays and enlivening intercourse with agreeable surprises.

"She was the best dresser I ever knew. Her appearance pleased numbers of people before they saw her face... She managed through all the changes of fashion to respect herself and her own figure and face: in the fashion she would always be; but still she would modulate it so as to be the queen and not the slave.

"Her manners in society were captivating. With what graceful attention she heard what you had to say. How modestly she gave her own opinion... She tried to please. She knew that a woman ought to be an object of admiration and affection, and she ruled her whole life with a view to this fact. Her religion gave a richness, a sweetness, a seriousness to all her charms.

"You will laugh when I tell you that Lady Beauty at the age of fifty-three had a new lover."

"BEAUTY RULES."

"Rule One.—A woman's power in the world is measured by her power to please. Whatever she will wish to accomplish, she will manage it best by pleasing. A woman's grand social aim should be to please.

"Rule Two.—Modesty is the ground on which all a woman's charms appear to the best advantage. In manner, dress, conversation, remember always that modesty must not be forgotten... Not prudery. Modesty is of the soul. Prudery is on the surface.

"Rule Three.—So the woman's aim is to please, and modesty is the first principle.

"Rule Four.—Always dress up to your age or a little beyond it. Let your face be the youngest thing about you, not the oldest.

"Rule Five.—Remember that what women admire in themselves is seldom what men admire in them.

"Rule Six.—Women's beauties are seldom men's beauties.

"Rule Seven.—Gayety tempered by seriousness is the happiest manner in society.

"Rule Eight.—Always speak low.

"Rule Nine.—A plain woman can never be pretty. She can always be fascinating if she takes pains. I remember well a man who was a great admirer of our sex telling me that one of the most fascinating women he ever knew was not only not pretty, but as to her face decidedly plain. 'Her figure,' he said, 'was neat, her dressing faultless, her every movement graceful; her conversation was clever and animated, and she always tried to please. She was one of the most acceptable women in society I ever knew. She married brilliantly.

"Rule Ten.—Every year a woman lives, the more pains she must take with her dress.

"Rule Eleven.—In all things, let a woman ask what will please a man of sense before she asks what will please the men of fashion. You see, if a woman lives for the commendation of men of fashion, she will, if pretty, piquant, or what not, have a reign of ten years. But if she remembers that she has charms of mind and character and taste, as well as charms of figure and complexion, the men of sense will follow her for a half century; and in the long run the men of fashion will be led by the men of sense.

"I have often asked myself, 'What is the secret of her character?' and I have always come to the same conclusion: that if her religious faith were deducted from her, she would not be what she is, but must become a less agreeable and not so good a woman."

CHAPTER IX.
THE LOVED WIFE.

Our life-story does not end, as it does in the novel, when the wedding-bells ring. After that comes the real life. The wedding-bells are but the call to more faithful duties, more earnest, unselfish love, greater effort to be attractive, more pains to make the husband happy than were taken to win his love. They ring out the birth of a love that is until death. They ring out the knell of all coyness and romance. The hero becomes the very human man: the shy girl is a woman who is to be his helpmeet. They ring out the beginning of a battle where man and woman must stand shoulder to shoulder if they would win. They tell of a conflict where there will be strength in union, but in division weakness, destruction of happiness, complete failure, disgrace, and sometimes even death.

A girl rarely considers the deep responsibilities she takes upon herself when she marries. She is more often thinking of the happiness it will give her than of what she is to be to the man. She does not stop to think whether or not she is going to make her husband happy. She forgets that from that time his whole happiness, his success in life, almost his soul, are in her keeping. "A man must ask his wife's leave to thrive" is altogether true. A wife may be a dead weight or an inspiration. The dead weight drags even the strongest down, and an inspiration helps him to conquer every time. I have heard a man with a bad wife say: "Oh, I have no heart in me to do anything. She takes it all out of me." I have known a man with less ability, but with a true wife to inspire him, to conquer where the other failed.

Marriage itself is not happiness unalloyed. Life never is in any state. You are happier married than single, but marriage has its hard places. The romance soon dies out. Real life comes. The every day living together brings friction. It is for better and for worse. It seems a light thing to say at the time when you are sure it will all be for the better. You fancy you have only half learned his goodness. In many cases that is so. In many more it is not: it is for the worse. Then the break comes. Gradually his weaknesses will be revealed to you. The golden idol shows clay feet. Slowly the gilding is all rubbed off, and the idol is seen to be clay all through. Many a woman meets with this disappointment. It is the great disappointment of her life. God help the woman who finds that her husband is unworthy of her love! A weak woman sinks under the blow, and drags him even farther down. A strong woman will stand up bravely and in the end draw him up to her heights.

She must gather together all her love for him. She must allow religion to take the helm with this love or all is lost. Sometimes love reels: sometimes the senses do. Then, of all times, a woman must watch herself well. She is fighting a terrible battle with her disappointment as well as with his faults. They must be silent battles: the more silent the stronger they will be, and the more sure she will be of victory. She must never by hint or word let any one outside know of his failings. If they are of the kind which go before or which are well known by the community, she must show the world that she is blind to them. She must never speak against her husband even to her own mother. She must never admit that he has a fault. She has entered into a partnership where one partner cannot be untrue to the other. She has promised before God to honor him. Her loyalty may save him. It is certain that if she does talk about him, and it comes to his ears, it will drive him away from her. When a breach is made between husband and wife, it widens continually. What in the beginning is a tiny thread soon becomes a broad gulf. It is really wonderful what a little while it takes for this breach to widen, and how disastrous are the effects. Our daily papers are a continual illustration of that fact.

A perfect wife will never allow her opinion of her unworthy husband to be known. If he is unkind to her, she hides it as she hides her own misdeeds.

Indeed, she would rather take upon herself the blame for any trouble others may have seen. She is pleased always with any kind attention he receives. A lady wrote her sister, with whom her husband was stopping for a few days: "He writes me you are doing every thing to make his visit pleasant. Thank you. Whatever kindness you bestow upon him you bestow upon me."

You will find plenty of listeners when you tell of your husband's faults and your own wrongs. They will be your apparent sympathizers. Not one, however, will respect you for doing so. No one will care about you. Almost all will repeat it to some one else. It will be generally said that you live unhappily with your husband. You will have as much blame as he has. It is the way of the world. It knows pretty well that the wife who so far forgets herself as to talk against her husband is as much to blame for the trouble as he is. She cannot be a good, loving, Christian wife, who is trying to lead him to better things. Such a woman would hold her tongue. In telling, you have simply opened all the doors and windows of your house and invited the community to look their fill at your most private affairs. The rest of the doors and windows of the community are closed. You have noticed—have you not?—that your confidence has not been returned. No, indeed. It is well known that the woman who cannot guard her husband's honor cannot respect another's confidence. If only in the sight of men then, the untrue wife is the loser. She sends him into greater wrong. She undoes herself as she undoes him. Together they must rise or fall. Many a woman in her blind anger at her husband has tried to crush him. Like Samson, when he would crush the Philistines, she has succeeded, but only to bury herself in the ruins with him.

That her husband is not what she thought him, is no excuse: she took him for worse as well as better. She is simply showing that she is not one whit above him, and that he has been decidedly deceived in her. He has gotten the worse too.

Unfortunately true, good men have bad wives, too—they are not confined to bad husbands only. There are wives of good men who forget that the husband's whole happiness depends upon them. Many a wife forgets this great responsibility. His business may be successful and everything outside going along satisfactorily, but if he has no peace at home he has no happiness. A woman who does not make her husband happy fails in her great life-work. She is unworthy to be the mother of his children. God gave woman to man to be his helpmeet; she is no helpmeet if she makes his life wretched. It is her highest pleasure, her great "rights," to smooth his path. If she fail there, she far better never have married.

What a man wants in his wife is companionship, sympathy, and love. He wants to feel that she is his best friend. He never wants to look anywhere else for sympathy and help: he never will if he can get all he needs from her. His life has many hard places: he needs a companion to go over them with him. He is often overtaken by misfortunes: he needs some one to stand by him and sympathize as she helps him to bear them. He has to fight with poverty often, and he needs a woman whom he feels, when he puts his arms about her, is worth fighting for. He has many enemies: he needs a wife whose loving words will make up for the bitter ones he hears from them. He needs a wife who will make him forget, when he is in her presence, that there is an unkind world outside. He meets sin everywhere: he wants a wife who will give him words of counsel, and who will take his hands and lead him to greater faith in, and love for, the Father. Storms will come all through life, he must encounter them. He needs a woman who will cling to him through the hardest. He needs her love through sunshine and victory as well.

He wants to feel through all that his refuge is in her arms as hers is in his. He wants a wife upon whose breast he can lay his head, when sorrows come, and weep. He wants one who will make him feel that no matter where else death strikes, as long as he has her he can endure life. I remember a man who, when his dearly-beloved sister died, laid his head on his wife's shoulder, weeping, and said, "If it were you I should die."

There are in history women upon whose strong hearts strong men have leaned and have become more strengthened in that leaning. Weak men have become manly through a womanly wife. Strong men have been weakened by a weak, wicked wife. Truly a man is made or marred when he marries. He must indeed ask his wife leave to thrive.

It is in every woman's power to be a well-loved wife. She cannot exact it: she must win it. She has his affection to start upon. She must increase it, instead of allowing it to decrease. She must not go upon the principle that because she is his wife it is his duty to worship her. If she does, she will be bankrupt as far as his affection is concerned. Men are not made in that way, as I have said before, and you must take them as you find them if you take one at all. Many a wife has allowed her husband's affection to die. She has fancied, maybe, that she was lowering her dignity to try to keep what she considered was her due. Nothing is our due of which we are not worthy. We are not worthy of a love we do not try to keep. Women who are exacting after marriage are generally the ones who tried the hardest to attract the man at first. It is generally the girl who runs after a man till she gets him who makes no effort after marriage to retain his love, and who talks the loudest about her "rights, and not grovelling at his feet," if it is suggested that she do better.

Before she married she dressed for him. Nothing she owned was too pretty to put on when she knew he would see her. She was careful to be tidy in her person. She would never let him see a room in her home which was in disorder. She was courteous always. She never said an impatient word to him or before him. If he was cross, she bore it like an angel. She greeted him always when he came with a sweet smile and caress. She had loving words for him as she told him how she wanted to see him every minute since they had parted. She desired in every way to appear at her best before him. She hid every defect of temper or disposition.

After marriage she does not care how untidy she is when he comes home. She never thinks of dressing for him. She is not courteous to him. She has no loving word, and she never hesitates to speak a cross one to him. She has smiles yet for the outside world, but none for the man whom she has promised to love and honor. She talks to him as she would be ashamed to have any one hear her speak. She never bears with him. If he is cross, she is crosser. Is it any wonder she loses his love? She is not what he thought she was, or what he thought he was marrying. If he had seen her in her true colors before the fatal words were spoken, he never would have bound himself to her. The beautiful soul, the sweet smile that won him, are gone. The gentle spirit he fancied he detected, was a delusion. What he loved, he does not possess. He possesses an unwomanly wife, and that he did not woo. With a weak man there comes a break. He often seeks his happiness with another woman. A strong man endures in silence, growing old and sad, broken in his youth.

Ought this to be? There is no reason, because you have grown familiar to each other, you should not try to hide your temper as you did before. There is no reason, because he is "caught" and cannot get away from you, that you should cease to be attractive to him. You spread your net well. Now make the nest so attractive that he will be glad that he was "caught." Be all that you led him to fancy you were.

Why should not a woman dress for her husband? Why should she not cultivate a sweet disposition for him and endeavor to make his home the happiest spot on earth? Why not try to banish from it every cloud, everything that will annoy or irritate? Is it of no use? It is of the greatest earthly use. It is a means of helping you both on to Heaven. If you must be selfish, remember it is making yourself happier to have your husband love you as he loves no other earthly being. Men, after all, are easily pleased—you found that out in your courtship days. They are easily managed too. A man will do almost everything for the wife that makes him happy. He is almost too much of a slave to her. She can do what she will to him. With him, getting her own way is only a matter of tact and sweetness. Husbands are almost all like the man in the fable of the wind and sun. The sun beat in the end. Warmth of love and sweetness of manner will gain a victory, where an ill-tempered insisting upon "rights" fails completely.

Ward McAllister says in his "Society as I Have Found It," "My advice to all married women is to keep up flirting with their husbands as much after marriage as before; to make themselves as attractive after their marriage as they were when they captivated them; not to neglect their toilet, but rather to improve it: to be as coquettish and coy after they are bound together as before when no ties held them."

THE
LADIES' BOOK OF ETIQUETTE,
AND
MANUAL OF POLITENESS.

A COMPLETE HAND BOOK FOR THE USE
OF THE LADY IN POLITE SOCIETY.

CONTAINING

FULL DIRECTIONS FOR CORRECT MANNERS, DRESS,
DEPORTMENT, AND CONVERSATION; RULES FOR THE DUTIES
OF BOTH HOSTESS AND GUEST IN MORNING RECEPTIONS,
DINNER COMPANIES, VISITING, EVENING PARTIES AND BALLS;
A COMPLETE GUIDE FOR LETTER WRITING AND CARDS OF
COMPLIMENT; HINTS ON MANAGING SERVANTS, ON THE
PRESERVATION OF HEALTH, AND ON ACCOMPLISHMENTS.

AND ALSO

USEFUL RECEIPTS FOR THE COMPLEXION, HAIR, AND WITH
HINTS AND DIRECTIONS FOR THE CARE OF THE WARDROBE.

BY
FLORENCE HARTLEY,
AUTHOR OF THE "LADIES' HAND BOOK OF
FANCY AND ORNAMENTAL WORK."

INTRODUCTION.

I N PREPARING A BOOK OF ETIQUETTE for ladies, I would lay down as the first rule, "Do unto others as you would others should do to you." You can never be rude if you bear the rule always in mind, for what lady likes to be treated rudely? True Christian politeness will always be the result of an unselfish regard for the feelings of others, and though you may err in the ceremonious points of etiquette, you will never be impolite.

Politeness, founded upon such a rule, becomes the expression, in graceful manner, of social virtues. The spirit of politeness consists in a certain attention to forms and ceremonies, which are meant both to please others and ourselves, and to make others pleased with us; a still clearer definition may be given by saying that politeness is goodness of heart put into daily practice; there can be no *true* politeness without kindness, purity, singleness of heart, and sensibility.

Many believe that politeness is but a mask worn in the world to conceal bad passions and impulses, and to make a show of possessing virtues not really existing in the heart; thus, that politeness is merely hypocrisy and dissimulation. Do not believe this; be certain that those who profess such a doctrine are practising themselves the deceit they condemn so much. Such people scout politeness, because, to be truly a lady, one must carry the principles into every circumstance of life, into the family circle, the most intimate friendship, and never forget to extend the gentle courtesies of life to every one. This they find too much trouble, and so deride the idea of being polite and call it deceitfulness.

True politeness is the language of a good heart, and those possessing that heart will never, under any circumstances, be rude. They may not enter a crowded saloon gracefully; they may be entirely ignorant of the *forms* of good society; they may be awkward at table, ungrammatical in speech; but they will never be heard speaking so as to wound the feelings of another; they will never be seen making others uncomfortable by seeking solely for their own *personal* convenience; they will always endeavor to set every one around them at ease; they will be self-sacrificing, friendly, unselfish; truly in word and deed, *polite*. Give to such a woman the knowledge of the forms and customs of society, teach her how best to show the gentle courtesies of life, and you have a *lady*, created by God, only indebted for the *outward* polish to the world.

It is true that society demands this same unselfishness and courtesy, but when there is no heart in the work, the time is frittered away on the mere ceremonies, forms of etiquette, and customs of society, and this politeness seeks only its own ends; to be known as courteous, spoken of as lady-like, and not beloved as unselfish and womanly.

Etiquette exists in some form in all countries, has existed and will exist in all ages. From the rudest savage who dares not approach his ignorant, barbarous ruler without certain forms and ceremonies, to the most polished courts in Europe, or the home circles of America, etiquette reigns.

True politeness will be found, its basis in the human heart, the same in all these varied scenes and situations, but the outward forms of etiquette will vary everywhere. Even in the same scene, time will alter every form, and render the exquisite polish of last year, obsolete rudeness next year.

Politeness, being based upon real kindness of heart, cannot exist where there is selfishness or brutality to warp its growth. It is founded upon love of the neighbor, and a desire to be beloved, and to show love. Thus, where such pure, noble feelings do not exist, the mere forms of politeness become hypocrisy and deceit.

Rudeness will repel, where courtesy would attract friends.

Never by word or action notice the defects of another; be charitable, for all need charity. Remember who said, "Let him that is without fault cast the first stone." Remember that the laws of politeness require the consideration of the feelings of others; the endeavor to make every one feel at ease; and frank courtesy towards all. Never meet rudeness in others with rudeness upon your own part; even the most brutal and impolite will be more shamed by being met with courtesy and kindness, than by any attempt to annoy them by insolence on your part.

Politeness forbids any display of resentment. The polished surface throws back the arrow.

Remember that a favor becomes doubly valuable if granted with courtesy, and that the pain of a refusal may be softened if the manner expresses polite regret.

Kindness, even to the most humble, will never lose anything by being offered in a gentle, courteous manner, and the most common-place action will admit of grace and ease in its execution.

Let every action, while it is finished in strict accordance with etiquette, be, at the same time, easy, as if dictated solely by the heart.

To be truly polite, remember you must be polite at *all* times, and under *all* circumstances.

CHAPTER I.
CONVERSATION.

THE ART OF CONVERSATION CONSISTS IN the exercise of two fine qualities. You must originate, and you must sympathize; you must possess at the same time the habit of communicating and of listening attentively. The union is rare but irresistible. None but an excessively ill-bred person will allow her attention to wander from the person with whom she is conversing; and especially she will never, while seeming to be entirely attentive to her companion, answer a remark or question made to another person, in another group. Unless the conversation be general among a party of friends, confine your remarks and attention entirely to the person with whom you are conversing. Steele says, "I would establish but one great general rule in conversation, which is this—that people should not talk to please themselves, but those who hear them. This would make them consider whether what they speak be worth hearing; whether there be either wit or sense in what they are about to say; and whether it be adapted to the time when, the place where, and the person to whom, it is spoken."

Be careful in conversation to avoid topics which may be supposed to have any direct reference to events or circumstances which may be painful for your companion to hear discussed; you may unintentionally start a subject which annoys or troubles the friend with whom you may be conversing; in that case, do not stop abruptly, when you perceive that it causes pain, and, above all, do not make the matter worse by apologizing; turn to another subject as soon as possible, and pay no attention to the agitation your unfortunate remark may have excited. Many persons will, for the sake of appearing witty or smart, wound the feelings of another deeply; avoid this; it is not only ill-bred, but cruel.

Remember that having all the talk sustained by one person is not conversation; do not engross all the attention yourself, by refusing to allow another person an opportunity to speak, and also avoid the other extreme of total silence, or answering only in monosyllables.

If your companion relates an incident or tells a story, be very careful not to interrupt her by questions, even if you do not clearly understand her; wait until she has finished her relation, and then ask any questions you may desire. There is nothing more annoying than to be so interrupted. I have heard a story told to an impertinent listener, which ran in this way:—

"I saw a fearful sight—"

"When?"

"I was about to tell you; last Monday, on the train—"

"What train?"

"The train from B———. We were near the bridge—"

"What bridge?"

"I will tell you all about it, if you will only let me speak. I was coming from B———"

"Last Monday, did you say?"

and so on. The story was interrupted at every sentence, and the relator condemned as a most tedious story-teller, when, had he been permitted to go forward, he would have made the incident interesting and short.

Never interrupt any one who is speaking. It is very ill-bred. If you see that a person to whom you wish to speak is being addressed by another person, never speak until she has heard and replied; until her conversation with that person is finished. No truly polite lady ever breaks in upon a conversation or interrupts another speaker.

Never, in speaking to a married lady, enquire for her *husband*, or, if a gentleman, ask for his *wife*. The elegant way is to call the absent party by their name; ask Mr. Smith how Mrs. Smith is, or enquire of Mrs. Jones for Mr. Jones, but never for "your husband" or "your wife." On the other hand, if you are married, never speak of your husband as your "lord," "husband," or "good man," avoid, also, unless amongst relatives, calling him by his Christian name. If you wish others to respect him, show by speaking of him in respectful terms that you do so yourself. If either your own husband or your friend's is in the army or navy, or can claim the Dr., Prof., or any other prefix to his name, there is no impropriety in speaking of him as the colonel, doctor, or whatever his title may be.

It is a mark of ill-breeding to use French phrases or words, unless you are sure your companion is a French scholar, and, even then, it is best to avoid them. Above all, do not use any foreign word or phrase, unless you have the language perfectly at your command. I heard a lady once use a Spanish quotation; she had mastered that one sentence alone; but a Cuban gentleman, delighted to meet an American who could converse with him in his own tongue, immediately addressed her in Spanish. Embarrassed and ashamed, she was obliged to confess that her knowledge of the language was confined to one quotation.

Never anticipate the point or joke of any anecdote told in your presence. If *you* have heard the story before, it may be new to others, and the narrator should always be allowed to finish it in his own words. To take any sentence from the mouth of another person, before he has time to utter it, is the height of ill-breeding. Avoid it carefully.

Never use the phrases, "What-d-ye call it," "Thingummy," "What's his name," or any such substitutes for a proper name or place. If you cannot recall the names you wish to use, it is better not to tell the story or incident connected with them. No lady of high breeding will ever use these substitutes in conversation.

Be careful always to speak in a distinct, clear voice; at the same time avoid talking too loudly, there is a happy medium between mumbling and screaming. Strive to attain it.

Overlook the deficiencies of others when conversing with them, as they may be the results of ignorance, and impossible to correct. Never pain another person by correcting, before others, a word or phrase mispronounced or ungrammatically constructed. If your intimacy will allow it, speak of the fault upon another occasion, kindly and privately, or let it pass. Do not be continually watching for faults, that you may display your own superior wisdom in correcting them. Let modesty and kind feeling govern your conversation, as other rules of life. If, on the other hand, your companion uses words or expressions which you cannot understand, do not affect knowledge, or be ashamed of your ignorance, but frankly ask for an explanation.

In conversing with professional gentlemen, never question them upon matters connected with their employment. An author may communicate, voluntarily, information interesting to you, upon the subject of his works, but any questions from you would be extremely rude. If you meet a physician who is attending a friend, you may enquire for their progress, but do not expect him to give you a detailed account of the disease and his manner of treating it. The same rule applies to questioning lawyers about their clients, artists on their paintings, merchants or mechanics of their several branches of business. Professional or business men, when with ladies, generally wish for miscellaneous subjects of conversation, and, as their visits are for recreation, they will feel excessively annoyed if obliged to "talk shop." Still many men can converse on no other subject than their every day employment. In this case listen politely, and show your interest. You will probably gain useful information in such conversation.

Never question the veracity of any statement made in general conversation. If you are certain a statement is false, and it is injurious to another person, who may be absent, you may quietly and courteously inform the speaker that he is mistaken, but if the falsehood is of no consequence, let it pass. If a statement appears monstrous, but you do not *know* that it is false, listen, but do not question its veracity. It may be true, though it strikes you as improbable.

Never attempt to disparage an absent friend. It is the height of meanness. If others admire her, and you do not, let them have their opinion in peace; you will probably fail if you try to lower her in their esteem, and gain for yourself the character of an ill-natured, envious person.

In conversing with foreigners, if they speak slightingly of the manners of your country, do not retort rudely, or resentfully. If their views are wrong, converse upon the subject, giving them frankly your views, but never retaliate by telling them that some custom of their own country is worse. A gentleman or lady of true refinement will always give your words candid consideration, and admit that an American may possibly know the customs of her country better than they do, and if your opponent is not well-bred, your rudeness will not improve his manners. Let the conversation upon national subjects be candid, and at the same time courteous, and leave him to think that the *ladies* in America are well-bred, however much he may dislike some little national peculiarity.

Avoid, at all times, mentioning subjects or incidents that can in any way disgust your hearers. Many persons will enter into the details of sicknesses which should be mentioned only when absolutely necessary, or describe the most revolting scenes before a room full of people, or even at table. Others speak of vermin, noxious plants, or instances of uncleanliness. All such conversation or allusion is excessively ill-bred. It is not only annoying, but absolutely sickening to some, and a truly lady-like person will avoid all such topics.

I cannot too severely censure the habit of using sentences which admit of a double meaning. It is not only ill-bred, but indelicate, and no person of true refinement will ever do it. If you are so unfortunate as to converse with one who uses such phrases, never by word, look, or sign show that you understand any meaning beyond the plain, outspoken language.

Avoid always any discussion upon religious topics, unless you are perfectly certain that your remarks cannot annoy or pain any one present. If you are tête-à-tête with a friend, and such a discussion arises, inquire your companion's church and mention your own, that you may yourself avoid unpleasant remarks, and caution him.

Never, when advancing an opinion, assert positively that a thing "*is so,*" but give your opinion *as* an opinion. Say, "I think this is so," or "these are *my* views," but remember that your companion may be better informed upon the subject under discussion, or, where it is a mere matter of taste or feeling, do not expect that all the world will feel exactly as you do.

Never repeat to a person with whom you converse, any unpleasant speech you may have heard concerning her. If you can give her pleasure by the repetition of a delicate compliment, or token of approval shown by a mutual friend, tell her the pleasant speech or incident, but do not hurt her feelings, or involve her in a quarrel by the repetition of ill-natured remarks.

Amongst well-bred persons, every conversation is considered in a measure confidential. A lady or gentleman tacitly confides in you when he (or she) tells you an incident which may cause trouble if repeated, and you violate a confidence as much in such a repetition, as if you were bound over to secrecy. Remember this.

Never criticise a companion's dress, or indeed make any remark whatever upon it. If a near friend, you may, if sincere, admire any article, but with a mere acquaintance let it pass unnoticed. If, however, any accident has happened to the dress, of which she is ignorant, tell her of it, and assist her in repairing the mischief.

To be able to converse really well, you must read much, treasure in your memory the pearls of what you read; you must have a quick comprehension, observe passing events, and listen attentively whenever there is any opportunity of acquiring knowledge. A quick tact is necessary, too, in conversation. To converse with an entirely uneducated person upon literature, interlarding your remarks with quotations, is ill-bred. It places them in an awkward situation, and does not add to your popularity. In conversing with persons of refinement and intelligence, do not endeavor to attract their admiration by pouring forth every item of your own information upon the subject under consideration, but listen as well as talk, and modestly follow their lead. I do not mean, to assent to any opinion they may advance, if you really differ in your own tastes, but do not be *too* ready to show your superior judgment or information. Avoid argument; it is not conversation, and frequently leads to ill feeling. If you are unfortunately drawn into an argument, keep your temper under perfect control, and if you find your adversary is getting too warm, endeavor to introduce some other topic.

Avoid carefully any allusion to the age or personal defects of your companion, or any one who may be in the room, and be very careful in your language when speaking of a stranger to another person. I have heard a lady inquire of a gentleman, "who that frightful girl in blue could be," and receive the information that the lady in question was the gentleman's own sister.

Be careful, when traveling, not to wound the feelings of your friends in another country or city, by underrating their native place, or attempting to prove the superiority of your own home over theirs.

Very young girls are apt to suppose, from what they observe in older ones, that there is some particular manner to be put on, in talking to gentlemen, and, not knowing exactly what it is, they are embarrassed and reserved; others observe certain airs and looks, used by their elders in this intercourse, and try to imitate them, as a necessary part of company behaviours, and, so become affected, and lose that first of charms, simplicity, natural grace. To such, let me say, your companions are in error; it requires no peculiar manner, nothing to be put on, in order to converse with gentlemen, any more than with ladies; and the more pure and elevated your sentiments are, and the better cultivated your intellect is, the easier will you find it to converse pleasantly with all. One good rule can be always followed by young ladies; to converse with a lady friend as if there were gentlemen present, and to converse with a gentleman as if in the room with other ladies.

Avoid affectation; it is the sure test of a deceitful, vulgar mind. The best cure is to try to have those virtues which you would affect, and then they will appear naturally.

CHAPTER II.
DRESS.

"A lady is never so well dressed as when you cannot remember what she wears."

No truer remark than the above was ever made. Such an effect can only be produced where every part of the dress harmonizes entirely with the other parts, where each color or shade suits the wearer's style completely, and where there is perfect neatness in each detail. One glaring color, or conspicuous article, would entirely mar the beauty of such a dress. It is, unfortunately, too much the custom in America to wear any article, or shape in make, that is fashionable, without any regard to the style of the person purchasing goods. If it is the fashion it must be worn, though it may greatly exaggerate a slight personal defect, or conceal or mar what would otherwise be a beauty. It requires the exercise of some judgment to decide how far an individual may follow the dictates of fashion, in order to avoid the appearance of eccentricity, and yet wear what is peculiarly becoming to her own face or figure. Another fault of our fair countrywomen is their extravagance in dress. No better advice can be given to a young person than to dress always according to her circumstances. She will be more respected with a simple wardrobe, if it is known either that she is dependent upon her own exertions for support, or is saving a husband or father from unnecessary outlay, than if she wore the most costly fabrics, and by so doing incurred debt or burdened her relatives with heavy, unwarrantable expense. If neatness, consistency, and good taste, preside over the wardrobe of a lady, expensive fabrics will not be needed; for with the simplest materials, harmony of color, accurate fitting to the figure, and perfect neatness, she will always appear well dressed.

GENERAL RULES.

NEATNESS—This is the first of all rules to be observed with regard to dress. Perfect cleanliness and careful adjustment of each article in the dress are indispensable in a finished toilet. Let the hair be always smooth and becomingly arranged, each article exquisitely clean, neat collar and sleeves, and tidy shoes and stockings, and the simplest dress will appear well, while a torn or soiled collar, rough hair, or untidy feet will entirely ruin the effect of the most costly and elaborate dress. The many articles required in a lady's wardrobe make a neat arrangement of her drawers and closets necessary, and also require care in selecting and keeping goods in proper order. A fine collar or lace, if tumbled or soiled, will lose its beauty when contrasted with the same article in the coarsest material perfectly pure and smooth. Each article of dress, when taken off, should be placed carefully and smoothly in its proper place. Nice dresses should be hung up by a loop on the inside of the waistband, with the skirts turned inside out, and the body turned inside of the skirt. Cloaks should hang in smooth folds from a loop on the inside of the neck. Shawls should be always folded in the creases in which they were purchased. All fine articles, lace, embroidery, and handkerchiefs, should be placed by themselves in a drawer, always laid out smoothly, and kept from dust. Furs should be kept in a box, alone, and in summer carefully packed, with a quantity of lump camphor to protect from moths. The bonnet should always rest upon a stand in the band-box, as the shape and trimming will both be injured by letting it lie either on the face, sides, or crown.

ADAPTIVENESS—Let each dress worn by a lady be suitable to the occasion upon which she wears it. A toilet may be as offensive to good taste and propriety by being too elaborate, as by being slovenly. Never wear a dress which is out of place or out of season under the impression that "it will do for once," or "nobody will notice it." It is in as bad taste to receive your morning calls in an elaborate evening dress, as it would be to attend a ball in your morning wrapper.

HARMONY—To appear well dressed without harmony, both in color and materials, is impossible. When arranging any dress, whether for home, street, or evening, be careful that each color harmonizes well with the rest, and let no one article, by its glaring costliness, make all the rest appear mean. A costly lace worn over a thin, flimsy silk, will only make the dress appear poorer, not, as some suppose, hide its defects. A rich trimming looks as badly upon a cheap dress, as a mean one does upon an expensive fabric. Observe this rule always in purchasing goods. One costly article will entirely ruin the harmony in a dress, which, without it, though plain and inexpensive, would be becoming and beautiful. Do not save on the dress or cloak to buy a more elaborate bonnet, but let the cost be well equalized and the effect will be good. A plain merino or dark silk, with a cloth cloak, will look much better than the most expensive velvet cloak over a cheap delaine dress.

FASHION—Do not be too submissive to the dictates of fashion; at the same time avoid oddity or eccentricity in your dress. There are some persons who will follow, in defiance of taste and judgment, the fashion to its most extreme point; this is a sure mark of vulgarity. Every new style of dress will admit of adaptation to individual cases, thus producing a pleasing, as well as fashionable effect. Not only good taste, but health is often sacrificed to the silly error of dressing in the extreme of fashion. Be careful to have your dress comfortable and becoming, and let the prevailing mode come into secondary consideration; avoiding, always, the other extreme of oddity or eccentricity in costume.

STYLE AND FORM OF DRESS—Be always careful when making up the various parts of your wardrobe, that each article fits you accurately. Not in the outside garments alone must this rule be followed, an ill-fitting pair of corsets, or wrinkles in any other article of the under-clothes, will make a dress set badly, even if it has been itself fitted with the utmost accuracy. A stocking which is too large, will make the boot uncomfortably tight, and too small will compress the foot, making the shoe loose and untidy. In a dress, no outlay upon the material will compensate for a badly fitting garment. A cheap calico made to fit the form accurately and easily, will give the wearer a more lady-like air than the richest silk which either wrinkles or is too tightly strained over the figure. Collars or sleeves, pinned over or tightly strained to meet, will entirely mar the effect of the prettiest dress.

ECONOMY—And by economy I do not mean mere cheapness. To buy a poor, flimsy fabric merely because the price is low, is extravagance, not economy; still worse if you buy articles because they are offered cheap, when you have no use for them. In purchasing goods for the wardrobe, let each material be the best of its kind. The same amount of sewing that is put into a good material, must be put into a poor one, and, as the latter will very soon wash or wear out, there must be another one to supply its place, purchased and made up, when, by buying a good article at first, this time and labor might have been saved. A good, strong material will be found cheapest in the end, though the actual expenditure of money may be larger at first.

COMFORT—Many ladies have to trace months of severe suffering to an improper disregard of comfort, in preparing their wardrobe, or in exposure after they are dressed. The most exquisite ball costume will never compensate for the injury done by tight lacing, the prettiest foot is dearly paid for by the pain a tight boot entails, and the most graceful effects will not prevent suffering from exposure to cold. A light ball dress and exquisite arrangement of the hair, too often make the wearer dare the inclemency of the coldest night, by wearing a light shawl or hood, to prevent crushing delicate lace or flowers. Make it a fixed rule to have the head, feet, and chest well protected when going to a party, even at the risk of a crushed flower or a stray curl. Many a fair head has been laid in a coffin, a victim to consumption, from rashly venturing out of a heated ball room, flushed and excited, with only a light protection against keen night air. The excitement of the occasion may prevent immediate discomfort in such cases, but it adds to the subsequent danger.

DETAILS—Be careful always that the details of your dress are perfectly finished in every point. The small articles of a wardrobe require constant care to keep in perfect order, yet they will wofully revenge themselves if neglected. Let the collar, handkerchief, boots, gloves, and belts be always whole, neat, and adapted to the dress. A lace collar will look as badly over a chintz dress, as a linen one would with velvet, though each may be perfect of its kind. Attention to these minor points are sure tests of taste in a lady's dress. A shabby or ill fitting boot or glove will ruin the most elaborate walking dress, while one of much plainer make and coarser fabric will be becoming and lady-like, if all the details are accurately fitted, clean, and well put on. In arranging a dress for every occasion, be careful that there is no missing string, hook, or button, that the folds hang well, and that every part is even and properly adjusted. Let the skirts hang smoothly, the outside ones being always about an inch longer than the under ones; let the dress set smoothly, carefully hooked or buttoned; let the collar fit neatly, and be fastened firmly and smoothly at the throat; let shoes and stockings be whole, clean, and fit nicely; let the hair be smooth and glossy, the skin pure, and the colors and fabric of your dress harmonize and be suitable for the occasion, and you will always appear both lady-like and well-dressed.

HOME DRESSES.

MORNING DRESS—The most suitable dress for breakfast, is a wrapper made to fit the figure loosely, and the material, excepting when the winter weather requires woolen goods, should be of chintz, gingham, brilliante, or muslin. A lady who has children, or one accustomed to perform for herself light household duties, will soon find the advantage of wearing materials that will wash. A large apron of domestic gingham, which can be taken off, if the wearer is called to see unexpected visitors, will protect the front of the dress, and save washing the wrapper too frequently. If a lady's domestic duties require her attention for several hours in the morning, whilst her list of acquaintances is large, and she has frequent morning calls, it is best to dress for callers before breakfast, and wear over this dress a loose sack and skirt of domestic gingham. This, while protecting the dress perfectly, can be taken off at a moment's notice if callers are announced. Married ladies often wear a cap in the morning, and lately, young girls have adopted the fashion. It is much better to let the hair be perfectly smooth, requiring no cap, which is often worn to conceal the lazy, slovenly arrangement of the hair. A few moments given to making the hair smooth and presentable without any covering, will not be wasted. Slippers of embroidered cloth are prettiest with a wrapper, and in summer black morocco is the most suitable for the house in the morning.

DRESS FOR MORNING VISITS—A lady should never receive her morning callers in a wrapper, unless they call at an unusually early hour, or some unexpected demand upon her time makes it impossible to change her dress after breakfast. On the other hand, an elaborate costume before dinner is in excessively bad taste. The dress should be made to fit the figure neatly, finished at the throat and wrists by an embroidered collar and cuffs, and, unless there is a necessity for it, in loss of the hair or age, there should be no cap or head dress worn. A wrapper made with handsome trimming, open over a pretty white skirt, may be worn with propriety; but the simple dress worn for breakfast, or in the exercise of domestic duties, is not suitable for the parlor when receiving visits of ceremony in the morning.

EVENING DRESS—The home evening dress should be varied according to circumstances. If no visitor is expected, the dress worn in the morning is suitable for the evening; but to receive visitors, it should be of lighter material, and a light head-dress may be worn. For young ladies, at home, ribbon or velvet are the most suitable materials for a head-dress. Flowers, unless they be natural ones in summer, are in very bad taste, excepting in cases where a party of invited guests are expected. Dark silk in winter, and thin material in summer, make the most suitable dresses for evening, and the reception of the chance-guests ladies in society may usually expect.

WALKING DRESSES—Walking dresses, to be in good taste, should be of quiet colors, and never conspicuous. Browns, modes, and neutral tints, with black and white, make the prettiest dresses for the street. Above all, avoid wearing several bright colors. One may be worn with perfect propriety to take off the sombre effect of a dress of brown or black, but do not let it be too glaring, and wear but little of it. Let the boots be sufficiently strong and thick to protect the feet from damp or dust, and wear always neat, clean, nicely fitting gloves.

The entire effect of the most tasteful costume will be ruined if attention is not paid to the details of dress. A soiled bonnet cap, untidy strings, or torn gloves and collar will utterly spoil the prettiest costume. There is no surer mark of vulgarity than over dressing or gay dressing in the street. Let the materials be of the costliest kind, if you will, but do not either wear the exaggerations of the fashion, or conspicuous colors. Let good taste dictate the limits where fashion may rule, and let the colors harmonize well, and be of such tints as will not attract attention.

For Morning Calls—The dress should be plain, and in winter furs and dark gloves may be worn.

For Bridal Calls—The dress should be of light silk, the bonnet dressy, and either a rich shawl or light cloak; no furs, and light gloves. In summer, a lace or silk mantle and white gloves should be worn.

Shopping Dresses—Should be of such material as will bear the crush of a crowded store without injury, and neither lace or delicate fabrics should ever be worn. A dress of merino in winter, with a cloth cloak and plain velvet or silk bonnet is the most suitable. In summer, a dress and cloak of plain mode-colored Lavella cloth, or any other cool but strong fabric, with a simply trimmed straw bonnet, is the best dress for a shopping excursion.

Storm Dresses—A lady who is obliged to go out frequently in bad weather, will find it both a convenience and economy to have a storm dress. Both dress and cloak should be made of a woolen material, (varying of course with the season,) which will shed water. White skirts are entirely out of place, as, if the dress is held up, they will be in a few moments disgracefully dirty. A woolen skirt, made quite short, to clear the muddy streets, is the proper thing. Stout, thick-soled boots, and gloves of either silk, beaver-cloth, or lisle thread, are the most suitable. The bonnet should be either of straw or felt, simply trimmed; and, above all, carry a *large* umbrella. The little light umbrellas are very pretty, no doubt, but to be of any real protection in a storm, the umbrella should be large enough to protect the whole dress.

Marketing—Here a dress of the most inexpensive kind is the best. There is no surer mark of vulgarity, than a costly dress in the market. A chintz is the best skirt to wear, and in winter a dark chintz skirt put on over a delaine dress, will protect it from baskets, and the unavoidable soils contracted in a market, while it looks perfectly well, and can be washed if required.

Traveling—Traveling dresses should be made always of some quiet color, perfectly plain, with a deep mantle or cloak of the same material. When traveling with a young babe, a dress of material that will wash is the best, but it should be dark and plain. A conspicuous traveling dress is in very bad taste, and jewelry or ornaments of any kind are entirely out of place. Let the dress be made of dark, plain material, with a simple straw or felt bonnet, trimmed with the same color as the dress, and a thick barege veil. An elastic string run through a tuck made in the middle of the veil, will allow one half to fall over the face, while the other half falls back, covering the bonnet, and protecting it from dust. If white collars and sleeves are worn, they should be of linen, perfectly plain. Strong boots and thick gloves are indispensable in traveling, and a heavy shawl should be carried, to meet any sudden change in the weather. Corsets and petticoats of dark linen are more suitable than white ones, as there is so much unavoidable dust and mud constantly meeting a traveler.

EVENING DRESSES—Must be governed by the number of guests you may expect to meet, and the character of the entertainment to which you are invited. For small social companies, a dark silk in winter, and a pretty lawn, barege, or white muslin in summer, are the most appropriate. A light head-dress of ribbon or velvet, or a plain cap, are the most suitable with this dress. For a larger party, low-necked, short-sleeved silk, light colored, or any of the thin goods made expressly for evening wear, with kid gloves, either of a color to match the dress or of white; black lace mittens are admissible, and flowers in the hair. A ball dress should be made of either very dressy silk, or light, thin material made over silk. It should be trimmed with lace, flowers, or ribbon, and made dressy. The *coiffure* should be elaborate, and match the dress, being either of ribbon, feather, or flowers. White kid gloves, trimmed to match the dress, and white or black satin slippers, with silk stockings, must be worn.

MOURNING—There is such a variety of opinion upon the subject of mourning, that it is extremely difficult to lay down any general rules upon the subject. Some wear very close black for a long period, for a distant relative; whilst others will wear dressy mourning for a short time in a case of death in the immediate family. There is no rule either for the depth of mourning, or the time when it may be laid aside, and I must confine my remarks to the different degrees of mourning.

For deep mourning, the dress should be of bombazine, Parramatta cloth, delaine, barege, or merino, made up over black lining. The only appropriate trimming is a deep fold, either of the same material or of crape. The shawl or cloak must be of plain black, without border or trimming, unless a fold of crape be put on the cloak; the bonnet should be of crape, made perfectly plain, with crape facings, unless the widow's cap be worn, and a deep crape veil should be thrown over both face and bonnet. Black crape collar and sleeves, and black boots and gloves. The next degree is to wear white collar and sleeves, a bow of crape upon the bonnet, and plain white lace facings, leaving off the crape veil, and substituting one of plain black net. A little later, black silk without any gloss, trimmed with crape, may be worn, and delaine or bombazine, with a trimming of broad, plain ribbon, or a bias fold of silk. The next stage admits a silk bonnet trimmed with crape, and lead color, dark purple, or white figures on the dress. From this the mourning passes into second mourning. Here a straw bonnet, trimmed with black ribbon or crape flowers, or a silk bonnet with black flowers on the outside, and white ones in the face, a black silk dress, and gray shawl or cloak, may be worn. Lead color, purple, lavender, and white, are all admissible in second mourning, and the dress may be lightened gradually, a white bonnet, shawl, and light purple or lavender dress, being the dress usually worn last, before the mourning is thrown aside entirely, and colors resumed. It is especially to be recommended to buy always the best materials when making up mourning. Crape and woolen goods of the finest quality are very expensive, but a cheaper article will wear miserably; there is no greater error in economy than purchasing cheap mourning, for no goods are so inferior, or wear out and grow rusty so soon.

CHAPTER III.
TRAVELING.

There is no situation in which a lady is more exposed than when she travels, and there is no position where a dignified, lady-like deportment is more indispensable and more certain to command respect. If you travel under the escort of a gentleman, give him as little trouble as possible; at the same time, do not interfere with the arrangements he may make for your comfort. It is best, when starting upon your journey, to hand your escort a sufficient sum of money to cover all your expenses, retaining your pocket book in case you should wish to use it. Have a strong pocket made in your upper petticoat, and in that carry your money, only reserving in your dress pocket a small sum for incidental expenses. In your traveling satchel carry an oil skin bag, containing your sponge, tooth and nail brushes, and some soap; have also a calico bag, with hair brush and comb, some pins, hair pins, a small mirror, and some towels. In this satchel carry also some crackers, or sandwiches, if you will be long enough upon the road to need a luncheon.

In your carpet bag, carry a large shawl, and if you will travel by night, or stop where it will be inconvenient to open your trunks, carry your night clothes, and what clean linen you may require, in the carpet bag. It is best to have your name and address engraved upon the plate of your carpet bag, and to sew a white card, with your name and the address to which you are traveling, in clear, plain letters upon it. If you carry a novel or any other reading, it is best to carry the book in your satchel, and not open the carpet bag until you are ready for the night. If you are to pass the night in the cars, carry a warm woolen or silk hood, that you may take off your bonnet at night. No one can sleep comfortably in a bonnet. Carry also, in this case, a large shawl to wrap round your feet.

One rule to be always observed in traveling is punctuality. Rise early enough to have ample time for arranging everything needful for the day's journey. If you sleep upon the boat, or at a hotel, always give directions to the servant to waken you at an hour sufficiently early to allow ample time for preparation. It is better to be all ready twenty minutes too soon, than five minutes late, or even late enough to be annoyed and heated by hurrying at the last moment.

A lady will always dress plainly when traveling. A gay dress, or finery of any sort, when in a boat, stage, or car, lays a woman open to the most severe misconstruction. Wear always neutral tints, and have the material made up plainly and substantially, but avoid carefully any article of dress that is glaring or conspicuous. Above all, never wear jewelry, (unless it be your watch,) or flowers; they are both in excessively bad taste. A quiet, unpretending dress, and dignified demeanor, will insure for a lady respect, though she travel alone from Maine to Florida.

If you are obliged to pass the night upon a steamboat, secure, if possible, a stateroom. You will find the luxury of being alone, able to retire and rise without witnesses, fully compensates for the extra charge. Before you retire, find out the position and number of the stateroom occupied by your escort, in case you wish to find him during the night. In times of terror, from accident or danger, such care will be found invaluable.

You may not be able to obtain a stateroom upon all occasions when traveling, and must then sleep in the ladies' cabin. It is best, in this case, to take off the dress only, merely loosening the stays and skirts, and, unless you are sick, you may sit up to read until quite a late hour. Never allow your escort to accompany you into the cabin. The saloon is open always to both ladies and gentlemen, and the cabin is for ladies *alone*. Many ladies are sufficiently ill-bred to ask a husband or brother into the cabin, and keep him there talking for an hour or two, totally overlooking the fact that by so doing she may be keeping others, suffering, perhaps, with sickness, from removing their dresses to lie down. Such conduct is not only excessively ill-bred, but intensely selfish.

There is scarcely any situation in which a lady can be placed, more admirably adapted to test her good breeding, than in the sleeping cabin of a steamboat. If you are so unfortunate as to suffer from sea-sickness, your chances for usefulness are limited, and patient suffering your only resource. In this case, never leave home without a straw-covered bottle of brandy, and another of camphor, in your carpet-bag. If you are not sick, be very careful not to keep the chambermaid from those who are suffering; should you require her services, dismiss her as soon as possible. As acquaintances, formed during a journey, are not recognized afterwards, unless mutually agreeable, do not refuse either a pleasant word or any little offer of service from your companions; and, on the other hand, be ready to aid them, if in your power. In every case, selfishness is the root of all ill-breeding, and it is never more conspicuously displayed than in traveling. A courteous manner, and graceful offer of service are valued highly when offered, and the giver loses nothing by her civility.

When in the car if you find the exertion of talking painful, say so frankly; your escort cannot be offended. Do not continually pester either your companion or the conductor with questions, such as "Where are we now?" "When shall we arrive?" If you are wearied, this impatience will only make the journey still more tedious. Try to occupy yourself with looking at the country through which you are passing, or with a book.

If you are traveling without any escort, speak to the conductor before you start, requesting him to attend to you whilst in the car or boat under his control. Sit quietly in the cars when they reach the depot until the first bustle is over, and then engage a porter to procure for you a hack, and get your baggage. If upon a boat, let one of the servants perform this office, being careful to fee him for it. Make an engagement with the hackman, to take you only in his hack, and enquire his charge before starting. In this way you avoid unpleasant company during your drive, and overcharge at the end of it.

If you expect a friend to meet you at the end of your journey, sit near the door of the steam-boat saloon, or in the ladies' room at the car depot, that he may find you easily.

There are many little civilities which a true gentleman will offer to a lady traveling alone, which she may accept, even from an entire stranger, with perfect propriety; but, while careful to thank him courteously, whether you accept or decline his attentions, avoid any advance towards acquaintanceship. If he sits near you and seems disposed to be impertinent, or obtrusive in his attentions or conversation, lower your veil and turn from him, either looking from the window or reading. A dignified, modest reserve is the surest way to repel impertinence. If you find yourself, during your journey, in any awkward or embarrassing situation, you may, without impropriety, request the assistance of a gentleman, even a stranger, and he will, probably, perform the service requested, receive your thanks, and then relieve you of his presence. Never, upon any account, or under any provocation, return rudeness by rudeness. Nothing will rebuke incivility in another so surely as perfect courtesy in your own manner. Many will be shamed into apology, who would annoy you for hours, if you encouraged them by acts of rudeness on your own part.

In traveling alone, choose, if possible, a seat next to another lady, or near an elderly gentleman. If your neighbor seems disposed to shorten the time by conversing, do not be too hasty in checking him. Such acquaintances end with the journey, and a lady can always so deport herself that she may beguile the time pleasantly, without, in the least, compromising her dignity.

Any slight attention, or an apology made for crushing or incommoding you, is best acknowledged by a courteous bow, in silence.

CHAPTER IV.
HOW TO BEHAVE AT A HOTEL.

In America, where the mania for traveling extends through all classes, from the highest to the lowest, a few hints upon deportment at a hotel will not be amiss, and these hints are especially addressed to ladies traveling alone.

When you arrive at the hotel, enquire at once for the proprietor. Tell him your name and address, and ask him to conduct you to a good room, naming the length of time you purpose occupying it. You may also request him to wait upon you to the table, and allot you a seat. As the hours for meals, at a large hotel, are very numerous, it is best to mention the time when you wish to break-fast, dine, or sup. If you stay more than one day at the hotel, do not tax the pro-prietor with the duty of escorting you to the table more than once. Request one of the waiters always to meet you as you enter, and wait upon you to your seat. This saves the embarrassment of crossing the room entirely unattended, while it shows others that you are a resident at the house. The waiter will then take your order for the dishes you wish. Give this order in a low tone, and do not harass the man by contradicting yourself several times; decide what you want before you ask for it, and then give your order quietly but distinctly. Use, always, the butter-knife, salt-spoon, and sugar-tongs, though you may be entirely alone in the use of them. The attention to the small details of table etiquette is one of the surest marks of good breeding. If any trifling civility is offered by the gentleman beside you, or opposite to you, thank him civilly, if you either accept or decline it. Thank the waiter for any extra attention he may offer.

Remember that a lady-like deportment is always modest and quiet. If you meet a friend at table, and converse, let it be in a tone of voice sufficiently loud for him to hear, but not loud enough to reach ears for which the remarks are not intended. A boisterous, loud voice, loud laughter, and bold deportment, at a hotel, are sure signs of vulgar breeding.

When you have finished your meal, cross the room quietly; if you go into the parlor, do not attract attention by a hasty entrance, or forward manner, but take the seat you may select, quietly.

The acquaintances made in a hotel may be dropped afterwards, if desirable, without rudeness, and a pleasant greeting to other ladies whom you may recognize from meeting them in the entries or at table, is courteous and well-bred; be careful, however, not to force attentions where you see they are not agreeably received.

A lady's dress, when alone at a hotel, should be of the most modest kind. At breakfast let her wear a close, morning dress, and never, even at supper, appear alone at the table with bare arms or neck. If she comes in late from the opera or a party, in full dress, she should not come into the supper-room, unless her escort accompanies her. A traveling or walking-dress can be worn with perfect propriety, at any meal at a hotel, as it is usually travelers who are the guests at the table.

After breakfast, pass an hour or two in the parlor, unless you are going out, whilst the chambermaid puts your room in order. You should, before leaving the room, lock your trunk, and be careful not to leave money or trinkets lying about. When you go out, lock your door, and give the key to the servant to hand to the clerk of the office, who will give it to you when you return. You may do this, even if you leave the room in disorder, as the chambermaids all carry duplicate keys, and can easily enter your room in your absence to arrange it. The door should not be left open, as dishonest persons, passing along the entry, could enter without fear of being questioned.

If you see that another lady, though she may be an entire stranger, is losing her collar, or needs attention called to any disorder in her dress, speak to her in a low tone, and offer to assist her in remedying the difficulty.

Be careful always in opening a door or raising a window in a public parlor, that you are not incommoding any one else.

Never sit down to the piano uninvited, unless you are alone in the parlor. Do not take any book you may find in the room away from it.

It is best always to carry writing materials with you, but if this is not convenient, you can always obtain them at the office.

In a strange city it is best to provide yourself with a small map and guide book, that you may be able to find your way from the hotel to any given point, without troubling any one for directions.

If you wish for a carriage, ring, and let the waiter order one for you.

When leaving a hotel, if you have been there for several days, give the waiter at table, and the chambermaid, a fee, as your unprotected situation will probably call for many services out of their regular routine of duties.

On leaving, ring, order your bill, pay it, state the time at which you wish to leave, and the train you will take to leave the city. Request a man to be sent, to carry your baggage to the hack; and if you require your next meal at an unusual hour, to be ready for your journey, order it then.

CHAPTER V.
EVENING PARTIES.
ETIQUETTE FOR THE HOSTESS.

The most fashionable as well as pleasant way in the present day, to entertain guests, is to invite them to evening parties, which vary in size from the "company," "sociable," "soirée," to the party, *par excellence*, which is but one step from the ball.

The entertainment upon such occasions, may vary with the taste of the hostess, or the caprice of her guests. Some prefer dancing, some music, some conversation. Small parties called together for dramatic or poetical readings, are now fashionable, and very delightful.

In writing an invitation for a small party, it is kind, as well as polite, to specify the number of guests invited, that your friends may dress to suit the occasion. To be either too much, or too little dressed at such times is embarrassing.

For large parties, the usual formula is:

Miss S——'s compliments to Miss G——, and requests the pleasure of her company for Wednesday, March 8th, at 8 o'clock.

Such an invitation, addressed either to an intimate friend or mere acquaintance, will signify full dress.

If your party is a musical soiré, or your friends meet for reading or conversation alone, say so in your invitation, as—

Miss S—— requests the pleasure of Miss G——'s company, on Thursday evening next, at 8 o'clock, to meet the members of the musical club, to which Miss S—— belongs;

or,

Miss S—— expects a few friends, on Monday evening next, at 8 o'clock, to take part in some dramatic readings, and would be happy to have Miss G—— join the party.

Always date your note of invitation, and put your address in one corner.

Having dispatched these notes, the next step is to prepare to receive your guests. If the number invited is large, and you hire waiters, give them notice several days beforehand, and engage them to come in the morning. Give them full directions for the supper, appoint one to open the door, another to show the guests to the dressing rooms, and a third to wait in the gentlemen's dressing-room, to attend to them, if their services are required.

If you use your own plate, glass, and china, show the waiters where to find them, as well as the table cloths, napkins, and other things they may require. If you hire the service from the confectioner's or restaurateur's where you order your supper, you have only to show your waiters where to spread supper, and tell them the hour.

You will have to place at least four rooms at the disposal of your guests— the supper room, and two dressing-rooms, beside the drawing-room.

In the morning, see that the fires in your rooms are in good order; and in the drawing-room, it is best to have it so arranged that the heat can be lessened towards evening, as the crowd, and dancing, will make it excessively uncomfortable if the rooms are too warm. See that the lights are in good order, and if you propose to have music instead of dancing, or to use your piano for dancing music, have it put in good tune in the morning. If you intend to dance, and do not wish to take up the carpets, you will find it economical, as well as much pleasanter, to cover them with coarse white muslin or linen; be sure it is fastened down smoothly, firmly, and drawn tightly over the carpets.

Do not remove all the chairs from the parlor; or, if this is necessary, leave some in the hall, for those who wish to rest after dancing.

In the dining-room, unless it will accommodate all your guests at once, have a silk cord so fastened that, when the room is full, it can be drawn across the door-way; those following the guests already in the room, will then return to the parlor, and wait their turn. A still better way, is to set the supper table twice, inviting the married and elderly people to go into the first table, and then, after it is ready for the second time, let the young folks go up.

Two dressing-rooms must be ready; one for the ladies, and the other for the gentlemen. Have both these rooms comfortably heated, and well lighted. Nothing can be more disagreeable than cold, ill-lighted rooms to dress in, particularly if your guests come in half-frozen by the cold of a winter's night, or still worse, damp from a stormy one.

Be sure that there is plenty of water, soap and towels on the washstand, two or three brushes and combs on the bureau, two mirrors, one large and one small, and a pin cushion, well filled with large and small pins.

In the ladies' room, have one, or if your party is large, two women to wait upon your guests; to remove their cloaks, overshoes, and hoods, and assist them in smoothing their dresses or hair. After each guest removes her shawl and hood, let one of the maids roll all the things she lays aside into a bundle, and put it where she can easily find it. It is an admirable plan, and prevents much confusion, to pin to each bundle, a card, or strip of paper, (previously prepared,) with the name of the person to whom it belongs written clearly and distinctly upon it.

Upon the bureau in the ladies' room, have a supply of hair-pins, and a workbox furnished with everything requisite to repair any accident that may happen to the dress of a guest. It is well, also, to have Eau de Cologne, hartshorn, and salts in case of sudden faintness.

In the gentlemen's room, place a clothes brush and boot-jack.

It is best to send out your invitations by your own servant, or one hired for that purpose especially. It is ill-bred to send invitations either by the dispatch, or through the post-office; and besides being discourteous, you risk offending your friends, as these modes of delivery are proverbially uncertain.

Be dressed and ready to receive your guests in good season, as some, in their desire to be punctual, may come before the time appointed. It is better to be ready too soon, than too late, as your guests will feel painfully embarrassed if you are not ready to receive them.

For the early part of the evening, take a position in your parlor, near or opposite to the door, that each guest may find you easily. It is not necessary to remain all the evening nailed to this one spot, but stay near it until your guests have all or nearly all assembled. Late comers will of course expect to find you entertaining your guests.

As each guest or party enter the room, advance a few steps to meet them, speaking first to the lady, or if there are several ladies, to the eldest, then to the younger ones, and finally to the gentlemen. If the new comers are acquainted with those already in the room, they will leave you, after a few words of greeting, to join their friends; but if they are strangers to the city, or making their first visit to your house, introduce them to a friend who is well acquainted in your circle, who will entertain them till you can again join them and introduce them to others.

Do not leave the room during the evening. To see a hostess fidgeting, constantly going in and out, argues ill for her tact in arranging the house for company. With well-trained waiters, you need give yourself no uneasiness about the arrangements outside of the parlors.

The perfection of good breeding in a hostess, is perfect ease of manner; for the time she should appear to have no thought or care beyond the pleasure of her guests.

Have a waiter in the hall to open the front door, and another at the head of the first flight of stairs, to point out to the ladies and gentlemen their respective dressing-rooms.

Never try to outshine your guests in dress. It is vulgar in the extreme. A hostess should be dressed as simply as is consistent with the occasion, wearing, if she will, the richest fabrics, exquisitely made, but avoiding any display of jewels or gay colors, such as will be, probably, more conspicuous than those worn by her guests.

Remember, from the moment your first guest enters the parlor, you must forget yourself entirely to make the evening pleasant for others. Your duties will call you from one group to another, and require constant watchfulness that no one guest is slighted. Be careful that none of the company are left to mope alone from being unacquainted with other guests. Introduce gentlemen to ladies, and gentlemen to gentlemen, ladies to ladies.

It requires much skill and tact to make a party for conversation only, go off pleasantly. You must invite only such guests as will mutually please, and you must be careful about introductions. If you have a literary lion upon your list, it is well to invite other lions to meet him or her, that the attention may not be constantly concentrated upon one person. Where you see a couple conversing slowly and wearily, stir them up with a few sprightly words, and introduce a new person, either to make a trio, or, as a substitute in the duet, carrying off the other one of the couple to find a more congenial companion elsewhere. Never interrupt an earnest or apparently interesting conversation. Neither party will thank you, even if you propose the most delightful substitute.

If your party meet for reading, have a table with the books in the centre of the apartment, that will divide the room, those reading being on one side, the listeners on the other. Be careful here not to endeavor to shine above your guests, leaving to them the most prominent places, and taking, cheerfully, a subordinate place. On the other hand, if you are urged to display any talent you may possess in this way, remember your only desire is to please your guests, and if they are really desirous to listen to you, comply, gracefully and promptly, with their wishes.

If you have dancing, and have not engaged a band, it is best to hire a pianist for the evening to play dancing music. You will find it exceedingly wearisome to play yourself all the evening, and it is ill-bred to ask any guest to play for others to dance. This victimizing of some obliging guest is only too common, but no true lady will ever be guilty of such rudeness. If there are several members of the family able and willing to play, let them divide this duty amongst them, or, if you wish to play yourself, do so. If any guest, in this case, offers to relieve you, accept their kindness for *one* dance only. Young people, who enjoy dancing, but who also play well, will often stay on the piano-stool all the evening, because their own good-nature will not allow them to complain, and their hostess wilfully, or through negligence, permits the tax.

See that your guests are well provided with partners, introducing every gentleman and lady who dances, to one who will dance well with them. Be careful that none sit still through your negligence in providing partners.

Do not dance yourself, when, by so doing, you are preventing a guest from enjoying that pleasure. If a lady is wanted to make up a set, then dance, or if, late in the evening, you have but few lady dancers left, but do not interfere with the pleasure in others. If invited, say that you do not wish to take the place of a guest upon the floor, and introduce the gentleman who invites you to some lady friend who dances.

It is very pleasant in a dancing party to have ices *alone*, handed round at about ten o'clock, having supper set two or three hours later. They are very refreshing, when it would be too early to have the more substantial supper announced.

It is very customary now, even in large parties, to have no refreshments but ice-cream, lemonade, and cake, or, in summer, fruit, cake, and ices. It is less troublesome, as well as less expensive, than a hot supper, and the custom will be a good one to adopt permanently.

One word of warning to all hostesses. You can never know, when you place wine or brandy before your guests, whom you may be tempting to utter ruin. Better, far better, to have a reputation as strict, or mean, than by your example, or the temptation you offer, to have the sin upon your soul of having put poison before those who partook of your hospitality. It is not necessary; hospitality and generosity do not require it, and you will have the approval of all who truly love you for your good qualities, if you resolutely refuse to have either wine or any other intoxicating liquor upon your supper-table.

If the evening of your party is stormy, let a waiter stand in the vestibule with a *large* umbrella, to meet the ladies at the carriage door, and protect them whilst crossing the pavement and steps.

When your guests take leave of you, it will be in the drawing-room, and let that farewell be final. Do not accompany them to the dressing-room, and never stop them in the hall for a last word. Many ladies do not like to display their "sortie du soirée" before a crowded room, and you will be keeping their escort waiting. Say farewell in the parlor, and do not repeat it.

If your party is mixed, that is, conversation, dancing, and music are all mingled, remember it is your place to invite a guest to sing or play, and be careful not to offend any amateur performers by forgetting to invite them to favor the company. If they decline, never urge the matter. If the refusal proceeds from unwillingness or inability on that occasion, it is rude to insist; and if they refuse for the sake of being urged, they will be justly punished by a disappointment. If you have guests who, performing badly, will expect an invitation to play, sacrifice their desire to the good of the others, pass them by. It is torture to listen to bad music.

Do not ask a guest to sing or play more than once. This is her fair share, and you have no right to tax her too severely to entertain your other guests. If, however, the performance is so pleasing that others ask for a repetition, then you too may request it, thanking the performer for the pleasure given.

CHAPTER VI.
EVENING PARTIES.
ETIQUETTE FOR THE GUEST.

Upon receiving an invitation for an evening party, answer it immediately, that your hostess may know for how many guests she must provide. If, after accepting an invitation, any unforeseen event prevents your keeping the engagement, write a second note, containing your regrets. The usual form is:—

Miss G—— accepts with pleasure Miss S——'s polite invitation for Monday next;

or,

Miss G—— regrets that a prior engagement will prevent her accepting Miss S——'s kind invitation for Monday evening.

Punctuality is a mark of politeness, if your invitation states the hour at which your hostess will be ready to welcome you. Do not be more than half an hour later than the time named, but if unavoidably detained, make no apology when you meet your hostess; it will be in bad taste to speak of your want of punctuality.

When you arrive at your friend's house, do not stop to speak to any one in the hall, or upon the stairs, but go immediately to the dressing room. The gentleman who accompanies you will go to the door of the lady's room, leave you, to remove his own hat and over-coat, and then return to the door to wait for you.

In the dressing-room, do not push forward to the mirror if you see that others are before you there. Wait for your turn, then perform the needful arrangements of your toilette quickly, and re-join your escort as soon as possible.

If you meet friends in the lady's-room, do not stop there to chat; you keep your escort waiting, and your friends will join you in the parlor a few moments later.

Avoid all confidential communications or private remarks in the dressing-room. You may be overheard, and give pain or cause annoyance by your untimely conversation.

When you enter the parlor, go immediately to your hostess, and speak to her; if the gentleman attending you is a stranger to the lady of the house, introduce him, and then join the other guests, as by delaying, to converse too long with your hostess, you may prevent her speaking to others who have arrived later than yourself.

If you have no escort, you may with perfect propriety send for the master of the house, to wait upon you from the dressing-room to the parlor, and as soon as you have spoken to the hostess, thank your host and release him, as the same attention may be required by others. Again, when alone, if you meet a friend in the dressing-room, you may ask the privilege of entering the parlor with her and her escort; or, if she also is alone, there is no impropriety in *two* ladies going into the room unattended by a gentleman.

While you maintain a cheerful deportment, avoid loud talking and laughing, and still more carefully avoid any action or gesture that may attract attention and make you conspicuous.

When dressing for a party, while you show that you honor the occasion by a tasteful dress, avoid glaring colors, or any conspicuous ornament or style of costume.

Avoid long tête-à-tête conversations; they are in bad taste, and to hold confidential communication, especially with gentlemen, is still worse.

Do not make any display of affection for even your dearest friend; kissing in public, or embracing, are in bad taste. Walking with arms encircling waists, or such demonstrative tokens of love, are marks of low breeding.

Avoid crossing the room alone, and never run, even if you feel embarrassed, and wish to cross quickly.

If you are a musician, and certain that you will confer pleasure by a display of your talents, do not make a show of reluctance when invited to play or sing. Comply gracefully, and after one piece, leave the instrument. Be careful to avoid the appearance of wishing to be invited, and, above all, never hint that this would be agreeable. If your hostess has requested you to bring your notes, and you are dependent upon them, bring them, and quietly place them on the music stand, or, still better, send them in the afternoon. It is a better plan, if you are called upon frequently to contribute in this way to the evening's amusement, to learn a few pieces so as to play them perfectly well without notes.

Never attempt any piece before company, unless you are certain that you can play it without mistake or hesitation. When you have finished your song or piece, rise instantly from the piano stool, as your hostess may wish to invite another guest to take the place. If you have a reason for declining to play, do so decidedly when first invited, and do not change your decision.

If your hostess or any of the family play for the guests to dance, it is both polite and kind to offer to relieve them; and if truly polite themselves, they will not take advantage of the offer, to *over* tax your good nature.

When others are playing or singing, listen quietly and attentively; to laugh or talk loudly when there is music in the room, is rude, both toward the performer and your hostess. If you are conversing at the time the music begins, and you find that your companion is not disposed to listen to the performer at the harp or piano, converse in a low tone, and take a position at some distance from the instrument.

If the rooms are not large enough for all the guests to dance at one time, do not dance every set, even if invited. It is ill-bred and selfish.

When you go up to supper, do not accept anything from any gentleman but the one who has escorted you from the parlor. If others offer you, as they probably will, any refreshment, say that Mr. —— (naming your escort) has gone to get you what you desire. He has a right to be offended, if, after telling him what you wish for, he returns to find you already supplied. It is quite as rude to offer what he brings to another lady. Her escort is probably on the same errand from which yours has just returned. It may seem trivial and childish to warn a lady against putting cakes or bonbons in her pocket at supper, yet it is often done by those who would deeply resent the accusation of rudeness or meanness. It is not only ill-bred, but it gives rise, if seen, to suspicions that you are so little accustomed to society, or so starved at home, that you are ignorant of the forms of etiquette, or are forced to the theft by positive hunger.

If you are obliged to leave the company at an earlier hour than the other guests, say so to your hostess in a low tone, when you have an opportunity, and then stay a short time in the room, and slip out unperceived. By a formal leave-taking, you may lead others to suppose the hour later than it is in reality, and thus deprive your hostess of other guests, who, but for your example, would have remained longer. French leave is preferable to a formal leave-taking upon such occasions.

If you remain until the usual hour for breaking up, go to your hostess before you leave the room, express the pleasure you have enjoyed, and bid her farewell.

Within the next week, you should call upon your hostess, if it is the first party you have attended at her house. If she is an intimate friend, the call should be made within a fortnight.

CHAPTER VII.
VISITING.
ETIQUETTE FOR THE HOSTESS.

When you write to invite a friend to visit you, name a time when it will be convenient and agreeable for you to receive her, and if she accepts your invitation, so arrange your duties and engagements that they will not interfere with your devoting the principal part of your time to the entertainment of your guest. If you have certain duties which must be performed daily, say so frankly when she first arrives, and see that during the time you are so occupied she has work, reading, music, or some other employment, to pass the time away pleasantly.

Have a room prepared especially for her use, and let her occupy it alone. Many persons have a dislike to any one sleeping with them, and will be kept awake by a companion in the room or bed. Above all, do not put a child to sleep in the chamber with your guest.

The day before your friend arrives, have her room swept, dusted, and aired; put clean, fresh linen upon the bed, see that the curtains are in good order, the locks in perfect repair, and the closet or wardrobe and bureau empty for her clothes. Have upon the bureau a pin cushion well filled, hair pins, brush and comb, and two mirrors, one large, and one small for the hand, as she may wish to smooth her hair, without unpacking her own toilet articles. Upon the wash-stand, have two pitchers full of water, a cup, tumbler, soap-dish and soap, basin, brush-dish, and a sponge, wash rag, and plenty of clean towels.

Have both a feather bed and a mattress upon the bedstead, that she may place whichever she prefers uppermost. Two sheets, a blanket, quilt, and counterpane, should be on the bed, and there should be two extra blankets in the room, should she require more covering in the night.

On the mantel piece, place a few books that she may read, if she wishes, before sleeping. Have upon the mantel piece a box of matches, and if the room is not lighted by gas, have also a supply of candles in a box, and a candlestick.

If the room is not heated by a furnace, be careful that the fire is made every morning before she rises, and keep a good supply of fuel in the room.

Besides the larger chairs, have a low one, to use while changing the shoes or washing the feet.

Upon the table, place a full supply of writing materials, as your guest may wish to send word of her safe arrival before unpacking her own writing-desk. Put two or three postage stamps upon this table.

Be sure that bells, locks, hinges, and windows, are all in perfect order.

Before your guest arrives, go to her room. If it is in winter, have a good fire, hot water on the washstand, and see that the windows are tightly closed, and the room cheerful with sunshine, or plenty of candle or gas light. If in summer, draw the curtains, bow the shutters, open the windows, and have a fan upon the table. It is well to have a bath ready, should your guest desire that refreshment after the dust and heat of traveling.

When the time arrives at which you may expect your guest, send a carriage to the station to meet her, and, if possible, go yourself, or send some member of the family to welcome her there. After her baggage is on the carriage, drive immediately to the house, and be certain all is ready there for her comfort.

As soon as she is at your house, have her trunks carried immediately to her own room, and lead her there yourself. Then, after warmly assuring her how welcome she is, leave her alone to change her dress, bathe, or lie down if she wishes. If her journey has been a long one, and it is not the usual hour for your next meal, have a substantial repast ready for her about half an hour after her arrival, with tea or coffee.

If she arrives late at night, after she has removed her bonnet and bathed her face, invite her to partake of a substantial supper, and then pity her weariness and lead the way to her room. She may politely assert that she can still sit up and talk, but be careful you do not keep her up too long; and do not waken her in the morning. After the first day, she will, of course, desire to breakfast at your usual hour, but if she has had a long, fatiguing journey, she will be glad to sleep late the first day. Be careful that she has a hot breakfast ready when she does rise, and take a seat at the table to wait upon her.

After the chambermaid has arranged the guest-chamber in the morning, go in yourself and see that all is in order, and comfortable, and that there is plenty of fresh water and towels, the bed properly made, and the room dusted. Then do not go in again through the day, unless invited. If you are constantly running in, to put a chair back, open or shut the windows, or arrange the furniture, you will entirely destroy the pleasantest part of your guest's visit, by reminding her that she is not at home, and must not take liberties, even in her own room. It looks, too, as if you were afraid to trust her, and thought she would injure the furniture.

If you have children, forbid them to enter the room your friend occupies, unless she invites them to do so, or they are sent there with a message.

If your household duties will occupy your time for some hours in the morning, introduce your guest to the piano, book-case, or picture-folio, and place all at her service. When your duties are finished, either join her in her own room, or invite her to sit with you, and work, chatting, meanwhile, together. If you keep your own carriage, place it at her disposal as soon as she arrives.

If she is a stranger in the city, accompany her to the points of interest she may wish to visit, and also offer to show her where to find the best goods, should she wish to do any shopping.

Enquire of your visitor if there is any particular habit she may wish to indulge in, such as rising late, retiring early, lying down in the daytime, or any other habit that your family do not usually follow. If there is, arrange it so that she may enjoy her peculiarity in comfort. If there is any dish which is distasteful to her, avoid placing it upon the table during her visit, and if she mentions, in conversation, any favorite dish, have it frequently placed before her.

If she is accustomed to eat just before retiring, and your family do not take supper, see that something is sent to her room every night.

If your friend has intimate friends in the same city, beside yourself, it is an act of kindly courtesy to invite them to dinner, tea, or to pass a day, and when calls are made, and you see that it would be pleasant, invite the caller to remain to dinner or tea.

Never accept any invitation, either to a party, ball, or public entertainment, that does not include your guest. In answering the invitation give that as your reason for declining, when another note will be sent enclosing an invitation for her. If the invitation is from an intimate friend, say, in answering it, that your guest is with you, and that she will accompany you.

It is a mistaken idea to suppose that hospitality and courtesy require *constant* attention to a guest. There are times when she may prefer to be alone, either to write letters, to read, or practice. Some ladies follow a guest from one room to another, never leaving them alone for a single instant, when they would enjoy an hour or two in the library or at the piano, but do not like to say so.

The best rule is to make your guest feel that she is heartily welcome, and perfectly at home.

When she is ready to leave you, see that her trunks are strapped in time by the servants, have a carriage ready to take her to the station, have the breakfast or dinner at an hour that will suit her, prepare a luncheon for her to carry, and let some gentleman in the family escort her to the wharf, check her trunks, and procure her tickets.

If your guest is in mourning, decline any invitations to parties or places of amusement whilst she is with you. Show her by such little attentions that you sympathize in her recent affliction, and that the pleasure of her society, and the love you bear her, make such sacrifices of gayety trifling, compared with the sweet duty of comforting her.

CHAPTER VIII.
VISITING.
ETIQUETTE FOR THE GUEST.

As a first rule with regard to paying a visit, the best one is, never to accept a *general* invitation. Instances are very common where women (I cannot say *ladies*) have, upon a slight acquaintance, and a "When you are in C—— I should be very happy to have you visit me," actually gone to C—— from their own home, and, with bag and baggage, quartered themselves upon the hospitality of their newly made friend, for weeks at a time.

Even where there is a long standing friendship it is not well to visit uninvited. It is impossible for you, in another city, to know exactly when it will be convenient for your friend to have you visit her, unless she tells you, and that will, of course, be a special invitation.

If your friends are really desirous to have you pay them a visit, they will name a time when it will be convenient and agreeable to have you come, and you may accept the invitation with the certainty that you will not incommode them.

Self-proposed visits are still worse. You, in a manner, force an invitation from your friend when you tell her that you can come at a certain time, unless you have previously arranged to let her know when you can be her guest. In that case, your own time is understood to be the most agreeable for her.

If, whilst traveling, you pass through a town where you have friends whom you wish to visit, and who would be hurt if you omitted to do so, go first to a hotel, and either call or send word that you are there. Then, it is optional with them to extend their hospitality or not. Do not be offended if it is not done. The love for you may be undiminished, and the desire to entertain you very great, yet family reasons may render such an invitation as you expect, impossible. Your friend may have engagements or duties at the time, that would prevent her making the visit pleasant for you, and wish to postpone the invitation until she can entertain you as she wishes.

To drive, trunks and all, in such a case, to your friend's house, without a word of warning, is unkind, as well as ill-bred. You force her to invite you to stay, when it may be inconvenient, and, even if she is really glad to see you, and wishes you to make a prolonged visit, you may feel certain she would have preferred to know you were coming. If she really loves you, her natural desire would be to have everything ready to give you a comfortable reception, and not have to leave you, perhaps with your traveling costume on, for an hour or two, while she prepares a room for you. It is not enough to say, at such a time, "Don't mind me," or, "Treat me as one of the family." However much her politeness or love may conceal annoyance, be sure, in her secret heart she *does* mind you, and remember you are *not* one of her private family.

To take the liberty of going to the house of a mere acquaintance, for a night or two, while traveling, without invitation, is making a convenience of them, and wears the appearance of wishing to save the customary hotel-bill, so, while it is extremely ill-bred and impertinent, it is also excessively mean.

In case of relationship, or long intimate friendship, an unexpected visit may be pardoned and give pleasure, but it is better to avoid it, as the pleasure will surely be increased if your relative or friend has time to prepare for your reception as her love will prompt, and arrange her duties and engagements to really enjoy your company.

When you receive an invitation by letter to visit a friend, answer it immediately, thanking her for her proffered hospitality, and say decidedly then whether you can accept or decline.

If you accept the invitation, state in your letter by what train, and at what hour you will arrive, that she may meet you, and let nothing but positive necessity keep you from being punctually at the time and place appointed. To linger by the way, for mere pleasure, and make her come several times to meet you, is unkind, as well as ill-bred. If you are unavoidably detained, write to her, state the reason that will prevent your keeping the appointment, and name another time when you can come.

It is well in answering a letter of invitation, to state the limits of your visit, and then to keep them. If she is unwilling to let you go, and you are tempted to stay, that very fact promises well for the pleasure of a second visit. It is better to leave while all will regret you, than to linger on until you have worn out your welcome.

Inquire, as soon as possible after your arrival, what are the regular habits of the family; the hours for rising, for meals, and for retiring, and then be punctual in your attendance. Many ladies are very ceremonious about waiting for a guest, and by delay in your room, or inattention to the time, when you are out, you will keep the whole family waiting.

If you do not wake early enough for the usual breakfast hour, request the chambermaid to knock at your door in time for you to be ready to go down with the family. Before you leave your room in the morning, take the clothes off your bed, throw the upper bed over the foot-board, and then open all the windows (unless it storms), that room and bed may be thoroughly aired before you sit there again.

After breakfast, ask your hostess if you can be of any assistance to her in the household duties. If she declines your services, do not follow her from room to room whilst she is thus engaged, but take your work, books, or music to the sitting room or parlor, until your own room is ready for you. By thus proving that you can occupy yourself pleasantly, while she is away, you make it less annoying to her to feel the obligation to leave you.

As soon as you see that she is ready to sew and chat, leave your book, or, if in your own room, come to the sitting room, where she is, and work with her. It is polite and kind, if you see that she has a large supply of family sewing, to offer to assist her, but if she positively declines your aid, then have some work of your own on hand, that you may sew with her. Many pleasant mornings may be spent while visiting, by one lady reading aloud whilst the other sews, alternating the work.

It is a pretty compliment to repay the hospitality of your hostess, by working whilst with her upon some piece of fancy work, a chair cover, sofa cushion, or pair of ottomans, presenting them to her when finished, as a keepsake. They will be duly appreciated, and remind her constantly of the pleasures of your visit.

If you pass the morning out of the house, remember your time is hers, and have no engagement to interfere with the plans she has laid for entertaining you. Observe this rule during your whole visit, and do not act independent of her plans. By constantly forming engagements without her knowledge, going out without her, or staying in when she has made some excursion or party for your pleasure, you insult her, by intimating that her house is no more to you than a hotel, to sleep and eat in, while your pleasures lie elsewhere.

After dinner, retire for an hour to your own room, that your hostess may lie down if she is accustomed to do so. If the hours kept are later than you have been accustomed to, or if the gayety of the family keeps you out at party or opera, it is best to sleep after dinner, even if you do not always do it. To give signs of weariness in the evening will be excessively rude, implying want of enjoyment, and making your hostess feel hurt and annoyed.

If you have shopping to do, find out where the best stores are, and then go to them alone, unless your hostess will accompany you upon similar business of her own. Do not tax her good nature to go, merely for the sake of aiding you as guide. If one of the children in the family is familiar with the stores and streets, ask her to accompany you, and be careful to acknowledge the kindness by buying something especially for the child whilst she is out with you, if it is only some cakes or bonbons. Choose an hour when you are certain your hostess has made no other engagement for you, or while she is busy in her domestic duties, for these shopping excursions. Offer, when you are going, to attend to any shopping she may want, and ask if there is any commission you can execute for her while you are out.

While on a visit to one friend, do not accept too many invitations from others, and avoid spending too much time in paying calls where your hostess is not acquainted. You owe the greater portion of your time and society to the lady whose hospitality you are accepting, and it is best to decline invitations from other houses, unless they inclose one for your hostess also.

Avoid paying any visits in a family not upon good terms with your hostess. If such a family are very dear friends of your own, or you can claim an acquaintance, pleasant upon both sides, with them, write, and state candidly the reason why you cannot visit them, and they will appreciate your delicacy.

If, while on a visit to one friend, you receive an invitation to spend some time with another friend in the same place, accept it for the period which you have named as the termination of your first visit. You insult your hostess by shortening your visit to her to accept another invitation, and quite as much of an insult is it, to take the time from the first visit to go to pay another, and then return to your first hostess, unless such an arrangement has been made immediately upon your arrival.

Never invite any friend who may call upon you to stay to dinner or tea; you will be taking a most unwarrantable liberty in so doing. This is the right of your hostess, and if, by her silence, she tacitly declines extending this courtesy, you will be guilty of impertinence in usurping her privilege.

Never take any one who calls upon you into any room but the parlor, unless invited to do so by your hostess. You have, of course, the *entrée* of other rooms, but you have no right to extend this privilege to others.

If you have many gentlemen visiters, check too frequent calls, and make no appointments with them. If they show you any such attention as to offer to drive you to places of interest, or visit with you picture galleries or public places, always consult your hostess before accepting such civilities, and decline them if she has made other engagements for you. If you receive an invitation to visit any place of public amusement, decline it, unless one of the family with whom you are staying is also invited. In that case you may accept. If the gentleman who invites you is a stranger to the family, introduce him to your hostess, or mention her name in conversation. He will then, if he really desires you to accept his proffered attention, include her in the invitation.

When visiting in a family where the members are in mourning, decline all invitations to parties or places of public amusement. It is an insult to them to leave them to join in pleasure from which their recent affliction excludes them. Your visit at such a time will be prompted by sympathy in their trouble, and for the time it is thoughtful and delicate to make their sorrows yours.

If sudden sickness or family trouble come to your friend whilst you are with her, *unless you can really be useful*, shorten your visit. In time of trouble families generally like to be alone, all in all to each other; and a visitor is felt a constant restraint.

If death comes while you are with your friend, endeavor to take from her as much of the care as you can, a really sympathizing friend is an inexpressible comfort at such a time, as the trying details which must be taken in charge by some one, will be less trying to her than to a member of the family. Do the necessary shopping for your friend, and relieve her of as much family care as you can. Let her feel that you are really glad that you are near her in her affliction, and repay the hospitality she offered in her season of joy by showing her that her sorrow makes her still more dear, and that, while you can enjoy the gayety of her house, you will not flee from its mourning. When your presence can be of no further service, then leave her.

Put out your washing and ironing when on a visit. It is annoying and ill-bred to throw your soiled clothes into the family wash.

Take with you, from home, all the writing and sewing materials you may require while paying your visit. It is annoying to be constantly requested by a visitor to lend her scissors, pins, needles, or paper; no lady should be without her own portfolio and work-box.

Be very careful not to injure any article of furniture in your sleeping apartment, and if, unfortunately, anything suffers from your carelessness, have the accident repaired, or the article replaced, at your own expense.

When your visit is over, give a present to each of the servants, varying its value, according to the length of your visit or the services you may have required. You will add to the pleasure by presenting such gifts yourself, with a few pleasant words.

Never compare the house you may be visiting with your own, or any other you may visit. Avoid also speaking of any house where you may have been a guest in terms of overpraise, giving glowing pictures of its splendor. Your hostess may imagine you are drawing comparisons unfavorable to your present residence. Also avoid speaking unfavorably of any former visit, as your hostess will naturally conclude that her turn for censure will come as soon as your visit is over.

If any family secret comes to your knowledge while you are on a visit in that family, remember the hospitality extended to you binds you to the most inviolable secrecy. It is mean, contemptible, rude, and ill-bred to make your entertainers regret their hospitality by betraying any such confidence; for it is as sacred a confidence as if you were bound over to silence in the most solemn manner.

After paying a visit, you should write to your hostess as soon as you reach home again; thank her in this letter for her hospitality, speak warmly of the enjoyment you have had in your recent visit, and mention by name every member of the family, desiring to be remembered to all.

CHAPTER IX.
MORNING RECEPTIONS OR CALLS.
ETIQUETTE FOR THE HOSTESS.

If your circle of visiting acquaintance is very large, while at the same time your time is fully occupied, or your home duties make it inconvenient to dress every morning to receive visitors, it is a good plan to set aside one morning in the week for a reception day.

Upon your own visiting cards, below the name, put the day when it will be proper to return the visit, thus:

Mrs. James Hunter.
　　　AT HOME WEDNESDAYS.
No. 1718 *C——— st.*

Your friends will, unless there is some especial reason for a call in the interval, pay their visit upon the day named.

Let nothing, but the most imperative duty, call you out upon your reception day. Your callers are, in a measure, invited guests, and it will be an insulting mark of rudeness to be out when they call. Neither can you be excused, except in case of sickness.

Having appointed the day when you will be at home to see your friends, you must, for that day, prepare to give your time wholly to them. The usual hours for morning receptions are from twelve to three, and you should be dressed, and ready for callers, at least half an hour before that time.

To come in, flushed from a hurried toilette, to meet your first callers, is unbecoming as well as rude.

Your dress should be handsome, but not showy. A silk or cashmere wrapper, richly trimmed, over an embroidered skirt, with a pretty cap, or the hair neatly arranged without head-dress, is a becoming and appropriate dress. Still better is a rich but plain silk, made high in the neck, with long sleeves. Wear a handsomely embroidered, or lace collar, and sleeves, and a rather dressy cap, or, still better, the hair alone, prettily arranged.

As each visitor arrives, rise, and advance part of the way to meet her. If gentlemen, rise, but do not advance.

It is not customary now to introduce callers at these morning receptions, though you can do so with perfect propriety where you know such an introduction will be agreeable to both parties.

In introducing a gentleman to a lady, address her first, as—

"Miss Jones, permit me to introduce Mr. Lee;" and, when introducing a young lady to a matron, you introduce the younger one to the elder, as—

"Mrs. Green, allow me to introduce to you my friend, Miss Brown."

In introducing strangers in the city it is well to name the place of their residence, as—Mr. James of Germany, or, Mr. Brown of New York, or, if they have recently returned from abroad, it is well to say so, as, Mr. Lee, lately from India; this is useful in starting conversation.

Be careful, when introducing your friends, to pronounce the name of each one clearly and distinctly, that there may be no mistake or necessity for repetition.

It is a good plan, if your receptions are usually largely attended, to have books and pictures on the centre table, and scattered about your parlors. You must, of course, converse with each caller, but many will remain in the room for a long time, and these trifles are excellent pastime, and serve as subjects for conversation.

It requires much tact to know when to introduce friends, when to take refuge under the shield fashion offers, and not make them acquainted with each other. It is a positive cruelty to force a talented, witty person, to converse with one who is ignorant and dull, as they will, of course, be obliged to do, if introduced.

A well-bred lady, who is receiving several visitors at a time, pays equal attention to all, and attempts, as much as possible, to generalize the conversation, turning to all in succession. The last arrival, however, receives a little more attention at first, than the others.

If it is not agreeable to you to set aside a day for the especial reception of callers, and you have a large circle of acquaintances, be ready to receive them each day that you are at home.

If you are engaged, let the servant say so when she opens the door, and do not send down that message after your friend has been admitted. If she is told when she arrives that you are engaged, she will understand that you are denied to *all* callers, but if that message comes after she has sent up her card, she may draw the inference that you will not see *her*, though you may see other friends.

Never keep a caller waiting whilst you make an elaborate toilette. If you are not ready for visitors, it is best to enter the parlor in your wrapper, apologizing for it, than to keep your friend waiting whilst you change your dress.

If a stranger calls, bringing a letter of introduction, and sends the letter, you may read it before going down stairs, but if they wait till you are in the parlor before presenting the letter, merely glance at the signature and at the name of your caller; do not read the letter through, unless it is very short, or you are requested by the bearer to do so.

If you have a friend staying with you, invite her to join you in the parlor when you have callers, and introduce her to your friends.

If you wish to invite a caller to stay to luncheon or dinner, give the invitation as soon as you have exchanged greetings, not after she has been seated for some time. In the latter case it appears like an after thought, not, as in the former, as if from a real desire to have the pleasure of her company.

If you have but one caller at a time, rise when she does, and accompany her to the vestibule; but, if there are several in the room, rise when each one does, but only accompany them to the parlor door; there take leave of them, and return to those who still remain seated.

If, after affliction, your friends call before you are able to see them, do not fear to give offence by declining to receive them. They will respect your sorrow, and the call is made more to show their sympathy than from a desire to converse with you.

Visits of condolence, paid between the death of one of your family and the day of the funeral, you may always excuse yourself from, with perfect propriety. They are made in kindness, and show interest, but if you decline seeing such callers, there is no offence given.

In parting from a gentleman caller, rise when he does, and remain standing until he leaves the room, but do not go towards the door.

When a gentleman calls in the morning he will not remove his outside coat, and will hold his hat in his hand. Never offer to take the latter, and do not invite him to remove his coat. Take no notice of either one or the other.

If strangers in the city call upon you, enquire at what hotel they are staying, and how long they will be there, that you may return their call before they leave town.

CHAPTER X.
MORNING RECEPTIONS OR CALLS.
ETIQUETTE FOR THE CALLER.

The usual hours for paying morning calls are between eleven and two, or twelve and three, and all calls of ceremony should be made between these hours.

Never, in paying a ceremonious call, stay more than twenty minutes, or less than ten. If your hostess has several other visitors at the same time that you are in her parlor, make your visit short, that she may have more attention to bestow upon others.

After you have received an invitation to a party, call within a week or fortnight after the evening, whether you have accepted or declined the invitation. If you have declined on account of mourning, the excuse extends also to the call.

When the servant answers your ring, hand in your card. If your friend is out or engaged, leave the card, and if she is in, send it up. Never call without cards. You may offend your friend, as she may never hear of your call, if she is out at the time, and you trust to the memory of the servant.

If your friend is at home, after sending your card up to her by the servant, go into the parlor to wait for her. Sit down quietly, and do not leave your seat until you rise to meet her as she enters the room. To walk about the parlor, examining the ornaments and pictures, is ill-bred. It is still more unlady-like to sit down and turn over to read the cards in her card basket. If she keeps you waiting for a long time, you may take a book from the centre-table to pass away the interval.

Never, while waiting in a friend's parlor, go to the piano and play till she comes. This is a breach of good-breeding often committed, and nothing can be more ill-bred. You may be disturbing an invalid unawares, or you may prevent your friend, if she has children, from coming down stairs at all, by waking the baby.

If you are a stranger in the city, and bring a letter of introduction to your hostess, send this letter up stairs with your card, that she may read it, and know how to welcome you when she comes down stairs. In this case, write upon the card the name of the hotel at which you are staying, and mention in the course of conversation, how long you will be in the city.

If you have a visitor, and desire to introduce her to your friends, you may invite her to accompany you when paying calls.

In making a call for condolence, it is sufficient to leave a card with your enquiries for the health of your friend, and offers of service. The same if calling upon invalids, if they are too ill to see you.

In visits of congratulation, go in, and be hearty in your expressions of interest and sympathy. Pay visits, both of condolence and congratulation, within a week after the event which calls for them occurs.

It is proper, when you have already made your call of the usual length, and another caller is announced, to rise and leave, not immediately, as if you shunned the new arrival, but after a moment or two. Never out-sit two or three parties of visitors, unless you have private business with your hostess which cannot be postponed. Many denounce the system of morning calls as silly, frivolous, and a waste of time. They are wrong. It may be carried to an excess, and so admit of these objections, but in moderation the custom is a good and pleasant one. You have then an opportunity of making friends of mere acquaintances, and you can, in a pleasant chat with a friend at home, have more real enjoyment in her society than in a dozen meetings in large companies, with all the formality and restraint of a party thrown around you. There are many subjects of conversation which are pleasant in a parlor, tête-à-tête with a friend, which you would not care to discuss in a crowded saloon, or in the street. Personal inquiries, private affairs can be cosily chatted over.

In paying your visits of condolence, show, by your own quiet gravity, that you sympathize in the recent affliction of your friend. Though you may endeavor to comfort and cheer her, you must avoid a gay or careless air, as it will be an insult at such a time. Avoid any allusion to the past that may be trying for her to hear or answer, yet do not ignore the subject entirely, as that appears like a want of interest in it. Though you may feel happy, avoid parading your own joyousness at such a time; whatever your own feeling may be, respect the sorrow of another.

Never sit gazing curiously around the room when paying a call, as if taking a mental inventory of the furniture. It is excessively rude. It is still worse to appear to notice any disorder or irregularity that may occur.

If, while paying a call, you perceive that any unforeseen matter in the family, calls for the attention of the lady of the house, leave instantly, no matter how short your call has been. Your friend may not appear to notice the screams of a child, a noise in the kitchen, or the cry from the nursery that the fire board has caught fire, but you may be sure she does hear it, and though too well-bred to speak of it, will heartily rejoice to say good-bye.

Do not take a child with you to pay calls, until it is old enough to behave quietly and with propriety. To have a troublesome child constantly touching the parlor ornaments, balancing itself on the back of a chair, leaning from a window, or performing any of the thousand tricks in which children excel, is an annoyance, both to yourself and your hostess.

Make no remark upon the temperature of the room, or its arrangement, when you enter it. Never open or shut a window or door without asking permission, and unless really suffering from excessive heat or cold, refrain from asking leave to take this liberty.

If you are invited to go up stairs to your friend's private apartment, you will, of course, accept the invitation, but never go up stairs uninvited. When you reach her door, if the servant has not preceded and announced you, knock, and await her invitation to enter. Then, once in, take no notice of the room, but go instantly to your friend. If she is sewing, do not speak of the nature of her work, but request her to continue, as if you were not present.

In cases of long standing friendship, you will not, of course, stand upon the ceremony of waiting for each and every one of your calls to be returned before paying another, but be careful that you are not too lavish of your visits. The most cordial welcome may be worn threadbare, if it is called into use *too* often.

If you are visiting an invalid, or one confined by physical infirmity to one apartment, while you are cheerful and ready to impart all the news that will interest them, do not, by too glowing descriptions of out-door pleasures, make them feel more keenly their own deprivations. It is well, when making such calls, to converse upon literature, or such general subjects as will not remind them of their misfortune.

In cases where, from long illness or other infirmity, a gentleman friend is confined entirely to his room, you may, with perfect propriety, call upon him. It is both polite and kind to do so, as otherwise he would be deprived entirely of the society of his lady friends. Many thus unfortunately situated, from study and reading while so shut out from the world, become the most delightful companions.

If, when you make a call, you unfortunately intrude upon an early dinner hour, do not go in, but leave your card, and say that you will call again.

If you call upon two ladies who are boarding at the same house, do not send up your card to both at the same time. If one is out, send a card to her room, and then send up for the other. If the first one is in, wait till she comes down, and then chat as long as a call usually lasts. When you rise as if to take leave, accompany your friend to the parlor door, then tell her that you are going to send up for your other friend. She will bid you good-morning, and go to her own room; ring the bell after she leaves you, and send your card by the waiter to your other friend.

In calling at a hotel, enter by the ladies' door, and send your card to the room of your friend by the waiter. It is well, if you are calling upon an entire stranger, to choose a seat, and tell the waiter to say to the lady exactly where she will find you. She will probably enter with your card in her hand; then rise, greet her by name, and introduce yourself. If you speak to another stranger upon the same errand as the one you expect, the error will be instantly perceived by the difference in name. If a stranger, bringing a letter of introduction, sends the letter with her card, instead of calling, courtesy requires you to make the first call, immediately; the same day that you receive the letter, if possible, if not, the day after.

CHAPTER XI.
DINNER COMPANY.
ETIQUETTE FOR THE HOSTESS.

In issuing invitations for a large dinner party, the usual form is—

Mr. and Mrs. G—— request the favor of Mr. and Mrs. L——'s company to dinner, on Wednesday, March 8th, at —— o'clock.

If your husband is giving a party to gentlemen only, he will have a card printed or written for the occasion, but your duties as hostess, if he wishes you to preside, will still be as arduous as if your own friends were included in the invitation.

The directions given in the chapter on "Evening parties" for the arrangement of the parlor and the dressing-rooms, will apply here equally well, but the dining-room (in this case the centre of attraction) requires still more careful attention. Any fault here will mar your own comfort and the pleasure of your guests, and must be carefully avoided.

Send out your invitations by a servant, or man hired for the purpose; do not trust them to despatch or penny post.

Be careful in selecting the guests for a dinner party. Remember that conversation will be the sole entertainment for several hours, and if your guests are not well chosen, your dinner, no matter how perfect or costly the viands, will prove a failure. The most agreeable dinners are those whose numbers will allow all the guests to join in a common conversation, and where the host has spirit and intelligence to take the lead, and start a new subject when the interest in the old one begins to flag. Dinners where the guests depend entirely upon the person next them for conversation, are apt to be stupid, as it requires marvelous tact to pair off all the couples, so that every one will be entertaining in tête-à-tête conversation.

To give a good dinner, your means, room, and establishment must all be taken into consideration when you are preparing for a dinner company. If you invite a large number, you must increase your establishment for the occasion, as to sit down to a dinner badly served, with a scarcity of waiters, is tiresome, and shows little tact or grace on the part of the hostess.

One cook cannot prepare dinner properly for more than ten persons, and three waiters will find ample employment in waiting upon the same number. More than this number will require a table too large for general, easy conversation, and throw your company into couples or trios, for entertainment.

Have your table spread in a room that will accommodate all the guests comfortably, at the same time avoid putting a small social party in a large room, where they will appear lost in the space around them. Let the room be comfortably warmed, and if your dinner is late, have the apartments well lighted. If you sit down by daylight, but will remain in the room until after dark, have the shutters closed and the lights lit, before the dinner is announced, as nothing can be more awkward than to do this in the middle of the meal.

The shape of a table is a point of more importance than some people think. If you wish your dinner to be social—not a mere collection of tête-à-têtes—the table should be of a shape which will make it easy for each guest to address any one at the table. The long parallelogram, with the host at one end and the hostess at the other, is stiff, too broad, too long, and isolates the givers of the feast from the guests.

The round table, if large enough to accommodate many guests, has too large a diameter each way for easy conversation. The best table is the oval, and the host and hostess should sit in the middle of each side, facing each other.

The dining room, even in the heat of summer, should be carpeted, to deaden the noise of the servants' feet. The chairs should be easy, without arms, and with tall, slanting backs. It adds much to the comfort, if each person is provided with a foot-stool.

You must have, besides the waiters, one servant to carve, and he must be an adept. No dish should be carved upon the table, and that no guest shall wait too long for his meat, you must engage a rapid and dexterous carver.

For a party of ten, two waiters, and the carver, are amply sufficient. If you have too many servants, they will only interfere with each other, and stand staring at the guests. Give your orders before dinner, and through the meal never speak to the servants. Your whole attention must be given to the guests. Even if you see that matters are going wrong, do not let your annoyance appear, but gracefully ignore the painful facts. Let each servant have his regular position at the table. One should take the guests at the right of the hostess, and the left of the host; the other the guests on the other side. They should wear light, noiseless shoes, and white gloves, and each one carry a folded napkin over his right arm.

The main point in the arrangement of the table itself, is to secure beauty, without interfering with conversation. The table cover and napkins must be of snowy damask, the glass clear as crystal, and taste must preside over each detail. Let nothing high be placed on the table, that will effectually separate the guests from each other. There should be, first, a handsome centre piece, and this may be of glass, silver, or china, and not too high or large, and must be elegant as a work of art, or it is better omitted altogether. Preserve or fruit stands, tastefully decorated, with the fruit on fresh, green leaves, and flowers mingled with them, form exquisite centre pieces. A pyramid of flowers, or tasty vase or basket, forms, too, a beautiful ornament for the centre of the table. In addition to this, the French scatter vases of flowers all over the table, at the corners and in the centre. Some place a small, fragrant bouquet before the plate of each guest. Nothing can be more beautiful than this arrangement. Glasses of celery, dishes of clear, transparent jellies or preserves, exquisite little glass plates of pickles should stand in order on the table.

Place before each guest, the plate, knife, fork, spoon, four wine-glasses of various sizes, the goblet for water, napkin, small salt cellar, salt spoon, and roll of bread. Place none of the meats or vegetables upon the large table. These should all be served at a side-table, each guest selecting his own, to be handed by the servants. The first course is soup. As this is not meant to destroy the appetite for other viands, it should be light, not too rich or thick. Let the servant hand one ladlefull to each person. If you have more than one kind, he must first inquire which each guest prefers.

If you have wines, let them be handed round after the soup.

Next comes the fish. If you have large fish, let a slice, cut smoothly, not made into a hash by awkward carving, be placed upon the plate of the guest, with a slice of egg, and drawn butter. If the fish are small, one should be placed upon each plate.

Then come the patties of oysters, minced veal, or lobster; or, instead of these, you may have poultry or game.

Next the roast. With the meats have vegetables served on a separate plate, that the guest may take as much as he wishes with meat. You will, of course, have a variety of vegetables, but scarcely any guest will choose more than two.

The pastry and puddings come next in order, and these, too, are better served from a side table. Between the pastry and the dessert, have salad and cheese placed before each guest.

If you eat dessert in the same room that you dine in, it should be placed upon the table (with the exception of the ices) before the guests are seated, and this comes after the pastry has been discussed. It should consist of fruit and ices.

A pleasanter and more elegant way, is to have the fruit and ices spread in a separate room, and leave the dining room after the pastry has been eaten. The change of position, the absence of the meat flavor in the atmosphere, make the dessert much more delightful than if it is eaten in the same room as the dinner. In summer especially, the change to a cool, fresh room, where the ices and fruits are tastefully spread, and flowers are scattered profusely about the room, delights every sense.

Coffee follows the dessert, and when this enters, if your guests are gentlemen only, your duty is at an end. You may then rise, leave the room, and need not re-appear. If you have lady guests, you give the signal for rising after coffee, and lead the way to the parlor, where, in a few moments, the gentlemen will again join you.

Suppose your guests invited, servants instructed, every arrangement made, and the important day arrived. The next point to consider is the reception of your guests. Be dressed in good season, as many seem to consider an invitation to dinner as one to pass the day, and come early. Take a position in your drawing-room, where each guest will find you easily, and remain near it, until every guest has arrived. As each one enters, advance to meet him, and extend your hand.

Have plenty of chairs ready in the drawing-room, as an invitation to dinner by no means argues a "stand up" party. As you have already arranged every detail, your duty as hostess consists in receiving your guests gracefully, conversing and looking as charmingly as possible. Flowers in the drawing-room are as great a proof of taste as in the dining room.

As the time just before dinner is very apt to be tiresome, you should bring forward all the armor against stupidity that you possess. Display upon tables arranged conveniently about the room, curiosities, handsome books, photographs, engravings, stereoscopes, medallions, any works of art you may own, and have the ottomans, sofas, and chairs so placed that your guests can move easily about the room, or rooms.

The severest test of good breeding in a lady, is in the position of hostess, receiving dinner guests. Your guests may arrive all at once, yet you must make each one feel that he or she is the object of your individual attention, and none must be hurt by neglect. They may arrive very early, yet your duty is to make the time fly until dinner is announced. They may come late, and risk the ruin of your choicest dishes, yet you must not, upon pain of a breach of etiquette, show the least annoyance. If you know that the whole kitchen is in arms at the delay, you must conceal the anguish, as the Spartan boy did his pangs, to turn a cheerful, smiling face upon the tardy guests.

When dinner is announced, you will lead the way to the dining-room upon the arm of one of your gentlemen guests, having paired off the company in couples. The host comes in last with a lady upon his arm.

You may indicate to each couple, as they enter the dining-room, the seats they are to occupy, standing until all are seated, or you may allow them to choose their own places. The English fashion of placing a card upon each plate with the name of the person to take that seat upon it, is a good one. It enables the hostess to place those whom she is certain will be mutually entertaining, next each other. Place the gentleman who escorts you from the parlor at your right hand.

Having once taken your seat at table, you have nothing to do with the dinner but to partake of it. Not a word, or even a glance, will a well-bred hostess bestow upon the servants, nor will she speak to the guests of the dishes. Their choice rests between themselves and the waiters, and you must take no notice of what they eat, how much, or how little. Nay, should they partake of one dish only, you must ignore the fact.

The greatest tact is displayed where the hostess makes each guest feel perfectly at ease. She will aid her husband both in leading and supporting the conversation and will see that no guest is left in silence from want of attention. Whilst she ignores every breach of etiquette her guests may commit, she must carefully observe every rule herself, and this she must do in an easy, natural manner, avoiding every appearance of restraint. Her deportment, she may be sure, is secretly watched and criticised by each guest, yet she must appear utterly unconscious that she is occupying any conspicuous position.

To watch the servants, or appear uneasy, lest something should go wrong, is excessively ill-bred, and if any accident does occur, you only make it worse by noticing it. To reprove or speak sharply to a servant before your guests, manifests a shocking want of good breeding.

The rules given above are only applicable to large dinner parties, and where the guests are few, and the host himself carves, these rules will not apply. In this case, as you will only require the services of your own household domestics, you must, of course, attend personally to the wants of your guests.

Dinner not being served from a side table, you must, while putting tasteful ornaments upon it, be careful not to crowd them, and leave room for the substantial dishes.

You must watch the plate of each guest, to see that it is well provided, and you will invite each one to partake of the various dishes.

Have a servant to pass the plates from you to each guest, and from the host to you, after he has put the meat upon them, that you may add gravy and vegetables before they are set before your visitors.

At these smaller dinner companies, avoid apologizing for anything, either in the viands or the arrangement of them. You have provided the best your purse will allow, prepared as faultlessly as possible; you will only gain credit for mock modesty if you apologize for a well-prepared, well-spread dinner, and if there are faults they will only be made more conspicuous if attention is drawn to them by an apology.

Ease of manner, quiet dignity, cheerful, intelligent conversation, and gentle, lady-like deportment, never appear more charming than when they adorn a lady at the head of her own table.

CHAPTER XII.
DINNER COMPANY.
ETIQUETTE FOR THE GUEST.

When you receive an invitation to join a dinner-party, answer it immediately, as, by leaving your hostess in doubt whether you intend to accept or decline her hospitality, you make it impossible for her to decide how many she must prepare for. If you accept at first, and any unforeseen event keeps you from fulfilling your engagement, write a second note, that your hostess may not wait dinner for you. Such a note, if circumstances render it necessary to write it, may be sent with perfect propriety an hour before the time appointed for dinner, though, if you are aware that you cannot attend, earlier, you must send the information in good season.

You should enter the house of your hostess from a quarter to half an hour earlier than the time appointed for dining. Proceed at once to the dressing-room, and arrange your dress and hair, and then enter the drawing-room. By going to the house too early, you may hasten or interrupt the toilet arrangements of your hostess; while, by being late, you will establish a most disagreeable association in the minds of all present, as "the lady who kept dinner waiting at Mrs. L——'s."

Immediately upon entering the parlor find your hostess, and speak to her first. It is very rude to stop to chat with other guests before greeting the lady of the house. You may bow to any one you know, in passing, but do not stop to speak. Having exchanged a few words with your hostess, turn to the other guests, unless you are the first arrival. In that case, converse with your host and hostess until others come in.

Be careful, if dinner is delayed by the tardiness of the guests, or from any other cause, that you do not show by your manner that you are aware of such delay. To look towards the door often, consult your watch, or give tokens of weariness, are all marks of ill-breeding. Your hostess will probably be sufficiently annoyed by the irregularity itself; do not add to her discomfort by allowing her to suppose that her guests perceive the deficiencies. Look over the books and pictures with an air of interest, converse cheerfully, and in every way appear as if dinner were a matter of secondary importance, (as, indeed, it should be,) compared with the pleasure of the society around you.

When the signal for dinner is given, your hostess will probably name your escort to the table. If he is a stranger, bow in acknowledgement of the introduction, take his arm, and fall into your place in the stream of guests passing from the parlor to the dining-room.

Take the seat pointed out by your hostess, or the waiter, as soon as it is offered. Each one will do this upon entering, and it prevents the confusion that will result if those first entering the room, remain standing until all the other guests come in.

When you take your seat, be careful that your chair does not stand upon the dress of the lady next you, as she may not rise at the same instant that you do, and so you risk tearing her dress.

Sit gracefully at the table; neither so close as to make your movements awkward, nor so far away as to drag your food over your dress before it reaches your mouth. It is well to carry in your pocket a small pincushion, and, having unfolded your napkin, to pin it at the belt. You may do this quietly, without its being perceived, and you will thus really save your dress. If the napkin is merely laid open upon your lap, it will be very apt to slip down, if your dress is of silk or satin, and you risk the chance of appearing again in the drawing-room with the front of your dress soiled or greased.

If, by the carelessness or awkwardness of your neighbors or the servants, you have a plate of soup, glass of wine, or any dish intended for your mouth, deposited upon your dress, do not spring up, or make any exclamation. You may wipe off the worst of the spot with your napkin, and then let it pass without further notice. If an apology is made by the unlucky perpetrator of the accident, try to set him at his ease by your own lady-like composure. He will feel sorry and awkward enough, without reproach, sullenness, or cold looks from you.

Gloves and mittens are no longer worn at table, even at the largest dinner-parties.

To make remarks upon the guests or the dishes is excessively rude.

If the conversation is general, speak loudly enough to be heard by those around you, but, at the same time, avoid raising your voice *too* much. If the company is very large, and you converse only with the person immediately beside you, speak in a distinct, but low tone, that you may not interrupt other couples, but carefully avoid whispering or a confidential air. Both are in excessively bad taste. To laugh in a suppressed way, has the appearance of laughing at those around you, and a loud, boisterous laugh is always unlady-like. Converse cheerfully, laugh quietly, but freely, if you will, and while you confine your attention entirely to your neighbor, still avoid any air of secrecy or mystery.

Never use an eye-glass, either to look at the persons around you or the articles upon the table.

Eat your soup quietly. To make any noise in eating it, is simply disgusting. Do not break bread into your soup. Break off small pieces and put into your mouth, if you will, but neither bite it from the roll nor break it up, and eat it from your soup-plate with a spoon.

In eating bread with meat, never dip it into the gravy on your plate, and then bite the end off. If you wish to eat it with gravy, break off a small piece, put it upon your plate, and then, with a fork, convey it to your mouth.

When helped to fish, remove, with knife and fork, all the bones, then lay down the knife, and, with a piece of bread in your left hand and a fork in your right, eat the flakes of fish.

Need I say that the knife is to cut your food with, and must never be used while eating? To put it in your mouth is a distinctive mark of low-breeding.

If you have selected what you will eat, keep the plate that is placed before you; never pass it to the persons next you, as they may have an entirely different choice of meat or vegetables.

Never attempt to touch any dish that is upon the table, but out of your reach, by stretching out your arms, leaning forward, or, still worse, standing up. Ask the waiter to hand it, if you wish for it; or, if the gentleman beside you can easily do so, you may ask him to pass it to you.

Do not press those near you to take more or other things than are upon their plate. This is the duty of the hostess, or, if the company is large, the servants will attend to it. For you to do so is officious and ill-bred.

When conversing let your knife and fork rest easily upon your plate, even if still in your hand. Avoid holding them upright. Keep your own knife, fork, and spoon solely for the articles upon your own plate. To use them for helping yourself to butter or salt, is rude in the extreme.

When you do not use the salt-spoon, sugar tongs, and butter-knife, you may be sure that those around you will conclude that you have never seen the articles, and do not know their use.

You need not fear to offend by refusing to take wine with a gentleman, even your host. If you decline gracefully, he will appreciate the delicacy which makes you refuse. If, however, you have no conscientious scruples, and are invited to take wine, bow, and merely raise the glass to your lips, then set it down again. You may thus acknowledge the courtesy, and yet avoid actually drinking the wine.

No lady should drink wine at dinner. Even if her head is strong enough to bear it, she will find her cheeks, soon after the indulgence, flushed, hot, and uncomfortable; and if the room is warm, and the dinner a long one, she will probably pay the penalty of her folly, by having a headache all the evening.

If offered any dish of which you do not wish to partake, decline it, but do not assign any reason. To object to the dish itself is an insult to your entertainers, and if you assert any reason for your own dislike it is ill-bred.

Do not bend too much forward over your food, and converse easily. To eat fast, or appear to be so much engrossed as to be unable to converse, is ill-bred; and it makes those around you suspect that you are so little accustomed to dining well, that you fear to stop eating an instant, lest you should not get enough.

It is equally ill-bred to accept every thing that is offered to you. Never take more than two vegetables; do not take a second plate of soup, pastry, or pudding. Indeed, it is best to accept but *one* plate of any article.

Never use a spoon for anything but liquids, and never touch anything to eat, excepting bread, celery, or fruit, with your fingers.

In the intervals which must occur between the courses, do not appear to be conscious of the lapse of time. Wear a careless air when waiting, conversing cheerfully and pleasantly, and avoid looking round the room, as if wondering what the waiters are about.

Never eat every morsel that is upon your plate; and surely no lady will ever scrape her plate, or pass the bread round it, as if to save the servants the trouble of washing it.

Take such small mouthfulls that you can always be ready for conversation, but avoid playing with your food, or partaking of it with an affectation of delicate appetite. Your hostess may suppose you despise her fare, if you appear so very choice, or eat too sparingly. If your state of health deprives you of appetite, it is bad enough for you to decline the invitation to dine out.

Never examine minutely the food before you. You insult your hostess by such a proceeding, as it looks as if you feared to find something upon the plate that should not be there.

If you find a worm on opening a nut, or in any of the fruit, hand your plate quietly, and without remark, to the waiter, and request him to bring you a clean one. Do not let others perceive the movement, or the cause of it, if you can avoid so doing.

Never make a noise in eating. To munch or smack the lips are vulgar faults.

Sit quietly at table, avoid stiffness, but, at the same time, be careful that you do not annoy others by your restlessness.

Do not eat so fast as to be done long before others, nor so slowly as to keep them waiting.

When the finger-glasses are passed round, dip the ends of your fingers into them, and wipe them upon your napkin; then do not fold your napkin, but place it beside your plate upon the table.

To carry away fruit or bonbons from the table is a sign of low breeding.

Rise with the other ladies when your hostess gives the signal.

After returning to the parlor, remain in the house at least an hour after dinner is over. If you have another engagement in the evening, you may then take your leave, but not before. You will insult your hostess by leaving sooner, as it appears that you came only for the dinner, and that being over, your interest in the house, for the time, has ceased. It is only beggars who "eat and run!"

CHAPTER XIII.
TABLE ETIQUETTE.

In order to appear perfectly well-bred at table when in company, or in public, as at a hotel, you must pay attention, three times a day, to the points of table etiquette. If you neglect these little details at home and in private, they will be performed awkwardly and with an air of restraint when you are in company. By making them habitual, they will become natural, and appear easily, and sit gracefully upon you.

Even when eating entirely alone, observe these little details, thus making the most finished and elegant manners perfectly familiar, and thus avoiding the stiff, awkward air you will wear if you keep your politeness only for company, when you will be constantly apprehensive of doing wrong.

At breakfast or tea, if your seat is at the head of the table, you must, before taking anything upon your own plate, fill a cup for each one of the family, and pass them round, being careful to suit each one in the preparation of the cup, that none may return to you for more tea, water, sugar, or milk. If you have a visitor, pass the cup with the tea or coffee alone in it, and hand with the cup the sugar bowl and cream pitcher, that these may be added in the quantity preferred.

After all the cups have been filled and passed round, you may take the bread, butter, and other food upon your own plate. Train your children, so that they will pass these things to you as soon as they see you are ready to receive them.

If you are yourself at the side of the table, pass the bread, butter, etc., to the lady at the head, when you see that she has sent the cups from the waiter before her, to those seated at the table.

If you occupy the place of head of the table, you must watch the cups, offer to fill them when empty, and also see that each one of the family is well helped to the other articles upon the table.

Avoid making any noise in eating, even if each meal is eaten in solitary state. It is a disgusting habit, and one not easily cured if once contracted, to make any noise with the lips when eating.

Never put large pieces of food into your mouth. Eat slowly, and cut your food into small pieces before putting it into your mouth.

Use your fork, or spoon, never your knife, to put your food into your mouth. At dinner, hold in your left hand a piece of bread, and raise your meat or vegetables with the fork, holding the bread to prevent the pieces slipping from the plate.

If you are asked at table what part of the meat you prefer, name your favorite piece, but do not give such information unless asked to do so. To point out any especial part of a dish, and ask for it, is ill-bred. To answer, when asked to select a part, that "it is a matter of indifference," or, "I can eat any part," is annoying to the carver, as he cares less than yourself certainly, and would prefer to give you the piece you really like best.

Do not pour coffee or tea from your cup into your saucer, and do not blow either these or soup. Wait until they cool.

Use the butter-knife, salt-spoon, and sugar-tongs as scrupulously when alone, as if a room full of people were watching you. Otherwise, you may neglect to do so when the omission will mortify you.

Never put poultry or fish bones, or the stones of fruit, upon the table-cloth, but place them on the edge of your plate.

Do not begin to eat until others at the table are ready to commence too.

Sit easily in your chair, neither too near the table, nor too far from it, and avoid such tricks as putting your arms on the table, leaning back lazily in your chair, or playing with your knife, fork, or spoon.

Never raise your voice, when speaking, any higher than is necessary. The clear articulation and distinct pronunciation of each word, will make a low tone more agreeable and more easily understood, than the loudest tone, if the speech is rapid or indistinct.

Never pass your plate with the knife or fork upon it, and when you pass your cup, put the spoon in the saucer.

Never pile up the food on your plate. It looks as if you feared it would all be gone before you could be helped again, and it will certainly make your attempts to cut the food awkward, if your plate is crowded.

If there is a delicacy upon the table, partake of it sparingly, and never help yourself to it a second time.

If you wish to cough, or use your handkerchief, rise from the table, and leave the room. If you have not time to do this, cover your mouth, and turn your head aside from the table, and perform the disagreeable necessity as rapidly and quietly as possible.

Avoid gesticulation at the table. Indeed, a well-bred lady will never gesticulate, but converse quietly, letting the expression and animation of her features give force to her words.

Never, when at the home table, leave it until the other members of the family are also ready to rise.

CHAPTER XIV.
CONDUCT IN THE STREET.

A lady's conduct is never so entirely at the mercy of critics, because never so public, as when she is in the street. Her dress, carriage, walk, will all be exposed to notice; every passer-by will look at her, if it is only for one glance; every unlady-like action will be marked; and in no position will a dignified, lady-like deportment be more certain to command respect.

Let me start with you upon your promenade, my friend, and I will soon decide your place upon the list of well-bred ladies.

First, your dress. Not that scarlet shawl, with a green dress, I beg, and—oh! spare my nerves!—you are not so insane as to put on a blue bonnet. That's right.

If you wish to wear the green dress, don a black shawl, and—that white bonnet will do very well. One rule you must lay down with regard to a walking dress. It must never be conspicuous. Let the material be rich, if you will; the set of each garment faultless; have collar and sleeves snowy white, and wear neatly-fitting, whole, clean gloves and boots. Every detail may be scrupulously attended to, but let the whole effect be quiet and modest. Wear a little of one bright color, if you will, but not more than one. Let each part of the dress harmonize with all the rest; avoid the *extreme* of fashion, and let the dress suit *you*. If you are short and plump, do not wear flounces, because they are fashionable, and avoid large plaids, even if they are the very latest style. If tall and slight, do not add to the length of your figure by long stripes, a little mantilla, and a caricature of a bonnet, with long, streaming ribbons. A large, round face will never look well, staring from a tiny, delicate bonnet; nor will a long, thin one stand the test much better. Wear what is becoming to *yourself*, and only bow to fashion enough to avoid eccentricity. To have everything in the *extreme* of fashion, is a sure mark of vulgarity.

Wear no jewelry in the street excepting your watch and brooch. Jewelry is only suited for full evening dress, when all the other details unite to set it off. If it is real, it is too valuable to risk losing in the street, and if it is *not* real, no lady should wear it. Mock jewelry is utterly detestable.

What are you doing? Sucking the head of your parasol! Have you not break-fasted? Take that piece of ivory from your mouth! To suck it is unlady-like, and let me tell you, excessively unbecoming. Rosy lips and pearly teeth can be put to a better use.

Why did you not dress before you came out? It is a mark of ill-breeding to draw your gloves on in the street. Now your bonnet-strings, and now—your collar! Pray arrange your dress before you leave the house! Nothing looks worse than to see a lady fussing over her dress in the street. Take a few moments more in your dressing-room, and so arrange your dress that you will not need to think of it again whilst you are out.

Do not walk so fast! you are not chasing anybody! Walk slowly, gracefully! Oh, do not drag one foot after the other as if you were fast asleep—set down the foot lightly, but at the same time firmly; now, carry your head up, not so; you hang it down as if you feared to look any one in the face! Nay, that is the other extreme! Now you look like a drill-major, on parade! So! that is the medium. Erect, yet, at the same time, easy and elegant.

Now, my friend, do not swing your arms. You don't know what to do with them? Your parasol takes one hand; hold your dress up a little with the other. Not so! No lady should raise her dress above the ankle.

Take care! don't drag your dress through that mud-puddle! Worse and worse! If you take hold of your dress on both sides, in that way, and drag it up so high, you will be set down as a raw country girl. So. Raise it just above the boot, all round, easily, letting it fall again in the old folds. Don't shake it down; it will fall back of itself.

Stop! don't you see there is a carriage coming? Do you want to be thrown down by the horses? You can run across? Very lady-like indeed! Surely nothing can be more ungraceful than to see a lady shuffle and run across a street. Wait until the way is clear and then walk slowly across.

Do not try to raise your skirts. It is better to soil them. (You were very foolish to wear white skirts this muddy day.) *They* are easily washed, and you cannot raise *all*. You will surely be awkward in making the attempt, and probably fail, in spite of your efforts. True, they will be badly soiled, and you expose this when you raise the dress, but the state of the streets must be seen by all who see your share of the dirt, and they will apologize for your untidy appearance in a language distinctly understood.

Don't hold your parasol so close to your face, nor so low down. You cannot see your way clear, and you will run against somebody. Always hold an umbrella or parasol so that it will clear your bonnet, and leave the space before your face open, that you may see your way clearly.

If you are ever caught in a shower, and meet a gentleman friend who offers an umbrella, accept it, if he will accompany you to your destination; but do not deprive him of it, if he is not able to join you. Should he insist, return it to his house or store the instant you reach home, with a note of thanks. If a stranger offers you the same services, decline it positively, but courteously, at the same time thanking him.

Never stop to speak to a gentleman in the street. If you have anything important to say to him, allow him to join and walk with you, but do not stop. It is best to follow the same rule with regard to ladies, and either walk with them or invite them to walk with you, instead of stopping to talk.

A lady who desires to pay strict regard to etiquette, will not stop to gaze in at the shop windows. It looks countrified. If she is alone, it looks as if she were waiting for some one; and if she is not alone, she is victimizing some one else, to satisfy her curiosity.

Remember that in meeting your gentlemen friends it is your duty to speak first, therefore do not cut them by waiting to be recognized. Be sure, however, that they see you before you bow, or you place yourself in the awkward position of having your bow pass, unreturned.

You are not expected to recognize any friend on the opposite side of the street. Even if you see them, do not bow.

Avoid "cutting" any one. It is a small way of showing spite, and lowers you more than your enemy. If you wish to avoid any further intercourse bow, coldly and gravely, but do not look at any one, to whom you are in the habit of bowing, and pass without bowing. If you do this, they may flatter themselves that they were really unrecognized, but a distant, cold bow will show them that you speak from civility only, not from friendship.

In the street a lady takes the arm of a relative, her affianced lover, or husband, but of no other gentleman, unless the streets are slippery, or in the evening.

When a lady walks with two gentlemen, she should endeavor to divide her attention and remarks equally between them.

If you do stop in the street, draw near the walls, that you may not keep others from passing.

Loud talking and laughing in the street are excessively vulgar. Not only this, but they expose a lady to the most severe misconstruction. Let your conduct be modest and quiet.

If a gentleman, although a stranger, offers his hand to assist you in leaving a carriage, omnibus, or to aid you in crossing where it is wet or muddy, accept his civility, thank him, bow and pass on.

If you wish to take an omnibus or car, see that it is not already full. If it is, do not get in. You will annoy others, and be uncomfortable yourself.

It is best to carry change to pay car or omnibus fare, as you keep others waiting whilst the driver is making change, and it is apt to fall into the straw when passing from one hand to another.

If a gentleman gives you his seat, hands your fare, or offers you any such attention, *thank him*. It is not countrified, it is lady-like. If you do not speak, bow.

Be careful not to be alone in the streets after night fall. It exposes you to insult. If you are obliged to go out, have a servant, or another lady, if you cannot procure the escort of a gentleman, which is, of course, the best.

Walk slowly, do not turn your head to the right or left, unless you wish to walk that way, and avoid any gesture or word that will attract attention.

Never look back! It is excessively ill-bred.

Make no remarks upon those who pass you, while there is even a possibility that they may hear you.

Never stare at any one, even if they have peculiarities, which make them objects of remark.

In taking your place in an omnibus or car, do so quietly, and then sit perfectly still. Do not change your place or move restlessly. Make room for others if you see that the opposite side is full.

If you walk with a gentleman, when he reaches your door invite him in, but if he declines, do not urge him. If you are returning from a ball or party, and the hour is a very late (or early) one, you are not bound in politeness to invite your escort to enter; the hour will be your apology for omitting the ceremony.

CHAPTER XV.
LETTER WRITING.

There is no branch of education called so universally into requisition as the art of letter writing; no station, high or low, where the necessity for correspondence is not felt; no person, young or old, who does not, at some time, write, cause to be written, and receive letters. From the President in his official capacity, with the busy pens of secretaries constantly employed in this branch of service, to the Irish laborer who, unable to guide a pen, writes, also by proxy, to his kinsfolks across the wide ocean; all, at some time, feel the desire to transmit some message, word of love, business, or sometimes enmity, by letter.

Yet, in spite of the universal need, and almost universal habit, there are really but very few persons who write a *good* letter; a letter that is, at the same time long enough to interest, yet not long enough to tire; sufficiently condensed to keep the attention, and not tedious, and yet detailed enough to afford satisfaction; that is correct in grammatical construction, properly punctuated, written in a clear, legible hand, with the date, address, signature, all in the proper place, no words whose letters stand in utter defiance to spelling-book rules; in short, a well-written letter.

Thousands, millions are sent from post to post every day. The lightning speed of the telegraph takes its messages from city to city; the panting steamer carries from continent to continent its heavy mail-bags, laden with its weight of loving messages; the "iron horse" drags behind it, its measure of the many missives; while, in the far-distant Western wilds, the lumbering wagon bears its paper freight, with its pen eloquence, to cheer and comfort, or sadden and crush, the waiting emigrants, longing for news of home.

To some, who, with hearts desolated by the separation from the home circle, could read, with an eager interest, volumes of the most common-place, trivial incidents, if only connected with the loved ones there, will come pages, from the pen of the dearest relative, full of learning, wit, and wisdom, wholly uninteresting to the receiver.

Why is this? Not from any desire upon the part of the writer to display learning or talent, but because, writing a letter being to them a great undertaking, and the letter being destined to go a long distance, they look upon it as an event too unusual to be wasted in detailing the simple, every-day details of domestic life, and ransack memory and learning for a subject worthy of the long journey and unusual labor.

Others will have, from mere acquaintances, long, tedious details of uninteresting trivialities, and from the near relatives, short, dry epistles, which fall like stones upon the heart longing for little, affectionate expressions, and home memories.

From some letter writers, who are in the midst of scenes and events of the most absorbing interest, letters arrive, only a few lines long, without one allusion to the interesting matter lying so profusely around them; while others, with the scantiest of outward subjects, will, from their own teeming brain, write bewitching, absorbing epistles, read with eagerness, laid aside with the echo of Oliver Twist's petition in a sigh; the reader longing for "more."

It is, of course, impossible to lay down any distinct rule for the *style* of letter writing. Embracing, as it does, all subjects and all classes, all countries and associations, and every relation in which one person can stand to another, what would be an imperative rule in some cases, becomes positive absurdity in others. Every letter will vary from others written before, in either its subject, the person addressed, or the circumstances which make it necessary to write it.

Letter writing is, in fact, but conversation, carried on with the pen, when distance or circumstances prevent the easier method of exchanging ideas, by spoken words. Write, therefore, as you would speak, were the person to whom your letter is addressed seated beside you. As amongst relatives and intimate friends you would converse with a familiar manner, and in easy language, so in your letters to such persons, let your style be simple, entirely devoid of effort.

Again, when introduced to a stranger, or conversing with one much older than yourself, your manner is respectful and dignified; so let the letters addressed to those on these terms with yourself, be written in a more ceremonious style, but at the same time avoid stiffness, and above all, pedantry. A letter of advice to a child, would of course demand an entirely different style, from that written by a young lady to a friend or relative advanced in life; yet the general rule, "write as you would converse," applies to each and every case.

Neatness is an important requisite in a letter. To send a fair, clean sheet, with the words written in a clear, legible hand, will go a great way in ensuring a cordial welcome for your letter. Avoid erasures, as they spoil the beauty of your sheet. If it is necessary to correct a word, draw your pen through it, and write the word you wish to use as a substitute, above the one erased; do not scratch out the word and write another over it: it is untidy, and the second word is seldom legible. Another requisite for a good letter is a clear, concise style. Use language that will be easily understood, and avoid the parenthesis. Important passages in letters are often lost entirely, by the ambiguous manner in which they are worded, or rendered quite as unintelligible by the blots, erasures, or villainously bad hand-writing. A phrase may, by the addition or omission of one word, or by the alteration of one punctuation mark, convey to the reader an entirely different idea from that intended by the writer; so, while you write plainly, use good language, you must also write carefully, and punctuate properly.

If you are in doubt about the correct spelling of a word, do not trust to chance, hoping it may be right, but get a dictionary, and be certain that you have spelt it as it ought to be.

Simplicity is a great charm in letter-writing. What you send in a letter, is, as a general rule, intended for the perusal of one person only. Therefore to cumber your epistles with quotations, similes, flowery language, and a stilted, pedantic style, is in bad taste. You may use elegant language, yet use it easily. If you use a quotation, let it come into its place naturally, as if flowing in perfect harmony with your ideas, and let it be short. Long quotations in a letter are tiresome. Make no attempt at display in a correspondence. You will err as much in such an attempt, as if, when seated face to face with your correspondent, alone in your own apartment, you were to rise and converse with the gestures and language of a minister in his pulpit, or a lecturer upon his platform.

As everything, in style, depends upon the subject of the letter, and the person to whom it is addressed, some words follow, relating to some of the various kinds of correspondence:

Business Letters should be as brief as is consistent with the subject; clear, and to the point. Say all that is necessary, in plain, distinct language, and say no more. State, in forcible words, every point that it is desirable for your correspondent to be made acquainted with, that your designs and prospects upon the subject may be perfectly well understood. Write, in such a letter, of nothing but the business in hand; other matters will be out of place there. Nowhere is a confused style, or illegible writing, more unpardonable than in a business letter; nowhere a good style and hand more important. Avoid flowery language, too many words, all pathos or wit, any display of talent or learning, and every merely personal matter, in a business letter.

Letters of Compliment must be restricted, confined entirely to one subject. If passing between acquaintances, they should be written in a graceful, at the same time respectful, manner. Avoid hackneyed expressions, commonplace quotations, and long, labored sentences, but while alluding to the subject in hand, as if warmly interested in it, at the same time endeavor to write in a style of simple, natural grace.

LETTERS OF CONGRATULATION demand a cheerful, pleasant style, and an appearance of great interest. They should be written from the heart, and the cordial, warm feelings there will prompt the proper language. Be careful, while offering to your friend the hearty congratulations her happy circumstances demand, that you do not let envy at her good fortune, creep into your head, to make the pen utter complaining words at your own hard lot. Do not dampen her joy, by comparing her happiness with the misery of another. There are many clouds in the life of every one of us. While the sun shines clearly upon the events of your friend›s life let her enjoy the brightness and warmth, unshadowed by any words of yours. Give her, to the full, your sympathy in her rejoicing, cheerful words, warm congratulations, and bright hopes for the future. Should there be, at the time of her happiness, any sad event you wish to communicate to her, of which it is your duty to inform her, write it in another letter. If you must send it the same day, do so, but let the epistle wishing her joy, go alone, unclouded with the news of sorrow. At the same time, avoid exaggerated expressions of congratulation, lest you are suspected of a desire to be satirical, and avoid underlining any words. If the language is not forcible enough to convey your ideas, you will not make it better by underlining it. If you say to your friend upon her marriage, that you wish her "*joy* in her new relations, and *hope* she may be *entirely happy* in her domestic life," you make her doubt your wishes, and think you mean to ridicule her chances of such happiness.

LETTERS OF CONDOLENCE are exceedingly trying, both to read and to write. If the affliction which calls for them is one which touches you nearly, really grieving and distressing you, all written words must seem tame and cold, compared with the aching sympathy which dictates them. It is hard with the eyes blinded by tears, and the hand shaking, to write calmly; and it is impossible to express upon paper all the burning thoughts and words that would pour forth, were you beside the friend whose sorrow is yours. If you do not feel the trial, your task is still more difficult, for no letters demand truth, spoken from the heart, more than letters of condolence. Do not treat the subject for grief too lightly. Write words of comfort if you will, but do not appear to consider the affliction as a trifle. Time may make it less severe, but the first blow of grief must be heavy, and a few words of sincere sympathy will outweigh pages of mere expressions of hope for comfort, or the careless lines that show the letter to be one of mere duty, not feeling. Let your friend feel that her sorrow makes her dearer to you than ever before, and that her grief is yours. To treat the subject with levity, or to wander from it into witticisms or every-day chit-chat, is a wanton insult, unworthy of a lady and a friend. Do not magnify the event, or plunge the mourner into still deeper despondency by taking a despairing, gloomy view of the sorrow, under which she is bent. Show her the silver lining of her cloud, try to soothe her grief, yet be willing to admit that it *is* a cloud, and that she *has* cause for grief. To throw out hints that the sorrow is sent as a punishment to an offender; to imply that neglect or imprudence on the part of the mourner is the cause of the calamity; to hold up the trial as an example of retribution, or a natural consequence of wrong doing, is cruel, and barbarous. Even if this is true, (indeed, if this is the case, it only aggravates the insult); avoid such retrospection. It is as if a surgeon, called in to a patient suffering from a fractured limb, sat down, inattentive to the suffering, to lecture his patient upon the carelessness which caused the accident. One of the most touching letters of condolence ever written was sent by a literary lady, well known in the ranks of our American authoresses, to her sister, who had lost her youngest child. The words were few, merely:—

"Sister Darling:

"I cannot write what is in my heart for you to-day, it is too full. Filled with a double sorrow, for you, for my own grief. Tears blind me, my pen trembles in my hand. Oh, to be near you! to clasp you in my arms! to draw your head to my bosom, and weep with you! Darling, God comfort you, I cannot.

"S."

That was all. Yet the sorrowing mother said that no other letter, though she appreciated the kind motive that dictated all, yet none comforted her as did these few lines. Written from the heart, their simple eloquence touched the heart for which they were intended. Early stages of great grief reject *comfort*, but they long, with intense longing, for sympathy.

Letters written to gentlemen should be ceremonious and dignified. If the acquaintance is slight, write in the third person, if there is a necessity for a letter. If a business letter, be respectful, yet not servile. It is better to avoid correspondence with gentlemen, particularly whilst you are young, as there are many objections to it. Still, if a friend of long standing solicits a correspondence, and your parents or husband approve and permit compliance with the request, it would be over-prudish to refuse. Write, however, such letters as, if they were printed in the newspapers, would cause you no annoyance. If the acquaintance admits of a frank, friendly style, be careful that your expressions of good will do not become too vehement, and avoid any confidential communications. When he begins to ask you to keep such and such passages secret, believe me, it is quite time to drop the correspondence.

LETTERS OF ENQUIRY, especially if they request a favor, should contain a few lines of compliment. If the letter is upon a private subject, such as enquiry with regard to the illness or misfortune of a friend, avoid making it too brief. To write short, careless letters upon such subjects, is unfeeling, and they will surely be attributed to motives of obligation or duty, not to interest. Letters of enquiry, referring to family matters, should be delicately worded, and appear dictated by interest, not mere curiosity. If the enquiry refers to matters interesting only to yourself, enclose a postage-stamp for the reply. In answering such letters, if they refer to your own health or subjects interesting to yourself, thank the writer for the interest expressed, and answer in a satisfactory manner. If the answer interests your correspondent only, do not reply as if the enquiry annoyed you, but express some interest in the matter of the letter, and give as clear and satisfactory reply as is in your power.

LETTERS OFFERING FAVORS—Be careful in writing to offer a favor, that you do not make your friend feel a heavy weight of obligation by over-rating your services. The kindness will be duly appreciated, and more highly valued if offered in a delicate manner. Too strong a sense of obligation is humiliating, so do not diminish the real value of the service by forcing the receiver to acknowledge a fictitious value. Let the recipient of your good will feel that it affords you as much pleasure to confer the favor as it will give her to receive it. A letter accompanying a present, should be short and gracefully worded. The affectionate spirit of such little epistles will double the value of the gift which they accompany. Never refer to a favor received, in such a letter, as that will give your gift the appearance of being payment for such favor, and make your letter of about as much value as a tradesman's receipted bill.

LETTERS OF THANKS for enquiries made, should be short, merely echoing the words of the letter they answer, and contain the answer to the question, with an acknowledgement of your correspondent's interest. If the letter is your own acknowledgement of a favor conferred, let the language be simple, but strong, grateful, and graceful. Fancy that you are clasping the hand of the kind friend who has been generous or thoughtful for you, and then write, even as you would speak. Never hint that you deem such a favor an obligation to be returned at the first opportunity; although this may really be the case, it is extremely indelicate to say so. In your letter gracefully acknowledge the obligation, and if, at a later day, you can return the favor, then let actions, not words, prove your grateful recollection of the favor conferred upon you. If your letter is written to acknowledge the reception of a present, speak of the beauty or usefulness of the gift, and of the pleasant associations with her name it will always recall.

LETTERS OF RECOMMENDATION should be truthful, polite, and carefully considered. Such letters may be business letters, or they may be given to servants, and they must be given only when really deserved. Do not be hasty in giving them; remember that you are, in some measure responsible for the bearer; therefore, never sacrifice truth and frankness, to a mistaken idea of kindness or politeness.

LETTERS OF INTRODUCTION must be left unsealed. They must not contain any allusion to the personal qualities of the bearer, as such allusion would be about as sure a proof of ill-breeding as if you sat beside your friend, and ran over the list of the virtues and talents possessed by her. The fact that the person bearing the letter is your friend, will be all sufficient reason for cordial reception by the friend to whom the letter is addressed. The best form is:—

PHILADELPHIA, *June* 18*th*, 18—.

MY DEAR MARY:

This letter will be handed to you by Mrs. C., to whom I am pleased to introduce you, certain that the acquaintance thus formed, between two friends of mine, of so long standing and so much beloved, will be pleasant to both parties. Any attention that you may find it in your power to extend to Mrs. C. whilst she is in your city, will be highly appreciated, and gratefully acknowledged, by

Your sincere friend

A——.

LETTERS OF ADVICE should not be written unsolicited. They will, in all probability, even when requested, be unpalatable, and should never be sent unless they can really be of service. Write them with frankness and sincerity. To write after an act has been committed, and is irrevocable, is folly, and it is also unkind. You may inform your friend that, "had you been consulted, a different course from the one taken would have been recommended," and you may really believe this, yet it will probably be false. Seeing the unfavorable result of the wrong course will enable you fully to appreciate the wisdom of the right one, but, had you been consulted when the matter was doubtful, you would probably have been as much puzzled as your friend to judge the proper mode of action. You should word a letter of advice delicately, stating your opinion frankly and freely, but giving it *as* an opinion, not as a positive law. If the advice is not taken, do not feel offended, as others, more experienced than yourself upon the point in question, may have also been consulted. Let no selfish motive govern such a letter. Think only of the good or evil to result to your friend, and while you may write warmly and earnestly, let the motive be a really disinterested one.

LETTERS OF EXCUSE should be frank and graceful. They must be written promptly, as soon as the occasion that calls for them admits. If delayed, they become insulting. If such a letter is called forth by an act of negligence on your own part, apologize for it frankly, and show by your tone that you sincerely desire to regain the confidence your carelessness has periled. If you have been obliged by positive inability to neglect the fulfilment of any promise you have given, or any commission you have undertaken, then state the reason for your delay, and solicit the indulgence of your friend. Do not write in such stiff, formal language that the apology will seem forced from you, but offer your excuse frankly, as if with a sincere desire to atone for an act of negligence, or remove a ground of offence.

LETTERS OF INTELLIGENCE are generally the answer to letters of enquiry, or the statement of certain incidents or facts, interesting both to the writer and reader of the letter. Be careful in writing such a letter that you have all the facts in exact accordance with the truth. Remember that every word is set down against you, if one item of your information prove to be false; and do not allow personal opinion or prejudice to dictate a single sentence. Never repeat anything gathered from mere hearsay, and be careful, in such a letter, that you violate no confidence, nor force yourself upon the private affairs of any one. Do not let scandal or a mere love of gossip dictate a letter of intelligence. If your news is painful, state it as delicately as possible, and add a few lines expressive of sympathy. If it is your pleasant task to communicate a joyful event, make your letter cheerful and gay. If you have written any such letter, and, after sending it, find you have made any error in a statement, write, and correct the mistake immediately. It may be a trivial error, yet there is no false or mistaken news so trifling as to make a correction unnecessary.

INVITATIONS are generally written in the third person, and this form is used where the acquaintance is very slight, for formal notes, and cards of compliment. The form is proper upon such occasions, but should be used only in the most ceremonious correspondence. If this style is adopted by a person who has been accustomed to write in a more familiar one to you, take it as a hint, that the correspondence has, for some reason, become disagreeable, and had better cease.

AUTOGRAPH LETTERS should be very short; merely acknowledging the compliment paid by the request for the signature, and a few words expressing the pleasure you feel in granting the favor. If you write to ask for an autograph, always inclose a postage stamp for the answer.

Date every letter you write accurately, and avoid postscripts.

Politeness, kindness, both demand that every letter you receive must be answered. Nothing can give more pleasure in a correspondence, than prompt replies. Matters of much importance often rest upon the reply to a letter, and therefore this duty should never be delayed. In answering friendly letters, it will be found much easier to write what is kind and interesting, if you sit down to the task as soon as you read your friend's letter. Always mention the date of the letter to which your own is a reply.

Never write on a half sheet of paper. Paper is cheap, and a *half* sheet looks both mean and slovenly. If you do not write but three lines, still send the whole sheet of paper. Perfectly plain paper, thick, smooth, and white, is the most elegant. When in mourning, use paper and envelopes with a black edge. Never use the gilt edged, or fancy bordered paper; it looks vulgar, and is in bad taste. You may, if you will, have your initials stamped at the top of the sheet, and on the seal of the envelope, but do not have any fancy ornaments in the corners, or on the back of the envelope.

You will be guilty of a great breach of politeness, if you answer either a note or letter upon the half sheet of the paper sent by your correspondent, even though it may be left blank.

Never write, even the shortest note, in pencil. It looks careless, and is rude.

Never write a letter carelessly. It may be addressed to your most intimate friend, or your nearest relative, but you can never be sure that the eye for which it is intended, will be the *only* one that sees it. I do not mean by this, that the epistle should be in a formal, studied *style*, but that it must be correct in its grammatical construction, properly punctuated, with every word spelt according to rule. Even in the most familiar epistles, observe the proper rules for composition; you would not in conversing, even with your own family, use incorrect grammar, or impertinent language; therefore avoid saying upon paper what you would not say with your tongue.

Notes written in the third person, must be continued throughout in the same person; they are frequently very mysterious from the confusion of pronouns, yet it is a style of correspondence much used and very proper upon many occasions. For compliment, inquiry where there is no intimacy between the parties, from superiors to inferiors, the form is elegant and proper. If you receive a note written in the third person, reply in the same form, but do not reply thus to a more familiar note or letter, as it is insulting, and implies offence taken. If you wish to repel undue familiarity or impertinence in your correspondent, then reply to the epistle in the most formal language, and in the third person.

It is an extraordinary fact, that persons who have received a good education, and who use their pens frequently, will often, in writing notes, commence in the third person and then use the second or first personal pronoun, and finish by a signature; thus—

Miss Claire's compliments to Mr. James, and wishes to know whether you have finished reading my copy of "Jane Eyre," as if Mr. James had finished it, I would like to lend it to another friend.

Sincerely yours,
ELLA CLAIRE.

The errors in the above are too glaring to need comment, yet, with only the alteration of names, it is a copy, *verbatim*, of a note written by a well educated girl.

Never sign a note written in the third person, if you begin the note with your own name. It is admissible, if the note is worded in this way:—

Will Mr. James return by bearer, the copy of "Jane Eyre" he borrowed, if he has finished reading it, and oblige his sincere friend,

ELLA CLAIRE.

If you use a quotation, never omit to put it in quotation marks, otherwise your correspondent may, however unjustly, accuse you of a desire to pass off the idea and words of another, for your own.

Avoid postscripts. Above all, never send an inquiry or compliment in a postscript. To write a long letter, upon various subjects, and in the postscript desire to be remembered to your friend's family, or inquire for their welfare, instead of a compliment, becomes insulting. It is better, if you have not time to write again and place such inquiries above your signature, to omit them entirely. Nobody likes to see their name mentioned as an afterthought.

Punctuate your letters carefully. The want of a mark of punctuation, or the incorrect placing of it, will make the most woful confusion. I give an instance of the utter absurdity produced by the alteration of punctuation marks, turning a sensible paragraph to the most arrant nonsense:

"Cæsar entered; on his head his helmet; on his feet armed sandals; upon his brow there was a cloud; in his right hand his faithful sword; in his eye an angry glare; saying nothing, he sat down."

By using precisely the same words, merely altering the position of the punctuation marks, we have—

"Cæsar entered on his head; his helmet on his feet; armed sandals upon his brow; there was a cloud in his right hand; his faithful sword in his eye; an angry glare saying nothing; he sat down."

Be careful, then, to punctuate properly, that you may convey to the reader the exact sense of what is in your mind.

If you receive an impertinent letter, treat it with contempt; do not answer it.

Never answer a letter by proxy, when you are able to write yourself. It is a mark of respect and love, to answer, in your own hand, all letters addressed to you. If you are obliged to write to a friend to refuse to grant a favor asked, you will lessen the pain of refusal by wording your letter delicately. Loving words, if it is a near friend, respectful, kind ones if a mere acquaintance, will make the disagreeable contents of the letter more bearable. Try to make the *manner* smooth and soften the hardness of the *matter*.

Every letter must embrace the following particulars: 1st. The date. 2d. The complimentary address. 3d. The body of the letter. 4th. The complimentary closing. 5th. The signature. 6th. The address.

There are two ways of putting the date, and the address. The first is to place them at the top of the sheet, the other is to place them after the signature.

When at the top, you write the name of your residence, or that of the city in which you reside, with the day of the month and the year, at the right hand of the first line of the sheet. Then, at the left hand of the next line, write the address, then the complimentary address below the name; thus—

WILLOW GROVE, NEW YORK,
June 27th, 1859.

MRS. E. C. HOWELL,
    My dear Madam,
        I received your letter, etc.

At the end of the letter, on the right hand of the sheet, put the complimentary closing, and then the signature; thus—

I remain, my dear Madam,
With much respect,
Yours sincerely,
S. E. LAW.

If you place the date and address after the signature, put it at the left of the sheet; thus—

I remain, my dear Madam,
With much respect,
Yours sincerely,
S. E. LAW.

MRS. E. C. HOWELL.
 June 27th, 1859.

For a long letter, it is better to put the date and address at the top of the page. For a letter of only a few lines, which ends on the first page, the second form is best. In a letter written to a person in the same city, you need not put the address under the signature; if not, write it—

S. E. LAW,
WILLOW GROVE, NEW YORK.

In writing to a dear friend or relative, where there is no formality required, you may omit the name at the top of the letter; put the date and address thus—

WILLOW GROVE, NEW YORK,
June 27th, 1859.

DEAR ANNA:
 I write, etc.

It is best, however, to put the full name at the bottom of the last page, in case the letter is mislaid without the envelope; thus—

E. C. LAW.

MISS ANNA WRIGHT.

If you use an envelope, and this custom is now universal, fold your letter neatly to fit into it; then direct on the envelope. Put first the name, then the name of the person to whose care the letter must be directed, then the street, the city, and State. If the town is small, put also the county.

This is the form:—

MISS ANNA WRIGHT,
 Care of Mr. John C. Wright,
  No. 40, Lexington street,
   Greensburg—Lee County.
    Mass.

If the city is a large one, New York, Philadelphia, Baltimore, or any of the principal cities of the Union, you may omit the name of the county. If your letter is to go abroad, add the name of the country: as, England, or France, in full, under that of the city.

The name of the state is usually abbreviated, and for the use of my readers, I give the names of the United States with their abbreviations:

Maine, Me. New Hampshire, N. H. Vermont, Vt. Massachusetts, Mass. Rhode Island, R. I. Connecticut, Conn. New York, N. Y. New Jersey, N. J. Pennsylvania, Pa., or, Penn. Delaware, Del. Maryland, Md. Virginia, Va. North Carolina, N. C. South Carolina, S. C. Georgia, Ga., or, Geo. Alabama, Ala. Mississippi, Miss. Missouri, Mo. Louisiana, La. Tennessee, Tenn. Kentucky, Ky. Indiana, Ind. Ohio, O. Michigan, Mich. Illinois, Ill. Wisconsin, Wis. Arkansas, Ark. Texas, Tex. Iowa, Io. Florida, Flo. Oregon, O. California, Cal. Minnesota, Minn. District of Columbia, D. C. If you are writing from another country to America, put United States of America after the name of the state.

On the upper right hand corner of your envelope, put your postage-stamp.

If you send a letter by private hand, write the name of the bearer in the lower left hand corner, thus:

Mrs. E. A. Howell,
Clinton Place,
Boston.

Mr. G. G. Lane.

In directing to any one who can claim any prefix, or addition, to his proper name do not omit to put that "republican title." For a clergyman, Rev. for Reverend is put before the name, thus:—

Rev. James C. Day.

For a bishop:

Right Reverend E. Banks.

For a physician:

Dr. James Curtis.

or,

James Curtis, M.D.

For a member of Congress:

Hon. E. C. Delta.

For an officer in the navy:

Capt. Henry Lee, U. S. N.

For an officer in the army:

Col. Edward Holmes, U. S. A.

For a professor:

Prof. E. L. James.

If the honorary addition, LL.D., A. M., or any such title belongs to your correspondent, add it to his name on the envelope, thus:—

J. L. PETERS, LL.D.

If you seal with wax, it is best to put a drop under the turn-over, and fasten this down firmly before you drop the wax that is to receive the impression.

Cards of compliment are usually written in the third person. I give a few of the most common and proper forms.

For a party:

Miss Lee's compliments to Mr. Bates, for Wednesday evening, Nov. 18th, at 8 o'clock.

Addressed to a lady:

Miss Lee requests the pleasure of Miss Howard's company on Wednesday evening, Nov. 18th, at 8 o'clock.

For a ball, the above form, with the word *Dancing*, in the left hand corner. Invitations to dinner or tea specify the entertainment thus:

Mrs. Garret's compliments to Mr. and Mrs. Howard and requests the pleasure of their company to dine (or take tea) on Wednesday, Nov. 6th, at 6 o'clock.

The form for answering, is:—

Miss Howard accepts with pleasure Miss Lee's polite invitation for Wednesday evening.

or,

Miss Howard regrets that a prior engagement will prevent her accepting Miss Lee's polite invitation for Wednesday evening.

Mr. and Mrs. Howard's compliments to Mrs. Garret, and accept with pleasure her kind invitation for Wednesday.

or,

Mrs. Howard regrets that the severe illness of Mr. Howard will render it impossible for either herself or Mr. Howard to join Mrs. Garret's party on Wednesday next.

Upon visiting cards, left when the caller is about to leave the city, the letters *p. p. c.* are put in the left hand corner, they are the abbreviation of the French words, *pour prendre congé*, or may, with equal propriety, stand for *presents parting compliments*. Another form, *p. d. a., pour dire adieu*, may be used.

No accomplishment within the scope of human knowledge is so beautiful in all its features as that of epistolary correspondence. Though distance, absence, and circumstances may separate the holiest alliances of friendship, or those who are bound together by the still stronger ties of affection, yet the power of interchanging thoughts, words, feelings, and sentiments, through the medium of letters, adds a sweetness to the pain of separation, renovating to life, and adding to happiness.

The wide ocean may roll between those who have passed the social years of youth together, or the snow-capped Alps may rise in sublime grandeur, separating early associates; still young remembrances may be called up, and the paradise of memory made to bloom afresh with unwithered flowers of holy recollection.

Though we see not eye to eye and face to face, where the soft music of a loved voice may fall with its richness upon the ear, yet the very soul and emotions of the mind may be poured forth in such melody as to touch the heart "that's far away," and melt down the liveliest eye into tears of ecstatic rapture.

Without the ability to practice the refined art of epistolary correspondence, men would become cold and discordant: an isolated compound of misanthropy. They would fall off in forsaken fragments from the great bond of union which now adorns and beautifies all society. Absence, distance, and time would cut the silken cords of parental, brotherly, and even connubial affection. Early circumstances would be lost in forgetfulness, and the virtues of reciprocal friendship "waste their sweetness on the desert air."

Since, then, the art and practice of letter-writing is productive of so much refined and social happiness, a laudable indulgence in it must ever be commendable. While it elevates the noble faculties of the mind, it also chastens the disposition, and improves those intellectual powers which would otherwise remain dormant and useless.

Notwithstanding the various beauties and pleasures attendant upon the accomplishment, yet there are many who have given it but a slight portion of their attention, and have, therefore, cause to blush at their own ignorance when necessity demands its practice. There is no better mode by which to test the acquirements of either a young lady or gentleman than from their letters.

Letters are among the most useful forms of composition. There are few persons, who can read or write at all, who do not frequently have occasion to write them; and an elegant letter is much more rare than an elegant specimen of any other kind of writing.

The more rational and elevated the topics are, on which you write, the less will you care for your letters being seen, or for paragraphs being read out of them; and where there is no need of any secrecy, it is best not to bind your friend by promises, but to leave it to her discretion.

CHAPTER XVI.
POLITE DEPORTMENT, AND GOOD HABITS.

Lord Chesterfield says, "Good sense and good nature suggest civility in general; but in good breeding there are a thousand little delicacies which are established only by custom."

It is the knowledge and practice of such "little delicacies" which constitutes the greatest charm of society.

Manner may be, and, in most cases, probably is, the cloak of the heart; this cloak may be used to cover defects, but is it not better so to conceal these defects, than to flaunt and parade them in the eyes of all whom we may meet?

Many persons plead a love of truth as an apology for rough manners, as if truth was never gentle and kind, but always harsh, morose, and forbidding. Surely good manners and a good conscience are no more inconsistent with each other than beauty and innocence, which are strikingly akin, and always look the better for companionship. Roughness and honesty are indeed sometimes found together in the same person, but he is a poor judge of human nature who takes ill-manners to be a guarantee of probity of character. Some persons object to politeness, that its language is unmeaning and false. But this is easily answered. A lie is not locked up in a phrase, but must exist, if at all, in the mind of the speaker. In the ordinary compliments of civilized life, there is no intention to deceive, and consequently no falsehood. Polite language is pleasant to the ear, and soothing to the heart, while rough words are just the reverse; and if not the product of ill temper, are very apt to produce it. The plainest of truths, let it be remembered, can be conveyed in civil speech, while the most malignant lies may find utterance, and often do, in the language of the fishmarket.

Many ladies say, "Oh, I am perfectly frank and outspoken; I never stop to mince words," or, "there is no affectation about me; all my actions are perfectly natural," and, upon the ground of frankness, will insult and wound by rude language, and defend awkwardness and ill-breeding by the plea of "natural manners."

If nature has not invested you with all the virtues which may be desirable in a lady, do not make your faults more conspicuous by thrusting them forward upon all occasions, and at all times. "Assume a virtue if you have it not," and you will, in time, by imitation, acquire it.

By endeavoring to *appear* generous, disinterested, self-sacrificing, and amiable, the opposite passions will be brought into subjection, first in the manner, afterwards in the heart. It is not the desire to deceive, but the desire to please, which will dictate such a course. When you hear one, who pretends to be a lady, boast that she is rough, capricious, and gluttonous, you may feel sure that she has never tried to conquer these faults, or she would be ashamed, not proud, of them.

The way to make yourself pleasing to others, is to show that you care for them. The whole world is like the miller at Mansfield, "who cared for nobody— no, not he—because nobody cared for him." And the whole world will serve you so, if you give them the same cause. Let every one, therefore, see that you do care for them, by showing them, what Sterne so happily calls, "the small, sweet courtesies of life," those courtesies in which there is no parade; whose voice is too still to tease, and which manifest themselves by tender and affectionate looks, and little, kind acts of attention, giving others the preference in every little enjoyment at the table, in the field, walking, sitting, or standing.

Thus the first rule for a graceful manner is unselfish consideration of others.

By endeavoring to acquire the habit of politeness, it will soon become familiar, and sit on you with ease, if not with elegance. Let it never be forgotten, that genuine politeness is a great fosterer of family love; it allays accidental irritation, by preventing harsh retorts and rude contradictions; it softens the boisterous, stimulates the indolent, suppresses selfishness, and by forming a habit of consideration for others, harmonizes the whole. Politeness begets politeness, and brothers may be easily won by it, to leave off the rude ways they bring home from school or college. Sisters ought never to receive any little attention without thanking them for it, never to ask a favor of them but in courteous terms, never to reply to their questions in monosyllables, and they will soon be ashamed to do such things themselves. Both precept and example ought to be laid under contribution, to convince them that no one can have really good manners abroad, who is not habitually polite at home.

If you wish to be a well-bred lady, you must carry your good manners everywhere with you. It is not a thing that can be laid aside and put on at pleasure. True politeness is uniform disinterestedness in trifles, accompanied by the calm self-possession which belongs to a noble simplicity of purpose; and this must be the effect of a Christian spirit running through all you do, or say, or think;

and, unless you cultivate it and exercise it, upon all occasions and towards all persons, it will never be a part of yourself.

It is not an art to be paraded upon public occasions, and neglected in every-day duties; nor should it, like a ball-dress, be carefully laid aside at home, trimmed, ornamented, and worn only when out. Let it come into every *thought*, and it will show forth in every *action*. Let it be the rule in the homeliest duties, and then it will set easily when in public, not in a stiff manner, like a garment seldom worn.

I wish it were possible to convince every woman that politeness is a most excellent good quality; that it is a necessary ingredient in social comfort, and a capital assistant to actual prosperity. Like most good things, however, the word politeness is often misunderstood and misapplied; and before urging the practical use of that which it represents, it may be necessary to say what it means, and what it does not mean.

Politeness is not hypocrisy:—cold-heartedness, or unkindness in disguise. There are persons who can smile upon a victim, and talk smoothly, while they injure, deceive, or betray. And they will take credit to themselves, that all has been done with the utmost *politeness*; that every tone, look, and action, has been in perfect keeping with the rules of good breeding. "The words of their mouth are smoother than butter, but war is in their heart: their words are softer than oil, yet are they drawn swords." Perish for ever and ever such spurious politeness as this!

Politeness is not servility. If it were so, a Russian serf would be a model of politeness. It is very possible for persons to be very cringing and obsequious, without a single atom of politeness; and it often happens that men of the most sturdy independence of character, are essentially polite in all their words, actions, and feelings. It were well for this to be fully understood, for many people will abstain from acts of real politeness, and even of common civility, for fear of damaging their fancied independence.

True politeness, as I understand it, is kindness and courtesy of feeling brought into every-day exercise. It comprehends hearty good will towards everybody, thorough and constant good-humor, an easy deportment, and obliging manners. Every person who cultivates such feelings, and takes no pains to conceal them, will necessarily be polite, though she may not exactly know it; while, on the other hand, a woman essentially morose and selfish, whatever may be her pretensions, must be very far from truly polite.

It is very true there are those whose position in society compels them to observe certain rules of etiquette which pass for politeness. They bow or courtesy with a decent grace; shake hands with the precise degree of vigor which the circumstances of the case require; speak just at the right time, and in the required manner, and smile with elegant propriety. Not a tone, look, or gesture, is out of place; not a habit indulged which etiquette forbids; and yet, there will be wanting, after all, the secret charm of sincerity and heart kindness, which those outward signs are intended to represent; and, wanting which, we have only the form, without the essence, of politeness.

Let me recommend, therefore, far beyond all the rules ever penned by teachers of etiquette, the cultivation of kind and loving feelings. Throw your whole soul into the lesson, and you will advance rapidly towards the perfection of politeness, for "out of the abundance of the heart the mouth speaketh," and the movements of your form and the words you utter will follow faithfully the hidden springs of action within.

There cannot be genuine good breeding to any happy degree, where there is not self-respect. It is that which imparts ease and confidence to our manners, and impels us, for our own sake, as well as for the sake of others, to behave becomingly as intelligent beings.

It is a want of true politeness that introduces the discord and confusion which too often make our homes unhappy. A little consideration for the feelings of those whom we are bound to love and cherish, and a little sacrifice of our own wills, would, in multitudes of instances, make all the difference between alienation and growing affection. The principle of genuine politeness would accomplish this; and what a pity it is that those whose only spring of rational enjoyment is to be found at *home*, should miss that enjoyment by a disregard of little things, which, after all, make up the sum of human existence!

What a large amount of actual discomfort in domestic life would be prevented, if all children were trained, both by precept and example, to the practice of common politeness! If they were taught to speak respectfully to parents, and brothers, and sisters, to friends, neighbors, and strangers, what bawlings, and snarlings would be stilled! If their behavior within doors, and especially at the table, were regulated by a few of the common rules of good breeding, how much natural and proper disgust would be spared! If courtesy of demeanor, towards all whom they meet in field or highway, were instilled, how much more pleasant would be our town travels, and our rustic rambles! Every parent has a personal interest in this matter; and if every parent would but make the needful effort, a great degree of gross incivility, and consequent annoyance, would soon be swept away from our hearths and homes.

Whilst earnestly endeavoring to acquire true politeness, avoid that spurious imitation, affectation. It is to genuine politeness and good breeding, what the showy paste is to the pure diamond. It is the offspring of a sickly taste, a deceitful heart, and a sure proof of low breeding.

The certain test of affectation in any individual, is the looking, speaking, moving, or acting in any way different when in the presence of others, especially those whose opinion we regard and whose approbation we desire, from what we should do in solitude, or in the presence of those only whom we disregard, or who we think cannot injure or benefit us. The motive for resisting affectation is, that it is both unsuccessful and sinful. It always involves a degree of hypocrisy, which is exceedingly offensive in the sight of God, which is generally detected even by men, and which, when detected, exposes its subject to contempt which could never have been excited by the mere absence of any quality or possession, as it is by the false assumption of what is not real. The best cure for affectation is the cultivation, on principle, of every good, virtuous, and amiable habit and feeling, not for the sake of being approved or admired, but because it is right in itself, and without considering what people will think of it. Thus a real character will be formed instead of a part being assumed, and admiration and love will be spontaneously bestowed where they are really deserved. Artificial manners are easily seen through; and the result of such observations, however accomplished and beautiful the object may be, is contempt for such littleness.

Many ladies, moving, too, in good society, will affect a forward, bold manner, very disagreeable to persons of sense. They will tell of their wondrous feats, when engaged in pursuits only suited for men; they will converse in a loud, boisterous tone; laugh loudly; sing comic songs, or dashing bravuras in a style only fit for the stage or a gentleman's after-dinner party; they will lay wagers, give broad hints and then brag of their success in forcing invitations or presents; interlard their conversation with slang words or phrases suited only to the stable or bar-room, and this they think is a dashing, fascinating manner. It may be encouraged, admired, in their presence, by gentlemen, and imitated by younger ladies, but, be sure, it is looked upon with contempt, and disapproval by every one of good sense, and that to persons of real refinement it is absolutely disgusting.

Other ladies, taking quite as mistaken a view of real refinement, will affect the most childish timidity, converse only in whispers, move slowly as an invalid, faint at the shortest notice, and on the slightest provocation; be easily moved to tears, and profess never to eat, drink, or sleep. This course is as absurd as the other, and much more troublesome, as everybody dreads the scene which will follow any shock to the dear creature's nerves, and will be careful to avoid any dangerous topics.

Self-respect, and a proper deference for our superiors in age or intellect, will be the best safeguards against either a cringing or insolent manner.

Without self-respect you will be apt to be both awkward and bashful; either of which faults are entirely inconsistent with a graceful manner. Be careful that while you have sufficient self-respect to make your manner easy, it does not become arrogance and so engender insolence. Avoid sarcasm; it will, unconsciously to yourself, degenerate into pertness, and often downright rudeness. Do not be afraid to speak candidly, but temper candor with courtesy, and never let wit run into that satire that will wound deeply, whilst it amuses only slightly.

Let your carriage be at once dignified and graceful. There are but few figures that will bear quick motion; with almost every one its effect is that of a jerk, a most awkward movement. Let the feet, in walking or dancing, be turned out slightly; when you are seated, rest them both on the floor or a footstool. To sit with the knees or feet crossed or doubled up, is awkward and unlady-like. Carry your arms, in walking, easily; never crossing them stiffly or swinging them beside you. When seated, if you are not sewing or knitting, keep your hands perfectly quiet. This, whilst one of the most difficult accomplishments to attain, is the surest mark of a lady. Do not fidget, playing with your rings, brooch, or any little article that may be near you; let your hands rest in an easy, natural position, perfectly quiet.

Never gesticulate when conversing; it looks theatrical, and is ill-bred; so are all contortions of the features, shrugging of shoulders, raising of the eyebrows, or hands.

When you open a conversation, do so with a slight bow and smile, but be careful not to simper, and not to smile too often, if the conversation becomes serious.

Never point. It is excessively ill-bred.

Avoid exclamations; they are in excessively bad taste, and are apt to be vulgar words. A lady may express as much polite surprise or concern by a few simple, earnest words, or in her manner, as she can by exclaiming "Good gracious!" "Mercy!" or "Dear me!"

Remember that every part of your person and dress should be in perfect order before you leave the dressing-room, and avoid all such tricks as smoothing your hair with your hand, arranging your curls, pulling the waist of your dress down, or settling your collar or sleeves.

Avoid lounging attitudes, they are indelicate, except in your own private apartment. Nothing but ill health will excuse them before company, and a lady had better keep her room if she is too feeble to sit up in the drawing-room.

Let your deportment suit your age and figure; to see a tiny, fairy-like young girl, marching erect, stiff, and awkwardly, like a soldier on parade, is not more absurd than to see a middle-aged, portly woman, aping the romping, hoydenish manners of a school-girl.

Let the movements be easy and flexible, and accord with the style of the lady.

Let your demeanor be always marked by modesty and simplicity; as soon as you become forward or affected, you have lost your greatest charm of manner.

You should be quite as anxious to *talk* with propriety as you are to think, work, sing, paint, or write, according to the most correct rules.

Always select words calculated to convey an exact impression of your meaning.

Let your articulation be easy, clear, correct in accent, and suited in tone and emphasis to your discourse.

Avoid a muttering, mouthing, stuttering, droning, guttural, nasal, or lisping, pronunciation.

Let your speech be neither too loud nor too low; but adjusted to the ear of your companion. Try to prevent the necessity of any person crying, "What? What?"

Avoid a loquacious propensity; you should never occupy more than your share of the time, or more than is agreeable to others.

Beware of such vulgar interpolations as "You know," "You see," "I'll tell you what."

Pay a strict regard to the rules of grammar, even in private conversation. If you do not understand these rules, learn them, whatever be your age or station.

Though you should always speak pleasantly, do not mix your conversation with loud bursts of laughter.

Never indulge in uncommon words, or in Latin and French phrases, but choose the best understood terms to express your meaning.

Above all, let your conversation be intellectual, graceful, chaste, discreet, edifying, and profitable.

CHAPTER XVII.
CONDUCT IN CHURCH.

In entering a church of a different denomination from the one you have been in the habit of frequenting, ask the sexton to show you to a seat. It is the height of rudeness to enter a pew without invitation, as the owner may desire, if her family do not require all the seats, to invite her own personal friends to take the vacant places. If you are not perfectly familiar with the manner of conducting the worship, observe those around you, rise, kneel, and sit, as you see they do. It is a mark of disrespect for the pastor as well as irreverence for the Most High, to remain seated through the whole service, unless you are ill, or otherwise incapacitated from standing and kneeling.

Enter the sacred edifice slowly, reverentially, and take your seat quietly. It is not required of you to bow to any friend you may see in passing up the aisle, as you are supposed yourself to be, and suppose her to be entirely absorbed in thought proper for the occasion. To stare round the church, or if you are not alone, to whisper to your companion, is irreverent, indelicate, and rude. If your own feelings will not prompt you to silence and reverence, pay some regard to the feelings of others.

Be careful not to appear to notice those around you. If others are so rude as to talk or conduct improperly, fix your own mind upon the worship which you come to pay, and let the impertinence pass unheeded.

If there is another person in the same pew with yourself, who, more familiar with the service, hands you the book, or points out the place, acknowledge the civility by a silent bow; it is not necessary to speak.

In your own pew, extend this courtesy to a stranger who may come in beside you, and even if it is a gentleman you may, with perfect propriety, hand him a book, or, if there is but one, offer him a share of your own.

Endeavor always to be in your seat before the service commences, and after it is over do not hurry away, and, above all, do not begin your preparations for departure, by shutting up your book, or putting on any article of dress you have removed, before the benediction.

If you are invited to accompany a friend to church, be sure you are ready in good season, that you may not keep her waiting when she calls, or cause her to lose any part of the service by detaining her at your house. If you invite a friend to take a seat in your pew, call for her early, give her the most comfortable place, and be sure she has a prayer and hymn-book.

If you are invited to stand as god-mother to a friend's child, be at the house of the parents in season to accompany the family to church, and send, the day before, the gift you design for the babe. A silver cup is the usual present, with your little namesake's initials, or full name, engraved upon it.

In assisting at a wedding at church, if you are one of the bridesmaids, wear white, a white bonnet but no veil. If you occupy the first place, the bride's, it is in better taste to be married in a simple dress and bonnet, and don your full dress when you return home to receive your friends. In such ceremonies the wedding-party all meet in the vestry, and go to the altar together.[*]

At a funeral, enter the church quietly, and, unless you belong to the mourners, wait until they leave the church before you rise from your seat. Never attempt to speak to any of the afflicted family. However heartfelt your sympathy, it will not be welcome at that time.

* For further particulars, see chapter on Bridal Etiquette.

If, when entering a crowded church, a gentleman sees you and offers his seat, acknowledge his civility, whether accepted or declined, by a bow, and a whispered "thank you." Many, who claim the name of lady, and think they are well-bred, will accept such an act of politeness without making the slightest acknowledgement. If the service has commenced, do not speak; a courteous inclination of the head will convey your sense of obligation.

Remember, as an imperative, general rule, in whatever church you may be, whether at home or abroad, conform to the mode of worship whilst you are in that church. If you find, in these modes, forms which are disagreeable to you, or which shock your own ideas of religion, avoid a second visit, but do not insult the congregation, by showing your contempt or disapproval, whilst you are among them. Silence, quiet attention, and a grave, reverential demeanor, mark the Christian lady in church.

CHAPTER XVIII.
BALL ROOM ETIQUETTE.
FOR THE HOSTESS.

When you have decided upon what evening you will give your ball, send out your invitations, a fortnight before the evening appointed. To ladies, word them:—

Mrs. L—— requests the pleasure of Miss G——'s company on Wednesday evening, Jan. 17th, at 9 o'clock.
Dancing.
The favor of an early answer is requested.

To gentlemen:—

Mrs. L——'s compliments to Mr. R—— for Wednesday evening, Jan. 17th, at 9 o'clock.
Dancing.
The favor of an early answer is requested.

If you are unmarried, put your mother's name with your own upon the cards. If you have a father or grown-up brother, let the invitations to the gentlemen go in his name.

In making your list for a ball, do not set down *all* of your "dear five hundred friends." The middle-aged, (unless they come as chaperons,) the serious, and the sober-minded, will not accept your invitation, and the two last named may consider it insulting to be invited to so frivolous an amusement. By the way, I do not agree with the straight-laced people, who condemn all such amusements. I agree with Madame Pilau. When the curé of her parish told her he was writing a series of sermons against dancing, she said to him:

"You are talking of what you do not understand. *You* have never been to a ball, *I* have; and I assure you there is no sin in the matter worthy of mention or notice."

If you really wish for dancing, you will accommodate your guests to your rooms, inviting one third more than they will hold, as about that number generally disappoint a ball-giver. If you wish to have a rush of people, and do not mind heat, crowding, and discomfort, to insure an immense assembly, (a ball to be talked about for its size only,) then you may invite every body who figures upon your visiting list.

Over one hundred is a "large ball," under that a "ball," unless there are less than fifty guests, when it is merely a "dance."

The directions given in chapter 5th for the arrangement of the dressing-rooms will apply here, but your parlor, or ball room, requires some attention. Have the carpets taken up two days before the evening of the ball, and the floor waxed. A smooth, polished floor is an absolute necessity for pleasant dancing. At one end of your ball room, have a space partitioned off for the musicians. Leave, for their use, plenty of room, as silence or discord will come from a crowded orchestra. If your house is double, and you use the rooms on each side, place the musicians in the hall.

Four pieces of music is enough for a private ball, unless your rooms are very large. For one room a piano, violin, and violoncello makes a good band.

You must have your rooms well ventilated if you wish to avoid fainting and discomfort.

To secure a really brilliant ball, pay considerable attention to the arrangement of your ball room. In Paris this arrangement consists in turning the room, for the evening, into a perfect garden. Every corner is filled with flowers. Wreaths, bouquets, baskets, and flowering-plants in moss-covered pots. With brilliant light, and taste in the details of arranging them, this profusion of flowers produces an exquisitely beautiful effect, and harmonizes perfectly with the light dresses, cheerful faces, and gay music. The pleasure of your guests, as well as the beauty of the rooms, will be increased by the elegance of your arrangements; their beauty will be heightened by brilliant light, and by judicious management a scene of fairy-like illusion may be produced.

Not only in the ball room itself, but in the hall, supper-room, and dressing-rooms, place flowers. A fine effect is produced, by placing a screen, covered with green and flowers, before the space set apart for the musicians. To hear the music proceeding from behind this floral embankment, and yet have the scraping and puffing men invisible, adds very much to the illusion of the scene.

In the dressing-rooms have, at least, two servants for each. Let them take the cloaks and hoods, and put a numbered ticket upon each bundle, handing the duplicate number to the lady or gentleman owning it.

It is best to have the supper-room upon the same floor as the ball room. The light dresses, worn upon such occasions, suffer severely in passing up and down a crowded staircase.

Have a number of double cards written or printed with a list of the dances, arranged in order, upon one side, and a space for engagements upon the other. Attach a small pencil to each. Let a waiter stand at the entrance to the ball room, and hand a card to each guest as they pass in.

The first strain of music must be a march; then follows a quadrille, then a waltz. Other dances follow in any order you prefer until the fourteenth, which should be the march which announces supper. If you throw open the supper-room, early, and the guests go out when they wish, the march may be omitted. Twenty-one to twenty-four dances are sufficient. Have an interval of ten minutes after each one.

The supper-room should be thrown open at midnight, and remain open until your last guest has departed. Let it be brilliantly lighted, and have plenty of waiters in attendance.

There can be no rule laid down for the supper. It may be hot or heavily iced. It may consist entirely of confectionary, or it may include the bill of fare for a hotel table. One rule you must observe; have abundance of everything. Other entertainments may be[162] given upon economical principles, but a ball cannot. Light, attendance, supper, every detail must be carefully attended to, and a ball must be an expensive luxury.

At a ball-supper every one stands up. The waiters will hand refreshment from the tables to the gentlemen, who, in turn, wait upon the ladies.

You must bring forth your whole array of smiles, when you perform the part of hostess in a ball room. As your guests will come dropping in at all hours, you must hover near the door to greet each one entering. There will be many strangers amongst the gentlemen. Miss G. will bring her fiancée. Miss L., her brother, just returned, after ten years' absence, from India. Miss R. introduces her cousin, in the city for a week. Miss M., as a belle, will, perhaps, take the liberty of telling some ten or twelve of her most devoted admirers where she may be seen on the evening of your ball, and, though strangers, they will, one after another, bow over your hand. To each and every one you must extend the amiable greeting due to an invited guest. If you are the only lady of the house, your duties will, indeed, be laborious. You must be everywhere at the same moment. Not a guest must pass unwelcomed. You must introduce partners to all the wall-flowers. You must see that every set is made up before the music commences. Each guest must be introduced to a proper partner for every dance, and not one frown, one pettish word, one look of fatigue, one sigh of utter weariness must disturb your smiling serenity. You must be ready to chat cheerfully with every bore who detains you, when crossing the room, to make up a set of quadrilles in a minute's time; listen patiently to the sighing lover, whose fair one is engaged fifty times during twenty dances; secure a good dancer for each longing belle; do the same for the beaux; yet you must never be hurried, worried, or fatigued.

If there are several ladies, a mother and two or three daughters, for instance, divide the duties. Let one receive the guests, another arrange the sets, a third introduce couples, and a fourth pair off the talkers. A brother or father will be a treasure in a ball room, as the standing of sets can be better managed by a gentleman than a lady.

None of the ladies who give the ball should dance until every fair guest has a partner.

One of your duties will be to see that no young ladies lose their supper for want of an escort to ask them to go out. You may give the hint to an intimate gentleman friend, if there is no brother or father to take the duty, introduce him to the disconsolate damsel, and send her off happy. If all the guests go to the supper-room when it is first thrown open, you must be the last to leave the ball room. For the hostess to take the lead to the supper-room, leaving her guests to pair off, and follow as they please, is in very bad taste.

If you announce supper by a march, many of your guests will remain in the ball room, to promenade, avoid the crowd at the first table, and indulge in a tête-à-tête conversation. These will afterwards go out, in pairs, when the first crush in the refreshment-room is over.

If, by accident or negligence, you miss an introduction to any of your gentlemen guests, you may still speak to them if you wish. It is your privilege as hostess to introduce yourself, and invite any gentleman to dance with you, or offer to introduce him to a partner. In the latter case he ought to mention his name, but if he omits to do so, you may ask it.

There has been a custom introduced in some of our large cities lately, which is an admirable one for a private ball. It is to hire, for the evening, a public hall. This includes the dressing-room, supper-room, every comfort, and saves you from the thousand annoyances which are certain to follow a ball in a private house. You hire the hall and other rooms, the price including light, hire a band of music, and order a supper at a confectioners, hiring from his establishment all the china, glass, and silver you will want. In this case you must enclose in every invitation a ticket to admit your friend's party, to prevent loungers from the street coming in, uninvited.

You will, perhaps, find the actual outlay of money greater, when you thus hire your ball room, but you will save more than the difference in labor, annoyance, and the injury to your house. You secure a better room than any parlor, you have the floor waxed and polished without the trouble of taking up your carpets. You save all the dreadful labor of cleaning up the house the next day, as well as that of preparation.

You can, if you wish, invite a few friends to a late dinner with you, and all proceed to the ball room together. You must be the first to enter the room, the last to leave it, and every duty is the same as if you were at home; the ball room is, in fact, your own house, for the evening.

If you wish your guests to come in costume for a fancy ball, name the character of the entertainment in your invitation.

CHAPTER XIX.
BALL ROOM ETIQUETTE.
FOR THE GUEST.

As in every other case where hospitality is extended to you by invitation, you must send your answer as soon as possible, accepting or declining the civility.

In preparing a costume for a ball, choose something very light. Heavy, dark silks are out of place in a ball room, and black should be worn in no material but lace. For a married lady, rich silk of some light color, trimmed with flowers, lace, or tulle; white silk plain, or lace over satin, make an exquisite toilette. Jewels are perfectly appropriate; also feathers in the *coiffure*.

For the young lady, pure white or light colors should be worn, and the most appropriate dress is of some thin material made over silk, white, or the same color as the outer dress. Satin or velvet are entirely out of place on a young lady. Let the *coiffure* be of flowers or ribbons, never feathers, and but very little jewelry is becoming to an unmarried lady. All ladies must wear boots or slippers of satin, white, black, or the color of the dress. White are the most appropriate; black, the most becoming to the foot. White kid gloves, full trimmed, a fine lace trimmed handkerchief, and a fan, are indispensable. Be very careful, when dressing for a ball, that the hair is firmly fastened, and the *coiffure* properly adjusted. Nothing is more annoying than to have the hair loosen or the head-dress fall off in a crowded ball room.

Your first duty, upon entering the room, is to speak to your hostess. After a few words of greeting, turn to the other guests.

At a private ball, no lady will refuse an introduction to a gentleman. It is an insult to her hostess, implying that her guests are *not gentlemen*. It is optional with the lady whether to continue or drop the acquaintance after the ball is over, but for that evening, however disagreeable, etiquette requires her to accept him for *one* dance, if she is disengaged, and her hostess requests it. At a public ball, it is safest to decline all introductions made by the master of ceremonies, though, as before, such acquaintances are not binding after the evening is over.

Be very careful how you refuse to dance with a gentleman. A prior engagement will, of course, excuse you, but if you plead fatigue, or really feel it, do not dance the set with another gentleman; it is most insulting, though sometimes done. On the other hand, be careful that you do not engage yourself twice for the same quadrille. In a polka or valse, you may do this, saying, "I will dance the second half with you, but have a prior engagement for the first." Then, after a few rounds with your first partner, say to him that you are engaged for the remainder of the dance, resume your seat, and your second partner will seek you.

Let your manner in a ball room be quiet. It looks very badly to see a lady endeavoring to attract attention by her boisterous manner, loud talking, or over-active dancing. Do not drag through dances as if you found them wearisome; it is an insult to your partner, but while you are cheerful and animated, be lady-like and dignified in your deportment.

At the end of each dance, your partner will offer his arm, and conduct you to a seat; then bow, and release him from further attendance, as he may be engaged for the next dance.

When invited to dance, hand your ball card to the gentleman, who will put his name in one of the vacant places.

If you wish to go to the supper-room, accept the invitation that will be made, after the dances whilst it is open, but do not remain there long. You may be keeping your escort from other engagements.

If you are accompanied by a gentleman, besides your father or brother, remember he has the right to the first dance, and also will expect to take you in to supper. Do not let any one else interfere with his privilege.

If you wish, during the evening, to go to the dressing-room to arrange any part of your dress, request the gentleman with whom you are dancing to escort you there. He will wait for you at the door, and take you back to the ball-room. Do not detain him any longer than is necessary. Never leave the ball room, for any such purpose, alone, as there are always gentlemen near and round the door, and it looks very badly to see a lady, unattended, going through a crowd of gentlemen.

It is best at a ball, to dance only every other dance, as over-fatigue, and probably a flushed face, will follow too much dancing. Decline the intermediate ones, on the plea of fatigue, or fear of fatigue.

Never go into the supper-room with the same gentleman twice. You may go more than once, if you wish for an ice or glass of water, (surely no lady wants two or three *suppers*,) but do not tax the same gentleman more than once, even if he invites you after each dance.

No lady of taste will carry on a flirtation in a ball room, so as to attract re-mark. Be careful, unless you wish your name coupled with his, how you dance too often with the same gentleman.

If you are so unfortunate as, forgetting a prior engagement, to engage your-self to two gentlemen for the same dance, decline dancing it altogether, or you will surely offend one of them.

Never press forward to take the lead in a quadrille, and if others, not un-derstanding the figures, make confusion, try to get through without remark. It is useless to attempt to teach them, as the music, and other sets, will finish the figure long before you can teach and dance it. Keep your temper, refrain from all remark, and endeavor to make your partner forget, in your cheerful conver-sation, the annoyances of the dance.

There is much that is exhilarating in the atmosphere of a ball room. The light, music, company, and even dancing itself, are all conducive to high spir-its; be careful that this flow of spirits does not lead you into hoydenism and rudeness. Guard your actions and your tongue, that you may leave the room as quietly and gracefully as you enter it.

Avoid confidential conversation in a ball room. It is out of season, and in excessively bad taste.

Be modest and reserved, but avoid bashfulness. It looks like a school-girl, and is invariably awkward.

Never allow your partner, though he may be your most intimate friend, to converse in a low tone, or in any way assume a confidential or lover-like air at a ball. It is in excessively bad taste, and gives annoyance frequently, as others suppose such low-toned remarks may refer to them.

Dance as others do. It has a very absurd look to take every step with dancing-school accuracy, and your partner will be the first one to notice it. A quadrille takes no more steps than a graceful walk.

Never stand up to dance in a quadrille, unless you are perfectly familiar with the figures, depending upon your partner to lead you through. You will probably cause utter confusion in the set, annoy the others forming it, and make yourself appear absurd.

No young lady should go to a ball, without the protection of a married lady, or an elderly gentleman.

Never cross a ball room alone.

Never remain in a ball room until all the company have left it, or even until the last set. It is ill-bred, and looks as if you were unaccustomed to such pleasures, and so desirous to prolong each one. Leave while there are still two or three sets to be danced. Do not accept any invitation for these late dances, as the gentleman who invites you may find out your absence too late to take another partner, and you will thus deprive him of the pleasure of dancing.

CHAPTER XX.
PLACES OF AMUSEMENT.

Do not accept an invitation to visit any place of public amusement, with a gentleman with whom you are but slightly acquainted, unless there is another lady also invited. You may, as a young lady, go with a relative or your fiancée, without a chaperon, but not otherwise.

Having received an invitation which it is proper for you to accept, write an answer immediately, appointing an hour for your escort to call for you, and be sure that you are ready in good season. To arrive late is not only annoying to those near your seat, whom you disturb when you enter, but it is ill-bred; you will be supposed to be some one who is unable to come early, instead of appearing as a lady who is mistress of her own time.

If the evening is cloudy, or it rains, your escort will probably bring a carriage; and let me say a few words here about entering and leaving a carriage.

How to get in is difficult, but of less importance than getting out; because if you stumble in, no one sees you, but some one who may happen to be in the carriage; but how to get out is so important, that I will illustrate it by a short diplomatic anecdote:—

"The Princess of Hesse-Darmstadt," says M. Mercy d'Argenteau, an ambassador of the last century, "having been desired by the Empress of Austria to bring her three daughters to court, in order that her Imperial Majesty might choose one of them for a wife to one of her sons, drove up in her coach to the palace gate. Scarcely had they entered the presence, when, before even speaking to them, the empress went up to the second daughter, and, taking her by the hand, said, 'I choose this young lady.' The mother, astonished at the suddenness of her choice, inquired what had actuated it. 'I watched the young ladies get out of their carriage,' said the empress. 'Your eldest daughter stepped on her dress, and only saved herself from falling by an awkward scramble; the youngest jumped from the coach to the ground, without touching the steps; the second, just lifting her dress in front, so as she descended to show the point of her shoe, calmly stepped from the carriage to the ground, neither hurriedly nor stiffly, but with grace and dignity: she is fit to be an empress; her eldest sister is too awkward, her youngest too wild.'"

THE THEATRE—Here you must wear your bonnet, though you may throw aside your cloak or shawl, if you desire it. Your escort will pass to your seats first, and then turn and offer his hand to lead you to your own. Once seated, give your attention entirely to the actors whilst the curtain is up—to your companion when it is down.

Do not look round the house with your glass. A lady's deportment should be very modest in a theatre. Avoid carefully every motion, or gesture that will attract attention. To flirt a fan, converse in whispers, indulge in extravagant gestures of merriment or admiration, laugh loudly or clap your hands together, are all excessively vulgar and unlady-like. Never turn your head to look at those seated behind you, or near you.

If you speak to your companion while the curtain is up, lower your voice, that you may not disturb others interested in the conversation on the stage.

THE OPERA—Here you should wear full dress, an opera cloak, and either a head-dress, or dressy bonnet of some thin material. Your gloves must be of kid, white, or some very light tint to suit your dress. Many dress for the opera as they would for the theatre; but the beauty of the house is much enhanced by each lady contributing her full dress toilette to the general effect.

If you go to the dressing-room, leave your hood and shawl in the care of the woman in waiting, whom you must fee when she returns them to you.

If you do not wish to go to the dressing-room, allow your escort to take off your shawl or cloak, and throw it over the back of the seat. As your opera cloak must be light enough to keep on all the evening, though you may throw it open, you must wear over it a heavier cloak or a shawl. Throw this off in the lobby, just before you enter your box. Your gloves you must keep on all the evening.

Avoid handling the play bills, as the printing ink will soil your gloves in a few minutes, making your hands appear very badly for the rest of the evening.

You should be in your seat at the opera before the overture commences.

Never converse during the performance. Even the lowest toned remark will disturb a real lover of music, and these will be near you on all sides. Exclamations of admiration, "Exquisite!" "Beautiful!" or "Lovely!" are in the worst taste. Show your appreciation by quiet attention to every note, and avoid every exclamation or gesture.

In our new opera houses there are rooms for promenade, and between the acts your escort may invite you to walk there. You may accept the invitation with perfect propriety. He will leave the box first and then offer his hand to you. In the lobby take his arm, and keep it until you return to the box. If you have taken your cloak or shawl to your seat, leave them there during your promenade. Return to your seat when the gong sounds the recall, that you may not disturb others after the next act commences.

In walking up and down in the promenading saloon, you may pass and repass friends. Bow the first time you meet them, but not again.

If you meet your gentlemen friends there, bow, but do not stop to speak. They may join you for once round the room, then allow them to leave you. Your escort will feel justly offended if you allow any other gentlemen to engross your attention entirely when he has invited you to the entertainment.

CONCERTS—Here, as at the opera, you may wear a bonnet or not, as you will. Go early to the hall, unless you have secured a seat, and then, be in time for the first song. If you are unavoidably late, enter quietly, and take a seat near the door. It is very rude to push forward to the front of the hall, and either crowd those upon the benches, or force some gentleman to offer you his place. If the hall is so crowded that even the back seats are full, and a gentleman offers you his place, you should thank him before accepting it.

Again, I repeat, do not converse, or disturb those around you by exclamations or gesticulations.

LECTURES—Two ladies may attend a lecture, unaccompanied by a gentleman, without attracting attention.

The dress, bonnet, and cloak, worn in the street, should be worn in a lecture-room, as these are, by no means, occasions for full dress.

If you return at an early hour from any place of amusement, invite your escort into the house upon your arrival there, and lay aside your bonnet and shawl. If you keep them on, he will conclude that you expect him to shorten his visit. If it is late when you reach home, he will probably decline your invitation to enter. If, however, he accepts it, do not lay aside your shawl, and he will soon leave you.

If he asks permission to call in the morning, you must, unless prevented by an imperative engagement, remain at home to see him.

Upon your way home from the theatre, concert, or opera, speak warmly of the pleasure of the evening, and, at parting, thank him for that pleasure. Show by your manner that you have heartily enjoyed the entertainment you owe to his civility. If you are weary, do not allow him to see it. If disappointed, conceal that also. You will be able to find *some* good points in the performance; speak of these and ignore the bad ones.

If at the theatre, opera, or in a concert-room, you see an acquaintance, you are not expected to recognize her, unless near enough to speak. A lady must not bow to any one, even her own sister, across a theatre or concert-room.

CHAPTER XXI.
ACCOMPLISHMENTS.

In the present age, when education is within the reach of all, both rich and poor, every lady will endeavor to become, not only well educated, but accomplished. It is not, as some will assert, a waste of time or money. Not only the fingers, voice, and figure are improved, but the heart and intellect will become refined, and the happiness greatly increased.

Take the young lady after a solid basis has been laid in her mind of the more important branches of education, and rear upon that basis the structure of lighter education—the accomplishments. To cultivate these, disregarding the more solid information, is to build your castle without any foundation, and make it, not only absurd, but unsteady. The pleasure of hearing from a lady a *cavatina* executed in the most finished manner, will be entirely destroyed, if her first spoken words after the performance are vulgar, or her sentence ungrammatical.

A lady without her piano, or her pencil, her library of French, German, or Italian authors, her fancy work and tasteful embroideries, is now rarely met with, and it is right that such arts should be universal. No woman is fitted for society until she dances well; for home, unless she is perfect mistress of needlework; for her own enjoyment, unless she has at least one accomplishment to occupy thoughts and fingers in her hours of leisure.

First upon the list of accomplishments, comes the art of conversing well. It is always ready. Circumstances in society will constantly throw you into positions where you can use no other accomplishment. You will not have a musical instrument within reach, singing would be out of place, your fancy work at home, on many occasions, and then you can exert your most fascinating as well as useful accomplishment, the art of conversing well.

Little culture, unfortunately, is bestowed upon this accomplishment, which, beyond all others, promotes the happiness of home, enlivens society, and improves the minds of both speaker and listener. How many excellent women are deficient in the power of expressing themselves well, or, indeed, of expressing themselves at all! How many minds "cream and mantle" from the want of energy to pour themselves out in words! On the other hand, how some, equally well-intentioned, drown the very senses in their torrent of remarks, which dashes, like a water-fall, into a sombre pool of *ennui* below!

One lady will enter society, well-dressed, well-looking, polite; she does not intend to chill it by her presence; yet her absence is found a relief. She takes her place as if she considered it sufficient to dress and look well. She brings no stock to the community of ideas. Her eyes return no response to the discourse which is going on. When you have once glanced at her, she becomes a mere expletive in the company.

Another one will be found a talker. She is like a canary bird; when others begin to speak, she hurries in her remarks, in an accompaniment. Her voice must be uppermost; conversation becomes a contest who can speak the most rapidly. The timid and modest retire from the encounter—she has the field to herself. She goes on, without mercy; the voice of a syren would fatigue, if heard continually. Others revolt at the injustice of the monopoly, and the words fall on ears that would be deaf if they could.

These are extreme cases; there are many other minor errors. The higher qualities of conversation must undoubtedly be based upon the higher qualities of the mind; then it is, indeed, a privilege to commune with others.

To acquire the power of thus imparting the highest pleasure by conversational powers, attention must be paid to literature. I am supposing the solid foundation of a good education already laid, but by literature, I do not mean only that class of it which is taught at school.

Reading, at the present day, is too much confined to light literature. I would not speak against this. The modern novels, and the poets of all ages, are good reading, but let them be taken in moderation, and varied by something more solid. Let them be the dessert to the more substantial *dinner* of history, travels, and works of a like nature.

Independent of the strength and polish given to the mind by a thorough course of reading, there is another reason why a lady should devote some portion of her time to it; she cannot do without it. She may, lacking this, pass through life respectably, even elegantly; but she cannot take her part in a communing with superior minds; she may enjoy, in wondering, the radiance of their intelligence; but the wondering must be composed, in part, of amazement at her own folly, in not having herself sought out the treasure concealed in the fathomless depths of books. She cannot truly enjoy society, with this art neglected. She may, for a few brief years, be the ornament of the drawing-room; but it must be, like many other ornaments there, in still life; she can never be the companion of the intellectual; and the time is gone by, when women, with all their energies excited, will be contented to be the mere plaything of brother, husband, or father.

Still it is not to the erudite, nor to the imaginative only, that it is given to please in conversation.

The art of imparting our ideas easily and elegantly to others, may be improved by ourselves, if there are opportunities of mingling in good society, with little study. The mind must first be cultivated; but it should not abash those who are conscious of moderate talents, or imperfect cultivation, from taking a due part in conversation, on account of their inferiority. It is a very different thing to shine and to please; to shine in society is more frequently attempted than compassed: to please is in the power of all. The effort to shine, when fruitless, brings a certain disgrace, and engenders mortification; all good people are inclined to take the will for the deed, when they see a desire to please. A gentle, deferential, kind manner, will disarm even the most discerning from criticising too severely the deficiencies of the inexperienced; confidence, disrespect of others, volubility, eagerness to dispute, must irritate the self-love of others, and produce an averseness to acknowledge talent or information, where they may even happen to exist.

It is wiser and safer for a young lady, in general, to observe the good, old-fashioned rule of being addressed first; but then she must receive the address readily, meeting it half way, repaying it by enlarging a little upon the topic thus selected, and not sinking into a dull silence, the moment after a reply is given. Some young ladies start, as if thunderstruck, when spoken to, and stare as if the person who pays them that attention, had no right to awaken them from their reverie. Others look affronted, possibly from shyness, and begin a derogatory attack upon the beauty of their dress by twitching the front breadth—or move from side to side, in evident distress and consternation. Time remedies these defects; but there is one less curable and less endurable—that of pertness and flippancy—the loud remarks and exclamations—the look of self-sufficiency and confidence. But these offensive manifestations spring from some previous and deep-seated defects of character, and are only to be repelled by what, I fear, they will frequently encounter—the mortification of inspiring disgust.

Neither is the lengthy, prosy, didactic reply, consistent with the submission and simplicity of youth; egotism, and egotism once removed, that is, the bringing into the topic one's own family and relations, are also antidotes to the true spirit of conversation. In general, it is wiser, more in good taste, safer, more becoming, certainly more in accordance with good breeding, to avoid talking of persons. There are many snares in such topics; not merely the danger of calumniating, but that of engendering a slippery conscience in matters of fact. A young girl, shy and inexpert, states a circumstance; she feels her deficiency as a narrator, for the power of telling a story, is a power to be acquired only by practice. She is sometimes tempted to heighten a little the incidents, in order to get on a little better, and to make more impression. She must of course defend her positions, and then she perils the sanctity of truth. Besides, few things narrow the intellect more than dwelling on the peculiarities, natural or incidental, of that small coterie of persons who constitute our world.

It is, in general, a wise rule, and one which will tend much to insure your comfort through life, to avoid disclosures to others of family affairs. I do not mean to recommend reserve, or art; to friends and relations, too great frankness can hardly be practised; but, with acquaintance, the less our own circumstances are discussed, the happier, and the more dignified will our commerce with them continue. On the same principle, let the concerns of others be touched upon with delicacy, or, if possible, passed over in silence; more especially those details which relate to strictly personal or family affairs. Public deeds are, of course, public property. But personal affairs are private; and there is a want of true good breeding, a want of consideration and deference, in speaking freely of them, even if your friend is unconscious of the liberty taken.

It seems paradoxical to observe that the art of listening well forms a part of the duty of conversation. To give up the whole of your attention to the person who addresses himself to you, is sometimes a heavy tax, but it is one which we must pay for the privileges of social life, and an early practice will render it an almost involuntary act of good breeding; whilst consideration for others will give this little sacrifice a merit and a charm.

To listen well is to make an unconscious advance in the power of conversing. In listening we perceive in what the interest, in what the failure of others consists; we become, too, aware of our own deficiencies, without having them taught through the medium of humiliation. We find ourselves often more ignorant than we could have supposed possible. We learn, by a very moderate attention to the sort of topics which please, to form a style of our own. The "art of conversation" is an unpleasant phrase. The power of conversing well is least agreeable when it assumes the character of an *art*.

In listening, a well-bred lady will gently sympathize with the speaker; or, if needs must be, differ, as gently. Much character is shown in the act of listening. Some people appear to be in a violent hurry whilst another speaks; they hasten on the person who addresses them, as one would urge on a horse—with incessant "Yes, yes, very good—indeed—proceed!" Others sit, on the full stare, eyes fixed as those of an owl, upon the speaker. Others will receive every observation with a little hysterical giggle.

But all these vices of manner may be avoided by a gentle attention and a certain calm dignity of manner, based upon a reflective, cultivated mind.

Observation, reading, and study, will form the groundwork for good powers of conversation, and the more you read, study, and see, the more varied and interesting will be your topics.

A young lady should consider music as one branch of her education, inferior, in importance, to most of those studies which are pointed out to her, but attainable in a sufficient degree by the aid of time, perseverance, and a moderate degree of instruction. Begun early, and pursued steadily, there is ample leisure in youth for the attainment of a science, which confers more cheerfulness, and brings more pleasure than can readily be conceived.

A young lady should be able to play with taste, correctness, and readiness, upon the general principle that a well educated woman should do all things well. This, I should suppose, is in the power of most persons; and it may be attained without loss of health, of time, or any sacrifice of an important nature. She should consider it as an advantage, a power to be employed for the gratification of others, and to be indulged with moderation and good sense for her own resource, as a change of occupation.

Consider in this light, music is what Providence intended it to be—a social blessing. The whole creation is replete with music,—a benignant Power has made the language of the feathered tribe harmony; let us not suppose that He condemns his other creatures to silence in the song.

Music has an influence peculiar to itself. It can allay the irritation of the mind; it cements families, and makes a home, which might sometimes be monotonous, a scene of pleasant excitement. Pursued as a recreation, it is gentle, rational, lady-like. Followed as a sole object, it loses its charm, because we perceive it is then over-rated. The young lady who comes modestly forward, when called upon as a performer, would cease to please, were she, for an instant, to assume the air and confidence of a professional musician. There is a certain style and manner—confined now to second-rate performers, for the highest and most esteemed dispense with it—there is an effort and a dash, which disgust in the lady who has bad taste enough to assume them.

And, whilst I am on this topic, let me remark that there is a great deal in the *choice* of music, in the selection of its character, its suitability to your feelings, style, and taste, and this especially with respect to vocal music.

There is no doubt that a good Italian style is the best for instruction, and that it produces the most careful and accomplished singers. Suppose a case. Your parents, most fair reader, have paid a high price to some excellent professor, to instruct you—and, with a fair ear, and a sufficient voice, you have been taught some of those elaborate songs which are most popular at the opera. A party is assembled—music is one of the diversions. Forth you step, and, with a just apprehension of the difficulties of your task, select one of those immortal compositions which the most eminent have made their study; you execute it wonderfully, only just falling a *little* short of all the song should be; only just provoking a comparison, in every mind, with a high standard, present in the memory of every cultivated musician near you. A cold approval, or a good-natured "bravo!" with, believe me, though you do not hear it, a thorough, and, often, expressed conviction that you had better have left the thing alone, follows the effort which has merely proclaimed the fact that, spite of time and money spent upon the cultivation of your voice, you are but a second-rate singer.

But, choose a wiser, a less pretending, a less conspicuous path. Throw your knowledge into compositions of a less startling, less aspiring character. Try only what you can compass. Be wise enough not to proclaim your deficiencies, and the critics will go away disarmed, even if they are not charmed. But if there be *any* voice, *any* feeling, *any* science, the touching melody, made vocal by youth and taste, will obtain even a far higher degree of encomium than, perhaps, it actually merits. You will please—you will be asked to renew your efforts. People will not be afraid of cadenzas five minutes long, or of bravuras, every note of which makes one hope it may be the last.

It is true that, to a person who loves music, the performance of one of the incomparable songs of Bellini, Rosini, Flotow, or Mozart, is an actual delight—but, when attempted by a young amateur, it should be, like many other delights, confined to the private circle, and not visited upon society in general.

Do not suppose that I mean to recommend poor music, or feeble, ephemeral compositions. What is good need not, of necessity, be always difficult. Ballad music is rich in songs adapted for the private performer—and there are many, in Italian, of great beauty, which, though they would not be selected for a concert-room, or for brilliant display, are adapted for ladies.

Music is the greatest, best substitute for conversation. It has many merits, in this light. It can never provoke angry retort; it can never make enemies; it can injure no one's character by slander; and in playing and singing one can commit no indiscretion.

Music is a most excellent amusement, and, in society, an indispensable one. It aids conversation by occasionally interrupting it for a short period, to be renewed with a new impetus. It makes the most delightful recreation for the home circle, varying the toil and trouble of the father's or husband's working day, by the pleasures of the evening made by music's power to glide smoothly and swiftly.

There are but few persons who are entirely without a love for music, even if they do not understand it. They will be borne along upon the waves of a sweet melody to high, pure thoughts, often to delicious memories.

The piano is, at the present day, the most popular instrument in society. The harp has ceased to be fashionable, though it is sometimes heard. The latter is a most beautiful accompaniment for the voice, but requires a large room, as, in a small one, it will sound stringy and harsh.

The guitar, while it makes a very pleasant accompaniment for the voice, has also the advantage of being easily carried from place to place.

It requires as much judgment to select proper instrumental pieces for a parlor performance, as you would display in a choice of songs. Page after page of black, closely printed notes, will drive those who see them from the piano. They may be executed in the most finished style, but they are not suited to general society. In their place, for practice, or for a musical soirée, where every one puts forth her best musical powers, they are appropriate, and will give pleasure, but they are not suited for a mixed party. When asked to play, choose, if you will, a brilliant, showy piece, but let it be short. It is better still to make no attempt at display, but simply try to please, selecting the music your own judgment tells you is best suited to your audience.

Avoid the loud, thumping style, and also the over-solemn style.

Be sure, before you accept any invitation to play, that you know perfectly the piece you undertake. It is better to play the simplest airs in a finished, faultless manner, than to play imperfectly the most brilliant variations.

Avoid movement at the piano. Swinging the body to and fro, moving the head, rolling the eyes, raising the hands too much, are all bad tricks, and should be carefully abstained from.

With respect to drawing, modeling, or any pursuits of the same nature, so much depends on taste and opportunity, and they are so little the accomplishments of society that they require but few of those restrictions which music, in its use and abuse, demands. Drawing, like music, should be cultivated early. Its advantages are the habits of perseverance and occupation, which it induces; and the additional delight which it gives to the works, both of nature and of art. Like music, it gives independence—independence of society. The true lover of the arts has a superiority over the indifferent, and, if she be not better prepared for society, is much better fitted for retirement than those who are not so happily endowed with tastes, when in moderation, so innocent and beneficial.

There is no accomplishment more graceful, pleasing, healthy, and lady-like, than that of riding well. Avoiding, at the same time, timidity and the "fast" style, keeping within the bounds of elegant propriety, gracefully yielding to the guidance of your escort, and keeping your seat easily, yet steadily, are all points to be acquired.

To ride well is undoubtedly an admirable qualification for a lady, as she may be as feminine in the saddle as in the ball room or home circle. It is a mistaken idea to suppose that to become an accomplished horse-woman a lady must unsex herself. But she must have a reserve in her manner, that will prevent contamination from the intercourse which too much riding may lead to. To hunt, or follow the field sports, in a pursuit which is the track of blood, disgusts the true admirer of gentle breeding. And such diversions will certainly result in a coarseness of manner and expression, growing upon the fair equestrian slowly but surely. A harsh voice, loud tone, expressions suited only to manly lips, but unconsciously copied, will follow her devotion to the unfeminine pursuit.

Nothing is more revolting than a woman who catches the tone and expressions of men. To hear the slang of jockeyism from female lips, is very offensive, yet ladies who mix in field sports are liable, nay, almost certain, to fall into a style of conversation which is ten times worse than the coarsest terms from the lips of a man. Instances there are, of the fairest of our sex, from a fondness for such diversions, and a habitual participation in such society, becoming hard, bold, and disgusting, even whilst retaining all their female loveliness of person.

A lady, unless she lives in the most retired parts of the country, should never ride alone, and even then she will be awkwardly placed, in case of accident, without an escort. In the cities, not only is it unfeminine, but positively dangerous, for a lady to ride unaccompanied by a gentleman, or a man servant.

Although it is impossible, within the limits of this little volume, to give many hints upon riding, a few may not be amiss. Like many other accomplishments, a teacher is necessary, if you wish to attain perfection, and no written directions can make you a finished horse-woman, unless you have had tuition and practice.

1. In mounting you are desired, gentle Amazon, to spring gracefully into your saddle, with the slight assistance of a hand placed beneath the sole of the shoe, instead of scrambling uncouthly to your "wandering throne," as Miss Fanshawe wittily calls it, from a high chair, as is frequently done by those who have not been properly instructed. To mount in the orthodox manner, you should stand nearly close to the horse, level with the front of the saddle, and taking the reins slackly in your right hand, you should place that hand on the nearest pommel, to secure your balance in rising, and with your left hand gather up the front of the habit, so as to leave the feet clear. The gentleman should place himself firmly, near, but not so near to you as to impede your rising, and with the same view must hold his head well back, as should he lose his hat from a whisk of your habit the effect produced is not good. You should then present your left foot, and the gentleman placing one hand beneath its sole, and the other above, so as to possess a safe hold, should, with nice judgment, give just such assistance as will enable you easily, with a spring, to vault gracefully into the saddle. You will then arrange your right leg comfortably over the pommel, your cavalier will then place your left foot in the stirrup and arrange the flow of the habit-skirt, and all is complete. All this, though so seemingly simple and easy, requires some little practice to effect neatly and gracefully.

2. Secondly, when riding with a gentleman, remember that you are best placed on the *left* side; because in that position the graceful flow of your habit is seen to the greatest advantage, while it does not inconvenience the gentleman by getting entangled with his stirrup, nor does it receive the splashes of his horse.

3. But when you have a double attendance of cavaliers, if you be at all a timid rider, it may become discreet to "*pack*" you (forgive the homely phrase) between the two, since, in this position, you are the most thoroughly protected from your own horse's shying, or from other horses or vehicles approaching you too closely, being thus forced to take that part of the road to which the better judgment of your companions inevitably guides you. If you be an accomplished equestrian, you will prefer being outside, and (as has been said) to the left.

Sit erect in the middle of your saddle, turning your face full towards the head of your horse. Cling as closely as possible to the saddle, but avoid stooping forward, or using your hands to keep you in your seat. Nervous motions on horseback are not only ungraceful, but dangerous, as your horse will not make any allowance for the delicacy of your nerves, and may prove his objections to a jerking hand, or a twitching rein, in a most decided and disagreeable manner.

The riding-dress, or habit, is best made to fit the figure tightly, with tight sleeves. It may be open in the front, over a neatly fitting chemisette, or buttoned close to the throat, with a neat linen collar and cuffs. The loose sacque is ungraceful, but a basque is most becoming on horseback. Gauntlet gloves, of leather, are the most suitable, and must be loose enough to give your hand perfect freedom, yet not so loose as to interfere with its motions. Do not wear the skirt too long; it will be dangerous in case of accident, and it may prove annoying to your horse. Your habit must be made of a material sufficiently heavy to hang gracefully, and not move too much with the wind. For a winter habit, a warmly-lined basque, trimmed at the throat and hands with fur, is an elegant and appropriate dress, and a round cap of the same cloth as the habit, with a band, and pieces to cover the ears, of fur to match the dress trimmings, makes a handsome and appropriate dress.

In summer, your hat should be of fine straw, and slouched to shade the face; in winter, of felt, or, if you prefer, a close cap of cloth. The hat may be trimmed with feathers or knots of ribbon, and the shape should be one to protect the complexion, at the same time graceful and becoming.

Avoid any display in a riding dress. Choose a material of some dark or neutral tint, and never use showy trimmings.

Curls, or any flowing loose style of wearing the hair, will be found exceedingly troublesome on horseback. Arrange it neatly and compactly under your hat, for if a stray curl or lock annoys you, or is blown across your eyes by the wind, your hands will be too fully occupied to remedy the difficulty.

Your whip should be light and small, tasteful if you will, but not showy.

At the period for which these hints are intended, the Modern Languages should form a portion of acquirement. As in music, an intelligent and assiduous girl may, I believe, acquire an adequate degree of proficiency in French, German, and Italian, without having been abroad, though a foreign tour will be of the greatest use in the acquisition of the accent and niceties of each tongue. With respect to French, it is no doubt essential to comfort to understand it; it is one of the attributes of a lady to speak it well; still, it is not indispensable to speak it so well that the American lady is mistaken for a Parisian. This, which but seldom happens, can only be acquired, in most cases, by a residence abroad. But French is thoroughly and grammatically taught in America. It is only the habit of speaking, the idioms and niceties, which cannot be acquired except by converse with a native.

There are hundreds of competent instructors in this country, French ladies and gentlemen amongst the number, who form classes for conversation and familiarizing their pupils with these very idioms. After availing herself of such advantages, a young lady will find that a very short residence abroad will improve and facilitate her French conversation.

Much, however, will depend upon how you use the opportunities within your reach. There are many opportunities of practice in large towns; and foreigners give all facilities, by their readiness to converse, their good-nature in listening, and in helping the beginner by kind hints. If a young lady, with simplicity, good breeding, and good taste, endeavors to speak whenever she has an opportunity, words will come as if by intuition. Do not think of by-standers and lookers-on; think only of the individual to whom you are addressing yourself. If possible, be not abashed by one or two errors at the first plunge—swim on till you have confidence. The effort, I grant, is great, and it may be obviated by a foreign education; but where this is impossible, the freedom acquired will more than repay the exertion.

In foreign literature, walk carefully, and if you have an older, wiser head than your own to point out the best paths, improve the advantage.

One cannot help deeming it a great era in education that German is cultivated as well as Italian and French, and that stores of literature are opened, to vary the delights of intellect, and to give freshness and interest to the studies of youth.

The rapture with which the works of Schiller are perused in the original, seems to repay the hours devoted to German; and I am sure the perusal of Tasso, or of the Aristodemo of Monti, would reward the study of Italian, were not the acquisition of that exquisite language of itself a source of poetic pleasure.

The modern French writers have increased an everlasting responsibility in corrupting the sources of amusement, open to the young readers, and it is remarkable that most of the distinguished French authors seem to have felt that they had erred, and to have retrieved in some of their works the tendencies of their other productions. Take for instance, Madame de Stael; her books cannot be judged altogether; the effect of some of her eloquent and almost incomparable writings varies in an extraordinary degree. Whilst "Delphine" is unfit for the perusal of a modest woman, her "L'Allemagne" is finely written throughout, and her criticisms and analyses of German writers are full of instruction as well as interest.

Still the works open to readers of French are numerous. The tragedies of Corneille and Racine are forcible and finished, and should be read because classical. The "Alzire" of Voltaire and his "Zaire" with the dramas of Casimir de la Vigne are also worthy of perusal. It is not an inspiriting kind of reading, but it is rich in sentiment, and perfectly unexceptionable in moral tone.

Although the scepticism of most German writers renders this literature dangerous to a young mind, there are fields of pure, noble writing open in that language. The works of Schiller, for example. His mind was originally noble, his heart good, his love to mankind, and his enquiry after truth were sincere. In early life, he wavered; and the besetting scepticism of the Germans dimmed, for a time, his perceptions of all that is most sublime, as well as true, in our finite knowledge. He was chastened—he suffered—he believed. He died an early but a bright instance that great genius may exist with true and humble piety, and that the mind is never so powerful as when illumined by divine light. His works are a magnificent library in themselves—and I could almost say, be contented to learn German and to read Schiller. Some of his works are open to objection, his "Bride of Messina," portions of "The Robbers," are better omitted from your collection, but "Wallenstein" and "Maria Stuart" are noble and admirable productions. On this subject, and, indeed, on the whole of German literature, Madame de Stael is an excellent guide in her "L'Allemagne," to which I refer the young German student, who is sincerely desirous of gleaning the good, and avoiding the evil in German compositions.

Italian literature furnishes a delightful theme for comment. It is singular that an enslaved, and, during many ages, a depraved and degraded people, should have possessed the purest poetry, the least exceptionable drama, in Europe. There is little to exclude, and much to recommend, in this beautiful language. The works of Tasso abound with high sentiment; the "Inferno" of Dante is a sublime picture of eternal retribution, softened with most touching pictures of human woe. Happy are those who have leisure to pursue extensively the acquisition of Italian literature, they may read and commit to memory without fear of an insidious meaning beneath the polished verse, or the prose which has all the charm of poetry.

Spanish literature will require the same judicious pruning which is necessary in French and German, but of all languages, it is the most musical for speech, and singing.

A lady in society must, if she would not grow utterly weary in company, know how to dance. It has been the practice among many excellent people to represent the ball room as a "pitfall covered with flowers;" a sheet of breaking ice; above, all gayety and motion; below, all darkness and danger. It may be that to some minds the ball room may be replete with temptations; but there are minds which find temptations everywhere. The innocent may be innocent, nay, the pious may feel devout, even in a ball room. There is nothing immoral or wrong in dancing; it is the tendency of youth to dance—it is the first effort of a child—the first natural recreation. It seems so natural that I confess I am always doubtful of the sincerity of those young ladies who profess to dislike the ball room.

In the present day, you must understand how to move gracefully through quadrilles, to dance polka, Schottische, Varsovienne, and waltz. To these you may add great variety of dances, each season, probably, bringing a new one.

"Dancing," says Mr. Sheldrake, "is one of the most healthy, as well as one of the most pleasing amusements that can be practised by the young. If it is learned from those who are well qualified to teach it, and practised, as it ought to be, consistently with the instructions given, it will contribute more to improve the health, as well as the form of the human frame, than any other exercise. For the discovery and promulgation of the true and correct principles according to which dancing should be taught, the world is indebted to France, a country which has long taken the lead in the elegant arts. In France, dancing was first raised to the dignity of a science, a royal academy being founded for the purpose of teaching and perfecting it, in the reign of Louis Quatorze. In this academy were trained many of the most distinguished dancers of both sexes." One of the most celebrated, Madame Simonet, gave the following account to Mr. Sheldrake of the mode of instruction pursued in the academy:—"All the pupils, before they were permitted to attempt to dance, were completely instructed in what were called the *preparatory exercises*; that is, a system of exercises, which endued all their limbs with strength, firmness, elasticity, and activity; when they had acquired these properties, they began to dance.

"In these preparatory exercises, the motions were of the most simple kind, the object being to teach the pupil, gradually and separately, all those movements which, when combined, and rapidly executed, constitute dancing." Madame Simonet thus described those elementary instructions, as gone through by herself:—"She successively learned to stand flat and firm upon both her feet, with her limbs quite straight, and the whole person perfectly upright, but not stiff; then to lift one foot from the ground, and to keep it so for some time without moving any part of her body; she then replaced that foot on the ground, and raised the other in the same manner. These simple actions were repeated till the pupils were quite familiar with them; they were then directed to keep the body quite erect, but not stiff, and bearing firmly upon one leg, to raise the other from the ground, gradually and slowly, by bending the upper joint of the limb, at the same time making the knee straight, and putting the toe to its proper extent, but *no more*. The foot, after it had been kept in this state for some time, was returned to the ground from whence it was taken, and the other foot treated in the same manner; when quite familiarized to these actions, they were directed to walk (march, as some people will call it) slowly, performing the same motions with the feet alternately." The exercises which followed these, were upon the turning out of the feet, the balancing of the body, and other attitudes, which need not be particularized.

Mr. Sheldrake gives several examples of persons trained upon these initiatory principles to the profession of dancing, who have lived in health to a great age. "This," says he, "is not the chance lot of a few; for I have, through life, been accustomed to see many persons of the same profession; I have communicated my own observations to many others, and all have agreed in remarking, that those who follow this profession have, very generally, excellent health, which very many of them carry into extreme old age. This indisputable fact can only be accounted for by supposing that the preparatory exercises which these persons go through, are a modification of what I have called regulated muscular tension, or action, and the early and constant practice of which lays a firm foundation for that high health which accompanies them through life. It is upon the same principle that a soldier is never seen with spinal curvature, or other personal deformity, or a stage dancer of either sex with a deformed person; it is, perhaps, impossible that such things should exist, for the plain reason, that the exercises which they begin to practice early in life, and continue regularly through its whole course, render it impossible for them to become so.

"The inference to be drawn from these incontrovertible facts is, that if we, in very early life, teach young children to practice similar exercises, and follow them steadily afterwards, we shall confirm them in excellent health, and prevent the accession of those evils which so often cause deformity to the figure, and destruction to the constitution, at later periods of life. I do not propose to make every boy a soldier, or every girl a dancer upon the stage, but to adopt the principles, by the application of which those persons are trained to the successful practices of their several occupations, and so to modify them, that they may qualify other classes of society to follow *their* different pursuits with equal success; and I am not without hopes that this undertaking will contribute something towards producing this desirable effect."

Dancing is an exercise which has been practiced by mankind from the most remote ages. With the Egyptians, Assyrians, and Persians, the founders of the three great empires of the ancient world, dancing was the favorite exercise or accomplishment, and the practice was not less prevalent among their successors in power and importance, the Greeks and Romans. The Jews, also, we learn from Scripture, were strongly attached to the exercise at all periods of their history.

At the present day, almost every people that exist, whether barbarous or civilized, has its own form of dancing. It is this universality of the exercise that makes dancing a subject of importance. Being so extensively practiced, it must be the instrument either of good or evil to the human race.

It is one of the most healthful and elegant amusements, and cannot be too highly recommended. Among a rude and dissolute people it may degenerate into something worthy of condemnation; but all the blessings we have are similarly liable to abuse, and it would be most unjust to condemn a cheerful domestic amusement, merely because it has, at times, been degraded by people of low, vulgar, immoral tastes. By all physicians, dancing, when pursued in moderation, is recommended as highly conducive to bodily health; and it may be truly said, that, allied with music, nothing is more conducive to *mental* health, more calculated to drive away melancholy, and put the whole temper into good humor.

Dancing is the poetry of motion. It must be performed with ease and grace, and always with a perfect regard for propriety of movement.

As an art it is taught by professed masters; and one of the leading rules given to the learner is to raise and lower herself gracefully on the elastic part of her feet, and to keep perfect time to the music. Dancing is really a simple and elegant gliding on the toes, which bend more or less to accommodate the steps, and prevent harsh, ungraceful motion.

The most popular dances of the present day, are, first, the quadrille.

These are of French origin, comparatively tranquil in their character, and generally danced once or more in every party. They are danced by four couples, one standing on each side of a square. There are many sets of quadrilles, the figures in each varying from the others. But there are five figures in each set. The plain, fancy, Lancers, Polka, Mazourka, and German, are among the most popular.

In plain quadrilles, a lady takes no steps, merely walking gracefully through the figures, but her feet must keep perfect time to the music, and she must know the changes of position perfectly.

A quadrille may be very properly described as a conversation dance, as there are long pauses between the figures, when the dancers must have a fund of small talk ready for their partners.

When moving in the figures, hold out your skirt a little with the right hand, merely to clear the ground, and prevent the possibility of treading upon it.

Next come the round dances, the *Valse*, Polka, Schottische, Varsovienne, and Redowa.

The Waltz is danced both *à troistemps* and *deuxtemps*. In the waltz, the position is a most important point. You may so lean upon your partner's arm, and so carry your figure, that the prudish can find but little fault, but you can also make the dance a most immodest one. I cannot, within the limits of my book, go into a long argument as to the propriety of these round dances. Opinions differ, and I am not writing a sermon, but giving, as far as is in my power, hints to ladies in society. It is, therefore, enough for me to know that these dances are tolerated, and that, even were I so inclined, *I* could not exclude them.

To return to the position. Stand a little to the right of your partner, that, in clasping your waist, he may draw you upon his arm to his shoulder, not his breast; the last position is awkward. By observing the first, you have your head free; turn it a little towards the left shoulder; need I say, never lay it upon your partner's shoulder? Throw the head and shoulders a little back, not too much to be consistent with easy grace, place one hand upon your partner's shoulder, and the other in his disengaged hand. So, you are ready to start.

The waltz may be danced to very fast time, or to slow music. The last is the most graceful, and there is not so much danger of giddiness. Grace can only be gained by a perfect timing of the steps to the music, and also evenness of step. It is, when properly timed with perfect step, and easy, gliding motion, the most graceful of dances. The Germans, who dance for the sake of *dancing*, will only allow a certain number of waltzers on the floor at one time, and these waltz in streams, all going down one side of the room and up the other, thus rendering collisions impossible.

An English writer, in a recent work published on etiquette, speaks of waltzing thus:—

"It is perhaps useless to recommend flat-foot waltzing in this country, where ladies allow themselves to be almost hugged by their partners, and where men think it necessary to lift a lady almost off the ground, but I am persuaded that if it were introduced, the outcry against the impropriety of waltzing would soon cease. Nothing can be more delicate than the way in which a German holds his partner. It is impossible to dance on the flat foot unless the lady and gentleman are quite free of one another. His hand, there-fore, goes no further round her waist than to the hooks and eyes of her dress, hers, no higher than to his elbow. Thus danced, the waltz is smooth, graceful, and delicate, and we could never in Germany complain of our daughter's languishing on a young man's shoulder. On the other hand, nothing is more graceless and absurd, than to see a man waltzing on the tips of his toes, lifting his partner off the ground, or twirling round and round with her like the figures on a street organ. The test of waltzing in time, is to be able to stamp the time with the left foot. The waltz is of German origin, but where it is still danced in Germany in the original manner, (as, for instance, among the peas-ants of the Tyrol,) it is a very different dance. It is there very slow and graceful; the feet are thrown out in a single long step, which Turveydrop, I presume, would call a *jeté*. After a few turns, the partners waltz alone in the same step, the man keeping the time by striking together his iron-shod heels, until with a shout and clapping of hands he again clasps his partner and continues in the same slow measure with her."

The position for the polka, redowa, and other round dances, should be the same as that for the waltz, and for the steps, they can only be acquired from a dancing teacher, and are impossible to describe properly.

One of the most delightful accomplishments which a lady can possess, and one which is unfortunately but little cultivated, is the art of reading aloud well; reading with expression, taste, animation, and correctness; and this art once acquired, let her also be able to recite well.

Long lectures may be given upon elocution, but the advice can be condensed into two directions. First, be sure you pronounce, accent, and enunciate every word correctly; then, throw your whole soul into the words. Study your author carefully, that you may know precisely what he means by each expression, and then try to bury your personal identity, to become, for the time, the character you represent.

One of the most delightful ways to spend a social evening, is to devote it to dramatic literature. Invite only guests who read well, or who are really interested listeners, and select a play, or scenes from several plays, and cast the parts among your guests. All jealousy must be put aside, and to-night's Hamlet must condescend to direct Richard to

"Stand by, my lord, and let the coffin pass,"

to-morrow.

After a few meetings, the peculiar talent of each reader will be recognized, and you can select your tragedy hero, comedy hero, queen, chambermaid, and other members of the force, with a view to the display of each one's best powers. Vary the entertainment by reciting monologues and dialogues. A whole play will often be found tiresome; it is best to select several scenes, keeping up the thread of the plot, and introducing the best characters, and leave out what is mere interlude, and dispense with some of the subordinate characters.

Leave one end of the room entirely vacant for the readers. You will find it more interesting to have the readers stand, and use some little motion; the words will flow more easily, the expressions come more forcibly if the appropriate gesture is made. Love scenes will, of course, require delicate handling, and embracing can be easily omitted; neither would I recommend the action of a dueling scene, or a murder, but merely to add gesture enough to give interest to both readers and audience.

You will find some little difficulty from bashfulness, and the "don't like to" people at first, but soon you will discover with delight how many of your friends possess the talent for reading well, and never knew it themselves.

You will do well to take a few lessons in elocution, but you need not fear to read if you have never made the accomplishment a study. With a correct knowledge of your own language, and a love for fine writing, you will soon read well.

Give to every part you undertake, the full effect intended by the writer. Do not throw all your energy, your whole soul, into a leading part at one time, and slight a subordinate character at another. If you have but five words to read, read them as they would be spoken were you the character you represent for the time. To hear a splendidly written, tragic burst of passion read in a weak, whining voice, is no worse than to have a few simple words from a servant's lips delivered with the gesture and emphasis suited to a Medea or Lady Macbeth.

I shall be condemned by many serious and well-judging persons, if I say one word in favor of private theatricals; yet, as it appears to me, there are in these diversions some advantages which are not to be found to excuse the waltz, or the polka, or the ballet, or the hunting field. In private theatricals there is the possibility of *some* benefit. The study of the finest dramatists, especially of Shakespeare, is not likely to demoralize the mind, or to cool the enthusiasm for what is good. We can scarcely know too well those works which have tended more to form character than any collection of any kind whatsoever.

Shakespeare, Sheridan, Bulwer,—but I cannot go through the list of fine dramatic writers whose works elevate the mind and taste. The plays of Sheridan, Knowles, and Bulwer, are, in most instances, well adapted for private representations—the most exquisite delineations of female character may be found in the dramatic library, and high, pure, manly thoughts, may be traced, line after line, to the same source.

Private theatricals should, however, be regulated with much judgment. I see no reason to restrict too severely talent of this kind where it exists, any more than to crush a dawning taste for the other fine arts. What we have to do is to raise and direct it; never to let it occupy too much time, nor to become the business of life; never to let it infringe upon duties; never to allow it to lead us into an unreasonable, and, therefore, criminal expense. Our ancestors were content to strew their stage at the end of their halls with rushes, and to hang up the name of the scene, instead of a scene, before each act. The best preparations, which generally render private theatricals both laborious and expensive, add but little to the pleasure of the beholders, whose attention is fixed upon the actors, and who can always see far finer scenes at a minor theatre than at any private theatricals. Were we content with greater simplicity in our amusements, how much vain ostentation, heart-sickening expense, self-recrimination, and trouble, might be avoided!

As a valid objection to private theatricals, it has been urged that they are apt to encourage a taste for the green-room of the public theatre in young men and boys; in women the risk is less, for few women are ever known to go on the stage except from necessity. I own this objection to theatricals is the greatest that can be urged. It can only be answered in mitigation that, where there exists a taste of the kind, it is better that it should be indulged at home, instead of at the theatre, with the modest inmates of a well-governed house, instead of with professional actors. Like all other amusements, the abuse is probable, but the power of restraint rests within ourselves.

Under the same head as private theatricals may come dramatized charades and proverbs, so much in fashion at the present time. These last have some great advantages over the standard plays; they are better suited to a parlor; they do not provoke comparison between the young actors, and the favorite public idols; they require but little scenery and arrangement; they are short; and they do not require so many subordinate characters.

Impromptu charades and proverbs are delightful, and are the occasion for much merriment; the mistakes, the absurd contrasts between character and costume, the scenery—a deep, hanging wood, the court of Louis Quatorze or the deck of a man of war, being improvised at a moment's notice, only add to the merry enjoyment.

One rule you must observe if you join in these amusements: never to carry your gayety into romping. Merry and laughing you may be, yet never forget you are a lady. You may personate a newly-caught Irish chambermaid, use the broadest brogue, wear the commonest dress, throw yourself heartily and thoroughly into the part, losing your personal identity almost entirely, and yet you may retain that nameless charm, which will place you in the mind of each of the audience as a lady of refinement.

You must also be perfectly good-natured and self-sacrificing; ready to play the smallest parts with the same interest you would throw into the principal ones. Try to throw out all the good points in the parts taken by the other members of the company. If you play an insignificant part, play it well, with all the grace you can, make the most of it, but do not try to raise it to the first place. Yield gracefully the prominent position to those who claim it in the plot of the play, and never try by conspicuous dress or by play, to go beyond the position set down for you.

Another delightful accomplishment, and one which will aid you if you are studying drawing and painting, is that of arranging *tableaux vivants.*

Mrs. Severn gives the following hints upon this subject:

"Perhaps there is no intellectual amusement in fashionable life, the nature of which is so little understood, as the *tableau vivant*; it being generally considered as only a vehicle for display, whereas its real purpose is to arrange scientifically a combination of natural objects, so as to make a good picture according to the rules of art.

"A *tableau vivant* is literally what its name imports—a living picture composed of living persons; and, when skilfully arranged and seen at a proper distance, it produces all the effect of a real picture. It is said, that the first living picture was contrived by a profligate young German nobleman, who having, during the absence of his father, sold one of the celebrated pictures belonging to the old castle, which was an heir-loom, to conceal the deficiency, placed some of his companions behind the frame, so as to imitate the missing picture, and to deceive his father, who passed through the room without being conscious of his loss.

"A *tableau vivant* may be formed in two ways: it may consist of a group of persons, who take some well-known subject in history or fiction to illustrate, and who form a group to tell the story according to their own taste; or, it may be a copy, as exact as circumstances will permit, of some celebrated picture. The first plan, it may be easily imagined, is very rarely effective; since, as we find that even the best masters are often months, or even years, before they can arrange a group satisfactorily on canvas, it is not probable that persons who are not artists should succeed in making good impromptu pictures. Indeed, it has been observed, that artists themselves, when they have to arrange a *tableau vivant*, always prefer copying a picture to composing one.

"Copying a real picture, by placing living persons in the positions of the figures indicated in the picture, appears, at first sight, an easy task enough; and the effect ought to be easily attained, as there can be no bad drawing, and no confused light and shade, to destroy the effect of the grouping. There are, however, many difficulties to conquer, which it requires some knowledge of art to be aware of. Painting being on a flat surface, every means are taken to give roundness and relief to the figures, which qualities of course are found naturally in a *tableau vivant*. In a picture the light is made effective by a dark shadow placed near it; diminished lights or demi-tints are introduced to prevent the principal light appearing a spot; and these are linked together by artful shades, which show the outline in some places, and hide it in others. The colors must also be carefully arranged, so as to blend or harmonize with each other. A want of attention to these minute points will be sufficient to destroy the effect of the finest picture, even to those who are so unacquainted with art as to be incapable of explaining why they are dissatisfied, except by an involuntary liking or disliking of what they see.

"The best place for putting up a *tableau vivant* is in a door-way, with an equal space on each side; or, at least, some space on both sides is necessary; and if there is a room or a passage between the door selected for the picture and the room the company is to see it from, so much the better, as there should be a distance of at least four yards between the first row of the spectators and the picture. It must be remembered that, while the tableau is being shown, nearly all the lights must be put out in the room where the company is assembled; and, perhaps, only one single candle, properly placed, in the intervening space between the company and the tableau, must be left slightly to illuminate the frame. In the above-mentioned door-way a frame, somewhat smaller than the original picture, must be suspended, three, four, or even five feet from the floor, as may suit the height of the door; or, if the door is not very high, the frame may be put one or two feet behind, to gain space; but care must be taken to fill up the opening that would, in that case, show between the door-way and the frame; also a piece of dark cloth ought to be put from the bottom of the frame to the ground, to give the appearance of the picture hanging on the wall. The most important thing is, that the chairs or tables ought to be placed behind the frame, so that the persons who are to represent the tableau may sit or stand as nearly in the position, with regard to the frame, as the figures appear to do in the real picture they are trying to imitate, and at about two feet from the frame, so that the light which is attached to the back of the frame may fall properly on the figures. In order to accomplish this, great study and contrivance are required, so that the shades may fall in precisely the same places as in the original picture; and sometimes the light is put on one side, sometimes on the other, and often on the top; and sometimes shades of tin or paper are put between the lights and the tableaux, to assist in throwing a shadow over any particular part. The background is one of the most important parts, and should be made to resemble that of the picture as nearly as possible; if it is dark, coarse cloth absorbs the light best; but whether it is to be black, blue, or brown, must depend on the tint of the picture; should the background be a light one, colored calico, turned on the wrong side, is generally used. If trees or flowers form the background, of course real branches or plants must be introduced to imitate those in the picture. Even rocks have been imitated; and spun glass has often successfully represented water. A thin, black gauze, black muslin, or tarlatan veil, should be fastened to the top of the frame, on the *outside* of it, through which the tableau is to be seen.

"Care ought to be taken to conceal the peculiarities of the different materials used in the draperies, and it is even sometimes necessary to cover the stuffs used for the purpose with a gauze of a different color, so as to imitate the broken and transparent colors found in most good pictures. This, carefully attended to, will give a quietness and simplicity to the whole, which will greatly add to the illusion."

The next subject upon the list of accomplishments, should be filled by some words upon fancy sewing. Under this head will come—Crochet, Knitting, Tapestry work, Embroidery, Chenille work, Netting, Canvas work, Berlin wool work, Frame work, Braiding, Bead work, etc.

Small social gatherings will be much more entertaining, the time will pass much more quickly, and the conversation flows more freely if the fingers are employed with some light work.

Pretty presents—nay, beautiful ones—may be made in this way, when the fingers would otherwise be idle, and these will have an additional value in being the work of your own hands.

From the most remote ages needlework has been, not only a source of pecuniary advantage for poor women, but also of pleasant pastime for the rich. It is one of the most elegant of the imitative art, and from time immemorial it has been an amusement for otherwise idle fingers, from the cottage to the palace.

I have not space for a long disquisition upon the uses and pleasures of fancy work; every woman has moments when such pretty playwork will be a valuable recreation. The taste for fancy work increases daily, and can be made not only ornamental, but useful. A ladies' wardrobe consists of so many, and such varied objects, that the evenings of an entire winter may be spent in making various useful garments, which are, at the same time, suitable for company sewing. Opera hoods, wool shawls, sleeves, Sontags, and other ladies' articles, may be varied by embroidering smoking caps, slippers, or handkerchiefs for gentlemen.

Embroidering on canvas, or tapestry work, opens a large field for taste and skill in execution. Beautiful articles for presents, chair covers, sofa cushions, slippers, may be worked in the otherwise idle moments spent in familiar society, and the fingers will soon acquire skill and astonishing rapidity.

The German ladies have constantly on hand a piece of netting or other fancy work, which they carry from place to place, and take out when conversing; and so far from entirely engrossing their thoughts, they chat more readily and freely with their fingers thus employed.

American ladies will find the custom worth imitating. Many tedious hours will be smoothly, pleasantly passed, with the mind free, but the fingers pleasantly occupied.

An evening passed in sewing or knitting, with one good reader to entertain the industrious workers, will be found very pleasant. I have known a circle of young people meet every week to work in this way, the reader being changed twice or three times in the course of the evening, and these meetings have proved so pleasant, that scarcely any member failed to plead "prior engagement" if invited out upon the evening appointed to read and sew.

It was formerly objected by the adversaries to mental cultivation in women, that the acquirement of book learning would make them neglect needlework; but so far from this being the case, the present, which is often called the age of learning, is preëminently a working age. Never were fingers more actively engaged than those of the rising female generation; braiding, embroidery, Berlin work, knitting, netting, and crochet, are all in full play. A long neglected work has been recently revived, called by the French "La Frivolité." It is very pretty evening work, partly because it does not impede conversation, for it may be carried on almost without looking at it, and partly because no other work shows to so much advantage the grace and delicacy of the hands. The most simple form of this work was anciently known under the name of Tatting, but that only consisted of a series of loops in a straight line, which were used for trimming linen articles, and which was not so pretty as La Frivolité, which has varieties which are a good imitation of point, and may be used for collars and sleeves.

I give a few specimens of pretty work for evening sewing, and refer the reader to "The Ladies' Handbook of Embroidery," published by G. G. Evans, for a full, complete description of every kind of fancy work, with specimens, patterns, and clear, plain directions.

NETTED CUFFS—These cuffs are very pretty, and easy to make. They are in plain netting, and will require white, and five shades of scarlet wool.

Set on thirty-five stitches of the white wool. Net five rows, then take a mesh a very little larger, and widen by netting two stitches in every stitch. Then net with the smallest mesh the two lightest shades, one row of each, and two rows of the other three shades. Then graduate the shades back again to white, narrowing the first row of white with the larger mesh. Net ten rows with the smaller mesh, widen again, repeat the shades of red, narrow again, and finish with the five rows of white.

KNITTED OPERA CAP.

MATERIALS REQUIRED—Half an ounce of white and half an ounce of shaded Berlin wool will be sufficient.

Cast on a hundred stitches with white wool, and knit and pearl alternately for four rows.

Shaded wool—Knit one row plain; next row bring forward, and take two together to the end.

White wool—Knit and pearl alternately four rows.

Shaded wool—Knit plain six rows.

White wool—Knit a row, decreasing it by taking the first two stitches together, and the last two. Pearl a row. Knit a row, decreasing it as before. Pearl a row.

Shaded wool—Knit a row, decreasing at the beginning and end. Next row, bring forward and take two together to the end.

White wool—Knit a row, decreasing at both ends. Pearl a row. Knit a row, decreasing as before. Pearl a row.

FOR THE PATTERN IN THE CENTRE OF THE CAP.

SHADED WOOL—*1st row*—Slip one. Knit two plain stitches (*a.*) Wool forward. Knit one. Wool forward. Knit two together. Knit one. Knit two together. Repeat from (*a.*)

2nd row—Pearled.

3rd row—Slip one. Knit two plain stitches (*b.*) Wool forward. Knit three plain stitches. Wool forward. Slip one. Knit two together. Pass the slipped stitch over the knitted ones. Repeat from (*b.*)

4th row—Pearled.

5th row—Slip one. Knit two plain stitches, (*c.*) Wool forward. Knit two together. Knit one. Knit two together. Wool forward. Knit one. Repeat from (*c.*)

6th row—Pearled.

7th row—Slip one. Knit two plain stitches (*d.*) Wool forward. Slip one. Knit two together. Pass the slipped stitch over the knitted ones. Wool forward. Knit three plain stitches. Repeat from (*d.*)

8th row—Pearled. Repeat the last eight rows.

White wool—Knit and pearl alternately for four rows; decrease at the beginning and ending of the two plain rows.

Shaded wool—Knit one plain row; decrease at the beginning and ending. Next row; bring the wool forward, knit two together to the end of the row.

White wool—Knit and pearl alternately for four rows; decrease at the beginning and ending of the two plain rows.

Knit eighteen plain stitches, run a piece of cotton through the remaining sixty-two stitches. Pearl and knit alternately, decreasing at the beginning and ending of every plain row, until you have four stitches remaining; cast them off; then take up eighteen stitches on the opposite sides, and work a piece to correspond; leaving forty-four centre stitches on the cotton.

Take up the centre stitches on a needle pointed at both ends, draw the cotton out; then pick up fourteen stitches at each end of the needle.

Shaded wool—Knit two plain rows.

White wool—Knit one plain row. Next row; wool forward, knit two together to the end of the row.

Shaded wool—Knit two plain rows and cast off. Join the two points together at the back of the cap. Fold the front at the first pattern row, and hem it to form the scallop at the edge. Pick up eighty stitches at the back of the cap.

AN ECONOMICAL POINT COLLAR.

It is well known that worked muslin collars, particularly if the work is good, very soon wear out; as the work is too heavy for the muslin, which, when it has been washed two or three times, becomes full of slits and holes, though the work is still as good as ever. When this is the case, cut the muslin off the work with a pair of sharp scissors, and lay the work on the pattern of a collar cut in paper, so as to fill the whole of the pattern. The work may be taken from two or three collars; the arrangement of it must depend upon taste. When the cut-out work is properly arranged, it must be tacked or basted to the paper pattern; and this is best done with colored thread, that no mistake may arise when the basting threads are to be drawn out. Four or six threads are then drawn from one piece of work to another, with a needle and cotton, so as to attach them together, and the loose threads are then overcast like button-holes, so as to imitate the uniting threads of point lace. When well done, with a sufficient quantity of the uniting threads, to make the work firm, these collars are handsome, and will wash and wear well.

KNITTED VEILS.

It is now customary to knit white veils of what is called Lady Betty's wool, for babies to put over their faces when they are carried out in cold weather, instead of pocket-handkerchiefs, which were formerly used for the purpose, though they were very unfit for it. Knitted veils in black silk or worsted are also worn by grown-up persons. The veils for babies are very simple in their construction; they consist of oblong pieces of knitting of any width and depth that may be required, with knitted lace at the bottom and sides, and a string case at the top. The following pattern is the most common:

Knit and pearl alternately four rows, so that there may be two of each; then bring forward and take two together an entire row. This pattern is repeated through the entire veil; and it must be observed, that as many stitches must be cast on as will make it of the necessary width. The needles should be of the smallest size, of bone. Any lace will do; but the following pattern, though not new, is both pretty and suitable; and has, besides, the important recommendation of being very easy.

Cast on eleven stitches and knit a row plain, then begin the pattern.

1st row—Knit three; bring forward and take two together; knit one, take two together; put the thread twice round the needle, take two together, and knit one.

2nd row—Knit two, pearl one, knit one, put the thread twice round the needle, take two together, bring forward, and knit five.

3rd row—Knit three, bring forward, take two together, knit one, bring forward, knit two, pearl one, bring forward, take two together, and knit two.

4th row—Knit two, bring forward, knit five, bring forward, take two together, knit five.

5th row—Knit three, bring forward, and take two together, knit the rest plain.

6th row—Cast off four, and knit the rest plain.

HINTS TO CROCHET-WORKERS.

Examine carefully the form of the needle, and *try* the hook, to ascertain that it is perfectly smooth. Some are so sharp and ill-made as to tear the cotton. Select those which are not of uniform thickness up to the hook; the best are those which are thinner there than an inch farther up. Where the needle is not proportionally fine near the hook, it is almost impossible to keep the work even.

Chain stitch ought to be done rather loosely, as working on it afterwards contracts it, and is apt to give it a puckered appearance. It is often advisable to use a needle one size larger for making the chain than for the rest of the work, especially in edgings. It will be found much easier to work the succeeding rows when this precaution is taken. Crochet needles should be kept in a housewife similar to those used for ordinary needles. The slightest soil or rust should be effaced with fine sandpaper.

ORNAMENTAL NET FOR THE HAIR.

Take two pieces of fine silk braid, scarlet or royal blue, and a No. 3 bone crochet hook.

Make a chain of eight stitches, unite the ends, and then D. C. the first round, putting two stitches into each loop; there will now be sixteen stitches and in the next round one long must be worked into every stitch, and two chain between each long; the round will now consist of forty-eight stitches, and we commence the pattern, or diamonds.

3rd round—Three long, two chain, four long with two chain after each, and these long put into every second loop; repeat.

4th round—Five long, two chain, five long with two chain after each, and these long put into every second loop with the exception of the fifth or last of them, which must skip two stitches instead of one; repeat.

5th round—Seven long, two chain, seven long with two chain after each, and each of these long put into every second stitch; repeat.

6th round—Five long, two chain, five long with two chain after each, and each of these long put into every other stitch, three long, two chain, five long again with two chain after each, and each put into every second stitch; repeat from beginning.

7th round—Three long, two chain, five long with two chain after each and worked in every third loop, five long, two chain, five long again with two chain after each, and these long worked as aforesaid in every third loop; repeat from beginning.

8th round—One long, two chain, five long with two chain after each and these long put into every third stitch, seven long, two chain, again five long, &c. &c. repeat from beginning.

9th round—Six long with two chain after each and work in every third stitch, (five long, twelve long with two chain after each, these long put in every third stitch); repeat the pattern in brackets.

10th round—Nine long with two chain after them, these long being worked in every second loop, (three long, two chain, nineteen long with two chain after them, and the long worked in every second loop); repeat the pattern in brackets.

11th, 12th, and 13th rounds—A long and two chain all round, and the long being worked alternately in every second and third loop; care being taken to bring one into the position to complete each diamond as it is come to.

A crochet edging, begun with braid, and the last two or three rows worked with gold twist as nearly the size of the braid as may be, and a cord and tassels, finish off this elegant head-dress.

The cord should be run in and out through the thirteenth round. We, however, prefer a single-crochet band of some fifty stitches long and six or eight wide, worked in the same material as the net, to a cord, and this band may be finished off with a piece of gold fringe instead of tassels at the ends, or with a scallop of edging crocheted in gold twist.

DRESS GLOVE BANDS; FULL OR FRILLED SHAPE.

Take three pieces of fine embroidery chenille, and a No. 3 bone crochet hook.

Make a chain of about forty stitches, or one long enough to go round the wrist; Dc one row.

3rd row—Two long, one chain and miss a stitch—repeat this all along. Then one row Dc.

6th row—Long crochet worked *very* loosely, so much so as to leave these stitches *at least* half an inch high; two stitches to be put into every second or third loop and one in each of the others all the way along; fasten off.

Join the chenille now on to the first row, and work a similar row or frill to the one just directed, so that there be one on each side.

Run a narrow velvet through the holes of the third row and affix wider velvet ends, or chenille tassels to each extremity. Finish off with a button and loop, and flute the frill on each side over the finger to make it set.

We need scarcely say that the chenille used should be selected to match or agree with the evening dress, and that the velvet must match the chenille.

These bands may be made to look very handsome by working a row of Dc loosely and evenly along the edge of each frill with gold or silver twist, and running a band of gold or silver braid or trimming through the holes in the third row instead of velvet. Then small bullion tassels to match the twist will form a suitable and elegant finish.

These bands may be worked round and slid over the hand like muffatees, or made open as we have directed and buttoned, like the glove. The buttons should be covered with crochet, and the loops crocheted.

KNITTED UNDER HABIT SHIRT.

Three ounces of Three thread White Fleecy Wool. Pair of No. 10 Bone Knitting Pins. Cast on forty-five stitches.

Knit three rows.

4th row—Knit ten; × make two and knit two together; knit one; × knit the last six stitches.

5th row—Knit, dropping the second of each of the two made stitches all along. Knit eight rows.

14th row—Knit ten; × make one and knit two together × repeat until six remain; knit three; make one; knit three.

15th row—Knit six; × make one and knit two together × repeat until ten remain, which knit.

Repeat these two rows three times more each, only not enlarging one (as in the end of row fourteen), *every* time, but only once in four rows, merely knitting the six in the intervening rows.

22nd row—Knit. Knit the next seven rows.

30th row—Same as *14th.*

31st row—Same as *15th.*

Keep on alternately knitting eight open, and then eight knitted rows, and enlarging one stitch at the end in every fourth row until there are a hundred and twenty-four rows.

Then decrease one stitch at the beginning or front in every other row for thirty-two rows, still continuing the pattern as before, and still enlarging one stitch in every fourth row, at the end or back. This shapes one side of the neck.

Now knit forty-eight rows without increase or decrease at either end, continuing the pattern or alternation of eight open and eight plain knitted rows. This forms the back of the neck and the bottom of the back of the habit-shirt.

In the next thirty-two rows we diminish one in every fourth row, by knitting two together at the back, while at the same time in every fourth row, at the back, we knit two together, and make one in order to form a series of holes, or pattern parallel to that on the other side caused by enlarging in every fourth row. We also cast on one, at the opposite end, in every other row, to shape the second side of the neck. We then knit one hundred and twelve rows, having each ten knitted stitches in the front of the habit-shirt, as on the opposite side, and six at the back, and decreasing one in every fourth row, at the back, and continuing the pattern, and also the series of holes at the back.

Knit eight rows.

Knit ten stitches, × make two and knit two together; × knit six at end.

Knit all, dropping the second of each of the two made stitches. Knit two rows; cast off.

Now, with same needles, pick up the stitches all along the right front of the habit-shirt; knit two rows and cast off. Do the same on the left front. Then pick up those of the neck, and do the same, shaping it, if necessary, by knitting two together occasionally. These finishing-off rows look pretty done in pale pink or blue wool. Button-holes may be made thus:—in the front or where the ten stitches are, and about once in thirty rows, knit three; cast off four; knit three instead of knitting the ten as usual. Next row, when we get back to the ten stitches, knit three; cast on four; knit three.

INFANT'S KNITTED SOCKS.

Half an ounce of White Lamb's Wool. Three No. 13 Knitting Needles. Cast on Thirty stitches.

1st row—Knit.

2nd row—Knit two; make or enlarge one stitch by picking up one from the previous row and knitting it; knit all the rest.

3rd row—Knit. Repeat second and third rows alternately four times more each of them.

12th row—Knit two; make a stitch according to directions above given; knit rest until four remain; knit two together; knit two.

13th row—Knit. Repeat these two rows alternately three times more each.

20th row—Knit two; enlarge one as before directed; knit rest until two remain; enlarge one; knit two.

21st row—Knit. Repeat these two rows alternately three more times each.

28th row—Knit.

29th row—Knit fourteen stitches, and leave the other upon the needle. Take up the third needle and knit twenty rows more, of fourteen stitches each.

49th row—Knit two together; knit twelve; on same needle, and with same wool, cast on twenty-seven stitches.

50th row—Knit.

51st row—Knit two; knit two together; knit rest until four remain; knit two together; knit two.

52nd row—Knit. Repeat these two rows alternately twice more each.

57th row—Knit two; make one in manner directed; knit rest until four remain; knit two together; knit two.

58th row—Knit. Repeat these two rows alternately three times more each.

65th row—Knit all until four remain; knit two together; knit two.

66th row—Knit. Repeat these two rows alternately four more times each.

75th row—Knit.

76th row—Cast off.

This completes the slipper portion of the sock. We now begin the instep-piece. Take the wool and knit off ten stitches from the needle on which the twenty-seven stitches were left; knit these ten from the toe-end, or that where the twenty rows of fourteen stitches each has been made; leave the remaining seventeen stitches still on the same needle. Knit twenty rows of ten stitches, and in every other one pick up the edge-stitch of the toe-piece and knit it with the tenth stitch, so as to unite these two portions, viz: the toe and the instep. With each stitch of the twentieth row, an edge-stitch of the side at the toe-end of the slipper must be picked up, knitted and cast off, and a neat and entire union of the toe of the slipper and the instep piece formed.

This instep piece is to be ribbed in rows of four, viz. four rows in which the plain side is uppermost, and four rows in which the pearled side is uppermost.

We now commence the leg portion of the sock.

With the needle which has been left in the first side of the slipper carefully pick up the edge-stitches all along the instep-piece and side of the slipper; when this is done, there should be about fifty on the needle. Take the wool and knit all along, including the picked up stitches, and the seventeen originally on the needle. Knit two rows.

4th row—Knit two; × make two (not by picking up, but in the ordinary way, by passing the wool twice over the needle), and knit two together; knit one; × repeat.

5th row—Knit all; casting off one of each of the double made stitches. Now knit twenty rows ribbed like the instep-piece.

26th row—× Knit one; make one and knit two together; × repeat all round.

27th row—Knit.

28th row—Knit two; × make one and knit two together; knit one; × repeat.

29th, 30th, and 31st rows—Knit.

32nd row—Cast off.

Take a wool needle, thread it with wool, and sew up the sock neatly, stitch for stitch, from the top of the leg to the point of the sole; then sew the toe; turn it; put on a little rosette of raveled wool; run a ribbon in and out through the holes at rows 4 and 5, of the leg portion, and it is completed.

As this is intended for an Infant's Sock, we have ordered white wool, that being most useful; should it, however, be wished to knit socks for an older baby, the slipper may be made of Cerise, Scarlet, Pale Blue, Green, or Straw-colored wool; and the 26th, 27th, and 28th rows, of the leg portion, and the casting-off done in the color of the slipper; while the instep-piece and the rest of the sock are made in white wool.

The sock may also be enlarged by casting on extra stitches in the beginning, and adding a couple of rows to each of the divisions of the slipper part, and enough to the toe to preserve its form and symmetry.

Almost any of the open anti-maccassar patterns may be used for knitting the sock and instep-piece, if a light lace-like appearance is desired. The well-known rose-leaf pattern looks particularly pretty.

CHAPTER XXII.
SERVANTS.

An English writer, speaking of servants, says:—

"There is no question but that we should seek to perform *all* our duties without hope of recompense; and yet, as regards our treatment of servants, we should be especially careful that, in endeavoring to make their bodily comfort and mental improvement an object of consideration, we do not allow ourselves to dwell on the hope of gratitude or affection from them in return. Many have done so, and having, with that view, been tempted to accord unwise indulgences and to overlook serious faults, they have found that, far from gaining the love of their servants, they have incurred their contempt; and when they have perceived that their favors, unappreciated, have led but to new encroachments, they have hardened their hearts and rushed into an opposite extreme. Then they have considered their servants as mere machines, from which labor must be extorted by all available means.

"A man servant is rarely grateful, and seldom attached. He is generally incapable of appreciating those advantages which, with your cultivated judgment, you know to be the most conducive to his welfare. Do you accord to him regular hours, a stated allowance of work; do you refrain from sending him out because it is wet and he is unwell; do you serve yourself rather than ring for him at dinner time; he will rarely have the grace to thank you in his heart for your constant consideration. Hear him! He will thus describe a comfortable place:—'There were very few in the family; when they went out of a night, we made it up of a morning; we had nice hot suppers, and the cook made a good hash for breakfast, and we always got luncheon between that and dinner; and we were all very comfortable together, and had a friend in when we liked. Master swore at us sometimes, but often made us a present for it when he had been very violent; a good-hearted man as ever lived, and mistress was quite the lady, and never meddled with servants. It was a capital place!'

"Servants' sympathies are with their equals. They feel for a poor servant run off his legs, and moped to death; they have no feeling for a pains-taking mistress, economical both from principle and scanty means; they would (most of them) see her property wasted, and her confidence abused without compunction. It is the last effort of a virtue in a servant if, without any *private reason*, he should discharge his duty by informing you of the injury which you are enduring at the hands of his fellow servant. It is an effort of virtue, for it will bring down many a bitter taunt and hard word upon his faithful head. '*I* never got a servant out of a place by telling tales on him,› will be said to him. Directly a servant departs, we all know, tongues, tied before, are loosed, to gain our favor by apparent candor. When it can avail us nothing, we are told. We all know this, and have said, ‹Be silent now, you should have mentioned this at the time.› Supposing, then, you have the *rara avis*, the servant that 'speaks at the time,' be chary of him, or let me say *her* (the best servants are women). Oh! as you value her, let her not suppose you cannot part with her. Treat her with confidence, but with strict impartiality; reprove when necessary, mildly, but decidedly; lest she should presume (power is so tempting), and compel you, if you would retain your freedom, to let her go.

"There is one thing a man servant values beyond all that your kindness and your consideration can do for him—his liberty; liberty to eat, drink, and be merry, with your things in the company of his own friends; liberty to get the housemaid to clean his candlesticks, and bring up his coals; and the housemaid wishes for liberty to lie in bed in the morning, because she was up so late talking to John in the pantry; liberty to wear flounces and flowers. The cook desires liberty too. For this liberty, if you grant it, they will despise you; if you deny it, they will respect you. Aim at their esteem; despair of their love or gratitude; make your place what the best class of servants will value, and, though in their heart, they may not thank you for it, you will gain, perhaps, one servant out of twenty who will keep gross imposition and gross immorality at bay.

"These remarks can never be intended to deny the warm attachment of female servants to the children of their employers. Deep love, no doubt, is lavished by many a woman on the babe she has nursed. There is a great deal to be said on the chapter of nurses which would require to be dealt with by itself. Much wisdom is required in the administration of a nursery, to which few general rules would apply. Cruel is the tyranny the nurse frequently practises on the parent, who often refrains from entering her nursery, not from want of love to her children, but positive dread of the sour looks which greet her. Let her be firm, let no shrinking from grieving her darling, who would 'break his heart if his Nanna went,' deter her from discharging the encroaching servant.

"I know a lady who was quietly informed by her nurse that she must have a 'specified hour' for visiting her children, for that her entering without ceremony was most inconvenient. The poor young lady, who was fully persuaded her delicate infant would die, if removed to a stranger's hands, meekly obeyed, and though tortured by the cries of the poor sickly baby, never dared to intrude lest the nurse should abandon it. This is a true history, and the sequel may as well be given: that the nurse remained seven years, at the end of which time, having become insupportable, though really devoted to the children, she gave warning, and, though it cost her mistress bitter tears and much resolution, she was suffered to depart, and then peace entered that house.

"On the choice of servants much of the comfort of the young housekeeper depends. It often happens that her choice has been determined by appearance rather than the value of character. If such be the case, she will have many difficulties to encounter. It is, in the present day, hardly safe to take a servant if there be a single objection to character, however it may be glossed over by the person referred to on this point; for there is now an unhealthy disposition to pass over the failings of servants who have left their places, and to make them perfect in the eyes of others. In respect to sobriety, many people will not acknowledge that a servant had had the vice of drinking, but will cover the unpleasant truth in such gentle and plausible terms that it becomes difficult to comprehend how far the hint is grounded, or not. Be assured when a lady or gentleman hesitates on this point, or on that of honesty, it is wiser not to engage a servant. Nor are you deviating from Christian charity in not overlooking a dereliction of so material a sort. The kindest plan to the vast community of domestic servants is to be rigid in all important points, and having, after a due experience, a just confidence in them, to be somewhat indulgent to errors of a more trivial nature.

"If all young housekeepers were strict upon the subject of dress, much misery to servants would be saved, much temptation avoided, and self-reproach prevented. Instead of this kind, and wise, and matronly particularity, a type of the good, old-fashioned common sense of our grandmothers, ladies now countenance their ladies'-maids in discontinuing caps, or, if they have caps, in wearing flowers and lace, flowered gowns, and other items of little apparent moment in detail, but of much importance to a community as serviceable to the public when well managed and respectable, as they are odious and noxious when immoral or insolent. After these cruel indulgences, ladies marvel when they find servants rise above their station and that they will not bear even a mild reproof; they wonder that a plain, useful servant is nowhere to be met with. There is now no medium between the fine lady with mittens and flowers who dresses your hair, and the dirty sloven of a lodging-house. All housemaids must now be upper housemaids; cooks must be cooks and housekeepers. The homely housemaid—that invaluable character in her way—is indeed difficult to be found; and, at a time when cleanliness is at its zenith, the rarity is to discover any one who will clean. All, except the raw country girl, expect to have deputies; and, if we go on to perfection in this unhealthy system, we shall soon have no working servants above twenty years of age. The consequence is, that a greater number of servants are kept in every household than formerly in similar families; many of these menials are corrupted by congregating together and by idleness. The loud and crying complaints of the worthlessness of this class are but too justly founded. That they are more mercenary than ever, is owing to the pernicious system which lifts them up above their condition, but fails to elevate them in the moral standard. In the scale of virtue they sink every day lower and lower; in the outward attributes they are, as they consider it, raised in character and improved in appearance.

"But is it so? The beauty of every thing is fitness. Is the half-fine, unlady-like, yet lady-like creature, who answers to your dressing-room bell, half so respectable as the old-fashioned, plainly dressed, careful, homely maiden of your young days? Is it not with a feeling of disgust that you turn from the attempted finery, and sigh for plain collars, and caps undecked by flowers, again? I think, among the best-bred, the most sensible, and, indeed, the most highly born people of a superior stamp, this disgust is so strong that, in some families, a grave and suitable costume is introduced for the female servants, and the effect is satisfactory, both on the appearance and on the mode of thinking of these persons. But this wise, and therefore kind plan, is far from being general; and I have heard that a lady's-maid complained to her mistress that she found herself the subject of ridicule, owing to her not wearing silks, and indeed satins, as the other ladies'-maids did.

"It becomes the duty of ladies of influence to rise above the silly vanity which, I fear, affects some of them, of seeing their ladies'-maids as smart as ladies, and to oppose innovations on the decencies of society, so pernicious to the class upon whom much of our comfort depends. In setting out in life, a young married lady ought to be more than ordinarily strict in these matters, for her inexperience will certainly be taken advantage of to some extent. If she be rich enough to have a housekeeper, let her endeavor to select one of strict religious faith, plain in attire, grave, but kind, and of good sense, and even intelligence; for cultivation of mind will never, whatever may be stated, detract from the utility of a servant. It is absurd to attribute to the diffusion of knowledge the deterioration of servants; it is rather owing to the scanty amount of knowledge among them. Most superficial is the education about which so much is said and written; were servants more thoroughly grounded in many branches of knowledge, they would be wiser, less rapacious, more systematic, and better contented than they are. They are wretched reasoners, generally losing sight of their own true interest, and grasping at that which is unreal and visionary. If they were better educated, this would not be the case; they would be less vain, less credulous; they would know what qualities to respect; they would weigh better the advantage of their lot; and they would work better as servants. They would give mind, where now they only give hands; and their acquirements, taken from school as they are in very early youth, are not ever likely to be such as to make the routine of their work distasteful to them, from over refinement or cultivation.

"It is always desirable to have, if possible, servants of one faith. But if it so happens that you have a Roman Catholic servant and a Protestant in your service, you are bound to allow each the free exercise of her religion, and you ought not to respect them if, out of interest, they will conform to yours. An exercise of authority on this point amounts, in my opinion, to an act of tyranny, and it can only tend to promote insincerity, and, perhaps, engender scepticism in its object. Nothing is, indeed, so dangerous as to unsettle the faith of the lower classes, who have neither time nor opportunity of fairly considering subjects of religious controversy.

"While on the subject of servants, I must deprecate the over-indulgence of the present system towards them. Formerly they were treated with real kindness, but it was the kindness that exacted duty in return, and took a real interest in the welfare of each servant. The reciprocal tie in former times between servant and master was strong, now it is wholly gone. The easy rule of masters and mistresses proceeds far more from indifference than from kindness of heart; for the real charity is to keep servants steadily to their duties. They are a class of persons to whom much leisure is destruction; the pursuits of their idle hours are seldom advantageous to them, and theirs are not minds which can thrive in repose. Idleness, to them, is peculiarly the root of all evil, for, if their time is not spent in vicious amusements, it is often passed in slander, discontent, or vanity. In writing thus, I do not recommend a hard or inconsiderate system to servants. They require, and in many instances they merit, all that can be done to alleviate a situation of servitude. They ought not to be the slaves of caprice or the victims of temper. Their work should be measured out with a just hand; but it should be regularly exacted in as much perfection as can be expected in variable and erring human nature.

"Another point on which I would recommend firmness is that of early hours. In this respect example is as important as precept; but, however uncertain you may be yourself, I would not relax a rule of that kind. For every comfort during the day depends upon the early rising of your servants. Without this, all their several departments are hurried through or neglected in some important respect.

"Your mode of address to servants must be decisive, yet mild. The authoritative tone I do not recommend. It is very unbecoming to any young person, and it rarely attains the end desired; but there is a quiet dignity of deportment which few servants ever can resist. This should be tempered with kindness, when circumstances call it forth, but should never descend to familiarity. For no caution is more truly kind than which confines servants strictly to their own sphere.

"Much evil results from the tendency, more especially of very young, or of very old mistresses of families, to partiality. Commonly, one servant becomes the almost avowed favorite; and it is difficult to say whether that display of partiality is the more pernicious to the servant who is the object of it, or to the rankling and jealous minds of the rest of the household. It is true that it is quite impossible to avoid entertaining a greater degree of confidence in some servants than in others; but it should be shown with a due regard to the feelings of all. It is, of course, allowable towards those who take a decidedly responsible and confidential situation in a household. Still, never let such persons assume the reins of government; let them act the part of helmsman to the vessel, but not aspire to the control of the captain.

"It is generally wise and right, after a due experience of the principles and intentions of servants, to place confidence in their honesty, and to let them have the comfort of knowing that you do so. At the same time, never cease to exercise a system of supervision. The great principle of housekeeping is regularity; and without this (one of the most difficult of the minor virtues to practice) all efforts to promote order must be ineffectual. I have seen energetic women, clever and well-intentioned, fail in attaining a good method, owing to their being uncertain in hours, governed by impulse, and capricious. I have seen women, inferior in capacity, slow, and apathetic, make excellent heads of families, as far as their household was concerned, from their steadiness and regularity. Their very power of enduring monotony has been favorable to their success in this way, especially if they are not called upon to act in peculiar and difficult cases, in which their actual inferiority is traceable. But these are not the ordinary circumstances of life.

"In closing these remarks on the management of servants, let me exhort you never to forget that they are fellow-laborers, in the life of probation, with ourselves; let us not embitter their lives by harshness, or proffer to them temptation from carelessness and over-indulgence. Since all that is given us of this world's goods is but in trust, let us regard our servants as beings for whose conduct, while under our control, we are more or less responsible. It is true that, if they come to us with morals wholly depraved, it is not likely that the most strenuous exertions can amend them; but many waver between good and evil. Let us endeavor to excite in their minds a respect for virtue, to give them motives for industry, inducements to save their wages. Those who have large households should not deem the morals of the meanest of their servants beneath their investigation, or too obscure for their influence to reach."

Some attention is absolutely necessary, in this country, to the training of servants, as they come here from the lowest ranks of English and Irish peasantry, with as much idea of politeness as the pig domesticated in the cabin of the latter.

Opening the door seems a simple act, yet few servants perform it in a proper, respectful manner. Let your servant understand that the door must be opened immediately after the bell rings. Visitors, from neglect of this rule, will often ring several times, and finally leave the door. I have known an instance when in a case of severe illness the patient lost the visit of the doctor, who, after ringing some minutes, was obliged to pay other visits, and could not return to the sufferer's house until several hours later.

When opening the door some servants hold it ajar and hold a long parley with the person on the steps, as if afraid they wished to enter for the purpose of murder or theft.

Train them to answer the door promptly, speak politely to any one who may be there, excuse you, if necessary, to visitors in courteous terms, or, if you are in, show the callers into the parlor, take their card, and come back quickly with your answer.

CHAPTER XXIII.
ON A YOUNG LADY'S CONDUCT WHEN CONTEMPLATING MARRIAGE.

The following chapter, met with in a recent perusal of an English work for young ladies, strikes me as so admirable, and so appropriate in this place, that I quote the chapter entire:

"The difficulties and trials of life have only just begun when a young lady fancies herself to be of sufficient importance to become the theme of animadversion. She knows little of the true importance of self-control, until she experiences the first indications of preference shown her by the other sex.

"Such indications are often manifested, whilst she to whom they are directed, is wholly unprepared to analyze her own feelings, before her opinions upon what she has seen are by any means developed; before she has even considered adequately, on what her happiness depends; before she has discernment to reject what is frivolous, or wisdom to prefer what is good. This is more especially the case in the highest and lowest classes, in which, by a strange analogy, they either rush into the marriage state whilst children, or wait until the bloom and hopes of youth have forever passed away, in order to form interested matches. The matured period of five-and-twenty to thirty, is passed by the lower classes in the single state in labor to gain subsistence; after thirty, or even forty, we often find them marrying. But the majority have sealed their own fate before the age of twenty.

"In high life, the same haste to dispose of daughters prevails as among the lowest classes. At seventeen, most of our belles of fashion expect to receive proposals. If they do not marry within a few years after their introduction, they have a mortified sense of having lost time—that the expectations of friends and of parents have not been fulfilled; that others have 'gone off' before them. The next ten years are often a period of subdued vexation, and the sweetness and contentment of the original character is impaired. About seven or eight and twenty, the views of life are sobered—the expectations chastened—a renovation takes place—women again become agreeable; their minds must in the lapse of time, even with a miserable store of observation, have improved. They then often marry—and, if the union be not a mere effort of despair, if it be based on sound and holy principles, and on good sense, there is, for both parties engaged, a great likelihood of happiness.

"But, it may be naturally contended, that there come not to *all* young ladies the opportunities of which I write; that indications of preference arrive not to all. I am inclined to believe that, with good temper, pleasing manners, and respectable connections, there exists, in modern society, very few young ladies who have not received under various circumstances, some marks of preference, more or less decided. Beauty and plainness are arbitrary, not positive, terms. Unless there be any actual deformity, any great infirmity, in which case I think it were cruel to pre-suppose the likelihood of such indications, there is no one, that I hardly ever met with, who has not had, on some grounds, her partizans and admirers. The plain are often particularized as elegant; tastes vary: even a sour look I have heard admired as sensible, cold manners eulogized as correct. Opinion, however it may generally verge to the correct, springs from so many sources, it is so governed by association of ideas, such trifles may guide it, that I am never surprised at the latitude given to personal encomium nor at the endless variety and incongruity of human judgment. It is well that all have a chance of being approved, admired, beloved, and it remains for them to avail themselves of those possibilities which contribute so much to happiness. For we are sympathizing beings, and a law of our nature makes us look for a return of sympathy. We are sent here to form ties, and to love, and to be loved, whether the term applies to parental, or filial, or fraternal love—or whether it respects the less sure and more fitful experiences of love, in its ordinary sense.

"I do not blame the parents who instil into their children of both sexes a desire to be married. I think those who teach the young a different lesson deceive them. Marriage, with all its chances, its infelicities, its sacrifices, is seldom so infelicitous, so uncertain, so full of sacrifice, as the single state. Life must have some objects, and those objects must be progressive. The mind is happier and healthier with such interests, even if sorrow comes along with them, than in its solitude, its desolate freedom from care, when having, as the phrase is, no troubles of the conjugal sort to disturb its tranquillity. I therefore do not censure those who desire to see their daughters happily and suitably established in life. It is the indiscreet and vulgar haste, the indelicacy, the low mercenary views, and the equally low ambition to compass a splendid match, which is blameable and revolting in the parental conduct.

"Many are, however, blessed with guides and guardians of very different characters; with parents, whose lofty natures not only reject such unworthy notions, but somewhat incline to the extreme of repelling all advances for their daughters. In either case, the conduct of a young lady may be the same. It is she who must form her own destiny in points on which none can effectually aid her. It is she who is to be the happy wife, or the wretched victim; and it is to her that these observations of admonition and of warning are addressed. Let us suppose her young, of course, attractive in appearance, of good birth, and some fortune. I here except heiresses, who, being anomalies, deserve a particular paragraph for themselves. But let us suppose that no obstacle of family or connection interferes to check the approach of a suitor.

"The eyes of her family and of her young friends are upon her, when a young lady receives the first indications of preference. She is generally ashamed of it. This is the first sentiment of a modest and ingenuous mind, and it is one indication, in my opinion, of the impropriety of early marriages. Nature seems still to wish to keep the young and blushing girl apart from that connection which entails grave and arduous duties. But Nature's voice is far less often heard than that of her adversary, expediency. I must, therefore, shape my injunctions to that which exists, not to that which we would wish to exist.

"Almost sinking under this painful sense of shame, this novel disturbance of her usual set of feelings, a young girl catches at the first reed to save herself from observation and detection. I mean detection of her perception of that which others may or may not see. She seizes upon ridicule. She pretends to laugh at one, whom sometimes her youthful romantic fancy dwells upon in a very different sense. She laughs at the foibles, supposed or real, of her admirer: she plays a dangerous game. If any of those to whom she imparts her witticisms are malevolently disposed or thoughtless, she runs a risk either of wounding the feelings of a man whom she does not like, or of losing the regard of one whom she might in time not only esteem, but love.

"Another effect of such attentions as awaken a consciousness in a young lady's mind, is the gratification of vanity, perhaps until then latent in her heart. The first preference is apt to upset the reason of its object as of him who shows it. The word vanity does not seem to imply danger. Vanity is generally considered an innocent failing; but it is innocent only as some kinds of food are to a healthy subject. On a weak, or even on an inexperienced mind, it acts, sometimes, fatally for the vain. A girl is either carried away by admiration so as to be flippant and foolish, or she is blinded by her vanity to the failings of the man who first admires her. She is intoxicated with the notion of an offer of marriage; she imagines, in her simplicity, effervesced as it is by the infusion of flattered vanity, that she has inspired such an attachment as will never be recovered, should she prove adverse to it. Many an engagement has been formed under this conviction, and fulfilled only to prove its fallacy, for the love which was supposed too strong to survive disappointment, has expired in the fruition of its hopes.

"To guard against either of these risks to happiness, a well-educated girl should endeavor, in this, to exercise her judgment. She should be sincere. She is blameable to ridicule the attentions which are meant as complimentary to her. They ought to be at least regarded with respect.

"Should they not be acceptable, she is inexcusable to requite them with levity and disdain. Let her reflect how she would like such conduct herself. Besides, she is often making a bitter enemy; perhaps she is exciting fierce and unamiable sentiments in one who otherwise might have been regarded as a mild and worthy individual. Let her be undeceived if she supposes that in thus doing she is carrying herself with dignity, or acquiring any added admiration from others. She ceases, in thus acting, to support the characteristics of a gentlewoman, which are mildness, courtesy, and reserve. If she cherishes, in spite of her pretended disgust, a secret partiality for the individual who distinguishes her, if she is lowering the esteem of a man whom she prefers, she not only incurs the hazard of losing his regard, but she is scattering ridicule on one whom she afterwards avows as her choice. In that case, she is lowering herself, or she is sowing the seeds of distrust in the minds of those who know her—she is, perhaps, frustrating and delaying her own happiness. Let her act with candor, with consideration, with good sense, and all this web which her folly would weave around her will not embarrass her. Let her not madly and obstinately resist the advice of those on whose affection to her, and on whose good judgment, experience has taught her to rely. Let her be a child in nothing except humility; let her listen to counsels; yet her own heart must decide for her—none can know so well as herself its secret throbs, or the impression of dislike or of regard which has been made upon it.

"I am, I confess, an enemy to trying to like a person, as I have rarely seen such a mental process end in happiness to either party. If an advantageous proposal offer itself, it is wiser decidedly to refuse it, than to trust to the slow growth of affection, upon a foundation of original dislike. And the trials of married life are such,—its temptations to irritability and contention are so manifold, its anxieties so unforseen and so complicated, that few can steer their difficult course safely and happily, unless there be a deep and true attachment, to contend with all the storms which may arise in the navigation.

"Deeply impressed with this conviction, should it be the lot of any young lady in whom I were interested to form a real, well-grounded attachment to a man whose circumstances were indifferent, I should counsel her, provided she can depend on the character and exertions of the object so beloved, to risk the event of an engagement—to trust to time and Providence, and to marry whenever means were afforded,—convinced as I am, that patience, and trust, and true affection, raise the character, and are acceptable in the eyes of our Heavenly Father. But in such a case, she must school her mind to meet the anxieties which attend limited means. She must prepare herself, by habits of diligence and economy, to become a poor man's wife. She must learn the difficult art of doing well upon a little. She must not, be she in any rank of life, think to indulge with impunity to herself in every refinement and luxury when she is single; and, upon her marriage, imagine that she can attain the practice of economy by wishing it. Such metamorphoses are out of reason—out of nature. She must endeavor before the bond which ties her to poverty is framed, to understand the duties of housekeeping, the mysteries of needle-work. She must lay down to herself rules of expenditure suitable, in part, to her future condition in life. Many a wife, thus commencing, has laid the foundations of future fortune, at least independence, to her husband, by keeping his mind at peace, during his progress up the steep ascent to professional, or clerical, or literary fame. Many a home has been cheered by domestic forbearance, and placid submission to circumstances, even in the higher classes, during the life-time of a father, or in the course of those long expectancies, in which the fortitude and principle of many of the aristocracy are tried and proved. But the self-denial, the cheerfulness, the good management, the strict principle, are formed at an earlier period than that in which a young lady gives her hand to him whom she has chosen, in spite of the frown of fortune, as her husband.

"Of this let the young be assured; there are few situations in life, in which a man, young, and in health, cannot meliorate his circumstances, if he possess energy and if he be stimulated by a true affection. The clergyman, with humble stipend, often hopeless from want of interest, has leisure—he has had education. He may, if he desires to assist himself, have recourse to literary labor, or to tuition. If he make not such exertion, during the course of an engagement, what hope can there be of him in future life?

"The young lawyer, however tedious his advancement, however few his opportunities, may also distinguish himself in a literary career. Innumerable are the subjects open to one of such a profession. How few avail themselves of the chance! Upon this rely, the man truly in love will make the effort. To the military man, though perhaps he may be less qualified, the same course is open, in a degree. Some of our best travels, some of our most amusing literary productions, have been the compositions of military men. And the advantage of this mode of aiding a small fortune is, that a man not only does not lower, but he raises his position by it, if his works are moral, written in a gentlemanly spirit, and affording information. However deep the attachment, however agreeable the object, if a man be indisposed to help himself to independence and competence, I should counsel no woman to continue an engagement formed in the expectation of 'times mending.' When I advocate the indulgence of attachment, it is to worthy, not to unworthy, objects.

"I now come to speak of moral character. Hard is the contest between affection and expediency, when it is raised by the question of circumstances. But harder still is it, when its result is to be decided upon an inquiry into moral conduct. I know not a more cruel situation than that when the heart is bestowed on one whom the judgment could not approve. I know not one which should be more strictly guarded against, not only by parents and friends, but (for I would impress on every young lady how much she may prove the best guardian of her own happiness) by the female heart itself.

"With every vigilance, with little to blame, little to repent, such cases will occur in this world. The feelings are interested, but the judgment distrusts. Happy is it for those who know the combat between affection and principle only in single life, and have not the misery of encountering so severe a destiny when it can no longer be remedied—who know not how to fulfill the vow to honor what is proved to be unworthy—and yet still must love,—for the affections once given, are little in our own power.

"In such a case occurring to the young, in, perhaps, a first attachment, I think they must be guided by friends. I am *not* an advocate for the interference of friends: where it is much a question of a long and contingent engagement—a question of being married at once, or of waiting, in some uncertainty—a question of ease or discomfort, of limited means or luxury—in such instances, if the moral character be unexceptionable, it is the duty of parents to point out all the risk, all the disadvantages, but to leave the heart to form its own decisions. Let them not seek to wrench the affections from the channel in which they flowed, when fresh from their source. They cannot know how deep the channel is—they cannot know if ever those pure and beautiful waters will flow in peace again when once hastily turned aside. But in cases of moral character, of right or wrong, the affair is wholly different, and the strictest parental authority ought, upon due inquiry, to be exercised.

"Submission and self-control are then the duty of the young sufferer—for a sufferer she truly *is*;—no page of her after-history could unfold a bitterer pang. But peace and hope come at last—the struggle, though violent, leaves behind it none of that corroding sorrow, which would have accompanied the acquiescence of parents in a union unblessed by a Providence, whose will is that all should be pure, even as He above is pure. Had your fond wishes been granted, young and trusting being, how fearful would have been your condition! For there is no suspicion so revolting to an innocent mind as that which unseats love from his throne in our affections, and places another in his stead. Be assured of this—little can you know of the moral conduct of the other sex; little is it desirable that you should know. But whenever improprieties are so flagrant as to be matters of conversation; when the good shun, and the pitying forbear to excuse; be assured some deeper cause than you can divine exists for the opprobrium. Think not that your empire over affections thus wasted can be a real one. It is transient, it will not last—it will not bring reformation—it will never be adequately requited. Throw yourself on the judgment of those whose interest in you has been life-long, or of such as you know truly regard your happiness; conquer the unhallowed preference; pray for support and guidance; trust in Him who 'catereth for the sparrow.'

"But, when the commencement of life is chilled by so cruel a sorrow—when the blight has fallen on the bud—we must not only look up to heavenly aid, we must take every means of care for an unfortunate, and, when once the judgment is convinced of the unworthiness of the object, a blameable attachment. How often, in the Psalms, in the Gospels, the word 'Help' is reiterated! We are to help ourselves—we must work for our heavenly peace on earth—the mental discipline, to prosper, must be aided by divine grace, but its springs must be from our own hearts. And, to fulfill the will of God in this, as in the other events of life, let us take such means as may aid us in the work of self-government.

"In the first place, let employment be resorted to by the sorrowing, do not indulge in tears; do not sit alone: abstain, for a time, from music; abstain from the perusal of poetry, or works of imagination. They still more soften the feelings and open up the sources of grief. Read works of *fact*—endeavor to occupy yourself with the passing events of the world. And, when the overburdened heart cannot be comforted, or its thoughts diverted—for there will be moments too mournful to be resisted—go forth into the fields, go to the houses of the poor—see the goodness and mercy of God—see too, the patience and long-suffering of the poor, who may often set the rich an example of fortitude. Occupy yourself, if you can, with children; their freshness, their joyful unconsciousness, the elasticity of their spirits, will sustain and draw you from yourself, or have recourse to the soothing calmness of the aged. Hear them converse upon the affairs of life; how they appreciate the importance of each passing event, as a traveler does the ruts and inequalities of the road he has traversed. How their confidence in the effect of time sustains you! and you turn from them, reflecting on all that the happiest of them must necessarily have endured. Be assured of your own recovery, under an influence so certain.

"Avoid young persons of your own age. If possible, except to a sister, whose deep interest in you will probably teach her a superior lesson, never confide in young friends, a similar trial as that to which I have referred. In general, your resolution will be weakened, your feelings re-excited, your confidence in your best advisers will be shaken. For the young usually take the part of the rejected lover—they delight in that dangerous species of sympathy which flatters with hope. They are naturally incredulous as to the delinquencies of a man who is agreeable, and in love; they incline to the notion of the hard-heartedness of fathers, uncles, and elder brothers; and even, if they happen to possess good sense, or to exercise the rare quality of prudence in such matters, the very communication of any sorrow, or the recital of any feelings, gives not only a merely temporary relief, but deadens that sorrow and strengthens those feelings, which grow every time they are imparted. If you wish to recover—and, if you have a sound and well-disposed mind, you *will* wish to recover—you must, after the first burst of grief is over, speak but rarely of a theme too painful and delicate to bear the contact of rude minds—too dangerous to dwell upon with those of a kindlier and loftier nature.

"To your female relations—to your mother, more especially, too great an openness cannot be practiced on these points, but openness does not imply a perpetual recurrence to a theme, which must wear out patience and exhaust all but maternal sympathy, in time. For maternal sympathy is exhaustless; be generous, and restrain, from that very reflection, the continual demand upon its flow. The first person to consult, the last to afflict—a mother—should not be the victim of her daughter's feelings. Her judgment should not be weakened by the incessant indulgence of a daughter's sorrows.

"I would, on many grounds, caution the young against hasty engagements. It seems extraordinary that the welfare of a life should often be determined upon the acquaintance of a few weeks. The principles, it is true, may be ascertained from the knowledge of others, the manners may please, the means and expectations may all be clearly understood. But the temper—that word of unspeakable import—the daily habits, the power of constancy—these are not to be known without a long and severe examination of the motives, and a daily observation of the conduct, of others. Very little suffices to mar the happiness of married life, if that little proceed in the character of a man, from a rooted selfishness.

"It is true, in regard to this defect, that much may be done by a wife to meliorate a vice of character which is, in some, only the result of never having had their feelings developed. But if there exist not this excuse—if, in spite of ties, which are dearer to an affectionate mind than existence; you find a man preferring his own comfort to that of those whom he professes to love—if you find him imperious to his servants, dictatorial to sisters, on cool terms with brothers, there is little hope that the mental disease will ever be rooted out, so as to leave a healthy character of mind. Examine well into this point; for a hasty temper may be remedied, and even endured—but the deep, slow, sullen course of a selfish nature wears away hope, imparts a cankering care, and, with it, often disgust. No defect is so little to be resisted as selfishness. It creeps into every detail; it infects the minutest affairs of life as well as the greatest concerns. It depresses the humble sufferer from its baneful effects; it irritates the passions of the unamiable. Study well the character in trifles; nor venture to risk your bark on the sea of matrimony, unless you know well how far this man, whom you might prefer, is free from this deadly infection. View him, if possible, in his home, before you pledge your faith with his—or, if that be not practicable, reflect upon the general course of his actions, of his sentiments, and endeavor dispassionately to judge them, as best you may."

CHAPTER XXIV.
BRIDAL ETIQUETTE.

In preparing a bridal outfit, it is best to furnish the wardrobe for at least two years, in under-clothes, and one year in dresses, though the bonnet and cloak, suitable for the coming season, are all that are necessary, as the fashions in these articles change so rapidly. If you are going to travel, have a neat dress and cloak of some plain color, and a close bonnet and veil. Avoid, as intensely vulgar, any display of your position as a *bride*, whilst traveling.

Take, first, the weddings at church. In this case none are invited to the ceremony excepting the family, and the reception is at the house of the bride's mother, or nearest relative, either on the wedding-day or upon her return from the bridal tour.

In sending out the invitations, let the card of the bridegroom and that of the bride be tied together with a white ribbon, and folded in the note paper upon which is printed the name of the bride's mother, with the date of the reception-day, thus:—

Mrs. John Saunders.

> At home, Thursday, Oct. 16th,
>   from 11 till 2.
> No. 218, —— st.

Of course the hours and dates vary, but the form is the same.

If there is no bridal reception upon the wedding day, the cards are worded:—

> MR. AND MRS. JAMES SMITH.
>   At home, Wednesdays,
>   On, and after, June 6th.
> No. 17, —— st.

Tie the card with the bride's maiden name upon it to this one.

Enclose the invitation in a white envelope, and tie it with white satin ribbon. If you send cake, have it put in a white box, and place the note outside the cover, tying it fast with white satin ribbon.

The bride's dress must be of white entirely. If she is married in the morning, a plain white silk, white mantle, and white bonnet, full trimmed with orange flowers, with a plain veil, is the most suitable dress, and she may wear a richer one at her reception, when she returns from her bridal tour.

As soon as the carriages come, let the bridesmaids, and relatives set off first.—Last, the bride with her parents. The bride, her parents, and the bridesmaids go immediately to the vestry, where they meet the bridegroom, and the groomsmen. The father of the bride gives her his arm and escorts her to the altar, the bridegroom walking on the other side. Then follow the bridesmaids and groomsmen in couples.

When they reach the altar the bridegroom removes his right hand glove, but the bride keeps hers on until the clergyman takes the ring. The first bridesmaid then removes the left hand glove, and it is not resumed. The bridesmaids should wear white dresses, white mantles, and bonnets, but not veils or orange flowers.

The bride and groom leave the church first, after the ceremony is over, and take the carriage with the parents of the bride, and the others follow in the order in which they came.

If there is a breakfast or morning reception, the bride will not change her dress until she retires to put on her traveling attire. If the wedding takes place in the evening at church, to be followed by a full dress reception at home, the bride should wear a white lace dress over satin, or any other material to suit her own taste, a veil, falling from her head to her feet, fastened to the hair by a coiffure of orange flowers; white kid gloves, and white satin slippers. A bouquet, if carried, should contain only white flowers.

The bridesmaids may wear white, or some thin, light-colored material over white, a head-dress of flowers, and carry bouquets of mixed flowers.

When the wedding takes place at home, let the company assemble in the front drawing-room, and close the doors between that and the back room. In the back room, let the bride, bridegroom, bridesmaids, and groomsmen, the parents of the bride, and the clergyman, assemble. The clergyman should stand in the centre of the room, the bride and groom before him, the brides-maids ranged beside the bride, the groomsmen beside the bridegroom. Then open the doors and let the ceremony begin. This arrangement saves that awk-wardness attendant upon entering the room and taking the position before a large company.

After the ceremony is over, the parents of the bride speak to her first; then her near relatives, and not until then the other members of the company.

It is not usual now to have dancing, or even music, at a wedding, and the hour is named upon the cards, at which the guests are expected to retire.

A very pretty effect is produced in the wedding group, if the bride wears pure white, and the bridesmaids white, with flowers and trimmings of a differ-ent color. Thus, one in white, with a head-dress and trimming of green leaves; another, white, with blue ribbons and forget-me-nots; another, white, with pink roses and ribbons.

If the wedding is in the morning, the bride and family may wear full dress; in that case the shutters should be closed and the rooms lighted as in the evenings.

Let the supper be laid early, and ready when the ceremony is over, that the guests may pass into the dining-room, if they wish, as soon as they have spoken to the bride. If a morning wedding, let the table be set as for an evening wedding.

If the bride gives a reception at her own house, after her return from her bridal tour, she should not wear her wedding-dress. If in the evening, a supper should be set. If a morning reception, let her wear a handsome light silk, col-lar and sleeves of lace. Wine and cake are sufficient to hand to each guest at a morning reception. At an evening reception let the bride wear full dress, but not her wedding-dress.

At parties given to a newly married couple, the bridesmaids and grooms-men are always invited, and the whole party are expected to wear the same dresses as at the wedding.

CHAPTER XXV.
HINTS ON HEALTH.

The universal remark of travelers visiting America, as well as the universal complaint of Americans themselves, relates to the ill health of the fairer portion of the community. Look where you will, go to any city in the vast Union, the remark and complaint will be made everywhere. With every natural advantage of climate, yet from North to South, East to West the cry resounds.

Foreigners, admiring the dark-eyed girls of the southern states or the blondes of the northern ones, will remark, with comments upon beauty:—

"But she looks delicate, poor thing!—Not strong? Ah! I thought not, none of the American women are, and how soon these young beauties fade!"

It seems to me, amongst the subjects treated of in my present work, that a few words on health will not come amiss.

"Light and sunshine are needful for your health. Get all you can; keep your windows clean. Do not block them up with curtains, plants, or bunches of flowers;—these last poison the air, in small rooms.

"Fresh air is needful for your health. As often as you can, open all your windows, if only for a short time in bad weather; in fine weather, keep them open, but never sit in draughts. When you get up, open the windows wide, and throw down the bed-clothes, that they may be exposed to fresh air some hours, daily, before they are made up. Keep your bed-clothes clean; hang them to the fire when you can. Avoid wearing at night what you wear in the day. Hang up your day-clothes at night. Except in the severest weather, in small, crowded sleeping-rooms, a little opening at the top of the window-sash is very important; or you will find one window pane of perforated zinc very useful. You will not catch cold half so easily by breathing pure air at night. Let not the beds be directly under the windows. Sleeping in exhausted air creates a desire for stimulants.

"Pure water is needful for your health. Wash your bodies as well as your faces, rubbing them all over with a coarse cloth. If you cannot wash thus every morning, pray do so once a week. Crying and cross children are often pacified by a gentle washing of their little hands and faces—it soothes them. Babies' heads should be washed carefully, every morning with soap. No scurf should be suffered to remain upon them. Get rid of all slops and dirty water at once. Disease, and even death, is often the consequence of our own negligence. Wash your rooms and passages at least once a week, use plenty of clean water; but do not let your children stay in them while they are wet, it may bring on croup or inflammation of the chest. If you read your Bibles, which it is earnestly hoped you do, you will find how cleanliness, both as to the person and habitation, was taught to the Jews by God himself; and we read in the 4th chapter of Nehemiah that when they were building their second temple, and defending their lives against their foes, having no time for rest, they contrived to put off their clothes for washing. It is a good old saying, that *cleanliness is next to godliness.* See Heb. x. 22.

"Wholesome food is needful for your health. Buy the most strengthening. Pieces of fresh beef and mutton go the farthest. Eat plenty of fresh salt with food; it prevents disease. Pray do not let your children waste their pennies in tarts, cakes, bull's eyes, hardbake, sour fruit, &c., they are very unwholesome, and hurt the digestion. People would often, at twenty years of age, have a nice little sum of money to help them on in the world, if they had put in the savings' bank the money so wasted. Cocoa is cheaper and much more nourishing than *tea*. None of these liquids should be taken *hot*, but lukewarm; when hot they inflame the stomach, and produce indigestion.

"We are all made to breathe the pure air of heaven, and therefore much illness is caused by being constantly in-doors. Let all persons make a point, whenever it is possible, of taking exercise in the *open air* for at least an hour and a half *daily*. *Time* would be saved in the long run by the increased energy and strength gained, and by the warding off of disease."

Let it not be supposed that it is not the duty of every young lady to take due care of her health, and to preserve in all its power of utility every portion of vigor which has been bestowed on her.

With many young ladies, it appears to be a maxim to do everything in their power to destroy the health which is so much wanted in the real business of life, and which forms so important a requisite to happiness. In the first place, as to hours—they never leave the ball-room until utterly exhausted, and scarcely fit to crawl to bed. The noon-day sleep, the scarcely touched breakfast, that most important meal, are followed by preparations for the succeeding night's pleasures, or in head-aching morning calls, driving about in a close carriage, or lounging on a sofa, in an over-heated room, reading novels.

Dressing follows; the warm wrapper or dress is thrown aside; over the tightly drawn corsets is fastened a flimsy dress, with an inch of sleeve; the neck laid bare; thin stockings drawn on, in place of thick ones, and the consumption-seeker goes forth to the ball-room again.

"At times, you miss from the gay assemblage some former ornament—you inquire about her—she has taken cold. Inflammation of the lungs, caught it in an accidental draught of air by one of these fair half-dressed beings, carried off, not long since, one of the gayest and fairest of the belles of the season—after an illness of three days.

"Preservation of the health ought, from an early stage of existence, to be enforced as a duty upon the young. To walk daily; to have daily recourse, in summer, even twice a day, to the sponging with cold water, or the shower-bath;—to eat sufficiently of plain, nutritious food; to keep the mind calm—these are *duties*;—they should be habitually exercised. Care should be taken not to come out heated, with a shawl just pinned across the shoulders, from a heated room. Where there is delicacy of the lungs or windpipe, yet not sufficient to render a withdrawal from evening parties necessary, the use of a respirator at night is desirable. It is usual to have recourse to this valuable invention only when disease is actually existing—as a preventive, it is neglected. Yet, preserving the temperature of a warm room, it is an excellent precaution, and can easily be assumed when the shawl or cloak is put on. The atmosphere of a city is destructive where there is any pulmonary delicacy, and who shall say, where there is *not* pulmonary delicacy? In this climate, there is a tendency to it, more or less, in almost every family,—at all events, it is too easily induced in our predisposed constitutions, by cold, aided by the debilitating effect of heated rooms and an artificial mode of existence, and accelerated also, most decidedly, by bared shoulders. For, in this climate, it is scarcely ever safe to lay bare that portion of the frame, the back and chest in which the lungs are seated; and, although custom may greatly lead to diminish the injurious effects, the sudden chill may strike, and may never be recovered.

"During every season, certain people have 'head colds,' coughs, and 'feverish colds.' These are produced by certain states of climate acting on certain states of constitution. At particular seasons such complaints abound—at others they abound still more; and again, from some singularity, they prevail so much that people say, there is an *Influenza*.

"Influenza has been long known in the world. It has often visited Europe; and made its appearance on our shores with greater severity than at present. It has sometimes been very severe, and left many persons ill for a year or two.

"The symptoms of influenza need not be dwelt on, as they have been so generally felt by our readers or their friends. It varies in different people, to be sure, both in kind and in degree. Considering the number of people it attacks, it may be looked on as an innocent disease; but, on the other hand, looking at the increase it has made in the number of deaths, it is an exceedingly serious one after all.

"In simple cases—confinement to a pure and temperate air, warm drinks, and a warm bath, or, at least, a warm foot-bath, with an extra blanket, and a little more rest than usual, keeping to mild food, and toast and water, and taking, if necessary, a dose of aperient medicine,—is all that is required. In serious cases, the domestic treatment must become professional. Mustard plasters to the back relieve the headache. Squills and other medicines 'loosen' the outstanding cough. Bark and wine, and even cold baths are sometimes requisite for the weakness left behind. But these things can only be used with discrimination by a regular professional man.

"Supposing that the seeds of disease have not been laid in childhood, and that there is no particular predisposition to any malady in the constitution, a young woman enters life with every fair prospect of enjoying tolerable health;—yet, how variable, and delicate, and complaining, do the majority of women become! What a vast expense is incurred, during the course of their lives, in physicians, medicine, change of air, baths abroad and at home, and journeys! How few women can walk,—or can suppress nervous feelings,—or can eat like reasonable beings: how many suffer, or say they suffer from debility, headaches, dyspepsia, a tendency to colds, eternal sore throats, rheumatic attacks, and the whole list of polite complaints! With all our modern wisdom, with all our books on health, our smatterings of physiological science, our open carriages, sponging baths, and attention to diet, women now are a far more feeble race than our grandmothers, or even our mothers, were. What daughter can walk half as far as her mother can? What young woman can take the active part that her mother did? In most families, the order of things is reversed. It is not a child trembling for her mother's health, and fearing, lest her parent, no longer young, should be fatigued; but it is the mother who is always striving to spare her child exertions which she can herself perfectly well undergo, but which the enfeebled child of modern self-indulgence dare not encounter.

"Yes! we are a self-indulgent race, this present generation. Witness our easily excited feelings; witness our late hours of rising, our sofas and easy chairs, our useless days and dissipated nights! Witness our pallid faces, our forms, sometimes attenuated and repulsive while yet in early life, age marching, not creeping, on before his time; or witness our over-fed and over-expanded forms, enfeebled by indolence, and suffering the worst species of debility—the debility of *fat*. Witness our doing those things by deputy which our grandmothers did themselves; witness our host of scents and perfumed waters on our dressing-tables; our over-refinement, which amounts to an enervating puerility, and our incapacity of parting with one accustomed indulgence, even at the bidding of the learned and disinterested adviser?

"'In the education of women,' writes a modern physician, 'too little attention is given to subdue the imaginative faculty, and to moderate sensibility; on the contrary, they are generally fostered; and, instead of a vigorous intellect and healthy condition of mind, we find imagination and sentiment predominant over the reasoning faculties, and laying the foundation of hysterical, hypochondriacal, and even maniacal diseases.'* It is, in fact, this want of judgment in the management of early life that produces so much misery when women are called upon to perform an important part in society, and when all that exertion can do is required at their hands.

"The duration of sleep should not, in the adult, exceed six or eight hours; women injure their health greatly by excess in this respect. On rising, all women should use some mode of cold or tepid bath; and, indeed, in this respect the practice of the present day is admirable; there is every facility for the bath. To some, the use of the shower-bath is deleterious, and to all inconvenient, and not likely to be resorted to except when positively ordered. Dr. Combe recommends for *general* use the tepid or warm bath, as being much more suitable than the cold bath, ‹especially in the winter for those who are not robust, and full of animal heat.› When the constitution is not sufficiently vigorous to ensure reaction after the cold bath, by producing a warm glow over the surface, ‹its use,› observes the same admirable writer, ‹inevitably does harm.› But he enforces, that ‹in order to promote a due exhalation from the skin, the warm, the tepid, or the shower-bath, as a means of preserving health, ought to be in as common use as a change of apparel, for it is equally a measure of necessary cleanliness.› He inclines to the use of the tepid bath, as likely to be the most generally efficacious.

"I have known the most beneficial effects from a modification of this advice, namely, from using a sponging-bath, into which you pour a jug of warm water, and in which you stand, whilst you sponge the body and limbs profusely with cold water. A strong friction should be employed after this process, either with horsehair gloves or with a large coarse towel, and few persons will find the use of the sponging-bath disagree with them when thus employed. It is, indeed, incredible, when we consider the importance of the exhalation performed by the skin, to what extent ablution is neglected, not only, as Dr. Combe specifies, in charitable institutions and seminaries for the young, but by ladies, in ordinary circumstances, to whom the use of the bath could be productive of no inconvenience. In nervous complaints, which are more or less the besetting evil of womankind, the bath, in its various forms, becomes an invaluable aid.

"In the formation of those habits which are necessary for the preservation of health, another circumstance, which, from its importance to health, cannot be deemed trifling should be mentioned. It is a general practice that beds should be made as soon as the occupants have left their rooms, and before the air has

* "The Sick-Room," by Dr. A. T. Thomson.

been freely admitted to play upon the recent depositary of the human frame; but this should be avoided. The bed-linen and blankets should be taken off, and the windows opened, so that, for an hour or more, a thorough ventilation should be procured.

"Upon another point, the inconsistency and mental blindness of women are almost inconceivable—the insufficiency of their dress to resist the attacks of our variable climate. How few women clothe themselves like rational beings! Although, in latter years, they have wisely adopted the use of warm dresses, and, more especially, of the valuable Scottish plaid, yet how commonly they neglect the aid of flannel in preserving them not only from cold, but in securing a necessary circulation of vitality in the skin! 'The necessary effect of deficient circulation in the skin,' remarks Dr. Combe, 'is to throw a disproportionate mass of blood inwards; and when this condition exists, insufficient clothing perpetuates the evil, until internal disease is generated, and health is irrecoverably lost.' How common is the complaint among young women, especially those of sedentary habits, of chilliness, cold feet, and other symptoms of deficient circulation! and yet how impossible would it often be—for women are usually obstinate on this head—to induce them to exchange the thin silk stocking for a warm merino one, or to substitute a proper walking shoe for the paper-like articles which they designate by that name! Hence arise many diseases, which are, by insensible degrees, fostered in the system by the unequal distribution of the blood oppressing the internal organs. The habitual tendency to that chilliness which has been referred to should never be disregarded, 'laying, as it does,' says Dr. Combe, 'the foundation of tubercles in the lungs, and other maladies, which show themselves only when arrived at an incurable stage.' 'All those who value health, and have common sense, will therefore take warning from signs like these, and never rest until equilibrium of action be restored.' Warm clothing, exercise in the open air, sponging with tepid water and vinegar, or the warm bath, the use of a flesh-brush or hair-glove, are adapted to remedy these serious and threatening evils.

"But, whilst insufficiency of clothing is to be deprecated, excessive wrapping up should also be avoided. Great differences exist between the power of generating heat and resisting cold in individuals, and it is therefore impossible to prescribe general rules upon the subject of clothing. The best maxim is, not to dress in an invariable way in all cases, but to put on clothing sufficient in the individual case, to protect the body effectively against the sensation of cold.*

"The insufficiency of warmth in the clothing of females constitutes only one part of its injurious effects. The tightness of dress obstructs the insensible

---

* Dr. Combe.

perspiration hurtfully, and produces an irregular circulation. Every part and function of the human frame are linked together so closely, that we cannot act wrongly towards one organ without all suffering, nor act rightly without all sharing the benefit of our judgment and good sense.

"The mischief arising from cold or wet feet is admitted by all persons who have given the subject of health even the most casual consideration. In conversing with very aged people, you will generally find a disregard of diet, and very different notions and practices upon the subject of exercise and ablution; but they all agree in the necessity of keeping the feet dry. I remember inquiring of a venerable clergyman, who, up to the age of ninety-six, had enjoyed a fair proportion of health, after a youth of delicacy. I asked him what system he pursued. 'Now,' was his reply, 'I never took much care what I ate; I have always been temperate. I never minded the weather; but I always took care to keep my feet dry and well shod.' Wet and damp are, indeed, more unwholsome when applied to the feet than when they affect other parts; 'because they receive a greater supply of blood to carry on a high degree of perspiration, and because their distance from the heart, or centre of circulation, diminishes the force with which this is carried on, and thus leaves them more susceptible from external causes.'*

"God, in his infinite benevolence, has given to his creatures other means of acquiring a healthy warmth than by clothing; he has endowed us with the power of exercise—that blessing which women of weak judgment and indolent natures are so prone to neglect and disparage. Most ladies appear to think that the privilege of walking is only intended for persons of inferior condition. They busy themselves, in their in-door occupations all the morning, take a hearty luncheon, and drive out in their carriages until dinner-time. It is partly owing to such customs as these that a rapid deterioration takes place in the physical state of our sex, in their looks, and in their power of utility, and enjoyment of happiness. God never intended us to be inactive.

"The chief purpose of the muscles with which we are endowed, is to enable us to carry into effect the volitions of the mind; and, whilst fulfilling this grand object, the active exercise of the muscles is conducive to the well-being of many other important functions. The processes of digestion, respiration, secretion, absorption, and nutrition, are promoted, and the healthful condition of the whole body influenced. The mind also is depressed or exhilarated by the proper or improper use of muscular exercise; for man is intended for a life of activity: nor can his functions ever go on so properly as when he duly exercises those organs with which Nature has endowed him. The evils arising from want of exercise are numerous:—the circulation, from the absence of due stimulus,

---

* Dr. Combe.

becomes languid, the appetite and digestion are weakened, the respiration is imperfect, and the blood becomes so ill-conditioned, that when distributed through the body it is inadequate to communicate the necessary stimulus to healthy and vigorous action. These points being established, it now becomes a consideration in what mode, or at what periods, ladies, in society, can most advantageously avail themselves of that privilege which is granted to so many, denied, comparatively, to so few.

"Much is said on the benefits of walking before breakfast, and to a person in full vigor it may, there is no doubt, be highly salutary; whilst, to the delicate, it will prove more hurtful than beneficial, producing a sense of weariness which destroys all the future pleasures of the day. I am disposed to think, however, from observation, that walking before breakfast may be rendered beneficial almost to any one by degrees. Most persons walk too far the first day; they are proud of the effort, become, nevertheless, exhausted, and dare not repeat it. A first walk before breakfast should not exceed a quarter of a mile; it should be extended very gradually, and, in delicate women, with great care, lest over-fatigue should ensue. It is, however, so valuable a habit, such a saving of time, so refreshing, so soothing, that many sacrifices of inclination should be made to procure it; in a gay season the freshness and seclusion of a morning's walk is peculiarly needed, and when it becomes so difficult to take exercise in the subsequent part of the day, the afternoon being too short, and the evening too much occupied. And the morning's walk, stolen from the hour given to a species of repose which seldom rests, may be, without the reproach of indolence, followed by the after-noon's siesta—a practice much to be commended, and greatly conducive to rest of nerves and invigoration of the frame, when used in moderation.

"Exercise may be taken, by the robust, at any time, even after eating heart-ily, but the delicate ought to avoid that risk; they should resort to it only when the frame is vigorous enough to bear it, and this is usually from one to four or five hours after eating. The morning is, therefore, the best time; but exercise ought not to be delayed until some degree of exhaustion has taken place from want of food, as in that case it dissipates rather than renovates the remaining strength, and impairs digestion. Exercise immediately before meals is therefore, unless very gentle, injurious; if it has been violent, before eating rest should intervene. 'Appetite,' says Dr. Combe, 'revives after repose.'

"Of all modes of exercise, that which nature has bestowed upon us, walk-ing, is decidedly the most salutary; and the prevailing system of substituting horse and carriage exercise almost entirely for it, is far from being advantageous to the present generation. Walking, which has for its aim some pleasing pursuit, and, therefore, animates the mind, is efficacious to the majority. Gardening, which is a modification of walking, offers many advantages both to the delicate and the strong, and it is a species of exercise which we can adjust to our powers. In a continued walk you must go on—you must return; there is no appeal, even if you have gone too far, and would willingly give up any further exertion. But, while gardening, you are still at home—your exertions are devoted to objects the most interesting, because progressive; hope and faith form a part of your stimulus. The happy future, when flowers shall bloom around you, supersedes in your thoughts the vexatious present or the mournful past. About you are the budding treasures of spring, or the gorgeous productions of summer, or the rich hues of those beauties which autumn pours forth most lavishly before it departs,—and is succeeded by winter. Above you are the gay warblers, who seem to hail you as you mingle in the sylvan scenes which are not all theirs, but which you share and appropriate. The ruffled temper, the harassed mind, may find a solace in the occupation of gardening, which aids the effect of exercise and the benign influence of fresh air. Stores of future and never-dying interest are buried in the earth with every seed, only to spring up again redoubled in their value. A lady, as a writer in the 'Quarterly Review' observes, should 'not only *have* but know her plants.' And her enjoyment of those delights is truly enhanced by that personal care, without which few gardens, however superintended by the scientific gardener, can prosper, and which bless as they thrive; her plants bestow health on the frame which is bowed down to train them—they give to her the blessing of a calm and rational pleasure—they relieve her from the necessity of excitement—they promote alike, in the wealthy and the poor, these gentle exertions which are coupled with the most poetical and the sweetest of associations.

"Exercise on horseback is not equally attainable with the two modes which I have just specified; when it is, the accelerated circulation, the change of scene and of ideas, are highly beneficial. Where the lungs are weak, it is thought by the learned to possess a great advantage over walking, as it does not hurry the breathing. The gentleness of the exercise enables a delicate person to enjoy the advantage of open air and motion for a much longer period than could be endured in the action of walking. From the tendency of horse exercise to equalize the circulation and stimulate the skin, it is invaluable, too, for the nervous and dyspeptic portion of young women, among whom, unhappily, such complaints are but too prevalent.

"Dancing, which is the most frequent mode of exercise with ladies in great cities, practiced, as it is, in heated rooms, and exhausting from its violence, often does more harm than good, from producing languor and over-fatigue. Unhappily there are but few modes of exercise in-doors adapted for women. If,

from any circumstances, they are confined to their homes, and they become feverish and languid from want of exercise, it never occurs to them to throw open
the windows and to walk about, or to make use of battledore and shuttlecock,
or any other mode of exertion. They continue sitting, reading, or walking, or
lounging, or sleeping, or gossiping,—whilst the bloom of health is rapidly giving place to the wanness and debility of the imprisoned frame.

"It is often the custom of young women to declare that they cannot walk,
sometimes from indolence, no doubt, and want of habit, occasionally from real
inability. But if we investigate the causes of this real inability, we shall often find
it to proceed from an improper choice of time in taking exercise, or from a defective judgment in the manner of taking it. Many women exhaust and fatigue
themselves with the duties of their house, and by a thousand trying occupations,
including that which forms a serious item in the day's work, namely, running up
and down stairs, and then discover that they cannot walk. Others go to extremes,
and walk for a certain distance, whether they feel fatigued or not by such exertions. 'It is only,' observes Dr. Combe, 'by a diffusion of the laws of exercise as a
part of useful education, that individuals can be enabled to avoid such mistakes,'
To be beneficial, exercise should always be proportioned to the strength and to the
constitution of an individual. When it causes extreme fatigue or exhaustion, it is
hurtful; it ought to be resumed always after a period of rest, and adopted regularly,
not, as too many persons are in the habit of doing, once in four or five days. The
average walk which a young woman in good health and in ordinary circumstances, may take, without undue and injurious fatigue, is from four to five miles a-day.
From this rule I except the *very* young. It has been found by experience that until
twenty-two or three the strength is not completely matured. The rate of mortality,
as it has been proved by statistical tables, increases in all classes of society from
fourteen until the age of twenty-three, when it begins to decrease.

"Another precaution which I would recommend to those who have the
regulation of families under their care, relates to the subject of ventilation. The
heated state of our rooms in ordinary occupation is one great source of all
those mischiefs which arise from catching cold, a subject on which Mr. Aber-
nethy was wont to declare, that 'a very useful book might be written.' There are
some houses into which one can never enter with impunity, from the want of
due ventilation. Housemaids, more especially, have an insupportable objection
to opening windows, on account of the dust which flies in and settles upon
the furniture. This evil—for the soiling of furniture certainly may be called an
evil—may easily be obviated by fastening a muslin blind against the open window, or by pinning a large piece of coarse muslin against it, so that the dusty
particles will be excluded.

"Generally our ordinary sitting-rooms are tolerably well ventilated by the opening and shutting of doors, the size of the fire-place, &c., but in our bed-rooms the vitiation of the air is far greater, owing to these rooms being wholly closed during the seven or eight hours in which we sleep in them, and, also, owing to the mass of curtains with which we usually take care to surround our beds. In this respect we are, indeed, improved, by the introduction of French bedsteads, which are among the most valuable of modern suggestions. But, not-withstanding this improvement, and many others which reflection and science have contributed to introduce, we incur much suffering from our ignorance and prejudice on the subject of ventilation. For generations, society has experi-enced the evil effects of the want of ventilation, and has felt in towns its results in the form of fevers, general ill-health, cutaneous and nervous diseases; and yet the most direful ignorance continues on this subject. Hospitals are among the few well-ventilated buildings which are erected, because an idea prevails that ventilation is essential for the sick, but it seems to have been forgotten that what is essential for the recovery of health is equally necessary for its preser-vation. 'Were,' says Dr. Combe, 'a general knowledge of the structure of man to constitute a regular part of a liberal education, such inconsistencies as this would soon disappear, and the scientific architect would speedily devise the best means for supplying our houses with pure air, as he has already supplied them with pure water.'"

CHAPTER XXVI.
MISCELLANEOUS.

There are many little pieces of rudeness, only too common, which, while they evince ill-breeding, and are many of them extremely annoying, yet they are met with every day, and in persons otherwise well-bred.

As they come under no particular head, they will merely be mentioned here, as habits carefully to avoid.

It is rude to look over the shoulder of a person who is either reading or writing, yet it is done every day.

To stand with the arms a-kimbo, the hands on the hips, or with the arms crossed, while conversing, is exceedingly unlady-like.

Avoid restless movements either with the hands, or feet; to sit perfectly quiet, without stiffness, easily, yet at the same time almost motionless, is one of the surest proofs of high-breeding.

If you wish to make yourself agreeable to any one, talk as much as you please about his or her affairs, and as little as possible about your own.

Avoid passing before persons seated in the same room with yourself. If you must rise to move from place to place, endeavor to pass behind the chairs of your companions. Above all, never pass between two persons who are conversing together.

Avoid personal remarks; they evince a want of judgment, good taste, kindness, and politeness. To exchange glances or significant smiles with a third person, whilst engaged in a conversation with a second, is a proof of low-breeding. Suppressed laughter, shrugging of the shoulders, rolling of the eyes, and significant glances are all marks of ill-breeding.

If you meet a gentleman at the foot of a flight of stairs, do not go up before him. Stop, bow, and motion to him to precede you. He will return your bow, and run up, leaving you to follow him.

Never whisper, or make any confidential communication in company. Keep private remarks for private occasions.

Accepting presents from gentlemen is a dangerous thing. It is better to avoid any such obligations, and, if you make it a rule *never* to accept such presents, you will avoid hurting any one›s feelings, and save yourself from all further perplexity.

In meeting your elderly friends in the street, look at them long enough to give them an opportunity of recognizing you; and if they do so, return their salutations respectfully, not with the familiar nod you would give to one of your own age.

Never remain seated, whilst a person older than yourself is standing before you, talking to you.

Never lounge on a sofa, while there are those in the room, whose years give them a better claim to this sort of indulgence.

Never tease a person to do what she has once declined.

Never refuse a request or invitation in order to be urged, and accept afterwards. Comply at once. If the request is sincere, you will thus afford gratification; if not, the individual making it deserves to be punished for insincerity, by being taken at her word.

It is not polite when asked what part of a dish you will have, to say, "Any part—it is quite indifferent to me;" it is hard enough to carve for one's friends, without choosing for them.

It is not polite to entertain a visitor with your own family history, or the events of your own household.

It is not polite for married ladies to talk, in the presence of gentlemen, of the difficulty they have in procuring domestics, and how good-for-nothing they are when procured.

It is not polite to put food upon the plate of a guest without asking leave, or to press her to eat more than she wants.

It is not polite to stare under ladies' bonnets, as if you suspected they had stolen the linings from you, or wore something that was not their own.

Never affect a foolish reserve in a mixed company, keeping aloof from others as if in a state of mental abstraction. If your brain is so full and so busy that you cannot attend to the little civilities, cheerful chit-chat, and light amusements of society, keep out of it.

Never read in company. You may open a book to look over the engravings, if you will, but do not attend to the letter-press until you are alone.

Never jest upon serious subjects. Avoid scandal. If another person attempts to open a conversation upon scandalous matters, check her. Say gravely that it is painful for you to hear of the faults or misfortunes of others, where your counsel and assistance can be of no service.

Many persons, whose tongues never utter a scandalous word, will, by a significant glance, a shrug of the shoulders, a sneer, or curl of the lip, really make more mischief, and suggest harder thoughts than if they used the severest language. This is utterly detestable. If you have your tongue under perfect control, you can also control your looks, and you are cowardly, contemptible, and wicked, when you encourage and countenance slander by a look or gesture.

Never speak of gentlemen by their first name unless you are related to them. It is very unlady-like to use the surname, without the prefix, Mr. To hear a lady speak of Smith, Brown, Anderson, instead of Mr. Anderson or Mr. Smith sounds extremely vulgar, and is a mark of low breeding.

Avoid eccentricity either in dress, conversation, or manner. It is a form of vanity, as it will attract attention, and is therefore in bad taste.

Never act as if in a hurry. Ease of action need not imply laziness, but simply polite self-possession.

Never laugh at your own wit. That is the part of those who hear you, and if you take their duty from them, they may omit to join you in your laugh.

Do not indulge in ridicule. It is coarse and unlady-like as well as unfeeling. Like every other personality, it should be carefully avoided.

Never handle any ornament or article of furniture in the room in which you are a visitor.

Do not lean your head against the wall. You leave an indelible mark upon the paper, or, if the wall is whitewashed, you give your hair a dingy, dusty look, by bringing it into contact with the lime.

Never lean forward upon a table. Let neither hands nor arms rest there heavily.

To bestow flattery upon a person to his face, betrays a want of delicacy; yet, not less so, rudely to rebuke his errors or mention his faults, and not have a tender regard for his feelings. It is not improper, and may sometimes be very kind to mention to an individual what yourself and others think of his conduct or performances, when it is for his interest or usefulness to know it. To express to a friend deserved approbation is generally proper.

Nothing but a quick perception of the feelings of others, and a ready sympathy with them, can regulate the thousand little proprieties that belong to visits of condolence and congratulation. There is one hint, however, as regards the former, which may perhaps be useful, and that is, not to touch upon the cause of affliction, unless the mourner leads the way to it; and if a painful effort is made to appear cheerful, and to keep aloof from the subject, do not make the slightest allusion that could increase this feeling.

When at table to *press* your guests to take more than they have inclination for, is antiquated and rude. This does not, however, prevent your recommending particular dishes to their attention. Everything like compulsion is quite exploded.

It is a great mistake to suppose that the best music is the most difficult of execution. The very reverse, generally speaking, is the case. Music of a high order certainly demands high gifts and attainments on the part of the performer. But the gifts of nature may be possessed by the amateur as well as by the professor; and the attainments of art may be the result of moderate study and application. A young lady possessed of a sweet and tunable voice, a good ear, intelligence, and feeling, may cultivate music in its grandest and most beautiful forms, and may render its practice a source of the purest enjoyment, not only to herself but to her domestic and social circle.

The various ceremonies observed in refined society are very useful in settling little points, on which there might otherwise be much doubt and perplexity; but they should never be so strenuously insisted upon as to make an accidental omission of them a ground of resentment, and an apology should always be accepted in their place.

Your enjoyment of a party depends far less on what you find there, than on what you carry with you. The vain, the ambitious, the designing, will be full of anxiety when they go, and of disappointment when they return. A short triumph will be followed by a deep mortification, and the selfishness of their aims defeats itself. If you go to see, and to hear, and to make the best of whatever occurs, with a disposition to admire all that is beautiful, and to sympathize in the pleasures of others, you can hardly fail to spend the time pleasantly. The less you think of yourself and your claims to attention, the better. If you are much attended to, receive it modestly, and consider it as a happy accident; if you are little noticed, use your leisure in observing others.

It were unjust and ungrateful to conceive that the amusements of life are altogether forbidden by its beneficent Author. They serve, on the contrary, important purposes in the economy of human life, and are destined to produce important effects both upon our happiness and character. They are, in the first place, in the language of the Psalmist, "the wells of the desert;" the kind resting-places in which toil may relax, in which the weary spirit may recover its tone, and where the desponding mind may resume its strength and its hopes. It is not, therefore, the use of the innocent amusements of life which is dangerous, but the abuse of them; it is not when they are occasionally, but when they are constantly pursued; and when, from being an occasional indulgence, it becomes an habitual desire.

Women in the middle rank are brought up with the idea that if they engage in some occupations, they shall lose "their position in society." Suppose it to be so; surely it is wiser to quit a position we cannot honestly maintain, than to live dependent upon the bounty and caprice of others; better to labor with our hands, than eat the bread of idleness; or submit to feel that we must not give utterance to our real opinions, or express our honest indignation at being required to act a base or unworthy part. And in all cases, however situated, every female ought to learn how all household affairs are managed, were it only for the purpose of being able to direct others. There cannot be any disgrace in learning how to make the bread we eat, to cook our dinners, to mend our clothes, or even to clean the house. Better to be found busily engaged in removing the dust from the furniture, than to let it accumulate there until a visitor leaves palpable traces where his hat or his arm have been laid upon a table.

Never put temptation in a servant's way; never be severe for trifling offences, such as accidentally breaking anything, but reserve your severity for those offences which are moral evils, such as a want of truth, general laxity of principle, &c. The orders given to servants should be clear and definite; and they should be trained as much as possible to perform their duties regularly, so that every morning they may know pretty nearly what will be expected of them during the day. It is a great point to live, when you are alone, as if you expected company; that is to say, to have everything so neat and orderly that you need not be ashamed of any one seeing your table. It is very little more trouble, and certainly no more expense; and the advantages in point of comfort are unspeakable.

If a foolish girl, by dint of squeezing and bracing with busk and bones, secures the conventional beauty of a wasp waist, she is tolerably certain to gain an addition she by no means bargained for, a *red nose*, which, in numberless instances, is produced by no other cause than the unnatural girth, obstructing circulation, and causing stagnation of the blood, in that prominent and important feature. Often, in assemblages of the fair, we have seen noses faultless in form, but tinged with the abhorred hue, to which washes and cosmetics have been applied in wild despair; but in vain! If the lovely owners had known the cause, how speedily the effect would have vanished! for surely the most perverse admirer of a distorted spine and compressed lungs, would deem the acquisition of a dram-drinker's nose, too heavy a condition to be complied with.

A well-bred woman will not demand as a right what she may have a claim to expect from the politeness of the other sex, nor show dissatisfaction and resentment if she fancies herself neglected. For want of good breeding some females are exorbitant in their expectations, and appear unthankful even when everything is done which true politeness demands. Young women should guard against this unamiable defect.

A well-bred person will take care not to use slang words and expressions. There never has been a time, at least in late years, when there have not been some two or three cant vulgarisms in vogue among all the blackguards of the country. Sometimes these phrases have been caught up from some popular song or farce; sometimes, we believe, they have had their origin "where assembles the collective wisdom of the country." A dozen of these terse but meaningless sayings now dance before our recollection, for who has not heard them, even to loathing? But from whatever source they may have been drawn, or whatever wit there might be in their original position, the obtrusion of them into decent society is an unwarrantable piece of impertinence.

A habit of inserting into familiar conversation such phrases as "You know," "You perceive," "You understand," "Says he," "Says she," is, so far as those matters extend, a sign of a want of good breeding.

With regard to any specific rules for dressing, we do not pretend to arbitrate in such matters. Let a true sense of propriety, of the fitness of things, regulate all your habits of living and dressing, and it will produce such a beautiful harmony and consistency of character as will throw a charm around you that all will feel, though few may comprehend. Always consider well whether the articles of dress, which you wish to purchase, are suited to your age, your condition, your means; to the climate, to the particular use to which you mean to put them; and let the principles of good taste keep you from the extremes of the fashion, and regulate the form, so as to combine utility and beauty, whilst the known rules of harmony in colors save you from shocking the eye of the artist by incongruous mixtures.

"Manners," says the eloquent Edmund Burke, "are of more importance than laws. Upon them, in a great measure, the laws depend. The law can touch us here and there, now and then. Manners are what vex or sooth, corrupt or purify, exalt or debase, barbarise or refine, by a constant, steady, uniform, insensible operation, like that of the air we breathe in. They give their whole form and colors to our lives. According to their quality they aid morals, they supply them, or they totally destroy them."

FOUR IMPORTANT RULES.

"Order is heaven's first law."

1. A suitable place for everything, and everything in its place.
2. A proper time for everything, and everything done in its time.
3. A distinct name for everything, and everything called by its name.
4. A certain use for everything, and everything put to its use.

Much time would be saved; many disputes avoided; numerous articles kept from being lost or injured, and constant confusion and disorder prevented, by the strict observance of these four important rules.

Dispense with ornaments altogether rather than wear mock jewelry.

Depend upon it, silvery hair is better adapted to the faded cheeks of middle age, than are tresses of nut-brown or coal-black, or any of the mysterious shades produced by a dirty decoction called Hair-dye.

The habitual use of very thin shoes invariably makes the feet tender, and a host of other inconveniences arise therefrom. If you are tempted to purchase tight shoes, don't, for several reasons; but one may suffice—you will not wear them more than twice.

If you are not quite certain of the line between neatness and the reverse, be over-scrupulous about your under garments. The edge of a soiled petticoat, or the glimpse of a rent stocking is singularly disenchanting.

Men of sense—I speak not of boys of eighteen to five and twenty, during their age of detestability—men who are worth the trouble of falling in love with, and the fuss and inconvenience, of being married to, and to whom one might, after some inward conflicts, and a course perhaps of fasting and self-humiliation, submit to fulfil those ill-contrived vows of obedience which are exacted at the altar, such men want, for their wives, companions, not dolls; and women who would suit such men are just as capable of loving fervently, deeply, as the Ringlettina, full of song and sentiment, who cannot walk, cannot rise in the morning, cannot tie her bonnet-strings, faints if she has to lace her boots, never in her life brushed out her beautiful hair, would not for the world prick her delicate finger with plain sewing; but who can work harder than a factory girl upon a lamb's-wool shepherdess, dance like a dervise at balls, ride like a fox-hunter, and, whilst every breath of air gives her cold in her father's house, and she cannot think how people can endure this climate, she can go out to parties in February and March, with an inch of sleeve and half-a-quarter of boddice.

All circumstances well examined, there can be no doubt Providence has willed that man should be the head of the human race, even as woman is its heart; that he should be its strength, as she is its solace; that he should be its wisdom, as she is its grace; that he should be its mind, its impetus, and its courage, as she is its sentiment, its charm, and its consolation. Too great an amelioration could not be effected, in our opinion, in the system generally adopted, which, far from correcting or even compensating the presumed intellectual inequality of the two sexes, generally serves only to increase it. By placing, for example, dancing and needle-work at the extreme poles of female study, the one for its attraction and the other for its utility, and by not filling the immense interval with anything more valuable than mere monotonous, imperfect, superficial, and totally unphilosophical notions, this system has made of the greater number of female seminaries, establishments which may be compared alike to nursery-grounds for coquettes and sempstresses. It is never remembered that in domestic life conversation is of more importance than the needle or choregraphy; that a husband is neither a pacha nor a lazzarone, who must be perpetually intoxicated or unceasingly patched; that there are upon the conjugal dial many long hours of calm intimacy, of cool contemplation, of cold tenderness; and that the husband makes another home elsewhere if his own hearth offers him only silence; or what is a hundred times worse, merely frivolous and monotonous discourse. Let the woman play the gossip at a given moment, that is all very well; let her superintend the laundry or the kitchen at another, that is also very well; but these duties only comprise two-thirds of her mission. Ought care not to be taken that during the rest of her time she could also be capable of becoming to her husband a rational friend, a cheerful partner, an interesting companion, or, at least, an efficient listener, whose natural intelligence, even if originally inferior to his own, shall, by the help of education, have been raised to the same level!

Pascal says: "Kind words do not cost much. They never blister the tongue or lips. And we have never heard of any mental trouble arising from this quarter. Though they do not cost much. 1. They help one's own good nature. Soft words soften our own soul. Angry words are fuel to the flame of wrath, and make it blaze more fiercely. 2. Kind words make other people good natured. Cold words freeze people, and hot words scorch them, and bitter words make them bitter, and wrathful words make them wrathful. There is such a rush of all other kinds of words in our days, that it seems desirable to give kind words a change among them. There are vain words, and idle words, and hasty words, and spiteful words, and silly words, and empty words, and profane words, and boisterous words, and warlike words. Kind words also produce their own image on men's souls. And a beautiful image it is. They smooth, and quiet, and comfort the hearer. They shame him out of his sour, morose, unkind feelings. We have not yet begun to use kind words in such abundance as they ought to be used."

A writer in the New York Observer, speaking of the necessity of guarding the tongue, says:—

"It is always well to avoid saying everything that is improper; but it is especially so before children. And here parents, as well as others, are often in fault. Children have as many ears as grown persons, and they are generally more attentive to what is said before them. What they hear, they are very apt to repeat; and, as they have no discretion, and not sufficient knowledge of the world to disguise anything, it is generally found that 'children and fools speak the truth.' See that boy's eyes glisten while you are speaking of a neighbor in a language you would not wish to have repeated. He does not fully understand what you mean, but he will remember every word; and it will be strange if he does not cause you to blush by the repetition.

"A gentleman was in the habit of calling at a neighbor's house, and the lady had always expressed to him great pleasure from his calls. One day, just after she had remarked to him, as usual, her happiness from his visit, her little boy entered the room. The gentleman took him on his knee, and asked, 'Are you not glad to see me, George?' 'No, sir,' replied the boy. 'Why not, my little man?' he continued. 'Because mother don't want you to come,' said George. 'Indeed! how do you know that, George?' Here the mother became crimson, and looked daggers at her little son. But he saw nothing, and therefore replied, 'Because, she said yesterday, she wished that old bore would not call here again.' That was enough. The gentleman's hat was soon in requisition, and he left with the impression that 'great is the truth, and it will prevail.'

"Another little child looked sharply in the face of a visitor, and being asked what she meant by it, replied, 'I wanted to see if you had a drop in your eye; I heard mother say you had frequently.'

"A boy once asked one of his father's guests who it was that lived next door to him, and when he heard his name, inquired if he was not a fool. 'No, my little friend,' replied the guest, 'he is not a fool, but a very sensible man. But why did you ask that question?' 'Because,' replied the boy, 'mother said the other day, that you were next door to a fool; and I wanted to know who lived next door to you.'"

The best way to overcome the selfishness and rudeness you sometimes meet with on public occasions, is, by great politeness and disinterestedness on your part; overcome evil with good, and you will satisfy your own conscience, and, perhaps, touch theirs. Contending for your rights stirs up the selfish feelings in others; but a readiness to yield them awakens generous sentiments, and leads to mutual accommodation. The more refined you are, and the greater have been your advantages, the more polite and considerate you should be toward others, the more ready to give place to some poor, uneducated girl, who knows no better than to push herself directly in your way.

Politeness is as necessary to a happy intercourse with the inhabitants of the kitchen, as with those of the parlor; it lessens the pains of service, promotes kind feelings on both sides, and checks unbecoming familiarity; always thank them for what they do for you, and always ask rather than command their services.

Of late years, the wearing of jewelry, in season and out of season, both by matrons and unmarried females, has increased vastly. It is an indication that the growing wealth of the people is not accompanied by a corresponding refinement; but that the love of vulgar show, the low pride of ostentation, takes the place of a pure and elevated taste. The emulation with fashionable dames, now-a-days, so far from being, as with the Spartan women, to excel each other in household virtues, is to wear the largest diamonds. And, in this ambition, they forget fitness, beauty, taste, everything but the mere vulgar desire to shine. To be gracefully and elegantly attired, in short, is secondary to the desire to be a sort of jeweler's walking show-card. We do not oppose the use of diamonds and pearls altogether, as some persons might imagine from these remarks. A few diamonds, judiciously worn, look well, on proper occasions, on married women. But young girls rarely, or never, improve their appearance by the use of these dazzling jewels; and, as a general rule, the simpler the costume of a woman in her teens, the better. Women are usually pretty, up to the age of twenty, at least. Consequently, at this period of life, there are few whom an elaborate attire does not injure; a simple dress, or a rose-bud in the hair, is frequently all that is required; and more only spoils that combination of youthfulness, grace, and modesty, which it should be the highest ambition of the girl to attain; because, if she did but know it, it is her highest charm. Instead of this, however, we see gay females, scarcely freed from the nursery, wearing enormous jeweled ear-drops, or sporting on the finger, a diamond ring as large as a sixpence. Sometimes, too, ladies pretending to be well-bred, descend to receive a morning visitor of their own sex, glittering like a jeweler's case, with costly gems. In all this, we repeat, there is neither refinement nor elegance, but simply vulgar ostentation. Female dress has ceased to be a means of beautifying the person or displaying the wearer's taste, and has become instead, a mere brag of the husband's or father's wealth.

A knowledge of domestic duties is beyond all price to a woman. Every one of the sex ought to know how to sew, and knit, and mend, and cook, and superintend a household. In every situation of life, high or low, this sort of knowledge is of great advantage. There is no necessity that the gaining of such information should interfere with intellectual acquirement or even elegant accomplishment. A well-regulated mind can find time to attend to all. When a girl is nine or ten years old, she should be accustomed to take some regular share in household duties, and to feel responsible for the manner in which her part is performed—such as her own mending, washing the cups and putting them in place, cleaning silver, or dusting and arranging the parlor. This should not be done occasionally, and neglected whenever she finds it convenient—she should consider it her department. When older than twelve, girls should begin to take turns in superintending the household—making puddings, pies, cakes, &c. To learn effectually, they should actually do these themselves, and not stand by and see others do them. Many a husband has been ruined for want of these domestic qualities in a wife—and many a husband has been saved from ruin by his wife being able to manage well the household concerns.

It is a mark, not only of ill-breeding, but of positive want of feeling and judgment, to speak disparagingly of a physician to one of his patients. Many persons, visiting an invalid friend, will exclaim loudly against the treatment pursued, recommend a different doctor, and add to the sufferings of the patient by their injudicious remarks upon the medicines or practice used.

It is too much the fashion, in conversation, to use exaggerated expressions which are opposed to *truth*, without the person employing them being aware of it, from the mere force of habit. Why need we say splendid for pretty, magnificent for handsome, horrid for unpleasant, immense for large, thousands, or myriads, for any number more than two? This practice is pernicious, for the effect is to deprive the person who is guilty of it, from being believed, when she is in earnest. No one can trust the testimony of an individual who, in common conversation, is indifferent to the import, and regardless of the value of words.

Politeness is very essential to the right transaction of that great business of woman's life, *shopping*. The variety afforded by the shops of a city renders people difficult to please; and the latitude they take in examining and asking the price of goods, which they have no thought of buying, is so trying to the patience of those who attend upon them, that nothing but the most perfect courtesy of demeanor can reconcile them to it. Some persons behave, in shopping, as if no one had any rights, or any feelings, but the purchasers; as if the sellers of goods were mere automatons, put behind the counter to do their bidding; they keep them waiting, whilst they talk of other things, with a friend; they call for various goods, ask the price, and try to cheapen them, without any real intention of buying. A lady who wants decision of character, after hesitating and debating, till the poor trader's patience is almost exhausted, will beg him to send the article to her house, for her to examine it there; and, after giving him all this trouble, she will refuse to purchase it, without any scruple or apology. Some think they have a right to exchange articles at the place where they were bought; whereas that privilege should be asked as a favor, only by a good customer,—and then but rarely.

RECEIPTS.
FOR THE COMPLEXION.

COLD CREAM, 1.—Take 2½ ounces of sweet oil of almonds, 3 drachms of white wax, and the same of spermaceti, 2½ ounces of rose-water, 1 drachm of oil of bergamot, and 15 drops each of oil of lavender, and otto of roses. Melt the wax and spermaceti in the oil of almonds, by placing them together in a jar, which should be plunged into boiling water. Heat a mortar (which should, if possible, be *marble*) by pouring boiling water into it, and letting it remain there until the mortar is uniformly heated; the water is to be poured away, and the mortar dried well. Pour the melted wax and spermaceti into the warm mortar, and add rose-water gradually, while the mixture is constantly stirred or whisked with an egg-whisp, until the whole is cold, and, when nearly finished, add the oils and otto of roses.

In the absence of a mortar, a basin plunged into another containing boiling water will answer the purpose.

COLD CREAM, 2.—Take 10 drachms of spermaceti, 4 drachms of white wax, half a pound of prepared lard, 15 grains of subcarbonate of potash, 4 ounces of rose-water, 2 ounces of spirits of wine, and ten drops of otto of roses.

Proceed as above. Some persons prefer orange-flower-water instead of rose-water, in which case use the same proportions.

Cold cream is a useful local application to hard and dry parts of the skin, to abrasions and cracks. When spread thickly upon rag, it is an excellent application to blistered surfaces or burns, or may be used to protect exposed parts from the influence of the sun.

GRANULATED COLD CREAM.—Take white wax and spermaceti, of each one ounce; almond oil 3 ounces, otto of rose, as much as you please. Dissolve the wax and spermaceti in the almond oil, by means of heat, and when a little cool, pour the mixture into a large wedgwood mortar previously warmed, and containing about a pint of warm water. Stir briskly until the cream is well divided, add the otto, and *suddenly* pour the whole into a clean vessel containing 8 or 12 pints of *cold water*. Separate the cream by straining through muslin, and shake out as much water as possible.

WHITE CAMPHORATED OINTMENT, 1.—Take 3 ounces 2 drachms of powdered carbonate of lead (cerussa), 45 grains of powdered camphor. Mix, and then stir into 5 ounces of melted lard.

This is applied to burns and contusions with very good effect, and is much used in Austria. The surface must not be abraded when it is applied.

WHITE CAMPHORATED OINTMENT, 2.—Take 4 ounces of olive oil, 1 ounce of white wax, 22 grains of camphor, and 6 drachms of spermaceti. Melt the wax and spermaceti with the oil, and when they have cooled rub the ointment with the camphor, dissolved in a little oil. Sometimes the white wax is omitted, and lard substituted for it.

It is useful in chaps, fissures, abrasions, and roughness of the skin.

PITCH POMADE, 1.—Take 1 drachm of pitch, and 1 ounce of lard. Mix well, and apply twice a day to the affected parts.

This is used for ringworm, and scald head.

TO SOFTEN THE SKIN, AND IMPROVE THE COMPLEXION.—If flowers of sulphur be mixed in a little milk, and, after standing an hour or two, the milk (without disturbing the sulphur) be rubbed into the skin, it will keep it soft, and make the complexion clear. It is to be used before washing.

TO REMOVE BLACK STAINS FROM THE SKIN.—Ladies that wear mourning in warm weather are much incommoded by the blackness it leaves on the arms and neck, and which cannot easily be removed, even by soap and warm water. To have a remedy always at hand, keep, in the drawer of your wash-stand, a box, containing a mixture in equal portions of cream of tartar, and oxalic acid (POISON). Get, at a druggist's, half an ounce of each of these articles, and have them mixed and pounded together in a mortar. Put some of this mixture into a cup that has a cover, and if, afterwards, it becomes hard, you may keep it slightly moistened with water. See that it is always closely covered. To use it, wet the black stains on your skin with the corner of a towel, dipped in water (warm water is best, but is not always at hand). Then, with your finger, rub on a little of the mixture. Then *immediately* wash it off with water, and afterwards with soap and water, and the black stains will be visible no longer. This mixture will also remove ink, and all other stains from the fingers, and from *white* clothes. It is more speedy in its effects if applied with warm water. No family should be without it, but care must be taken to keep it out of the way of young children, as, if swallowed, it is poisonous.

PASTES.

ALMOND.—Take 1 ounce of bitter almonds, blanch and pound them to a fine powder, then add 1 ounce of barley flour, and make it into a smooth paste by the addition of a little honey. When this paste is laid over the skin, particularly where there are freckles, it makes it smooth and soft.

PALATINE.—Take 8 ounces of soft-soap, of olive oil, and spirits of wine, each 4 ounces, 1½ ounce of lemon-juice, sufficient silver-sand to form into a thick paste, and any perfume that is grateful to the person. Boil the oil and soap together in a pipkin, and then gradually stir in the sand and lemon-juice. When nearly cool add the spirit of wine, and lastly the perfume. Make into a paste with the hands, and place in jars or pots for use.

This paste is used instead of soap, and is a valuable addition to the toilette, as it preserves the skin from chapping, and renders it smooth and soft.

AMERICAN COSMETIC POWDER.—Calcined magnesia applied the same as ordinary toilette powders, by means of a swan's-down ball, usually called a "puff."

MALOINE.—Take 4 ounces of powdered marsh-mallow roots, 2 ounces of powdered white starch, 3 drachms of powdered orris-root, and 20 drops of essence of jasmine. Mix well, and sift through fine muslin.

This is one of the most agreeable and elegant cosmetics yet known for softening and whitening the skin, preserving it from chapping, and being so simple that it may be applied to the most delicate or irritable skin.

This receipt has never before been published, and we know that only six bottles of it have been made.

OXIDE OF ZINC is sprinkled into chaps and fissures to promote their cure.

YAOULTA.—Take 1 ounce of white starch, powdered and sifted, ½ a drachm of rose pink, 10 drops of essence of jasmine, and 2 drops of otto of roses. Mix and keep in a fine muslin bag.

This exquisite powder is to be dusted over the face, and, being perfectly harmless, may be used as often as necessity requires. It also imparts a delicate rosy tinge to the skin preferable to rouge.

CRÈME DE L'ENCLOS.—Take 4 ounces of milk, 1 ounce of lemon-juice, and 2 drachms of spirit of wine. Simmer over a slow fire, and then bring it to the boil, skim off the scum, and when cold apply it to the skin.

It is much used by some persons to remove freckles and sun-burnings.

WASHES AND LOTIONS.

MILK OF ROSES, 1.—Take 2 ounces of blanched almonds; 12 ounces of rose-water; white soft-soap, or Windsor soap; white wax; and oil of almonds, of each 2 drachms; rectified spirit, 3 ounces; oil of bergamot, 1 drachm; oil of lavender, 15 drops; otto of roses, 8 drops. Beat the almonds well, and then add the rose-water gradually so as to form an emulsion, mix the soap, white wax, and oil together, by placing them in a covered jar upon the edge of the fire-place, then rub this mixture in a mortar with the emulsion. Strain the whole through very fine muslin, and add the essential oils, previously mixed with the spirit.

This is an excellent wash for "sunburns," freckles, or for cooling the face and neck, or any part of the skin to which it is applied.

MILK OF ROSES, 2.—This is not quite so expensive a receipt as the last; and, at the same time is not so good.

Take 1 ounce of Jordan almonds; 5 ounces of distilled rose-water; 1 ounce of spirit of wine; ½ a drachm of Venetian soap, and 2 drops of otto of roses. Beat the almonds (previously blanched and well dried with a cloth) in a mortar, until they become a complete paste, then beat the soap and mix with the almonds, and afterwards add the rose-water and spirit. Strain through a very fine muslin or linen, and add the otto of roses.

The common milk of roses sold in the shops, frequently contains salt of tartar, or pearlash, combined with olive oil and rose-water, and therefore it is better to make it yourself to ensure it being good.

FRENCH MILK OF ROSES.—Mix 2½ pints of rose-water with ½ a pint of rosemary-water, then add tincture of storax and tincture of benzoin, of each 2 ounces; and *esprit de rose*, ½ an ounce. This is a useful wash for freckles.

GERMAN MILK OF ROSES.—Take of rose-water and milk of almonds, each 3 ounces; water 8 ounces; rosemary-water 2 ounces; and spirit of lavender ½ an ounce. Mix well, and then add ½ an ounce of sugar of lead.

This is a dangerous form to leave about where there are children, and should never be applied when there are any abrasions, or chaps on the surface.

MILK OF ALMONDS.—Blanch 4 ounces of Jordan almonds, dry them with a towel, and then pound them in a mortar; add 2 drachms of white or curd soap, and rub it up with the almonds for about ten minutes or rather more, gradually adding one quart of rose-water, until the whole is well mixed, then strain through a fine piece of muslin, and bottle for use.

This is an excellent remedy for freckles and sunburns, and may be used as a general cosmetic, being applied to the skin after washing by means of the corner of a soft towel.

ANTI-FRECKLE LOTION, 1.—Take tincture of benzoin, 2 ounces; tincture of tolu, 1 ounce; oil of rosemary, ½ a drachm. Mix well and bottle. When required to be used, add a teaspoonful of the mixture to about a wine-glassful of water, and apply the lotion to the face or hands, &c., night and morning, carefully rubbing it in with a soft towel.

ANTI-FRECKLE LOTION, 2.—Take 1 ounce of rectified spirit of wine; 1 drachm of hydrochloric acid (spirit of salt); and 7 ounces of water. Mix the acid gradually with the water, and then add the spirit of wine; apply by means of a camel's-hair brush, or a piece of flannel.

GOWLAND'S LOTION.—Take 1½ grains of bichloride of mercury, and 1 ounce of emulsion of bitter almonds; mix well. Be careful of the bichloride of mercury, because it is a poison.

This is one of the best cosmetics for imparting a delicate appearance and softness to the skin, and is a useful lotion in acne, ringworm, hard and dry skin, and sun-blisterings.

COLD CREAM.—Sweet almond oil, 7 lbs. by weight, white wax, ¾ lb., spermaceti, ¾ lb., clarified mutton suet, 1 lb., rose-water, 7 pints, spirits of wine, 1 pint. Directions to mix the above:—Place the oil, wax, spermaceti, and suet in a large jar; cover it over tightly, then place it in a saucepan of boiling water, (having previously placed two or more pieces of fire-wood at the bottom of the saucepan, to allow the water to get underneath the jar, and to prevent its breaking) keep the water boiling round the jar till all the ingredients are dissolved; take it out of the water, and pour it into a large pan previously warmed and capable of holding 21 pints; then, with a wooden spatula, stir in the rose-water, cold, as quickly as possible, (dividing it into three or four parts, at most,) the stirring in of which should not occupy above five minutes, as after a certain heat the water will not mix. When all the water is in, stir unremittingly for thirty minutes longer, to prevent its separating, then add the spirits of wine, and the scent, and it is finished. Keep it in a cold place, in a white glazed jar, and do not cut it with a *steel* knife, as it causes blackness at the parts of contact. Scent with otto of roses and essential oil of bergamot to fancy. For smaller quantities, make ounces instead of pounds.

PALM SOAP.—I make it in the following manner:—Cut thin two pounds of yellow soap into a double saucepan, occasionally stirring it till it is melted, which will be in a few minutes if the water is kept boiling around it; then add quarter of a pound of palm oil, quarter of a pound of honey, three pennyworth of true oil of cinnamon; let all boil together another six or eight minutes; pour out and stand it by till next day; it is then fit for immediate use. If made as these directions it will be found to be a very superior soap.

CURE FOR CHAPPED HANDS.—Take 3 drachms of gum camphor, 3 drachms of white beeswax, 3 drachms of spermaceti, 2 ounces of olive oil,—put them together in a cup upon the stove, where they will melt slowly and form a white ointment in a few minutes. If the hands be affected, anoint them on going to bed, and put on a pair of gloves. A day or two will suffice to heal them.

To WHITEN THE NAILS.—Diluted sulphuric acid, 2 drachms; tincture of myrrh, 1 drachm; spring water, 4 ounces. Mix. First cleanse with white soap, and then dip the fingers into the mixture.

To WHITEN THE HANDS.—Take a wine-glassful of eau de Cologne, and another of lemon-juice; then scrape two cakes of brown Windsor soap to a powder, and mix well in a mould. When hard, it will be an excellent soap for whitening the hands.

FOR THE TEETH.

To REMOVE TARTAR FROM THE TEETH.—1st. The use of the tooth-brush night and morning, and, at least, rinsing the mouth after every meal at which animal food is taken. 2nd. Once daily run the brush lightly two or three times over soap, then dip it in salt, and with it clean the teeth, working the brush up and down rather than—or as well as—backwards and forwards. This is a cheap, safe, and effectual dentrifice. 3rd. Eat freely of common cress, the sort used with mustard, under the name of small salad; it must be eaten with salt only. If thus used two or three days in succession it will effectually loosen tartar, even of long standing. The same effect is produced, though perhaps not in an equal degree, by eating strawberries and raspberries, especially the former. A leaf of common green sage rubbed on the teeth is useful both in cleansing and polishing, and probably many other common vegetable productions also.

CARE OF THE TEETH.—The water with which the teeth are cleansed should be what is called lukewarm. They should be well but gently brushed both night and morning; the brush should be neither too hard nor too soft. The best tooth-powders are made from cuttle-fish, prepared chalk, and orris-root commingled together in equal quantities.

SIMPLE MEANS OF REMOVING TARTAR FROM THE TEETH.—In these summer months, tartar may be effectually removed from the teeth, by partaking daily of strawberries.

TOOTH POWDER.—Powdered orris-root, ½ an ounce; powdered charcoal, 2 ounces, powdered Peruvian bark, 1 ounce; prepared chalk, ½ an ounce; oil of bergamot, or lavender, 20 drops. These ingredients must be well worked up in a mortar, until thoroughly incorporated. This celebrated tooth-powder possesses three essential virtues, giving an odorous breath, cleansing and purifying the gums, and preserving the enamel; the last rarely found in popular tooth-powders.

TOOTH-POWDER.—One of the best tooth-powders that can be used may be made by mixing together 1½ ounces prepared chalk, ½ ounce powder of bark, and ¼ ounce of camphor.

A CHEAP BUT GOOD TOOTH-POWDER.—Cut a slice of bread as thick as may be, into squares, and burn in the fire until it becomes charcoal, after which pound in a mortar, and sift through a fine muslin; it is then ready for use.

CHEAP AND INVALUABLE DENTIFRICE.—Dissolve 2 ounces of borax in three pints of water; before quite cold, add thereto one tea-spoonful of tincture of myrrh, and one table-spoonful of spirits of camphor; bottle the mixture for use. One wine-glass of the solution, added to half a pint of tepid water, is sufficient for each application. This solution, applied daily, preserves and beautifies the teeth, extirpates all tartarous adhesion, produces a pearl-like whiteness, arrests decay, and induces a healthy action in the gums.

INVALUABLE DENTIFRICE.—Dissolve two ounces of borax in three pints of boiling water; before quite cold, add one tea-spoonful of tincture of myrrh, and one table-spoonful of spirits of camphor; bottle the mixture for use. One wine-glassful of this solution, added to half a pint of tepid water, is sufficient for each application.

FOR THE HAIR.

LOSS OF HAIR.—The most simple remedy for loss of hair, is friction to the scalp of the head, using for the purpose an old tooth-brush, or one of which the bristles have been softened by soaking in boiling water. The shape of the instrument adapts it to be inserted readily and effectually between the hair, where it should be rubbed backwards and forwards over the space of an inch or so at a time. In addition to the friction, which should be used once or twice a day, the head may be showered once a day with cold water, carefully drying it with soft, spongy towels.

POMATUM.—Take of white mutton suet 4 pounds, well boiled in hot water, (3 quarts,) and washed to free it from salt. Melt the suet, when dried, with 1½ pounds of fresh lard, and 2 pounds of yellow wax. Pour into an earthen vessel, and stir till it is cold; then beat into it 30 drops of oil of cloves, or any other essential oil whose scent you prefer. If this kind of pomatum is too hard, use less wax.

At times numbers of loose hairs come away in the brushing or combing. Such cases as these will generally be found remedial. Wilson recommends women with short hair to dip their heads into cold water every morning, and afterwards apply the brush until a glow of warmth is felt all over the scalp. Those who have long hair are to brush it till the skin beneath becomes red, when a lotion is to be applied, as here specified.

Eau de Cologne	2 oz.
Tincture of Cantharides	½ oz.
Oil of Nutmegs	½ drachm.
Oil of Lavender	10 drops.

To be well mixed together.

Another is composed of:—

Mezereon bark in small pieces	1 oz.
Horse-Radish root in small pieces	1 oz.
Boiling distilled Vinegar	½ pint.

Let this infusion stand for a week, and then strain through muslin for use.

If irritating to the skin, these lotions can be made weaker, or less frequently applied than might otherwise be necessary. Either of them, or distilled vinegar alone, may be rubbed into a bald patch with a tooth-brush. The same lotions may also be used if the hair is disposed to become gray too early; as they invigorate the apparatus situated beneath the skin, and enable it to take up coloring matter. Dyeing of the hair is a practice which ought never to be resorted to. Those who are unwilling or unable to discontinue the practice of applying some kind of dressing to the hair, should, at least, content themselves with a simple, yet good material. The best olive oil is most suitable for the purpose, scented with otto of roses or bergamot; the latter, as many persons know, is the essence of a species of mint. The same scents may also be used for pomatum, which should be made of perfectly pure lard, or marrow.

HAIR OILS, &c.—When used moderately, oils, ointments, &c., tend to strengthen the hair, especially when it is naturally dry. When used in excess, however, they clog the pores, prevent the escape of the natural secretions, and cause the hair to wither and fall off. The varieties of "oils," "Greases," "ointments," rivaling each-other in their high sounding pretensions, which are daily imposed upon public credulity, are interminable. We add one or two of the most simple.

FOR THICKENING THE HAIR.—To one ounce of Palma Christi oil, add a sufficient quantity of bergamot or lavender to scent it. Apply it to the parts where it is most needed, brushing it well into the hair.

AN OINTMENT FOR THE HAIR.—Mix two ounces of bear's grease, half an ounce of honey, one drachm of laudanum, three drachms of the powder of southernwood, three drachms of the balsam of Peru, one and a half drachms of the ashes of the roots of bulrushes, and a small quantity of the oil of sweet almonds.

MACASSAR OIL.—It is said to be compounded of the following ingredients:—To three quarts of common oil, add half-a-pint of spirits of wine, three ounces of cinnamon powder, and two ounces of bergamot; heat the whole in a large pipkin. On removing from the fire, add three or four small pieces of alkanet root, and keep the vessel closely covered for several hours. When cool, it may be filtered through a funnel lined with filtering paper.

Whether oils are used or not, the hair ought night and morning to be carefully and elaborately brushed. This is one of the best preservatives of its beauty.

The following is recommended as an excellent Hair Oil:—Boil together half-a-pint of port wine, one pint and a-half of sweet oil, and half-a-pound of green southernwood. Strain the mixture through a linen rag several times; adding, at the last operation, two ounces of bear's grease. If fresh southernwood is added each time it passes through the linen, the composition will be improved.

POMADE VICTORIA.—This highly-praised and excellent pomade is made in the following way—and if so made, will be found to give a beautiful gloss and softness to the hair:—Quarter of a-pound of honey and half-an-ounce of bees' wax simmered together for a few minutes and then strain. Add of oil of almonds, lavender, and thyme, half-a-drachm each. Be sure to continue stirring till quite cold, or the honey and wax will separate.

LEMON POMATUM.—Best lard, two pounds; suet, half-a-pound; dissolve with a gentle heat, and mix them well together. Then add four ounces of orange-flower water, and four ounces of rose-water, and mix them well together before adding, or they will separate. Having done this, add a quarter of an ounce of essence of lemon; half-a-drachm of musk, and half-a-drachm of oil of thyme.

TO COLOR POMATUM.—Yellow, by palm oil or annatto; red, by alkanet root; and green, by guaiacum, or the green leaves of parsley.

BANDOLINE FOR THE HAIR, (A FRENCH RECEIPT).—To one quart of water put ½ ounce of quince pips, boil it nearly an hour, stirring it well, strain it through a fine muslin, let it stand twenty-four hours, and then add fourteen drops of the essential oil of almonds. A dessert-spoonful of brandy may be added, if required to keep a long time.

BANDOLINE FOR THE HAIR.—Take of castor oil, two ounces; spermaceti, one drachm; oil of bergamot, one drachm; mix with heat and strain; then beat in six drops otto of roses. If wished colored, add half-a-drachm of annatto.

ANOTHER.—I furnish you with an excellent form of Bandoline, much more quickly made than others. Have a small packet of powdered gum dragon by you, and when you require any fresh Bandoline, take a tea-spoonful of the powder, and pour enough of boiling water on it to make a small bottle full. Scent with otto of roses.

CURLING FLUID.—Place two pounds of common soap, cut small, into three pints of spirits of wine, with eight ounces of potash, and melt the whole, stirring it with a clean piece of wood. Add, on cooling, essence of amber, vanilla, and neroli, of each quarter of an ounce. The best method of keeping *ringlets* in curl, is the occasional application of the yolk of an egg, and the hair, afterwards, well washed in lukewarm water. Apply the egg with a tooth or hair-brush.

FOR THE LIPS.

VERY EXCELLENT LIP-SALVE.—Take four ounces of butter, fresh from the churn, cut it small, put it into a jar, cover it with good rose-water, and let it remain for four or five days; then drain it well, and put it into a small and very clean saucepan, with one ounce of spermaceti, and one of yellow beeswax sliced thin, a quarter of an ounce of bruised alkanet root, two drachms of gum benzoin, and one of storax, beaten to powder, half an ounce of loaf sugar, and the strained juice of a moderate sized lemon. Simmer these gently, keeping them stirred all the time, until the mixture looks very clear, and sends forth a fine aromatic odour; then strain it through a thin doubled muslin, and stir to it from twelve to twenty drops of essential oil of roses, and pour it into small gallipots, from which it can easily be turned out when cold, and then be rubbed against the lips, which is the most pleasant way of using it, as it is much firmer than common lip-salve, and will be found more healing and infinitely more agreeable. When butter cannot be had direct from the churn, any which is quite fresh may be substituted for it, after the salt has been well washed and soaked out of it, by working it with a strong spoon in cold water, in which it should remain for a couple of days or more, the water being frequently changed during the time.

ROSE LIP-SALVE.—8 ounces sweet almond oil, 4 ounces prepared mutton suet, 1½ ounces white wax, 2 ounces spermaceti, 20 drops otto; steep a small quantity of alkanet root in the oil, and strain before using. Melt the suet, wax, and spermaceti together, then add the coloric oil and otto.

LIP-SALVES.—A good lip-salve may be made as follows:—Take an ounce of the oil of sweet almonds, cold drawn; a drachm of fresh mutton suet; and a little bruised alkanet root: and simmer the whole together in an earthen pipkin. Instead of the oil of sweet almonds you may use oil of Jasmin, or oil of any other flower, if you intend the lip-salve to have a fragrant odour.—2. Take a pound of fresh butter; a quarter of a pound of beeswax; four or five ounces of cleansed black grapes, and about an ounce of bruised alkanet root. Simmer them together over a slow fire till the wax is wholly dissolved, and the mixture becomes of a bright red color; strain, and put it by for use. 3. Oil of almonds, spermaceti, white wax, and white sugar-candy, equal parts, form a good white lip-salve.

SUPERIOR LIP-SALVE.—White wax, two and a half ounces; spermaceti, three quarters of an ounce; oil of almonds, four ounces. Mix well together, and apply a little to the lips at night.

ANOTHER.—A desert spoonful of salad oil in a saucer, hold it over a candle, and drop melted wax over it till the oil is thinly covered, when they are incorporated, pour it into boxes.—(Wax taper will do.)

FOR CORNS.

CURE FOR CORNS.—Place the feet for half an hour, two or three nights successively, in a pretty strong solution of common soda. The alkali dissolves the indurated cuticle, and the corn falls out spontaneously, leaving a small excavation, which soon fills up.

TO REMOVE CORNS.—Get four ounces of white diachylon plaster, four ounces of shoemaker's wax, and sixty drops of muriatic acid or spirits of salt. Boil them for a few minutes in an earthen pipkin, and when cold, roll the mass between the hands and apply a little on a piece of white leather.

A CERTAIN CURE FOR SOFT CORNS.—Dip a piece of soft linen rag in turpentine, and wrap it round the toe on which the soft corn is, night and morning; in a few days the corn will disappear; but the relief is instantaneous.

PERFUMES.

TO MAKE EAU DE COLOGNE.—Rectified spirits of wine, four pints; oil of bergamot, one ounce; oil of lemon, half an ounce; oil of rosemary, half a drachm; oil of Neroli, three quarters of a drachm; oil of English lavender, one drachm; oil of oranges, one drachm. Mix well and then filter. If these proportions are too large, smaller ones may be used.

EAU DE COLOGNE.—Oil of neroli, citron, bergamot, orange, and rosemary, of each twelve drops; cardamom seeds, one drachm; spirits of wine, one pint. Let it stand for a week.

LAVENDER WATER.—Oil of lavender, 2 drachms; oil of bergamot, ½ drachm; essence of musk, 1 drachm; spirits of wine, 13 ounces; water, 5 ounces. Let it stand for a week.

FOR KEEPING THE WARDROBE IN ORDER.

TO CLEAN KID GLOVES.—Make a strong lather with curd soap and warm water, in which steep a small piece of new flannel. Place the glove on a flat, clean, and unyielding surface—such as the bottom of a dish, and having thoroughly soaped the flannel (when squeezed from the lather), rub the kid till all dirt be removed, cleaning and resoaping the flannel from time to time. Care must be taken to omit no part of the glove, by turning the fingers, &c. The gloves must be dried in the sun, or before a moderate fire, and will present the appearance of old parchment. When quite dry, they must be gradually "pulled out," and will look new.

ANOTHER.—First see that your hands are clean, then put on the gloves and wash them, as though you were washing your hands, in a basin of spirits of turpentine, until quite clean; then hang them up in a warm place, or where there is a good current of air, which will carry off all smell of the turpentine. This method was brought from Paris, and thousands of dollars have been made by it.

TO CLEAN COLORED KID GLOVES.—Have ready on a table a clean towel, folded three or four times, a saucer of new milk, and another saucer with a piece of brown soap. Take one glove at a time, and spread it smoothly on the folded towel. Then dip in the milk a piece of clean flannel, rub it on the soap till you get off a tolerable quantity, and then, with the wet flannel, commence rubbing the glove. Begin at the wrist, and rub lengthways towards the end of the fingers, holding the glove firmly in your right-hand. Continue this process until the glove is well cleaned all over with the milk and soap. When done, spread them out, and pin them on a line to dry gradually. When nearly dry, pull them out evenly, the crossway of the leather. When quite dry, stretch them on your hands. White kid gloves may also be washed in this manner, provided they have never been cleaned with India-rubber.

TO CLEAN WHITE OR COLORED KID GLOVES.—Put the glove on your hand, then take a small piece of flannel, dip it in camphene, and well, but gently, rub it over the glove, *taking care not to make it too wet*, when the dirt is removed, dip the flannel (or another piece if that is become too dirty) into pipe-clay and rub it over the glove; take it off, and hang it up in a room to dry, and in a day or two very little smell will remain; and if done carefully they will be almost as good as new. In colored ones, if yellow, use gamboge after the pipe-clay, and for other colors match it in dry paint.

TO CLEAN WHITE KID GLOVES.—Stretch the gloves on a clean board, and rub all the soiled or grease-spots with cream of tartar or magnesia. Let them rest an hour. Then have ready a mixture of alum and Fuller's earth (both powdered), and rub it all over the gloves with a brush (a clean tooth-brush or something similar), and let them rest for an hour or two. Then sweep it all off, and go over them with a flannel dipped in a mixture of bran and finely powdered whiting. Let them rest another hour; then brush off the powder, and you will find them clean.

TO CLEAN LIGHT KID GLOVES.—Put on one glove, and having made a strong lather with common brown soap, apply it with a shaving brush, wiping it off immediately with a clean towel, then blow into the glove, and leave it to dry.

AN EXCELLENT PASTE FOR GLOVES.—Liquor of ammonia half an ounce, chloride of potash ten ounces, curd soap one pound, water half a pint; dissolve the soap in the water, with a gentle heat, then as the mixture cools, stir in the other ingredients. Use it, by rubbing it over the gloves until the dirt is removed.

TO WASH THREAD LACE.—Rip off the lace, carefully pick out the loose bits of thread, and roll the lace very smoothly and securely round a clean black bottle, previously covered with old white linen, sewed tightly on. Tack each end of the lace with a needle and thread, to keep it smooth; and be careful in wrapping not to crumple or fold in any of the scallops or pearlings. After it is on the bottle, take some of the *best* sweet oil and with a clean sponge wet the lace thoroughly to the inmost folds. Have ready in a wash-kettle, a strong *cold* lather of clear water and white Castile soap. Fill the bottle with cold water, to prevent its bursting, cork it well, and stand it upright in the suds, with a string round the neck secured to the ears or handle of the kettle, to prevent its knocking about and breaking while over the fire. Let it boil in the suds for an hour or more, till the lace is clean and white all through. Drain off the suds, and dry it on the bottle in the sun. When dry, remove the lace from the bottle and roll it round a wide ribbon-block; or lay it in long folds, place it within a sheet of smooth, white, paper, and press it in a large book for a few days.

TO WASH A WHITE LACE VEIL.—Put the veil into a strong lather of white soap and very clear water, and let it simmer slowly for a quarter of an hour. Take it out and squeeze it well, but be sure not to rub it. Rinse it in two cold waters, with a drop or two of liquid blue in the last. Have ready some very clear and weak gum-arabic water, or some thin starch, or rice-water. Pass the veil through it, and clear it by clapping. Then stretch it out even, and pin it to dry on a linen cloth, making the edge as straight as possible, opening out all the scallops, and fastening each with pins. When dry, lay a piece of thin muslin smoothly over it, and iron it on the wrong side.

TO WASH A BLACK LACE VEIL.—Mix bullock's gall with sufficient hot water to make it as warm as you can bear your hand in. Then pass the veil through it. It must be squeezed, and not rubbed. It will be well to perfume the gall with a little musk. Next rinse the veil through two cold waters, tinging the last with indigo. Then dry it. Have ready in a pan some stiffening made by pouring boiling water on a very small piece of glue. Pat the veil into it, squeeze it out, stretch it, and clap it. Afterwards pin it out to dry on a linen cloth, making it very straight and even, and taking care to open and pin the edge very nicely. When dry, iron it on the wrong side, having laid a linen cloth over the ironing-blanket. Any article of black lace may be washed in this manner.

To CLEAN WHITE SATIN AND FLOWERED SILKS.—1. Mix sifted stale bread crumbs with powder blue, and rub it thoroughly all over, then shake it well, and dust it with clean, soft cloths. Afterwards, where there are any gold or silver flowers, take a piece of crimson ingrain velvet, rub the flowers with it, which will restore them to their original lustre. 2. Pass them through a solution of fine hard soap, at a hand heat, drawing them through the hand. Rinse in lukewarm water, dry and finish by pinning out. Brush the flossy or bright side with a clean clothes-brush, the way of the nap. Finish them by dipping a sponge into a size, made by boiling isinglass in water, and rub the wrong side. Rinse out a second time, and brush, and dry near a fire, or in a warm room. Silks may be treated in the same way, but not brushed.

To CLEAN WHITE SILK.—Dissolve some of the best curd soap in boiling water, and when the solution is as hot as the hand can bear, pass the silk through it thoroughly, handling it gently, not to injure the texture. If there are any spots, these may be rubbed carefully until they disappear. The article must then be rinsed in lukewarm water.

To IRON SILK.—Silk cannot be ironed smoothly, so as to press out all the creases, without first sprinkling it with water, and rolling it up tightly in a towel, letting it rest for an hour or two. If the iron is in the least too hot, it will injure the color, and it should first be tried on an old piece of the same silk.

To WASH SILK.—Half a pint of gin, four ounces of soft soap, and two ounces of honey, well shaken; then rub the silk, with a sponge (wetted with the above mixture), upon a table, and wash through two waters, in which first put two or three spoonfuls of ox gall, which will brighten the colors, and prevent their running. The silks should not be wrung, but well shaken and hung up smoothly to dry, and mangled while damp. The writer has had *green* silk dresses washed by this receipt, and they have looked as well as new.

To RENOVATE BLACK SILK.—Slice some uncooked potatoes, pour boiling water on them; when cold sponge the right side of the silk with it, and iron on the wrong.

To KEEP SILK.—Silk articles should not be kept folded in white paper, as the chloride of lime used in bleaching the paper will probably impair the color of the silk. Brown or blue paper is better—the yellowish smooth India paper is best of all. Silk intended for a dress should not be kept in the house long before it is made up, as lying in the folds will have a tendency to impair its durability by causing it to cut or split, particularly if the silk has been thickened by gum. We knew an instance of a very elegant and costly thread-lace veil being found, on its arrival from France, cut into squares (and therefore destroyed) by being folded over a pasteboard card. A white satin dress should be pinned up in blue paper, with coarse brown paper outside, sewed together at the edges.

To RESTORE VELVET.—When velvet gets plushed from pressure, holding the reverse side over a basin of boiling water will raise the pile, and perhaps it may also succeed in the case of wet from rain.

To IRON VELVET.—Having ripped the velvet apart, damp each piece separately, and holding it tightly in both hands, stretch it before the fire, the wrong side of the velvet being towards the fire. This will remove the creases, and give the surface of the material a fresh and new appearance. Velvet cannot be ironed on a table, for, when spread out on a hard substance, the iron will not go smoothly over the pile.

To CLEAN ERMINE AND MINIVAR FUR.—Take a piece of soft flannel, and rub the fur well with it (but remember that the rubbing must be always against the grain); then rub the fur with common flour until clean. Shake it well, and rub again with the flannel till all the flour is out of it. I have had a Minivar boa for four years. It has never been cleaned with anything but flour, and is not in the least injured by the rubbing. It was a school companion who told me that her aunt (a Russian lady) always cleaned her white furs with flour, and that they looked quite beautiful. It has one advantage—the lining does not require to be taken out, and it only requires a little trouble. Ermine takes longer than Minivar. The latter is very easily done.

To PERFUME LINEN.—Rose-leaves dried in the shade, or at about four feet from a stove, one pound; cloves, carraway-seeds, and allspice, of each one ounce; pound in a mortar, or grind in a mill; dried salt, a quarter of a pound; mix all these together, and put the compound into little bags.

To RESTORE SCORCHED LINEN.—Take two onions, peel and slice them, and extract the juice by squeezing or pounding. Then cut up half an ounce of white soap, and two ounces of fuller's earth; mix with them the onion juice, and half a pint of vinegar. Boil this composition well, and spread it, when cool, over the scorched part of the linen, leaving it to dry thereon. Afterwards wash out the linen.

To WHITEN LINEN THAT HAS TURNED YELLOW.—Cut up a pound of fine white soap into a gallon of milk, and hang it over the fire in a wash-kettle. When the soap has entirely melted, put in the linen, and boil it half an hour. Then take it out; have ready a lather of soap and warm water; wash the linen in it, and then rinse it through two cold waters, with a very little blue in the last.

To WASH CHINA CRAPE SCARFS, &c.—If the fabric be good, these articles of dress can be washed as frequently as may be required, and no diminution of their beauty will be discoverable, even when the various shades of green have been employed among other colors in the patterns. In cleaning them, make a strong lather of boiling water—suffer it to cool; when cold, or nearly so, wash the scarf quickly and thoroughly, dip it immediately in cold hard water, in which a little salt has been thrown (to preserve the colors), rinse, squeeze, and hang it out to dry in the open air; pin it at its extreme edge to the line, so that it may not in any part be folded together; the more rapidly it dries, the clearer it will be.

To Clean Embroidery and Gold Lace.—For this purpose no alkaline liquors are to be used; for while they clean the gold, they corrode the silk, and change its color. Soap also alters the shade, and even the species of certain colors. But spirit of wine may be used without any danger of its injuring either color or quality; and, in many cases, proves as effectual for restoring the lustre of the gold as the corrosive detergents. But, though spirits of wine is the most innocent material employed for this purpose, it is not in all cases proper. The golden covering may be in some parts worn off; or the base metal with which it has been alloyed may be corroded by the air, so as to leave the particles of the gold disunited; while the silver underneath, tarnished to a yellow hue, may continue a tolerable color to the whole, so it is apparent that the removal of the tarnish would be prejudicial, and make the lace or embroidery less like gold than it was before. It is necessary that care should be taken.

To Remove Stains of Wine or Fruit from Table Linen.—A wine stain may sometimes be removed by rubbing it, while wet, with common salt. It is said, also, that sherry wine poured immediately on a place where port wine has been spilled, will prevent its leaving a stain. A *certain* way of extracting fruit or wine stains from table-linen is to tie up some cream of tartar in the stained part (so as to form a sort of bag), and then to put the linen into a lather of soap and cold water, and boil it awhile. Then transfer it wet to a lukewarm suds, wash and rinse it well, and dry and iron it. The stains will disappear during the process. Another way, is to mix, in equal quantities, soft soap, slackened lime, and pearl-ash. Rub the stain with this preparation, and expose the linen to the sun with the mixture plastered on it. If necessary, repeat the application. As soon as the stain has disappeared, wash out the linen immediately, as it will be injured if the mixture is left in it.

Stain Mixture.—Take an ounce of sal-ammoniac (or hartshorn) and an ounce of salt of tartar—mix them well, put them into a pint of soft water, and bottle it for use, keeping it very tightly corked. Pour a little of this liquid into a saucer, and wash in it those parts of a white article that have been stained with ink, mildew, fruit, or red wine. When the stains have, by this process, been removed, wash the article in the usual manner.

CHEMICAL RENOVATING BALLS—for taking out grease, paint, pitch, tar, from silks, stuffs, linen, woolen, carpets, hats, coats, &c., without fading the color or injuring the cloth:—¼ ounce of fuller's earth, ¼ ounce of pipe-clay, 1 ounce salt of tartar, 1 ounce beef gall, 1 ounce spirits of wine. Pound the hard parts and mix the ingredients well together. Wet the stain with cold water, rub it well with this ball, then sponge it with a wet sponge and the stain will disappear.

TO PREVENT COLORED THINGS FROM RUNNING.—Boil ¼ pound of soap till nearly dissolved, then add a small piece of alum and boil with it. Wash the things in this lather, but do not soap them. If they require a second water put alum to that also as well as to the rinsing and blue water. This will preserve them.

TO REMOVE STAINS FROM MOURNING DRESSES.—Take a good handful of fig-leaves, and boil them in two quarts of water until reduced to a pint. Squeeze the leaves and put the liquor into a bottle for use. The articles, whether of bombasin, crape, cloth, &c., need only be rubbed with a sponge dipped in the liquor, when the effect will be instantly produced. If any reason exists to prevent the substance from being wetted, then apply French chalk, which will absorb the grease from the finest texture without injury.

TO SHRINK NEW FLANNEL.—New flannel should always be shrunk or washed before it is made up, that it may be cut out more accurately, and that the grease which is used in manufacturing it may be extracted. First, cut off the list along the selvage edges of the whole piece. Then put it into warm (not boiling) water, without soap. Begin at one end of the piece, and rub it with both hands till you come to the other end; this is to get out the grease and the blue with which new white flannel is always tinged. Then do the same through another water. Rinse it through a clean, lukewarm water; wring it lengthways, and stretch it well. In hanging it out on a line do not suspend it in festoons, but spread it along the line straight and lengthways. If dried in festoons, the edges will be in great scollops, making it very difficult to cut out. It must be dried in the sun. When dry let it be stretched even, clapped with the hands, and rolled up tight and smoothly, till wanted.

GUM ARABIC STARCH.—Get two ounces of fine, white gum arabic, and pound it to powder. Next put it into a pitcher, and pour on it a pint or more of boiling water (according to the degree of strength you desire), and then, having covered it, let it set all night. In the morning, pour it carefully from the dregs into a clean bottle, cork it, and keep it for use. A table-spoonful of gum water stirred into a pint of starch that has been made in the usual manner, will give to lawns (either white or printed) a look of newness to which nothing else can restore them after washing. It is also good (much diluted) for thin white muslin and bobinet.

To Wash White Thread Gloves and Stockings.—These articles are so delicate as to require great care in washing, and they must not on any account be rubbed. Make a lather of white soap and *cold* water, and put it into a saucepan. Soap the gloves or stockings well, put them in, and set the saucepan over the fire. When they have come to a hard boil, take them off, and when cool enough for your hand, squeeze them in the water. Having prepared a fresh cold lather, boil them again in that. Then take the pan off the fire, and squeeze them well again, after which they can be stretched, dried, and then ironed on the wrong side.

To Clean Silk Stockings.—First wash the stockings in the usual manner, to take out the rough dirt. After rinsing them in clean water, wash them well in a fresh soap liquor. Then make a third soap liquor, which color with a little stone-blue; then wash the stockings once more, take them out, wring them, and particularly dry them. Now stove them with brimstone, and draw on a wooden leg two stockings, one upon the other, observing that the two fronts or outsides are face to face. Polish with a glass bottle. The two first liquors should be only lukewarm, but the third as hot as you can bear your hand in. Blondes and gauzes may be whitened in the same manner, but there should be a little gum put in the last liquor before they are stoved.

To Take out Mildew from Clothes.—Mix some soft soap with powdered starch, half as much salt, and the juice of a lemon, lay it on the part with a brush, let it be exposed in the air day and night, until the stain disappears. Iron-moulds may be removed by the salt of lemons. Many stains in linen may be taken out by dipping linen in sour buttermilk, and then drying it in the sun; afterwards wash it in cold water several times. Stains caused by acids may be removed by tying some pearlash up in the stained part; scrape some soap in cold, soft water, and boil the linen till the stain is out.

Bleaching Straw.—Straw is bleached, and straw bonnets cleaned, by putting them into a cask into which a few brimstone matches are placed lighted. The fumes of the sulphur have the effect of destroying the color, or whitening the straw. The same effect may be produced by dipping the straw into the chloride of lime dissolved in water.

To Wash Mouseline-de-Laine.—Boil a pound of rice in five quarts of water, and, when cool enough, wash in this, using the rice for soap. Have another quantity ready, but strain the rice from this and use it with warm water, keeping the rice strained off for a third washing which, at the same time, stiffens and also brightens the colors.

To BLEACH A FADED DRESS.—Wash the dress in hot suds, and boil it until the color appears to be gone; then rinse it and dry it in the sun. Should it not be rendered white by these means, lay the dress in the open air, and bleach it for several days. If still not quite white, repeat the boiling.

INDELIBLE MARKING INK, WITHOUT PREPARATION.—1½ drachms nitrate of silver (lunar caustic), 1 ounce distilled water, ½ ounce strong mucilage of gum arabic, ¾ drachm liquid ammonia; mix the above in a clean glass bottle, cork tightly, and keep in a dark place till dissolved, and ever afterwards. Directions for use:—Shake the bottle, then dip a clean quill pen in the ink, and write or draw what you require on the article; immediately hold it close to the fire, (without scorching) or pass a hot iron over it, and it will become a deep and indelible black, indestructible by either time or acids of any description.

MIXTURE FOR REMOVING INK STAINS AND IRON-MOULDS.—Cream of tartar and salts of sorrel, one ounce each; mix well, and keep in a stoppered bottle.

To WASH HAIR-BRUSHES.—Never use soap. Take a piece of soda, dissolve it in warm water, stand the brush in it, taking care that the water only covers the bristles; it will almost immediately become white and clean; stand it to dry in the open air with the bristles downwards, and it will be found to be as firm as a new brush.

To CLEAN HEAD AND CLOTHES-BRUSHES.—Put a table-spoonful of pearl-ash into a pint of boiling water. Having fastened a bit of sponge to the end of a stick, dip it into the solution, and wash the brush with it; carefully going in among the bristles. Next pour over it some clean hot water, and let it lie a little while. Then drain it, wipe it with a cloth, and dry it before the fire.

Lola Montez in her "Arts of Beauty" gives the following receipts for complexion, hair, &c:—

FOR THE COMPLEXION.—"Infuse wheat-bran, well sifted, for four hours in white wine vinegar, add to it five yolks of eggs and two grains of ambergris, and distill the whole. It should be carefully corked for twelve or fifteen days, when it will be fit for use.

"Distill two handfuls of jessamine flowers in a quart of rose-water and a quart of orange-water. Strain through porous paper, and add a scruple of musk and a scruple of ambergris."

To GIVE ELASTICITY OF FORM.—

"Fat of the stag or deer	8 oz.
Florence oil (or olive oil)	6 oz.
Virgin wax	3 oz.
Musk	1 grain.

| White brandy | ½ pint. |
| Rose-water | 4 oz. |

"Put the fat, oil, and wax into a well glazed earthen vessel, and let them simmer over a slow fire until they are assimilated; then pour in the other ingredients, and let the whole gradually cool, when it will be fit for use. There is no doubt but that this mixture, frequently and thoroughly rubbed upon the body on going to bed, will impart a remarkable degree of elasticity to the muscles. In the morning, after this preparation has been used, the body should be thoroughly wiped with a sponge, dampened with cold water."

FOR THE COMPLEXION.—"Take equal parts of the seeds of the melon, pumpkin, gourd, and cucumber, pounded till they are reduced to powder; add to it sufficient fresh cream to dilute the flour, and then add milk enough to reduce the whole to a thin paste. Add a grain of musk, and a few drops of the oil of lemon. Anoint the face with this, leave it on twenty or thirty minutes, or overnight if convenient, and wash off with warm water. It gives a remarkable purity and brightness to the complexion.

"Infuse a handful of well sifted wheat bran for four hours in white wine vinegar; add to it five yolks of eggs and two grains of musk, and distill the whole. Bottle it, keep carefully corked fifteen days, when it will be fit for use. Apply it over night, and wash in the morning with tepid water."

TOOTH-POWDER.—

"Prepared chalk	6 oz.
Cassia powder	½ oz.
Orris-root	1 oz.

"These should be thoroughly mixed and used once a day with a firm brush.

"A simple mixture of charcoal and cream of tartar is an excellent tooth-powder."

TO WHITEN THE HAND.—"Both Spanish and French women—those, at least, who are very particular to make the most of these charms—are in the habit of sleeping in gloves which are lined or plastered over with a kind of pomade to improve the delicacy and complexion of their hands. This paste is generally made of the following ingredients:—

"Take half a pound of soft soap, a gill of salad oil, an ounce of mutton tallow, and boil them till they are thoroughly mixed. After the boiling has ceased, but before it is cold, add one gill of spirits of wine, and a grain of musk.

"If any lady wishes to try this, she can buy a pair of gloves three or four sizes larger than the hand, rip them open and spread on a thin layer of the paste, and then sew the gloves up again. There is no doubt that by wearing them every night they will give smoothness and a fine complexion to the hands. Those who have the means, can send to Paris and purchase them ready made.

"If the hands are inclined to be rough and to chap, the following wash will remedy the evil.

Lemon-juice	3 oz.
White wine vinegar	3 oz.
White brandy	½ oz.

FOR THE HAIR.—"Beat up the white of four eggs into a froth, and rub that thoroughly in close to the roots of the hair. Leave it to dry on. Then wash the head and hair clean with a mixture of equal parts of rum and rose-water."

"HONEY-WATER.—

"Essence of ambergris	1 dr.
Essence of musk	1 dr.
Essence of bergamot	2 drs.
Oil of cloves	15 drops.
Orange-flower water	4 oz.
Spirits of wine	5 oz.
Distilled water	4 oz.

"All these ingredients should be mixed together, and left about fourteen days, then the whole to be filtered through porous paper, and bottled for use.

"This is a good hair-wash and an excellent perfume."

"TO REMOVE PIMPLES.—There are many kinds of pimples, some of which partake almost of the nature of ulcers, which require medical treatment; but the small red pimple, which is most common, may be removed by applying the following twice a-day:—

"Sulphur water	1 oz.
Acetated liquor of ammonia	¼ oz.
Liquor of potassa	1 gr.
White wine vinegar	2 oz.
Distilled water	2 oz."

"TO REMOVE BLACK SPECKS OR 'FLESHWORMS.'—Sometimes little black specks appear about the base of the nose, or on the forehead, or in the hollow of the chin which are called 'fleshworms,' and are occasioned by coagulated lymph that obstructs the pores of the skin. They may be squeezed out by pressing the skin, and ignorant persons suppose them to be little worms. They are permanently removed by washing with warm water, and severe friction with a towel, and then applying a little of the following preparation:—

"Liquor of potassa	1 oz.
Cologne	2 oz.
White brandy	4 oz.

"The warm water and friction alone are sometimes sufficient."

"To REMOVE FRECKLES.—The most celebrated compound ever used for the removal of freckles was called Unction de Maintenon, after the celebrated Madame de Maintenon, mistress and wife of Louis XIV. It is made as follows:—

"Venice soap	1 oz.
Lemon-juice	½ oz.
Oil of bitter almonds	¼ oz.
Deliquidated oil of tartar	¼ oz..
Oil of rhodium	3 drops.

"First dissolve the soap in the lemon-juice, then add the two oils, and place the whole in the sun till it acquires the consistence of ointment, and then add the oil of rhodium. Anoint the freckly face at night with this unction, and wash in the morning with pure water, or, if convenient, with a mixture of elder-flower and rose-water.

"To REMOVE TAN.—An excellent wash to remove tan is called Crème de l'Enclos, and is made thus:—

"New milk	½ pint.
Lemon-juice	¼ oz.
White brandy	½ oz.

"Boil the whole, and skim it clear from all scum. Use it night and morning.

"A famous preparation with the Spanish ladies for removing the effects of the sun and making the complexion bright, is composed simply of equal parts of lemon-juice and the white of eggs. The whole is beat together in a varnished earthen pot, and set over a slow fire, and stirred with a wooden spoon till it acquires the consistence of soft pomatum. This compound is called Pommade de Seville. If the face is well washed with rice-water before it is applied, it will remove freckles, and give a fine lustre to the complexion."

TRUE POLITENESS

A
HAND-BOOK OF ETIQUETTE
FOR
LADIES

BY AN AMERICAN LADY

INTRODUCTIONS.

I.

NEVER INTRODUCE PERSONS TO EACH OTHER without a knowledge that it will be agreeable to both parties; this may sometimes be ascertained without a formal question: very great intimacy with and knowledge of each party may be a sufficient assurance that the introduction will be agreeable.

II.

The inferior should always be introduced to the superior—ladies take precedence of gentlemen; you will present the gentleman to the lady, not the lady to the gentleman.

III.

An introduction at a ball for the purpose of dancing does not compel you to recognise the person in the street or in any public place; and except under very peculiar circumstances such intimacies had better cease with the ball.

IV.

When introducing one to another, mention the name of each distinctly. A failure to do this is often the cause of much embarrassment. If you have been introduced, and have not caught the name, it is better to say at once, "I beg pardon; I did not hear the name;" it will save much unpleasant feeling.

V.

As a general rule, avoid all proffers of introduction, unless from those in whom, from relationship or other causes, you can place implicit confidence. A lady cannot shake off an improper acquaintance with the same facility as a gentleman can do, and her character is more easily affected by contact with the worthless and dissipated.

VI.

Upon a first introduction to a lady or gentleman, make a slight but gracious inclination of the head and body. The old style of curtsying has given place to the more easy and graceful custom of bowing. It is ill-bred to shake hands.

VII.

If you meet a lady for the second or subsequent times, the hand may be extended in addition to the inclination of the head; but never extend the hand to a gentleman, unless you are very intimate.

VIII.

Bow with slow and measured dignity; never hastily.

IX.

If you wish to avoid the company of a gentleman who has been properly introduced, treat him with respect, at the same time shunning his company. But few will mistake you.

X.

If, in travelling, any one introduces himself to you in a proper and respectful manner, conduct yourself toward him with reserve and dignity, yet with ease and politeness; and thank him for any attentions he may render you. If he is a gentleman he will appreciate your behavior; if he is not, he will be deterred from annoying you. All such acquaintances cease with the occasion. Converse only upon topics of general interest; it is necessary only to be civil. If he should betray the least want of respect, turn from him in dignified silence; a lady by her behavior always has it in her power to silence the boldest.

XI.

If on paying a morning visit you meet strangers at the house of your friend and are introduced, it is a mere matter of form, and does not entitle you to future recognition by such persons.

XII.

Be very cautious of giving a gentleman a letter of introduction to a lady,—it may be the means of settling the weal or woe of the persons for life.

XIII.

If you have an introductory letter, do not deliver it yourself, unless upon cases of urgent business, but send it with your card and the number of your lodging, enclosed in an envelope, as soon as you have made yourself comfortable after arriving at your destination.

XIV.

On receiving a letter introducing any person, so soon as convenient wait upon her, and show such attention as the nature of the introduction may require: upon meeting the party introduced, you will easily perceive whether any further INTIMACY will be desirable.

XV.

A lady, who receives a letter introducing a gentleman, may answer it by a note to the bearer, inviting him to pay a morning or evening visit.

XVI.

When introduced to another lady, you may say, "I am very happy to make your acquaintance;" but there are few cases where this remark can be addressed with propriety to a gentleman. It is a favor for him to be presented to her, therefore the pleasure is on his side.

RECOGNITIONS AND SALUTATIONS.

XVII.

THE superior in rank and station should first salute the inferior. Therefore, if you meet a gentleman in the street with whom you are acquainted, recollect that it is your province to recognise him before he presumes to salute you. Another reason is, he may bow to you, when you do not recognise him, and there is no remedy; but if you recognise him first, no gentleman would fail to return the salute. Though etiquette is quite definite on the subject, it is often waived with advantage when intimacy, equality of station and circumstances, and a known appreciation of each other, warrant the liberty.

XVIII.

If a person whom you have met as specified in Nos. IV. and XI., should presume to salute you, do not recognise the salute, but pass on, and leave him to suppose that you imagined it was intended for another.

XIX.

On meeting a friend in any public place, do not boisterously salute, or proclaim her name aloud.

XX.

It is, in general, bad taste for ladies to kiss each other in the presence of gentlemen, with whom they are but slightly acquainted.

XXI.

It is proper to vary the phraseology of questions concerning another's health as much as possible, and to abstain from them entirely toward a superior or a person with whom we are but little acquainted, as such inquiries presuppose some degree of intimacy. Custom forbids a lady to make these inquiries of a gentleman, unless he is very ill or aged.

XXII.

After we are informed of the health of the persons we are visiting, it is proper to inquire of them in relation to that of their families; and in case of absence of near relations, if they have heard from them lately, and if the news is favorable. They on their part usually ask the same of us.

XXIII.

If in a public promenade you repeatedly pass persons of your acquaintance, salute them only on the first occasion.

XXIV.

It is unladylike to cut a person; if you wish to rid yourself of any one's society, a cold bow in the street, and particular ceremony in the circles of your mutual acquaintance, is the best mode to adopt.

XXV.

Always bow when meeting acquaintances in the street. To curtsy is not gracefully consistent with locomotion.

DRESS AND FASHION.

XXVI.

The plainest dress is always the most genteel, and a lady that dresses plainly will never be dressed unfashionably. Next to plainness, in every well-dressed lady, is neatness of dress and taste in the selection of colors.

XXVII.

Let your dress harmonize with your complexion, your size, and the circumstances in which you may be placed: for instance, the dress for walking, for a dinner or an evening party, each requires a different style of both material and ornament.

XXVIII.

Avoid the extreme mode; and, in adopting the style of your friend, be careful that it will suit your figure, your complexion, and stature: the dress which may be adapted to her may be absurd in you.

XXIX.

If your stature be short, you should not allow a superfluity of flounces upon the skirt of your dress: if you are tall, they may be advantageously adopted when fashion does not forbid them.

XXX.

A very high head-dress would not be suitable for a very tall or short person; the latter may venture upon a higher dress than the former. A person with a short neck should be careful as to the sort of frill she wears, if she considers one necessary; while a person with a very long one may relieve the awkwardness of the appearance by judiciously adopting this article of dress.

XXXI.

A hostess should not dress so richly as when she is a guest: it is good taste in a lady not to appear to vie with her guests in the richness of her attire.

XXXII.

Be not ostentatious in the display of jewelry: if, however, you have superb jewelry, your dress and your establishment should harmonize therewith, or the world will either not give you credit for their real worth, or it will charge you with ostentatious extravagance.

XXXIII.

Never wear mosaic gold or paste diamonds; they are representatives of a mean ambition to appear what you are not, and most likely what you ought not to wish to be.

XXXIV.

Let your ornaments be, then, more remarkable for their intrinsic worth, and for the taste with which they are chosen and worn, than for profusion.

XXXV.

Ladies of good taste seldom wear jewelry in the morning, and when they do, confine themselves to trinkets of gold, or those in which opaque stones only are introduced. Ornaments with brilliant stones are unsuited for a morning costume.

XXXVI.

In large parties do not exhibit any remarkable anxiety for the care of your dress, nor, if an accident should happen thereto, exhibit peculiar or violent emotion; if you are so distraite, many will believe that you have exhibited the best portion of your wardrobe.

XXXVII.

Adapt your head-dress, or the style of your hair, to the character of your face. If you have your own maid, she will soon ascertain what style suits you best; if, however, you intrust to a friseur this important portion of your appearance, give him complete directions, or he will not regard the character of the physiognomy, but arrange your hair according to the last importation of blocks from Paris or London.

XXXVIII.

Gloves should harmonize with your dress; and must always be clean. Nothing can be more vulgar than high-coloured gloves: the primrose (and the white for evening parties) are the most elegant, if your dress will admit of their being worn.

XXXIX.

Perfumes are a necessary appendage to the toilet; let them be delicate, not powerful; the Atta of roses is the most elegant; the Heduesmia is at once fragrant and delicate. Many others may be named; but none must be patronized which are so obtrusive as to give the idea that they are not indulged in as a luxury but used from necessity.

XL.

Keep your finger-nails scrupulously clean, and avoid the disagreeable habit of allowing them to grow to an unnatural length.

XLI.

Singularity of dress and ostentatious ornament are by no means character-istic of a lady, but their adoption proves a primâ facie case against the wearer of being a nouveau riche striving after notoriety. Station and refinement of manner will make those vulgarisms bearable, or even pleasing; but the parties are then bearable or pleasing in spite of, not in consequence of them.

CONVERSATION,—TATTLING.

XLII.

CONVERSATION is a difficult art, but do not despair of acquiring it. It consists not so much in saying something different from the rest, but in extending the remarks of others; in being willing to please and be pleased; and in being attentive to what is said and to what is passing around you. Talking is not conversation, it is the manner of saying things which gives them their value.

XLIII.

One of the greatest requisites, also, is the art of listening discreetly. To listen is a delicate piece of flattery, and a compliment so gratifying as to surely recom-mend you.

XLIV.

Cultivate a soft tone of voice and a courteous mode of expression.

XLV.

It is better to say too little than too much in company: let your conversa-tion be consistent with your sex and age.

XLVI.

Cautiously avoid relating in one house any follies or faults you may hear or see in another.

XLVII.

Never converse with strangers or mere acquaintances upon family circum-stances or differences.

XLVIII.

Do not look for faults in the characters or habits of your friends—the crit-ic generally likes to communicate her opinions or discoveries—hence arises a habit of detraction.

XLIX.

Never encourage tattling or detraction; if there were no listeners this petty vice could not exist; besides, the habit of listening to this sort of gossip will soon induce you to participate, by similar communications.

L.

Abjure punning, and exercising even the most refined RAILLERY: the latter requires both observation and talent, and most people mistake satire for raillery; the one may be the offspring of a vicious, the former must be of an enlightened and benevolent mind.

LI.

Do not appear abstracted while another person is speaking; and never interrupt another by intruding a remark of your own.

LII.

Avoid pedantry and dogmatism. Be not obtrusively positive in the assertion of your opinions—modesty of speech, as well as manner, is highly ornamental in a woman.

LIII.

Double entendre is detestable in a woman, especially when perpetrated in the presence of men; no man of taste can respect a woman who is guilty of it: though it may create a laugh, it will inevitably excite also disgust in the minds of all whose good opinions are worth acquiring. Therefore not only avoid all indelicate expressions, but appear not to understand any that may be uttered in your presence.

LIV.

Rather be silent than talk nonsense, unless you have that agreeable art, possessed by some women, of investing little nothings with an air of grace and interest; this most enviable art is indeed very desirable in a hostess, as it often fills up disagreeable pauses, and serves as a prelude for the introduction of more intellectual matter.

LV.

Flattery is a powerful weapon in conversation; all are susceptible to it. It should be used skilfully, never direct, but inferred; better acted than uttered. Let it seem to be the unwitting and even the unwilling expression of genuine admiration, the honest expression of the feelings.

LVI.

Do not (except with a view to improvement) introduce subjects with which you are but superficially acquainted. If you should do so with the idea that all others present are equally or more ignorant than yourself, you may be very disagreeably undeceived, by some quiet, unpresuming person, who may have been listening to the development of your ignorance.

LVII.

Do not use the terms "genteel people;" "This, that, or the other, is very genteel." Substitute for them, "They are highly accomplished;" "he is a gentlemanly man;" "that has a gentlemanly appearance;" "she has the manners of a gentlewoman."

LVIII.

It is not good taste for a lady to say "Yes, Sir," and "No, Sir," to a gentleman, or frequently to introduce the word "Sir" at the end of her sentence, unless she desire to be exceedingly reserved toward the person with whom she is conversing.

LIX.

Do not introduce proverbs and cant phrases; a well educated lady can always find words to express her meaning, without resorting to these.

LX.

Never introduce your own affairs for the amusement of the company; such discussions cannot be interesting to others, and the probability is that the most patient listener is laying the foundation for some tale to make you appear ridiculous.

LXI.

It is not contrary to good-breeding to laugh in company, and even to laugh heartily when there is anything amusing going on; this is nothing more than being sociable. To remain prim and precise on such occasions, is sheer affectation. Avoid, however, what is called the "horse-laugh."

LXII.

Never laugh at your own remarks; it may be a very agreeable excitation, but it invariably spoils what you are saying.

LXIII.

If you are a wit, do not let your witty remarks engross the whole conversation, as it wounds the self-love of your hearers, who also wish to be heard, and becomes excessively fatiguing.

LXIV.

Do not address persons by the initial of their names; "Mrs. A. says this;" "Mrs. B. does that;" it is a mark of vulgarity.

VISITS.

LXV.

A LADY's visiting card should be of small size, glazed, but not gilt. It should be engraved in script characters, small and neat, not in German text or Old English. Never have your card printed; a written card, though passable, is not perfectly au fait. If you write them, never first draw a line across the card to guide you,—it betokens ill-breeding.

LXVI.

A morning call should not exceed from a quarter of an hour to twenty minutes in duration; the most proper time for such visits is between eleven and two o'clock; if your friends are people of fashion, from twelve to three will be the best hours.

LXVII.

If the persons called on be not at home, leave a card for each person to whom the visit was designed, or beg the servant to mention that you inquired for so many persons.

LXVIII.

The subjects for conversation should harmonize with the character of your visit, and prevent your introducing a gay conversation, when paying a visit of condolence; or subjects requiring deep thought, upon casual visits or calls of ceremony.

LXIX.

In making friendly calls almost all ceremony should be dispensed with. They are made at all hours, without much preparation or dressing.

LXX.

Visits of ceremony should be paid after a nearly similar interval has elapsed from when they were made. People in this way give you notice whether they wish to see you seldom or often.

LXXI.

Never display the visiting cards you may receive, by placing them in the frame of your looking-glass. It is usual to have an ornamental card-basket on the centre table.

LXXII.

If the person you call upon is preparing to go out, or to sit down at table, you ought, although asked to remain, to retire as soon as possible. The person visited so unseasonably, should on her part be careful to conceal her knowledge that the other wishes the visit ended quickly.

LXXIII.

Ceremonious visits should be short; if the conversation ceases without being again continued by the person you have come to see, and if she rises from her seat under any pretext whatever, custom requires you to make your salutation and withdraw. If other visitors are announced, you should leave soon after without saying much. If a letter is brought in, entreat your hostess to read it; she will probably not do so, and this circumstance will warn you to shorten your visit.

LXXIV.

A lady is at liberty to take either a gentleman or another lady to pay a morning visit to a friend, without asking permission; but she should never allow a gentleman the same liberty; if he desires to make any of his friends known to her, he must first ask if the acquaintance would be agreeable.

LXXV.

When a lady visits another for the first time, her visit should be returned within a week.

LXXVI.

If when paying an evening visit you should find a party assembled, enter as you would otherwise have done, but remain only a few minutes, and escape in as quiet a way as possible. Let it be known shortly after, in such a way that it will reach the family, that you were unaware of company being assembled.

LXXVII.

In calling upon a person staying at a hotel, if she is not at home add your address to your name, else your visit may be fruitless.

LXXVIII.

When about to be absent a long time, make your farewell visit short, announcing the fact; if necessary to leave your card, mark on it T. T. L. or P. P. C. When you return, those upon whom you have called will pay you the first visit; those whom you have neglected, will properly conclude the acquaintance is discontinued. If you are married while abroad, this is especially the case.

LXXIX.

Visits after a party or dinner should be paid within the week.

LXXX.

Upon the death of any member of a family with which you have associated, visits of condolence should not be personally made until after a week or two has elapsed.

RECEIVING VISITS.

LXXXI.

IN receiving morning visits, lay aside any employment in which you may be occupied; this will enable you to pay those little attentions, and to say those elegant but appropriate nothings, which make your guests immediately at home, and tend to the establishment of your character as one of the mode. When your visitors rise to depart, ring the bell for a servant to open the street door.

LXXXII.

Avoid all appearance of anxiety; yet let nothing escape your attention.

LXXXIII.

When visitors enter, rise immediately, advance toward them, and request them to be seated. If it is an elderly person, insist upon his occupying the arm-chair; if a lady, beg her to be seated on the sofa.

LXXXIV.

In winter the most honorable place is the corner of the fireplace; therefore, if a married lady enters, offer her that seat. If this place is occupied by a young lady, she ought to rise and offer her seat to the other, taking for herself a chair in another part of the room.

LXXXV.

In proportion as the visitor is a stranger, you will rise, and any persons already there, should do the same. If any withdraw, conduct them as far as the door of the parlor.

LXXXVI.

As hostess, in your attentions, consider all your guests equal; the greatest stranger or person of least rank should, if any, receive more attention than others.

LXXXVII.

If your guests are about to remain on a visit of any length, see before their arrival that their room is furnished with everything which can contribute to neatness, and their comfort. Congratulate them upon their arrival, and express the pleasure it gives you; inquire kindly about the incidents of their journey, and request them to make your house their home. Be assiduous in your attentions, and show them every object of interest about the house and neighborhood.

LXXXVIII.

If your guests express an intention of leaving you, affectionately endeavor to detain them; if not successful, renew your invitation for another visit, and express your regret at parting so soon.

LXXXIX.

The art of receiving company can only be acquired by education, experience, or close observation. Have a determination to act naturally, not hurried, and let a desire to please be a ruling principle; you will then generally act correctly.

THE BALL-ROOM.

XC.

INVITATIONS to a ball or evening party should be given in the lady's name, and answers to such invitations should be addressed to her. Cards of invitation are usually issued from one to three weeks previous to the entertainment.

XCI.

The hours for the arrival of the guests vary from nine to twelve o'clock: in this you will be guided by the usages of the circle in which you move.

XCII.

Never go early to a public ball; and do not be frequently seen at such. When you do attend, do not dance from the time you enter the room until you leave; it may leave the impression that you have few opportunities of dancing except at such balls.

XCIII.

As the fashion for a lady's dress for a ball is so constantly changing, it is impossible to prescribe. But we may remark, that the handkerchief should be "fine as a snowy cobweb," and perfumed just sufficiently to render it agreeable. Your gloves should be of white kid, your shoes small and fitting with the nicest exactness.

XCIV.

When you enter the drawing-room, immediately advance and pay your respects to the ladies of the house; until this is done, do not recognise any one you may know. If, as it sometimes happens, the lady is not in the room when you enter, though the position may be rather embarrassing if you do not meet any acquaintances, do not show that it is so, but enter into conversation with your partner or the lady nearest you, until the lady returns, when you immediately pay your respects; which should be a little more marked than when paying a morning visit.

XCV.

If possible, do not enter a room alone. If you have no brother or near relation, you may at any time request a gentleman of your acquaintance, who has not been invited by the lady of the house, to accompany you.

XCVI.

The lady of the house should dance, if at all, but little, unless there is a distinguished stranger present to whom it is desirable to pay a compliment. This is necessary, that you may be enabled to attend to your guests, and make the evening agreeable to them. If you do dance, you may select your partner, who should feel honored by the act.

XCVII.

If the hostess intends to dance, it is customary for her to open the ball: if she does not, the host opens it with the lady of the highest rank present.

XCVIII.

When a gentleman who has been properly introduced requests the honor of dancing with you, you will not refuse unless you have a previous engagement.

XCIX.

At the ordinary public balls, it is desirable to make up a party sufficiently large to render you independent of the introductions of the master of the cere- monies, as, in spite of his best efforts, objectionable individuals will gain access to such. When a party is thus formed, you can easily and without rudeness refuse to be introduced to any gentleman, by stating that you are engaged; as of course you would be to your friends for that evening.

C.

If a gentleman presumes to ask you to dance without an introduction, you will of course refuse. It is hardly necessary to supply the fair reader with words to repel such a rudeness; a man must have more than ordinary impertinence if he was not satisfied by your saying, "I must decline, sir, not having the honor of your acquaintance;" and recollect that his previous rudeness ought to be punished by your refusing to be introduced.

CI.

Draw on your gloves in the dressing-room, and do not take them off during the evening, except at supper-time, when it should be invariably done.

CII.

Let your dancing be quiet and unobtrusive; let your movements in the dance be characterized by elegance and gracefulness, rather than by activity and complexity of steps.

CIII.

In giving the hand for "ladies' chain," or any other figures, you should wear a smile, and accompany it with a polite inclination of the head in the manner of a salutation.

CIV.

Pay attention to the dance, but not so marked as to appear as if that atten- tion was necessary to prevent a mistake. A lively manner harmonizes with the scene; but, to preserve this, it is not necessary to be boisterous. Refinement of manners has, in woman, an unspeakable charm.

CV.

Recollect that your partner is for the time being your very humble servant, and that he will be honored by acquiescing in any of your wishes: for instance, you may wish to promenade, to walk from one room to another, to join your friends; you may require a jelly, ice, wine, or any other refreshment; your dress may have become disarranged; in short, he will feel honored by receiving your commands, and ought to anticipate your wishes on most of the above, and many more ordinary occasions. On no account be seen parading a ball-room by yourself.

CVI.

When you are dancing, you will consider yourself engaged to your partner, therefore not at liberty to hold a flirtation between the figures with some other gentleman.

CVII.

Do not mistake affectation for refinement: it would be no less an error than confounding vice with virtue.

CVIII.

Do not make a public room the arena for torturing any simple swain who perchance may admire you a little more than you deserve. Recollect that while you are wounding another's heart you may be trifling with your own peace.

CIX.

When you leave a party before the others, do so quietly and as little seen as possible; first making your parting curtsy to the ladies of the house, if convenient. During the week, make them a visit of thanks, at which you may converse of the pleasure of the ball, and the good selection of the company.

CX.

If you are engaged to a gentleman, do not let your attention be paid exclusively to him—the object of your love should alone perceive it.

CXI.

If you have accepted an invitation, do not fail to keep it unless for the most unavoidable reasons.

CXII.

The members of an invited family should not be seen conversing often together at a party.

MUSIC.

CXIII.

Never exhibit any particular anxiety to sing or to play. You may have a fine voice, have a brilliant instrumental execution; but your friends may by possibility neither admire nor appreciate either.

CXIV.

If you intend to sing, do not affect to refuse when asked, but at once accede. If you are a good singer, your prompt compliance will add to the pleasure of your friends, and to their regard; if you are not, the desire to amuse will have been evinced, and will be appreciated.

CXV.

Do not sing songs descriptive of masculine passion or sentiment; there is an abundance of superior songs for both sexes.

CXVI.

If you are singing second, do not drag on, nor as it were tread upon the heels of your prima; if you do not regard your friend's feelings, have mercy on your own reputation, for nine out of ten in every party will think you in the wrong, and those who know that you are singing in correct time, will believe you ill-natured or not sufficiently mistress of the song to wait upon your friend.

CXVII.

If playing an accompaniment to a singer, do not forget that your instrument is intended to aid, not to interrupt: that it is to be subordinate to the song.

CXVIII.

If nature has not given you a voice, do not attempt to sing, unless you have sufficient taste, knowledge, and judgment, to cover its defects by an accompaniment.

CXIX.

Never sing more than one or two songs consecutively.

CXX.

When at concerts or private parties where music is being performed, never converse, no matter how anxious you may be to do so, or how many persons you may see doing so; and refrain from beating time, humming the airs, applauding, or making ridiculous gestures of admiration.

THE DINNER-TABLE.

CXXI.

INVITATIONS to dinner must of course be answered to the lady. Cards of invitation to a dinner party are usually issued from three days to a fortnight previous to the entertainment; they should specify the hour of meeting. The proper number for such a party is somewhat in dispute: the happy medium may be considered ten.

CXXII.

As persons are necessarily introduced at a dinner party, only such persons as are known to each other, or who mutually desire to be acquainted should be invited, except under the circumstances alluded to in No. I.

CXXIII.

Be punctual to the hour appointed.

CXXIV.

When an invitation is accepted, let nothing but imperative necessity compel you to break the engagement, or at the last moment to send an excuse.

CXXV.

When your guests enter, present them to the others, and if any delay occur, let the conversation be light and on commonplace topics.

CXXVI.

It is usual for the host or hostess to point out to the gentlemen the ladies they are to conduct to the dining-room, according to some real or imaginary standard (age or distinction). If persons of distinction are present, it is desirable that this should be done—of course giving them precedence.

CXXVII.

The hostess follows her guests to the dining-room, the host having led the way with the lady of most consideration; the gentleman of the greatest distinction accompanies the hostess to the dining-room.

CXXVIII.

The hostess takes the head of the table: the seat of honor for a gentleman is at her right hand; for a lady, it is to the right of the host.

CXXIX.

Ladies do not wear gloves during dinner.

CXXX.

In the best houses, the operation of carving is performed at the side tables; i. e. the principal joint, or joints, which require strength in the operation, are there carved.

CXXXI.

Table napkins are indispensable at the dinner table; and silver forks are now met with in almost every respectable house. Steel forks, except for carving, are now seldom placed upon the dinner table.

CXXXII.

It is usual to commence with soup, which never refuse; if you do not eat it, you can toy with it until it is followed by fish; of either of which never take more than once.

CXXXIII.

When all are seated, send a plate of soup to every one. Do not ask any one if they will be helped, as every one takes it, of course.

CXXXIV.

Always feed yourself with the fork; a knife is only used as a divider. Use a dessert spoon in eating tarts, puddings, curries, &c., &c.

CXXXV.

If what you are eating before the dessert has any liquid, sop the bread and then raise it to the mouth. For articles of the dessert having liquid, a spoon is usually provided.

CXXXVI.

In helping sauce or vegetables, place them upon the side of the viands on the plate.

CXXXVII.

If anything is sent you from the host or hostess, do not offer it to any other person; and when helped do not wait until others are served, but at once arrange your napkin, and proceed to the important business of the moment.

CXXXVIII.

In helping a joint, do not overload a person's plate; and if game, or any particularly select dish is placed before you, serve it with discretion.

CXXXIX.

In helping, wherever a spoon can be conveniently used, it is preferable to the use of a knife and fork.

CXL.

Fish must be helped with a fish slice: you may carve it more dexterously by taking a spoon in your left hand.

CXLI.

Soup must be eaten from the side, not the point of the spoon; and, in eating it, be careful not to make a noise, by strongly inhaling the breath: this habit is excessively vulgar; you cannot eat too quietly.

CXLII.

In helping soup, recollect that a little more than a ladle full is sufficient.

CXLIII.

As hostess, do not press people to eat more than they appear inclined to take, nor force upon them any particular dish which you may think super-excellent. If any difficulty occurs in carving, you should feel no diffidence in requesting the gentleman to your right or left to assist you: it is a part of their duty and privilege.

CXLIV.

Do not ask any one at the table to help you to anything, but apply to the servant.

CXLV.

The hostess should never send away her plate until all the guests have finished.

CXLVI.

When you send your plate for anything, leave your knife and fork upon it. When you have done, place both together on one side of the plate.

CXLVII.

Servants wait at table in white gloves, or have a fine napkin in their hand, which prevents its contact with your plate.

CXLVIII.

Finger-glasses come on with the dessert; wet a corner of your napkin and wipe your mouth; then immerse your fingers in the water and dry them with the napkin.

CXLIX.

As hostess, you will give the signal for retiring by rising from the table. The time for so doing varies in different companies, and must be left to your discretion.

CL.

Should your servants break anything while you are at table, do not appear to notice it. If they betray stupidity or awkwardness, avoid reprimanding them publicly, as it only draws attention to their errors, and adds to their embarrassment.

CLI.

During the week which follows the entertainment, each of the guests owes a visit to the entertainer. Converse about the dinner, the pleasure you have enjoyed, and of the persons whom you have met there.

CLII.

The mistress of the house should never appear to pride herself regarding what is on her table, nor confuse herself with apologies for the bad cheer which she may offer you; it is much better for her to observe silence in this respect, and leave it to her guests to pronounce eulogiums on the dinner.

CLIII.

Ladies should not leave the table before the end of the entertainment, unless from urgent necessity. If it is a married lady, she requests some one to accompany her; if unmarried, she goes with her mother.

COURTSHIP AND MARRIAGE.

CLIV.

WHEN about to be married send your card with the gentleman's in an envelope to the circle which you intend to visit. They are usually sent by your connexions, or your bridesmaid and groomsman, with your assistance. The lady's should have engraved on it: "At home, ——, —th inst. at — o'clock." They should be sent at least one week previous.

CLV.

The styles of card and envelope are so varied that none are more fashionable than others. The cards are sometimes united by a white ribbon, or silken cord.

CLVI.

After marriage you need not retain the whole of your previous acquaintance; those only to whom you send cards are for the future, considered in the circle of your visiting acquaintance. The bridegroom selects those persons among his former associates whom he wishes to retain as such.

CLVII.

When the married pair receive company call upon them, offer your compliments, and wish them much happiness in their new sphere. Address the bride first. Do not remain longer than a few minutes, unless it is an evening party; when, after paying your respects, mingle with the rest of the company. Retire early from a wedding party.

CLVIII.

Newly married persons should abstain in public from every mark of affection too conspicuous, and every exclusive attention.

SERVANTS.

CLIX.

Do not imagine that you will increase your importance by hauteur to your own or to other people's servants.

CLX.

At the house of your friend always preface your request to a servant by the words, "I would thank you for so and so;" and do not omit the usual courtesy on receiving it.

CLXI.

Do not scold your servants; you had better turn them away at once. When they need reproof, give them it in a calm, dignified, and firm manner; but on no account, if you can possibly avoid it, find fault with them in the presence of strangers, even though they should let fall the tray with your best set of china upon it.

CLXII.

If you have only one servant, speak of her by her Christian name; if you have more, talk of them by the names of their offices, such as nurse, cook, housemaid, footman, &c., but always address them by their Christian names.

LETTERS AND NOTES.

CLXIII.

In writing, endeavor to make your style clear, concise, elegant, and appropriate for all subjects. Avoid repetitions, erasures, insertions, omissions, and confusion of ideas, or labored construction. If your letter is to an equal or friend, these blemishes may remain; if otherwise, it must be commenced again.

CLXIV.

To write on very coarse paper is allowable only for the most indigent; to use gilt-edged and perfumed paper for letters of business, would be ridiculous. The very best paper, but plain or without much ornament, is most to be recommended.

CLXV.

It is extremely impolite to write upon a single leaf of paper, even if it is a billet; it should always be double, although we write only two or three lines. Envelopes are now used almost as much as the paper itself is.

CLXVI.

Use a lofty style towards persons to whom you owe respect; an easy, trifling, or even jesting style toward a friend, and a courteous style toward one another generally.

CLXVII.

The date is often necessary to the understanding of many passages of your letter, therefore never omit it. It may be put at the right hand of the commencement of the letter, if writing to an equal; but in writing to a superior, it should be at the end, in order that the title at the head of the letter may be entirely alone.

CLXVIII.

Seal your communications with wax: bronze or other colors are more suitable than red; use black wax when in mourning. Let the seal be small; large ones are in very bad taste.

CLXIX.

Ceremonious notes and social letters should always be in the third person, and of course not signed.

CLXX.

Letters of introduction should be concise and brief, and enclosed in an envelope, unsealed.

FUNERALS.

CLXXI.

WHEN any of your acquaintances are deceased, be at the house at not quite an hour after the time specified, as the procession moves exactly one hour after the time announced.

CLXXII.

It is optional whether you go to the grave or not; it is customary now, to go merely to the house, until the procession has moved, when you are at liberty to return to your ordinary pursuits.

CLXXIII.

Returning cards "of thanks" after a death for visits of condolence, implies that the bereaved parties are prepared to receive visitors; it must, therefore, be with them entirely a matter of feeling, as to how soon it is done.

CARDS.

CLXXIV.

NEVER be too punctilious and exacting with regard to the penalties incurred through mistakes.

CLXXV.

Lose without any exhibition of ill-humor, and win without any symptoms of exultation.

CLXXVI.

Never lose your temper at cards, and avoid the exhibition of anxiety or of vexation at want of success. If you are playing whist, not only keep your temper, but hold your tongue; any intimation to your partner is not ladylike.

CLXXVII.

Women should never play, unless they can retain the command of their temper. She who wishes to win a heart or retain one, should never permit her admirers to behold her at cards, as the anxiety they produce is as destructive to beauty as to sentiment.

PRESENTS.

CLXXVIII.

Ladies' gifts to gentlemen should be of the most refined nature possible; little articles not purchased, but those deriving a priceless value as being the offering of their gentle skill, such as a trifle from their needle, or a picture from their pencil. But such offerings, though invaluable among friends, are not used on occasions of ceremony.

CLXXIX.

In the eyes of persons of delicacy, presents are of no worth, except from the manner in which they are bestowed. Strive, then, to give them this value.

CLXXX.

Never give away a present which you have received from another; or at least, so arrange it, that it may never be known.

CLXXXI.

Endeavor always to present an article which the recipient has not. This in many cases may be difficult; but where it is possible, it should always be done. I have known gentlemen to receive half a dozen purses, only one of which did they use.

GENERAL OBSERVATIONS.

CLXXXII.

In entering any public room with a gentleman, let him precede you and obtain a seat.

CLXXXIII.

If at another's house you should break anything, do not appear to notice it. Your hostess, if a lady, would take no notice of the calamity, nor say, as is sometimes done by ill-bred persons, "Oh! it is of no consequence."

CLXXXIV.

Do not beat the "devil's tattoo," by drumming with your fingers on a table. Never read in an audible whisper; it disturbs those near you.

CLXXXV.

You should never take the arms of two gentlemen, one being upon either side.

CLXXXVI.

A lady ought not to present herself alone in a library or museum, unless she goes there to study or work as an artist.

CLXXXVII.

Perfect order, exquisite neatness and elegance, which easily dispense with being sumptuous, ought to mark the entrance of the house, the furniture, and the dress of the lady.

CLXXXVIII.

The most obvious mark of good breeding and good taste is a sensitive regard for the feelings of others.

CLXXXIX.

Dean Swift, I think, remarks, that good breeding does not consist so much in the observance of particular forms, as in bringing the dictates of refined sense and taste to bear upon the ordinary occurrences of life.

THE END.

THE LADIES' GUIDE TO TRUE POLITENESS AND PERFECT MANNERS;

OR,

MISS LESLIE'S BEHAVIOUR BOOK

A GUIDE AND MANUAL FOR LADIES, AS REGARDS THEIR

CONVERSATION; MANNERS; DRESS; INTRODUCTIONS; ENTRE TO SOCIETY; SHOPPING; CONDUCT IN THE STREET; AT PLACES OF AMUSEMENT; IN TRAVELING; AT THE TABLE, EITHER AT HOME, IN COMPANY, OR AT HOTELS; DEPORTMENT IN GENTLEMEN'S SOCIETY; LIPS; COMPLEXION; TEETH; HANDS; THE HAIR; ETC., ETC.

WITH FULL INSTRUCTIONS AND ADVICE IN

LETTER WRITING; RECEIVING PRESENTS; INCORRECT WORDS; BORROWING; OBLIGATIONS TO GENTLEMEN; OFFENCES; CHILDREN; DECORUM IN CHURCH; AT EVENING PARTIES; AND SUGGESTIONS IN BAD PRACTICES AND HABITS EASILY CONTRACTED, WHICH NO YOUNG LADY SHOULD BE GUILTY OF, ETC., ETC.

BY MISS LESLIE
AUTHOR OF "MISS LESLIE'S CELEBRATED NEW COOKERY BOOK," "MISS LESLIE'S NEW RECEIPTS FOR COOKING," ETC.

PREFACE.

IT IS SAID THAT SOON AFTER the publication of Nicholas Nickleby, not fewer than six Yorkshire schoolmasters (or rather six principals of Yorkshire institutes) took journeys to London, with the express purpose of prosecuting Dickens for libels—"each one and severally" considering himself shown up to the world as Mr. Squeers of Dotheboys Hall.

Now, if Dickens had drawn as graphic a picture of Dothe*girls* Hall, we firmly believe that none of the lady principals of similar institutes would have committed themselves by evincing so little tact, and adopting such impolitic proceedings. They would wisely have held back from all appropriation of the obnoxious character, and passed it over unnoticed; as if it could not possibly have the slightest reference to *them*.

Therefore we wish that those of our fair readers whom certain hints in the following pages may awaken to the consciousness of a few habitual misbehavements, (of which they were not previously aware,) should pause, and reflect, before they allow themselves to "take umbrage too much." Let them keep in mind that the purpose of the writer is to amend, and not to offend; to improve her young countrywomen, and not to annoy them. It is with this view only that she has been induced to "set down in a note-book" such lapses from *les bienséances* as she has remarked during a long course of observation, and on a very diversified field.

She trusts that her readers will peruse this book in as friendly a spirit as it was written.

ELIZA LESLIE.

CHAPTER I.
SUGGESTIONS TO VISITERS.

AN AMUSING WRITER OF THE LAST century, justly complains of the want of definite words to express, distinctly and unmistakably, the different degrees of visits, with reference to their length. Whether the stay of the guest comprises ten minutes, an hour, an evening, a day, a week, or a month, still it goes under the vague and general term of a visit.

We propose, humourously, that if the stay of the guest exceeds a week, it should be called "a visitation." If it includes a dining, or a tea-drinking, or evening-spending, it may be termed "a visit;" while a mere call can be mentioned as "a vis."

The idea is a very convenient one, and we should like to see it carried out by general adoption. Meanwhile, we must, for the present, be contented with the old uncertain practice of saying only "visit" and "visiter." We think it our duty to explain that this chapter is designed for the benefit of such inexperienced females as may be about to engage in what we should like to call "a visitation."

To begin at the beginning:—

Do not *volunteer* a visit to a friend in the country, or in another town, unless you have had what is called "a standing invitation," with every reason to believe that it was sincerely and cordially given. Many invitations are mere "words of course," without meaning or motive, designed only to make a show of politeness, and not intended to be taken literally, or ever acted upon. Even when convinced that your friend is really your friend, that she truly loves you, has invited you in all sincerity, and will be happy in your society, still, it is best to apprize her, duly, of the exact day and hour when she may expect you; always with the proviso that it is convenient to herself to receive you at that time, and desiring her to let you know, candidly, if it is not. However close your intimacy, an unexpected arrival may possibly produce inconvenience to your hostess; particularly if her family is numerous, or her bedchambers few. The case is somewhat different, where the house is large, and where there is no scarcity of apartments for guests, of servants to wait on them, or of money to furnish the means of entertaining them liberally. But even then, the time of arrival should be previously intimated, and observed as punctually as possible. Such are now the facilities of travelling, and the rapidity of transmitting intelligence, that there is no excuse for unexpected or ill-timed visits; and when unexpected, they are too frequently ill-timed. When attempted as "agreeable surprises," they are seldom very agreeable to the surprised. Also the improvement in manners has rendered these incursions old-fashioned and ungenteel. Above all, never volunteer visits to families whose circumstances are so narrow that they can ill afford the expense of a guest.

Having received an invitation, reply to it immediately; and do not keep your friends waiting, day after day, in uncertainty whether you mean to accept or decline it; causing them, perhaps, to delay asking other visiters till they have ascertained if you are to be expected or not.

Excuse yourself from accepting invitations from persons whom you do not like, and whose dispositions, habits, feelings, and opinions are in most things the reverse of your own. There can be no pleasure in daily and familiar intercourse where there is no congeniality. Such visits never end well; and they sometimes produce irreconcilable quarrels, or at least a lasting and ill-concealed coolness. Though for years you may have always met on decent terms, you may become positive enemies from living a short time under the same roof; and there is something dishonourable in laying yourself under obligations and receiving civilities from persons whom you secretly dislike, and in whose society you can have little or no enjoyment.

When you arrive, take occasion to mention how long you intend to stay; that your hostess may plan her arrangements accordingly. It is rude and inconsiderate to keep her in ignorance of the probable duration of your visit. And when the allotted time has expired, do not be persuaded to extend it farther, unless you are earnestly, and with undoubted sincerity invited to do so. It is much better that your friends should part with you reluctantly, than you should give them reason to wish your visit shorter. Even if it *has* been very pleasant on both sides, it may not continue so if prolonged too far. Take care of wearing out your welcome. Besides, your room may be wanted for another guest.

On your first evening, enquire the hours of the house, that you may always be ready to comply with them. Rise early enough to be washed and dressed in time for breakfast; but if you are ready too early, remain in your own apartment, or walk about the garden, or go to the library till the cleaning and arranging of the sitting-room has been completed. Meanwhile, you can occupy yourself with a book, if you stay in your own room.

As soon as you quit your bed, take off the bedclothes, (each article separately,) and spread them widely over the chairs, turning the mattrass or bed as far down as it will go. This will give the bedding time to air; and in all houses it should be done every morning, the whole year round. Before you leave the room, raise the windows as high as they will go, (unless it should be raining, or snowing,) that the apartment may be well ventilated. Fortunate are those who have been accustomed to sleeping always with the sash more or less open, according to the weather, or the season. Their health will be much the better for the excellent practice of constantly admitting fresh air into their sleeping-room. See Dr. Franklin's essay on the "Art of Sleeping Well." Mr. Combe, who has written copiously on this subject, says it not only improves the health, but the complexion; and that ladies who follow this practice continue to look young long after those who sleep in close rooms have faded and shrivelled. Except in a very unhealthy climate, or in the neighbourhood of marshes, no external air can be so unwholesome, or productive of such baneful effects on the constitution, as the same air breathed over and over again in a close room, and returning continually to the lungs, till before morning it becomes unfit to be breathed at all. Sleeping with the windows closed in a room newly painted has produced fatal diseases. To some lungs the vapour of white lead is poisonous. To none is it quite innoxious. Its dangerous properties may be neutralized by placing in newly-painted rooms, large tubs of water, into each of which has been mixed an ounce of vitriol. The tubs must be set near the walls, and the water and vitriol renewed every day. The introduction of zinc-paint promises to put that of white lead out of use; as zinc is quite as cheap, and not at all pernicious to health.

At sleeping hours the air of a bedroom should be perfectly free from all scents, either pleasant or otherwise. Many persons cannot sleep with flowers in their chamber, or with any sort of perfume. It is best not.

If when on a visit, you find that the chambermaid does not make your bed so that you can sleep comfortably, show her how to do it, (privately,) but say nothing to your hostess. There is but one way of making a bed properly; and yet it is surprising how little that way is known or remembered. First, shake up the bed high and evenly; turning it over, and see that the foot is not higher than the head. If there is a mattrass above the bed, turn the mattrass half up, and then half down, till you have shaken up the bed beneath. Next spread on the under-sheet, laying it well over the bolster to secure it from dragging down and getting under the shoulders. However, to most beds now, there is a bolster-case. Then tuck in the under-sheet, well, at both sides, to prevent its getting loose and disordered in the night. For the same reason tuck in the upper-sheet, well, at the foot, leaving the sides loose. Tuck in the blankets at bottom, but not at the sides. Lay the counterpane smoothly over the whole. Turn it down at the top; and turn down the upper-sheet above it, so as to conceal the blankets entirely.

Should the chambermaid neglect your room, or be remiss in filling your pitchers, or in furnishing you with clean towels, speak to her on the subject when alone. She will hardly, for her own sake, inform her mistress that you have had occasion to find fault with her; unless she is very insolent or sulky, she will say she is sorry, and will promise to do better in future. Complaining to her mistress of these neglects will probably give offence to the lady, who may be of that wayward (though too common) disposition which will allow no one except herself, to find any deficiency in *her* servants. As mistresses are frequently very touchy on these points, your hostess may hint that your statement is incredible, and that "no one ever complained before." Above all things, avoid letting her know that you have found or felt insects in your bed; a circumstance that may chance sometimes to happen even in the best kept houses. In a warm climate, or in an old house, the utmost care and the most vigilant neatness cannot always prevent it. It may be caused by the bringing of baggage from boats, or ships, and by servants neglecting their own beds; a too common practice with them, unless the mistress or her housekeeper compels them to be cleanly, and sees that they are so.

If you have proof positive that your bed is not free from these intolerable nuisances, confide this fact to the chambermaid only, and desire her to attend to it speedily. She will do so the more readily, if you promise her a reward in case of complete success. Enjoining her to manage this as quietly as possible, and to say nothing about it to any one, may spare you a scene with your hostess; who, though you have always regarded her as your warm friend, may, notwithstanding, become your enemy for life, in consequence of your having presumed to be incommoded in *her* house, where "nobody ever complained before." A well-bred, sensible, good-tempered woman will not, of course, take offence for such a cause; and will believe that there must have been good reason for the complaint, rather than suppose that her guest and her friend would mention so delicate a subject even to a servant, unless there was positive proof. And she will rightly think it was well to make it known, and have it immediately remedied. But all women who invite friends to visit them, are not sensible and good-tempered. Therefore, take care.

For similar reasons, should a servant purloin any article belonging to you, (and servants, considered quite honest, will sometimes pilfer from a visiter when they would not dare to do so from their mistress,) it is safest to pass it over, unless the article stolen is of consequence. You may find your hostess very unwilling to believe that a servant of *hers* could possibly be dishonest; and much may be said, or evidently *thought*, that will be very painful to you, her guest.

Notwithstanding all that may be said to you about "feeling yourself perfectly at home," and "considering your friend's house as your own," be very careful not literally to do so. In fact, it is impossible you *should* with any propriety—particularly, if it is your first visit. You cannot possibly know the real character and disposition of any acquaintance, till after you have had some experience in living under the same roof. If you find your hostess all that you can desire, and that she is making your visit every way agreeable, be very grateful to her, and let her understand that you are exceedingly happy at her house; but avoid staying too long, or taxing her kindness too highly.

Avoid encroaching unreasonably upon her time. Expect her not to devote an undue portion of it to you. She will probably be engaged in the superintendence of household affairs, or in the care of her young children, for two or three hours after breakfast. So at these hours do not intrude upon her,—but amuse yourself with some occupation of your own, till you see that it is convenient to the family for you to join them in the sitting-room. In summer afternoons, retire for an hour or more, soon after dinner, to your own apartment, that you may give your friends an opportunity of taking their naps, and that you may do the same yourself. You will be brighter in the evening, from indulging in this practice; and less likely to feel sleepy, when you ought to be wide awake, and ready to assist in entertaining your entertainers. A silent visiter, whether silent from dulness or indolence, or a habit of taciturnity, is never an agreeable one.

Yet, however pleasant the conversation, have sufficient self-denial to break off in seasonable time, so as not to keep the family up by continuing in the parlour till a late hour. Some of them may be tired and sleepy, though you are not. And between ten and eleven o'clock it is well to retire.

If you have shopping to do, and are acquainted with the town, you can be under no necessity of imposing on any lady of the family the task of accompanying you. To shop *for* others, or *with* others, is a most irksome fatigue. Even when a stranger in the place, you can easily, by enquiring of the family, learn where the best stores are to be found, and go to them by yourself.

While you are a guest at the house of a friend, do not pass too much of your time in visiting at *other* houses, unless she is with you. You have no right to avail yourself of the conveniences of eating and sleeping at her mansion, without giving her and her family the largest portion of your company.

While a guest yourself, it is taking an unwarrantable liberty to invite any of your friends or relatives to come there and spend a day or days.*

Refrain from visiting any person with whom your hostess is at enmity, even if that person has been one of your own intimate friends. You will in all probability be regarded as "a spy in the camp." There is nothing so difficult as to observe a strict neutrality; and on hearing both sides, it is scarcely possible not to lean more to the one than to the other. The friend whose hospitality you

---

* So it is to order the carriage without first asking permission of your hostess.

are enjoying will soon begin to look coldly upon you, if she finds you seeking the society of her enemy; and she may evince that coldness whenever you come home from these visits. However unjust her suspicions, it is too probable she may begin to think that you are drawn in to make her, and her house, and family, subjects of conversation when visiting her adversary; therefore, she will cease to feel kindly toward you. If you understand, soon after your arrival, that there is no probability of a reconciliation, send at once a concise note to the lady with whom your hostess is at variance; express your regret at the circumstance, and excuse yourself from visiting her while you remain in your present residence. This note should be polite, short, and decisive, and so worded as to give no offence to either side; for, before sending, it is proper for you to show it, while yet unsealed, to the friend with whom you are staying. And then let the correspondence be carried no further. The lady to whom it is addressed, will, of course, return a polite answer; such as you may show to your hostess.

It is to be presumed, she will not be so lost to all delicacy and propriety, as to intrude herself into the house of her enemy for the purpose of visiting you. But, if she does, it is your place civilly to decline seeing her. A slight coolness, a mere offence on a point of etiquette, which, if let alone, would die out like a tinder-spark, has been fanned, and blown into a flame by the go-betweening of a so-called *mutual friend*. We repeat, while you are a visiter at a house, hold no intercourse with any foe of that house. It is unkind and disrespectful to the family with whom you are staying, and very unsafe for yourself.

If you know that your friends are hurried with their sewing, or with preparations for company, offer to assist them, as far as you can. But if you are conscious of an incapacity to do such things well, it is better to excuse yourself by candidly saying so, than to attempt them and spoil them. At the same time, express your willingness to learn, if permitted. And you *may* learn, while staying at the house of a clever, notable friend, many things that you have hitherto had no opportunity of acquiring.

When called on by any of your own acquaintances, they will not expect you to ask them to stay to tea, or to dinner. That is the business of your hostess—not yours.

If you are a young lady that has beaux, remember that you have no right to encourage the over-frequency of their visits in any house that is not your home, or to devote much of your time and attention to flirtation with them. Above all, avoid introducing to the family of your entertainers, young men whom they are likely in any respect to disapprove. No stranger who has the feelings of a gentleman, will make a *second* visit to any house unless he is invited by the head of the family, and he will take care that his visits shall not begin too early, or continue too late. However delightful he may find the society of his lady-fair, he has no right to incommode the family with whom she is staying, by prolonging his visits to an unseasonable hour. If he seems inclined to do so, there is nothing amiss in his fair-one herself hinting to him that it is past ten o'clock. Also, there should be "a temperance" even in his morning calls. It is rude in a young lady and gentleman to monopolize one of the parlours nearly all the forenoon—even if they are *really* courting—still more if they are only pretending to court; for instance, sitting close to each other, and whispering on subjects that might be discussed aloud before the whole house, and talked of across the room.

Young ladies noted for abounding in beaux, are generally rather inconvenient visiters; except in very spacious houses, and in gay, idle families. They should not take the liberty of inviting the said beaux to stay to dinner or to tea. Leave that civility to the head of the house,—without whose invitation no *gentleman* ought to remain.

It is proper for visiters to put out and pay for their own washing, ironing, &c. Therefore, carry among your baggage two clothes-bags; one to be taken away by the laundress, the other to receive your clothes in the interval. You may always hear of a washerwoman, by enquiring of the servants of the house.

On no consideration question the servants, or talk to them about the family, particularly if they are slaves.

Take with you a small writing-case, containing whatever stationery you may be likely to want during your visit; including post-office stamps. Thus you will spare yourself, and spare the family, the inconvenience of applying to them whenever you have occasion for pen, ink, paper, &c. If you have no ink with you, the first time you go out, stop in at a stationer's store, and buy a small sixpenny bottle that will stand steadily alone, and answer the purpose of an inkstand. Also, take care to be well supplied with all sorts of sewing articles. There are young ladies who go from home on long visits, quite unprovided with even thimbles and scissors; depending all the time on borrowing. Many visiters, though very agreeable in great things, are exceedingly troublesome in little ones.

Take care not to slop your washing-stand, or to lay a piece of wet soap upon it. Spread your wet towels carefully on the towel-rail. See that your trunks are not placed so near the wall as to injure the paper or paint when the lid is thrown back.

If, when travelling, you are to stop but one night at the house of a friend, it is not necessary, for that one night, to have *all* your baggage carried up-stairs, particularly if your trunks are large or heavy. Before leaving home, put into your carpet-bag all the things you will require for that night; and then no other article of your baggage need be taken up to your chamber. They can be left down-stairs, in some safe and convenient place, which your hostess will designate. This will save much trouble, and preclude all the injury that may otherwise accrue to the banisters and staircase-wall, by the corners of trunks knocking against them. It is possible to put into a carpet-satchel (that can be carried in your own hand) a night-gown and night-cap, (tightly rolled,) with hair-brush, combs, tooth-brush, &c. It is surprising how much these hand-satchels may be made to contain, when packed closely. No lady or gentleman should travel without one. In going from home for one night only, a satchel is, frequently, all that is requisite.

On concluding your visit, tell your entertainers that it has been pleasant, and express your gratitude for the kindness you have received from them, and your hope that they will give you an opportunity of returning their civilities. Give a parting gratuity to each of the servants—the sum being according to your means, and to the length of your visit. Give this to each servant *with your own hands*, going to them for the purpose. Do not tempt their integrity, by intrusting (for instance) to the chambermaid the fee intended for the cook. She may dishonestly keep it to herself, and make the cook believe that you were "so mean as to go away without leaving any thing at all for her." Such things have happened, as we know. Therefore, give all your fees in person.

After you get home, write very soon (within two or three days) to the friend at whose house you have been staying, tell her of your journey, &c., and allude to your visit as having been very agreeable.

The visit over, be of all things careful not to repeat any thing that has come to your knowledge in consequence, and which your entertainers would wish to remain unknown. While inmates of their house, you may have unavoidably become acquainted with some particulars of their way of living not general-ly known, and which, perhaps, would not raise them in public estimation, if disclosed. Having been their guest, and partaken of their hospitality, you are bound in honour to keep silent on every topic that would injure them in the smallest degree, if repeated. Unhappily, there are ladies so lost to shame, as, after making a long visit, to retail for the amusement of their cronies, all sorts of in-vidious anecdotes concerning the family at whose house they have been staying; adding by way of corroboration—"I assure you this is all true, for I stayed five or six weeks at their house, and had a good chance of knowing." More shame then to tell it!

Whatever painful discoveries are made during a visit, should be kept as closely secret as if secrecy was enjoined by oath. It is not sufficient to refrain from "mentioning names." No clue should be given that could possibly enable the hearers even to hazard a guess.

CHAPTER II.
THE VISITED.

Having invited a friend to pass a few days or weeks at your house, and expecting her at a certain time, send a carriage to meet her at the rail-road depôt or the steamboat wharf, and if her host or hostess goes in it, so much the better; but do not take the children along, crowding the vehicle, for the sake of giving them a ride. Arriving at your house, have her baggage taken at once to the apartment prepared for her, and when she goes up-stairs, send a servant with her to unstrap her trunks. Then let her be left *alone* to arrange her dress. It is to be supposed that before her arrival, the mistress of the house has inspected the chamber of her guest, to see that all is right—that there are *two* pitchers full of fresh water on the stand, and three towels on the rail, (two fine and one coarse,) with a china mug for teeth-cleaning, and a tumbler to drink from; a slop jar of course, and a foot-bath. We conclude that in all genteel and well-furnished houses, none of these articles are wanting in every bedroom. On the mantel-piece a candle or lamp, with a box of lucifer matches beside it—the candle to be replaced by a new one every morning when the chambermaid arranges the room—or the lamp to be trimmed daily; so that the visiter may have a light at hand whenever she pleases, without ringing the bell and waiting till a servant brings one up.

By-the-bye, when a guest is expected, see previously that the bells and locks of her room are in order; and if they are not, have them repaired.

If it is cold weather, let her find a good fire in her room; and the shutters open, that she may have sufficient light. Also an extra blanket, folded, and laid on the foot of the bed. If summer, let the sashes be raised, and the shutters bowed. The room should have an easy chair with a heavy foot-cushion before it,—a low chair also, to sit on when shoes and stockings are to be changed, and feet washed. In a spare chamber there should be both a mattrass and a feather-bed, that your visiters may choose which they will have uppermost. Though you and all your own family may like to sleep hard, your guests may find it difficult to sleep at all on a mattrass with a paillasse under it. To many constitutions hard sleeping is not only intolerable, but pernicious to health.

Let the centre-table be furnished with a writing-case well supplied with all that is necessary, the inkstand filled, and with *good black ink*; and some sheets of letter-paper and note-paper laid near it. Also, some books, such as you think your friend will like. Let her find, at least, one bureau vacant; *all* the drawers empty, so that she may be able to unpack her muslins, &c., and arrange them at once. The same with the wardrobe or commode, so that she may have space to hang up her dresses—the press-closet, likewise, should be for her use while she stays.

By giving up the spare bedroom *entirely* to your visiter you will very much oblige her, and preclude the necessity of disturbing or interrupting her by coming in to get something out of drawers, closets, &c.

Every morning, after the chambermaid has done her duty, (the room of the visiter is the first to be put in order,) the hostess should go in to see that all is right. This done, no further inspection is necessary for that day. There are ladies who, when a friend is staying with them, are continually slipping into her chamber when she is out of it, to see if the guest has done nothing amiss—such as moving a chair to suit her own convenience, or opening a shutter to let in more light, at the possible risk of hastening imperceptibly the fading of the carpet. There are families who condemn themselves to a perpetual twilight, by living in the dimness of closed shutters, to the great injury of their eyes. And this is endured to retard awhile the fading of furniture too showy for comfort. We have seen staircase-windows kept always shut and bolted, (so that visiters had to grope their way in darkness,) lest the small portion of stair-carpet just beneath the window should fade before the rest.

It is not pleasant to be a guest in a house where you perceive that your hostess is continually and fretfully on the watch, lest some almost imperceptible injury should accrue to the furniture. We have known ladies who were always uneasy when their visiters sat down on a sofa or an ottoman, and could not forbear inviting them to change their seats and take chairs. We suppose the fear was that the more the damask-covered seats were used, the sooner they would wear out. Let no visiter be so rash as to sit on a pier-divan with her back near a mirror. The danger is imminent—not only of breaking the glass by inadvertently leaning against it, but of certainly fretting its owner, with uneasiness, all the time. Children should be positively interdicted taking these precarious seats.

It is very kind and considerate to enquire of your guest if there is any dish, or article of food that she particularly likes, so that you may have it on the table while she stays; and also, if there is any thing peculiarly disagreeable to her, so that you may refrain from having it during her visit. A well-bred and sensible woman will not encroach upon your kindness, or take an undue advantage of it, in this respect or any other.

For such deficiencies as may be avoided or remedied, refrain from making the foolish apology that you consider her "no stranger"—and that you regard her "just as one of the family." If you invite her at all, it is your duty, for your own sake as well as hers, to treat her well in every thing. You will lose nothing by doing so.

If she desires to assist you in sewing, and has brought no work of her own, you may avail yourself of her offer, and employ her in moderation—but let it be in moderation only, and when sitting in the family circle. When alone in her own room, she, of course, would much rather read, write, or occupy herself in some way for her own benefit, or amusement. There are ladies who seem to expect that their guests should perform as much work as hired seamstresses.

Let the children be strictly forbidden to run into the apartments of visiters. Interdict them from going thither, unless sent with a message; and then let them be made to understand that they are always to knock at the door, and not go in till desired to do so. Also, that they are not to play and make a noise in the neighbourhood of her room. And when she comes into the parlour, that they are not to jump on her lap, put their hands into her pockets, or rummage her work-basket, or rumple and soil her dress by clinging to it with their hands. Neither should they be permitted to amuse themselves by rattling on the lower keys when she is playing on the piano, or interrupt her by teazing her all the time to play "for them to dance." All this we have seen, and the mothers have never checked it. To permit children to ask visiters for pennies or sixpences is mean and contemptible. And, if money *is* given them by a guest, they should be made to return it immediately.

Enquire on the first evening, if your visiter is accustomed to taking any refreshment before she retires for the night. If she is, have something sent up to her room every night, unless your own family are in the same habit. Then let sufficient for all be brought into the parlour. These little repasts are very pleasant, especially at the close of a long winter evening, and after coming home from a place of public amusement.

To "welcome the coming—speed the parting guest"—is a good maxim. So when your visiter is about to leave you, make all smooth and convenient for her departure. Let her be called up at an early hour, if she is to set out in the morning. Send a servant up to strap and bring down her trunks, as soon as she has announced that they are ready; and see that an early breakfast is prepared for her, and some of the family up and dressed to share it with her. Slip some cakes into her satchel for her to eat on the road, in case, by some chance, she should not reach the end of her journey at the usual hour. Have a carriage at the door in due time, and let some male member of the family accompany her to the starting-place and see her off, attending to her baggage and procuring her tickets.

CHAPTER III.
TEA VISITERS.

When you have invited a friend to take tea with you, endeavour to render her visit as agreeable as you can; and try by all means *to make her comfortable*. See that your lamps are lighted at an early hour, particularly those of the entry and stair-case, those parts of the house always becoming dark as soon as the sun is down; and to persons coming in directly from the light of the open air, they always seem darker than they really are. Have the parlours lighted rather earlier than usual, that your guest, on her entrance, may be in no danger of running against the tables, or stumbling over chairs. In rooms heated by a furnace, or by any other invisible fire, it is still more necessary to have the lamps lighted early.

If there is a coal-grate, see that the fire is burning clear and brightly, that the bottom has been well-raked of cinders and ashes, and the hearth swept clean. A dull fire, half-choked with dead cinders, and an ashy hearth, give a slovenly and dreary aspect to the most elegantly furnished parlour. A sufficiently large grate (if the fire is well made up, and plenty of fresh coal put on about six o'clock) will generally require no further replenishing during the evening, unless the weather is unusually cold; and then more fuel should be added at eight or nine o'clock, so as to make the room comfortable.

In summer evenings, let the window-sashes be kept up, or the slats of the venetian blinds turned open, so that your guest may find the atmosphere of the rooms cool and pleasant. There should always be fans (feather or palm-leaf) on the centre-tables.

The domestic that attends the door should be instructed to show the guest up-stairs, as soon as she arrives; conducting her to an unoccupied apartment, where she may take off her bonnet, and arrange her hair, or any part of her dress that may require change or improvement. The lady should then be left to her-self. Nothing is polite that can possibly incommode or embarrass—therefore, it is a mistaken civility for the hostess, or some female member of the family to follow the visiter up-stairs, and remain with her all the time she is preparing for her appearance in the parlour. We have seen an inquisitive little girl per-mitted by her mother to accompany a guest to the dressing-table, and watch her all the while she was at the glass; even following her to the corner in which she changed her shoes; the child talking, and asking questions incessantly. This should not be. Let both mothers and children understand that, on all occasions, over-officiousness is not politeness, and that nothing troublesome and inconvenient is ever agreeable.

The toilet-table should be always furnished with a clean hair-brush, and a nice comb. We recommend those hair-brushes that have a mirror on the back, so as to afford the lady a glimpse of the back of her head and neck. Better still, as an appendage to a dressing-table, is a regular hand-mirror, of sufficient size to allow a really *satisfactory* view. These hand-mirrors are very convenient, to be used in conjunction with the large dressing-glass. Their cost is but trifling. The toilet-pincushion should always have pins in it. A small work-box properly furnished with needles, scissors, thimble, and cotton-spools, ought also to find a place on the dressing-table, in case the visiter may have occasion to repair any accident that may have happened to her dress.

For want of proper attention to such things, in an ill-ordered, though perhaps a very showy establishment, we have known an *expected* visiter ushered first into a dark entry, then shown into a dark parlour with an ashy hearth, and the fire nearly out: then, after groping her way to a seat, obliged to wait till a small hand-lamp could be procured to light her dimly up a steep, sharp-turning stair-case; and then, by the same lamp, finding on the neglected dressing-table a broken comb, an old brush, and an empty pincushion,—or (quite as probably) nothing at all—not to mention two or three children coming to watch and stare at her. On returning to the parlour, the visiter would probably find the fire just then making up, and the lamp still unlighted, because it had first to be trimmed. Meanwhile, the guest commences her visit with an uncomfortable feeling of self-reproach for coming too early; all things denoting that she was not expected so soon. In such houses everybody comes too early. However late, there will be nothing in readiness.

The hostess should be in the parlour, prepared to receive her visiter, and to give her at once a seat in the corner of a sofa, or in a fauteuil, or large comfortable chair; if a rocking-chair, a footstool is an indispensable appendage. By-the-bye, the dizzy and ungraceful practice of rocking in a rocking-chair is now discontinued by all genteel people, except when entirely alone. A lady should never be seen to rock in a chair, and the rocking of a gentleman looks silly. Rocking is only fit for a nurse putting a baby to sleep. When children get into a large rocking-chair, they usually rock it over backward, and fall out. These chairs are now seldom seen in a parlour. Handsome, stuffed easy chairs, that are moved on castors, are substituted—and of these, half a dozen of various forms are not considered too many.

Give your visiter a fan to cool herself, if the room is warm, or to shade her eyes from the glare of the fire or the light—for the latter purpose, a broad hand-screen is generally used, but a palm-leaf fan will do for both. In buying these fans, choose those whose handle is the firm natural stem, left remaining on the leaf. They are far better than those with handles of bamboo, which in a short time become loose and rickety.

There are many persons who, professing never to use a fan themselves, seem to think that nobody can by any chance require one; and therefore they selfishly keep nothing of the sort in their rooms.

If, in consequence of dining very late, you are in the custom of also taking tea at a late hour—or making but slight preparations for that repast—waive that custom when you expect a friend whom you know to be in the practice of dining early, and who, perhaps, has walked far enough to feel fatigued, and to acquire an appetite. For her accommodation, order the tea earlier than usual, and let it be what is called "a *good* tea." If there is ample room at table, do not have the tea carried round,—particularly if you have but one servant to hand the whole. It is tedious, inconvenient, and unsatisfactory. There is no comfortable way of eating bread and butter, toast, or buttered cakes, except when seated at table. When handed round, there is always a risk of their greasing the dresses of the ladies—the greasing of fingers is inevitable—though that is of less consequence, now that the absurd practice of eating in gloves is wisely abolished among genteel people.

Still, if the company is too numerous for all to be commodiously seated at the usual family table, and if the table cannot be enlarged—it is better to have tea carried round by *two* servants, even if an extra one is hired for the occasion, than to crowd your guests uncomfortably. One person too many will cause inconvenience to all the rest, however the hostess may try to pass it off, by assuring the company that there is quite room enough, and that she has seen a still larger number seated round that very table. Everybody knows that "what's impossible a'n't true."

In setting a tea-table, see that there is not only enough, but *more than enough* of cups and saucers, plates, knives and forks, spoons, napkins, &c. Let the *extra* articles be placed near the lady of the house,—to be distributed, if wanted. We have known families who had the means and the inclination to be hospitable, that never sat down to table without several spare *covers*, as the French call them, ready for accidental guests.

Unless you have domestics on whom you can implicitly rely, it is well to go into the eating-room about ten minutes before the announcement of tea, and to see that all is right; that the tea is strong and properly made, and the pot (which should be scalded twice) is not filled nearly to overflowing with a superabundance of water. The practice of drowning away all the flavour of the tea is strangely prevalent with servants; who are also very apt to neglect scald-ing the tea-pot; and who do not, or will not, remember that the kettle should be boiling hard at the moment the water is poured on the tea—otherwise the infusion will be insipid and tasteless, no matter how liberally the Chinese plant has been afforded.

If your cook is not *habitually* a good coffee-maker, the coffee will most probably be sent in cold, thick, and weak—for want of some previous supervision. Let it have that supervision.

We have heard of tea-tables (even in splendid establishments) being left en-tirely to the *mis*management of incompetent or negligent servants; so that when the company sat down, there was found a deficiency in some of the indispens-able appendages; such as spoons, and even forks, and napkins—butter-knives forgotten, and (worse than all) *cooking-butter* served in mistake for the better sort. By-the-bye, the use of cooking-butter should be abolished in all genteel-houses. If the butter is not good enough to eat on the surface of cold bread or on warm cakes, it is not good enough to eat in the inside of sweet cakes, or in pastry, or in any thing else; and is totally unfit to be mixed with vegetables or sauces. The use of butter is to make things taste well; if it makes them taste ill, let it be entirely omitted: for bad butter is not only unpalatable, but unwholesome. There are houses in which the money wasted on one useless bauble for the drawing-room would furnish the family with excellent fresh butter for a whole year—enough for all purposes.

We know, *by experience*, that it is possible to make very fine butter even in the State of New York, and to have it fresh in winter as in summer, though not so rich and yellow. Let the cows be well fed, well sheltered, and *kept fat* and clean—the dairy utensils always in perfect order—churning done twice or thrice every week—all the milk worked well out—and the butter will surely be good.

If cakes for tea have been made at home, and they have turned out failures, (as is often the case with home-made cakes where there is not much practice in baking them,) do not have them brought to table at all, but send to a shop and get others. It is rude to set before your guests what you know is unfit for them to eat. And heavy, tough, ill-baked things are discreditable to any house where the means of obtaining better are practicable.

In sending for cakes to a confectioner, do not *a second time* allow him to put you off with stale ones. This many confectioners are in the practice of doing, if it is passed over without notice. Stale cakes should at once be sent back, (with a proper reproof,) and fresh ones required. Let the confectioner with whom you deal understand that he is *not* to palm off his stale cakes upon *you*, and that you will not keep them when sent. You will then find that fresh ones will generally be forthcoming. It is always well to send for cakes in the early part of the afternoon.

Have a pitcher of ice-water on the side-table, and a tumbler beside every plate—as most persons like to finish with a glass of water.

Do not, on sitting down to table, inform your guest that "you make no stranger of her," or that you fear she will not be able to "make out" at your plain table. These apologies are ungenteel and foolish. If your circumstances will not allow you *on any consideration* to make a little improvement in your usual family-fare, your friend is, in all probability, aware of the fact, and will not wish or expect you to incur any inconvenient expense on her account. But if you are known to possess the means of living well, you ought to do so; and to consider a good, though not an extravagantly luxurious table as a necessary part of your expenditure. There is a vast difference between laudable economy and mean economy. The latter (whether it shows itself in bad food, bad fires, bad lights, bad servants) is never excused in persons who dress extravagantly, and live surrounded by costly furniture, and who are universally known to be wealthy, and fully able to afford comfort, as well as show.

If you invite a friend to tea, in whose own family there is no gentlemen, or no man-servant, it is your duty previously to ascertain that you can provide her on that evening with an escort home; and in giving the invitation, you should tell her so, that she may know on what to depend. If you keep a carriage, it will be most kind to send her home in it.

Even if it is your rule to have the entry-lamp extinguished at a certain hour, let your servants understand that this rule must be dispensed with, as long as an evening-visiter remains in the house. Also, do not have the linen covers put on the furniture, and the house audibly shut up for the night, before she has gone. To do this is rude, because she cannot but receive it as a hint that she has staid too long.

If your visiter is obliged to go home with no other escort than your ser-vant-man, apprize him, in time, that this duty will be expected of him; desiring that he takes care to be at hand before ten o'clock.

A lady that has no escort whose services she can command, ought not to make unexpected tea-visits. In many cases these visits produce more inconve-nience than pleasure. If you wish to "take tea sociably" with a friend, inform her previously of your intention. She will then let you know if she is disengaged on that evening, or if it is in any way inconvenient to receive you; and she will herself appoint another time. Generally, it is best not to volunteer a tea-visit, but to wait till invited.

If you are engaged to take tea with an intimate friend, who assures you that you will see none but the family; and you afterward receive an invitation to join a party to a place of public amusement, which you have long been desirous of visiting, you may retract your first engagement, provided you send an apology in due time, telling the exact truth, and telling it in polite terms. Your intimate friend will then take no offence, considering it perfectly natural that you should prefer the concert, the play, or the exhibition, to a quiet evening passed at her house with no other guests. But take care to let her know as early as possible.* And be careful not to disappoint her again in a similar manner.

If you are accustomed to taking coffee in the evening, and have an insuperable dislike to tea, it is best not to make an *unexpected* visit—or at least, if you go at all, go early—so as to allow ample time for the making of coffee—a much slower process than that of tea; particularly as there may chance to be no roasted coffee in the house. Much inconvenience has been caused by the "sociable visiting" of determined coffee-drinkers. It is very easy to make green or black tea at a short notice—but not coffee.

In inviting "a few friends," which means a small select company, endeavour to assort them suitably, so as not to bring together people who have no community of tastes, feelings, and ideas. If you mix the dull and stupid with the bright and animated, the cold and formal with the frank and lively, the professedly serious with the gay and cheerful, the light with the heavy, and above all, those who pride themselves on high birth (high birth in America?) with those who boast of "belonging to the people," none of these "few friends" will enjoy each other's society; the evening will *not* go off agreeably, and you and the other members of your family will have the worst of it. The pleasantest people in the room will naturally congregate together, and the task of entertaining the unentertainable will devolve on yourself and your own people.

Still, it is difficult always to assort your company to your satisfaction and theirs. A very charming lady may have very dull or very silly sisters. An intelligent and refined daughter may be unfortunate in a coarse, ignorant mother, or a prosing, tiresome, purse-proud father. Some of the most delighted persons you may wish to invite, may be encumbered with relations totally incapable of adding any thing to the pleasure of the evening;—for instance, the numerous automatons, whom we must charitably believe are speechless merely from diffidence, and of whom we are told, that "if we only knew them," we should discover them, on intimate acquaintance, to be "quite intelligent people." Perhaps so. But we cannot help thinking that when a head is full of ideas, some of them will involuntarily ooze out and be manifest. Diffidence is very becoming to

---

* Where the city-post is to be depended on, a note can always be sent in that way.

young people, and to those who are new to the world. But it is hardly credible that it should produce a painful taciturnity in persons who have passed from youth into maturity; and who have enjoyed the advantages of education and of living in good society. Still those who, as the French say, have "a great talent for silence," may redeem themselves from suspicion of stupidity, by listening attentively and understandingly. A good talker is never displeased with a good hearer.

We have often met with young ladies from whom it was scarcely possible for one of their own sex to extract more than a few monosyllables at long intervals; those intervals being passed in dozing, rather than in hearing. And yet, if any thing in the shape of a beau presented itself, the tongues of these "dumb belles" were immediately loosened, and the wells of their minds commenced running as glibly as possible. To be sure, the talk amounted to nothing definite; but still they *did* talk, and often became quite lively in a few minutes. Great is the power of beaux!

To return to the tea-table.—Unless you are positively sure, when you have a visiter, that she drinks the same tea that is used in your own family, you should have both black and green on the table. Either sort is often extremely disagreeable to persons who take the other. Drinkers of green tea, for instance, have generally an unconquerable aversion to black, as tasting like hay, herbs, &c., and they find in it no refreshing or exhilarating property. In some, it produces nausea. Few, on the other hand, dislike the taste of *good* green tea, but they assign as a reason for not drinking it, that it is supposed from its enlivening qualities to affect the nerves. Judge Bushrod Washington, who always drank green, and avoided black, said that "he took tea as a beverage, not as a medicine." And there are a vast number of sensible people in the same category. If your guest is a votary of green tea, have it made for her, in time for the essence of the leaves to be well drawn forth. It is no compliment to give her green tea that is weak and washy. And do not, at your own table, be so rude as to lecture her upon the superior wholesomeness of black tea. For more than a century, green tea was universally drunk in every house, and there was then less talk of nervous diseases than during the reign of Souchong,—which, by-the-bye, is nearly exploded in the best European society.

In pouring out, do not fill the cups to the brim. Always send the cream and sugar round, that each person may use those articles according to their own taste. Also, send round a small pot of hot water, that those who like their tea weak may conveniently dilute it. If tea is handed, a servant should, at the last, carry round a water-pitcher and glasses.

Whether at dinner or tea, if yourself and family are in the habit of eating fast, (which, by the way, is a very bad and unwholesome one, and justly cited against us by our English cousins,) and you see that your visiter takes her food deliberately, endeavour (for that time at least) to check the rapidity of your own mastication, so as not to finish before she has done, and thus compel her to hurry herself uncomfortably, or be left alone while every one round her is sitting unoccupied and impatient. Or rather, let the family eat a little more than usual, or seem to do so, out of politeness to their guest.

When refreshments are brought in after tea, let them be placed on the centre-table, and handed round from thence by the gentlemen to the ladies. If there are only four or five persons present, it may be more convenient for all to sit round the table—which should not be cleared till after all the visiters have gone, that the things may again be offered before the departure of the guests.

If a friend makes an afternoon call, and you wish her to stay and take tea, invite her to do so at once, as soon as she has sat down; and do not wait till she has risen to depart. If she consents to stay, there will then be ample time to make any additional preparation for tea that may be expedient; and she will also know, at once, that you have no engagement for the evening, and that she is not intruding on your time, or preventing you from going out. If you are intimate friends, and your guest is disposed to have a long chat, she will do well to ask you, at the beginning, if you are disengaged, or design going out that afternoon.

We knew a very sensible and agreeable lady in Philadelphia, who liking better to have company at home than to go out herself, made a rule of invit-ing every day, half a dozen friends (not more) to take tea with her—just as many as could sit round the table, "with ample room and verge enough." These friends she assorted judiciously. And therefore she never asked a whole family at once; those who were left out understanding that they would be invited another time. For instance, she would send a note for the father and mother only—to meet another father and mother or two. A few weeks after, a billet would come for the young people only. But if there were *several* young people, some were delayed—thus—"I wish James and Eliza to take tea with me this evening, to meet so-and-so. Another time I promise myself the pleasure of Edward's company, and Mary's."

This distribution of invitations never gave offence.

Those who were honoured with the acquaintance of such a lady were not likely to be displeased at so sensible a mode of receiving them. These little tea-drinkings were always pleasant, and often delightful. The hostess was well qualified to make them so.

Though the refreshments were of the best kind, and in sufficient abun-dance, and the fires, lights, &c. all as they should be, there was no ostentatious display, and the ladies were dressed no more than if they were spending a quiet evening at home—party-finery being interdicted—also, such needle-work as required constant attention to every stitch.

If you have a friend who is in somewhat precarious health, and who is afraid of being out in the night air, or who lives in a distant part of the town, invite her to dinner, or to pass the day, rather than to tea. She will then be able to get home before twilight.

There is in Boston a very fashionable and very distinguished lady, who, since her return from Europe, has relinquished the custom of giving large parties; and now entertains her friends by, almost every day, having two or three to dine with her,—by invitation. These dinners are charming. The hour is according to the season—earlier in winter, later in summer—the guests departing before dark, and the lady always having the evening to herself.

We know a gentleman in Philadelphia, who every Monday has a family-dinner at his house, for all his children and grandchildren, who there meet and enjoy themselves before the eyes of the father and mother—a friend or two being also invited. Nothing can be more pleasant than to see them all there together, none staying away—for parents, children, sons-in-law, daughters-in-law, sisters-in-law, brothers-in-law, are all at peace, and all meeting in friendship—unhappily, a rare case, where there is a large connection, and considerable wealth.

We wish that social intercourse was more frequently conducted on the plan of the few examples above cited.

Should chance-visiters come in before the family have gone to tea, let them at once be invited to partake of that repast; which they will of course decline, if they have had tea already. In a well-provided house, there can be no difficulty in adding something to the family tea-table, which, in genteel life, should never be discreditably parsimonious.

It is a very mean practice, for the members of the family to slip out of the parlour, one by one at a time, and steal away into the eating-room, to avoid inviting their visiter to accompany them. The truth is always suspected by these separate exits, and the length of absence from the parlour—and is frequently betrayed by the rattle of china, and the pervading fumes of hot cakes. How much better to meet the inconvenience (and it cannot be a great one) by decently conducting your accidental guest to the table, unless he says he has already taken tea, and will amuse himself with a book while the family are at theirs.

Casual evening visiters should avoid staying too late. Ten o'clock, in our country, is the usual time to depart, or at least to begin departing. If the visit is unduly prolonged, there may be evident signs of irrepressible drowsiness in the heads of the family, which, when perceived, will annoy the guest, who must then feel that he has stayed too long—and without being able to excuse himself with any approach to the elegance of William Spencer's apology to the charming Lady Anne Hamilton.

> Too late I stay'd—forgive the crime;
> Unheeded flew the hours,
> For noiseless falls the foot of Time
> That only treads on flowers.
> Ah! who with clear account remarks
> The ebbing of the glass,
> When all its sands are diamond sparks,
> That dazzle as they pass!

CHAPTER IV.
THE ENTRÉE.

A lady is said to have the *entrée* of her friend's room, when she is allowed or assumes the privilege of entering it familiarly at all times, and without any previous intimation—a privilege too often abused. In many cases, the visited person has never really granted this privilege, (and after growing wise by experience, she rarely will;) but the visiter, assuming that she herself must, under all circumstances, be welcome, carries her sociability so far as to become troublesome and inconvenient. Consequently, their friendship begins to abate in its warmth. No one likes to be annoyed, or be intruded on at all hours. So the visited begins to think of the adage, "My room is my castle," and the visiter finds that seeing a friend under all circumstances somewhat diminishes respect, and that "familiarity brings contempt."

There are few occasions on which it is well, on entering a house, to run directly to the chamber of your friend, and to bolt into her room without knocking; or the very instant *after* knocking, before she has time to desire you to enter, or to make the slightest arrangement for your reception. You may find her washing, or dressing, or in bed, or even engaged in repairing clothes,—or the room may be in great disorder, or the chambermaid in the act of cleaning it. No one likes unseasonable interruptions, even from a very dear friend. That friend would be dearer still, if she had sufficient tact and consideration to refrain from causing these annoyances. Also, friendships are not always lasting—particularly those that become inordinately violent, and where both parties, by their excessive intimacy, put themselves too much into each other's power. Very mortifying disclosures are sometimes made after a quarrel between two Hermias and Helenas, when recrimination begins to come, and mutual enmity takes the place of mutual kindness.

A familiar visit will always begin more pleasantly, if the visiter enquires of the servant at the door if the lady she wishes to see is at home, and then goes into the parlour, and stays there till she has sent her name, and ascertained that she can be received up-stairs.* Then (and not till then) let her go to her friend's room, and still remember to knock at the door before she enters. Let her have patience till her friend bids her come in, or has time to rise, cross the room, and come to open the door, if it is fastened.

It is extremely rude, on being admitted to a private apartment, to look curiously about, as if taking an inventory of all that is to be seen. We have known ladies whose eyes were all the time gazing round, and even slily peering under tables, sofas, &c.; turning their heads to look after every person who chanced to be moving about the room, and giving particular attention to whatever seemed to be in disorder or out of place. Nay, we have known one who prided herself upon the gentility of her forefathers and foremothers, rise from her seat when her hostess opened a bureau-drawer, or a closet-door, and cross the room, to stand by and inspect the contents of said bureau or closet, while open—a practice very common with ill-taught *children*, but which certainly should be rebuked out of them long before they are grown up.

Make no remark upon the work in which you find your friend engaged. If she lays it aside, desire her not to quit it because of your presence; but propound no questions concerning it. Do not look over her books, and ask to borrow them. In short, meddle with nothing.

Some ladies never enter the room of an intimate friend without immediately exclaiming against its heat or its cold—seldom the latter, but very frequently the former, as it is rather fashionable to be always too warm; perhaps because it makes them seem younger. If they really are uncomfortably warm on a very cold day, we think it can only be from the glow produced by the exercise of walking. This glow must naturally subside in a few minutes, if they would sit down and wait with a little patience, or else avail themselves of the fan which ought to be at hand in every room. We have known ladies of this warm temperament, who had sufficient consideration always to carry a pocket-fan in winter as well as summer. This is far better than to break out instantly with a complaint of the heat of the room, or to run and throw up a window-sash, or fling open the door,

---

* If the visiter has been properly announced, a well-trained servant will, in all probability, run up before her, and open the room-door.

at the risk of giving cold to others. No intimacy can authorize these freedoms in a cold day, unless permission has first been asked, and sincerely granted.

If you are perfectly certain that you have really the entrée of your friend's room, and even if she has the same of yours, you have no right ever to extend that privilege to any other person who may chance to be with you when you go to see her. It is taking an unjustifiable liberty to intrude a stranger upon the privacy of her chamber. If another lady is with you, waive your privilege of entrée for that time, take your companion into the parlour, and send up the names of both, and do not say, "Oh! come up, come up—I am on no ceremony with her, and I am sure she will not *mind you.*" And how can you be sure? Perhaps in reality, she *will* mind her very much, and be greatly discomfited, though too polite to appear so.

There are certain unoccupied females so over-friendly as to take the entrée of the whole house. These are, generally, ultra-neighbourly neighbours, who run in at all hours of the day and evening; ferret out the ladies of the family, wherever they may be—up-stairs or down; watch all their proceedings when engaged, like good housewives, in inspecting the attics, the store-rooms, the cellars, or the kitchens. Never for a moment do they seem to suppose that their hourly visits may perhaps be inconvenient or unseasonable; or too selfish to abate their frequency, even when they suspect them to be so, these inveterate sociablists make their incursions at all avenues. If they find that the front-door is kept locked, they glide down the area-steps, and get in through the basement. Or else, they discover some back-entrance, by which they can slip in at "the postern-gate"—that is, alley-wise:—sociablists are not proud. At first, the sociablist will say, on making her third or fourth appearance for the day, "Who comes to see you oftener than I?" But after awhile even this faint shadow of an apology is omitted—or changed to "Nobody minds *me.*" She is quite domesticated in your house—an absolute *habitué.* She sees all, hears all, knows all your concerns. Of course she does. Her talk *to* you is chiefly gossip, and therefore her talk *about* you is chiefly the same. She is *au-fait* of every thing concerning your table, for after she has had her dinner at her own home, she comes bolting into your dining-room and "sits by," and sees you eat yours. It is well if she does not begin with "a look in" upon you before breakfast. She finds out everybody that comes to your house; knows all your plans for going to this place or that; is well acquainted with every article that you wear; is present at the visits of all your friends, and hears all their conversation. Her own is usually "an infinite deal of nothing."

A sociablist is commonly what is called good-natured, or else you would not endure her at all—and you believe, for a time, that she really has an extraordinary liking for you. After awhile, you are undeceived. A coolness ensues, if not a quarrel, and you are glad to find that she carries her sociability to another market, and that a new friend is now suffering all that you have experienced. To avoid the danger of being overwhelmed by the sociability of an idle neighbour, discourage the first indications of undue intimacy, by making your own visits rather few, and rather far between. A young lady of good sense, and of proper self-respect, will never be too lavish of her society; and if she has pleasant neighbours, will visit them always in moderation. And their friendship will last the longer.

CHAPTER V.
INTRODUCTIONS.

Fashion, in its various unmeaning freaks, sometimes decrees that it is not "stylish to introduce strangers." But this is a whim that, whenever attempted, has neither become general nor lasted long. It has seldom been adopted by persons of good sense and good manners—and very rarely by that fortunate class whose elevated standing in society enables them to act as they please, in throwing aside the fetters of absurd conventionalities, and who can afford to do so.

Non-introduction has been found, in many instances, to produce both inconvenience and vexation. Persons who had long known each other by reputation, and who would have rejoiced in an opportunity of becoming personally acquainted, have met in society, without being aware of it till afterward; and the opportunity has never recurred. One of our most distinguished literary Americans was seated at a dinner-party next to an European lady equally distinguished in literature; but as there were no introductions, he was not aware of her presence till the party was over and the lady gone. The lady knew who the gentleman was, and would gladly have conversed with him; but as he did not speak, because he was not introduced, she had not courage to commence—though she might have done so with perfect propriety, considering who *he* was, and who *she* was.

Still worse—from not knowing who are present, you may inadvertently fall upon a subject of conversation that, for private reasons, may be extremely irksome or painful to some of the company; for instance, in discussing a public character. Severe or mortifying remarks may unintentionally be made on the near relative, or on the intimate companion, of one whom you would on no account desire to offend. And in this way you may make enemies, where, under other circumstances, you would have made friends. In such cases, it is the duty of the hostess, or of any mutual acquaintance, immediately to introduce both parties, and thus prevent any further animadversions that, may be *mal-a-propos*, or in any way annoying. It is safest, when among strangers, to refrain from bitter animadversions on anybody.

In introducing a gentleman to a lady, address *her* first, as for instance— "Miss Smith, permit me to make you acquainted with Mr. Jones"—or, "Mrs. Farley, allow me to present Mr. Wilson"—that is, you must introduce the gentleman to the lady, rather than the lady to the gentleman. Also, if one lady is married and the other single, present the single lady to the matron, as—"Miss Thomson, let me introduce you to Mrs. Williams."*

In introducing a foreigner, it is proper to present him as "Mr. Howard from England"—"Mr. Dupont from France"—"Mr. Wenzel from Germany." If you know of what European city he is a resident, it is better still, to say that he is "from London,"—"Paris,"—"Hamburg." Likewise, in introducing one of your own countrymen very recently returned from a distant part of the world, make him known as "Mr. Davis, just from China"—"Mr. Edwards, lately from Spain"—"Mr. Gordon, recently from South America." These slight specifications are easily made; and they afford, at once, an opening for conversation between the two strangers, as it will be perfectly natural to ask "the late arrived" something about the country he has last visited, or at least about his voyage.

When presenting a member of Congress, mention the State to which he belongs, as, "Mr. Hunter of Virginia"—"Mr. Chase of Ohio," &c. Recollect that both senators and gentlemen of the house of representatives are members of Congress—Congress including the two legislative bodies. In introducing a governor, designate the state he governs—as, "Governor Penington of New Jersey." For the chief magistrate of the republic, say simply—"The President."

In introducing an officer, tell always to which service he belongs—as "Captain Turner of the Navy"—"Captain Anderson of the Army."

We regret the custom of continuing to give military titles to militia officers. Foreigners are justly diverted at finding *soi-disant* generals and colonels among men who fill very subordinate stations in civil life—men that, however respectable in their characters, may be deficient in the appearance, manners, or education that should belong to a regular officer. This foolish practice can only be done away by the militia officers themselves (those that really are gentlemen— and there are many) magnanimously declining to be called generals, colonels, &c. except on parade occasions; and when actually engaged in militia duty. Let

---

* It is well to present a lady or gentleman from another city, as "Miss Ford of New York"—"Mrs. Stephens of Boston"—"Mr. Warren of New Orleans."

them omit these titles on their cards, and request that no letters be directed to them with such superscriptions; and that in introductions or in conversation they may be only addressed as plain Mr. It is still more absurd to continue these military titles long after they have ceased to hold the office,—and above all, to persist in them when travelling in foreign countries, tacitly permitting it to be supposed that they own commissions in the regular service.

English tourists (even when they know better) make this practice a handle for pretending, in their books, that the officers of the American army are so badly paid, or so eager to make additional money, that they exercise all sorts of trades, and engage in the humblest occupations to help themselves along. They tell of seeing a captain stitching coats, a major making shoes, a colonel driving a stage, and a general selling butter in market—sneeringly representing them as regular officers of the United States army. Is it true that we republicans have such a hankering after titles? If so, "reform it altogether." And let one of the first steps be to omit the "Esq." in directing a letter to an American citizen, for whom the title can have no meaning. In England it signifies the possessor of an estate in the country, including the office of justice of peace. In America, it means a magistrate only; who may live in a city, and own not an inch of ground anywhere. But why should all manner of men, of all trades, and professions, expect to see an "Esq." after their name, when with reference to *them*, it can have no rational application?

An introduction should always be given in a distinct and audible voice, so that the name may be clearly understood. The purpose is defeated, if it is murmured over in so low a tone as to be unintelligible. And yet how often is this the case; for what reason it is difficult to divine. It is usual for the introducee to repeat the name of the introduced. This will prove that it has really been heard. For instance, if Mrs. Smith presents Miss Brook to Miss Miles, Miss Miles immediately says, "Miss Brook"—or better still—"Miss Brook, I am glad to meet you," or something similar. Miss Miles then begins a talk.

If you introduce yourself to a lady whom you wish to know, but who does not know *you*, address her by her name, express your desire to make her acquaintance, and then give her your card. Replying that it affords her pleasure to meet you, she will give you her hand, and commence a conversation, so as to put you quite at ease after your self-introduction.

In introducing members of your own family, always mention, audibly, the name. It is not sufficient to say "my father," or "my mother"—"my son," "my daughter"—"my brother," or "my sister." There may be more than one surname in the same family. But say, "my father, Mr. Warton,"—"my daughter, Miss Wood"—or "my daughter-in-law, Mrs. Wood"—"my sister, Miss Mary

Ramsay"—"my brother, Mr. James Ramsay," &c. It is best in all these things to be explicit. The eldest daughter is usually introduced by her surname only—as "Miss Bradford"—her younger sisters, as "Miss Maria Bradford"—"Miss Harriet Bradford."

In presenting a clergyman, put the word "Reverend" before his name—unless he is a bishop, and then, of course, the word "Bishop" suffices. The head of a college-department introduce as "Professor"—and it is to them only that the title properly belongs, though arrogated by all sorts of public exhibitors, mesmerists and jugglers included.

Where the company is large, the ladies of the house should have tact enough to avoid introducing and placing together persons who cannot possibly assimilate, or take pleasure in each other's society. The dull, and the silly, will be far happier with their compeers. To a woman of talent, and a good conversationist, it is a cruelty to put her unnecessarily in contact with stupid, or unmeaning people. She is wasted and thrown away upon such as are neither amusing nor amusable. Neither is it well to bring together a gay, lively woman of the world, and a solemn, serious, repulsive dame, who is a contemner of the world and all its enjoyments. There can be no conversation that is mutually agreeable, between a real lady of true delicacy and refinement, and a so-called lady whose behaviour and talk are coarse and vulgar,—or between a woman of highly cultivated mind, and one who is grossly ignorant of every thing connected with books, and who boasts of that ignorance. We have heard a lady of fashion say, "Thank God, I never read." The answer might well have been, "You need not tell us that."

In inviting but a small company, it is indispensable to the pleasure of all, that you ask none who are strikingly unsuitable to the rest—or whose presence will throw a damp on conversation. Especially avoid bringing into the same room, persons who are at notorious enmity with each other, even if, unhappily, they should be members of the same family. Those who are known as adversaries should be invited on different evenings.

Avoid giving invitations to bores. They will come without.

The word "bore" has an unpleasant and an inelegant sound. Still, we have not, as yet, found any substitute that so well expresses the meaning,—which, we opine, is a dull, tiresome man, or "a weariful woman," either inveterately silent, or inordinately talkative, but never saying any thing worth hearing, or worth remembering—people whom you receive unwillingly, and whom you take leave of with joy; and who, not having perception enough to know that their visits are always unwelcome, are the most sociable visiters imaginable, and the longest stayers.

In a conversation at Abbotsford, there chanced to be something said in reference to bores—those beings in whom "man delights not, nor woman neither." Sir Walter Scott asserted, humourously, that bores were always "good respectable people." "Otherwise," said he, "there could be no bores. For if they were also scoundrels or brutes, we would keep no measures with them, but at once kick them out the house, and shut the door in their faces."

When you wish an introduction to a stranger lady, apply to your hostess, or to some of the family, or to one of the guests that is acquainted with that lady: you will then be led up and presented to her. Do not expect the stranger to be brought to you; it is your place to go to her.

If you are requested by a female friend to introduce her to a distinguished gentleman, a public character, be not so ungenerous as to go *immediately* and conspicuously to inform him of the fact. But spare her delicacy, by deferring the ceremony for a while; and then take an opportunity of saying to him, "I shall be glad to make you acquainted with my friend Miss Morris. Come with me, and I will introduce you." When the introduction has thus taken place, you may with propriety leave them together to entertain each other for awhile; particularly if both parties are capable of doing so. And then, after a quarter of an hour's conversation, let the lady release the gentleman from further attendance, by bowing to him, and turning to some other acquaintance who may not be far off. She can leave *him* much more easily than he can leave *her*, and it will be better to do so in proper time, than to detain him too long. It is generally in his power to return to her before the close of the evening, and if he is pleased with her society, he will probably make an opportunity of doing so.

If he is what is called a lion, consideration for the rest of the company should admonish her not to monopolize him. But lions usually know how to get away adroitly. By-the-bye, she must not talk to him of his professional celebrity, or ask him at once for his autograph.

We saw no less a person than Charles Dickens compelled, at a large party, to devote the whole evening to writing autographs for a multitude of young ladies—many of whom, not satisfied with obtaining one of his signatures for themselves, desired half a dozen others for "absent friends." All conversation ceased with the first requisition for an autograph. He had no chance of saying any thing. We were a little ashamed of our fair townswomen.

Should it fall to your lot to introduce any of the English nobility, take care (before hand) to inform yourself exactly what their titles really are. Americans are liable to make sad blunders in these things. It may be well to know that a duke is the highest title of British nobility, and that his wife is a duchess. His eldest son is a marquis as long as his father lives, on whose demise the marquis becomes a duke. The wife of a marquis is a marchioness. There are a few marquises whose fathers were not dukes. The younger sons are termed Lord Henry, Lord Charles, Lord John, &c. The daughters Lady Caroline, Lady Augusta, Lady Julia. The family name is generally quite different from the title. Thus, the name of the Duke of Richmond is Lenox—that of the Duke of Rutland, Manners. The family name of the Duke of Norfolk (who ranks first of the English nobility) is Howard. The present Duke of Northumberland's name is Algernon Percy. Arthur Wellesley was that of the great Duke of Wellington. His eldest son was Marquis of Douro, and his second son Lord Charles Wellesley. The children of a marquis are called Lord Frederick, or Lord Henry, and Lady Louisa, or Lady Harriet.

The next title is viscount, as Viscount Palmerston. The next is earl, whose wife is a countess, and the children may be Lord Georges and Lady Marys.

After the viscounts come the barons, whose children are denominated the Honourable Miss, or Mr. John Singleton Copley, (whose father was Copley, the celebrated American painter,) is now Baron Lyndhurst. His eldest daughter is the Hon. Miss Copley. In common parlance, barons are always termed lords. Some few have two titles—as Lord Say and Sele—Lord Brougham and Vaux. After William the Fourth had suddenly dissolved the parliament that held out so long against passing the reform bill, and the king, appointing a new cabinet, had placed Lord Brougham at the head of the ministry, a ridiculous comic song came out at one of the minor theatres, implying that now his majesty has swept out the whole parliament, "he takes up his broom and valks" (Brougham and Vaux).

When the widow of a nobleman marries a man who has no title, she always retains hers. Thus when the widow of the Earl of Mansfield married Colonel Greville, (a nephew of the Earl of Warwick,)—on their door-plate the names were—"The Countess Dowager of Mansfield, and the Hon. Colonel Greville,"—a rather long inscription. A nobleman's daughter marrying a commoner, retains her original title of Lady, but takes his surname—thus, Lady Charlotte Campbell, whose father was Duke of Argyle, became, on her marriage with Dr. Bury, a clergyman, Lady Charlotte Bury. It will be understood that if a nobleman's daughter marries a nobleman, her title merges in his—but if she marries a commoner, she retains what title she had originally—her husband, of course, obtaining no rank by his marriage.

The title of a baronet is Sir—as Sir Francis Burdett, Sir Walter Scott. His children are Mr. and Miss, without any "Hon." affixed to their names. Baronets are a grade below barons, but the title is hereditary, descending to the eldest son or next male heir. In directing to a baronet, put "Bart." after his name. A knight is also called Sir, as Sir Thomas Lawrence, Sir Edwin Landseer, &c.; but his title being only for life, dies with him.* It is always conferred by the sovereign touching his shoulder with a sword, and saying, for instance, "Rise up, Sir Francis Chantry." In writing to a knight, put "Knt." The wives of both baronets and knights are called Lady. The wife of Sir John Franklin (who was knighted) is Lady Franklin—not Lady *Jane* Franklin, as has been erroneously supposed. She could not be Lady Jane unless her father was a nobleman.

A nobleman always signs his title only, without designating his exact rank—the Duke of Athol signing himself "Athol"—the Duke of Bedford, "Bedford"—the Marquis of Granby, "Granby"—the Earl of Chesterfield, "Chesterfield," &c. The wives of peers give their christian name with their title—as Isabella Buccleuch—Margaret Northampton—Elizabeth Derby, &c.

The English bishops are addressed in letters as the Lord Bishop of Rochester, the Lord Bishop of Bath and Wells. The Archbishop of Canterbury, who is Primate of England,—(Head of the English Church,) is called His Grace, or Your Grace. The bishops are all (by virtue of their office) members of the House of Peers or Lords. They sign their christian name with the title of their bishopric, as John Durham—William Oxford.

All full noblemen have an hereditary seat in the House of Peers, which they take on attaining the age of twenty-one, and it continues while they live. Their younger sons, the Lord Johns and Lord Fredericks, can only have a seat in the House of Commons, and to that they must be elected, like the other members. Baronets, not being peers, must also be elected as commons.

Americans going to England would do well to look over a book of the British Peerage, so as to save themselves from making blunders, which are much ridiculed in a country where little allowance is made for republican habits and for republican ignorance of what appertains to monarchical institutions.** It would not be amiss even to know that a full coat of arms, including shield, supporters, crest, and scroll with a motto, belongs only to the chief of a noble family; and that the younger branches are entitled only to the crest, which is the head of the same animal that stands erect on each side of the shield as if to support it, such as stags, foxes, bears, vultures, &c. A baronet has a shield only, with a bloody or wounded hand over the top.

Our countrymen abroad sometimes excite ill-concealed mirth, by the lavish use they make of titles when they chance to find themselves among the

---

*   Distinguished men of all professions, doctors, lawyers, artists, authors, and officers of the army and navy, frequently receive the honour of knighthood.

**   It would be well if all the public offices at Washington were furnished with copies of the British Peerage. Perhaps they are.

nobility. They should learn that none but servants or people of the lower classes make constant use of the terms "my lord," and "my lady"—"your lordship," or "your ladyship"—"your grace," &c., in conversing with persons of rank. Formerly it was the custom, but it is long since obsolete, except, as we have said, from domestics or dependants. Address them simply as Lord Derby, or Lord Dunmore—Lady Wilton, Lady Mornington, &c.

CHAPTER VI.
CONDUCT IN THE STREET.

When three ladies are walking together, it is better for one to keep a little in advance of the other two, than for all three to persist in maintaining one unbroken line. They cannot all join in conversation without talking across each other—a thing that, in-doors or out-of-doors, is awkward, inconvenient, ungenteel, and should always be avoided. Also, three ladies walking abreast occupy too much of the pavement, and therefore incommode the other passengers. Three young *men* sometimes lounge along the pavement, arm in arm. Three young *gentlemen* never do so.

If you meet a lady with whom you have become but slightly acquainted, and had merely a little conversation, (for instance, at a party or a morning visit,) and who moves in a circle somewhat higher or more fashionable than your own, it is safest to wait till she recognises you. Let her not see in you a disposition to obtrude yourself on her notice.

It is not expected that all intimacies formed at watering-places shall continue after the parties have returned to their homes. A mutual bow when meeting in the street is sufficient. But there is no interchanging of visits, unless both ladies have, before parting, testified a desire to continue the acquaintance. In this case, the lady who is eldest, or palpably highest in station, makes the first call. It is not customary for a young lady to make the first visit to a married lady.

When meeting them in the street, always speak first to your milliner, mantua-maker, seamstress, or to any one you have been in the practice of employing. To pass without notice any servant that you know, is rude and unfeeling, as they will attribute it to pride, not presuming to speak to you themselves, unless in reply. There are persons who having accepted, when in the country, much kindness from the country-people, are ashamed to recognise them when they come to town, on account of their rustic or unfashionable dress. This is a very vulgar, contemptible, and foolish pride; and is always seen through, and despised. There is no danger of plain country-people being mistaken for vulgar city-people. In our country, there is no reason for keeping aloof from any who are respectable in character and appearance. Those to be avoided are such as wear tawdry finery, paint their faces, and leer out of the corners of their eyes, *looking* disreputably, even if they are not disreputable in reality.

When a gentleman meets a lady with whom his acquaintance is very slight, (perhaps nothing more than a few words of talk at a party,) he allows her the option of continuing the acquaintance or not, at her pleasure; therefore, he waits till she recognises him, and till she evinces it by a bow,—he looking at her to give the opportunity. Thus, if she has no objection to numbering him among her acquaintances, she denotes it by bowing first. American ladies never curtsey in the street. If she has any reason to disapprove of his character or habits, she is perfectly justifiable in "cutting" him, as it is termed. Let her bow very coldly the first time, and after that, not at all.

Young ladies should yield the wall to old ladies. Gentlemen do so to all ladies.

In some cities it is the custom for all gentlemen to give their arm to all ladies, when walking with them. In others, a gentleman's arm is neither offered nor taken, unless in the evening, on slippery pavements, or when the streets are very muddy. A lady only takes the arm of her husband, her affianced lover, or of her male relatives. In the country the custom is different. There, a gentleman, when walking with a lady, always gives her his arm; and is much offended when, on offering his arm, the lady refuses to take it. Still, if it is contrary to the custom of her place, she can explain it to him delicately, and he will at once see the propriety of her declining.

When a lady is walking between two gentlemen, she should divide her conversation as equally as practicable, or address most of it to him who is most of a stranger to her. He, with whom she is least on ceremony, will excuse her.

A gentleman on escorting a lady to her own home, must not leave her till he has rung the bell, and waited till the servant has come and opened the door, and till she is actually in the house. Men who know no better, think it sufficient to walk with her to the foot of the steps and there take their departure, leaving her to get in as she can. This we have seen—but not often, and the offenders were not Americans.

If you stop a few minutes in the street to talk to an acquaintance, draw to one side of the pavement near the wall, so as not to impede the passengers—or you may turn and walk with her as far as the next corner. And never stop to talk in the middle of a crossing. To speak loudly in the street is exceedingly ungenteel, and foolish, as what you say will be heard by all who pass by. To call across the way to an acquaintance, is very unlady-like. It is best to hasten over, and speak to her, if you have any thing of importance to say.

When a stranger offers to assist you across a brimming gutter, or over a puddle, or a glair of slippery ice, do not hesitate, or decline, as if you thought he was taking an unwarrantable liberty. He means nothing but civility. So accept it frankly, and thank him for it.

When you see persons slip down on the ice, do not laugh at them. There is no fun in being hurt, or in being mortified by a fall in the public street; and we know not how a *lady* can see any thing diverting in so painful a circumstance. It is more feminine, on witnessing such a sight, to utter an involuntary scream than a shout of laughter. And still more so, to stop and ascertain if the person that fell has been hurt.

If, on stopping an omnibus, you find that a dozen people are already seated in it, draw back, and refuse to add to the number; giving no heed to the assertion of the driver, that "there is plenty of room." The *passengers* will not say so, and you have no right to crowd them all, even if you are willing to be crowded yourself—a thing that is extremely uncomfortable, and very injurious to your dress, which may, in consequence, be so squeezed and rumpled as never to look well again. None of the omnibuses are large enough to accommodate even twelve grown people *comfortably*; and that number is the utmost the law permits. A child occupies more than half the space of a grown person, yet children are brought into omnibuses *ad libitum*. Ten grown persons are as many as can be really well seated in an omnibus—twelve are too many; and a *lady* will always regret making the thirteenth—and her want of consideration in doing so will cause her to be regarded with unfavourable eyes by the other passengers. It is better for her to go into a shop, and wait for the next omnibus, or even to walk home, unless it is actually raining.

Have your sixpence ready in your fingers a few minutes before you are to get out; and you may request any gentleman near you to hand it up to the driver. So many accidents have happened from the driver setting off before a lady was entirely out of the vehicle and safely landed in the street, that it is well to desire the gentleman not to hand up the sixpence till after you are fairly clear of the steps.

When expecting to ride in an omnibus, take care to have sufficient small change in your purse—that is, sixpences. We have seen, when a quarter-dollar has been handed up, and the driver was handing down the change, that it has fallen, and been scattered among the straw. There was no stopping to search for it, and therefore the ride cost twenty-five cents instead of six: the driver, of course, finding the change himself, as soon as he got rid of all his passengers.

It is most imprudent to ride in an omnibus with much money in your purse. Pickpockets of genteel appearance are too frequently among the passengers. We know a gentleman who in this way lost a pocket-book containing eighty dollars; and various ladies have had their purses taken from them, by well-dressed passengers. If you are obliged to have money of any consequence about you, keep your hand all the time in that pocket.

If the driver allows a drunken man to come into an omnibus, the ladies will find it best to get out; at least those whose seats are near his. It is, however, the duty of the gentlemen to insist on such fellows being refused admittance where there are ladies.

No lady should venture to ride in an omnibus after dark, unless she is escorted by a gentleman whom she knows. She had better walk home, even under the protection of a servant. If alone in an omnibus at night, she is liable to meet with improper company, and perhaps be insulted.

CHAPTER VII.
SHOPPING.

When you go out shopping, it is well to take with you some *written* cards, inscribed with your residence as well as your name. For this purpose to use engraved visiting-cards is an unnecessary expense. That there may be no mistake, let your shopping-cards contain not only your street and number, but the side of the way, and between what streets your house is situated. This minuteness is particularly useful in Philadelphia, where the plan and aspect of the streets is so similar. Much inconvenience, disappointment, and delay have resulted from parcels being left at wrong places. If you are staying at a hotel, give also the number of your chamber, otherwise the package may be carried in mistake to the apartment of some other lady; the servants always knowing the number of the rooms, but not always remembering the names of the occupants; usually speaking of the ladies and gentlemen as No. 25, No. 42, &c.

There is another advantage in having cards with you when you go out shopping: if you should chance to forget your reticule, or handkerchief, and leave it on the counter, the shopkeeper will know exactly by the card where to send it, or for whom to keep it till called for.

If you intend to purchase none but small articles, take but little money in your purse, so that if you chance to lose it, the loss may not be great.* When you buy articles of any consequence, they will always be sent home at your

---

* When circumstances render it expedient to carry much money out with you, divide it; putting half in one purse or pocket-book, and half in another, and put these portions into two pockets.

request—and (unless you keep a standing account at that store) desire the bill to be sent along; and sent at an hour when you will certainly be at hand to pay it. Be careful to take receipts for the payment; and keep the receipts on a file or wire. We have known instances when, from the clerk or storekeeper neglecting or delaying to cross out an account as soon as paid, the same bill was inadvertently sent twice over; and then by having the receipt to show, the necessity of *paying it twice over* was obviated. Look carefully at every item of the bill, and see that all is correct. Sometimes (though these oversights are of rare occurrence) the same article may accidentally be set down twice in the same bill. But this is easily rectified by taking the bill to the storekeeper, and showing it to him.

In subscribing for a magazine or newspaper, and paying in advance, (as you always should,) be especially careful of the receipts given to you at paying. So many persons are in the habit of allowing these accounts to run on for years, that if you neglect preserving your receipts, and cannot produce them after-ward, you may be unintentionally classed among the delinquents, and have no means of proving satisfactorily that you have really paid.

Many ladies keep a day-book, in which they set down, regularly, all the money they have expended on that day; adding up the whole every week. An excellent plan, and of great importance to every one who is mistress of a family.

In making purchases for other persons, have bills made out; and send the bills (receipted) with the articles purchased, as an evidence of the exact price of the things, and that they were paid for punctually. The friends that have commissioned you to buy them, should *immediately* repay you. Much inconvenience may be felt by a lady whose command of money is small, when a friend living in a distant place, and probably in opulent circumstances, neglects or postpones the payment of these sums. She should, at the beginning, send money amply sufficient to make these purchases. It is enough that you take the trouble of going to the stores, selecting the desired articles, and having them packed and sent off. She has no right to put you to the slightest pecuniary inconvenience. There have been instances, where articles thus bought for a lady in a far-off place, have not been paid for by that lady till after the lapse of many months. For such remissness there is no excuse. To go shopping for a friend is rarely a pleasant business. Besides its encroaching on your time, there is always a danger of the purchases proving unsatisfactory, or not suiting the taste of her for whom they are intended. Also, circumstances may prevent the articles reaching her as soon as expected. Whenever practicable, it is best to send all such packages by the Transportation Line—that charge to be paid by the owner, on delivery.

It is not well to trouble a gentleman with the care of a parcel, unless it is quite small, and he has to pass the door of the house at which it is to be delivered; or unless his residence is in the immediate neighbourhood.

When visiting the shops, if you do not intend to buy at that time, but are merely looking round to see varieties of articles before you determine on what to purchase, candidly say so to the persons standing at the counter. They will (particularly if they know you) be perfectly willing to show you such things as you desire to see, in the hope that you may return to their store and buy of them afterward. At the same time, avoid giving unnecessary trouble; and do not, from mere curiosity, desire such things to be brought to you as you have no intention of buying at all.

The practice that is called cheapening, or beating down the price, is now nearly obsolete. Most tradesmen have a fixed price for every thing, and will not abate.

It is but rarely that you will meet with articles of really good quality on very low terms, unless near the close of the season, when the storekeepers, anxious to get rid of their old stock, generally put down the prices of the goods that are left on hand; knowing that by the return of next season, these will be superseded by things of a newer fashion. Economical ladies, who are not resolutely determined on wearing none but articles of the very latest fashion, may thus supply themselves with excellent silks, lawns, &c. in August and September, at prices far below what they would have given in May or June. And then they can lay them by till next summer. In the same way they can purchase merinoes, mousselines de laine, &c. in January, February, and March, much lower than in November and December. It is best always to buy rather too much than too little; and to have a piece left, rather than to get a scanty pattern, such as will barely hold out, leaving nothing for repairs or alterations. There is much advantage in getting an extra yard and a half, or two yards, and keeping it back for new sleeves. Unless you are small and slender, it is not well to buy a dress embroidered with a border pattern. They are always scanty in width, and have that look when made up. The skirts are never quite wide enough. A tall woman requires as full a skirt as a fat one; else her height will make her look lanky and narrow.

When bespeaking an article to be made purposely for you, ascertain from the maker what will be the cost, and then request him to write down the terms on a card, or a slip of paper, or on a leaf of your tablet. If he says he cannot tell how much it will be, or that he knows not what price to fix on it, or that he cannot decide till after it is finished, it will be safest and wisest for you to decline engaging it, till he *has* calculated the amount, or something very near it. Persist in this condition being a *sine qua non*. It is his place to know every thing connected with his business, and to be able to judge of his outlay, and his prof-its. If you do not insist on a satisfactory answer when making the bargain, you may in the end find yourself greatly overcharged, (as we know by experience;) the price in the bill, after the article is made, and sent home, proving infinitely higher than you would have been willing to give if previously aware of it. In dealing with foreigners whose language is not yours, take especial care that there is a correct understanding on both sides.

When on a visit to a city with which you are not familiar, enquire where the best shops are to be found, and make memorandums of them in your tab-lets. This will spare your friends the trouble of accompanying you on your shopping expeditions. And if you have a small pocket-map of the town, there will be no danger of losing your way. Except to ladies whose chief delight is in seeing things connected with dress, to go shopping with a stranger is usually very tiresome. Also, the stranger will feel less constraint by going alone; and more at liberty to be guided by her own taste in selecting, and to consult her pecuniary convenience in regard to the price. It is only when you feel that you have reason for distrusting your own judgment, as to the quality and gentility of the articles, that it is well to be accompanied by a person of more experience. And then you will, most probably, be unwilling to fatigue her by going to as many shops as you would like to visit. In most cases, it is best to go shopping without any companion, except, perhaps, a member of your immediate family. Gentlemen consider it a very irksome task to go on shopping expeditions, and their ill-concealed impatience becomes equally irksome to you.

If you have given the salesman or saleswoman unusual trouble in showing you articles which you find not to suit, make some compensation, by at least one or two small purchases before leaving the store; for instance, linen to lay by as a body-lining for a future dress, gloves, mits, a neck-ribbon, cotton spools, pins, needles, tape, black sewing-silk, &c.,—things that will always come into use.

Remember that in all American stores, the rule of "first come, first served," is rigidly observed. Therefore, testify no impatience if a servant-girl, making a sixpenny purchase, is served before you—which she certainly will be, if her entrance has preceded yours.

There are still some ladies who think that one of the great arts of shopping, is to disparage the articles shown to them, to exclaim at the price, and to assert that at other places they can get exactly such things infinitely lower. When shopping, (as well as under all other circumstances,) it is best to adhere to the truth. If you really like the article, why not gratify the salesman by saying so. If you know that the price is in conformity to the usual rate, you need not attempt to get it lower, for you will seldom succeed—unless, indeed, on that day the tradesman is particularly anxious to sell, having a sum of money to make up, and being somewhat at a loss. Perhaps then, he may abate something; but if he does not himself propose the abatement, and if he is largely in business, and sure of plenty of custom, there will be little use in your urging it.

If you are a stranger in the city, (Philadelphia for instance,) do not always be exclaiming at the prices, and declaring that you can buy the same articles much lower and much handsomer in New York, Boston, or Baltimore. For certain reasons, prices are different in different places. If an article is shown to you in Philadelphia as "something quite new," refrain from saying that it has been out of fashion these two years in New York. This may injure its sale with bystanders, chancing to hear you. You need only say "that it is very pretty, but you do not want it now."

It is strange, but no less strange than true, that though the distance between New York and Philadelphia is reduced to less than half a day's travel, it takes a year or more, for the New York fashions to get to Philadelphia, and many of them never arrive at all. There are certain dress-makers and milliners in the latter city, who, if you show them any thing quite fresh from New York, will habitually reply, "Oh! we made that, here in Philadelphia, a year or two ago." You need not believe them. Our American ladies derive all their ideas of costume from France; and as New York rejoices in the most extensive and the most speedy intercourse with that land of taste and elegance, the French fashions always get there first. The wonder is that so long a time elapses before they prevail in the other cities. We must say, however, that whatever is fantastic and extreme, is generally modified and softened down in Philadelphia. In provincial towns, and in remote new settlements, we often see a disposition to carry to the utmost a fashion already too showy or gaudy.

When you see on another lady a new article of dress that you admire, it is *not* ill-manners, (but rather the contrary,) to tell her so. But unless you really desire to get one exactly like it for yourself, and are sincerely asking for information, it is considered very rude to enquire where she bought it, and what was the cost. And it is peculiarly vulgar to preface the enquiry by the foolish words—"If it is a fair question." The very doubt proves that you know the question to be a very unfair one. And so it is. We have never known that expression used except to introduce something rude and improper. Any lady who is asked an impertinent question, would be perfectly justifiable in saying, "Excuse me from answering"—and then immediately changing the conversation. Yet there are ladies who are always catechising others about their dress. You are not bound to give explicit answers to these, or any other questions concerning your personal affairs. Much mischief accrues in society, from some ladies being too inquisitive, and others too communicative.

It is really a great fatigue, both of body and mind, to go shopping with a very close economist, particularly if you know that she can well afford a sufficiently liberal expenditure. The length of time she will ponder over every thing before she can "make up her mind;" the ever-besetting fear that she may possibly have to give a few cents more in one store than in another; her long deliberation as to whether a smaller than the usual quantity may not be "made to do;" her predilection for bargain-seeking in streets far off, and ungenteel; the immense trouble she gives to the persons behind the counter,—all will induce you to forswear trying a second time the experiment of attending on the progress of a shopper who sets out with the vain expectation of obtaining good articles at paltry prices.

In what are called "cheap shops," you will rarely find more than two or three things that are really cheap. If of bad quality, they are not *cheap*, but dear. Low-priced ribbons, for instance, are generally flimsy, tawdry, of ugly figures, and vulgar colours,—soon fading, and soon "getting into a string." Yet there are ladies who will walk two miles to hustle in the crowd they find squeezing toward the counter of the last new emporium of cheap ribbons; and, while waiting their turn, have nothing to look at around them but lots of trash, that if they bought they would be ashamed to wear. Coarse finery is trumpery.

On the other hand, for ladies of small means, it is not indispensable to their standing in society, that they should deal only at stores noted for selling *higher* than the usual price. It is a very poor boast; particularly when they cannot afford it.

Whatever may be the caprices of fashion, a lady of good taste (and we may add, good sense,) will not, in buying dresses, select those of large figures, and high glaring colours. There is something peculiarly ungenteel and ungraceful in a white ground with large red flowers and green leaves wandering over it. Even if the fabric is brocade, it has a look of calico. Red and green is only beautiful in real flowers. In a lady's dress, it somehow looks unlady-like. A great variety of bright colours is only suited to a carpet. For a dress, two are quite sufficient. And then if one is blue, pink, scarlet, or orange, let it be contrasted with brown, gray, olive, or some chaste and quiet tint that will set it off. Few silks are more becoming than those in which the figure is formed by a darker shade of the same colour as the ground. Silks of one colour only, trim the best—variegated trimming looks confused and ineffective. No colours are more ungenteel, or in worse taste, than reddish lilacs, reddish purples, and reddish browns. The original tint of aronetta, or anatto, is the contempt of ladies; but by previously washing the article in strong, warm pot-ash water, before it is put into the solution of aronetta, you will obtain a beautiful bird-of-paradise colour, entirely free from all appearance of the unpopular powder.

Buy no silk that is stiff and hard, however thick and heavy it may seem. It will crack and split, and wear worse than a soft silk that appears much thinner. Venture on no satin that is not of excellent quality. A thin satin frays and ravels, and is not worth making up. For common wear, a soft, thick India silk is generally excellent. We have never seen a *good one* for less than a dollar a yard. The figured or embossed India silks are not worth buying,—wearing rough and fuzzy, and fraying all over. For a serviceable, long-lasting home dress, there is nothing equal to a very thick, soft, double-width India black satin, such as is called two yards wide, and sells at two dollars a yard. But they have become very scarce. Never use satin to cover cord. It ravels too much. Velvet and satin should be corded with substantial silk. If you cannot match the exact shade, let it be darker rather than lighter. A belt-ribbon should always be darker than the dress. Cord merino with itself. A cording of silk will not wash.

If you cannot get lace that is tolerably fine, wear none at all, rather than have it coarse. We have seen lace called Brussels, so coarse that it looked as if made of cotton, though in truth it was of thread. There was no real beauty in it. Genuine Brussels lace is exquisitely fine.

Large showy ornaments, by way of jewellery, are exceedingly ungenteel. They always tell their own story, of glass stones set in gilding, not gold. If you cannot obtain real jewels, never attempt sham ones. It requires no practised eye to detect them—particularly false diamonds.

Do not interfere with the shopping of other customers, (who may chance to stand near you at the counter,) by either praising or deprecating any of the articles they are looking at. Leave them to the exercise of their own judgment; unless they ask your opinion. And then give it in a low voice, and sincerely.

If you meet an acquaintance unexpectedly in a store, it is not well to engage in a long conversation with her, and thus detain persons behind the counter from waiting on other customers. Finish your purchase-making first, and then you will have leisure to step aside and converse. A store is not the place for social intercourse, and you may chance to say something there, that bystanders should not hear. "Greetings in the market-place" should always be short.

It is not admissible to try on kid gloves in a store. After buying a pair, ask for the glove-stretcher, (which they keep in all good shops, for the convenience of customers,) and then stretch the gloves upon it, unless you have a glove-stretcher at home. This will render them easy to put on when you take them into wear. Glove-stretchers are to be bought at the variety stores; or ought to be. They will save many a new glove from tearing.

In buying stockings, whether silk or cotton, you will find it cheapest in the end, to get those of the best *English* manufacture, particularly those of fine quality. For winter, and to wear with boots, English stockings of unbleached cotton are very comfortable, feeling warmer than those that are perfectly white. It is to be lamented that all black stockings (even of silk) are painful and injurious to the feet, the copperas dye being poisonous.

In buying black mits, see that they are *really of silk*, otherwise they will stain your hands, and look brown and foxy. Much cotton is now substituted for silk; a way having been discovered of carding silk and cotton together, before the thread is spun. Linen also, is shamefully adulterated with cotton, and it is difficult for purchasers to discover the cheat before the article is washed. Linen is frequently injured in the piece by bad bleaching-salts; so that after the first washing, it drops into holes, such as are caused by vitriol. Of this we have had sad experience in several instances, when the linen was supposed to be of the best quality.

Always object to a parcel being put up in newspaper—as the printing-ink will rub off, and soil the article inclosed. If it is a little thing that you are going to take home in your own hand, it will smear your gloves. All shopkeepers in good business can afford to buy proper wrapping-paper, and they generally do so. It is very cheap. See also that they do not wrap your purchase in so small a bit of paper as to squeeze and crush it.

If you go out with much money, (which is never advisable,) divide it into two portions, putting part in your pocket-book or porte-monnaie, and the remainder into your purse, so that if you lose it, or have your pocket picked, the loss may be less. Do not carry notes in your purse, but keep them in your pocket-book. Little gold dollars had best go into your porte-monnaie. If kept in your purse with small change, you will be very likely to lose them, or to mistake them for three-cent pieces if the light is bad.

Once, on embarking in a New York steamboat, we saw a gentleman having bought a penny paper, give the news-boy a gold eagle in mistake for a cent. The gentleman was instantly apprized of his error by a bystander, who had seen it; but the boy had already sprung upon the wharf and was lost in the crowd.

We knew an instance of a lady in New York giving a hundred-dollar note to a strawberry woman, instead of a note of one dollar. Neither note nor woman were seen or heard of more.

In getting change see that three-cent pieces are not given to you for five cents.

And now a few words to saleswomen. They have always, when commencing that vocation, two important qualities to cultivate (exclusive of cleverness in business)—civility, and patience. In these two requisites, few of our American young women are deficient. Let them also learn activity in moving, and quickness in recollecting where all the articles called for are to be found, so as not to keep the customers waiting too long, while they, the sellers, are searching the shelves and boxes. Also, if a lady wishes to match something, (for instance, a piece of silk,) it is foolish and useless to bring her a piece that is not *exactly* like; trying to persuade her to take it, and calling it "as good a match as she is likely to get." Of course she will *not* take a piece that is only *tolerably* like, but not quite the same; for unless it matches exactly, it is no match at all. If a customer enquires for light blue ribbon it is absurd to bring her dark blue, saying "we have no light blue"—or to say "we have no pink, but we have scarlet—we have no lilac, but we have purple." Or still worse, to try to persuade the customer that deep crimson is a beautiful shade of scarlet; or worse than all, that those very unbecoming tints, called improperly rose-white and pearl-white, are really a pure dead white; when you know very well that they are no such thing. Both white and black are very difficult to match *precisely*.

Let the yard-measure be visible to the customers. In some shops the measure is at the back of the counter, hidden behind a glass case. This practice of measuring out of sight, sometimes gives rise to a suspicion that the measure is not true, as it is so easy to deceive where the brass nails that mark it are concealed from view of the customers.

Every female who keeps, or attends in a store, should discourage the visits of her friends at business hours. If she looks off to chat with her shop-visiters, she cannot attend properly to her customers; and those visiters may be inconsiderate and obtrusive enough to interfere, by putting in their word, and praising the beauty or cheapness of the articles, by way of promoting the interest of the seller, which it ultimately *will not*.

Show as much civility and attention to a customer plainly dressed, and walking on foot, or getting out of an omnibus, as you would to a lady elegantly attired, and coming in her own carriage. The former may prove the most profitable customer. Be careful to exhibit no temper, even if you have had the trouble of showing a variety of goods to one who goes away without buying any thing. Another time, perhaps, she may come and make large purchases: but if you offend her, she will assuredly never enter the store again. Recollect that no one feels under the least compulsion to buy what does not suit them. You would not yourself. Habitual courtesy is a valuable qualification, and always turns to good account.

CHAPTER VIII.
PLACES OF AMUSEMENT.

It would be well in *all* places of public amusement, if there could be an apartment appropriated to the ladies, in which they might deposit their cloaks, hoods, &c. in charge of a responsible attendant; her care to be rewarded by a small gratuity. Ladies would then be under no necessity of carrying warm outer-garments into a crowded and heated room; or of wearing their bonnets, and thereby intercepting the view of persons seated behind them; always a grievance where the benches are not sufficiently elevated, or where there is no difference at all in their respective elevation, as is sometimes the case. Also, the appearance of the female part of the company is always more elegant, when wearing bandeaus, caps, or other light head-dresses; young persons requiring their hair only, or the slight decoration of a flower or a ribbon. It is very painful and fatiguing to be for several hours continually dodging your head from side to side, and stretching your neck this way and that, and peeping wherever you can obtain a tantalizing glimpse between the bonnets of ladies seated immediately before you. This, in addition to the annoyance of being squeezed on a bench that is over-full, is enough to destroy nearly all the pleasure of the exhibition; and to make a large portion of the audience regret that they came.

If you wish to secure a good seat, go early. It is better to sit there an hour before the commencement of the performance, than to arrive after it has begun. The time of waiting will soon pass away, in conversation with the friends whom you have accompanied.

When invited to join a party to a place of amusement, begin to prepare in ample time; so as not to keep them waiting for you. When a *large* party is going to a place of amusement, (for instance, the theatre, or opera,) it is better that each family should go thither from their own home, (being provided with their own tickets,) than that they should all rendezvous at the house of one of the company; at the risk of keeping the whole party waiting, perhaps for the very youngest members of it. When a box has been taken, let the tickets be sent to all the persons who are to have seats in it, and not retained by the taker of the box till the whole party has assembled at the door of the theatre. If the tickets are thus distributed, the persons from each house can go when they please, without compelling any of the party to wait for them.

Still, to make an entrance after the performance has begun, is (or ought to be) very embarrassing to ladies. It excites the attention of all around, diverting that attention from the performance; and there is always, when the house is full, and the hour late, some delay and difficulty in reaching the seats, even when the seats have been secured.

If it is a concert, where places cannot be previously engaged, there are, of course, additional reasons for going in due time; and the most sensible and best-behaved part of the audience always endeavour to do so. But if you are unavoidably late, be satisfied to pay the penalty, by quietly taking back-seats, if no others are vacant. We have seen young ladies not arriving till after the entertainment had commenced, march boldly up to the front benches, and stand there looking steadfastly in the faces of gentlemen who with their parties had earned good seats by coming soon after the doors were opened. The ladies persevering in this determined stare, till they succeeded in dislodging these unfortunate gentlemen, and compelling them to quit their seats, to leave the ladies who belonged to them, and to stand for the remainder of the evening, perhaps in a distant part of the room. American *men* are noted, everywhere, for their politeness to females. We wish we could say the same of the politeness of our fair countrywomen in return. Yet frequently they will avail themselves of these civilities from strangers, without rewarding them with a word of thanks, or even a bow of acknowledgment.

English tourists remark (and with truth) that there is no position in which American ladies appear to such disadvantage as when crowding the galleries of our legislative assemblies; ejecting gentlemen to whom it is of importance to hear the debates; and still worse, intruding upon the floor of the senate-chamber, and compelling the senators to relinquish their places, and find others where they can, or else to stand all the time. And among these ladies, there may be very few who are really capable of enjoying or appreciating the eloquence of our distinguished orators, or of entering understandingly into the merits of the question. Often these damsels are whispering half the time about some nonsense of their own; and often, as is surmised, the chief object of the ladies whose visits to the capitol are most frequent, is the chance of a few words of flirtation with some of the most gallant among the members; or the possibility of being escorted home by a congressman, who has but little to do, or at least who does but little. We think the English parliament is right in excluding ladies from their halls, except when the queen goes there in state, to open or prorogue the session. Let them be satisfied with reading the debates in the newspapers.

We acknowledge that it is very interesting to see and hear the most eminent men of our country arranging the affairs of the nation; to become acquainted with their personal appearance, and to listen to their eloquence. But the privilege should not be abused as it is, by those who, after all, listen so badly, or comprehend so badly, that if questioned an hour afterward, they could scarcely repeat the purport of one single sentence,—nor perhaps even recollect the subject of debate. Such instances we have known—and not a few of them either.

To laugh deridingly, or to whisper unfavourable remarks during the performance of a concert or a play, is a rudeness of which few American ladies are guilty. Still, we occasionally see some of that few, who, much to the annoyance of those persons near them who really wish to enjoy what they came for, talk audibly in ridicule of the performers; the performers being, in all probability, near enough to hear these vexatious remarks, and to be disconcerted by them. We heard of a highly respectable actress who was so mortified by the unfeeling animadversions of some young ladies in a stage-box, that she forgot her part, was unable to utter a word, or to restrain her tears, and became so nervous that she played badly during the remainder of the piece, and was in consequence, severely handled next day by the newspaper critics. This was very hard.

Parents before taking their children to the theatre, should first ascertain whether the play is such as will amuse or interest them. Small children are invariably restless, troublesome, and finally sleepy at a performance that affords *them* no entertainment, and they will be better at home. Yet we have seen little girls brought to see the painful tragedy of the Gamester —or still worse, the dreary comedy of the Stranger. How is it that young ladies are frequently matronized to plays that even their mothers cannot witness without blushes?

CHAPTER IX.
TRAVELLING.

No lady should set out on a journey unprovided with an oiled-silk bag for the reception of tooth-brushes, soap, a hair-brush, and a towel. Let the bag be about half a quarter of a yard longer at the back than at the front; so as to leave a flap to turn over, and tie down, when all the articles are in. It should be square, (exclusive of the flap,) and about a quarter and half-quarter in length, and the same in breadth; stitched in compartments, something like an old-fashioned thread-case, only that the compartments differ much in size. The two smallest are for two tooth-brushes. Another should be broad enough to contain a hair-brush. For travelling, have a hair-brush with a mirror at the back, and if you can get one that has also a dressing-comb attached to it, so much the better.

The largest compartment (which should occupy the centre) is for a towel, and a cake of soap. If you are obliged to start in haste, all these things can be put in while wet from recent use, the towel being rolled or folded into as small a compass as possible. The oiled silk will prevent the wet from oozing through. When all are in, turn over the flap at the top, (which should be furnished with two long strings of broad, white tape,) and tie it securely down. Carry this bag in the square satchel which all ladies now keep in their hands when travelling, and which contain such things as they may want during the day, precluding the necessity of opening their large carpet-bag, till they stop for the night.

In a carpet-bag pack nothing but white articles, or such as can be washed, and will not be spoiled by the bag chancing to get wet. Have your name engraved on the lock of your carpet-bag, and also on the brass plate of your trunks. Besides this, write your full direction on several cards, make a small hole in each, and running a string through the hole, tie a card to the handle of each trunk, and sew one on the side of your carpet-bag—the direction designating the place to which you are going. Your name in full should be painted in white letters on every trunk. This costs but a trifle, and secures the recognition of your baggage when missing. It is also an excellent plan to tie round the handle of each trunk or bag, a bit of ribbon—blue, red, or yellow—all the bits being off the same piece.*

Write on a large card, a list and description of each trunk, box, &c. and give the card to the gentleman who escorts you. It will greatly assist him in identifying all the articles that comprise your baggage.

Be quite ready at least a quarter of an hour before the time for starting. Nelson said he traced all the most fortunate events of his life to his practice of being, on every occasion, quite prepared a quarter of an hour too early. It is a good rule.

Previous to departing, put into the hand of your escort rather more than a sufficient sum for the expenses of your journey, so as to provide for all possible contingencies. He will return you the balance when all is paid. Having done this, should any person belonging to the line come to you for your fare, refer them to the gentleman, (mentioning his name,) and take care to pay nothing more yourself.

Dress very plainly when travelling. Few ladies that *are* ladies wear finery in rail-cars, and steamboats—still less in stages—stage-roads being usually very dusty. Showy silks, and what are called dress-bonnets are preposterous—so are jewellery ornaments, which, if real, you run a great risk of losing, and if false,

---

* In a former work of the author's, The House Book, published by A. Hart, Philadelphia, will be found ample directions for packing trunks, &c.

are very ungenteel. Above all, do not travel in white kid gloves. Respectable women never do.

The best travelling-dresses are of merino, or alpaca; plain mousseline de laine, grey or brown linen; or strong India silk, senshaw for instance. In warm weather, gingham is better than printed lawn, which rumples and tumbles and "gets into a string" directly. The sleeves wide, for if tight to the arm, they will stain with perspiration. Your travelling-dress for summer should have a large cape or pelerine of the same. Beside which, carry on your arm a large shawl for chilly mornings and evenings. No lady should travel in cold weather, without a warm cloak, mantilla, or pelisse,—furs, &c. of course—and travelling-boots lined with fur or flannel; having also inner soles of lambs-wool, varnished on the leather side to make them water-proof. Take with you one of those very useful umbrellas, that are large enough to shelter one person from the rain, and can also be used as a parasol. Do not pack it away in a trunk, for you may want it in the transit from rail-car to steamboat. Keep it near you all the time, with your satchel and extra shawl. By all means wear a white collar.

If you are fortunately able to ride backward as well as forward, you will be less incommoded with flying sparks, by sitting with your back to the engine. A spark getting into the eye is very painful, and sometimes dangerous. It is possible to expel it by blowing your nose very hard, while with the other hand you wipe out the particle of cinder with a corner of your handkerchief, pulling down the lower eye-lid. We have seen this done successfully. Another way is to wrap the head of a pin in the corner of a fine, soft cambric handkerchief, and placing it beneath the lid, sweep all round the eye with it. If this does not succeed, get out at the first station-house where you can stop long enough, procure a bristle-hair from a sweeping-brush, tie it in a loop or bow with a bit of thread, and let some one insert it beneath your eye-lid, and move it slowly all round, so as to catch in it the offending particle of coal, and bring it out. Or if there is time, send to the nearest apothecary for an eye-stone, (in reality, a lobster's eye,) and soak it five minutes in a saucer of vinegar and water to give it activity, then, wiping it dry, and carefully inserting it beneath the eye-lid, bind a handkerchief over it. The eye-stone will go circling round the eye, and most likely take up the mote in its course. When the pain ceases, remove the handkerchief, and wash the eye with cold water.

To read in a rail-car is very injurious to the eyes, from the quivering, tremulous motion it seems to communicate to the letters of the page. It is best to abstain from your book till you are transferred to the steamboat.

Many persons cannot talk in a rail-car without a painful exertion of the voice. And it is not an easy task, even to those whose lungs are strong. You can easily excuse yourself from conversing with your escort, by telling him that your voice is not loud enough to be heard above the racket of the cars, and that though you will gladly listen to *him*, he must allow you to listen without replying, except in as few words as possible. If he finds a gentleman with whom he is acquainted, desire him to talk to his friend, and leave you to hear their conversation as a silent auditor.

If you pass the night in a steamboat, and can afford the additional expense of a *whole* state-room, by all means engage one as soon as you go on board. The chambermaid will give you the key and the number, and you can retire to it whenever you please, and enjoy the luxury of being alone, and of washing and dressing without witnesses. If you are constrained to take a berth in the ladies' sleeping-cabin, it is not the least necessary to retire to it immediately after supper. By doing so you will have a very long, tiresome night, and be awake many hours before morning. And if you are awake, do not be continually calling upon the poor chambermaid, and disturbing her with inquiries, such as "Where are we now?" and "How soon shall we arrive?"

The saloon is the place in which ladies and gentlemen sit together. If a lady is so inconsiderate or selfish as to violate the rules of the boat, by inviting her husband or lover to take a seat in the ladies' cabin, there is no impropriety in sending the chambermaid to remind him that he must leave the room. This is often done, and always should be. We once saw a gentleman (or a pretended one) so pertinacious in remaining, (it is true his lady-love urged him "not to mind,") that the captain had to be brought to threaten him with forcible expulsion. This had the desired effect.

Such are the facilities of travelling, that a lady evidently respectable, plainly dressed, and behaving properly, may travel very well without a gentleman. Two ladies still better. On commencing the journey she should speak to the conductor, requesting him to attend to her and her baggage, and to introduce her to the captain of the boat, who will of course take charge of her during the voyage.

Before arriving at the wharf, she had best engage one of the servants of the boat, (promising him a shilling or two,) to obtain for her a porter or a hack, and to see that her baggage is safe. She must stipulate with the hackman that no stranger is to be put into the carriage with her. This is against the law, but notwithstanding, is often done, and the lady who has first engaged the coach, is liable to have for her riding-companions persons of improper character and vulgar appearance, and to be carried with them to their places in remote parts of the city, before she is conveyed to her own home. Previous to getting in, take the number of the coach, by writing it on a card with your pencil, and make your bargain with him as to the charge for conveying you and your baggage.

It would be well if the imposition and insolence of hack-drivers were *always* followed with the punishments provided by law. Ladies are naturally unwilling to appear at a magistrate's office. But it is the duty of every gentleman, as a good citizen, to see that the municipal regulations are never violated with impunity.

All trouble may be avoided on arriving, by sending for the captain of the boat, and requesting him to see you on shore, or to depute his clerk to that office.

In arriving at a rail-road depôt, be careful not to quit the cars till after they have positively stopped quite still. The time gained is but an instant, and the risk is very imminent of serious injury by falling, should your ankle twist in stepping out while there is the least motion.

On arriving at a hotel, ask immediately to see the proprietor; give him your name and address, tell how long you purpose staying, and request him to see that you are provided with a good room. Request him also to conduct you to the dining-room at dinner-time, and allot you a seat near his own. For this purpose, he will wait for you near the door, (do not *keep him waiting*,) or meet you in the ladies' drawing-room. While at table, if the proprietor or any other gentleman asks you to take wine with him, politely refuse.

If, on arriving at the wharf, you expect a gentleman to meet you, take a seat either on deck near the cabin-door, or just inside of the door, so that he may find you easily.

If you are to pursue your journey early in the morning, desire, over-night, the waiter who attends your room, to knock hard at your door an hour before the time of starting. Before you go down-stairs, ask for the chambermaid who has attended you, and give her a fee, (not less than a quarter-dollar,) putting it into her own hand yourself, and not commissioning another to convey it to her. Do not omit giving a quarter-dollar at least, to the waiter who attended your room, and one also to him who has served you at table.

Refrain from making acquaintance with any strangers, unless you are certain of their respectability. If a gentleman of whom you know nothing, endeavours to get into conversation with you, turn away, and make no reply. Avoid saying any thing to women in showy attire, with painted faces, and white kid gloves. Such persons have frequently the assurance to try to be very sociable with respectable ladies who are travelling alone. Keep aloof from them always.

If you have breakfasted early, it will be well to put some gingerbread-nuts or biscuits into your satchel, as you may become very hungry before dinner.

Carry but little money in your pocket—not more than will suffice for the expenses of the day. But for travelling, have another pocket, concealed *beneath* your upper petticoat, and *in that* keep the main portion of your cash. Be cautious of taking bank-notes in change—they may be such as you cannot pass. If they are offered to you, refuse them, and insist upon gold or silver.

Travelling in America, ladies frequently meet with little civilities from gentlemen, so delicately offered, that to refuse them would be rude. These incidental acts of politeness should always be acknowledged with thanks; but they should not be construed into a desire of commencing an acquaintance. If a lady obliged to travel alone, wishes to be treated with respect, her own deportment must in all things be quiet, modest and retiring.

If you have a servant with you, see that she gets her meals, and has a comfortable sleeping-place, or in all probability she will be neglected and overlooked. In a steamboat or a hotel, speak yourself to the head-waiter, and desire him to take her to the servants' table and attend to her; and tell the chambermaid to see her provided with a bed. If their lady forgets to look out for them, coloured women in particular have often no courage to look out for themselves.

CHAPTER X.
DEPORTMENT AT A HOTEL,
OR AT A LARGE BOARDING-HOUSE.

Now that there is so much travelling in the summer, (and indeed at all seasons,) and so much living in public, to save the trouble and the expense of keeping house in private, it may be well to offer some hints on the propriety of manners that ought to be observed in places where you are always exposed to the inspection and to the remarks of strangers. These strangers, knowing you but slightly, or not at all, will naturally draw their inferences for or against you from what they see before their eyes; concluding that you are genteel or ungenteel, patrician or plebeian, according to the coarseness or the polish of your manners.

Yet strange to say, there are persons who indulge themselves in astounding acts of rudeness, from the supposition that a hotel is only a tavern, a sort of Liberty Hall, where every one has a right to "take their ease in their inn," if they pay for it. Have they no respect for themselves?

It is usual for members of the same party to meet in the ladies' drawing-room before they go in to breakfast, unless the party is large; and then it is not expected that half a dozen persons should be kept waiting for one or two late risers, or tardy dressers. When two or three of the party find themselves ready in the parlour, it will be best for them to proceed to the eating-room, and leave the others to follow at their convenience, by twos or by threes,—always seeing that a young lady, if a stranger, is not left to go in alone. Strangers at hotels can have no particular seats at breakfast and tea, as at these two repasts, they always come to table by instalments, and at no regular time. If a large party enters all at once and they are *determined* to sit all together, they may occasion much inconvenience to persons already seated, or to the regular boarders, who have their allotted seats. Neither is there any necessity or advantage in six, eight, or ten people, who travel as one party, resolving to establish themselves at a hotel-table all side by side, in a row; particularly when it causes inconvenience to others. Certainly not more than three or four persons ranged in a line can join in the same conversation, or attend to the wants of their friends. Why then should they make any extraordinary point of occupying chairs next to each other? It would be better to divide their forces; and if they can, for half to sit on one side of the table, and the other half directly opposite. Or they will find that if the table is full, and they have to disperse still more widely, they had best do so with a good grace, rather than make any disturbance on the subject. When they quit the table to return to the drawing-room they may be very sure of all meeting again near the door.

Nine o'clock (or half-past) is the latest hour that any guest at a hotel should come to breakfast; and few *Americans* have so little consideration as to detain the table and the servants till ten or eleven.* At a boarding-house, the guests are very soon made to understand that if they are late risers, they need expect nothing but the cold leavings of the breakfast. At a hotel they find more indulgence. You there choose from the bill of fare such dishes as you may prefer, and they will be brought to you, after you have been supplied with tea or coffee, and bread and butter to begin with. To each person is allowed a separate dish or plate of the articles selected; and it is understood to be for yourself alone, and that no other person has a right to partake of it, or to meddle with it in any way. Yet even from your own dish, never help yourself with the knife and fork or spoon you are eating with; but always use a spare one, with which the waiter will furnish you. Do not eat different sorts of relishes off the same plate. At a hotel there is no scarcity of plates, or of servants to change them. Always take butter with the butter-knife, and then do not forget to return that knife to the butter-plate. Carefully avoid cutting bread with your own knife, or taking salt with it from the salt-cellar. It looks as if you had not been accustomed to butter-knives and salt-spoons.

* Nevertheless, it is not good manners to make any remark (even to a friend) on their coming to breakfast late or early. It is no concern of yours, and they have reasons of their own, undoubtedly.

Ladies no longer eat salt-fish at a public-table. The odour of it is now considered extremely ungenteel, and it is always very disagreeable to those who *do not* eat it. If you breakfast alone, you can then indulge in it.

Speak to the waiter in a distinct, but not in too loud a voice, and always civilly. Thank him for any little extra attention he may show you. If you do not like what he has brought you, or find that you cannot eat it, make your objection in a low voice, so as not to be heard by the neighbouring guests; and quietly desire him to bring you something else.

It is usual at a hotel-table for each waiter to have charge of three or four persons, and to attend to *their* wants exclusively. If you are a stranger, ask the waiter his name when he first comes to you; and unless he is not at hand, and you see another standing idle, do not call on any one else to attend you.

If the servants are coloured men, refrain from all conversation in their presence that may grate harshly on their feelings, by reminding them of their unfortunate African blood. Do not talk of them as "negroes,"[*] or "darkies." Avoid all discussions of abolition, (either for or against,) when coloured people are by. Also, quote none of their laughable sayings while they are present.

When the domestics are Irish, and you have occasion to reprove them for their negligence, forgetfulness, or blunders, do so without any reference to their country. If you find one who is disrespectful or insolent, or who persists in asserting a falsehood, it is safest to make no reply yourself, but to have the matter represented to the proprietor of the house; desiring that another waiter may be allotted to you.

It is ungenteel to go to the breakfast-table in any costume approaching to full dress. There must be no flowers or ribbons in the hair. A morning-cap should be as simple as possible. The most genteel morning-dress is a close gown of some plain material, with long sleeves, which in summer may be white muslin. A merino or cashmere wrapper, (grey, brown, purple, or olive,) faced or trimmed with other merino of an entirely different colour, such as crimson, scarlet, green, or blue, is a becoming morning dress for winter. In summer, a white cambric-muslin morning-robe is the handsomest breakfast attire, but one of gingham or printed muslin the most convenient. The coloured dress may be made open in front, with short loose sleeves and a pointed body. Beneath it a white under-dress, having a chemisette front down to the belt, and long white sleeves down to the wrist. This forms a very graceful morning costume, the white skirt appearing where the coloured skirt opens.

The fashion of wearing black silk mittens at breakfast is now obsolete. It was always inconvenient, and neither useful nor ornamental.

---

[*] Americans never really say n——rs, though constantly accused of doing so by their British cousins. The word negor we have heard, but n——r never.

After breakfast, it is customary for the ladies to adjourn to the drawing-room, where they converse, or read the papers, or receive early visiters, while the chambermaids are putting the bed-chambers in order. Some who are not accustomed to hotels, go immediately from the breakfast-table to their own apartment, sitting there among the flue and dust during the whole process of bed-making and room-sweeping; afraid to trust the chambermaid alone, lest she should steal something. This is absurd. They should know that the chambermaids (being all considered honest and responsible) are furnished with duplicate keys, by which they can at any time unlock the chamber-doors, and let themselves in, when the occupant is absent. Also, this palpable suspicion of their honesty is an insult to the girls, and is always felt as such. It is sufficient to lock the bureau, the wardrobe, and your trunks. When you go out, (that is, out of the house,) *then* lock the door of your room, lest some one passing by, should have curiosity to stroll in and look about, and meddle with what they see there.

Should you perceive that the dress of another lady is, by some accident, out of order—for instance, that a hook or a button has become unfastened; or that a string is visibly hanging out; a collar unpinned, and falling off; the corner of a shawl dragging along the floor; a skirt caught up; or a sleeve slipping down, immediately have the kindness to apprize her of it in a low voice, and assist her in repairing the mischance; and, if necessary, leave the room with her for that purpose.

We have seen a lady who, finding that a cluster of her false curls was coming down, had the courage to say so to a gentleman with whom she was conversing at a party. And going openly, and at once, to the nearest mirror, she calmly adjusted her borrowed locks, and returned to her seat with a good grace. Consequently, nobody laughed at the untoward accident; as might perhaps have been the case, had she seemed excessively confused and mortified, and awkwardly tried to hold on her curls till she got out of the room.

If you do not wish to be encumbered by carrying the key in your pocket, let it be left during your absence, with the clerk in the office, or with the barkeeper; and send to him for it on your return. Desire the servant who attends the door to show no person up to your room during your absence. If visiters wish to wait for your return, it is best they should do so in the parlour.

In going in and out, be careful to shut the parlour-doors after you, except in summer. Young ladies are often very inconsiderate in this respect, and cause much inconvenience, in cold weather, to those who do not like to sit with a draught of keen air blowing upon them. Even if you feel too warm yourself, it is rude to throw open a door, (much more to raise a window-sash,) without first enquiring if other ladies have no objection.

There is no impropriety in a lady commencing conversation with a stranger of genteel appearance. You can easily take occasion to mention your own name, and then, in return, she will communicate hers. But, unless you are previously certain of her respectability, have little to say to a woman who is travelling without a companion, and whose face is painted, who wears a profusion of long curls about her neck, who has a meretricious expression of eye, and who is over-dressed. It is safest to avoid her. Also, you will derive no pleasure or advantage from making acquaintance with females who are evidently coarse and vulgar, even if you know that they are rich, live in a large house, and are of respectable character. Young girls who are loud, noisy, bold, and forward, (however fashionable they may be,) it is best also to avoid. They will not want your society, as they are generally all the time surrounded by "beaux," or else rattling over the keys of the piano.

In a public parlour, it is selfish and unmannerly to sit down to the instrument uninvited, and fall to playing or practising, without seeming to consider the probability of your interrupting or annoying the rest of the company, particularly when you see them all engaged in reading or in conversation. If you want amusement, you had better read, or occupy yourself with some light sewing or knitting-work.

If you have no book, you can ring the bell, and send to the reading-room to borrow a file of newspapers; but in most hotels, there are books belonging to the establishment, lying on a table in the ladies' parlour. Be sure not to carry any of these books up-stairs, as they are intended solely for the drawing-room; and their removal from thence is interdicted. Also, never carry away the Directory, the Atlas, the City Guide, or any other book placed there for the convenience of strangers.

If you want pen and ink, or any sort of stationery, you can obtain it immediately, by ringing for a servant to bring it you from the office. In ringing the bell, one pull is sufficient; and always pull the cord *downward*. If you jerk it out horizontally, and give successively several hard pulls in that direction, the cord is very likely to break, or the knob or tassel to come off in your hand. At the chief hotel in one of the New England cities, we saw a printed paper with directions in large type, pasted beside *every bell-pull in the house*; the directions specifying minutely the proper mode of bell-ringing. Could it be that this house was frequented by persons unaccustomed to bells?

To return to the too-prevalent evil of uninvited and ill-timed piano-playing, (much of which does not deserve the name of music,) we have always been at a loss to understand how a young stranger, (modest and unobtrusive in other things,) could walk up to the instrument, sometimes almost as soon as she arrives, and rattle "fast and furious" over the keys, drowning the voices of ladies and gentlemen who were talking, and therefore compelling them to cease their conversation; or if they pursued it, obliging them to raise their tone painfully; or to lose more than half, from the impossibility of hearing each other distinctly. To read when piano-playing is going on, is to most persons impossible. There are few readers who cannot so concentrate their attention on their book, as not to be disturbed by any *talking* that may occur in their vicinity; and if talking *does* withdraw their attention from the book, it is best that they should read only when alone in their apartment. But we have met with no one who could read in the neighbourhood of a played piano.

If the music is really very good, and accompanied by a fine voice, it is true that most readers will willingly close the book to listen. But if the playing is barely tolerable, or decidedly bad, and if the singing is weak and insipid, or harsh and screaming, or timeless and tasteless, who can possibly wish to hear it; except perhaps a doating father, or an injudicious mother, vain of her daughter because she is *hers*, and so anxious to show her off, that she encourages the girl to display even her deficiencies.

We believe that our beloved America is not yet the land of music; and that (with many exceptions) her children are generally not furnished with much capacity for it. If there was a true feeling for music, there would be more genius for that charming art, and there would be more composers of original airs, the number of which, in our country, is smaller than in any civilized nation in the world. It is true we have many excellent musicians, and many very good singers, but still, music is not the grand forte of Jonathan. Pity it were,—for he has "a nobler and a manlier one."

Now as "there is a time for all things," we persist in saying that the time and place for school-girls to hear their own music, or to prove that it is not worth hearing, is not in the drawing-room of a hotel, or in the presence of a company that can have no desire to hear them. What would be thought of a young lady, who in a public room, should suddenly come forward and "speak a speech;" or suddenly rise up, and commence, "loud and high," a reading of poetry, or recite a French fable, or repeat the multiplication table, or favour the company with a spontaneous *pas seul.* And yet we do not perceive that any of these feats would be a much greater evidence of deficiency in diffidence, (to call it by no bolder name,) than the practice of rattling, uninvited and unseasonably, over the keys of a piano. A really good musician is rarely obtrusive with her music, seldom playing unless she is asked; and then, of course, complying at once.*

* It is customary with professional or public musicians, when in private company, to volunteer a song or a piece; knowing that, out of delicacy, no one will ask them to give a gratuitous specimen of the art by which they live. This is polite and proper. It is always duly appreciated, and adds to the popularity of the performer.

We repeat that no lady should play or sing in company, unless she knows herself to be universally considered a good singer or player, and capable of something more than the mere series of lessons she has learnt from her music teacher. Also, some punishment should be devised for a young girl who cannot play, yet has the folly and assurance to seat herself at the piano of a public parlour, and annoy the company by an hour of tinking and tanking with one finger only. Yet this we have seen; and her mother present all the time.

The gratuitous exhibition of bad music is said by Europeans to be one of the peculiar characteristics of American young ladies. Let them then "reform it altogether."

Bring no large sewing into the ladies' drawing-room, and nothing that will produce clippings or litter. Whenever you have occasion to write more than a few lines, do it in your own apartment. It is well to have always there a small writing-case of your own, with paper, pens, ink, wafers, sealing-wax, envelopes, post-office stamps, &c. There are very neat little writing-cases, (to be purchased at the best stationers,) that are fitted with receptacles for all the above articles, excepting paper; the whole occupying no more space in your travelling-satchel than a needle-book. The ink is so secured, that there is no danger of its spilling. You may even carry these writing-cases in your pocket as conveniently as a card-case. As writing-paper should not be folded or rolled in packing, lay it flat in a small port-folio, and put it into your trunk. You will find great convenience, when from home, to have with you a little assortment of writing materials.

Except in cases of illness, it is well to decline invitations to visit ladies in their own apartments, unless you are very intimately acquainted with them, or have some particular business. Too much sociability may induce communications too confidential; and subsequent events may prove this confidence to be misplaced. Among the ladies staying at a hotel, there is always more harmony, when they all content themselves with meeting at table, or in the public drawing-room. Young ladies should not encourage daily morning visits from young men boarding at the same house, particularly if these visits are long. In our country, nearly every young man is obliged, in some way, to get his own living; and few can afford to idle away their mornings in loitering about parlours, and talking flirtation. A youth who passes his time in this manner, is a beau not worth having. A man that deserves to be called a *good match* has something else to do with his mornings. Ladies at hotels should be specially careful not to make acquaintance with gentlemen of whom they know nothing. If a man of notoriously dissipated or immoral character, presumes to request an introduction to a lady who is aware of his bad reputation, let her at once reply that not considering the acquaintance desirable, she must be excused for declining it. It is better thus to keep off an objectionable man, (even with the certainty of offending him,) than weakly to subject yourself to the annoyance and discredit (perhaps, still worse) of allowing him to boast of his intimacy with you.

In conversing with gentlemen at hotels, (and all other places,) try not to fall into the too common practice of talking to him nothing but nonsense. It is a problem difficult to solve, that so many ladies of good abilities and cultivated minds, and who always with their own sex talk like intelligent, sensible women, should, as soon as they get into conversation with a gentleman, seem immediately to take leave of rationality, and demean themselves like utter fools—giving way at once to something they call *excitement*, now the fashionable word for almost every feeling that is wrong.

We grieve to see a charming, modest, refined young lady, almost the moment a gentleman begins to talk to her, changing her whole demeanour, and quickly becoming bold, forward, noisy, and nonsensical; chattering at the top of her voice about nothing; and keeping up a continual laugh about nothing. Does she suppose he cannot understand her if she talks sense,—or does she think he will like her the better for regaling him with nothing but folly? She is, in all probability, egregiously mistaken, unless the gentleman is himself a simpleton.

Let it not be supposed that we have any objection to that sprightliness which is one of the most agreeable characteristics of youth. On the contrary, we are glad to see vivacity in women of all ages; and if they have a sprinkling of wit and humour, so much the better. But we wish them to do themselves justice; and not, when conversing with men, run wild, because it *is* with men; and give themselves up to all manner of folly, such as would be pointless, vapid, and insipid, if it was not seasoned with causeless laughter, and with eyes keeping time to the tongue, rolling about in perpetual motion at nothing. We do not wish ladies in conversing, even with men of sense, to confine themselves always to grave discussions on important subjects. On the contrary, gay and lively conversation is always pleasant, when well-timed. But those who have not a talent for wit and humour, had best not attempt it. Again, in listening to a woman of real wit, you will see that it is her hearers who laugh, and not herself.

Persons who have no turn for humour, and little perception of it, are apt to mistake mere coarseness for that amusing gift; and in trying to be diverting, often become vulgar—a word not too severe for things that are sometimes said and written by very good people who wish to be funny, and do not know how. For instance, there is no wit, but there is shocking ungentility, in a lady to speak of taking a "snooze" instead of a nap,—in calling pantaloons "pants," or gentlemen "gents,"—in saying of a man whose dress is getting old that he looks "seedy,"—and in alluding to an amusing anecdote, or a diverting incident, to say that it is "rich." All slang words are detestable from the lips of ladies.

We are always sorry to hear a young lady use such a word as "polking" when she tells of having been engaged in a certain dance too fashionable not long since; but happily, now it is fast going out, and almost banished from the best society. To her honour be it remembered, Queen Victoria has prohibited the polka being danced in her presence. How can a genteel girl bring herself to say, "Last night I was polking with Mr. Bell," or "Mr. Cope came and asked me to polk with him." Its coarse and ill-sounding name is worthy of the dance.

If you own a lap-dog or poodle, recollect that however charming it may be to yourself, others may regard it as an annoyance; therefore, try to do without it when you are in the parlour of a house that is not your own, and when the company present does not consist entirely of your own family. All but their infatuated mistresses soon become very tired of the society of these animals. Poodles are generally peevish, whining, and snappish, prone to get under chairs and bite at feet, and to writhe about the skirts of dresses. Their faces often look old, withered, cross, and blear-eyed, seeming as if constantly troubled by the hair that dangles uncomfortably in their eyes; and they are seldom healthy. They have none of the honest, grateful, affectionate character common to dogs of larger growth. Though they often inspire their mistress with a love that becomes such a mania as to weaken her affection for all other things, they seldom make friends of any one else. We include what is called a King Charles's dog in the same category. For instance Jip—whose character is as true to nature, and as admirably drawn as that of Dora herself.

Should a visiter come in to see one of the boarders who may be sitting near you, change your place, and take a seat in a distant part of the room. It is ill-manners to remain, and listen to the conversation. It is best for the visited lady to meet her friend as soon as she sees her enter the room, and conduct her to a sofa or ottoman where they can enjoy their talk without danger of being overheard. After the visiter is gone, do not enquire her name of the friend she has just called on.

It is *not* well to call at the same time on two ladies both living at the same house, (so as to make one visit suffice for both,) unless they are intimate friends of each other, or unless your stay in the city will be very short. If one is taciturn, and the other conversable, she that is silent may imagine herself neglected, by the dialogue being chiefly between those who can talk fluently, as it certainly will be, if the third person only speaks when spoken to, and replies in monosyllables.

It is better to make a separate visit to each lady, on different days. There is another way, and a very good one. For instance, should Mrs. Canning wish to call on Mrs. Austin and Miss Lovel, both inmates of the same house, let her, when shown into the parlour, send up her name to Mrs. Austin first. When that lady comes down, and she and her friend have conversed about as long as the usual term of a morning call, Mrs. Canning will rise to depart, and when Mrs. Austin has seen her to the parlour door, Mrs. C. may say, "I will detain you no longer," or "I will encroach no longer on your time, but I am going now to send up for Miss Lovel."

Mrs. Austin then takes her leave, and goes up-stairs, (*her* part of the visit being over;) while Mrs. Canning returns to her seat in the parlour, having first rung the bell, and sent for Miss Lovel.

In this manner, two distinct visits may be politely made to two ladies living in the same hotel—and it is very customary.

Any lady that lives at a hotel can in some degree make a return for the civilities received from private families, by occasionally inviting a friend to dine or take tea with her. These dinners or teas are of course always charged in her bill. If she expects a friend, she will previously send to apprize the head-waiter that she wishes him to reserve a seat next to her own, for a lady. She should give her arm to her guest, in going to the table.

If a friend chances to call, whom she really wishes to stay and dine or drink tea with her, she should ask her guest to take off her bonnet as soon as she comes in; giving her the invitation at once, and not delaying it till the visiter is about taking her leave.

Even in a private house, such extemporaneous invitations (which if evidently sincere, are always gratifying, whether accepted or not) should be given *immediately*, as soon as the hostess meets her guest. There will then be time to order any improvement in the table arrangements that may be deemed necessary.

We often have occasion to repeat, that whatever is done at all, should be done well.

If, while in the parlour of the hotel, you wish to know if a person you are desirous of seeing is staying at the house, the easiest way to obtain the information, is not to enquire round of the ladies present, but to ring the bell, and desire the waiter to go and ask at the office. You can then send a message accordingly. It should be a card with a message pencilled on it.

By sending to the office you may learn where all the public places in the city and its environs are to be found. Also, where the churches are situated.

You may be sure that the most fashionable shops are in the main street.

At any stationer's, you can buy a small pocket-map of the city, folded in a little morocco case. This will be an almost indispensable aid in finding your way. In Philadelphia, the arrangement of the long streets that run east and west from the Delaware to the Schuylkill, has given occasion to the old rhyme of

Market, Arch, Race and Vine,

Chestnut, Walnut, Spruce and Pine.

If when about to ascend the stairs, you find that a gentleman is going up at the same time, draw back and make a sign for him to precede you. He will bow, and pass on before you. When coming down, do the same, that the gentleman may descend in advance of you.

A very polished man will not wait for a signal from the lady, but will bow and run up-stairs, passing her as a thing of course.

Do not idly detain a parlour newspaper on your lap, for half an hour or more, after you have done reading it. As soon as you have read all you want, replace it on the table, or transfer it to another lady, who may wish to read it, and who may have been waiting anxiously to see you lay it out of your hand. You have no right to monopolize any thing that is intended for the convenience of the whole company.

CHAPTER XI.
HOTEL DINNER.

In dressing for a hotel dinner, it is not well to adopt a full evening costume, and to appear as if attired for a ball; for instance, with a coloured velvet gown; or one of a splendid brocade; or a transparent gauze material over a satin; or with short sleeves and bare neck in cold weather; or with flowers or jewels in the hair. Such costumes should be reserved for evening parties. If worn at the table d'hôte, it may be suspected you have no other place in which to display them. Your dress need not be more showy than you would wear when dining at a private house, particularly if you are a permanent boarder. There is no place where dress escapes with less scrutiny than at a great hotel. Still, it is bad taste to go to the dinner-table in ungenteel and unbecoming habiliments—such as a figured or party-coloured mousseline-de-laine, a thing which always has the effect of calico, and, like calico, gives an unlady-like look even to the most decided lady. In fact, what is it but woollen calico? And if it is accompanied by a very thin, flimsy collar, so small and narrow as to be scarcely visible, the neck and face will look dingy and ill-coloured for want of sufficient white to relieve it. No collar at all, but merely a coloured silk handkerchief, or a coloured dress, coming immediately against the neck, is disfiguring to all women, and men too.

Most American ladies beyond the age of thirty-five, look better in caps than without them, even if their hair shows no signs of middle age. Before that time, the females of our country begin to fade, evincing one effect of torrid summers and frozen winters. A tasteful and simply elegant cap (not one that is elaborate in its design, and loaded with ornament,) imparts a grace and softness to a faded face, and renders less conspicuous the inroads of time. A decidedly old lady, persisting in going with her head uncovered, is a pitiable object, and scarcely looks respectable. Worse still, when she takes to an auburn wig. Gray hair is seldom unbecoming to a man. To a woman it gives a masculine aspect, especially if worn without a cap; and if there is an attempt at long gray locks, or ringlets, the effect is strange, wild and ghastly. It is far more becoming for an elderly lady to give a dark shade to her temples, and the upper part of her forehead, by a plain, simple, and becoming dark-coloured braid, not intended to pass as her natural hair, (for it never does,) but merely that the face should be set off by a due proportion of shadow,—and not be all light or lightish. If a decidedly old lady prefers wearing her own gray hair, let her part it smoothly on her forehead, but make no attempt at curls, and be sure to add a cap to it. An elderly female should, as we have said, *always* wear a cap; and her cap should have tabs or broad strings to tie under her chin. There is no use or beauty in a lady looking older than is necessary, by wearing a short-eared or round-eared cap, set back from her head, and exposing all her cheeks even beyond her ears, with the crease in her chin, and the deep furrows or wrinkles on each side of her neck—all which can be concealed by bringing forward the bow of her cap tabs.

Let all ladies, old and young, avoid having their caps trimmed with ribbons or flowers of what are called high-colours; deep, heavy pinks and blues, and reddish lilacs. These colours vulgarize every thing they are intended to decorate. High-coloured ribbons, flowered or figured, are decidedly vulgar.

A profusion of jewels at a public table is in very bad taste, particularly if the jewellery is palpably false—for instance, a large brooch with great mock diamonds, or a string of wax beads meant for pearls. Still worse, glass things imitating topazes or garnets—or two or three gilt bracelets on one arm. A *large* imitation gem always betrays its real quality by its size.

Endeavour to make your arrangements so as to be dressed for dinner, and seated in the ladies' drawing-room, about ten or fifteen minutes before the dining-hour, that you may be ready to go in with the rest of the company.

If you and your party are strangers, recently arrived, do not at once take the lead, and walk up to the head of the table, regardless of dislodging and causing inconvenience among the regular boarders, to whom those seats have been allotted. But desire a servant to show you a place. The head-waiter is usually at hand to arrange seats for the strangers, and he will attend to you. Persons not accustomed to hotels, frequently show a great craving for the seats near the head of the table. This is foolish. There are no places of honour; neither are the eatables better at one part of the table than another.

Nobody "sits below the salt." And every one has an equal chance of obtaining a share of the nicest articles on the table. What is most desirable is to have a seat in the vicinity of agreeable people, and you will more frequently find them about the middle, or lower end of the table, than at the top—that being the place usually most coveted by the least genteel of the guests. We have seen the Chief Magistrate of the Union, "the ruler of millions," simply take a seat near the door, at the lower end of a hotel-table, in Philadelphia, having arrived unexpectedly.

As we have said before, we perceive not the propriety or the convenience of a large party of strangers, on entering in a body, pertinaciously making their way to the upper end of the table, with a determination to obtain seats all in a row; as if the whole row together could join in the same conversation, or even *see* each other, when they sit on the same side.

In seating yourself, look down for a moment to see if you have placed the foot of your chair on the dress of the lady sitting next to you; and if you have done so, remove it immediately, that her dress may be in no danger of tearing when she attempts to rise. Sit close to the table, but never lean your elbows upon it. To sit far from it, and reach out distantly, is very awkward. Having unfolded your napkin, secure it to your belt with a pin, to prevent its slipping down from your lap, and falling under the table. This may be done so that the pinning will not be perceptible. Bring with you a spare pin or two for this purpose,—or keep always a pincushion in your pocket. It is much better than to incur the risk of getting your dress greased or stained by the napkin deserting your lap. If such accidents *should* happen, pass them over slightly, and do not lose your temper. For the present, wipe the spot with your napkin, and dip the corner in water, and rub it lightly over the grease-mark. When dinner is over, you can finish repairing the injury in your own room. The coloured waiters are generally very clever at removing grease-spots from dresses. One of them will do it for you after dinner. The stain of wine or fruit may in most cases be taken out of a washable article by laying it immediately in cold water.

To eat in gloves or mittens was always foolish; fortunately it is no longer fashionable; but greatly the contrary.

Refrain from loud talking, or loud laughing. Young ladies truly genteel are never conspicuously noisy at a public table, or anywhere else. Still more carefully refrain from whispering, or exchanging significant glances. Whispers are always overheard, (even when the vulgar precaution is taken of screening your mouth with your hand,) and glances are always observed.* Joggings, nudgings, pinchings, sleeve-pullings, &c. are excessively unlady-like, and shamefully impudent when (as is often the case) the eye of the jogger is fixed upon the object of the jog. To put up an eye-glass at the face of a stranger, is very rude. So it is to make remarks in French.

When eating fish, first remove the bones carefully, and lay them on the edge of your plate. Then with your fork in your right hand, (the concave or hollow side held uppermost,) and a small piece of bread in your left, take up the flakes of fish. Servants, and all other persons, should be taught that the butter-sauce should not be *poured over* the fish, but put on one side of the plate, that the eater may use it profusely or sparingly, according to taste, and be enabled to mix it conveniently with the sauce from the fish-castors. Pouring butter-sauce *over* any thing is now ungenteel.

Do not attempt removing a cover from a dish, that you may help yourself before the rest of the company. Leave all that to the waiters. Tell them what you want in a distinct, but not in a loud, conspicuous voice. In asking a servant to bring you a thing, add not the useless and senseless words "*will* you?" for instance, "Bring me the bread, will you?"—"Give me some water, will you?" Of course he will. Has he the option of refusing? How you would be startled were he to answer, "*I will not.*" It is well always to say, even to servants, "I will thank you for the bread,—or the water." If you are a stranger in the house, ask, at the beginning, the servant who waits on you to tell you his name. This may save you some inconvenience. Where servants are numerous, they should always go by their surnames, and be called Wilson, Jackson, Thomson, or whatever it may be. This will prevent the confusion arising from half a dozen Johns, or as many Williams.

If the waiters are attentive, and in sufficient number, you will have, at a *good* hotel, little or no occasion to help yourself to any thing. Do not, under any circumstances, reach across the table, or rise on your feet to get at any particular dish you may want. Trouble no one of the company; but wait till you see a servant at hand. No man who is a gentleman ever puts the ladies in requisition to help him at table.

It is not customary at hotels for ladies to be assiduous in watching and supplying the plates of gentlemen. They can take care of themselves.

---

* A whisperer usually betrays herself by unconsciously fixing her eyes on the person she is secretly talking of. If you wish to inform your neighbour that a distinguished person is present say softly, "Mr. C. is here, but do not look at him just now."

If in turning to speak to a waiter, you find him in the act of serving some one else, say, "*When you are at leisure*, I will thank you for some water,"—or whatever you may want.

It is selfish to be continually sending out of the room the man who waits near you, for the purpose of bringing extra things for yourself. Try to be satisfied with what you find on the table, and recollect that you are depriving others of his services, while you are dispatching him back and forward on errands to the kitchen.

Many persons hold silver forks awkwardly, as if not accustomed to them. It is fashionable to use your knife only while cutting up the food small enough to be eaten with the fork alone. While cutting, keep the fork in your left hand, the hollow or concave side downward, the fork in a very slanting position, and your fore-finger extended far down upon its handle. When you have done cutting up what you are going to eat, lay aside your knife, transfer the fork to your right hand, and take a small piece of bread in your left. If eating any thing soft, use your silver fork somewhat as a spoon, turning up the hollow side that the cavity may hold the food. If engaged in talking, do not, meanwhile, hold your fork bolt upright, but incline it downward, so as to be nearly on a level with your plate. Remember, always, to keep your own knife, fork, and spoon out of the dishes. It is an insult to the company, and a disgrace to yourself, to dip into a dish any thing that has been even for a moment in your mouth. To take butter or salt with your own knife is an abomination. There is always a butter-knife and a salt-spoon. It is nearly as bad to take a lump of sugar with your fingers.

In eating bread at dinner, break off little bits, instead of putting the whole piece to your mouth and biting at it.

No lady looks worse than when gnawing a bone, even of game or poultry. Few *ladies* do it. In fact, nothing should be sucked or gnawed in public; neither corn bitten off from the cob, nor melon nibbled from the rind.* It is very ungraceful to eat an orange at table, unless, having cut a bit off the top, you eat the inside with a tea-spoon—otherwise reserve it for the privacy of your own room. Always pare apples and peaches; and crack no nuts with your teeth. In eating cherries, put your half-closed hand before your mouth to receive the stones; then lay them on one side of your plate. To spit out the stones one at a time as you proceed with the cherries is very ungenteel. Get rid of plumb-stones in the same manner.

Do not eat incongruous and unsuitable things from the same plate, telling the waiter that "he need not change it, as it will do very well." The washing of

---

* It is, however, customary in eating sweet potatoes of a large size, to break them in two, and taking a piece in your hand, to pierce down to the bottom with your fork, and then mix in some butter, continuing to hold it thus while eating it.

a plate (more or less) is no object whatever in a large establishment, and it is expected that the guests will have clean ones very frequently.

It is an affectation of ultra-fashion to eat pie with a fork, and has a very awkward and inconvenient look. Cut it up first with your knife and fork both; then proceed to eat it with the fork in your right hand.

Much of this determined fork-exercise may be considered foolish. But it is fashionable.

If a lady wishes to eat lobster, let her request the waiter that attends her, to extract a portion of it from the shell, and bring it to her on a clean plate—also to place a castor near her.

Novices in lobster sometimes eat it simply with salt, or with vinegar only, or with black pepper. This betrays great ignorance of the article. To prepare it according to the usual custom,—cut up, very small, the pieces of lobster, and on another plate make the dressing. First, mash together some hard-boiled yolk of egg, and some of the red coral of the lobster, with a little salt and cayenne. Mix in, with a fork, mustard to your taste; and then a liberal allowance of salad-oil, finishing with vinegar. Transfer the bits of lobster to the plate that has the dressing, and combine the whole with a fork. Lettuce salad is dressed in the same manner.

At a public table, a lady should never volunteer to dress salad for others of the company. Neither should she cut up a pie, and help it round. These things ought only to be done by a gentleman, or a servant.

If a gentleman with whom you are acquainted has dressed a salad, and offers the plate to you, take what you want, and immediately return to him the remainder; and do not pass it on to persons in your vicinity. It is *his* privilege, and not *yours* to offer it to others, as he has had the trouble of dressing it. And it is just that he should have a portion of it for himself, which will not be the case if you officiously hand it about to people around you. Leave it to him to dispose of as he pleases.

It was formerly considered ill-manners to refuse to take wine with a gentleman. Now that the fortunate increase of temperance has induced so many persons to abjure, entirely, the use of all liquors, it is no longer an offence to decline these invitations. If you have no conscientious scruples, and if you are acquainted with the gentleman, or have been introduced to him, (not else,) you may comply with his civility, and when both glasses are filled, look at him, bow your head, and taste the wine. If you are placed between a lady and gentleman who are taking wine together, lean back a little that they may see each other's faces. It is not customary, in America, for a lady to empty her glass,—or indeed, at a hotel, or boarding-house, to take wine with the same gentleman after the first day. Next time he asks, politely refuse, simply desiring him to excuse you. If he is a true gentleman, he will regard your refusal in its proper light, and not persist. We have often, at a public table, regretted to see ladies in the daily practice of taking wine with the same gentleman as often as invited. This "daily practice" is improper, indelicate, and we will say mean—for wine is expensive, and no lady should every day place herself under the same obligation to the same gentleman, even for a single glass. He will not respect her the more for doing so. On no consideration let any lady be persuaded to take *two* glasses of champagne. It is more than the head of an *American* female can bear. And she may rest assured that (though unconscious of it herself) all present will find her cheeks flushing, her eyes twinkling, her tongue unusually voluble, her talk loud and silly, and her laugh incessant. Champagne is very insidious; and two glasses may throw her into this pitiable condition.

If a stranger whom you do not know, and to whom you have had no introduction, takes the liberty of asking you to drink wine with him, refuse at once, positively and coldly, to prove that you consider it an unwarrantable freedom. And so it is.

If you are helped to any thing whose appearance you do not like, or in which you are disappointed when you taste it, you, of course, at a hotel table, are not obliged to eat it. Merely leave it on your plate, without audibly giving the reason; and then, in a low voice, desire the waiter to bring you something else. It is well, while at table, to avoid any discussion of the demerits of the dishes. On the other hand, you may praise them as much as you please.

In refusing to be helped to any particular thing, never give as a reason that "you are afraid of it," or "that it will disagree with you." It is sufficient simply to *refuse*; and then no one has a right to ask why? While at table, all allusions to dyspepsia, indigestion, or any other disorders of the stomach, are vulgar and disgusting. The word "stomach" should never be uttered at any table, or indeed anywhere else, except to your physician, or in a private conversation with a female friend interested in your health. It is a disagreeable word, (and so are all its associations,) and should never be mentioned in public to "ears polite." Also, make no remarks on what is eaten by persons near you, (except they are children, and under your own care,) such as its being unwholesome, indigestible, feverish, or in any way improper. It is no business of yours; and besides, you are not to judge of others by yourself. No two constitutions are alike, and what is very bad for *you*, may be perfectly innoxious to others. If persons are with you in whom you are much interested, and over whom you have influence, and they seem inclined to eat what is bad for them, refrain from checking them in presence of strangers. Above all, do not open your eyes, and hold up your hands, and exclaim against their folly, and want of self-control, and predict their certain sufferings from that cause. But if you *must* remonstrate, wait till you have quitted the table, and find yourself alone with the delinquent.

Never, while at table, (whether in public or private,) allow yourself to talk on painful or disgusting subjects. Avoid all discussions of sicknesses, sores, surgical operations, dreadful accidents, shocking cruelties, or horrible punishments. A love of such topics, evinces a coarse and unfeminine mind. It is rude in gentlemen at any time to introduce them before ladies; and a polished man never does so. The conversation at table should be as cheerful and pleasant as possible. Political and sectarian controversies ought to have no place there. Shakespeare truly says, "Unquiet meals make ill digestion."

Avoid the discussion at table of private affairs; either your own, or those of other people. Remember that "servants have ears," and frequently much more quickness of comprehension and retentiveness of memory than is generally supposed. So have children.

Abstain from picking your teeth at table. Notwithstanding that custom has allowed this practice in Europe, (even in fashionable society,) it is still a very disagreeable one, and to delicate spectators absolutely sickening to behold. Delay it till you are alone, and till you can indulge in it without witnesses. We know that it is quite possible to go on through a long life, and to have clean teeth, without ever once having been *seen* to pick them; and yet those teeth are really picked after every meal.

Should you chance to be extremely incommoded by some extraneous substance that has gotten between your teeth, you can remove it unperceived, by holding up your napkin or handkerchief before your mouth, so as effectually to conceal the process. When you take any thing out of your teeth, do not make the persons who are near you sick, by laying the disgusting particle on the side of your plate; but conceal it immediately. Still, nothing but "sheer necessity" can excuse any teeth-picking at table.

We have seen a young *lady*, at a very fashionable house in one of our great cities, pull a dish of stewed oysters close to her, and with a table-spoon fish out and eat the oysters one at a time; audibly sipping up their liquor from the said dish.

We have seen a young *gentleman* lift his plate of soup in both hands, hold it to his mouth and drink, or rather lap it up. This was at no less a place than Niagara.

We have heard of a well-dressed stranger at a great hotel in Boston, who having used his own knife for the butter, flew into a violent passion with the waiter for respectfully pointing out to him the silver butter-knife. Swearing that the knife he had been putting in his mouth was quite good enough, afterward, for any butter in the world, the *gentleman* flung the silver knife across the table, and broke it against the wall. For this exploit he had to pay five dollars.

A man that habitually rises on his feet to reach across the table for a dish, and pulls it to himself, instead of desiring the waiter to bring it to him, is unworthy the appellation of a gentleman. Ladies, of course, cannot be guilty of this abomination; but it is true that they sometimes extend their arms entirely too far, in trying to get at something which a servant would bring them if asked to do so.

Some persons behave coarsely at a public table because they are ignorant, and know no better. Some (far less excusable) are rude because they are too selfish to put any restraint on their inclinations, or to care for the convenience of others.

Some display, all the time, a vulgar determination to "get the full worth of their money." Some, who at a *private* dinner-table would be the most polite people imaginable, lay aside their good manners in a *public* dining-room; regarding a hotel as they would a tavern—a sort of Liberty Hall. And some are insolent by way of "showing their consequence,"—having, in reality, mixed so little with *true* people of consequence, as not to be aware that persons of high station are, with few exceptions, entirely free from the assumption of undue importance.

Servants are often very shrewd observers, and they always say that real gentlefolks "never take airs." Neither they do.

When the finger-glasses are sent round, dip a clean corner of your napkin into the water, and wet round your lips with it, but omit the disgusting foreign fashion of taking water into your mouth, rinsing and gurgling it round, and then spitting it back into the glass. Wait till you can give your mouth a regular and efficient washing up-stairs. Dip your fingers into the glass, rub them with the slice of lemon, or the orange-leaf that may be floating on the surface, and then wipe them on the napkin. We have heard of a man who saw finger-glasses for the first time in his life, when dining at one of the New York hotels. A slice of lemon floating on the top, he took up the bowl and drank the water, exclaiming as he set it down—"Well! if this isn't the poorest lemonade I ever tasted!"

On quitting the table, it is not necessary to fold up your napkin. Merely lay it on the table near your plate. The napkins will be immediately collected by the servants, carried to the laundry, and thrown at once into tubs of water, to take out the stains.

When dinner is over, and you see that nearly all the company, except two or three, have left the table, it is not well to be one of that two or three, and to remain to an indefinite period, loitering over the last pickings of a plate of nuts—nut-picking being always a tedious business. The waiters are, by this time, very tired of standing, and they (like all other people) are entitled to some consideration of their comfort. Even the attraction of a beau drinking his wine beside her, ought not to induce a young lady to outstay all the company, with the pretext of being passionately fond of nuts. She may indulge this passion at any time by keeping a bag of them in her own room.

The English travellers who visit America are often right in their remarks on many of our customs. And instead of resenting these remarks, we might profit by them, and reform.

For instance, it is true that the generality of Americans eat too fast, for their own health, and the comfort of those about them; masticating their food very slightly, and not allowing themselves time enough to enjoy their meals. The French, however, eat faster still, and can dispatch a surprising quantity of food in less time than any people in the civilized world. If we pattern after either nation in the customs of the table, the *genteel* English are far better models than most of their neighbours across the Channel. But the best class of Americans are unsurpassed in the essentials of all these observances. The English attach too much importance to ceremonies merely conventional, and for which there seems no motive but the ever-changing decrees of fashion. Yet, on going to England, let every American lady take care to make herself acquainted with these ceremonies; for her ignorance of them will find no quarter there—and she need not flatter herself that it will be passed over unnoticed.

In most hotels it is not customary to have hot cakes or any warm dishes on the tea-table, except in cold weather. We think, in a summer afternoon, they can be easily dispensed with, and that ladies might be satisfied with sweet cakes, fruit, preserves, and other things more delicate, and more suited to the hour, than the hot preparations they sometimes call for; and which, by not seeing them on the table, they may be assured do not come within scope of the tea-arrangements. It is expecting too much to suppose the cook will be willing to mix batter-cakes and bake them, or to scorch over the fire with broiling or stewing relishes, in a warm summer evening—or even to make toast, except for an invalid. Also, every one should know that a substantial meal (including tea and coffee) can generally be had at the nine o'clock supper-table. In houses where there is no nine o'clock supper, the tea-table is set out with greater profusion and variety.

At hotels, the interval between dinner and tea is usually short; the tea-hour being early, that the guests may have ample time to prepare for going to places of amusement. Yet there are ladies who, though spending all the evening at home, will remain sitting idly in the parlour till eight o'clock, (or later still,) keeping the table standing and servants waiting in attendance, that they may have a better appetite, and be able to make a heartier meal at their tea. This is selfish and inconsiderate, particularly as they might easily wait a little longer, and take their tea or coffee at the supper-table. Their appetites would then be still better. The servants certainly require rest, and should be exempt from all attendance in the ladies' eating-room, for an hour or two in the evening.

No lady can remain long in the drawing-room talking to a gentleman after all the rest have retired for the night, without subjecting herself to remarks which it would greatly annoy her to hear—whether merited or not. Neither is it well for her to be seen continually sitting at the same window with the same gentleman.

Ladies and gentlemen who wish to hold private dialogues, should not for that purpose monopolize a centre-table; thereby preventing persons who wish to read from availing themselves of the light of the chandelier above it. Lovers who have proper consideration, (a rare occurrence,) always sit as far as possible from the rest of the company, and so they should—unless they can bring themselves to join in general conversation. That is, if the lovership is real. In many cases the semblance is only assumed to produce effect, and the talk has really nothing secret or mysterious about it, and might just as well be uttered audibly.

In making acquaintance with a stranger at a hotel, there is no impropriety (but quite the contrary) in enquiring of her from what place she comes. In introducing yourself give your name *audibly*; or what is still better, if you have a card about you, present that; and she should do the same in return. Before you enter into conversation on any subject connected with religion, it will be well to ask her to what church she belongs. This knowledge will guard you from indulging, inadvertently, in sectarian remarks which may be displeasing to her, besides producing a controversy which may be carried too far, and produce ill-feeling between the parties. We have known the mere question, "Have you been to church to-day?" when asked of a stranger at a Sunday dinner-table, bring on a dialogue of great asperity, and very annoying to the hearers. As it cannot possibly concern yourself whether the strangers at a hotel have been to church or not, or what church they have visited, omit catechising them at table on this or any other religious subject. We have never known a clergyman guilty of this solecism in good sense and good manners.

When you give a gratuity to a servant—for instance, to the man who waits on you at table, or he that attends your room, or to the chambermaid or the errand-boy—give it at no regular time, but whenever you think proper, or find it convenient. It is injudicious to allow them to suppose that they are to do you no particular service without being immediately paid for it. It renders them mercenary, rapacious, and neglectful of other boarders who are less profuse; not reflecting that the servants are hired to wait on the company, and are paid wages for doing so, by the proprietor of the establishment, and that it is therefore their duty to him, and to his guests, to exert themselves so to give satisfaction. Still, it is right and customary to pay them extra for conveying your baggage up and down stairs when you are departing from the house or returning to it. Carrying heavy baggage is very hard work even for strong men. If you are a permanent boarder, and from ill-health require extra attendance, it is well to give a certain sum monthly to each of the servants who wait upon you; and then they will not expect any thing more, except on extraordinary occasions. And to each of them, separately, give the money with your own hand. In short, whatever you give to any one, (servants or others,) it is safest, when convenient, to bestow it in person. There will then be no mistakes, no forgettings, and no temptation to embezzlement.

If you live in Philadelphia, you will find it very convenient, in most cases, to send messages by a note with a stamp on it, put into the city-post. There is a mail-bag and a letter-box at all hotels, and at most of the large boarding-houses. The errand-boy of the hotel carries parcels, and takes such messages as require an *immediate* answer. For a distance of any consequence, he will expect from twelve to twenty-five cents. For little errands in the immediate neighbourhood, less will suffice. When a servant brings you small change, do not tell him to keep it. It is giving him the bad habit of expecting it always; and at times when you may have occasion, yourself, for that very change. It is the worst way of feeing them. On leaving the house, and at Christmas, it is customary to give a fee rather larger than usual, to the servants who have been your attendants. But as we have said before, give it with your own hands.

It is ungenerous and most unjustifiable to bribe the servants to neglect other boarders, (whose place is near yours,) for the purpose of their bestowing on you a double share of attention. It is taking an undue advantage, which in the end will come out badly.

All persons who go to hotels are not able to lavish large and frequent gratuities on the servants. But all, for the price they pay to the proprietor, are entitled to an ample share of attention from the domestics.

It is very mean and unladylike to gossip secretly with the servants, and question them about any of the other guests. Still worse, to repeat what they tell you, and give *them* as authority. Treat them always with kindness and civility, but have no confidential and familiar intercourse with them. To those you know, it is but common civility to bid good morning every day. Coloured people you may always gratify by saying a few words to them, now and then, in passing. They value this little kindness, and will not presume upon it like those from "the old country," who, if treated familiarly, will frequently take liberties, and lose all respect for you. Elderly coloured people, (particularly in the South,) like much to be called "aunt" or "uncle;" and it degrades no white lady to please them by doing so.

In all hotels, it is against the rule to take out of the ladies' drawing-room any books that may be placed there for the general convenience of the company, such as dictionaries, guide-books, directories, magazines, &c. If you borrow a file of newspapers from the reading-room, get done with them as soon as you can, lest they should be wanted there by the gentlemen; and as soon as you have finished, ring for a servant to carry them back.

Be careful, in cold weather, always to shut the parlour-doors after you. If you think the room too warm, do not throw open either door or window, without first enquiring if it will cause inconvenience to any one present. It is a good practice to carry a pocket fan even in winter, in case you should chance to feel the heat more sensibly than any other lady in the room. If the heat of the grate causes you inconvenience, enquire if there is any objection to having the blower brought in and stood up before it. If not, ring the bell and order it.

If you have an anthracite fire in your chamber, and wish to extinguish it on retiring for the night, take the tongs, and lifting off some of the largest coals from the top, lay them beneath the grate. Then, with the shut-tongs or the poker, make a deep hollow in the centre of the fire; raking it into two hills, one on each side, leaving a valley down in the middle. It will begin to blacken immediately, and go out in a few minutes. If you cannot do this yourself, ring for a servant.

This is *the only way* to put out an anthracite fire, whether in a grate or a stove.—There is no other. Try it.

CHAPTER XII.
SHIP-BOARD.

There are few places where the looks and manners of the company are more minutely scanned than on ship-board; and few where the agreeability of a lady will be more highly appreciated. There is little or no variety of objects to attract attention. The passengers are brought so closely into contact with each other, and confined to so small a neighbourhood, or rather so many neighbours are crowded into so small a space, that all their sayings and doings are noticed with unusual attention, by those who are well enough to regard any thing but themselves. Sea-sickness is a very selfish malady,—and no wonder that it is so. Fortunately it is less prevalent than formerly, thanks to the improvements in cabin-room, ventilation, lodging, food, and many other things connected with ocean-travelling. A lady who is not of a bilious or dyspeptic habit, and who has taken precautionary medicine a few days before commencing the voyage, frequently escapes sea-sickness altogether; or at least gets well after the first day or two.

It is best not to be over-officious in offering your aid to the sick ladies, unless they are your intimate friends. The stewardess of a packet-ship is generally all-sufficient; and much more capable of attending to their wants than you can be. Sea-sickness renders its victims very querulous; and few like to be continually reminded of their condition by enquiries too often repeated of—"How do you find yourself now?" "Do you feel any better?" or, "Do you think you could not eat something?" To one very much prostrated by the effects of the sea-motion, the mere replying to these questions is an additional misery. Whatever sympathy you may feel, at the time, for those afflicted with the marine malady, remember that it is a disorder which never kills, but very frequently cures.

If you are sick yourself, say as little about it as possible. And never allude to it at table, where you will receive little sympathy, and perhaps render yourself disgusting to all who hear you. At no time talk about it to gentlemen. Many foolish common-place sayings are uttered by ladies who attempt to describe the horrors of sea-sickness. For instance this—"I felt all the time as if I wished somebody to take me up, and throw me overboard." This is untrue—no human being ever really *did* prefer drowning to sea-sickness.

When the ship is actually in danger, this malady is always frightened away; the feelings of the mind entirely overpowering those of the body.

Try to avoid supposing that every fresh gale is a violent storm; but confide in the excellence of the ship, and the skill of its navigators. Yet, though not afraid yourself, remember that others may be so, and do not try to show your courage by indulging in undue gayety. Mirth is out of place when the sky is overcast with gloom, the wind blowing hard, and the waves "running mountains high," and foaming and roaring all round the vessel.

If there is truly a violent tempest, and if the danger is real and imminent, trust to that Almighty Power who is with you always,—on the sea, and on the land; and silently and fervently implore his protection.

No captain likes to be teazed with importunities concerning the probable length of the passage. You may be sure he will do all he can to make it as short as possible. In rough weather, refrain from asking, whenever you see him, "If there is any danger?" If there really is, he will certainly let you know it in time.

Endeavour to live harmoniously with your fellow-passengers. Avoid such national allusions as may give offence to the foreigners. If you find that any of them are in the frequent practice of sneering at your own country, or speaking of it disrespectfully, repress your resentment, resort to no recrimination, but refrain from further conversation with that individual, and leave him to the gentlemen. If a female foreigner is in the habit of gratuitously abusing America, endeavour calmly to convince her that her ideas of your country are erroneous. If she will not be convinced, (as is most likely, if she is an *ungenteel* Englishwoman,) give up the attempt, and leave her to herself. If you have a taste for the ridiculous, you will regard her prejudices and the expression of them only as objects of amusement.

Avoid all arguments with a woman of irritable disposition, lest you are drawn in yourself to defend your opinion too warmly. You will soon find whether or not you can convince her, or whether she is likely to convince you. And it is worse than useless for both to continue protracting the argument, when they know that the opinion of neither will be shaken. Also, it is foolish to keep on repeating the same ideas, with no change but in a few of the words.

Long and turbulent discussions are peculiarly annoying on ship-board, particularly in rainy weather, when for the weary and pent-up audience, "there's no door to creep out."

It is certainly advisable for every lady on ship-board to endeavour to make herself as agreeable as she can, and not to suppose that all her "whims and oddities" will be excused because she is suffering "the pains and penalties" of the sea, and is therefore not "a responsible being." If free from sickness, a lady may propose or promote many pleasant little amusements and occupations; such as playing children's games on deck, or taking a part in chess, chequers, and backgammon in the cabin. Ladies sometimes form a regular little coterie, for assembling at certain hours, and employing themselves in knitting, bead-work, light-sewing, &c. while a gentleman reads aloud to them in some entertaining book. In the evening, vocal concerts will be an agreeable variety, as there are always some persons on board who can sing. And when the weather is fine, and the ship steadily laying her course, a moonlight dance on deck is delightful.

A young lady should improve the opportunity of learning the names of the principal parts of the ship. It is a silly boast at the end of the voyage, (and yet we have heard such boasts,) to say that you do not know the fore-mast from the main-mast; and that you have no idea where the mizen-mast is, much less the bow-sprit. And even if a fair damsel should be able to distinguish the fore-topsail from the jib, and to know even the flying-jib, and have learnt the difference between the compass and the quadrant, and the log-line and the lead-line, we opine that "the gentlemen" will think none the worse of her; to say nothing of the satisfaction it will afford herself to listen with some comprehension to talk concerning the ship, and to read understandingly a few of the numerous excellent novels that treat of "life on the ocean wave."

If you have, unfortunately, the rude and unamiable habit of laughing whenever you see any one get a fall, leave it off when on ship-board,—where falls are of continual occurrence from the rolling of the vessel, and the steepness of the stairs. We never could tell why a fall, even on the ice, should be regarded as a subject of mirth, when the chance is that it may produce a serious hurt, and is always attended with some pain or some annoyance at least. Low-bred women always say they cannot help laughing at such sights. We think *ladies* ought always to help it, and hasten at once to the relief of the sufferer, to ascertain if they are hurt.

Be washed and dressed *neatly* every day. This can generally be managed with the assistance of the female servants—even if you *are* sick.

A piano never sounds well on ship-board—the cabins are too small, and the ceilings too low. To the sick and nervous, (and all who are sea-sick become *very* nervous,) this instrument is peculiarly annoying. Therefore be kind enough to spare them the annoyance. You can practise when the weather is fine; and the invalids are on deck. Pianos have been abolished in many of the finest ships. Such instruments as can be carried on deck, and played in the open air, are, on the contrary, very delightful at sea, when in the hands of good performers—particularly on a moonlight evening.

In going to England, take with you no American reprints of English books, unless you intend leaving them on board the ship. If you attempt to land them, they will be seized at the custom-house. American books by American authors are *not* prohibited.

Make no attempt to smuggle any thing. You may be detected and disgraced. The risk is too great, and the advantage too little.

When you leave your state-room to sit in the ladies' cabin, do not fall to relating the particulars of your sickness, or complaining of the smallness of your apartment, the rolling of the ship, or the roughness of the waves. These inconveniences are unavoidable, and must always be expected in a sea-voyage; and talking about them too much seems to magnify their evils.

If there is any deficiency in accommodations or attentions, either try as well as you can to do without them, or in a kind and considerate manner endeavour to obtain them of the servants, if not too inconvenient, or against the ship's regulations.

It is very inconsiderate to have things cooked at luncheon time purposely for yourself. Ladies who are quite well will sometimes order baked apples, stewed prunes, buttered toast, arrow-root, cups of tea or coffee, &c.,—notwithstanding that the lunch-table is always profusely spread with a variety of cold articles; and that when dinner is cooking at the same time, the small size of the kitchen renders any extra preparations very inconvenient to the preparers.

CHAPTER XIII.
LETTERS.

The practice of enclosing letters in envelopes is now universal; particularly as when the letter is single no additional postage is charged for the cover. The postage now is in almost every instance pre-paid, it being but three cents when paid by the writer, and five if left to the receiver. Therefore, none but very poor or very mean people send unpaid letters. Letter-stamps for the United States post should be kept in a little box on your writing-table. You can get them always by sending to the post-office—from a dollar's worth or more, down to fifty or twenty-five cents' worth, at a time. In a second box, keep stamps for the city or penny post, which transmits notes from one part of the town to another. And in a third, stamps to go on the covers of newspapers.

Sealing with wax is found to be very insecure for letters that are carried by steamers into warm climates—the wax melting with the heat, and sticking the letters to each other, so that they cannot be separated without tearing. Wafers are better.

It would be very convenient to use the post-office stamp as a seal, but the clerks in that establishment charge extra postage for the trouble of turning the letter to mark the stamp. This subjects the receiver to the payment of two additional cents.

In writing upon business exclusively your own, for instance to make a request, to ask for information, to petition for a favour, or to solicit an autograph, it is but right not only to pay the postage of your own letter, but to enclose a stamp for the answer. This is always done by really polite and considerate people. You have no right, when the benefit is entirely your own, to cause any extra expense to the receiver of the letter—not even the cost of three cents to pay the postage back again. It is enough to tax their time by requiring them to write to you and send off the reply. Also, in corresponding with a relative, or very intimate friend, to whom even a small expense is of more importance than to yourself, you may enclose a stamp for the answer. Do so always in writing to poor people. Be careful not to allow yourself to get entirely out of post-office stamps. Replenish your stock in time. If the gum on the back seems too weak, go over it afresh with that excellent cement, "Perpetual Paste." Embossed or bordered envelopes are not often used except in notes of ceremony—or when the acquaintance is slight. The same with ornamented note-paper. Intimate friends and relatives use paper that is handsome, but plain. Letters of business are generally enclosed in yellow or buff-coloured envelopes. Some of these yellow envelopes are large enough to contain a folio sheet when folded. Notes *not* to be sent by post, are usually sealed with wax—the seal very small. But a *small* wafer is admissible—a white one looks best for a note. In folding your note or letter, see that it is not too large to go into the envelope. It is customary to write the direction on the envelope only. Nevertheless, if the letter is to go a long distance by post, the envelope may be worn off, or torn off accidentally, or get so damaged in the letter-bag as to be rendered illegible. The surest and safest way is to put the address on the letter also; or if the sheet is full, to find a corner for the direction, either at the beginning or end.

We have seen no *good* letter-paper at less price than twenty-five cents per quire; and for that it ought to be *very* good. If of lower cost, you may find it soft and fuzzy, so that the pen will not move freely, (the nib wearing out directly,) or so thin that you cannot write on both sides of the sheet. In paper, as in most other things, the best is the cheapest. If the tint is bluish, the writing will not be so legible as on a pure white. The surface should be smooth and glossy. For letter writing *ruled* paper is rarely used, except by children. In writing for the press, no other is so convenient. A page of ruled lines to slip beneath, is indispensable to those who cannot otherwise write straight. They are to be had for a few cents at every stationer's. It is well to get three different sizes. If you write a small hand, the lines should be closer together than if your writing is large. If you are addressing a friend and have much to say, and expect to fill the sheet, begin very near the top of the first page. But if your letter is to be a short one, commence lower down, several inches from the top. If a *very* short letter of only a few lines, begin but a little above the middle of the page. Crossing a letter all over with transverse lines is obsolete. It is intolerable to read, and there is no excuse for it now, when postage is so low, and every body pays their own.

Write the date near the right-hand side of the first page, and place it about two lines higher than the two or three words of greeting or accosting with which letters usually commence. Begin the first sentence a little below those words, and farther toward the right than the lines that are to follow. It is well in dating *every* letter to give always your exact residence—that is, not only the town you live in, but the number and street. If your correspondent has had *but one* notification of your present place of abode, she may have forgotten the number, and even the street. Your letter containing it may not be at hand as a reference, and the answer may, in consequence, be misdirected—or directed in so vague a manner that it will never reach you. We have known much inconvenience (and indeed loss) ensue from not specifying with the date of *each* letter the exact dwelling-place of the writer. But if it is *always* indicated at the top of *every one*, a reference to *any* one of your letters will furnish your proper address. If you are in the country, where there are no streets or numbered houses, give the name of the estate and that of the nearest post-town; also the county and state. All this will occupy a long line, but you will find the advantage. If your letter fills more than one sheet, number each page. Should you have no envelope, leave, on the inside of the third page, two blank spaces where the seal is to come. These spaces should be left rather too large than too small. Lest you should tear the letter in *breaking* it open, it is best to *cut* round the seal. We have seen letters that were actually illegible from the paleness of the ink. If you write from your own house this is inexcusable, as you ought always to be *well* supplied with that indispensable article; and in a city you can easily send to a stationer's and buy it. It is still better to make it yourself; than which nothing is more easy. The following receipt *we know, by experience, to be superlative.* Try it.

Buy at a druggist's four ounces of the best blue Aleppo nut-galls; half an ounce of green copperas; and half an ounce of clean, white gum-arabic. These three articles must be pulverized in a mortar. Put them into a large, clean, white-ware pitcher, and pour on a quart of boiling water. Stir the whole with a stick that will reach to the bottom, and set the pitcher in a warm place; covering it lightly with a folded newspaper. In about an hour, stir it again very hard; and repeat the stirring several times during the day. Let it remain in the pitcher several days, or a week, till it becomes an excellent black; the blackening will be accelerated by keeping the pitcher in the sun; for instance, in a sunny balcony. Stir it, down to the bottom, two or three times a day—always with a stick. Use nothing of metal in making this ink. When it is very black, and writes well, pour it off carefully from the bottom, (which must have rested undisturbed for two or three hours previous,) passing it through a funnel into pint-bottles. Before you cork them, put into each a large tea-spoonful of brandy, to prevent moulding, or a few drops of lavender. A small tea-spoonful of cloves, (slightly broken,) placed in the bottom of each bottle, before the ink is poured in, will answer the same purpose. Scouring the pitcher with soap and sand, after throwing away the dregs of the ink, will completely clear off the stains.

Ink-stands should be washed out, before they are filled anew.

There is no ink superior to this in blackness or smoothness. You can make it at less than half the cost of that which you buy in the shops. It looks blacker the next day after using, and never fades. If it becomes rather too thick, dilute it slightly with water, and stir it down to the bottom.

Never use *blue* ink. If the letter chances to get wet, the writing will be effaced. Serious losses have resulted from business letters being written in blue ink.

If you make a mistake in a word, draw your pen through it, or score it so as to be quite illegible, and then interline the correction, placing a caret beneath. This will be better than scratching out the error with your pen-knife, and afterward trying to write a new word in the identical place; an attempt which rarely succeeds, even with the aid of pounce-powder, which is pulverized gum-sandarac.

At the end of the letter, somewhat lower than your signature, (which should be very near the right-hand edge of the page,) add the name and address of the person for whom the letter is designed, and to whom it will thus find its way, even if the envelope should be defaced, or torn off and lost. Write your own name rather larger than your usual hand, and put a dot or dash after it.

Some of the ensuing paragraphs are taken (with permission of the publisher) from a former work of the author's.

In folding a letter, let the breadth (from left to right) far exceed the height. A letter folded tall is ridiculous, and one verging towards squareness looks very awkward. It is well to use a folder (or paper-knife) to press along the edges of the folds, that they may be smooth and straight. If one is looser than another, or if there is the slightest narrowing in, or widening out, toward the edge of the turn-over, the letter will have an irregular, unsightly appearance. Pieces of ruled lines may be so cut that you can slip them under the back of a letter after it is folded, and then you will be in no danger of writing the direction crooked, or uneven.

Write the name of your correspondent about the middle of the back, and very clearly and distinctly. Then give the number and street on the next line, a little nearer to the right. Then the town in *large* letters, extending still nearer to the right. If a country-town, give next (in letters a little smaller) the name of the *county* in which it is situated. This is very necessary, as in some of our states there is more than one town of the same name, and "Washingtons" all over the Union. Lastly, at the very bottom, and close to the right, indicate the state or district by its usual abbreviation,—for instance, *Me.* for Maine*—*N. H.* New Hampshire—*Vt.* Vermont—*Mass.* Massachusetts—*R. I.* Rhode Island—

---

* When the name of the state is short, you may give all the letters that compose it, as Maine—Ohio—Iowa—Texas—Utah.

Ct. or *Conn.* Connecticut—*N.Y.* New York—*N. J.* New Jersey—*Pa.* or *Penna.* Pennsylvania—*Del.* Delaware—*Md.* Maryland—*Va.* Virginia—*N. C.* North Carolina—*S. C.* South Carolina—*Ga.* or *Geo.* Georgia—*Ala.* Alabama—*Miss.* Mississippi—*Mo.* Missouri—*La.* Louisiana—*Tenn.* Tennessee—*Ky.* Kentucky—*O.* Ohio—*Ind.* Indiana—*Ill.* Illinois—*Mich.* Michigan—*Ark.* Arkansas—*Wis.* Wisconsin—*Io.* Iowa—*Tex.* Texas—*Flo.* Florida—*Cal.* California—*Or.* Oregon—*Minn.* Minnesota—*Utah*—*D. C.* District of Columbia.

To these may be added the abbreviations of the British possessions in North America: *U. C.* Upper Canada—*L. C.* Lower Canada—*N. S.* Nova Scotia—*N. B.* New Brunswick—*N. P.* New Providence.

In directing a letter to a foreign country, give the whole name, as France, Spain, Belgium, England, Ireland, Scotland, &c. We have towns in America called after all manner of European towns. For instance, a letter directed to our Havre-de-Grace, might, if Maryland was not designated, find its way to Havre-de-Grace in France; Rome in the state of New York might be taken to Rome in Italy,—York in Pennsylvania to York in England, &c. We know an instance of a gentleman directing an important letter to Boston, and, forgetting to add *Mass.* (for Massachusetts) at the bottom, the letter actually went from Philadelphia to the small town of Boston in Lincolnshire, England. In writing *from* Europe, finish the direction with the words *United States of North America.*

When you send a letter by a private opportunity, (a thing which is already almost obsolete since the days of cheap postage,) it will be sufficient to introduce very near the lower edge of the left-hand corner of the back, simply the name of the gentleman who carries it, written small. It is now considered old-fashioned to insert on the back of such a letter—"Politeness of Mr. Smith"—"Favoured by Mr. Jones"—"Honoured by Mr. Brown." If the letter is to cross the sea, by mail or otherwise, write the name of the vessel on the left-hand corner of the outside.

When a letter is to go to New York city, always put the words New York *in full,* (and not N. Y.), written large. Much confusion is caused by the name of this state and its metropolis being the same. It has been well-suggested that the name of the state of New York should be changed to Ontario—a beautiful change. In directing to any of the towns in the state of New York, then put N. Y. after the name of the town, as Hudson, N. Y.,—Syracuse, N. Y., &c.

In sending a letter to the metropolis of the Union, direct for Washington, D. C.

In directing to a clergyman, put *Rev.* (Reverend) before his name. If a bishop, *Right Reverend.* To an officer, immediately after his name put U. S. A.

for United States Army, or U. S. N. for United States Navy—having preceded his name with *Gen.*, *Col.*, *Capt.*, *Lieut.*, according to his rank.

The title Hon. (Honourable) is always used in directing to a member of congress, a member of the cabinet, a judge of the supreme court, an ambassador, or the governor of a state. For the Chief Magistrate of the Union, you may direct simply to the President of the United States. The term "Excellency" is now but little used.

For a gentleman holding a professorship in a university, preface his name with *Prof.* or *Professor*. The title of "Professor" does not really belong to all men who teach any thing, or to every man that exhibits a show—or to mesmerists, and spiritual knockers. Do not give it to them.

For sealing letters no light is so convenient as a wax taper in a low stand. A lamp, or candle, may smoke or blacken the wax. To seal well, your wax should be of the finest quality. Red wax of a bright scarlet colour is the best. Low-priced wax consumes very fast; and when melted, looks purplish or brownish. When going to melt sealing-wax, rest your elbow on the table to keep your hand steady. Take the stick of wax between your thumb and finger, and hold it a little above the light, so that it barely touches the point of the flame. Turn the stick round till it is equally softened on all sides. Then insert a little of the melted wax *under* the turn-over part of the letter, just where the seal is to come. This will render it more secure than if the sole dependence was on the outside seal. Or instead of this little touch of wax, you may slip beneath the turn-over a small wafer, either white or of the same colour as the wax. Then begin at the outer edge of the place you intend for the seal; and move the wax in a circle, which must gradually diminish till it terminates in the centre. Put the seal exactly to the middle of the soft wax, and press it down hard, but do not screw it round. Then withdraw it suddenly. Do not use motto seals unless writing to a member of your own family, or to an intimate friend. For common service, (and particularly for letters of business,) a plain seal, with simply your initials, is best.

For a note always use a very small seal. In addressing one of your own family, it is not necessary to follow scrupulously all these observances. In writing to persons decidedly your inferiors in station, avoid the probability of mortifying them by sending mean, ill-looking notes.

Remember also (what, strange to say, some people calling themselves ladies seem not to know) that a note commenced in the first person must continue in the first person all through. The same when it begins in the third person. We have heard of invitations to a party being worded thus:—

Mrs. Welford's compliments to Mrs. Marley, and requests the pleasure of her company on Thursday evening.

> Yours sincerely,
> E. Welford.

Notes of invitation should always designate both the day of the week and that of the month. If that of *the month only* is specified, one figure may perhaps be mistaken for another; for instance, the 13th may look like the 18th, or the 25th like the 26th. We know instances where, from this cause, some of the guests did not come till the night *after* the party.

There are some very sensible people who, in their invitations, tell frankly what is to be expected, and if they really ask but *a few* friends, they at once give the names of those friends, so that you may know whom you are to see. If you are to meet no more than can sit round the tea-table, they signify the same. If they expect twenty, thirty, or forty persons, they say so—and do not leave you in doubt whether to dress for something very like a party, or for a mere family tea-drinking.

If it is a decided music-party, by all means specify the same, that those who have no enjoyment of what is considered fashionable music, may stay away.

Always reply to a note of invitation the day after you have received it. To a note on business send an answer the same day. After accepting an invitation, should any thing occur to prevent your going, send a second note in due time.

Do not take offence at a friend because she does not invite you every time she has company. Her regard for you may be as warm as ever, but it is probably inconvenient for her to have more than a certain number at a time. Believe that the omission is no evidence of neglect, or of a desire to offend you; but rest assured that you are to be invited on other occasions. If you are *not*, then indeed you may take it as a hint that she is no longer desirous of continuing the acquaintance. Be dignified enough not to call her to account; but cease visiting her, without taking her to task and bringing on a quarrel. But if you *must* quarrel, let it not be in writing. A paper war is always carried too far, and produces bitterness of feeling which is seldom entirely eradicated, even after apologies have been made and accepted. Still, when an offence has been given in writing, the atonement should be made in writing also.

Much time is wasted (particularly by young ladies) in writing and answering such epistles as are termed "letters of friendship,"—meaning long documents (frequently with crossed lines) filled with regrets at absence, asseverations of eternal affection, modest deprecations of your humble self, and enthusiastic glorifyings of your exalted correspondent; or else wonderments at both of you being so much alike, and so very congenial; and anticipations of rapture at meeting again, and lamentations at the slow progress of time, till the extatic hour of re-union shall arrive—the *postscript* usually containing some confidential allusion to a lover, (either real or supposed,) and perhaps a kind enquiry about a real or supposed lover of your friend's.

Now such letters as these are of no manner of use but to foster a sickly, morbid feeling, (very often a fictitious one,) and to encourage nonsense, and destroy all relish for such true friendship as is good and wholesome.

A still worse species of voluminous female correspondence is that which turns *entirely* upon love, or rather on what are called "beaux;" or entirely on hate—for instance, hatred of step-mothers. This topic is considered the more *piquant* from its impropriety, and from its being carried on in secret.

Then there are young ladies born with the organ of letter-writing amazingly developed, and increased by perpetual practice, who can scarcely become acquainted with a gentleman possessing brains, without volunteering a correspondence with him. And then ensues a long epistolary dialogue about nothing, or at least nothing worth reading or remembering; trenching closely on gallantry, but still not quite *that*; affected flippancy on the part of the lady; and unaffected impertinence on that of the gentleman, "which serves her right"— alternating with pretended poutings on her side, and half or whole-laughing apologies on his. Sometimes there are attempts at moralizing, or criticising, or sentimentalizing—but nothing is ever elicited that, to a third person, can afford the least amusement or improvement, or excite the least interest. Yet, strange to say, gentlemen have been inveigled into this sort of correspondence, even by ladies who have made a business of afterward selling the letters for publication, and making money out of them. And such epistles have actually been printed. We do not suppose they have been read. The public is very stubborn in refusing to read what neither amuses, interests, or improves—even when a publisher is actually so weak as to print such things.

No young lady ever engages in a correspondence with a gentleman that is neither her relative or her betrothed, without eventually lessening herself in his eyes. Of this she may rest assured. With some men, it is even dangerous for a lady to write a note on the commonest subject. He may show the superscription, or the signature, or both, to his idle companions, and make insinuations much to her disadvantage, which his comrades will be sure to circulate and exaggerate.

Above all, let no lady correspond with a married man, unless she is obliged to consult him on business; and from that plain, straight path let her not diverge. Even if the wife sees and reads every letter, she will, in all probability, feel a touch of jealousy, (or more than a touch,) if she finds that they excite interest in her husband, or give him pleasure. This will inevitably be the case if the married lady is inferior in intellect to the single one, and has a lurking consciousness that she is so.

Having hinted what the correspondence of young ladies ought *not* to be, we will try to convey some idea of what it ought. Let us premise that there is no danger of *any* errors in grammar or spelling, and but few faults of punctuation, and that the fair writers are aware that a sentence should always conclude with a period or full stop, to be followed by a capital letter beginning the next sentence; and that a new paragraph should be allotted to every change of subject, provided that there is room on the sheet of paper. And still, it is well to have always at hand a dictionary and a grammar, in case of unaccountable lapses of memory. However, persons who have read much, and read to advantage, generally find themselves at no loss in orthography, grammar, and punctuation. To spell badly is disgraceful in a lady or gentleman, and it looks as if they had quitted reading as soon as they quitted school.

To write a legible and handsome hand is an accomplishment not sufficiently valued. And yet of what importance it is! We are always vexed when we hear people of talent making a sort of boast of the illegibility of their writing, and relating anecdotes of the difficulty with which it has been read, and the mistakes made by its decipherers. There are persons who affect bad writing, and boast of it, because the worst signatures extant are those of Shakespeare, Bonaparte, and Byron. These men were great in spite of their autographs, not because of them. The caliph Haroun Alraschid, who was well imbued with Arabic learning, sent an elegantly written letter to Charlemagne, with a splendid cover and seals; not being aware that the European emperor's signature was made by dipping his thumb into the ink and giving a smear—sealing with the hilt of his dagger.

The "wording" of your letter should be as much like conversation as possible, containing (in a condensed form) just what you would be most likely to talk about if you saw your friend. A letter is of no use unless it conveys some information, excites some interest, or affords some improvement. It may be handsomely written, correct in spelling, punctuation, and grammar, and yet stiff and formal in style—affectedly didactic, and therefore tiresome—or mawkishly sentimental, and therefore foolish. It may be refined, or high-flown in words, but flat and barren in ideas, containing nothing that a correspondent cares to know.

Read over each page of your letter, as you finish it, to see that there are no errors. If you find any, correct them carefully. In writing a familiar letter, a very common fault is tautology, or a too frequent repetition of the same word—for instance, "Yesterday I received a letter from sister Mary, which was the first letter I have received from sister since she left." The sentence should be, "Yesterday I received a letter from my sister Mary, the first since she left us."

Unless you are writing to one of your own family, put always the pronoun "*my*" before the word "sister." Say also—"my father," "my mother," and not "father," "mother," as if they were also the parents of your correspondent.

To end the sentence with the word "left," (for departed,) is awkward and unsatisfactory—for instance, "It is two days since he left." Left what? It is one of the absurd innovations that have crept in among us of late years, and are supposed to be fashionable. Another is the ridiculous way of omitting the possessive S in words ending with that letter; for instance, "Sims' Hotel" instead of "Sims's Hotel"—"Jenkins' Bakery" for "Jenkins's Bakery." Would any one, in talking, say they had stayed at Sims' Hotel, or that they bought their bread at Jenkins' Bakery? This is ungrammatical, as it obliterates the possessive case, and is therefore indefinite; and moreover, it looks and sounds awkwardly.

Many persons who think themselves good grammarians put on their cards "The Misses Brown,"—"The Misses Smith." Those who *really* are so, write "The Miss Browns"—"The Miss Smiths"—the plural being always on the substantive, and never on the adjective. Would we say "the whites glove" instead of "the white gloves"—or the "blues ribbon" for the "blue ribbons." Does any lady in talking say, "The two Misses Brown called to see me?"

It is also wrong to say "two *spoons*ful," instead of two *spoon*fuls. Thus, "two spoonsful of milk" seems to imply two separate spoons with milk in each; while "two spoonfuls of milk" gives the true idea—one spoon twice filled.

Avoid in writing, as in talking, all words that do not express the true meaning. We are sorry to say that sometimes even among educated people, when attempting smartness or wit, we find a sort of conventional slang that has, in truth, a strong tinge of vulgarity, being the wilful substitution of bad words or bad phrases for good ones. When we find them issuing from the lips or the pen of a *lady*, we fear she is unfortunate in a reprobate husband, or brother, from whom she must have learnt them. Yet even reprobates dislike to hear their wives and sisters talking coarsely.

Unless you know that your correspondent is well versed in French, refrain from interlarding your letters with Gallic words or phrases.

Do not introduce long quotations from poetry. Three or four lines of verse are sufficient. One line, or two, are better still. Write them rather smaller than your usual hand, and leave a space at the beginning and end; marking their commencement and termination with inverted commas, thus " ".

One of our young relatives when seven or eight years old, tried her hand at story-writing. In finishing the history of a naughty girl, much addicted to falsehood, the terminating sentence ran thus:—

"Arabella did not cure herself of this fault; but when she grew up, and became an authoress, she never marked her quotations."

If your letter is longer than can be comprised in one sheet, number the pages, placing the number near the upper corner. If engaged in a regular correspondence on business or other things, or in writing from a foreign country to your family at home, number not only the pages, but the letter itself, putting that figure in the centre at the top of the first page. Thus, if your friend, having received No. 10, finds the next letter that comes to hand is No. 12, she will know that No. 11 is missing, and will tell you so in her reply. Keep a memorandum of the letters you have sent, that you may know how to number the next. Before commencing a long letter, it is well to put down on a slip of paper, a list of the subjects you intend to write on.

Unless to persons living in the same house, do not enclose one letter in another. And even then, it is not always safe to do so. Let each letter be transmitted on its own account, by mail, with its own full direction, and its own post-office stamp. We know an instance where the peace of a family was entirely ruined by one of its members suppressing enclosed letters. Confide to no one the delivery of an important letter intended for another person. It is better to trust to the mail, and send a duplicate by the next post.

To break the seal of a letter directed to another person is punishable by law. To read *secretly* the letter of another is morally as felonious. A woman who would act thus meanly is worse than those who apply their eyes or ears to key-holes, or door-cracks, or who listen under windows, or look down from attics upon their neighbours; or who, in a dusky parlour, before the lamps are lighted, ensconce themselves in a corner, and give no note of their presence while listening to a conversation not intended for them to hear.

We do not conceive that, unless he authorizes her to do so, (which he had best not,) a wife is justifiable in opening her husband's letters, or he in reading hers. Neither wife nor husband has any right to entrust to the other the secrets of their friends; and letters may contain such secrets. Unless under extraordinary circumstances, parents should not consider themselves privileged to inspect the correspondence of grown-up children. Brothers and sisters always take care that their epistles shall not be unceremoniously opened by each other. In short, a letter is the property of the person to whom it is addressed, and nobody has a right to read it without permission.

If you are shown an autograph signature at the bottom of a letter, be satisfied to look at *that only*; and do not open out, and read the whole—unless desired.

Some years ago, in one of our most popular magazines, were several pages containing fac-simile signatures of a number of distinguished literary women—chiefly English. We saw an original letter, from a lady, who complained that some mischievous person had taken *her* magazine out of the post-office before it reached her, and shamefully *scribbled women's names* in it, disfiguring it so as to render it unfit for binding; therefore she desired the publisher to send her a clean copy in place of it.

In putting up packets to send away, either tie them round and across, with red tape, (sealing them also where the tape crosses,) or seal them without any tape. If the paper is strong, the wax good, and the contents of the parcel not too heavy, sealing will in most cases be sufficient. Twine or cord may cut the paper, and therefore is best omitted. Never put up a parcel in newspaper. It looks mean and disrespectful, and will soil the articles inside.

Keep yourself provided with different sorts and sizes of wrapping-paper.

A large packet requires more than one seal; the seals rather larger than for a letter.

Put up newspapers, for transmission, in thin whitish or brownish paper, pasting the cover, and leaving one end open. Newspaper-stamps cost but one cent, and are indispensable to the transmission of the paper.

Avoid giving letters of introduction to people whose acquaintance cannot possibly afford any pleasure or advantage to those whose civilities are desired for them, or who have not leisure to attend to strangers. Artists, authors, and all other persons to whom "time is money," and whose income stops whenever their hands and eyes are unemployed, are peculiarly annoyed by the frequency of introductory letters, brought by people with whom they can feel no congeniality, and whom they never would have sought for. Among the children of genius, but few are in a situation to entertain strangers *handsomely*, as it is called, which means, *expensively*. Many are kept always in straitened circumstances, from the incessant demands on their time and attention. And in numerous instances, letters are asked and given with no better motive than the gratification of idle curiosity.

We advise all persons obtaining an introductory letter to a painter, to ascertain, before presenting it, what branch of the art he professes. We have been asked whether a certain artist (one of the most distinguished in London) painted "figures, flowers, or landscapes." Also, no one should presume to request an introduction to an authoress, if they are ignorant whether she writes prose or verse. Not that they are expected to talk to her, immediately, on literary subjects.

Far from it; but if they know nothing of her works, they deserve no letter. In America, books, or at least newspapers, are accessible to all who can read.

Bores are peculiarly addicted to asking letters of introduction, in accordance with their system of "bestowing their tediousness" upon as many people as possible. We pity the kind friends from whom these missives are required, and who have not courage to refuse, or address enough to excuse themselves plausibly from complying.

We have known instances of stupid, vulgar persons, on preparing to visit another city, obtaining letters to families of the really highest class, and receiving from them the usual civilities, which they knew not how to appreciate.

On the other hand, how pleasant it is, by means of an introductory letter, to bring together two kindred spirits, whose personal intercourse must inevitably produce mutual satisfaction, who are glad to know each other, glad to meet frequently, and grateful to the friend who has made them acquainted.

Letters of introduction should not be sealed. To do so is rude, and mean. If you wish to write on the same day to the same person, take another sheet, write as long an epistle as you please, seal it, and send it *by mail.*

It is best to deliver an introductory letter in person, as the lady or gentleman whose civilities have been requested in your behalf, may thus be spared the trouble of calling at your lodgings, with the risk of not finding you at home. This is very likely to happen, if you *send* instead of taking it yourself. If you *do* send it, enclose a card with your residence. Also, it is more respectful to go yourself, than to expect them to come to you.

As soon as you are shown into the parlour, send up the letter, and wait till the receiver comes to you.

When a letter is brought to you by a private hand, the usual ceremony is to defer reading it till the bringer has departed, unless he desires you to read it at once, which he will, if it is evidently a short letter. If a long one, request him to excuse you a moment while you look at the beginning, to see if your correspondent is well.

On farewell cards, it is usual to write with a pencil the letters "t. t. l.," "to take leave"—or "p. p. c.," "pour prendre congé." A lady complained to us that an acquaintance of hers, about to leave town, had left a card for her with "p. d. a." upon it. Not understanding the meaning of these letters, she had applied to a friend for explanation, who told her they meant "poor dear adieu." "Now," continued she—"I cannot understand why a mere acquaintance should be so familiar as to call me 'poor dear;' why am I a poor dear to her?" We relieved her by explaining that "pour dire adieu" was French for "to bid adieu."

To conclude—let nothing induce you to give a letter of introduction to any person whose moral character is disreputable.

CHAPTER XIV.
PRESENTS.

Having accepted a present, it is your duty, and ought to be your pleasure, to let the giver see that you make use of it as intended, and that it is not thrown away upon you. If it is an article of dress, or of personal decoration, take occasion, on the first *suitable* opportunity, to wear it in presence of the giver. If an ornament for the centre-table, or the mantel-piece, place it there. If a book, do not delay reading it. Afterward, speak of it to her as favourably as you can. If of fruit or flowers, refer to them the next time you see her.

In all cases, when a gift is sent to you, return a note of thanks; or at least a verbal message to that effect.

Never enquire of the giver what was the price of her gift, or where she bought it. To do so is considered exceedingly rude.

When an article is presented to you for a specified purpose, it is your duty to use it for *that* purpose, and for no other, according to the wish of the donor. It is mean and dishonourable to give away a present; at least without first obtaining permission from the original giver. You have no right to be liberal or generous at the expense of another, or to accept a gift with a secret determination to bestow it *yourself* on somebody else. If it is an article that you do not want, that you possess already, or that you cannot use for yourself, it is best to say so candidly, at once; expressing your thanks for the offer, and requesting your friend to keep it for some other person to whom it will be advantageous. It is fit that the purchaser of the gift should have the pleasure of doing a kindness with her own hand, and eliciting the gratitude of one whom she knows herself. It is paltry in you to deprive her of this pleasure, by first accepting a present, and then secretly giving it away as from yourself.

There are instances of women whose circumstances did not allow them to indulge often in delicacies, that on a present of early fruit, or some other nice thing being sent to them by a kind friend, have ostentatiously transferred the gift to a wealthy neighbour, with a view of having it supposed that they had bought it themselves, and that to *them* such things were no rarities. This is contemptible—but it is sometimes done.

Making a valuable present to a rich person is in most cases, a work of supererogation; unless the gift is of something rare or *unique*, which cannot be purchased, and which may be seen and used to more advantage at the house of your friend than while in your own possession. But to give an expensive article of dress, jewellery, or furniture to one whose means of buying such things are quite equal (if not superior) to your own, is an absurdity; though not a very uncommon one, as society is now constituted. Such gifts elicit no real gratitude, for in all probability, they may not suit the pampered taste of those to whom fine things are no novelties. Or they may be regarded (however unjustly) as baits or nets to catch, in return, something of still greater cost.

There are persons, who, believing that presents are generally made with some mercenary view, and being unwilling themselves to receive favours, or incur obligations, make a point of repaying them as soon as possible, by a gift of something equivalent. This at once implies that they suspect the motive. If sincere in her friendship, the donor of the first present will feel hurt at being directly paid for it, and consider that she has been treated rudely, and unjustly. On the other hand, if compensation *was* secretly desired, and really expected, she will be disappointed at receiving nothing in return. Therefore, we repeat, that among persons who can conveniently provide themselves with whatever they may desire, the bestowal of presents is generally a most unthankful business. If you are in opulent circumstances, it is best to limit your generosity to such friends only as do not abound in the gifts of fortune, and whose situation denies them the means of indulging their tastes. By them such acts of kindness will be duly appreciated, and gratefully remembered; and the article presented will have a double value, if it is to them a novelty.

Gratitude is a very pleasant sensation, both for those who feel and to those who excite it. No one who confers a favour can say *with truth*, that "they want no thanks." They always do.

We know not why, when a young lady of fortune is going to be married, her friends should all be expected to present her with bridal gifts. It is a custom that sometimes bears heavily on those whose condition allows them but little to spare. And from that little it may be very hard for them to squeeze out enough to purchase some superfluous ornament, or some bauble for a centre-table, when it is already glittering with the gifts of the opulent;—gifts lavished on one who is really in no need of such things; and whose marriage confers no benefit on any one but herself. Why should she be rewarded for gratifying her own inclination in marrying the man of her choice? Now that it is fashionable to display all the wedding-gifts arranged in due form on tables, and labelled with the names of the donors, the seeming necessity of giving something expensive, or at least elegant, has become more onerous than ever. For instance, poor Miss Cassin can barely afford a simple brooch that costs about five dollars; but she strains the utmost capacity of her slender purse to buy one at ten dollars, that it may not disgrace the brilliant assemblage of jewellery that glitters on the bridal table of her wealthy friend Miss Denham. And after all, she finds that her modest little trinket looks really contemptible beside the diamond pin given by Mrs. Farley the millionaire. After all, she sees no one notice it, and hears no one say that it is even neat and pretty. To be sure, the bride, when it was sent with a note on the preceding day, did vouchsafe a polite answer. But then, if poor Miss C. does not make a wedding present to rich Miss D., it might be supposed that Miss C. cannot afford it. Neither she can. And her making the effort elicits perhaps some satirical remarks, that would be very mortifying to Miss Cassin if she heard them.

We repeat, that we cannot exactly perceive why, when the union of a couple of lovers, in many cases, adds to the happiness, honour, and glory of the married pair alone, their friends should think it a duty to levy on themselves these contributions; so often inconvenient to the givers, and not much cared for by the receivers.

When the young couple are not abounding in what are called "the goods of this world," the case is altered; and it may then be an act of real kindness for the opulent friends of the bride to present her with any handsome article of dress, or of furniture, that they think will be acceptable. What we contend is, that on a marriage in a wealthy family, the making of presents should be confined to the immediate relatives of the lady, and only to such of *them* as can well afford it.

Much of the money wasted in making ostentatious gifts to brides whose fathers have already given them a splendid outfit, might be far better employed, in assisting to purchase the *trousseaus* and the furniture of deserving young women in humble life, on their marriage with respectable tradesmen or mechanics. How many ladies of fortune have it in their power to do this—yet how seldom it is done!

At christenings, it is fortunately the sponsors only that are expected to make gifts to the infant. Therefore, invite no persons as sponsors, who cannot well afford this expense; unless you are sufficiently intimate to request them, privately, not to comply with the custom; being unwilling that they should cause themselves inconvenience by doing so.

The presentation of Christmas and New-Year's gifts is often a severe tax on persons with whom money is not plenty. It would be well if it were the universal custom to expect and receive no presents from any but the rich.

In making gifts to children, choose for them only such things as will afford them somewhat of lasting amusement. For boys, kites, tops, balls, marbles, wheelbarrows, carts, gardening utensils, and carpenter's tools, &c. Showy toys, that are merely to look at, and from which they can derive no enjoyment but in breaking them to pieces, are not worth buying. Little girls delight in little tea-sets, and dinner-sets, in which they can "make feasts," miniature kitchen-utensils, to play at cooking, washing, &c.; and dolls so dressed that all the clothes can be taken off and put on at pleasure. They soon grow tired of a doll whose glittering habiliments are sewed fast upon her. A wax doll in elegant attire is too precarious and expensive a plaything to make them happy; as they are always afraid of injuring her. We knew a little girl for whom a magnificent wax doll, splendidly dressed, was brought from France; and for an hour she was highly delighted. But next morning she was found still more happy in carrying about her favourite baby, a sofa-pillow, with an old shawl pinned round it for a frock; feeling perfect freedom to toss it about as she pleased. Children like their doll-babies to be very substantial, and rather heavy than light. A large, well-made *rag*-doll is for a small child far better than any other—occasionally putting a clean new face upon it.

We have seen country children perfectly satisfied with a doll that was nothing but a hard ear of Indian corn, arrayed in a coarse towel pinned round it. A little farm-house boy, of three years old, made a pet of a large squash, which he dressed in a pocket-handkerchief, and called Phebe Ann. We heard him say, as he passed his hand over its lumpy neck, "Poor Phebe Ann! what hives she has!"

To an intelligent child, no gifts are so valuable as entertaining books—provided they really *are* entertaining. Children are generally wise enough to prefer an amusing book in a plain cover, to a dull one shining with gold. When children are able to read fluently, they lose much of their desire for mere picture-books. If the cuts are badly executed, and give ugly, disagreeable ideas of the characters in the stories, they only trouble and annoy the little readers, instead of pleasing them. Some of the most popular juvenile books have no pictures inside, and no gilding outside. Bad engravings, (beside uselessly enhancing the price,) spoil the taste of the children. We highly recommend to the publishers of juvenile books to omit the cuts entirely, if they cannot afford very good ones. Many children have better judgment in these things than their parents suppose; and some of them more than the parents themselves.

Children have less enjoyment than is supposed in being taken to shops to choose gifts for themselves, or even in laying out their own money. It is always a long time before they can decide on what to buy, and as soon as they have fixed upon one thing, they immediately see something they like better. And often, after getting home, they are dissatisfied with their choice, and sorry they bought it. Also, they frequently wear out the patience of the shopkeepers; being desirous of seeing every thing, and pondering so long before they can determine on buying any thing.

It is in every way better to go to the shops without them, buy what you think proper, and then give them an agreeable surprise by the presentation.

Young ladies should be careful how they accept presents from gentlemen. No truly modest and dignified woman will incur such obligations. And no gentleman who really respects her will offer her any thing more than a bouquet, a book, one or two autographs of distinguished persons, or a few relics or mementos of memorable places—things that derive their chief value from associations. But to present a young lady with articles of jewellery, or of dress, or with a costly ornament for the centre-table, (unless she is his affianced wife,) ought to be regarded as an offence, rather than a compliment, excusable only in a man sadly ignorant of the refinements of society. And if he is so, she should set him right, and civilly, but firmly, refuse to be his debtor.

Yet, we are sorry to say, that there are ladies so rapacious, and so mean, that they are not ashamed to give broad hints to gentlemen, (particularly those gentlemen who are either very young or very old,) regarding certain beautiful card-cases, bracelets, essence-bottles, &c. which they have seen and admired,—even going so far as to fall in love with elegant shawls, scarfs, splendid fans, and embroidered handkerchiefs. And their admiration is so violent, and so reiterated, that the gentleman knows not how to resist; he therefore puts them in possession of a gift far too costly for any woman of delicacy to accept. In such cases, the father or mother of the young lady should oblige her to return the present. This has been done.

There are ladies who keep themselves supplied with certain articles of finery, (for instance, white kid gloves,) by laying ridiculous wagers with gentlemen, knowing that, whether winning or losing, the gentleman, out of gallantry, always pays. No lady should ever lay wagers, even with one of her own sex. It is foolish and unfeminine—and no man likes her any the better for indulging in the practice.

Some young ladies, who profess a sort of daughterly regard for certain wealthy old gentlemen, are so kind as to knit purses or work slippers for them, or some other nick-nacks, (provided always that the "dear old man" has a character for generosity,) for they know that he will reward them by a handsome present of some bijou of real value. And yet they may be assured that the kind old gentleman (whom "they mind no more than if he was their pa") sees through the whole plan, knows why the purse was knit, or the slippers worked, and esteems the kind young lady accordingly.

Another, and highly reprehensible way of extorting a gift, is to have what is called a philopena with a gentleman. This very silly joke is when a young lady, in cracking almonds, chances to find two kernels in one shell; she shares them with a beau; which ever first calls out *"philopena,"* on their next meeting, is entitled to receive a present from the other; and she is to remind him of it till he remembers to comply. So much nonsense is often talked on the occasion, that it seems to expand into something of importance; and the gentleman thinks he can do no less, than purchase for the lady something very elegant, or valuable; particularly if he has heard her tell of the munificence of other beaux in their philopenas.

There is great want of delicacy and self-respect in philopenaism, and no lady who has a proper sense of her dignity *as a lady* will engage in any thing of the sort.

In presenting a dress to a friend whose circumstances are not so affluent as your own, and who you know will gladly receive it, select one of excellent quality, and of a colour that you think she will like. She will feel mortified, if you give her one that is low-priced, flimsy, and of an unbecoming tint. Get an ample quantity, so as to allow a piece to be cut off and laid by for a new body and sleeves, when necessary. And to make the gift complete, buy linen for the body-lining; stiff, glazed muslin for the facings; buttons, sewing-silk, and whatever else may be wanted. This will save her the cost of these things.

When you give a dress to a poor woman, it is far better to buy for her a substantial new one, than to bestow on her an old thin gown of your own. The poor have little leisure to sew for themselves; and second-hand fine clothes last them but a very short time before they are fit only for the rag-bag.

If you are going to have a party, and among your very *intimate* friends is one whose circumstances will not permit her to incur the expense of buying a handsome new dress for the occasion, and if she has no choice but to stay away, or to appear in a costume very inferior to that of the other ladies, you may (if you can well afford it) obviate this difficulty by presenting her with a proper dress-pattern, and other accessories. This may be managed anonymously, but it will be better to do it with her knowledge. It will be a very gratifying mark of your friendship; and she ought to consider it as such, and not refuse it from a feeling of false pride. Of course, it will be kept a secret from all but yourselves. In the overflow of gratitude *she* may speak of it to others, but for *you* to mention it would be ungenerous and indelicate in the extreme. We are glad to say that ladies of fortune often make gifts of party-dresses to their less-favoured friends.

In sending a present, always pay in advance the expense of transmitting it, so that it may cost nothing at all to the receiver. You may send by the Mail a package of any size, weighing not more than four pounds, paying the postage yourself at the office from whence it goes. It will then be delivered at the door of your friend, without further charge.

CHAPTER XV.
CONVERSATION.

Conversation is the verbal interchange of thoughts and feelings. To form a *perfect* conversationist, many qualifications are requisite. There must be knowledge of the world, knowledge of books, and a facility of imparting that knowledge; together with originality, memory, an intuitive perception of what is best to say, and best to omit, good taste, good temper, and good manners. An agreeable and instructive talker has the faculty of going "from gay to grave, from lively to serene," without any apparent effort; neither skimming so slightly over a variety of topics as to leave no impression of any, or dwelling so long upon one subject as to weary the attention of the hearers. Persons labouring under a monomania, such as absorbs their whole mind into one prevailing idea, are never pleasant or impressive talkers. They defeat their own purpose by recurring to it perpetually, and rendering it a perpetual fatigue. A good talker should cultivate a temperance in talking; so as not to talk too much, to the exclusion of other good talkers. Conversation is dialogue, not monologue. It was said of Madame de Stael that she did not converse, but delivered orations.

To be a perfect conversationist, a good voice is indispensable—a voice that is clear, distinct, and silver-toned. If you find that you have a habit of speaking too low, "reform it altogether." It is a bad one; and will render your talk unintelligible.

Few things are more delightful than for one intelligent and well-stored mind to find itself in company with a kindred spirit—each understanding the other, catching every idea, and comprehending every allusion. Such persons will become as intimate in half an hour, as if they had been personally acquainted for years.

On the other hand, the pleasure of society is much lessened by the habit in which many persons indulge, of placing themselves always in the opposition, controverting every opinion, and doubting every fact. They talk to you as a lawyer examines a witness at the bar; trying to catch you in some discrepancy that will invalidate your testimony; fixing their scrutinizing eyes upon your face "as if they would look you through," and scarcely permitting you to say, "It is a fine day," without making you prove your words. Such people are never popular. Nobody likes perpetual contradiction, especially when the subject of argument is of little or no consequence. In young people this dogmatic practice is generally based upon vanity and impertinence. In the old it is prompted by pride and selfishness. We doubt if in the present day the talk and manners of Johnson would have been tolerated in really good society.

Unless he first refers to it himself, never talk to a gentleman concerning his profession; at least do not question him about it. For instance, you must not expect a physician to tell you how his patients are affected, or to confide to you any particulars of their maladies. These are subjects that he will discuss only with their relatives, or their nurses. It is also very improper to ask a lawyer about his clients, or the cases in which he is employed. A clergyman does not like always to be talking about the church. A merchant, when away from his counting-house, has no wish to engage in business-talk with ladies; and a mechanic is ever willing "to leave the shop behind him." Every American is to be supposed capable of conversing on miscellaneous subjects; and he considers it no compliment to be treated as if he knew nothing but what the Scotch call his "bread-winner." Still, there are some few individuals who like to talk of their bread-winner. If you perceive this disposition, indulge them, and listen attentively. You will learn something useful, and worth remembering.

Women who have begun the world in humble life, and have been necessitated to give most of their attention to household affairs, are generally very shy in talking of housewifery, after their husbands have become rich, and are living in style, as it is called. Therefore, do not annoy them by questions on domestic economy. But converse as if they had been ladies always.

Lord Erskine, having lived a bachelor to an advanced age, finally married his cook, by way of securing her services, as she had frequently threatened to leave him. After she became Lady Erskine she lost all knowledge of cookery, and it was a mortal affront to hint the possibility of her knowing how any sort of eatable should be prepared for the table.

Never remind any one of the time when their situation was less genteel, or less affluent than at present, or tell them that you remember their living in a small house, or in a remote street. If they have not moral courage to talk of such things themselves, it is rude in you to make any allusion to them.

On the other hand, if invited to a fashionable house, and to meet fashionable company, it is not the time or place for you to set forth the comparative obscurity of your own origin, by way of showing that you are not proud. If *you* are not proud, it is most likely that your entertainers may be, and they will not be pleased at your ultra-magnanimity in thus lowering yourself before their aristocratic guests. These communications should be reserved for *tête-à-têtes* with old or familiar friends, who have no more pride than yourself.

When listening to a circumstance that is stated to have actually occurred to the relater, even if it strikes you as being very extraordinary, and not in conformity to your own experience, it is rude to reply, "Such a thing never happened to *me*." It is rude because it seems to imply a doubt of the narrator's veracity; and it is foolish, because its not having happened to *you* is no proof that it could not have happened to any body else. Slowness in belief is sometimes an evidence of ignorance, rather than of knowledge. People who have read but little, travelled but little, and seen but little of the world out of their own immediate circle, and whose intellect is too obtuse to desire any new accession to their own small stock of ideas, are apt to think that nothing can be true unless it has fallen under their own limited experience. Also, they may be so circumstanced that nothing in the least out of the common way is likely to disturb the still water of their pond-like existence.

A certain English nobleman always listens incredulously when he hears any person descanting on the inconveniences of travelling on the continent, and relating instances of bad accommodations and bad fare; uncomfortable vehicles, and uncomfortable inns; the short beds and narrow sheets of Germany; the slow and lumbering diligence-riding of France; the garlicky stews of Spain with a feline foundation; the little vine-twig fires in the chilly winters of Northern Italy; and various other ills, which the flesh of travellers is heir to;—the duke always saying, "Now really *I* never experienced any of these discomforts, much as I have traversed the continent. None of these inconveniences ever come in my way." And how should they, when, being a man of enormous wealth, he always travels with a cavalcade of carriages; a retinue of servants; a wagon-load of bedding and other furniture; a cook, with cooking-utensils, and lots of luxurious eatables to be cooked at stopping-places—his body-coach (as it is called) being a horse-drawn palace. What inconveniences can possibly happen to *him*?

When you hear a gentleman speak in praise of a lady whom you do not think deserving of his commendations, you will gain nothing by attempting to undeceive him; particularly if she is handsome. Your dissenting from his opinion he will, in all probability, impute to envy, or ill-nature; and therefore the only impression you can make will be against yourself.

Even if you have reason to dislike the lady, recollect that few are without some good points both of person and character. And it will be much better for you to pass over her faults in silence, and agree with him in commending what is really commendable about her. What he would, perhaps, believe implicitly if told to him by a man, he would attribute entirely to jealousy, or to a love of detraction if related by a woman. Above all, if a gentleman descants on the beauty of a lady, and in your own mind you do not coincide with his opinion, refrain, on your part, from criticizing invidiously her face and figure, and do not say that "though her complexion may be fine, her features are not regular;" that "her nose is too small," or "her eyes too large," or "her mouth too wide." Still less disclose to him the secret of her wearing false hair, artificial teeth, or tinging her cheeks with rouge. If she is a bold, forward woman, he will find that out as soon as yourself, and sooner too,—and you may be sure that though he may amuse himself by talking and flirting with her, he in reality regards her as she deserves.

If a foreigner chances, in your presence, to make an unfavourable remark upon some custom or habit peculiar to your country, do not immediately take fire and resent it; for, perhaps, upon reflection, you may find that he is right, or nearly so. All countries have their national character, and no character is perfect, whether that of a nation or an individual. If you know that the stranger has imbibed an erroneous impression, you may calmly, and in a few words, endeavour to convince him of it. But if he shows an unwillingness to be convinced, and tells you that what he has said he heard from good authority; or that, before he came to America, "his mind was made up," it will be worse than useless for you to continue the argument. Therefore change the subject, or turn and address your conversation to some one else.

Lady Morgan's Duchess of Belmont very properly checks O'Donnell for his ultra-nationality, and advises him not to be always running a tilt with every Englishman he talks to, continually seeming as if ready with the war-cry of "St. Patrick for Ireland, against St. George for England."

Dr. Johnson was speaking of Scotland with his usual severity, when a Caledonian who was present, started up, and called out, "Sir, *I* was born in Scotland." "Very well, sir," said the cynic calmly, "I do not see why so small a circumstance should make any change in the national character."

English strangers complain (and with reason) of the American practice of imposing on their credulity, by giving them false and exaggerated accounts of certain things peculiar to this country, and telling them, as truths, stories that are absolute impossibilities; the amusement being to see how the John Bulls swallow these absurdities. Even General Washington diverted himself by mystifying Weld the English traveller, who complained to him at Mount Vernon of musquitoes so large and fierce that they bit through his cloth coat. "Those are nothing," said Washington, "to musquitoes I have met with, that bite through a thick leather boot." Weld expressed his astonishment, (as well he might;) and, when he "put out a book," inserted the story of the boot-piercing insects, which he said *must* be true, as he had it from no less a person than General Washington.

It is a work of supererogation to furnish falsehoods for British travellers. They can manufacture them fast enough. Also, it is ungenerous thus to sport with their ignorance, and betray them into ridiculous caricatures, which they present to the English world in good faith. We hope these tricks are not played upon any of the best class of European travel-writers.

When in Europe, (in England particularly,) be not over sensitive as to remarks that may be made on your own country; and do not expect every one around you to keep perpetually in mind that you are an American; nor require that they should guard every word, and keep a constant check on their conversation, lest they should chance to offend your republican feelings. The English, as they become better acquainted with America, regard us with more favour, and are fast getting rid of their old prejudices, and opening their eyes as to the advantages to be derived from cultivating our friendship instead of provoking our enmity. They have, at last, all learnt that our language is theirs, and they no longer compliment newly-arrived Americans on speaking English "quite well." It is not many years since two young ladies from one of our Western States, being at a party at a very fashionable mansion in London, were requested by the lady of the house to talk a little American; several of her guests being desirous of hearing a specimen of that language. One of the young ladies mischievously giving a hint to the other, they commenced a conversation in what school-girls call *gibberish*; and the listeners, when they had finished, gave various opinions on the American tongue, some pronouncing it very soft, and rather musical; others could not help saying candidly that they found it rather harsh. But all agreed that it resembled no language they had heard before.

There is no doubt that by the masses, better English is spoken in America than in England.

However an Englishman or an Englishwoman may boast of their intimacy with "the nobility and gentry," there is one infallible rule by which the falsehood of these pretensions may be detected. And that is in the misuse of the letter H, putting it where it should not be, and omitting it where it should. This unaccountable practice prevails, more or less, in all parts of England, but is unknown in Scotland and Ireland. It is never found but among the middle and lower classes, and by polished and well-educated people is as much laughed at in England as it is with us. A relative of ours being in a stationer's shop in St. Paul's Church Yard, (the street surrounding the cathedral,) heard the stationer call his boy, and tell him to "go and take the babby out, and give him a *hairing*— the babby having had no *hair* for a week." We have heard an Englishman talk of "taking an *ouse* that should have an *ot* water pipe, and a *hoven*." The same man asked a young lady "if she had *eels* on her boots." We heard an Englishwoman tell a servant to "bring the *arth* brush, and sweep up the *hashes*." Another assured us that "the American ladies were quite *hignorant* of *hetiquette*."

We have actually seen a ridiculous bill sent seriously by a Yorkshireman who kept a livery-stable in Philadelphia. The items were, *verbatim*—

	D.C.
anosafada	2 50
takinonimome	0 37

No reader can possibly guess this—so we will explain that the first line, in which all the words run into one, signifies "An orse af a day,"—or "A horse half a day." The second line means "takin on im ome,"—or "Taking of him home."

English travellers are justly severe on the tobacco-chewing and spitting, that though exploded in the best society, is still too prevalent among the million. All American ladies can speak feelingly on this subject, for they suffer from it in various ways. First, the sickening disgust without which they cannot witness the act of expectoration performed before their faces. Next, the danger of tobacco-saliva falling on their dresses in the street, or while travelling in steamers and rail-cars. Then the necessity of walking through the abomination when leaving those conveyances; treading in it with their shoes; and wiping it up with the hems of their gowns. We know an instance of the crown of a lady's white-silk bonnet being bespattered with tobacco-juice, by a man spitting out of a window in one of the New York hotels. A lady on the second seat of a box at the Chestnut-street theatre, found, when she went home, the back of her pelisse entirely spoilt, by some man behind not having succeeded in trying to spit past her—or perhaps he did not try. Why should ladies endure all this, that men may indulge in a vulgar and deleterious practice, pernicious to their own health, and which they cannot acquire without going through a seasoning of disgust and nausea?

It is very unmannerly when a person begins to relate a circumstance or an anecdote, to stop them short by saying, "I have heard it before." Still worse, to say you do not wish to hear it at all. There are people who set themselves against listening to any thing that can possibly excite melancholy or painful feelings; and profess to hear nothing that may give them a sad or unpleasant sensation. Those who have so much tenderness for themselves, have usually but little tenderness for others. It is impossible to go through the world with perpetual sunshine over head, and unfading flowers under foot. Clouds will gather in the brightest sky, and weeds choke up the fairest primroses and violets. And we should all endeavour to prepare ourselves for these changes, by listening with sympathy to the manner in which they have affected others.

No person of good feelings, good manners, or true refinement, will entertain their friends with minute descriptions of sickening horrors, such as barbarous executions, revolting punishments, or inhuman cruelties perpetrated on animals. We have never heard an officer dilate on the dreadful spectacle of a battlefield; a scene of which no description can ever present an adequate idea; and which no painter has ever exhibited in all its shocking and disgusting details. Physicians do not talk of the dissecting-room.

Unless you are speaking to a physician, and are interested in a patient he is attending, refrain in conversation from entering into the particulars of revolting diseases, such as scrofula, ulcers, cutaneous afflictions, &c. and discuss no terrible operations—especially at table. There are women who seem to delight in dwelling on such disagreeable topics.

If you are attending the sick-bed of a friend, and are called down to a visiter, speak of her illness with delicacy, and do not disclose all the unpleasant circumstances connected with it; things which it would grieve her to know, may, if once told, be circulated among married women, and by them repeated to their husbands. In truth, upon most occasions, a married woman is not a safe confidant. She will assuredly tell every thing to her husband; and in all probability to his mother and sisters also—that is, every thing concerning her friends—always, perhaps, under a strict injunction of secrecy. But a secret entrusted to more than two or three persons, is soon diffused throughout the whole community.

A man of some humour was to read aloud a deed. He commenced with the words, "Know one woman by these presents." He was interrupted, and asked why he changed the words, which were in the usual form, "Know all men by these presents." "Oh!" said he, "'tis very certain that all men will soon know it, if one woman does."

Generally speaking, it is injudicious for ladies to attempt arguing with gentlemen on political or financial topics. All the information that a woman can possibly acquire or remember on these subjects is so small, in comparison with the knowledge of men, that the discussion will not elevate them in the opinion of masculine minds. Still, it is well for a woman to desire enlightenment, that she may comprehend something of these discussions, when she hears them from the other sex; therefore let her listen as understandingly as she can, but refrain from controversy and argument on such topics as the grasp of a female mind is seldom capable of seizing or retaining. Men are very intolerant toward women who are prone to contradiction and contention, when the talk is of things considered out of their sphere; but very indulgent toward a modest and attentive listener, who only asks questions for the sake of information. Men like to dispense knowledge; but few of them believe that in departments exclusively their own, they can profit much by the suggestions of women. It is true there are and have been women who have distinguished themselves greatly in the higher branches of science and literature, and on whom the light of genius has clearly descended. But can the annals of woman produce a female Shakespeare, a female Milton, a Goldsmith, a Campbell, or a Scott? What woman has painted like Raphael or Titian, or like the best artists of our own times? Mrs. Damer and Mrs. Siddons had a talent for sculpture; so had Marie of Orleans, the accomplished daughter of Louis Philippe. Yet what are the productions of these talented ladies compared to those of Thorwaldsen, Canova, Chantrey, and the master chisels of the great American statuaries? Women have been excellent musicians, and have made fortunes by their voices. But is there among them a Mozart, a Bellini, a Michael Kelly, an Auber, a Boieldieu? Has a woman made an improvement on steam-engines, or on any thing connected with the mechanic arts? And yet these things have been done by men of no early education—by self-taught men. A good tailor fits, cuts out, and sews better than the most celebrated female dress-maker. A good man-cook far excels a good woman-cook. Whatever may be their merits as assistants, women are rarely found who are very successful at the head of any establishment that requires energy and originality of mind. Men make fortunes, women make livings. And none make poorer livings than those who waste their time, and bore their friends, by writing and lecturing upon the equality of the sexes, and what they call "Women's Rights." How is it that most of these ladies live separately from their husbands; either despising them, or being despised by them?

Truth is, the female sex is really as inferior to the male in vigour of mind as in strength of body; and all arguments to the contrary are founded on a few anomalies, or based on theories that can never be reduced to practice. Because there was a Joan of Arc, and an Augustina of Saragossa, should females expose themselves to all the dangers and terrors of "the battle-field's dreadful array?" The women of the American Revolution effected much good to their country's cause, without encroaching upon the province of its brave defenders. They were faithful and patriotic; but they left the conduct of that tremendous struggle to abler heads, stronger arms, and sterner hearts.

We envy not the female who can look unmoved upon physical horrors— even the sickening horrors of the dissecting-room.

Yet women are endowed with power to meet misfortune with fortitude; to endure pain with patience; to resign themselves calmly, piously, and hopefully to the last awful change that awaits every created being; to hazard their own lives for those that they love; to toil cheerfully and industriously for the support of their orphan children, or their aged parents; to watch with untiring tenderness the sick-bed of a friend, or even of a stranger; to limit their own expenses and their own pleasures, that they may have something to bestow on deserving objects of charity; to smooth the ruggedness of man; to soften his asperities of temper; to refine his manners; to make his home a happy one; and to improve the minds and hearts of their children. All this women can—and do. And this is their true mission.

In talking with a stranger, if the conversation should turn toward sectarian religion, enquire to what church he belongs; and then mention your own church. This, among people of good sense and good manners, and we may add of true piety, will preclude all danger of remarks being made on either side which may be painful to either party. Happily we live in a land of universal toleration, where all religions are equal in the sight of the law and the government; and where no text is more powerful and more universally received than the wise and incontrovertible words—"By their fruits ye shall know them." He that acts well is a good man, and a religious man, at whatever altar he may worship. He that acts ill is a bad man, and has no true sense of religion; no matter how punctual his attendance at church, if of that church he is an unworthy member. Ostentatious sanctimony may deceive man, but it cannot deceive God.

On this earth there are many roads to heaven; and each traveller supposes his own to be the best. But they must all unite in one road at the last. It is only Omniscience that can decide. And it will then be found that no sect is excluded because of its faith; or if its members have acted honestly and conscientiously according to the lights they had, and molesting no one for believing in the tenets of a different church. The religion of Jesus, as our Saviour left it to us, was one of peace and good-will to men, and of unlimited faith in the wisdom and goodness, and power and majesty of God. It is not for a frail human being to place limits to his mercy, and say what church is the only true one—and the only one that leads to salvation. Let all men keep in mind this self-evident truth—"He can't be wrong whose life is in the right;" and try to act up to the Divine command of "doing unto all men as you would they should do unto you."

In America, no religious person of good sense or good manners ever attempts, in company, to controvert, uncalled for, the sectarian opinions of another. No clergyman that is a gentleman, (and they all are so, or ought to be,) ever will make the drawing-room an arena for religious disputation, or will offer a single deprecatory remark, on finding the person with whom he is conversing to be a member of a church essentially differing from his own. And if clergymen have that forbearance, it is doubly presumptuous for a woman, (perhaps a silly young girl,) to take such a liberty. "Fools rush in, where angels fear to tread."

Nothing is more apt to defeat even a good purpose than the mistaken and ill-judged zeal of those that are not competent to understand it in all its bearings.

Truly does the Scripture tell us—"There is a time for all things." We know an instance of a young lady at a ball attempting violently to make a proselyte of a gentleman of twice her age, a man of strong sense and high moral character, whose church (of which he was a sincere member) differed materially from her own. After listening awhile, he told her that a ball-room was no place for such discussions, and made his bow and left her. At another party we saw a young girl going round among the matrons, and trying to bring them all to a confession of faith.

Religion is too sacred a subject for discussion at balls and parties.

If you find that an intimate friend has a leaning toward the church in which you worship, first ascertain truly if her parents have no objection, and then, but not else, you may be justified in inducing her to adopt your opinions. Still, in most cases, it is best not to interfere.

In giving your opinion of a new book, a picture, or a piece of music, when conversing with a distinguished author, an artist or a musician, say modestly, that "so it appears to *you*"—that "it has given *you* pleasure," or the contrary. But do not positively and dogmatically assert that it *is* good, or that it *is* bad. The person with whom you are talking is, in all probability, a far more competent judge than yourself; therefore, listen attentively, and he may correct your opinion, and set you right. If he fail to convince you, remain silent, or change the subject. Vulgar ladies have often a way of saying, when disputing on the merits of a thing they are incapable of understanding, "Any how, *I* like it," or, "It is quite good enough for *me*."—Which is no proof of its being good enough for any body else.

In being asked your candid opinion of a person, be very cautious to whom you confide that opinion; for if repeated as yours, it may lead to unpleasant consequences. It is only to an intimate and long-tried friend that you may safely entrust certain things, which if known, might produce mischief. Even very intimate friends are not always to be trusted, and when they have actually told something that they heard under the injunction of secrecy, they will consider it a sufficient atonement to say, "Indeed I did not mean to tell it, but somehow it slipped out;" or, "I really intended to guard the secret faithfully, but I was so questioned and cross-examined, and bewildered, that I knew not how to answer without disclosing enough to make them guess the whole. I am very sorry, and will try to be more cautious in future. But these slips of the tongue will happen."

The lady whose confidence has been thus betrayed, should be "more cautious in future," and put no farther trust in she of the slippery tongue—giving her up, entirely, as unworthy of farther friendship.

No circumstances will induce an honourable and right-minded woman to reveal a secret after promising secrecy. But she should refuse being made the depository of any extraordinary fact which it may be wrong to conceal, and wrong to disclose.

We can scarcely find words sufficiently strong to contemn the heinous practice, so prevalent with low-minded people, of repeating to their friends whatever they hear to their disadvantage. By low-minded people, we do not exclusively mean persons of low station. The low-minded are not always "born in a garret, in a kitchen bred." Unhappily, there are (so-called) ladies—ladies of fortune and fashion—who will descend to meannesses of which the higher ranks ought to be considered incapable, and who, without compunction, will wantonly lacerate the feelings and mortify the self-love of those whom they call their friends, telling them what has been said about them by other friends.

It is sometimes said of a notorious tatler and mischief-maker, that "she has, notwithstanding, a good heart." How is this possible, when it is her pastime to scatter dissension, ill-feeling, and unhappiness among all whom she calls her friends? She may, perhaps, give alms to beggars, or belong to sewing circles, or to Bible societies, or be officious in visiting the sick. All this is meritorious, and it is well if there is some good in her. But if she violates the charities of social life, and takes a malignant pleasure in giving pain, and causing trouble—depend on it, her show of benevolence is mere ostentation, and her acts of kindness spring not from the heart. She will convert the sewing circle into a scandal circle. If she is assiduous in visiting her sick friends, she will turn to the worst account, particulars she may thus acquire of the sanctities of private life and the humiliating mysteries of the sick-chamber.

If indeed it can be possible that tatling and mischief-making may be only (as is sometimes alleged) a bad habit, proceeding from an inability to govern the tongue—shame on those who have allowed themselves to acquire such a habit, and who make no effort to subdue it, or who have encouraged it in their children, and perhaps set them the example.

If you are so unfortunate as to know one of these pests of society, get rid of her acquaintance as soon as you can. If allowed to go on, she will infallibly bring you into some difficulty, if not into disgrace. If she begins by telling you—"I had a hard battle to fight in your behalf last evening at Mrs. Morley's. Miss Jewson, whom you believe to be one of your best friends, said some very severe things about you, which, to my surprise, were echoed by Miss Warden, who said she knew them to be true. But I contradicted them warmly. Still they would not be convinced, and said I must be blind and deaf not to know better. How very hard it is to distinguish those who love from those who hate us!"

Instead of encouraging the mischief-maker to relate the particulars, and explain exactly what these severe things really were, the true and dignified course should be to say as calmly as you can—"I consider no person my friend, who comes to tell such things as must give me pain and mortification, and lessen my regard for those I have hitherto esteemed, and in whose society I have found pleasure. I have always liked Miss Jewson and Miss Warden, and am sorry to hear that they do not like *me*. Still, as I am not certain of the exact truth, (being in no place where I could myself overhear the discussion,) it will make no difference in my behaviour to those young ladies. And now then we will change the subject, never to resume it. My true friends do not bring me such tales."

By-the-bye, tatlers are always listeners, and are frequently the atrocious writers of anonymous letters, for which they should be expelled from society.

Let it be remembered that all who are capable of detailing unpleasant truths, (such as can answer no purpose but to produce bad feeling, and undying enmity,) are likewise capable of exaggerating and misrepresenting facts, that do not seem quite strong enough to excite much indignation. Tale-bearing always leads to lying. She who begins with the first of these vices, soon arrives at the second.

Some prelude these atrocious communications with—"I think it my duty to tell how Miss Jackson and Mrs. Wilson talk about you, for it is right that you should know your friends from your enemies." You listen, believe, and from that time become the enemy of Miss Jackson and Mrs. Wilson—having too much pride to investigate the truth, and learn what they really said.

Others will commence with—"I'm a plain-spoken woman, and consider it right, for your own sake, to inform you that since your return from Europe, you talk quite too much of your travels."

You endeavour to defend yourself from this accusation, by replying that "having seen much when abroad, it is perfectly natural that you should allude to what you have seen."

"Oh! but there should be moderation in all things. To be candid—your friend Mrs. Willet says she is tired of hearing of France and Italy."

"Why then does she always try to get a seat next to me, and ask me to tell her something more of those countries?"

"Well, I don't know. People are so deceitful! There is Mr. Liddard, who says you bore him to death with talking about England."

"And yet whenever I do talk about England, I always find him at the back of my chair. And when I pause, he draws me on to say more."

"Men are such flatterers! Well, I always tell the plain truth. So it is best you should know Colonel Greenfield declares that since your return from Europe you are absolutely intolerable. Excuse my telling you these things. It is only to show that every body else thinks just as I do. Mrs. Gray says it is a pity you ever crossed the Atlantic."

Do not excuse her—but drop her acquaintance as soon as you can, without coming to a quarrel, in which case you will most probably get the worst. A plain-spoken woman is always to be dreaded. Her cold-blooded affectation of frankness is only a pretext to introduce something that will wound your feelings; and then she will tell you "that Mrs. A. B. C. and D., and Mr. E. and Mr. F. also, have said a hundred times that you are a woman of violent temper, and cannot listen to advice without flying into a passion."

And she will quietly take her leave, informing you that she is your best friend, and that all she has said was entirely for your own good, and that she shall continue to admonish you whenever she sees occasion.

A plain-spoken woman will tell you that you were thought to look very ill at Mrs. Thomson's party, your dress being rather in bad taste; that you ought to give up singing in company, your best friends saying that your style is now a little old-fashioned; that you should not attempt talking French to French ladies, as Mr. Leroux and Mr. Dufond say that your French is not quite Parisian, &c. &c. She will say these things upon no authority but her own.

When any one prefaces an enquiry by the vulgarism, "If it is a fair question?" you may be very certain that the question is a most *un*fair one—that is, a question which it is impertinent to ask, and of no consequence whatever to the asker.

If a person begins by telling you, "Do not be offended at what I am going to say," prepare yourself for something that she knows will certainly offend you. But as she has given you notice, try to listen, and answer with calmness.

It is a delicate and thankless business to tell a friend of her faults, unless you are certain that, in return, you can bear without anger to hear her point out your own. She will undoubtedly recriminate.

It is not true that an irritable temper cannot be controlled. It can, and is, whenever the worldly interest of the *enragée* depends on its suppression.

Frederick the Great severely reprimanded a Prussian officer for striking a soldier at a review. "I could not refrain," said the officer. "I have a high temper, your majesty, and I cannot avoid showing it, when I see a man looking sternly at me." "Yes, you can," replied the king. "I am looking sternly at you, and I am giving you ten times as much cause of offence as that poor soldier—yet you do not strike *me*."

A naturally irritable disposition can always be tamed down, by a strong and persevering effort to subdue it, and by determining always to check it on its first approaches to passion. The indulgence of temper renders a man (and still more a woman) the dread and shame of the whole house. It wears out the affection of husbands, wives, and children—of brothers and sisters; destroys friendship; disturbs the enjoyment of social intercourse; causes incessant changing of servants; and is a constant source of misery to that most unhappy of all classes, poor relations.

That a violent temper is generally accompanied by a good heart, is a popular fallacy. On the contrary, the indulgence of it hardens the heart. And even if its ebullitions are always succeeded by "compunctious visitings," and followed by apologies and expressions of regret, still it leaves wounds that time cannot always efface, and which we may forgive, but cannot forget.

Ill-tempered women are very apt to call themselves nervous, and to attribute their violent fits of passion to a weakness of the nerves. This is not true. A real nervous affection shows itself "more in sorrow than in anger," producing tears, tremor, and head-ache, fears without adequate cause, and general depression of spirits—the feelings becoming tender to a fault.

When a woman abandons herself to terrible fits of anger with little or no cause, and makes herself a frightful spectacle, by turning white with rage, rolling up her eyes, drawing in her lips, gritting her teeth, clenching her hands, and stamping her feet, depend on it, she is not of a nervous, but of a furious temperament. A looking-glass held before her, to let her see what a shocking object she has made herself, would, we think, have an excellent effect. We have seen but a few females in this revolting state, and only three of them were ladies—but we have heard of many.

When the paroxysm is over, all the atonement she can make is to apologize humbly, and to pray contritely. If she has really any goodness of heart, and any true sense of religion, she will do this promptly, and prove her sincerity by being very kind to those whom she has outraged and insulted—and whose best course during these fits of fury is to make no answer, or to leave the room.

As out of nothing, nothing can come, to be a good conversationist, you must have a well-stored mind, originality of ideas, and a retentive memory. Without making a lumber-room of your head, and stuffing it with all manner of useless and unnecessary things not worth retaining, you should select only such as are useful or ornamental, interesting or amusing. Your talk must flow as if spontaneously; one subject suggesting another, none being dwelt upon too long. Anecdotes may be introduced with much effect. They should be short, and related in such words as will give them the most point. We have heard the same anecdote told by two persons. With one it became prosy and tiresome, and the point was not perceptible from its being smothered in ill-chosen words. With the other narrator, the anecdote was "all light and spirit; soon told, and not soon forgotten." Brevity is the soul of wit, and wit is the soul of anecdote. And where wit is wanting, humour is an excellent substitute. Every body likes to laugh, or ought to. Yet there is a time for all things; and after listening to a serious or interesting incident well related, it is exceedingly annoying to hear some silly and heartless girl follow it with a ridiculous remark, intended to be funny—such as "Quite solemncolly!"—or, "We are all getting into the doldrums."

You may chance to find yourself in a company where no one is capable of appreciating the best sort of conversation, and where to be understood, or indeed to keep them awake, you must talk down to the capacities of your hearers. You must manage this adroitly, or they may find you out, and be offended. So, after all, it is, perhaps, safest to go on and scatter pearls where wax beads would be equally valued. Only in such society, do not introduce quotations from the poets, especially from Shakespeare, or your hearers may wonder what queer words you are saying. Another time, and with congenial companions, you can indulge in "the feast of reason, and the flow of soul."

If placed beside a lady so taciturn that no effort on your part can draw her out, or elicit more than a monosyllable, and that only at long intervals, you may safely conclude that there is nothing in her, and leave her to her own dullness, or to be enlivened by the approach of one of the other sex. That will make her talk.

Few persons are good talkers who are not extensive and miscellaneous readers. You cannot attentively read the best authors without obtaining a great command of words, so that you can always, with ease and fluency, clothe your ideas in appropriate language.

Knowledge is of course the basis of conversation—the root whose deepened strength and vigour gives life to the tree, multiplicity to its branches, and beauty to its foliage.

Much that is bad and foolish in women would have no existence if their minds were less barren. In a waste field, worthless and bitter weeds will spring up which it is hard to eradicate; while a soil that is judiciously cultivated produces abundant grain, luxuriant grass, and beautiful flowers.

There are ladies so exceedingly satisfied with themselves, and so desirous of being thought the special favourites of Providence, that they are always desiring to hold out an idea "that pain and sorrow can come not near them," and that they enjoy a happy exemption from "all the ills that flesh is heir to." They complain of nothing, for they profess to have nothing to complain of. They feel not the cold of winter, nor the heat of summer. The temperature is always exactly what *they* like. To them the street is never muddy with rain, nor slippery with ice. Unwholesome food agrees perfectly with *them*. They sleep soundly in bad beds, or rather no beds are bad. Travelling never fatigues them. Nobody imposes on them, nobody offends them. Other people may be ill—they are always in good health and spirits. To them all books are delightful—all pictures beautiful—all music charming. Other people may have trouble with their children—*they* have none. Other people may have bad servants—*theirs* are always excellent.

Now if all this were true, the lot of such persons would indeed be enviable, and we should endeavour to learn by what process such complete felicity has been attained—and why they see every thing through such a roseate medium. But it is not true. This is all overweening vanity, and a desire "to set themselves up above the rest of the world." We have always noticed that these over-fortunate, over-happy women have, in reality, a discontented, care-worn look, resulting from the incessant painful effort to seem what they are not. And if any body will take the trouble, it is very easy to catch them in discrepancies and contradictions. But it is not polite to do so. Therefore let them pass.

As mothers are always on the *qui vive*, (and very naturally,) be careful what you say of their children. Unless he is a decidedly handsome man, you may give offence by remarking, "The boy is the very image of his father." If the mother is a vain woman, she would much rather hear that all the children are the very image of herself. Refrain from praising too much the children of another family, particularly if the two sets of children are cousins. It is often dangerous to tell a mother that "little Willy is growing quite handsome." She will probably answer, "I had hoped my child was handsome always." With some mothers it is especially imprudent to remark that "little Mary looks like her aunt, or her grandmother." Again, if you prudently say nothing about the looks of the little dears, you may be suspected and perhaps accused of taking no interest in children. Young ladies, when in presence of gentlemen, are too apt to go on the other extreme, and over-act their parts, in the excessive fondling and kissing and hugging of children not in the least engaging, or even good-looking. We cannot believe that any female, not the mother, can really fall into raptures with a cross, ugly child. But how pleasant it is to play with and amuse, an intelligent, affectionate, and good-tempered little thing, to hear its innocent sayings, and to see the first buddings of its infant mind.

When you are visiting another city, and receiving civilities from some of its inhabitants, it is an ill requital for their attentions to disparage their place, and glorify your own. In every town there is something to praise; and in large cities there is a great deal to amuse, to interest, and to give pleasure. Yet there are travellers who (like Smelfungus) are never satisfied with the place they are in—who exclaim all the time against the east winds of Boston, the sea-air of New York, the summer heats of Philadelphia, the hilly streets of Baltimore, and the dusty avenues of Washington. We have heard people from New Orleans call Philadelphia the hottest city in the Union, and people from Quebec call it the coldest. If there are two successive days of rain, then poor Philadelphia is the rainiest of all places. If it snows twice in two weeks, then it is the snowiest. If a fire breaks out, it is the city of fires. If there is an Irish fight in Moyamensing, it is the city of perpetual riots. By-the-bye, after that summer when we really had several successive riots up-town, and down-town, we saw an English caricature of the City of Brotherly Love, where the spirit of William Penn, in hat and wig, was looking down sadly from the clouds at the rioters, who were all represented as Quakers, in strait, plain clothes, and broad brims, knocking each other about with sticks and stones, firing pistols, and slashing with bowie-knives. Alas, poor Quakers! how guiltless ye were of all this! It is a common belief in England, that of this sect are *all* the people of Pennsylvania.

In talking to an elderly lady, it is justly considered very rude to make any allusion to her age; even if she is unmistakeably an old woman, and acknowledges it herself. For instance, do not say—"This silk of yours is very suitable for an elderly person"—or—"Will you take this chair?—an old lady like you will find it very comfortable"—or—"Look, baby—is not that grandma?"—or—"I told the servant to attend first to you, on account of your age"—or—"Children, don't make such a noise—have you no respect for old people?"

All this we have heard.

CHAPTER XVI.
INCORRECT WORDS.

Every one who sees much of the world must observe with pain and surprise various unaccountable instances of improper and incorrect words that sometimes disfigure the phraseology of females who have gone through a course of fashionable education, and mixed in what is really genteel society. These instances, it is true, are becoming every day more rare; but we regret that they should exist at all. Early impressions are hard to eradicate. Bad habits of speaking are formed in childhood: sometimes from the society of illiterate parents, but more frequently from that of nurses and servants; and if not corrected or shaken off in due time, will cling like burrs to the diction of women who are really ladies in every thing else. Such women will say "that there," and "this here"—"them girls"—"them boys"—"I don't want no more"—"I didn't hear nothing about it"—"I didn't see nobody there"—"I won't do so no more." And other similar violations of grammar; and grammar is never more palpably outraged than when two negatives are used for an affirmative. It is surely shorter and easier to say, "I want no more"—"I heard nothing about it"—"I saw nobody there"—"I will do so no more."

Another grammatical error, less glaring, but equally incorrect, is the too common practice of converting a certainty into an uncertainty by saying, "I have no doubt but he was there." As if his being there was your only doubt. You should say, "I have no doubt of his being there." "I have no doubt but that he wrote it," seems to signify that you do doubt his writing it, and that you are nearly sure he did not. The proper phrase is, "I have no doubt of his writing it." "I do not doubt but that she knew it long ago," implies that you do doubt her having known it. It should be, "I do not doubt her knowing it long ago." Leave out *but*, when you talk of doubting.

No word is proper that does not express the true meaning. For instance, it is not right to call a township a town. A township is a section of land that may consist entirely of forests and farms, and may not comprise even a small village or hamlet. A town resembles a city in being closely built up with streets of adjoining houses. Men cannot go fishing or hunting in a *town*, though they may in a township. We are surprised to find this misapplication of the word among some of the most distinguished of the New-England *literati*. Perhaps it explains Jonathan's perplexity in one of the old Yankee Doodle songs:

"He said he couldn't see the town,
There were so many houses."

We hope it is not necessary to caution our readers against the most provincial of Yankee provincialisms, such as, "I hadn't ought," or "I shouldn't ought"—or "It warn't," instead of "It was not"—or the exclamations, "Do tell!" or "I want to know," ejaculated as a token of surprise the moment after you have told, and made known. The common English habit, or rather a habit of the common English, of using continually the words "you know," and "you know," is very tiresome, particularly when they are talking of something that you cannot possibly be acquainted with. Check them by saying, "No, I do not know." They also make great use of the word "monstrous"—ugly as that word is. Do not imitate them in saying that you are "monstrous glad," or "monstrous sorry," or "monstrous tired," or that a young lady is "monstrous pretty." We have heard even "monstrous little."

We advise our New-England friends to eschew, both in speaking and writing, all Yankee phrases that do not convey the exact meaning of the words. For instance, to "*turn out* the tea," instead of to "*pour* it out." There can be no turn given, in this process, to the spout or handle of the tea-pot. On the contrary, it cannot pour well unless it is held straight. To "cut the eggs," instead of to beat them. The motion of beating eggs does not cut them. "Braiding eggs," is still worse. But we believe that this braiding is not the same as cutting. What is it?

Two young officers were travelling in the far West when they stopped to take supper at a small road-side tavern, kept by a very rough Yankee woman. The landlady, in a calico sun-bonnet, and bare feet, stood at the head of the table to pour out. She enquired of her guests, "if they chose long sweetening, or short sweetening in their coffee." The first officer, supposing that "long sweetening" meant a large portion of that article, chose it accordingly. What was his dismay when he saw their hostess dip her finger deep down into an earthen jar of honey that stood near her, and then stir it (the finger) round in the coffee. His companion, seeing this, preferred "short sweetening." Upon which the woman picked up a large lump of maple sugar that lay in a brown paper on the floor beside her, and biting off a piece, put it into his cup. Both the gentlemen dispensed with coffee that evening. This anecdote we heard from the sister of one of those officers.

"Emptyings" is not a good name for yeast. "Up chamber, up garret, down cellar," are all wrong. Why not say, "up in the chamber, up in the garret, down in the kitchen, down in the cellar" &c.? Why should a mirthful fit of laughter be called "a gale!" "Last evening we were all in such a gale!"

Snow and ice are not the same. Therefore a snowball should not be called an ice-ball, which latter might be a very dangerous missile.

Pincushions are pincushions, and not pin-balls, unless they are of a globular shape. If in the form of hearts, diamonds, &c., they are not balls.

When you are greatly fatigued, say so—and not that you are "almost beat out." When the Yankees are "beat out," the English are quite "knocked up." The English are "starved with cold"—Americans only starve with hunger. They may perish with cold; but unless hunger is added, they will not starve.

It is wrong to say that certain articles of food are healthy or unhealthy. Wholesome and unwholesome are the right words. A pig may be healthy or unhealthy while alive; but after he is killed and becomes pork, he can enjoy no health, and suffer no sickness.

If you have been accustomed to pronounce the word "does" as "doos," get rid of the custom as soon as you can. Also, give up saying "pint" for "point," "jint" for "joint," "anint" for "anoint," &c. Above all, cease saying "featur, creatur, natur, and raptur."

In New England it is not uncommon to hear the word "ugly" applied to a bad temper. We have heard, "He will never do for president, because he is so ugly." On our observing that we had always considered the gentleman in question, as rather a handsome man, it was explained that he was considered ugly in disposition.

A British traveller, walking one day in a suburb of Boston, saw a woman out on a door-step whipping a screaming child. "Good woman," said the stranger, "why do you whip that boy so severely?" She answered, "I *will* whip him, because he is so ugly." The Englishman walked on; but put down in his journal that "American mothers are so cruel as to beat their children, merely because they are not handsome."

No genteel Bostonian should call Faneuil Hall, "Old Funnel," or talk of the "Quinsey market," instead of Quincy, or speak of "Bacon street," or "Bacon Hill." That place was so called from a beacon, or signal-pole with a light at the top, and never was particularly celebrated for the pickling and smoking of pork.

The word "slump," or "slumped," has too coarse a sound to be used by a lady.

When you have exchanged one article for another, say so, and not that you have "traded it."

Do not say, "I should admire to read that book," "I should admire to hear that song," "I should admire to see the president." Substitute, "I should like to read that book," "I should like to hear that song," "I should like to see the president."

Using the word "love" instead of "like" is not peculiar to the ladies of any section of the Union. But they may assure themselves it is wrong to talk of *loving* any thing that is eatable. They may *like* terrapins, oysters, chicken-salad, or ice-cream; but they need not *love* terrapins or oysters, or *love* chicken-salad.

We remember, in the farce of Modern Antiques, laughing at an awkward servant-girl bringing in a dish of salad to a supper-table, before the company had assembled, and, after taking a large bite, turning her foolish face toward the audience, and saying, "I loves beet-root."

Even if you are a provincial New-Yorker, give up calling the door-step or porch by the ancient Dutch name of "stoop," (stoep,) and do not talk of going out on the stoop, or sitting in the stoop. When a load of wood or coal is put down at your door, say not that it is "dumped." Never speak of visiting friends that "live to Brooklyn," or "live to Newark." They live *at* those places, not *to* them. The word "muss" sounds badly, when a young lady says, "her scarf is mussed," or her collar is "mussed"—or that her bureau drawers are all in a muss. The English synonyme, "mess," has *rather* a better sound. Be it also remembered that a stool is not a bench. A bench holds several people, a stool but one.

When you mean that an article of dress (a bonnet or a cap) is neat and pretty, do not say that it is cunning. An inanimate object cannot be cunning.

To be cunning requires some mind. We are sorry to say that we have heard females who, when they intend to be witty, talk of taking a snooze, (which means a nap,) and speak of a comic anecdote as being "rich," and of a man in faded clothes as looking "seedy." We have heard Philadelphia ladies speak of a "great big" house, or a "great big" ship; and there are still some who *expect* what has already come to pass—as, "I expect it rained somewhere last night"—"I expect she arrived yesterday"—"I expect he went to Baltimore." In all these cases the proper term is "I suppose," and not "I expect."

The word "mayhap" (instead of perhaps) is a positive vulgarism. It is of English origin, but is only used in England by very low people—and by English writers, never.

We have little tolerance for young ladies, who, having in reality neither wit nor humour, set up for both, and having nothing of the right stock to go upon, substitute coarseness and impertinence, (not to say impudence,) and try to excite laughter, and attract the attention of gentlemen, by talking slang. Where do they get it? How do they pick it up? From low newspapers, or from vulgar books? Surely not from low companions?

We have heard one of these ladies, when her collar chanced to be pinned awry, say that it was put on drunk—also that her bonnet was drunk, meaning crooked on her head. When disconcerted, she was "floored." When submitting to do a thing unwillingly, "she was brought to the scratch." Sometimes "she did things on the sly." She talked of a certain great vocalist "singing like a beast." She believed it very smart and piquant to use these vile expressions. It is true, when at parties, she always had half a dozen gentlemen about her; their curiosity being excited as to what she would say next. And yet she was a woman of many good qualities; and one who boasted of having always "lived in society."

We think that gentlemen lose a particle of their respect for young ladies who allow their names to be abbreviated into such cognomens as Kate, Madge, Bess, Nell, &c. Surely it is more lady-like to be called Catharine, Margaret, Eliza, or Ellen. We have heard the beautiful name Virginia degraded into Jinny; and Harriet called Hatty, or even Hadge.

A very silly practice has been introduced of writing Sally, Sallie—Fanny, Fannie—Mary, Marie—Abby, Abbie, &c. What would our grand-parents have thought of Pollie, Mollie, Peggie, Kittie, Nancie? Suppose young men were to adopt it, and sign themselves, Sammie, Billie, Dickie, Tommie, &c.!

By-the-bye, unless he is a relation, let no young lady address a gentleman by his christian name. It is a familiarity which he will not like.

CHAPTER XVII.
BORROWING.

Any article you are likely to want on more than one occasion, it is better to buy than to borrow. If your own, you can have it always at hand: you will lay yourself under no obligation to a lender, and incur no responsibility as to its safety while in your possession. But when you *do* borrow, see that the article is speedily returned. And, under no consideration, take the liberty of lending it to any person whatever, before restoring it to the owner. Apologies and expressions of regret are no compensation, should it be out of your power to replace it if injured or lost.

When you ask to borrow a thing, do not say, "Will you *loan* it to me?" The word "loan" is, by good talkers, and good writers, never used but as a substantive: notwithstanding that Johnson gives it as a verb also, but only on one obscure authority—and Johnson is not now regarded as infallible. To *lend*, not to *loan*, is the usual and proper expression. As a substantive it is generally employed in a commercial and political sense, or to denote a large sum borrowed for a public and important purpose. It is true you can say, "May I request the loan of your fan?" "Will you permit me to ask the loan of this book?" But it is much easier and smoother to say simply, "Will you lend me your fan for a few minutes?" "Will you be kind enough to lend me this book?"

No articles, perhaps, are more frequently borrowed than umbrellas, and none are returned with so little punctuality. Frequently, a borrowed umbrella is never thought of by the borrower, till after the weather clears up; the lender, most probably, suffering inconvenience for want of it. Often it is detained till the next rain, when the lender has to take the trouble of sending for it. And then it is very possible it may not be found at all; some person in the mean time having nefariously carried it off. In such a case, it is a matter of common honesty for the careless borrower to replace that umbrella with a new one; as she is not to suppose that empty expressions of regret or unmeaning apologies will be sufficient compensation for a substantial loss.

To avoid any difficulties concerning umbrellas, it is safest, in cloudy weather, not to leave home without one. Many persons venture out beneath a threatening sky, unwilling to encumber themselves with an umbrella, which (possibly) they may not chance to require before they got home. Their dependance is on stopping in at the house of a friend, and borrowing one there. But is it not better to incommode yourself a little by carrying a closed umbrella, even if you should *not* find occasion to use it, than to hasten rapidly through the street to reach a shelter when you find the rain beginning to drop; and afterwards to deprive your friend, even temporarily, of an article which the wet weather may render it inconvenient to spare. Also, you may be caught by a sudden shower, at a considerable distance from the dwelling of the person with whom you are acquainted, and you may find the omnibuses all full, (as they generally are when it rains,) and no other vehicle in sight. Therefore, when the wind is in a rainy quarter, and the sky louring, be always on the safe side, and take an umbrella with you on leaving home.

Every lady should own a small light umbrella, or else a very large parasol, of extra size, covered with strong India silk that will not easily tear or fade, and that may be used, on occasion, for either sun or rain; and that will not be cumbrous to carry, though quite large enough to shelter *one* person. In truth, we have found but few umbrellas, however large, that could effectually cover *two* persons (unless they were people of very small size) so that the rain did not drop upon the off-shoulder of one or the other. You cannot be well screened by an umbrella, unless you carry it all the time steadily in your *own* hands, and over yourself alone. And politeness requires that you should give your companion the best of the shelter. So when two ladies go out together, the clouds portending rain, let each take an umbrella for herself, and then much injury to bonnets and shawls may be avoided.

These small light umbrellas are excellent to travel with, and especially useful in the transit from car to steamboat, or even from the house to the carriage. When not in "actual service," keep this umbrella beside you with your shawl and your travelling satchel. It will be useful during the journey, if packed away in a trunk.*

When you purchase an umbrella, desire that, before sending it home, your name be engraved on the little plate at the termination of the handle, or else on the slide. "To make assurance doubly sure," you may get the name painted in full in small white or yellow letters on the *inside* of one of the gores of silk. These letters will not be conspicuous on the outside, but they will always serve to identify the umbrella. Your residence (if permanent) may be added. When about to travel, sew a small card with your address near the bottom of one of the gores inside. This card may be changed when staying at a new place. With

---

* In buying a handsome parasol or umbrella, see that it has a folding-joint in the middle of the stick, and that this joint works easily, so that there may be no difficulty in packing it in a trunk or box. To prevent the silk being rubbed, tie up the parasol in a smooth linen case, previous to packing.

these precautions, and a little care, (unless you are habitually thoughtless and forgetful,) you may carry an umbrella from Maine to Florida without losing it.

All the members of a family should be provided with at least one rain-umbrella of their own, and these should be kept up-stairs when not likely to be wanted. There is always great danger of their being purloined, or *borrowed*, if left in the hall. Persons who would not, for the world, be known to pilfer a single cent, are by no means particular with regard to detaining an umbrella or a book.

Umbrellas for the kitchen can now be had as low as seventy-five cents, or one dollar. If of coloured cotton (brown or blue) and highly glazed, they will turn off a moderate rain very well, but a drenching shower may cause the dye or colouring to run in streams. For very common use, though higher in price, the best are of oil-cloth, or of brown unbleached linen. The handsomest umbrellas are of blue or brown India silk, with steel frames, and a small silver name-plate on the handle. A green silk umbrella will soon be spoiled by the rain, and none look so badly in a short time. We have known a lady's bonnet entirely ruined by the drippings from a green parasol, hastily put up as a small screen from a sudden shower. No colour stands the sun and damp so badly as green.

After borrowing an umbrella, fail not to send it back immediately, unless you have previously ascertained from the owner that it will not be wanted for two or three hours. In that case, you will have time to dry it before it goes home; and this should be done as soon as possible, that it may be returned in good order. If left in the entry or hall, it may be carried off; or, in plain words, stolen. Let it be dried under your own inspection, spreading it wide open, and standing it on the floor. If dried fast, and in an expanded position, the wetting will not perceptibly injure it. But if left shut and standing up closed, with the wet soaking into the umbrella, it will dry in discoloured streaks, and be spoiled. If the spring or any other part of a borrowed umbrella gets broken or injured while in your possession, be sure to have it repaired before sending home. There is a meanness verging on dishonesty in leaving this to be done by the owner.

If the cheap or common umbrellas are given up to the care of the domestics, and kept in the kitchen, in all probability they will soon disappear altogether, and be no longer forthcoming when wanted. They will lend them to their friends, and lose them in various ways. The umbrellas should be kept in some small room or closet up-stairs; and when required, the servants should come and ask for them; bringing them back when done with, and dried.

When you go out to tea, even in a summer evening, carry a shawl on your arm to throw over your shoulders before coming out into the night-air. This will preclude the necessity of borrowing one of your friend, should the weather have changed and grown cooler. Also, to prevent any risk from damp pavements, take with you a pair of over-shoes, (India-rubber, of course,) or else a pair of inside-soles, such as you can conveniently slip into your pocket. We have found no inside-soles equal to those of lamb-skin with the wool left on the upper-side; the under-side of the skin being coated with India-rubber varnish to render them water-proof. These soles are both warm and dry, and are far pleasanter than cork soles covered with flannel, and more lasting. But if you are obliged to borrow things to wear home, see that they are sent back next morning, if not the same evening, and in good order—the shawl well-dried from the damp, and folded smoothly, and the over-shoes cleaned nicely.

Always take a fan with you on going to a place of public amusement. You will be sure to require it, and it is better than to depend on fanning yourself with the bill or programme, or borrowing the fan of a more provident friend, and perhaps forgetting to return it.

With regard to the practice of borrowing articles of household use, it is generally a custom "more honoured in the breach than the observance," particularly when living in a place where all such things can be easily obtained by sending to the shops. There are persons who, with ample means of providing themselves with all that is necessary for domestic service, are continually troubling their neighbours for the loan of a hammer, a screw-driver, a gimlet, a carpet-stretcher, a bed-stead screw, a fluting-iron, a preserving kettle, jelly-moulds, ice-cream freezers, &c. &c. If these or any other articles *must* be borrowed, let them be returned promptly, and in good order.

If, in consequence of the unexpected arrival of company, any thing for the table is borrowed of a neighbour, such as tea, coffee, butter, &c., see that it is punctually returned; equal in quantity, and in quality; or rather superior. Habitual borrowers are very apt to forget this piece of honesty, either neglecting to return the things at all, or meanly substituting inferior articles—or perhaps laying themselves under such an imputation without actually deserving it, should the lender be ill-natured or untruthful. There is a homely proverb, "To go a-borrowing is to go a-sorrowing."

We have been told of a very aristocratic but very economical lady, in one of our large cities, who was in the almost daily practice of borrowing things of a neighbour to whom she never condescended to speak. On one occasion she borrowed the use of that neighbour's fire to roast a pair of fowls.

Avoid borrowing change, or small sums. It is possible that you may really forget to repay them; but then it is also possible that you may be suspected of forgetting wilfully. So do not trust much to your memory. It is a true remark, that there are few instances of a borrower being so oblivious as to offer twice over the return of a small loan, forgetting that it had been paid already.

In borrowing a dress as a pattern, it is safest not to try it upon yourself, lest some part of the body should be stretched or frayed. Also, in trying on a bonnet or cap that is not your own, refrain from tying the strings; as every tying will give them additional wrinkles or rumples, and perhaps somewhat soil them. Never put on another person's gloves.

Should you be staying at a boarding-house, do not depend on "the lady in the next room," or any other lady, to lend you things which you can procure quite as easily as she can. Keep yourself always provided with pen, ink, and paper, envelopes, wafers, sealing-wax, pencils, post-office stamps, &c. Also with sewing implements.

When a friend lends you a handkerchief, a collar, or any other washable article, see that it is nicely washed, and done up, before returning it to her,—and do so promptly. If an article of jewellery, carry it back to her yourself, and put it into her own hand, to preclude all risk of loss. She will not be so ungenerous as to tell any person that she has lent it to you; and will for a while afterward, refrain from wearing it herself, in any company where it may be recognized.

Should a visiter accidentally leave her handkerchief at your house, have it washed and ironed before restoring it to her.

On borrowing a book, immediately put a cover upon it—and let the cover be of clean, smooth, white or light-coloured paper. What is called nankeen paper is best and strongest for this purpose. Newspaper, or any paper that is printed, makes a vile book-cover. Beside its mean and dirty appearance, the printing-ink will not only soil your own hands while reading, but will do more injury to the binding than if it was left uncovered.

To cover a book neatly—take a sheet of nice paper of more than sufficient size, and lay the book open upon it. Cut a notch or indentation at the top and bottom of this paper, so as to admit the back of the book, making the notch exactly the width of the back, and two or three inches deep. Fold down the edges of the paper straightly, smoothly, and evenly, over the edges of the binding or cover. Fold the corners of the paper nicely underneath, (trimming off the superfluous paper that turns under,) making them lie as flat as possible. You may secure all the folds at the corners with small wafers, pins, or paste-cement. If you use pins, take care to stick them so as not to scratch the inside of the binding, or to prick and tear the fly-leaves. The paper-cover should not only be strong, but smooth also; if coarse and rough, it will injure the binding. When you send the book home, put it up neatly, so as to make a well-looking package; secured with either a string or a seal, and direct it to the owner.

If the book is a pamphlet, and the sewing-thread gives way, sew it again, with a large needle and a strong brown thread—not white cotton. If not sewed immediately, it will fall apart, and some leaves may drop out, and be lost. If, by any unlucky accident, a leaf is torn, lay the two pieces nicely together, and sew them, lightly, with a rather fine thread. But if one side of the torn page is blank, it will be best to mend it by pasting a small narrow slip of white paper underneath, so as to unite the torn edges neatly.

You may have excellent paste or cement, continually at hand, by buying at a druggist's an ounce of the *best and cleanest* gum tragacanth, with a little bit of corrosive sublimate not larger than a grain of corn, and dissolving them in a large half-pint of clear water, either warm or cold. Pick the gum tragacanth very clean, freeing it carefully from all dust and impurities. Put it with the corrosive sublimate into a white or queensware vessel having a close cover, and holding a pint, to allow for swelling. Pour on the water; cover it closely; and stir it *with a stick*, several times during the day. When sufficiently dissolved, the paste will be smooth throughout. The corrosive sublimate will cause it to keep good for a year or more; and it is an excellent and most convenient cement for all purposes, from wall-paper to artificial flowers. It must on no account be kept in a metal vessel or be stirred with a metal spoon, as it will then turn black. No house should be without this paste—and it should find a place in every library and office. When it is nearly used up, and becomes dry at the bottom, pour on a little water, and it will dissolve again.

Make no remarks with pen or pencil on the margin of any book that does not belong to yourself. Whatever may be your own opinion of certain passages, you have no right to disturb other readers by obtruding upon them these opinions, unasked for. The pleasure of reading a book from a public library, is frequently marred by finding, as you proceed, that some impertinent fools have been before you, and scribbled their silly comments all through; or indulged in sneers and vituperations directed at the author. You may lessen this annoyance by turning over all the leaves before you begin reading, and erasing all the marginal remarks with India rubber; and this will also be an act of kindness to the next reader after yourself. When written with ink, (as is often the case,) there is no remedy; and you must endure the infliction of being annoyed throughout the book by these gratuitous criticisms. In a book, even belonging to yourself, it is well to use the pencil sparingly; and only to correct an error of the press, or a chronological mistake of the author. All readers like to form their own opinions as they go along, without any prompting from those who have preceded them.

Never, on any consideration, allow yourself to lend a borrowed book. If requested to do so, it should be a sufficient excuse to say that "it is not your own." But if still urged, persist in declining steadily; for it is a liberty you have no right to take with any article belonging to another. Even if the owner is your sister, you should lend nothing of hers without first obtaining her permission. Whatever you borrow yourself, should pass safely from your hands to those of the owner. If a friend of yours is very desirous of reading a borrowed book, and has no other means of obtaining it, and you think you can depend on her carefulness and punctuality, (not else,) you may promise "to request for her the favour." And when the owner has consented, (and not till then,) you may transfer the book to the new borrower with strict injunctions to take great care of it, and to return it as soon as possible.

I have known a borrowed book travel round a whole circle of relations and acquaintances, till, when sent home at last, it was literally worn out by dint of use. And this when nearly the whole set were persons who could well afford to buy all they were desirous of reading. Many ladies like very well to read when they can do so at the cost of their friends; but they seem to regard the purchase of any thing to improve the mind, or amuse the fancy, as throwing away money which they would expend more to their satisfaction in articles of personal decoration. And is it not melancholy to see an intelligent child craving in vain for books, while bedizened with finery to gratify the vanity of an ostentatious mother?

If, with the permission of the owner, you have lent a borrowed book to a person who, having lost or injured it, still has the presumption to ask you to intercede for the loan of another, you are bound to refuse the request; and do so with civility but steadiness, assigning the true reason. It may be a salutary lesson to that borrower.

Remember never to send home any article in a wrapper of newspaper. Keep always in the house a supply of good wrapping-paper, bought for the purpose, and also of balls of twine. For putting up small things, what is called shoe-paper is very useful. It is both nice and cheap, selling from fifty to sixty cents per ream, according to the size, and there are twenty quires in a ream. There are varieties of stronger and larger wrapping-paper for articles that require such, and for parcels that are to be sent to far-off places, or to go by public conveyances. Such packages are best secured by red tape and sealing-wax. At every stationer's may be purchased all varieties of paper.

Be particularly careful of borrowed magazines, as the loss of one number spoils a whole set, and you may find great difficulty in replacing a lost number. Even a newspaper should be punctually returned. The owner may wish to file it, or to send it away to a friend. If lost or defaced while in your possession, send to the publishing-office and buy another. It is unsafe to leave the book you are reading in the parlour of a hotel. Always carry it away with you, whenever you quit the room—otherwise you will be likely to see it no more.

In America, books are so cheap (not to mention the numerous public libraries) that in most instances all who can afford it had better buy than borrow, particularly such works as are worth a second reading. If you find your books accumulating inconveniently, give away a portion of them to some lover of reading, who, less fortunate than yourself, is unable to expend much money with the booksellers.

I have often wondered to see a fair young stranger sitting day after day, idle and listless in the drawing-room of a hotel, when she might have known that there were bookstores in the immediate neighbourhood.

If, while in your possession, a borrowed book is irreparably injured, it is your duty to replace it by purchasing for the owner another copy. And, if that cannot be procured, all you can do is to buy a work of equal value, and to present *that*, as the only compensation in your power. Observe the same rule with all borrowed articles, lost or injured. The lender is surely not the person to suffer from the carelessness of the borrower. Leave no borrowed books in the way of children, and never give a young child a book to play with. Eat no cake or fruit over an open book, lest it be greased or stained. And take care not to blister or spoil the binding by putting it down in a wet place, for instance, on a slopped table.

Some young ladies have a bad habit of biting their fingers, especially if they rejoice in handsome hands; and the same ladies, by way of variety, are prone to bite the corners of books, and the edges of closed fans. So it is dangerous to trust these articles in their vicinity. We have seen the corners of an elegant Annual nearly bitten off at a centre-table in the course of one evening. And we have seen ice-cream eaten and wine drank over an open port-folio of beautiful engravings.

By-the-bye, in taking up a print to look at it, always extend it carefully with both hands, that the paper may be in no danger of cracking or rumpling, which it cannot escape if held but in one hand, particularly if there is a breeze blowing near it. To show a large engraving without risk of injury, spread it out smoothly on a table; keeping it flat by means of books or other weights, laid carefully down on the corners, and, if the plate is *very* large, at the sides also. And let no one lean their elbows upon it.

It is an irksome task to show any sort of picture to people who have neither taste, knowledge, nor enjoyment of the art. There are persons (ungenteel ones, it is true) who seem to have no other pleasure, when looking at a fine print or picture, than in trying to discover in the figures or faces, fancied resemblances to those of some individuals of their own circle: loudly declaring for instance, that, "Queen Victoria is the very image of Sarah Smith;" "Prince Albert an exact likeness of Dick Brown;" "the Duke of Wellington the very ditto of old Captain Jones," &c. &c. To those "who have no painting in their souls," there is little use in showing or explaining any fine specimen of that noblest of the fine arts. We have heard a gentleman doubting whether a capital portrait of Franklin was not General Washington in his everyday dress. We could fill pages with the absurd remarks we have heard on pictures, even from persons who have had a costly education put at them. There are ladies who can with difficulty be made to understand the difference between a painting and an engraving—others who think that "the same man always makes both." Some call a coloured print a painting—others talk* of themselves *painting pictures* in albums—not understanding that, properly speaking, they are water-colour drawings when done on paper and with transparent tintings—while *pictures* are painted with oil or opaque colours on canvas or board. Frescoes are painted on new walls before the plastering is quite dry, so that the colours incorporate at once with the plaster, and dry along with it; acquiring in that manner a surprising permanency.

There is another very common error, that of calling a diorama a panorama. A panorama, correctly speaking, is a large circular representation of one place only, (such as Rome, Athens, Thebes, Paris,) comprising as much as the eye can take in at a view. The spectators, looking from an elevated platform in the centre, see the painting all around them in every direction, and appearing the size of reality, but always stationary. The panoramas exhibited successively in London by Barker, Burford, Catherwood and others, are admirable and truthful views of the places they represent; and after viewing them a few minutes, you can scarcely believe that you are not actually there, and looking at real objects. A few of these triumphs of perspective and colouring, have been brought to America. It were much to be wished that an arrangement could be made for conveying every one of these fine panoramas

---

* We were a few years since, told by one of our principal booksellers that a young lady came into his store when he chanced to be at the counter himself, and, showing him a small English prayer-book elegantly bound, and with fine engravings, she enquired if he had any exactly like that. On his replying in the negative, she desired that he would get precisely such a prayer-book made for her, in time for church on Sunday morning—(it was then Friday)—as she had set her mind on it. It must have just such pictures, and just such a beautiful gilt cover. He endeavoured in vain to convince her of the utter impossibility of performing this feat of having one single book printed, and bound, with plates engraved purposely for it, and all in the space of a day and a half. She seemed much displeased, and went away, in search, as she said, of a bookseller that was more obliging.

successively across the Atlantic, and exhibiting them in all our principal cities. It would be a good speculation.

It is difficult to imagine whence originated the mistake of calling a diorama a panorama, which it is *not*. A diorama is one of those numerous flat-surface paintings of which we have had so many, (and some few of them very good,) and which, moving on unseen rollers, glide or slide along, displaying every few minutes a new portion of the scenery.

The error has grown so common that persons fall habitually into it, though knowing all the time that it *is* an error. To correct it, let the exhibiters of dioramas cease to call them *panoramas*, and give them their proper name, both in their advertisements and in their verbal descriptions. Sebron's magnificent representation of the departure of the Israelites, that looked so amazingly real, was not a diorama, for it did not move, and not a panorama, for it was not circular. But it was a colossal picture, so excellent that at the first glance it seemed to be no picture at all, but the real scene, with the real people.

CHAPTER XVIII.
OFFENCES.

If the visits of an acquaintance become less frequent than formerly, the falling off is not always to be imputed to want of regard for you, or to having lost all pleasure in your society. The cause may be want of time, removal to a distance, precarious health, care of children, absence from town, family troubles, depressed fortunes, and various other circumstances. Also, with none of these causes, visiting may gradually and almost insensibly decline, and neither of the parties have the slightest dislike to each other. If no offence has been intended, none should be taken; and when you chance to meet, instead of consuming the time in complaints of estrangement, meet as if your intercourse had never been interrupted, and you will find it very easy to renew it; and perhaps on a better footing than before. The renewal should be marked by a prompt interchange of special invitations—followed by visits.

Unless your rooms are spacious, you cannot have what is called a large general party. Some of your acquaintances must be omitted, and all that are left out, are generally offended. Therefore it is not well ever to have such parties, unless your accommodations are ample. *Squeezes* are out of fashion in the best American society. We have heard of parties at great houses in London, where, after the rooms were crowded to suffocation, a large portion of the company had to pass the evening on the stairs; and where coaches, unable to draw up from the immense number of these vehicles that were in advance, had to remain all night at the foot of the line, with ladies sitting in them. When morning came, they had to turn back, and drive home, the carriages being all they saw of the party.

It is better to give two or three moderate entertainments in the course of the season, than to crowd your rooms uncomfortably; and even then to risk giving offence to those who could not be added to the number.

If such offence has been given, try to atone for it by inviting the offended to dine with you, or to pass an evening, and asking at the same time a few pleasant people whom you know she likes.

You may have a very intimate and sincere friend who does not find it convenient to send for you every time she has company. If, in all things else, she treats you with uniform kindness, and gives reason to believe that she has a true affection for you, pass over these occasional omissions of invitation, and do not call her to account, or treat her coolly when you see her. True friendship ought not depend upon *parties*. It should be based on a better foundation.

If no answer is returned to a note of invitation, be not hasty in supposing that the omission has sprung from rudeness or neglect. Trust that your friend is neither rude nor neglectful; and believe that the answer was duly sent, but that it miscarried from some accidental circumstance.

A friend may inadvertently say something that you do not like to hear, or may make a remark that is not pleasant to you. Unless it is prefaced with a *previous* apology; or unless she desires you "not to be offended at what she is going to say;" or unless she informs you that "she considers it her duty always to speak her mind,"—you have no right to suppose the offence premeditated, and therefore you should restrain your temper, and calmly endeavour to convince her that she is wrong; or else acknowledge that she is right. She ought then to apologize for what she said, and you should immediately change the subject, and never again refer to it. In this way quarrels may be prevented, and ill-feeling crushed in the bud. When what is called "a coolness" takes place between friends, the longer it goes on the more difficult it is to get over. But "better late than never." If, on consideration, you find that *you* were in the wrong, let no false pride, no stubborn perverseness prevent you from making that acknowledgement. If your friend, on her part, first shows a desire for reconciliation, meet her half-way. A vindictive disposition is a bad one, and revenge is a most unchristian feeling. People of sense (unless the injury is very great, and of lasting consequences) are easy to appease, because they generally have good feelings, and know how to listen to reason. Dr. Watts most truly says—

"The wise will let their anger cool,
At least before 'tis night;
But in the bosom of a fool,
It burns till morning light."

Should you chance to be thrown into the presence of persons who have proved themselves your enemies, and with whom you can have no intercourse, say nothing either *to* them or *at* them; and do not place yourself in their vicinity. To talk *at* a person, is mean and vulgar. Those who do it are fully capable of writing anonymous and insulting letters; and they often do so. High-minded people will always be scrupulously careful in observing toward those with whom they are at variance, all the ceremonies usual in polite society—particularly the conventional civilities of the table.

If you have, unfortunately, had a quarrel with a friend, talk of it to others as little as possible; lest in the heat of anger, you may give an exaggerated account, and represent your adversary in darker colours than she deserves. You may be very sure these misrepresentations will reach her ear, and be greatly magnified by every successive relater. In this way a trifle may be swelled into importance; a mole-hill may become a mountain; and a slight affront may embitter the feelings of future years. "Blessed are the peacemakers,"—and a mutual friend, if well-disposed toward both opponents, generally has it in her power to effect a reconciliation, by repeating, kindly, any favourable remark she may chance to have heard one of the offended parties make on the other. In truth, we wish it were the universal custom for all people to tell other people whatever good they may hear of them—instead of the wicked and hateful practice of telling only the bad. Make it a rule to repeat to your friends all the pleasant remarks that (as far as you know) are made on them, and you will increase their happiness, and your own popularity. We do not mean that you should flatter them, by reciting compliments that are not true; but truth is not flattery, and there is no reason why agreeable truths should not always be told. There would then be far more kind feeling in the world. Few persons are so bad as not to have some good in them. Let them hear of the good. Few are so ugly as not to have about them something commendable even externally, if it is only a becoming dress. Let them hear of that dress. Flattery is praise without foundation. To tell a person with heavy, dull gray eyes, that her eyes are of a bright and beautiful blue; to talk of her golden locks to a woman with positive red hair of the tint called carroty; to tell a long, thin, stoop-shouldered girl, that she possesses the light and airy form of a sylph; or a short-necked, fat one that her figure has the dignity of an empress; to assure a faded matron that she looks like a young girl; to fall into raptures on listening to bad music, or when viewing a drawing that depicts nothing intelligible; or praising album poetry that has neither "rhyme nor reason,"—all this is gross flattery, which the object (if she has any sense) will easily detect, and suspect that you are trying experiments on her vanity and credulity.

Still where agreeable qualities *really* exist, it is not amiss to allude to them delicately. It will give pleasure without compromising veracity.

When any thing complimentary is said to you, acknowledge it by a bow and smile, but do not attempt an answer unless you can say something in return that will be equally sincere and pleasant. Most probably you cannot; therefore look gratified, and bow your thanks, but remain silent. Few ladies are distinguished, like the Harriet Byron of Grandison, "for a very pretty manner of returning a compliment." Do not reject the compliment by pretending to prove that you do not deserve it. But if it is a piece of bare-faced flattery, the best answer is to look gravely, and say or do nothing.

Should you chance accidentally to overhear a remark to your disadvantage, consider first if there may not be some truth in it. If you feel that there is, turn it to profitable account, and try to improve, or to get rid of the fault, whatever it may be. But never show resentment at any thing not intended for your ear, unless it is something of such vital importance as to render it necessary that you should come forward in self-defence. These instances, however, are of rare occurrence.

If you are so placed that you can hear the conversation of persons who are talking about you, it is very mean to sit there and listen. Immediately remove to a distance far enough to be out of hearing.

It is a proverb that listeners seldom hear any good of themselves. It were a pity if they should. Eavesdropping or listening beneath an open window, the crack of a door, or through a key-hole, are as dishonourable as to pick pockets.

CHAPTER XIX.
OBLIGATIONS TO GENTLEMEN.

In her intercourse with gentlemen, a lady should take care to avoid all pecuniary obligations. The civility that a gentleman conventionally owes to a lady is a sufficient tax—more she has no right to expect, or to accept. A man of good sense, and of true politeness, will not be offended at her unwillingness to become his debtor. On the contrary, he will respect her delicacy, and approve her dignity; and consent at once to her becoming her own banker on all occasions where expense is to be incurred. This is the custom in Europe; and is, in most cases, a very good one.

When invited to join a party to a place of amusement, let her consent, if she wishes; but let her state expressly that it is only on condition of being permitted to pay for her own ticket. If she steadily adheres to this custom, it will soon be understood that such is always her commendable practice; and she can then, with perfect propriety, at any time, ask for a seat among friends who intend going. To this accommodation she could not invite herself, if in the continual habit of visiting public places at the expense of others. The best time for a lady to pay for herself is to put her money into the hand of the gentleman *previous* to their departure for the place of performance. He will not be so rude as to refuse to take it. If he does refuse, she should evince her resentment by going with him no more.

Young men of limited means are frequently drawn into expenses they can ill afford, by being acquainted with young ladies who profess a passion for equestrian exercises—a most inconvenient passion for one who has not a horse of her own, or who lives in a family where no horses are kept. If her gentleman is obliged to hire, not only a horse for himself, but also one for the lady, let her have sufficient consideration *not* to propose to him that they should take rides together—and let her not draw him into an invitation, by her dwelling excessively on the delight of horseback excursions. In cities, these rides are expensive luxuries to those who keep no horses. Few city ladies ride well, (even if they have been at riding-school,) for want of daily practice out of doors. They are not exactly at ease on the horse, and always seem somewhat afraid of him; at least till they are "off the stones," and out in the open country. While in the streets, the rare sight of a lady on horseback attracts much attention, and a crowd of boys gathers round to see her mount her steed, or alight from it. This to a young lady of delicacy is very embarrassing, or ought to be.

In the country, the case is totally different. There, "practice makes perfect." The ladies, being accustomed to riding their own horses from childhood, acquire the art without any trouble, have no fear, feel perfectly at home in the saddle, and therefore sit gracefully, and manage their steeds easily. And as every country gentleman has a riding-horse of his own, he can accompany a lady without the expense of hiring.

Lay no wagers with gentlemen, and have no philopenas with them. In betting with a lady, it is customary for the gentleman to pay whether he wins or loses. What then does the wager imply, but a rapacious and mean desire on the part of the lady to "get a present out of him"—as such ladies would express it. No delicate and refined female ever bets at all. It is a very coarse and masculine way of asserting an opinion or a belief; and always reminds gentlemen of the race-course, or the gaming-table.

We disapprove of ladies going to charity-fairs in the evening, when they require a male escort—and when that escort is likely to be drawn into paying exorbitant prices for gifts to his fair companion—particularly, if induced to do so from the fear of appearing mean, or of being thought wanting in benevolence. In the evening, the young ladies who "have tables," are apt to become especially importunate in urging the sale of their goods—and appear to great disadvantage as imitation-shop-keepers, exhibiting a boldness in teazing that no real saleswoman would presume to display. Then the crowd is generally great; the squeezing and pushing very uncomfortable; and most of the company far from genteel. Ladies who *are* ladies, should only visit fancy-fairs in the day-time, when they can go without gentlemen; none of whom take much pleasure in this mode of raising money; or rather of levying contributions for special purposes. There are other ways that are more lady-like, more effective, less fatiguing, and more satisfactory to all concerned—and far less detrimental to the interests of the numerous poor women who get their living by their needles, or by their ingenuity in making ornamental nick-nacks for sale, and who ask but a fair price for them. Dress-makers are frequently induced to keep back portions of silk, the rightful property of their customers, who may afterwards be put to great inconvenience for want of them, when the dress is to be altered or repaired. And these pieces are given to the ladies who go about begging for materials to make pincushions, &c. for fancy-fairs. This is dishonest. Let them go to a store and buy small pieces of silk, velvet, ribbon, and whatever they want for these purposes.

If you have occasion to send by a gentleman a package to a transportation-office, give him along with it the money to pay for its carriage. If you borrow change, (even one cent,) return it to him punctually. He ought to take it as a thing of course, without any comment. When you commission him to buy any thing for you, if you know the price, give the money beforehand; otherwise, pay it as soon as he brings the article. Do all such things promptly, lest they should escape your memory if delayed.

When visiting a fancy-store with a gentleman, refrain from excessively admiring any handsome or expensive article you may chance to see there. Above all, express no wish that you were able to buy it, and no regret that you cannot, lest he should construe these extreme tokens of admiration into hints that you wish him to buy it for you. To allow him to do so, would on your part be very mean and indelicate, and on his very foolish.

It ought to be a very painful office (and is a very improper one) for young ladies to go round soliciting from gentlemen subscriptions for charitable purposes. Still it is done. Subscription-papers should only be offered by persons somewhat advanced in life, and of undoubted respectability—and then the application should be made, exclusively, to those whose circumstances are known to be affluent. People who have not much to give, generally prefer giving that little to objects of charity within their own knowledge. Who is there that does not know a poor family? And without actually giving money, (which in too many instances, is immediately appropriated by a drunken husband to supply himself with more drink,) much may be done to procure a few comforts for a miserable wife and children.

When you ask money for a charitable purpose, do so only when quite alone with the person to whom you apply. It is taking an undue advantage to make the request in presence of others—particularly if, as before observed, there is not wealth as well as benevolence. There is a time for all things—and young ladies are deservedly unpopular when, even in the cause of charity, they seize every opportunity to levy contributions on the purses of gentlemen.

It is wrong to trouble gentlemen with commissions that may cause them inconvenience or expense. In the awful days of bandboxes, unfortunate young men riding in stages were sometimes required to convey one of these cumbrous receptacles of bonnets and caps a day's journey upon their knees, to save it from rain outside. Sometimes an immense package containing an immense shawl. We knew an officer who, by particular desire, actually carried *three* great shawls several hundred miles; each bundle to be delivered at a different house in "the City of Magnificent Distances." But as to officers, "sufferance is the badge of all their tribe." Now these shawls should all have been sent by the public line, even if the transportation *did* cost something.

We repeat, that a lady cannot be too particular in placing herself under obligations to a gentleman. She should scrupulously avoid it in every little thing that may involve him in expense on her account. And he will respect her the more.

CHAPTER XX.
CONDUCT TO LITERARY WOMEN.

On being introduced to a female writer, it is rude to say that "you have long had a great *curiosity* to see her." Curiosity is not the right word. It is polite to imply that, "knowing her well by reputation, you are glad to have an opportunity of making her personal acquaintance." Say nothing concerning her writings, unless you chance to be alone with her. Take care not to speak of her first work as being her best; for if it is really so, she must have been retrograding from that time; a falling off that she will not like to hear of. Perhaps the truth may be, that you yourself have read only her *first* work; and if you tell her this, she will not be much flattered in supposing that you, in reality, cared so little for her first book, as to feel no desire to try a second. But she will be really gratified to learn that you are acquainted with most of her writings; and, in the course of conversation, it will be very pleasant for her to hear you quote something from them.

If she is a writer of fiction, and you presume to take the liberty of criticising her works, (as you may at her own request, or if you are her intimate friend,) refrain from urging that certain incidents are *improbable*, and certain characters *unnatural*. Of this it is impossible for you to judge, unless you could have lived the very same life that she has; known exactly the same people; and inhabited with her the same places. Remember always that "Truth is stranger than fiction." The French say—"Le vrai n'est pas toujours le plus vraisemblable,"—which, literally translated, means that "Truth is not always the most truth-like." Also, be it understood that a woman of quick perception and good memory can see and recollect a thousand things which would never be noticed or remembered by an obtuse or shallow, common-place capacity. And the intellect of a good writer of fiction is always brightened by the practice of taking in and laying up ideas with a view toward turning them to professional use. Trust in her, and believe that she *has* painted from life. A sensible fictionist always does. At the same time, be not too curious in questioning her as to the identity of her personages and the reality of her incidents. You have no right to expect that she will expose to you, or to any one else, her process of arranging the story, bringing out the characters, or concocting the dialogue. The machinery of her work, and the hidden springs which set it in motion, she naturally wishes to keep to herself; and she cannot be expected to lay them bare for the gratification of impertinent curiosity, letting them become subjects of idle gossip. Be satisfied to take her works as you find them. If you like them, read and commend them; but do not ask her to conduct you behind the scenes, and show you the mysteries of her art—for writing is really an art, and one that cannot be acquired, to any advantage, without a certain amount of talent, taste, and cultivation, to say nothing of genius. What right have you to expect that your literary friend will trust you with "the secrets of her prison-house," and put it into your power to betray her confidence by acquainting the world that a certain popular novelist has informed you with her own lips ("but it must on no account be mentioned, as the disclosure would give mortal offence, and create for her hosts of enemies,") that by her character of Fanny Gadfly she really means Lucy Giddings; that Mr. Hardcastle signifies Mr. Stone; that Old Wigmore was modelled on no less a person than Isaac Baldwin; that Mrs. Bastings was taken from Mrs. Sunning; and Mrs. Babes from Mrs. Childers—&c. &c. Also, do not expect her to tell you on what facts her incidents were founded, and whether there was any truth in them, or if they were mere invention.

Be not inquisitive as to the length of time consumed in writing this book or that—or how soon the work now on hand will be finished. It can scarcely be any concern of yours, and the writer may have reasons for keeping back the information. Rest assured that whenever a public announcement of a new book is expedient, it will certainly be made in print.

There are persons so rude as to question a literary woman (even on a slight acquaintance) as to the remuneration she receives for her writings—in plain terms, "How much did you get for that? and how much are you to have for this? And how much do you make in the course of a year? And how much a page do you get? And how many pages can you write in a day?"

To any impertinent questions from a stranger-lady concerning the profits of your pen, reply concisely, that these things are secrets between yourself and your publishers. If you kindly condescend to answer without evasion, these polite enquiries, you will probably hear such exclamations as, "Why, really—you must be coining money. I think I'll write books myself! There can't be a better trade," &c.

Ignorant people always suppose that popular writers are wonderfully well-paid—and must be making rapid fortunes—because they neither starve in garrets, nor wear rags—at least in America.

Never ask one writer what is her *real* opinion of a contemporary author. She may be unwilling to entrust it to you, as she can have no guarantee that you will not whisper it round till it gets into print. If she voluntarily expresses her own opinion of another writer, and it *is* unfavourable, be honourable enough not to repeat it; but guard it sedulously from betrayal, and avoid mentioning it to any one.

When in company with literary women, make no allusions to "learned ladies," or "blue stockings," or express surprise that they should have any knowledge of housewifery, or needle-work, or dress; or that they are able to talk on "common things." It is rude and foolish, and shows that you really know nothing about them, either as a class or as individuals.

Never tell an authoress that "you are afraid of her"—or entreat her "not to put you into a book." Be assured there is no danger.

An authoress has seldom leisure to entertain morning visiters; so much of her time being professionally occupied either in writing, or in reading what will prepare her for writing. She should apprize all her friends of the hours in which she is usually engaged; and then none who are really her friends and well-wishers, will encroach upon her convenience for any purpose of their own; unless under extraordinary circumstances. To tell her that you were "just passing by," or "just in the neighbourhood," and "just thought you would stop in," is a very selfish, or at least a very inconsiderate excuse. Is she to suppose that you do not consider her conversation worthy of a visit made on purpose?

Recollect that to a woman who gets her living by her pen, "time is money," as it is to an artist. Therefore, encroaching on her time is lessening her income. And yet how often is this done (either heedlessly or selfishly) by persons professing to be her friends, and who are habitually in the practice of interrupting her in her writing hours, which should always be in the morning, if possible. They think it sufficient to say, like Paul Pry, "I hope I don't intrude"—knowing all the time that they *do*, and pretending to believe her when civility obliges her to tell them they do *not*. Even if the visit is not a long one, it is still an interruption. In one minute it may break a chain of ideas which cannot be reunited, dispel thoughts that can never be recalled, disturb the construction of a sentence, and obliterate a recollection that will not return. And to all this the literary lady must submit, because her so-called friend "chanced to be out that morning shopping"—or "happened to be visiting in that part of the town"—and therefore has called on *her* by way of "killing two birds with one stone." Very likely, the visiter will say to the unfortunate visited, "I know it is inconvenient to you to see your friends in the morning, but I never feel like going out in the afternoon. As soon as dinner is over I must have my nap; and by the time that is finished, it is too late for any thing else."

In consequence of these ill-timed visits, the printer may have to send in vain for "copy" that is not yet ready; and an article written expressly for a magazine may arrive too late for the next month, and be therefore deferred a month later, which may subject her not only to inconvenience, but to actual pecuniary loss—loss of money. Or, at least, the interruption may compel her to the painful effort of trying to finish it even by sitting up late at night, and straining her weary eyes by lamp-light. Yet this she must endure because it suits an idle and thoughtless *friend* to make her a long and inopportune visit. The children of the pen and the pencil might say to these intruders, like the frogs in the pond when the boys were pelting them with stones—"This may be sport to you, but it is death to us."

If, when admitted into her study, you should find her writing-table in what appears to you like great confusion, recollect that there is really no wit in a remark too common on such occasions,—"Why, you look quite *littery*,"—a poor play on the words *literary* and *litter*. In all probability, she knows precisely where to lay her hand upon every paper on the table: having in reality placed them exactly to suit her convenience. Though their arrangement may be quite unintelligible to the uninitiated, there is no doubt method (her own method, at least) in their apparent disorder. It is not likely she may have time to put her writing table in nice-looking order every day. To have it done by servants is out of the question, as *they* would make "confusion worse confounded;" being of course unable to comprehend how *such a table* should be arranged.

If you chance to find an authoress occupied with her needle, express no astonishment, and refrain from exclaiming, "What! can *you* sew?" or, "I never supposed a literary lady could even hem a handkerchief!"

This is a false, and if expressed in words, an insulting idea. A large number of literary females are excellent needle-women, and good housewives; and there is no reason why they should not be. The same vigour of character and activity of intellect which renders a woman a *good* writer, will also enable her to acquire with a quickness, almost intuitive, a competent knowledge of household affairs, and of the art of needle-work. And she will find, upon making the attempt, that, with a little time and a little perseverance, she may become as notable a personage (both in theory and practice) as if she had never read a book, or written a page.

The Dora of David Copperfield is an admirable illustration of the fact that a silly, illiterate woman may be the worst of housewives. Dickens has unquestionably painted this character exactly from life. But that he always does. He must have known a Dora. And who has not?

If you find your literary friend in dèshabille, and she apologizes for it—(she had best *not* apologize)—tell her not that "authoresses are privileged persons, and are never expected to pay any attention to dress." Now, literary slatterns are not more frequent than slatterns who are not literary. It is true that women of enlarged minds, and really good taste, do not think it necessary to follow closely all the changes and follies of fashion, and to wear things that are inconvenient, uncomfortable, and unbecoming, merely because milliners, dress-makers, &c. have pronounced them "the last new style."

It is ill-manners to refer in any way to the profession of the person to whom you are talking, unless that person is an intimate friend, and you are alone with her; and unless she herself begins the subject. Still worse, to allude to their profession as if you supposed it rendered them different from the rest of the world, and marked them with peculiarities from which other people are exempt.

It is true that authorlings and poetizers are apt to affect eccentricity. Real authors, and even real poets, (by real we mean good ones,) have generally a large portion of common sense to balance their genius, and are therefore seldom guilty of the queernesses unjustly imputed to the whole fraternity.

When in company with a literary lady with whom you are not on very confidential terms, it is bad taste to talk to her exclusively of books, and to endeavour to draw out her opinion of authors with whom she is personally acquainted—and whom she will, of course, be unwilling to criticise, (at least in miscellaneous society,) lest her remarks should be invidiously or imprudently repeated, and even get into print. "Any thing new in the literary world?" is a question by which some people always commence conversation with an author. Why should it be supposed that they always "carry the shop along with them," or that they take no interest or pleasure in things not connected with books? On the contrary, they are glad to be allowed the privilege of unbending like other people. And a good writer is almost always a good talker, and fully capable of conversing well on various subjects. Try her.

It was beautifully said of Jane Taylor, the charming author of a popular and never-tiring little book of "Original Poems for Children," that "you only knew that the stream of literature had passed over her mind by the fertility it left behind it."

We have witnessed, when two distinguished lady-writers chanced to be at the same party, an unmannerly disposition to "pit them against each other"— placing them side by side, or *vis-à-vis*, and saying something about, "When Greek meets Greek," &c., and absolutely collecting a circle round them, to be amused or edified by the expected dialogue. This is rude and foolish.

It is not treating a talented woman with due consideration, to be active in introducing to her the silliest and flattest people in the room, because the said flats have been worked up into a desire of seeing, face to face, "a live author-ess"—though in all probability they have not read one of her works.

That notorious lion-hunter, the Countess of Cork, was so candid as to say to certain celebrated writers, "I'll sit by *you* because you are famous." To a very charming American lady whom she was persuading to come to her party, she frankly added, "My dear, you really must not refuse me. Don't you know you are my decoy-duck."

There are mothers (called pattern-mothers) who uphold the theory that every thing in the world must bend to the advantage (real or supposed) of chil-dren, that is, of their own children—and who have continually on their lips the saying, "a mother's first duty is to her children." So it is, and it is her duty not to render them vain, impertinent, conceited, and obtrusive, by allowing them to suppose that they must on all occasions be brought forward; and that their mother's visiters have nothing to do but to improve and amuse *them*. Therefore a literary lady often receives a more than hint from such a mother to talk only on edifying subjects when the dear little creatures are present; and then the conversation is required to take a Penny-Magazine tone, exclusively—the darlings being, most probably, restless and impatient all the time, the girls sitting uneasily on their chairs and looking tired, and the boys suddenly bolting out of the room to get back to their sports. It is true the children will be less impatient if the visiter will trouble herself to "tell them stories" all the time; but it is rude to ask her to do so.

When directing a letter to "a woman of letters," it is not considered polite to insert the word "Authoress" after her name. And yet we have seen this done by persons who ought to know better. If you are unacquainted with the number and street of her residence, direct to the care of her publisher; whose place you may always find, by referring to the title-page of one of her last works, and by seeing his advertisements in the newspapers. The booksellers always know where their authors are to be found. So do the printers—for their boys convey the proof-sheets.

Observe that the term "learned lady" is not correctly applied to a female, unless she has successfully cultivated what is understood to be the learning of colleges—for instance, the dead languages, &c. Unfortunately, the term is now seldom used but in derision, and to denote a woman whose studies have been entirely of the masculine order. You may speak of a well-informed, well-read, talented, intellectual, accomplished lady; but call her not *learned*, unless she is well-versed in the Greek and Latin classics, and able to discuss them from their original language. Even then, spare her the appellation of *learned*, if gentlemen are present. In the dark ages, when not every lady could read and write, the few that *were* entitled to the "benefit of clergy," frequently "drank deep in tasting the Pierian spring," and proceeded to study the learned languages with great success; for instance, Lady Jane Grey and Queen Elizabeth.

In desiring the autograph of a literary lady, do not expect her to write in your album "a piece of poetry." Be satisfied with her signature only. There is a spice of meanness in requesting from her, as a gift, any portion of her stock in trade. As well might you ask Mr. Stewart, or Mr. Levy, to present you with an embroidered collar, or a pair of gloves. For the same reason, never request an artist to "draw something" in your album. It is only amateur poets, and amateur artists, that can afford to write and draw in albums. Those who make a living by their profession, have no time to spare for gratuitous performances; and it is as wrong to ask them, as it is to invite public singers to "favour the company with a song" at private parties, where they are invited as guests. It is, however, not unusual for professional musicians to kindly and politely gratify the company by inviting themselves to sing; saying, "Perhaps you would like to hear my last song." And sometimes, if quite "in the vein," a real poet, when modestly asked for merely his signature, will voluntarily add a few lines of verse. But do not expect it.

There are pretty little books of fine paper, handsomely bound, that are used for the purpose of containing signature autographs; one on each page. A lady owning such a book, can send it to any distinguished person of whose hand-writing she wishes to possess a specimen.

When the name at the bottom of a letter is shown to you as an autograph, it is rude to take the letter into your own hand, and read the whole, or even to glance your eye over it. It is not intended that you shall see any thing but the signature.

We will now address a few words to beginners in the art of writing, with reference to their intercourse with women of well-established literary reputation. If these ladies of decided standing in the republic of letters have sufficient leisure, they will generally be very kind in assisting with their counsel a young aspirant, who shows any evidence of talent for the profession. Unluckily, too many novices in the art, mistake a mere desire to get into print, for that rarest of gifts—genius. And without genius, there is no possibility of gaining by the pen, either fame, or fortune.

Long manuscripts are frequently sent for the revisal "at leisure" of a person who has little or no leisure. Yet in the intervals of toiling for herself, she is expected to toil for some one else; probably for a stranger whom she does not know, in whom she can take no interest, and who has evidently "no writing in her soul." If, however, the modest request is kindly complied with, in all probability the corrections will only give offence, and may perhaps be crossed out before the manuscript is offered to the publisher, who very likely may reject it for want of these very corrections. We have known such incidents.

The least talented of the numerous females pretending to authorship, are generally the most conceited and the most obtrusive. They are frequently very great annoyances to women "well-up the ladder," who are expected, in many instances, not only to revise the manuscript, but immediately to find a purchaser for it—a purchaser of high rank among publishers—one who will bring it out handsomely, ensure it an immense circulation, pay promptly, and pay as much as is given to the standard authors. And besides being desired to "get it published," the reviser of the manuscript will, perhaps, be requested to correct the proofs; that is, if the literary novice should chance to know what proof-sheets are.

The work thus arrogantly thrust upon the time and attention of a deservedly-popular writer may be a book of "sweet poetry," on weak, worn-out, common-place subjects, done into feeble, halting, ill-rhyming verses, such as few read, and none remember. Or the aspirant after fame, may have chosen the easier path of prose, and produced a fiction without fancy, a novel without novelty, "a thrilling tale" that thrills nobody, a picture of fashionable life after no fashion that ever existed, or "a pathetic story of domestic life," neither pathetic nor domestic.

Yet if a practised and successful author ventures to pronounce an *unfavourable* verdict on such productions, because the writer desired her *candid* opinion, she will probably light up a flame of resentment, that may never be extinguished, and make an enemy for life; the objections being imputed to "sheer envy," and to a malignant design of "extinguishing a rising star."

A sufficient introduction to a publisher is to send him the manuscript, accompanied by a note requesting his opinion as soon as convenient. If he approves it, and believes it will be profitable, there is no doubt of his being willing to print the work. And if he thinks he shall make nothing by it, it is equally certain that he will decline the offer. It is too much to expect that he will be so regardless of his own interest as to publish a book, the sale of which will not remunerate him for the cost of paper and printing.

Ladies who live in the same house with an authoress, have opportunities enough of seeing her in the parlour, and at table; therefore they may dispense with visiting her in her own room. Spare her all interruptions of applying for the loan of books, paper, pens, ink, &c. Do not expect that, because she writes, she must necessarily keep a free circulating library, or a gratuitous stationer's shop. Supply yourself with all such conveniences from the regular sources. Buy them, and pay for them, instead of troubling one who has not time to be troubled. Above all, refrain from the meanness of asking her to lend you any book written by herself. If she volunteers the loan, then receive it thankfully; and take care to return it speedily, and in good condition. It is *her* interest, and the interest of her publishers, that a large number of copies shall be *sold*; not lent, or given away. Many persons erroneously suppose that an author has always on hand an unlimited number of her own books; or that the publisher will kindly give her as many as she can want for herself and friends. This is by no means the case. It is usual, when the first edition comes out, for the publisher to send the author half a dozen copies of the book, or a dozen, if it is a small one. After that, if she wants any more, she is expected to buy them of the bookseller. Therefore, she has none to *give away*, except to members of her own family, or to friends whose circumstances will not permit them to expend money in books, and who have an ardent love for reading without the means of gratifying it. We have known ladies, possessing diamonds and India shawls, and living in splendid houses, ask the author for the loan of a cookery-book, with the avowed purpose of "copying out the best receipts."

Apropos to cookery-books:—If you have faithfully followed a receipt, and the result is not quite satisfactory, there is nothing amiss in your acquainting the writer with that fact, provided it *is* a fact. On the contrary, you may do her a kindness, by enabling her to detect an error in the directions, and to rectify that error in a future edition.

Women often assert that the receipt was not a good one, and that upon trial it proved a failure, when, on investigation, you will find that, from false economy, some of the ingredients were left out; or the relative proportions diminished in quantity—too much of the cheapest articles being put in, and not enough of the more costly. Or else, that sufficient time and pains were not bestowed on the mixing and preparing; or that the thing was not sufficiently cooked.

By-the-bye, remember that a receipt for cookery, is not to be called a *recipe*. The word *recipe* belongs to pharmacy, and is only used with reference to medical prescriptions. The cook uses *receipts*, the apothecary *recipes*.

Whatever article you may wish to borrow from an inmate of the same house, apply first to persons whose time is of comparatively small importance to them, before you disturb and interrupt a literary lady. Do not trouble her for the loan of umbrellas, over-shoes, hoods, calashes, &c., or send to her for small change.

We once lived in a house where coal-fires were scarce, and wood-fires plenty. Our own fire-arrangement was wood in a Franklin stove, and no other person in the house was the fortunate owner of a pair of bellows. Liking always to be comfortable, we had bought a pair for ourselves.

Ten times a day we were disturbed by a knock at the door, from a coloured girl who came "a-borrowing" this implement to revive the fire of some other room. She called it by a pleasing variety of names—running through all the vowels. Sometimes she wanted the bellow*sas*; sometimes the bellow*ses*; or the bellow*sis*, the bellow*sos*, or the bellow*sus*. These frequent interruptions, with others that were similar, became a real grievance. We thought it would cost us less to present the bellows to the house, and buy another pair for ourselves. We did so—but very soon the first pair was somehow missing, and our own was again in requisition.

Since that winter we have burnt anthracite, and therefore have no bellow*sas* to lend.

CHAPTER XXI.
SUGGESTIONS TO INEXPERIENCED AUTHORS.

There is some economy and much convenience in buying your paper by the ream, (twenty quires,) having first tried a sample. The surface of the paper should be smooth, and somewhat glossy; particularly if you write with metallic pens. That which is soft and spongy, though a little lower in price, wears out the pen so fast that what is saved in paper is lost in pens; also, there is no possibility of writing on it with ease and expedition. You will find it best to use paper ruled in lines. If you write a large hand, take foolscap; if a small hand, use letter-paper size. But note-paper is too small, when you are writing for the press.

Before you commence your manuscript, take a quire, and prepare each sheet by splitting it all down the folded side, with a sharp paper-cutter, thus dividing it into half-sheets. You can do this better on a flat table than on the slope of a desk. Keep your left hand pressing down hard on the quire, while you are cutting it with your right.

The best paper-cutters are those of real ivory. A handle is of no advantage to them, but rather the contrary. They should be thin, plain, and perfectly straight, except being rounded off at the two ends. Ivory paper-knives of this form are generally used by the book-binders, an evidence that they are convenient and expeditious. Those of bone or horn are scarcely worth buying, though but half the price; the edges soon becoming blunt, and therefore useless. Wooden paper-knives are good for nothing. Paper-knives of mother of pearl, and other ornamental substances, are of little utility, being rarely sharp enough, (even when new,) and in a short time becoming quite dull. Also, they break very easily. Avoid cutting a sheet of paper, or the leaves of a book, with scissors; it is comparatively a slow and awkward process; and cannot, even with great care, be effected as smoothly and evenly as with a cutter of ivory.

Before you split or divide the sheet, press the paper-knife all along the fold, so as to flatten the crease, and make it cut evenly and easily. Having split your whole sheets into leaves or half-sheets, take each half-sheet separately, and fold over an inch or more all along the left-hand edge; so as to leave a margin or space for sewing the manuscript when finished. Do this with the paper-knife. Lay a pile of these half-sheets beside you when you sit down to write, and take them as you want them.

Write only on one side of the paper. If written on both sides, it will cause trouble and inconvenience to the printers, by obliging them to turn over at the end of every page. This rule, however, may be dispensed with, when a manuscript is so short that it may be comprised in one sheet, and is to be transmitted by mail. This may be the more easily managed, by drawing with a pencil or pen a straight perpendicular line down the middle of each page, so as to divide it into columns. When it is finished, enclose it in an envelope, direct, and seal it, and put on a post-office stamp. If the manuscript occupies two or three sheets, put two or three stamps side by side. There are large envelopes that will hold foolscap paper, properly folded.

Do not use *blue* ink; for if any part of your manuscript should chance to get wet, there is a risk of the blue ink being effaced or obliterated by the damp, so as to render the writing illegible; and this has frequently happened.

Let your writing be large enough, and plain enough to be read with ease, and the compositor will be less likely to make mistakes. Printers, though accustomed to read all sorts of writing, are sometimes completely at a loss in deciphering a very bad hand. There is no excuse for a person in respectable life persisting in writing illegibly, as it is never too late to improve. You have only to take lessons of a good instructor, and apply yourself sedulously to acquiring a new hand, and you will succeed in doing so.

Do not, in writing for the press, affect the crow-quill calligraphy that is fashionable for album verses and complimentary billets. When your manuscript is finished, sew the leaves *evenly* together, with nothing more than a strong thread; or, if it is very thick, it may be sewed with a fine twine put into a large needle. A handsome cover, daintily fastened with a pretty ribbon, is of no account in a printing-office, where the first thing that is done with a manuscript is to remove the cover, and cut the leaves loose from the fastening. The printers will gladly dispense with covers, ribbons, and fairy-like penmanship, in favour of a plain legible hand, pages regularly numbered, and leaves written on one side only.

In commencing a manuscript, write the title or caption in large letters, at some distance from the top of the first page; and if you are not anonymous, put your name a little below the title. Then begin the *first* line of the first paragraph, several inches distant from the left-hand side, or margin. In this manner commence every paragraph. The length of the paragraphs may be regulated by the time when you think a pause longer than that of a period or full stop may be effective; or to give the reader an opportunity of resting for a minute; or to denote the commencement of another subject.

In writing a dialogue, begin every separate speech with a capital, and commence each speech on a new line, and at some distance from the left-hand margin. Also mark the beginning and end of every speech with double commas. If the names of the speakers are given at the *commencement* of every speech, write those names in *large* letters, putting a dot and a dash after them. All these arrangements are the same in writing as in printing.

If you are, unfortunately, not familiar with the rules of punctuation, refresh your memory by referring to them in a grammar-book. They must be strictly observed; otherwise your meaning will be unintelligible. Always remember that every period or full stop, and every note of interrogation, or of admiration, must be followed by a capital letter, beginning the next word. Dashes, particularly in a dialogue, add much to the effect, if not used too lavishly.

Errors of orthography are rarely committed by any one who presumes to write for the press. It is scarcely possible for a person who reads much to spell incorrectly, as the appearance of the printed words becomes insensibly and indelibly fixed in the mind. Still it may be well to write with a dictionary on your table, in case you should have any doubt as to the proper spelling and meaning of a word with which you may not be very familiar.

Keep also a grammar on your table. Grammatical errors are annoying to the reader, and disgraceful to the writer, unless it is well known that she has not had the advantage of an education, even at a common school. Then she is to be pitied. But it is never too late to study grammar, and she had best do so before she ventures to write for the public. If she writes ungrammatically, how must she talk! In a work of fiction it is shocking to have lords and ladies, or the noble and dignified hero, and the elegant and refined heroine, conversing in "bad grammar," because the author knew no better. Yet such books we have seen. There are, luckily, not many of them. But there should be none.

Every morning, previous to commencing your task, revise carefully all that you have written on the preceding day, and correct and alter whatever you may deem susceptible of improvement. Some authors revise every page as soon as they have written it. But, unless you are much pressed for time, it is best to do this next morning, when your perceptions are fresh and clear. In crossing or blotting out, do it effectually, so that the original words may not appear through, and remain still legible. If you find that you have omitted a word, or if you wish to change one word for another, interline it; inserting the new word just above the line to which it belongs, and placing this mark ^ below. Lay aside each page as you finish it. Be particular in numbering every page; and it is best to do this before you begin, placing the number near the top of the right-hand corner. Let not your lines be too close, or there will not be space enough for legible interlining.

If the publisher lives in your own town, it will be sufficient to roll up the manuscript in clean white paper, twisted at each end, and wafered in the middle. But however short the distance, write on the outside of the paper the full direction of the publishing office; that, in case of its being dropped in the street, any person finding it may know exactly where to take it.

In putting up a large manuscript, in a packet for transmission to a distant place, use strong nankeen paper for the cover, and secure it with wafers, or paste, if it is to go a voyage in a steamer, as a wax seal may be melted by the heat of the fire. If it will reach its destination in a few hours, you may seal it with wax, having tied red tape about. Do not use twine, as that may cut the paper. Newspapers are generally put up in a brownish paper cover, pasted at the side and bottom, with one end left open.

Postage is now so cheap, that manuscripts had best always be transmitted by mail; putting a sufficient number of stamps on the outside, all close to each other.

Few women can write well enough for publication, without going twice over the subject; first in what is called the rough copy, and then making a fair copy with all the original errors corrected, and all proper alterations inserted. If you have time, make *two* fair copies; one for the printer, and one to keep for yourself, in case the other should be accidentally destroyed or lost— retaining it till after the work is actually in print. Much postage is wasted, and much annoyance is given to the editors of periodicals, by applications for the restoration of unpublished verses, and other "Rejected Addresses," consisting, perhaps, of a sheet of poetry, or a few pages of prose, of which it would have been very easy to have made another copy for the author's keeping.

In writing articles for Annuals, let it be remembered that the printing of these books is always completed some months before they are published or announced for sale. Therefore, all contributions should be sent to the publisher before February, or March at farthest. For a magazine, they should be transmitted at least two months in advance. For a weekly paper, two weeks ahead.

Those who write for periodicals should remember[281] that it is the custom to address all letters on compensations, copies of work, &c. to the publisher; and not to the editor, who seldom has any concern in the pecuniary affairs, his business being solely to receive, and read the manuscripts, to accept or reject them, and to arrange them for the press. It is not usual for the compensation to be paid till after the book is published. Some publishers send to every contributor one copy of the work. Others do not present a copy when the article is very short—for instance, a few stanzas of verse. Prose obtains a higher price than poetry, of which there is always a superabundance in the market. Much poetry is published without any pay at all; the writers being contented with seeing their effusions in print. No *good* author has any occasion to write gratuitously. A "merely passable" or "just tolerable" writer of poetry or fiction, should give up the inventive line, and try something else—something for which genius is not indispensable; and from which, by patience and industry, a sort of living may be wrought out.

In composing poetry, a common, but unpardonable fault is that of introducing a lame or halting line—a line with one syllable too many, or too few. And if the author does not understand that it is an intolerable blemish, and sends it uncorrected to the press, she is unworthy of being called a poetess. We are inclined to believe that no person devoid of an ear for music, can write poetry deserving of the name. The ideas may be good, but the lines will have no melody, and will move harshly and ruggedly, very much like rough prose.

Some writers seem to think that blank verse is nothing but prose with a capital at the beginning of each line; never having learnt or remembered that though the lines do not rhyme, they must all comprise ten syllables, (syllables, not words,) otherwise the effect when read, will, to even a tolerable ear, be absolutely painful. We saw a play, (the first attempt of a since distinguished dramatist,) the dialogue of which was unintelligible to the audience, and nearly impracticable to the actors, who found it absolutely beyond their skill to enunciate; or rather beneath it. We afterward heard the manager of the Chestnut-street Theatre explain, that the difficulty, both with the speakers and the hearers, was the execrable blank verse in which the play was written; some of the lines containing but seven or eight syllables, (instead of ten,) and some twelve or fourteen. A very few English authors write irregular blank verse; but we are sorry to say that a great many Americans do not seem to understand the process, simple as it is, of confining themselves to ten syllables only,—neither more nor less. Can they have read Shakespeare?

There is no blank verse in French poetry. That language seems incapable of it.

If you are writing for a periodical, and are desirous of ascertaining before-hand how many pages your manuscript will make when printed, take, at random, any printed page of the work, and copy it in your usual hand, and on a sheet of the same paper you intend using throughout. You will thus, by comparison, be able to judge with tolerable accuracy, how much of your writing will make a page when printed.

Keep a memorandum-book for the express purpose of setting down whatever relates to your literary affairs. Insert the day when you commenced a manuscript, the day when you finished it, and the day on which it went to the publisher. Also, the whole number of its pages. When you see it in print, put down the number of its printed pages. In this book, set down, *immediately on receiving them*, whatever sums are paid to you for your writings.

If you are a writer of fiction, have a large book for memorandums, of any amusing or remarkable things you may chance to hear, and which you may turn to account afterward. If you write truth only, keep a book for the reception of useful or interesting facts. A written book of names, alphabetically arranged, (surnames and christian names,) will be of great advantage in selecting appellations for your characters. Do not give elegant names to your common people; or to your patrician characters names that are coarse and vulgar. A fault in Dickens is that nearly all his names are rugged, uncouth, and ill-sounding, and seldom characteristic. Why should a very excellent and generous brother and sister be called Tom Pinch and Ruth Pinch. What did they pinch?

There is a proof-reader in every printing-office, but after he has done, the proofs are generally sent to the author for farther revisal.

In correcting proof-sheets, first see that they are quite dry. Draw your pen through any word you desire to change, and then write the new word on the margin, placing it even with the line of the rejected word. When you alter the punctuation, converting a comma into a semicolon, or a period into a note of admiration, make a slight mark on the margin of that line, that the printer may not overlook it. If you have occasion to change a whole sentence, cross it out, and put the new sentence on the margin at the bottom of the page.

If the printer's boy can wait, you had best correct the proofs while he stays.

CHAPTER XXII.
CHILDREN.

Miss Edgworth says that the education of a child begins at three months old. It is true that both bad and good habits may seem to commence at this early age; but we do not believe that in so slight a soil they take a very deep root, or that what is called a cross baby is sure to grow up an ill-tempered adult. Infants, when they are not really sick, frequently cry from some incidental annoyance, and not from a fretful disposition. If they feel comfortably they will usually be good-humoured and pleasant. Much of their comfort is sacrificed to the vanity of the mother in dressing them fashionably and expensively. We knew a baby that was very good in the morning, but very cross in the afternoon, or when dressed for show. And no wonder, for in her show-costume she was tortured with necklace, sleeve-loops, and bracelets of fine branchy, or rather briary coral, scratching and irritating her delicate skin, and leaving the print in red marks. On our representing this to the mother as the probable cause of the baby's fretfulness, the thorny ornaments were left off, and the child became amiable. Gold chains are also very irritating to the neck and arms of an infant. Coral beads of a smooth round form, strung evenly on a simple thread of silk, without any intermingling of gold chain, are, perhaps, the most comfortable necklaces for children, and are also very becoming; but as they are not expensive, they are of course not fashionable.

Fortunately, the days of worked caps are over. Young ladies are no longer expected to cover pieces of cambric with elaborate cotton embroidery for the babies of their married friends, and the tender heads of the babies are no longer chafed with rough needle-work rubbing incessantly upon them, or heated with a silk lining to the cambric already thickened all over with close, heavy patterns. We wish also that mothers, generally, were less proud of seeing their babies with "luxuriant heads of hair," which if it has no natural tendency to curl, disfigures the child and gives it a wild, ungenteel look. If it does curl, it still heats the head and neck, and is said to draw away much strength from the system. The most healthy infants we have seen, had very little hair, or it was judiciously kept closely cut. To curl children's hair in papers is barbarous. They pay dearly for the glory of appearing in ringlets during the day, if they are made to pass their nights lying upon a mass of hard, rough bobs, about as pleasant as if they had their heads in a bag of hickory-nuts. But then the mother has the gratification of hearing their curls admired!

Among other sufferings inflicted on babies is that of sending them out in bleak winter days with brimless hats, that, so far from screening their faces from the cold wind, do not even afford the slightest shade to their eyes, which are winking and watering all the time from the glare of the sun and snow. We have seen false curls pinned to these babies' hats, and dangling in their eyes.

Another detestable practice is that of making the waists of children's frocks ridiculously long and painfully tight; particularly over the chest and body, which are thus pressed flat, to the utter ruin of the figure, and the risk of producing incurable diseases—such as consumption of the lungs, and projection of the spine; to say nothing of the various complaints connected with the stomach, which is thus squeezed into half its natural compass. Also, the sleeve-holes are so small and tight as to push up the shoulders. Then the hips are pressed downward far below their proper place, and the legs are consequently in danger of becoming short and bandy. Is it possible this vile fashion can continue much longer?—and are "the rising generation" really to grow up with high shoulders, round backs, flat chests, bodies that seem longer than their legs, and hips almost where their knees ought to be?

Also, these limbs must suffer from cold in winter with no other covering than cotton stockings, the skirts of the dress scarcely reaching to the knees—the little boys disfigured with the ugliest of all garments, short knee-breeches.

Add to all the rest of these abominations, tight boots with peaked toes, and can we wonder that children, even beyond the period of infancy, should, at times, be cross, irritable, and unamiable. How can they be otherwise, when they seldom feel comfortably? Then, if the parents can afford it, (or whether or not,) the unhappy children are bedizened with all manner of expensive finery, and interdicted from romping, lest they should injure it. But, what matter if the children suffer—the mother's vanity *must* be gratified, and she *must* have the delight of seeing that her boys and girls are as fashionably dressed as the little Thomsons and Wilsons and Jacksons.

We look back with regret to the days when little girls, as well as boys, wore their hair closely cropped; convenient and cool, and showing to advantage the form of the head, till they were twelve or thirteen—and they wore only washable dresses, descending far below the knees, and with pantalets down to their ancles. In summer their frocks had short wide sleeves, and were *not* close up to the throat. The bodies were of a natural length, the outside gathered full upon a moderately tight lining. If there is no lining to a full frock-body it will puff out at the back and front, and give the waist a look of deformity before and behind. Then the little girls went out in close cottage-bonnets of straw in summer, and beaver in winter—shading and screening their faces—and were kept warm when out of doors with long wide cloaks or coats of cloth or merino, instead of the fantastic short things now worn, with open sleeves and open fronts. Then, when at home, how innocent and childlike they looked in their long-sleeved convenient bib-aprons!—so much better than the short silk ones now worn, trimmed and bordered and ribboned, and rendered so fine that the children are expected to be as careful of injuring their showy aprons as of soiling their showy frocks.

Formerly, children learned to play various amusing games, such as "Hot buttered beans," "Blind-man's bluff," &c. Now their play is chiefly running and squealing, and chasing each other about, without any definite object, except that of making a noise. Then, at a juvenile party, the amusement was chiefly in the varieties of these entertaining games. Now it is dancing—for as many as can find places to dance—and nothing at all for those who cannot, but to grow tired and sleepy. In former times, children's parties commenced at two o'clock in the afternoon in winter, and at four in summer. They played till they were summoned to a large and well-supplied tea-table, and were sent for to come home by eight o'clock, being then quite tired enough to go to bed and sleep soundly, and waken with pleasant recollections of yesterday. If the party was very large, the elder children sat round the room, and tea, &c. was handed to them, while the little ones were accommodated at a table where the hostess presided. The children of that time really enjoyed these parties, and so would those of the present time, if they could have such. The juvenile-party dress was then but a simple white muslin frock with a ribbon sash. We have since seen little girls at a summer party steadfastly refuse strawberries and cream, in obedience to the interdiction of their mothers; who had enjoined them to do so, lest they should stain or otherwise injure their elegant silk dresses.

Fortunately, it is no longer fashionable for mothers to take their children with them on morning visits. On these occasions small children rarely behave well. They soon grow tired, and restless, and begin teazing to go somewhere else. Their presence is (or ought to be) a restraint on conversation, as much may be said during a visit that is not well for them to hear. They comprehend certain things far more easily than is supposed. Great mischief has ensued from allowing children to sit and listen; and there is no dependence on their discretion or secrecy.

It is not well to put a small child "through its facings," by trying to make it exhibit any of its little feats before strangers. They are generally very reluctant to make this exhibition. Sometimes they are bashful, sometimes perverse; but if the mother persists in her attempt to show them off, it will probably prove a complete failure, and end in a cry, or that outbreak usually called a tantrum. By-the-bye, there is no better way of stopping a tantrum than quietly to divert the child's attention to something else.

Beware of trusting an infant, too confidingly, to an European nurse; and when she carries out the baby, it would be well if an older sister or the mother herself could go along. Instead of carrying it to one of the public squares, or to some other place where there is air and shade, she may take it into dirty alleys, on a visit to some of her own relations, perhaps newly arrived in an emigrant ship, with the filth and diseases of a steerage passage still about them. This we know to have been done, and the child has in consequence taken a disgusting disease. Or, believing it a meritorious act, an Irish nurse may secretly carry the infant to a priest, and have it baptized in the Catholic church, herself standing godmother. Of this there have been numerous instances. Young children frequently acquire, from being too much with ignorant and vulgar nurses, bad habits of talking that are exceedingly difficult to eradicate—so lasting are early impressions. We have heard an Irish brogue from infantine lips; and the letter H sadly misused by the American nursling of a low Englishwoman. Above all, do not permit your own children to play with the children of their nurse. No good ever accrues from it.

Children should not be brought to table till they are able to feed themselves, first with a spoon, and next with a fork. And not then, unless they can be depended on to keep quiet, and not talk. The chattering of children all dinner-time is a great annoyance to grown people. The shrill voice of a child can be distinguished annoyingly amid those of a whole company. They should be made to understand that if they talk at table, they are to be immediately taken away to finish their dinner in the nursery. On no consideration should they be admitted to table when there is a dinner-party. The foolish custom of having all the children dressed for the purpose, and brought in with the dessert, is now obsolete. It never was very prevalent, except in England.

We have seen children so well and so early trained that they could be trusted to come to table every day without the least fear of their misbehaving by talking or otherwise. They sat quietly, asked for nothing, took contentedly whatever was put on their plates, made no attempt at helping themselves, and neither greased nor slopped the table-cloth; and when done, wiped their mouths and hands on their napkins, before they quitted their chairs, which they did at a sign from their mother; going out without noise, and neither leaving the door open nor slamming it hard. It is very easy to accustom children to these observances. Also, they may be taught very early, how to behave to visiters. For instance, not to pass between them and the fire, not to hang on the back of a lady's chair; or to squeeze close to her; or to get on her lap; or to finger her dress; or to search her reticule, or her pocket; or to ask a stranger for pennies or sixpences; or to tell her that she is not pretty; or to enquire "why she wears such an ugly bonnet?"

We have known a fine little boy, not three years old, who, on the entrance of a friend of his mother's, would haul up a chair for her, and invite her to a seat near the fire, place a footstool at her feet, ask her to let him take her bonnet, and invite her to stay to dinner, to stay all day, and to "stay for ever," adding, "I try to be polite."

There are very little girls who, if their mother is from home, can do the honours in her place; seat the visiter on the sofa, and press her to stay till their mother comes in; and if the lady declines doing so, they will ask her at least to stay awhile, and rest herself, and have a glass of cool water; and while she stays, they will do their best to entertain her. Such children always grow up with polished manners, if not removed from the influence that made them so in early life.

Children should be early taught not to repeat the conversation of grown persons, and never to tell the servants any thing they have heard in the parlour. When they come home from school, they ought not to be encouraged in telling school-tales. If they dine out, never question them concerning what they had for dinner. Forbid their relating any circumstances concerning the domestic economy of the house at which they have been entertained.

If a child purloins cakes or sweetmeats, punish him by giving him none the next time they are on table.

At four years of age, a beginning should be made in teaching them to read, by hearing them the alphabet every day till they have learned it perfectly; and afterwards the first spelling-tables. With a quarter of an hour's daily instruction, a child of common capacity will, in six months, be able to spell in two or three syllables, and to read short easy stories with the syllables divided. At the end of the year, if her lessons are regular, and not so long as to tire her, she will, in all probability, take pleasure in reading to herself, when her lessons are over. Were they taught *out of story-books only*, there are few children that at the age of six years would find any difficulty in reading fluently. If *very* intelligent, they often can read well at five. When they can once read, encourage them in the love of books; but do not set them at any other branch of education till they are eight. Then, their hands being strong enough to guide the pen firmly, they may commence writing copies. They should be supplied with slates and pencils at three years old. If they have any dormant talent for drawing, this will call it out. Little girls may begin to sew at four or five, but only as an amusement, not as a task. The best and most satisfactory dolls for young children are those of linen or rag, made very substantially. Much money is wasted in toys that afford them no amusement whatever; and toys that, being merely to look at, they grow tired of immediately, and delight in breaking to pieces.

Never give an infant a book to play with. He will most assuredly tear it; that being the only amusement it can afford him. It is possible at a very early age to teach a tractable female child such a respect for books that she will never attempt to injure them. When they are old enough to take pleasure in looking at the pictures, it is easy to accustom them to be always satisfied with the books being shown to them in the hands of grown persons. Do not buy those books that have absurd and revolting prints of people with gigantic heads and diminutive bodies. Children always dislike them, and so they ought.

Rejoice when a little girl shows a fondness for reading, and by all means encourage it. Keep her well supplied with good and entertaining books, and you will have little trouble with her. Do not needlessly interrupt, and call her off— but let her read in peace. It will do her more good than any thing else, and lay the foundation of an intelligent mind. A taste for reading, if not formed in early childhood, may perhaps never come at all. And then what a solace it is in bodily illness! How patiently a reading child, whose mind is stored with "pleasant memories," can bear pain, and submit to the confinement of a sick-bed. We have known more than one instance of the illness of a reading child taking a turn for the better, from the time she was indulged with an amusing and interesting book.

There is no place in which children appear to greater disadvantage or are less ungovernable than at hotels or boarding-houses. We are always sorry when the circumstances of parents oblige them permanently to live thus in public, with their young families, who are consequently brought up in a manner which cannot but have an unfavourable effect in forming the characters of the future men and women. By way of variety, and that they may not always be confined up-stairs, the children are encouraged, or at least permitted by their mothers, to spend much of their time in the drawing-room, regardless of the annoyance which their noise and romping never fails to inflict upon the legitimate occupants of that apartment. The parents, loving their children too much to be incommoded themselves by any thing that their offspring can say or do, seem not aware that they can possibly interrupt or trouble the rest of the company. Or else, conscious of their own inability to control them, they are afraid to check the children lest they should turn restive, rebel, or break out into a tantrum. "Any thing for the sake of peace," is a very foolish maxim where juveniles are concerned. By being firm once or twice, and dismissing them from the room when they deserve it, you may have peace ever after. The noisiest and most inconvenient time to have children in a public parlour is in the interval between their tea and their bed-time. Some children have no bed-time. And when they are tired of scampering and shouting, they lie about sleeping on the sofas, and cry if they are finally wakened, to go up with their mother when she retires for the night.

Still worse is the practice that prevails in some hotels and boarding-houses, of the mothers sending the nurse-maids with the babies, to sit in the drawing-room among the ladies; who are thus liable to have a vulgar and obtrusive servant-girl, most probably "from the old country," boldly taking her seat in the midst of them, or conspicuously occupying one of the front-windows; either keeping up a perpetual undercurrent of fulsome, foolish talk to the baby, or listening eagerly to the conversation around her, and, perhaps, repeating it invidiously as soon as she gets an opportunity. If one lady sends her nurse-maid to sit in the drawing-room with the child, all the other mothers of babies immediately follow suit, and the drawing-room becomes a mere nursery.

Every hotel should have a commodious and airy parlour set apart entirely for the children and nurses. The proprietors could easily afford to keep one good room for that purpose, if they would expend a little less on the finery of the parlours, &c. We have heard of an embroidered piano-cover, in a great hotel, costing fourteen hundred dollars, and the children pulling it down and dragging it about the floor. With a piano-cover of the usual cost, and other things less ostentatious, a children's parlour might well have been afforded in this very establishment.

At a hotel, if the children come to the ladies' table, they are always in danger of eating food that is highly improper for them, and they very soon learn to help themselves to much more than they want, and to eat voraciously, in their desire to "have something of every thing." There is always a table purposely for those children whose parents pay half-price for them; and at which the housekeeper presides. However good this table may be, and though the pies and puddings may be excellent, the mothers are frequently dissatisfied with the absence of ice-cream, blanc-mange, charlotte-russe, &c., though certainly, were they in houses of their own, they would not have such things every day. Therefore, though it is "not in the bond," the mothers carry away from the table saucers of these delicacies, and the children learn to expect a daily supply of them from the ladies' dining-room. This, we must say, is a mean practice. We have, however, known some mothers, who, really being "honourable women," sent every day to a confectioner's to *buy* ice-cream for their children.

There is danger at a hotel of little boys loitering about the bar or office, encouraged by unthinking young men, who give them "tastes of drink," and even amuse themselves by teaching them to smoke segars.

And no children, either boys or girls, can live at a public house without hearing and seeing much that it is best they should not know. The English travellers deprecate the American practice of bringing up young people in hotels or boarding-houses. And they are right.

When a lady, having with her a young child, and no nurse-maid, stops for a day at a hotel, she can avoid the inconvenience of taking the child with her to table, and incommoding herself and all who sit near her. She has only to entrust the little traveller to a chambermaid up-stairs; directing the girl how to take care of it, and promising her a gratuity for her trouble. She will rarely have cause to regret such an arrangement. It will spare the annoyance and mortification of having the child make a noise at table, and perhaps compelling the mother to go away with it.

CHAPTER XXIII.
DECORUM IN CHURCH.

We wish it were less customary to go to church in gay and costly habiliments, converting its sacred precincts into a place for the display of finery, and of rivalry to your equally bedizened neighbours. In many Catholic countries,* a

* The author is a Protestant.

peculiar costume is universally adopted for visiting a place of worship—a very plain gown of entire black, with a long, black cloak, and a black hood finished with a veil that shades the face. This dress is kept for the purpose of wearing at church. We highly approve the custom, and wish that something similar could be introduced into the United States—particularly on the solemn occasions of taking the communion, or being confirmed as a christian member. We have known young ladies to have elegant dresses made on purpose, and to get their hair dressed by a barber when preparing for confirmation.

In a Sacred Melody of Moore's, St. Jerome tells us—

> "Yet worldly is that heart at best,
>   Which beats beneath a broider'd veil;
> And she who comes in glittering vest
>   To mourn her frailty—still is frail."

Endeavour always to be in your pew before the service commences, and do not hurry out of it, hastily, the moment the benediction is finished; or begin visibly to prepare for departure as soon as it commences. Stay quietly till the mass of the crowd has gone.

If you go into a strange church, or rather into a church where you are a stranger, wait in the vestibule till you see the sexton; and then request him to show you to a vacant seat, or rather to one which he believes will be that day un-occupied—for instance, if the family owning it is out of town. This is far better than to wander about the aisles alone, or to intrude yourself into a pew where you may cause inconvenience to its owners. If you see that a pew is full, you know, of course, that you cannot obtain a seat in it without dislodging somebody.

Yet we have seen many a lady, on entering a church in which she was a stranger, walk boldly up the middle aisle to one of the best pews near the pul-pit, and pertinaciously stand there, looking steadfastly at its rightful occupants, till one of them quitted his own seat, and gave it up to her, seeking for himself another place wherever he could find one. Those who go to strange churches should be contented with seats near the door; or at the lower end of the side-aisles; or up in the gallery.

If a family invites you to go to church with them, or to come thither, and have a seat in their pew, do not take the liberty of asking a friend of your own to accompany you; and above all, do not bring a child with you.

Should you (having a pew of your own) ask another lady to go with you, call for her in due time; and she ought to be quite ready. Place her in a cor-ner-seat, (it being the most comfortable,) and see that she is accommodated with a foot-stool; and be assiduous in finding the places for her in the prayer-book, or hymn-book.

In American churches there is much civility to strangers. We have often seen, when a person of respectable appearance was in quest of a seat, the doors of half a dozen pews kindly opened to admit him, and, as soon as he entered, a prayer-book offered to him open at the proper place.

No good can result from taking children to church when they are too young to read, or to understand. They are always eager to go, because they like to go everywhere; but when once seated in the pew, they soon become tired and restless; and frequently there is no way to keep them quiet, but to let them go to sleep in the lap of the mother or elder sister. And then they are apt to cry whenever they waken. If there are two little boys, they are prone to get to playing, or what is far worse, quarrelling. And then if they make a noise, some elder member of the family is subjected to the mortification of conveying them out of church—perhaps by desire of the minister audibly expressed from the pulpit. We know clergymen who do not permit their children to be taken to church till they can read—convinced that if their first recollections of a place of worship are rather painful than pleasant, they are the less likely to grow up with a due regard for religion—that is, for religion of the heart—the spirit, and not merely the letter.

We are sorry to see young ladies, on their way to church, laughing and talking loudly, and flirting with the beaux that are gallanting them thither. It is too probable that these beaux will occupy a large share of their thoughts during the hours of worship. Nay, there are some so irreverent, and so regardless of the sanctity of the place, as to indulge in frequent whispers to those near them, or to their friends in the adjoining pews.

A lady of high fashion and fortune, formerly a resident of Philadelphia, was noted for the scandalous lightness and levity of her behaviour in church—laughing and talking, in more than whispers, nearly all the time, to the idle young men whom she always brought with her, and who, to do them justice, sometimes seemed rather ashamed of her conduct. Her pew was directly in front of the pulpit. One Sunday morning, Bishop White gave her a severe and merited rebuke, by stopping in his sermon, fixing his eyes sadly upon her, and bowing to her, as an intimation that till she had ceased he could not go on. We are sorry to add that the reproof had no other effect than to excite her anger, and caused her immediately to go out of church, highly exasperated. That lady went to live in Europe, and has not yet become a good woman, but greatly the contrary.

"The Lord is in his holy temple; let all the earth keep silence before him," was the solemn and impressive inscription over the altar of St. Augustine's church in Philadelphia.

In visiting a church of a different denomination from your own, comply, as far as you can, with all the ceremonies observed by the congregation, particularly if you are in a foreign country. Even if some of these observances are not the least in conformity with your own opinions and feelings, remember that you are there as a guest, and have no right to offend or give displeasure to your hosts by evincing a marked disapprobation of their mode of worship. If you find it very irksome to refrain, (which it should not be,) you need not go a second time. Every religious sect believes its own faith to be the best; but God only knows which really is. Christ has said, "By their fruits ye shall know them."

CHAPTER XXIV.
EVENING PARTIES.

Having made out a list of the persons you intend to invite, proceed to write the notes; or have them written in a neat, handsome hand, by an experienced calligrapher. Fashion, in its various changes, sometimes decrees that these notes, and their envelopes, shall be perfectly plain, (though always of the finest paper,) and that the wax seals shall of course be very small. At other times, the mode is to write on embossed note paper, with bordered envelopes, secured by fancy wafers, transparent, medallion, gold or silver. If the seals are gold or silver, the edges or borders of the paper should be also gilt or silvered. Sometimes, for a very large or splendid party, the notes are engraved and printed on cards. Consult the Directory, to obtain the *exact* address of those to whom you send them.

These invitations may be transmitted by one of the City post offices; first putting a stamp on each. Let the stamps be such as will leave nothing additional to be paid by the receiver. If they go through the United States Post-Office, the carrier will require another cent for each, beside the stamp. In Philadelphia, Blood's Dispatch Post may be trusted, as to punctuality, (if faithfully put into the letter-box at the proper time;) and there is no cost but that of the penny stamp which you put on yourself.

Another way is to send round the notes by a reliable servant-man of your own; or to engage, for this purpose, one of the public waiters that are hired to attend at parties. The notes are usually sent either eight, seven, or six days before the party—if it is to be very large, ten days or two weeks. In the notes, always specify not only the day of the week, but also the day of the month, when the party is to take place. It is very customary now to designate the hour of assembling, and then the company are expected to be punctual to that time.

People, *really genteel*, do not go ridiculously late. When a ball is intended, let the word "Dancing" be introduced in small letters, at the lower left-hand corner of the note.

For a bridal party, subsequent to a wedding, the words now used are thus—

MR. AND MRS. S. M. MORLAND,
At Home, on Thursday evening, Sept. 22, 1853.

Their residence must be given beneath, in a corner, and in smaller letters.

Oblong slices of plumb-cake, iced all over, are now sent round in very pretty white card-board boxes, exactly fitting each slice, covered on the inside with lace-paper, and an engraved card of the bride and groom laid on the top of the cake. These boxes (to be had at the fancy stationers,) are of various prices; some of them are very elegant and costly.

At wedding-parties, it is usual for the bride and bridesmaids to appear in exactly the same dresses they wore at the marriage; all of them ranged in their respective stations before the company begin to arrive.

When the marriage-guests are not too numerous, it is customary to have all the company shown into the largest parlour, when they first arrive; the folding-doors being closed between. Meanwhile, the bride and groom, bridesmaids and groomsmen, with the heads of the family, arrange themselves in a line or a semi-circle; the most important personages in the centre, with the clergyman in front of them. When all is ready, the doors are thrown open, the guests advance, and the ceremony begins. When it is over, and the bride is receiving the compliments of her friends, we hope the silliest woman present will not go up and ask her the foolish question, "If she does not feel already like an old married woman?"

A crowd at a wedding is now obsolete. We once heard of a marriage in a great family, where the company was so numerous that all the doors were blocked up, and quite inaccessible; and the bride could only make her entrance by being taken round outside, and lifted through a back window—the groom jumping in after her.

Dancing at weddings is old-fashioned. A band of music playing in the hall is of no use, as on such occasions no one listens to it, and some complain of the noise. We think a marriage in church is not as fine a spectacle as may be imagined. The effect is lost in the size of the building, and broken up by the intervention of the aisles and pews; the wedding guests seated in the latter, and the former occupied by people out of the street, coming in to see the show. And this they will do, if not forcibly excluded; particularly idle boys, and nurse-maids with children, all trying to get as near the altar as possible.

If the bride and groom are to set out on a journey immediately after the ceremony, it is best for her to be married in a handsome travelling-dress—new for the occasion, of course. This is often done now. She can reserve the usual wedding costume for her first party after returning home.

In preparing for a party, it is well (especially if you have had but little experience yourself,) to send for one of the *best* public waiters, and consult with him on the newest style of "doing these things." A respectable coloured man will be found the most efficient for this purpose. He can also give you an idea of the probable expense. We do not, of course, allude to magnificent entertainments, such as are celebrated in the newspapers, and become a nine days' wonder; and are cited as costing, not hundreds, but thousands of dollars.

In case the required waiter should be pre-engaged, it is well to send for, and consult him, a week or two before your party.

We knew a lady who, some years ago, sent for Carroll, (a very excellent mulatto man, well known in Philadelphia,) to officiate at a projected party. Carroll, in very polite terms, expressed that he was engaged for that identical evening to attend at a ball. "Then," said the lady, "you must try to furnish me with some one else, in your place. Where is Bogle?" "I know Bogle can't come," answered Carroll; "he is bespoke that night for a wedding." "Shepherd, then?" said the lady; "see if you cannot send me Shepherd." "As to Shepherd," replied Carroll, "he is sick in his bed, and like to keep so." "Where is Solomon King, then?" pursued the lady; "Solomon King will do very well." "Indeed, ma'am," answered Carroll, "I don't think Solomon King will suit you now, anyhow; he's taken very much to drink, and besides he's dead!"

Apropos to the talk of coloured people.—We were told by a southern lady, that one of her girls being dressed for an entertainment given by a neighbour to the servants, came to her, and said: "Mistress, Becky has come for me to go with her; and she says *her* mistress has gave her two grand words to say at the party.—Now, I want you to give *me* two words that shall beat Becky's; for I know you are a heap smarter than *her* mistress."

"Tell me the words given by Becky's mistress," said my informant.

"Yes, ma'am.—One is *Desdemona*, and one is *Cataplasm!*"

No doubt, Becky, in some way, contrived to say them both.

In engaging your presiding genius, it is well to desire him to come on the morning of the party; he will be found of great advantage in assisting with the final preparations. He will attend to the silver, and china, and glass; and see that the lamps are all in order, and that the fires, coal-grates, furnaces, &c., are in proper trim for evening. He will bring with him (at whatever hour you indicate,) his "young men," as he calls them; (if coloured youths, they are too genteel to answer to the name of boys;) and these are his apprentices that he has in training for the profession.

One of these men should be stationed in the vestibule, or just within the front door. On that evening, (if not at other times,) let this door be furnished with a lamp, placed on a shelf or bracket in the fan-light, to illumine the steps, and shine down upon the pavement, where the ladies cross it on alighting from the carriages. If the evening proves rainy, let another man attend with an umbrella, to assist in sheltering them on their way into the house. The ladies should all wear over-shoes, to guard their thin slippers from the damp, in their transit from the coach to the vestibule.

At the top, or on the landing-place, of the first stair-case, let another man be posted, to show the female guests to their dressing-room; while still another waiter stays near the gentlemen's room till the company have done arriving.

In the apartment prepared as a fixing-room for the ladies two or more women should be all the evening in attendance; both rooms being well warmed, well lighted, and furnished with all that may be requisite for giving the last touches to head, feet, and figure, previous to entering the drawing-room. When ready to go down, the ladies meet their gentlemen in the passage between the respective dressing-rooms; the beaux being there already, waiting for the belles, who must not detain them long—men being very impatient on these, and all other occasions.

If any lady is without an escort, and has no acquaintances at hand to take her under their wing, she should send for the master of the house to meet her near the door, and give her his arm into the drawing-room. He will then lead her to the hostess, and to a seat. Let her then bow, as a sign that she releases him from farther attendance, and leaves him at liberty to divide his civilities among his other guests.

In the ladies' room, (beside two toilet glasses with their branches lighted,) let a Psyche or Cheval glass be also there. Likewise, a hand-mirror on each toilet to enable the ladies to see the back of their heads; with an ample supply of pins, combs, brushes, hair pins, &c.; and a work-box containing needles, thread, thimble, and scissors, to repair accidents to articles of dress. Let there be bottles of fine eau de cologne, and camphor and hartshorn, in case of faintings. Among the furniture, have a sofa and several foot-stools, for the ladies to sit on if they wish to change their shoes.

The women attending must take charge of the hoods, cloaks, shawls, over-shoes, &c.; rolling up together the things that belong to each lady, and putting each bundle in some place they can easily remember when wanted at the breaking up of the assembly.

It is now the custom for the lady of the house (and those of her own family,) to be drest rather plainly, showing no desire to eclipse any of her guests, on this her own night. But her attire, though simple, should be handsome, becoming, and in good taste. Her business is, without any bustle or apparent officiousness, quietly and almost imperceptibly to try and render the evening as pleasant as possible to all her guests; introducing those who, though not yet acquainted, ought to be; and finding seats for ladies who are not young enough to continue standing.

The custom that formerly prevailed in the absurd days of crowds and jams, when dense masses were squeezed into small apartments, of removing every seat and every piece of furniture from the room, is now obsolete. A hard squeeze is no longer a high boast. Genteel people no longer go to parties on the stair-case, or in the passages. The ladies are not now so compressed that nothing of them is seen but their heads; the sleeves, skirts, &c., undergoing a continual demolition down below. We knew of a lady, who, at a late hour, went to a crowded party in a real blonde dress, which was rubbed entirely off her before she reached the centre of the room, and it was hanging about her satin skirt in shreds, like transparent rags dissolving into "air—thin air!" For this blonde she had given two hundred dollars; and she was obliged to go home and exchange its tatters for a costume that was likely to last out the evening.

In houses where space is not abundant, it is now customary to have several *moderate* parties in the course of the season, instead of inviting all your "dear five hundred friends" on the self-same night.

When the hour of assembling is designated in the notes of invitation, (as it always should be,) the guests, of course, will take care to arrive as nearly as possible about that hour. At large parties, tea is usually omitted—it being supposed that every one has already taken that beverage at home, previous to commencing the business of the toilette. Many truly hospitable ladies still continue the custom, thinking that it makes a pleasant beginning to the evening, and exhilarates the ladies after the fatigue of dressing and arriving. So it does. For a large company, a table with tea, coffee, and cakes, may be set in the ladies-room, women being in attendance to supply the guests with those refreshments before they go down. Pitchers of ice-water and glasses should also be kept in this room.

If there is no tea, the refreshments begin with lemonade, macaroons, kisses, &c., sent round soon after the majority of the company has come. If there *is* tea, ice-water should be presented after it, to all; otherwise, there will be much inconvenience by numerous ladies dispatching the servants, separately, to bring them some.

After a little time allotted to conversation, music is generally introduced by one of the ladies of the family, if she plays well; otherwise, she invites a competent friend to commence. A lady who can do nothing "without her notes," or who cannot read music, and play at sight, is scarcely enough of a musician to perform in a large company—for this incapacity is an evidence that she has not a good ear, or rather a good memory for melody—or that her musical talent wants more cultivation. A large party is no time or place for practising, or for risking *attempts* at new things, or for vainly trying to remember old ones.

Some young ladies rarely sit down to a piano in any house but their own, without complaining that the instrument is out of tune. "It is a way they have." We have known a fair amateur to whom this complaint was habitual, and never omitted; even when we knew that, to provide against it, the piano had really been tuned that very day.

The tuning of a harp immediately before playing is sometimes a very tedious business. Would it not be well for the harpist to come a little earlier than the rest, and tune it herself previous to their arrival? And let her deem *that* tuning sufficient for a while, and not repeat the operation more than once again in the course of the evening, especially in the midst of her first piece. However delicate may be her own ear, or exquisitely fastidious her own taste, she may be assured that few of her audience would detect any deficiency, if she only went quietly on, and did not herself imply that deficiency.

Unless a gentleman is himself familiar with the air, let him not, on "mounting guard beside the piano," volunteer to turn over the pages for the lady who is playing. He will certainly turn them over too soon or too late, and therefore annoy and confuse her. Still worse, let him not attempt to accompany her with his voice, unless he is an excellent musician, or accustomed to singing with her.

For the hearers to crowd closely round the instrument, is smothering to the vocalist. Let them keep at a proper distance, and she will sing the better, and they will hear the better. It is so rude to talk during a song, that it is never done in company; but a little low conversation is sometimes tolerated in the adjoining room, during the performance of one of those interminable pieces of instrumental music, whose chief merit lies in its difficulty, and which (at least to the ears of the uninitiated,) is rather a bore than a pleasure. We have read a French novel, in which the only child of a farmer has just come home from a provincial boarding-school, and the seigneur, or lord of the manor, has volunteered a visit to these his respected tenants. The mother, amidst all the bustle of preparing a great dinner for the occasion, comes in to remind Annette that if the seigneur should ask her to play for him, she is to curtsey very low, and thank him for the honour. "And then, Annette," adds the good old dame, "be sure to play that tune which your father and I hate so much!"

By-the-bye, it is very old fashioned to return thanks to a lady for her singing, or to tell her she is very kind to oblige the company so often. If she is conscious of really singing well, and sees that she delights her hearers, she will not feel sensible of fatigue—at least till the agreeable excitement of conscious success is over.

It is ill-mannered, when a lady has just finished a song, for another lady to exclaim in her hearing—"Mary Jones sings that delightfully!"—or—"How charmingly Susan Smith gives us that ballad!" Let the glories of Mary Jones and Susan Smith rest, for that evening, within the limits of their own circle.

Do not ask any lady for a song that has already been sung on this very evening by another person.

People who have no idea of music sometimes make strange blunders in their requests. We know of a female who, at a large party, hearing a young lady accompany her voice on the national instrument of Spain, became very urgent to have the Battle of Prague performed on the guitar.

It is sometimes fashionable, when the company is not too large for what is called "a sitting party," to vary the amusements of the evening by introducing some of the numerous plays or games which are always the delight of fine children, and which, by way of variety, frequently afford much diversion to adults. It is not necessary that all these plays should become "a keen encounter of the wits," or that all the players should be persons of talent. But it is certainly desirable that the majority of the company should have some tact, and some quickness of parts; that they should have read some books, and mixed somewhat with the world—otherwise, they will not be clever even at playing plays. Those who are incapable of understanding, or entering into the spirit of a play, would do well to excuse themselves from joining in it, and prefer sitting by as spectators. Many young ladies can play nothing beyond "How do you like it?" and are not great at that—saying, when the question is put to them—"Me! I am sure I don't know how I like it—can't you pass me by?" You may as well take her at her word, pass her by, and proceed on to her next neighbour; for if she *does* concoct an answer, it will probably, if the word is "*brush*" be liked "to sweep the hearth with;" or if "*Hat*" is the word, it will be liked "*of Beaver*"—or something equally palpable.

Such plays as *The Lawyer*, and *The Secret Word*, are very entertaining in good hands, but complete failures when attempted by the dull or illiterate. The amusing game of Proverbs had best be given up for that evening, if, on trial, it is found that few of the ladies have any knowledge of those true, though homely aphorisms, that have been aptly called "the concentrated wisdom of nations."

We know a very ingenious gentleman who, in playing the Secret Word, contrives to introduce that word in some very short and very humorous anecdote.

A family, on one side of European origin, made a visit to the transatlantic continent, where they found, still living in a certain great city, a relative connected with an ancient branch of nobility. This rendered them more genteel than ever—and when, covered with glory, they returned to this poor republic of ours, the names of nobles, and even of princes, with whom they had associated, were "familiar in their mouths as household words." At a party where these personages were so engaged in talking, that they forgot to keep the run of the plays; a new game was commenced by a young gentleman slipping out of the room, and then returning with a very lugubrious visage, and announcing, in a melancholy tone, the death of a certain monarch, whom all the company were immediately to unite in lamenting loudly, on pain of paying forfeits unless they steadily persisted in their dismal faces. On the sad intelligence being proclaimed—"The king of Bohemia is dead!"—one of our travelled ladies mistaking it for a solemn truth, turned to her daughter with—"Ah! Caroline! did you hear that? The dear good king of Bohemia, who was so kind to us whenever we attended his court!" "Oh! mamma!" replied Caroline, putting her handkerchief to her eyes—"the news is really heart-breaking. He paid us so much attention all the time we were in ——, in his dominions. It will be long before we cease grieving for the king of Bohemia."

The gentleman who brought this deplorable news also had recourse to *his* handkerchief, and slipped out into the hall to indulge his mirth; and several others slipped out after him for the same purpose. No one, however, undeceived these ladies, and for several days at their morning calls they continued to mourn for the king of Bohemia.

Conundrums* afford infinite diversion at a small party, provided the company, like Billy Black's cat, "almost always gives up." Long guessing occupies too much time; a commodity of which we Americans seldom have any to spare.

Early in the Mexican war, a premium was awarded in Philadelphia for a very clever conundrum, alluding to a certain "Bold Dragoon" at Palo Alto. "In what manner did Captain May cheat the Mexicans?" "He charged them with a troop of horse which they never got."

Our confectioners, in making up the *bon bons* called "*secrets*," instead of enfolding with the sugar-plumb a printed slip containing a contemptible distich,

---

* Miss Leslie's American Girl's Book (published by C. S. Francis,) contains a great variety of amusing plays, ways to redeem forfeits, &c., with an unusual number of conundrums.

would do well to have good conundrums printed, (with the answer,) and enclosed in the ornamented papers. They would certainly be more popular than the old-fashioned mottoes—such, for instance, as

"My heart, like a candle of four to the pound,
Consumes all the day, and no comfort is found."

Yet the above is one of the least bad. Most of these mottoes are so flat as to be not even ridiculous.

At a dancing party, the ladies of the house decline joining in it, out of politeness to their guests, till towards the latter part of the evening, when the company begins to thin off, and the dancers are fatigued.

We admire a charming girl, who, in her own house, being asked to dance by an agreeable man, has the self-denial to say to him—"Being at home, and desirous that my friends shall share as much as possible in the enjoyments of the evening, I would rather refrain from dancing myself. Let me present you to Miss Lindley, or to Miss Darwood; you will find either of these young ladies a delightful partner."

These amiable refusals we have heard from our amiable and unselfish young friends, and such, we hope, are heard often in what is *truly* "the best society."

Ladies who are strangers in the place, are, by courtesy, entitled to particular attention from those who know them.

We have sometimes seen, at a private ball, the least attractive woman dancing every set, (though acquitting herself very ill,) while handsome and agreeable ladies were sitting still. The mystery was solved on finding that the lady of the house carried her ultra benevolence so very far, as to make a business of procuring partners all the time for this unlovely and unprepossessing female, lest she should feel neglected. Now a certain portion of this officiousness is highly praiseworthy, but too much of it is a great annoyance to the victimized gentlemen—especially to those who, as a backwoodsman would say, are certainly "some pumpkins."

Even the most humane man, whatever may be the kindness of his heart, would rather not exhibit himself on the floor with a partner *ni jeune ni jolie*, who is ill-dressed, looks badly, moves ungracefully, can neither keep time to the music nor understand the figure, and in fact has "no dancing in her soul." If, with all the rest, she is dull and stupid, it is cruel for any kind friend to inflict her on a gentleman as a partner. Yet such things we have seen.

On one occasion we threw away a great deal of good pity on a youth, whom we thought had been inveigled into quadrilling with a lady who made the worst figure we ever saw in a ball-room. We afterwards learned that he had actually solicited the introduction; and we saw that he devoted himself to her all the remainder of the evening. She was a rich heiress.

Self-knowledge is a rare acquirement. But when a lady *does* suspect herself to be deficient in all the essential qualifications of a ball-room, she should give up dancing entirely, and be magnanimous enough always to excuse herself positively, when asked to dance; especially if verging on "a certain age." Let all "trippings on the light fantastic toe" be left to the young and gay.

A deformed woman dancing is "a sorry sight." She should never consent to any such exhibition of her unhappy figure. She will only be asked out of mere compassion, or from some interested and unworthy motive. We are asked—"Why should not such a lady dance, if it gives her pleasure?" We answer—"It should *not* give her pleasure."

When a lady is so unfortunate as to have a crooked, or misshapen person, it is well for her to conceal it as much as possible, by wearing a shawl, a large cape, a mantilla, a long sacque, (not a polka jacket;) and on no account a tight-bodied pelisse; or still worse, a spencer—than which last, nothing is more trying to the form of the waist, except a riding-habit.

We saw Frederika Bremer at an evening assemblage, and she was so judiciously attired, that her personal defects did not prevent her from looking really well. Over a rich black satin dress, she wore a long loose sacque of black lace, lined with grey silk. From beneath the short sleeves of her sacque, came down long wide sleeves of white lace, confined with bracelets round her fair and delicate little hands. Her throat was covered closely with a handsome collar of French embroidered muslin, and her beautiful and becoming cap was of white lace, white flowers, and white satin ribbon—her light hair being simply parted on her broad and intellectual forehead. With her lively blue eyes, and the bright and pleasant expression of her countenance, no one seemed to notice the faults of her nose, mouth, and complexion—and those of her figure were so well concealed as to be scarcely apparent. And then her lady-like ease, and the total absence of all affectation, rendered her graceful and prepossessing. True it is, that with a good heart and a good mind no woman can be ugly; at least, they soon cease to be so considered, even if nature has been unkind to them in feature, figure, and complexion. An intelligent eye, and a good humoured mouth, are excellent substitutes for the want of regular beauty. Physiognomists say that the eye denotes the mind, and the mouth indicates the heart.

Now as a deformed lady may render herself very agreeable as a good conversationist, we repeat that she has no occasion to exhibit the defects of her person by treading the mazes of a cotillion, or above all, in going down a country dance, should those "never-ending, still beginning" performances come again into fashion. Young men say that an ugly, misshapen female, who waltzes, or joins in a polka, or redowa, or mazurka, deserves the penitentiary.

We deprecate the practice of keeping the small children of the family up all the evening, running and scampering in every one's way, or sleeping about on the chairs and sofas, and crying when wakened up to be carried to bed. Would it not be much better to have them sent to bed at their usual time? We knew two well-trained little boys, who submitted obediently to go to bed at their customary hour, on the night of their mother's party, of which they had seen nothing but the decorations of the parlours. They told their parents next morning, that still they had a great deal of pleasure, for after the carriages began to arrive, they had lain awake and "heard every ring."

At a large party, or at a wedding, there is generally a supper table; lemonade and cakes having been sent round during the evening. The host and hostess should see that *all* the ladies are conducted thither, and that none are neglected, particularly those that are timid, and stand back. It is the business of the host to attend to those himself, or to send the waiters to them.

If the party is so large that all the ladies cannot go to the table at once, let the matrons be conducted thither first, and the young ladies afterwards. If there is a crowd, it is not unusual to have a cord (a handsome one, of course,) stretched across the door of the supper-room, and guarded by a servant, who explains that no more are to pass till after that cord is taken down. Meanwhile, the younger part of the company amuse themselves in the adjacent rooms. No lady should take the liberty of meddling with the flowers that ornament the table, or of secreting "good things" to carry home to her children.

Apropos to flowers.—The stiff, hard bouquets are now obsolete, where the flowers (stripped of their natural green leaves,) were tied *en masse* on a wooden skewer, against a flat back-ground of cedar sprays. The more elegant arrangement is revived of arranging them in a full round cluster, with a fair portion of their real leaves; the largest and finest flowers in the centre, (large white ones particularly); those of middle size next; and the light, long, and branchy sprays and tendrils at the extremities, the smallest near the bottom of the bouquet, which is not so large and massy as formerly, but more graceful and select. The bouquet may be carried on the young lady's arm, suspended to a long and handsome white ribbon tied in a bow—a *coloured* ribbon will disturb the effect of the flowers. There should be nothing to interfere with their various and beautiful tints.

At a ball, let no *coloured* chalks or crayons be used for the floor. They will rub off on the white shoes of the ladies, and spoil them.

When, instead of *setting* a supper-table, refreshments are handed round to the ladies, the fashion has long since gone by of a gentleman walking beside each waiter, and "assisting the ladies." It is now found that if the articles are properly arranged, and of the proper sort, the ladies can much more conveniently help themselves, and with less risk of staining or greasing their dresses. Unless the gentleman was "a thorough-going party-man," and stereotyped as such, he often committed rather vexatious blunders, particularly if he was not *au-courant* to the new improvements, and accustomed to being "at good men's feasts;" or rather, at *women's good feasts*. One evening at a party, we saw an "ingenuous youth," whose experience in that line must have been rather limited, officiously undertake the portioning out to the ladies of a composition hitherto quite new to himself. This was "a trifle," being the contents of a very large glass bowl, filled with macaroons, &c., dissolved in wine, &c., with profuse layers of custard, sweetmeats, &c., and covered in at the top with a dome of whipt cream heaped high and thick over the whole. The pea-green youth assisted the ladies to nothing but saucers of froth from the top, thinking that was the right way. At last, the mulatto man, whose superior tact must have been all this time in a state of suffering, explained to the novice in trifles, that a portion of all the various contents of the glass bowl should be allotted to each saucer. "That!" said the surprised doer of honours, "I thought all that was only the grounds!" The coloured man relieved him by taking the silver server round a second time to all the ladies, who had hitherto missed the sediment of the syllabub.

At a summer evening party, the refreshments are of a much lighter description than at a winter entertainment; consisting chiefly of ice-creams, water-ices, fresh fruit, lady-cake, and almond sponge-cake. Also strawberry or raspberry charlottes, which are made by arranging in glass bowls slices of cake cut in even and regular forms, and spread thickly over with the fruit mashed to a jam with white sugar—the bowls being heaped with whipt cream.

The dresses of the ladies are of clear muslin, or some other light material, and without any elaborate trimming. The hair is simply arranged—curls being inconvenient in warm weather; and the only head ornaments are ribbons, or *real* flowers.

At summer evening-parties the veranda is always put into requisition, being cooler than any part of the house.

At summer dinner-parties, let the dessert be served in another and cooler apartment; the company quitting the dining-room as soon as they have done with the meats, &c. The beauties of the dessert appear to greater advantage, when seen all at one view on a fresh table.

We will introduce a minute account of a very fashionable English dinner-party, obtained from a friend who was one of the guests. It may afford some hints for the routine of an elegant entertainment, *à l'Anglais*, in our own country.

The guests were twenty-four in number, and they began to assemble at half past seven, punctually. They were received in the library, where the host and hostess were standing ready to receive them, introducing those who were strangers to each other. When all had arrived, the butler entered, and going up to the lady of the house, told her in a low voice that "dinner was served." The hostess then arranged those that were not previously acquainted, and the gentlemen conducted the ladies to the dining-room; the principal stranger taking the mistress of the house, and the master giving his arm to the chief of the female guests. In England, these arrangements are made according to the rank of the ladies—that of the gentlemen is not considered. A duchess takes precedence of a marchioness, a viscountess of a countess, a baroness of a baron*et's* lady, &c.,—for a baron is above a baronet. Going into the dining-room, the company passed by the butler and eight footmen, all of whom were stationed in two rows. The butler was dressed entirely in black—the footmen in their livery. According to a new fashion, they may now wear long gaiters. White kid gloves are indispensable to the footmen.

The table was set for twenty-six—and standing on it were elegant gilt candelabras. *All* the lights were wax candles. Chandeliers were suspended from the ceiling. In the middle of the table was a magnificent plateau, or centre ornament of gold; flowers surmounted the summit; and the circular stages below were covered with confectionery elegantly arranged. On each side of the plateau, and above and below, were tall china fruit-baskets. In the centre of each basket were immense pine-apples of hot-house growth, with their fresh green leaves. Below the pine-apples were large bunches of purple and white hot-house grapes, beautifully disposed, with leaves and tendrils hanging over the sides of the baskets. Down each side of the whole long table, were placed large, round, saucer-shaped fruit-dishes, heaped up with peaches, nectarines, pears, plumbs, ripe gooseberries, cherries, currants, strawberries, &c. All the fruits not in season were supplied from hot-houses. And alternating with the fruit were all the *entreméts* in covered dishes, placed on long slips of damask the whole length of the table. All the plate was superb. The dinner-set was of French china, gilt, and painted with roses. At every plate was a caraffe of water, with a tumbler turned down over it, and several wine-glasses. The napkins were large. The side-board held only the show-silver and the wine. The side-tables were covered with elegant damask cloths. On these were ranged, laid along in numerous rows, the knives, forks, and spoons to be used at dinner. The dessert-spoons were in the form of hollow leaves, the stems being the handles. They were beautifully engraved in tasteful patterns. The fruit-knives had silver blades and pearl handles. There were two soups (white and brown,) standing on a side-table. Each servant handed the things in his white kid gloves, and with a damask napkin under his thumb. They offered (mentioning its name in a low voice,) a plate of each soup to each guest. After the soup, Hock and Moselle wine were offered to each guest, that they might choose either. A dish of fish was then placed at each end of the table—one was salmon, the other turbot. These dishes were immediately taken off to be helped by the servants, both sorts of fish being offered to each person. Then the appropriate sauce for the fish—also cucumbers to eat with the salmon. No castors were on the large table, but they were handed round by the servants. Directly after the fish came the *entreméts,* or French dishes. The wine following the fish was Madeira and Sherry.

Afterwards, a saddle or haunch of Welsh mutton was placed at the master's end of the table, and at the lady's end a boiled turkey. These dishes being removed to the side-tables, very thin slices of each were handed round. The poultry was not dissected—nothing being helped but the breast. Ham and tongue was then supplied to those who took poultry; and currant-jelly to the eaters of mutton. Next came the vegetables, handed round on dishes divided into four compartments, each division containing a different sort of vegetable.

Next, two dishes of game were put on—one before the master of the house, and the other before the mistress. The game (which was perfectly well-done,) was helped by them, and sent round with the appropriate sauce. Then, placed along the table, were the sweet things—charlottes, jellies, frozen fruit, &c. A lobster salad, drest and cut up large, was put on with the sweets. On a side-table were stilton and cream cheese, to be eaten with the salad. After this, port wine—the champagne being early in the dinner. Next the sweets were handed round. With the sweets were frozen fruits—fruits cut up, and frozen with isinglass-jelly (red, in moulds).

Next, a dessert plate was given to each guest, and on it a ground glass plate, about the size of a saucer. Between these plates was a crochet-worked white doyly, of the size of the under-plate; the crochet-work done with thread, so as to resemble lace. These doylies were laid under the ground-glass plate, to deaden the noise of their collision. Then was brought from the side-table a ground-glass plate of ice-cream, or water-ice, which you took in exchange for that before you. The water-ice was frozen in moulds, in the form of fruit, and suitably coloured. The baskets containing the fruit were then removed to the side-tables, where the servants had silver scissors, with which they clipped off small bunches of the grapes, and the green tops of the pine-apples, and a portion of the flesh of the fruit. The middle part was then pared and sliced. On each dessert-plate was placed a slice of pine-apple, and small bunches of white and blue grapes. After the grapes and pine-apples were thus handed round, the dishes of the other fruits were then offered successively to every guest. After the ground-glass and doylies, there was no farther change of plates.

After sitting a while over the fruit, the lady of the house gives the signal, by looking and bowing to the ladies on each side, and the ladies at this signal prepare to retire. The gentlemen all rise, and remain standing while the ladies depart—the master of the house holding the door open. The servants then all retire, except the butler, who remains to wait on the gentlemen, while they linger awhile (not more than a quarter of an hour,) over the fruit and wine.

CHAPTER XXV.
MISCELLANIES.

It may be well to caution our young friends against certain bad practices, easily contracted, but sometimes difficult to relinquish. The following are things not to be done:—Biting your nails. Slipping a ring up and down your finger. Sitting cross-kneed, and, jogging your feet. Drumming on the table with your knuckles; or, still worse, tinking on a piano with *your fore-finger only*. Humming a tune before strangers. Singing as you go up and down stairs. Putting your arm round the neck of another young girl, or promenading the room with arms encircling waists. Holding the hand of a friend all the time she sits beside you; or kissing and fondling her before company. Sitting too closely.

Slapping a gentleman with your handkerchief, or tapping him with your fan. Allowing him to take a ring off your finger, to look at it. Permitting him to unclasp your bracelet, or, still worse, to inspect your brooch. When these ornaments are to be shown to another person, always take them off for the purpose. Pulling at your own ringlets, or your own ear-rings—or fingering your neck ribbon. Suffering a gentleman to touch your curls. Reading with a gentleman off the same book or newspaper. Looking over the shoulder of any person who is reading or writing. Taking up a *written* paper from the table, and examining it.

To listen at door-cracks, and peep through key-holes, is vulgar and contemptible. So it is to ask children questions concerning their parents, though such things are still done.

If you mean that you were angry, do not say you were "mad."—"It made me so mad"—"I was quite mad at her," are phrases not to be used by people considering themselves genteel. Anger and madness are not the same, or should not be; though it is true that ungoverned rage, is, sometimes, carried so far as to seem like insanity.

Enter into no freaks of fashion that are silly, unmeaning, and unlady-like; even if they *have* been introduced by a belle, and followed by other belles. Commit no absurdity because a public singer or dancer has done so in her ignorance of good behaviour. During the Jenny Lind fever, there were young ladies who affected to skuttle into a drawing-room all of a sudden, somewhat as the fair Swede came skuttling in upon the concert stage, because in reality she knew not how to make her entrance gracefully. Other demoiselles twined and waved about, with body, head, and eyes, never a moment quiet. This squirming (as it was called) originated in a very bad imitation of Fanny Elssler's dancing motions. At one time there were girls at parties, who stood on one foot, and with the other kicked up their dresses behind, while talking to gentlemen. This fashion began with a celebrated beauty who "dared do any thing." Luckily, these "whims and oddities" are always of short duration, and are never adopted by young ladies of good taste and refinement.

Do not nod your head, or beat time with fan or foot while listening to music.

Never at a party consent to accompany another lady in a duet, unless you are accustomed to singing with her. Still worse—do not volunteer to "assist" her in a song that is not a duet. Each voice will interrupt and spoil the other. A lady who sings by ear only, cannot accompany one that sings by note.

One of the most horrible sounds imaginable is that produced by several fine voices all singing different songs. This cats' concert (as school-girls call it) results in a shocking and yet ludicrous discord, equally frightful and laughable. And yet all the performers are singing individually well. Try it.

Raising a window-sash, in cold weather, without first ascertaining if the rest of the company are, like yourself, too warm. Leaving the parlour door open in winter—a perpetual occurrence at hotels and boarding-houses.

Talking so loudly that you can be heard all over the room. Or so low that you cannot be heard at all, even by those who are conversing with you. This last fault is the worst. To talk with one who has a habit of muttering unintelligibly, is like trying to read a letter illegibly written.

Using too often the word "madam" or "ma'am," which in fact, is now nearly obsolete in familiar conversation. In the old French tragedies the lovers addressed their mistresses as "madam." But then the stage Alexander wore a powdered wig, and a laced coat, knee-breeches, and a long-skirted waistcoat; and Roxana figured in a hoop-petticoat, a brocade gown, a flowered apron, and a towering gauze cap. The frequent use of "sir" is also out of fashion. "Yes, ma'am," "No, ma'am," "Yes, sir," "No, sir," no longer sounds well, except from children to their elders. If you have not distinctly heard what another lady has just said to you, do not denote it by saying, "Ma'am?" but remark to her, "Excuse me, I did not exactly hear you!"

Never, in a public parlour, place yourself in a position where you can secretly hear conversation that is not intended for you—for instance in a corner behind a pillar. If you hear yourself talked of, it is mean to stay and listen. It is a true adage that "Listeners seldom hear any good of themselves."

However smart and witty you may be considered, do not exercise your wit in rallying and bantering your friends. If you do so, their friendship will soon be worn out, or converted into positive enmity. A jest that carries a sting with it can never give a pleasant sensation to the object. The bite of a musquito is a very little thing, but it leaves pain and inflammation behind it, and the more it is rubbed the longer it rankles in the blood. No one likes to have their foibles or mishaps turned into ridicule—before other persons especially. And few can cordially join in a laugh that is raised against themselves.

The slightest jest on the personal defects of those you are conversing with, is an enormity of rudeness and vulgarity. It is, in fact, a sneer at the Creator that made them so. No human creature is accountable for being too small, or too large; for an ill-formed figure, or for ill-shaped limbs; for irregular features, or a bad complexion.

Still worse, to rally any person (especially a woman) on her age, or to ask indirect questions with a view of discovering what her age really is. If we continue to live, we must continue to grow old. We must either advance in age, or we must die. Where then is the shame of surviving our youth? And when youth departs, beauty goes along with it. At least as much beauty as depends on complexion, hair, and teeth. In arriving at middle age, (or a little beyond it,) a lady must compound for the loss of either face or figure. About that period she generally becomes thinner, or fatter. If thin, her features shrink, and her skin shrivels and fades; even though she retains a slender and perhaps a girlish form. If she grows fat, her skin may continue smooth, and her complexion fine, and her neck and arms may be rounder and handsomer than in girlhood; but then symmetry of shape will cease—and she must reconcile herself to the change as best she can. But a woman with a good mind, a good heart, and a good temper, can never at any age grow ugly—for an intelligent and pleasant expression is in itself beauty, and the best sort of beauty.

Sad indeed is the condition of women in the decline of life when "No lights of age adorn them." When, having neglected in the spring and summer to lay up any stores for the winter that is sure to come, they find themselves left in the season of desolation with nothing to fall back upon—no pleasant recollections of the acquisition of knowledge or the performance of good deeds, and nothing to talk about but the idle gossip of the day—striving painfully to look younger than they really are; still haunting balls and parties, and enduring all the discomforts of crowded watering-places, long after all pleasure in such scenes must have passed away. But then they must linger in public because they are miserable at home, having no resources within themselves, and few enduring friends to enliven them with their society.

The woman that knows how to grow old gracefully, will adapt her dress to her figure and her age, and wear colours that suit her present complexion. If her neck and arms are thin, she will not expose them under any circumstances. If her hair is grey, she will not decorate it with flowers and flimsy ribbons. If her cheeks are hollow, she will not make her face look still longer and thinner by shadowing it with long ringlets; and setting her head-dress far back—but she will give it as much softness as she can, by a light cap-border tied under her chin. She will not squeeze herself out of all human shape by affecting a long tight *corsage*; and she will wear no dresses glaring with huge flowers, or loaded with gaudy trimmings. She will allude to her age as a thing of course; she will speak without hesitation of former times, though the recollection proves her to be really old. She will be kind and indulgent to the young; and the young will respect and love her, and gladly assemble near her chair, and be amused and unconsciously instructed. As long as she lives and retains her faculties she will endeavour to improve, and to become still a wiser and a better woman; never excusing herself by indolently and obstinately averring that "she is too old to learn," or that she cannot give up her old-fashioned habits. If she finds that those habits are unwarrantable, or that they are annoying to her friends, she ought to relinquish them. No one with a mind unimpaired, and a heart still fresh, is too old to learn.

This book is addressed chiefly to the young; but we shall be much gratified by finding that even old ladies have found in it some advantageous suggestions on points that had hitherto escaped their notice.

THE
LADIES' VASE

OR

POLITE MANUAL
FOR
YOUNG LADIES

BY AN AMERICAN LADY

PREFACE.

S O MANY VOLUMES HAVE ALREADY APPEARED before the public, similar in character to this little work, that it is with feelings of diffidence we bring our humble offering, especially when we consider the rich merit possessed by many of its predecessors. But our apology must be found in the fact that these publications are, from their size, and consequent expense, inaccessible to many of the class whose improvement they are so well adapted to promote. Considering the formation of female character and manners a matter of inestimable importance, especially at the present age, swayed as it is by moral [iv]rather than by physical force, we have carefully availed ourselves of the best advice of some of our most judicious writers on female education; and, by presenting our work in a cheaper form than any of this class which is now before the public, hope to render it attainable to all those for whom it is especially designed.

POLITENESS.

Politeness, like every thing else in one's character and conduct, should be based on Christian principle. "Honor all men," says the apostle. This is the spring of good manners; it strikes at the very root of selfishness: it is the principle by which we render to all ranks and ages their due. A respect for your fellow-beings—a reverence for them as God's creatures and our brethren—will inspire that delicate regard for their rights and feelings, of which good manners is the sign.

If you have truth—not the truth of policy, but religious truth—your manners will be sincere. They will have earnestness, simplicity, and frankness—the best qualities of manners. They will be free from assumption, pretense, affectation, flattery, and obsequiousness, which are all incompatible with sincerity. If you have sincerity, you will choose to appear no other, nor better, than you are—to dwell in a true light.

We have often insisted, that the Bible contains the only rules necessary in the study of politeness. Or, in other words, that those who are the real disciples of Christ, cannot fail to be truly polite. Thus, let the young woman who would possess genuine politeness, take her lessons, not in the school of a hollow, heartless world, but in the school of Jesus Christ. I know this counsel may be despised by the gay and fashionable; but it will be much easier to despise it, than to prove it to be incorrect.

"Always think of the good of the whole, rather than of your own individual convenience," says Mrs. Farrar, in her Young Ladies' Friend. A most excellent rule; and one to which we solicit your earnest attention. She who is thoroughly imbued with the Gospel spirit, will not fail to do so. It was what our Savior did continually; and I have no doubt that his was the purest specimen of good manners, or genuine politeness, the world has ever witnessed; the politeness of Abraham himself not excepted.

TRUE AND FALSE POLITENESS.

Every thing really valuable is sure to be counterfeited. This applies not only to money, medicine, religion, and virtue, but even to politeness. We see in society the truly polite and the falsely polite; and, although all cannot explain, all can feel the difference. While we respect the one, we despise the other. Men hate to be cheated. An attempt to deceive us, is an insult to our understandings and an affront to our morals. The pretender to politeness is a cheat. He tries to palm off the base for the genuine; and, although he may deceive the vulgar, he cannot overreach the cultivated. True politeness springs from right feelings; it is a good heart, manifesting itself in an agreeable life; it is a just regard for the rights and happiness of others in small things; it is the expression of true and generous sentiments in a graceful form of words; it regards neatness and propriety in dress, as something due to society, and avoids tawdriness in apparel, as offensive to good taste; it avoids selfishness in conduct and roughness in manners: hence, a polite person is called a gentle man. True politeness is the smoothness of a refined mind and the tact of a kind heart.

Politeness is a word derived from the Greek word polis, which means a city—the inhabitants of which are supposed, by constant intercourse with each other, to be more refined in manners than the inhabitants of the country. From polis, comes our English word polish, which signifies an effect produced by rubbing down roughnesses until the surface is smoothed and brightened: hence, we speak of polished minds and polished manners. Persons in good society rub against each other until their sharp points are worn down, and their intercourse becomes easy. The word urbanity comes from the Latin word urbs; that, also, means a city, and it signifies politeness, gentleness, polish, for a similar reason.

In mingling with our fellow-men, there is a constant necessity for little offices of mutual good will. An observing and generous-minded person notices what gives him offense, and what pleases him in the conduct of others; and he seeks at once to correct or cultivate similar things in himself. He acts upon the wise, Christian principle of doing to others as he would have them do to him. Hence, in dress and person, he is clean and neat; in speech, he is courteous; in behavior, conciliating; in the pursuit of his own interests, unobtrusive. No truly polite person appears to notice bodily defects or unavoidable imperfections in others; and, above all, he never sneers at religion, either in its doctrines, ordinances, or professors.

False politeness is but a clumsy imitation of all this. It is selfish in its object, and superficial in its character. It is a slave to certain forms of speech, certain methods of action, and certain fashions of dress. It is insincere; praising where it sees no merit, and excusing sin where it beholds no repentance. It is the offspring of selfishness; perverting the golden rule by flattering stupidity and winking at vice, with the hope of being treated in the same way by the community. It is a bed of flowers, growing over a sepulchre, and drawing its life from the loathsome putrefaction within.

Yet, insincere and wrong as are the motives to false politeness, it is, after all, better than vulgarity. It is the cotton batting, that keeps the glass vases of society from dashing against each other. «Familiarity," says the proverb, "breeds contempt;" and this is found true, whenever coarse minds with rude manners come in contact. Careless of the little decencies of society; selfish in selecting the best seat in the room, or the best dish at the table; unwashed in person, and slovenly in dress: what is this but an open proclamation of utter disregard for others? How soon contempt must follow!

Let the young polish their manners, not by attending to mere artificial rules, but by the cultivation of right feelings. Let them mingle with refined society as often as they can; and, by refined society, I do not mean those whom you find in the ball-room—in the theater—in the crowded party, or those—however wealthy, or richly dressed—you feel to be only artificially polite; but I mean those who make you feel at ease in their society, while, at the same time, they elevate your aims and polish your manners. What a good style is to noble sentiments, politeness is to virtue.

IMPORTANCE OF GOOD MANNERS.

There is something in the very constitution of human nature which inclines us to form a judgment of character from manners. It is always taken for granted, unless there is decisive evidence to the contrary, that the manners are the genuine expression of the feelings. And even where such evidence exists—that is, where we have every reason to believe that the external appearance does injustice to the moral dispositions; or, on the other hand, where the heart is too favorably represented by the manners—there is still a delusion practiced upon the mind, by what passes under the eye, which it is not easy to resist. You may take two individuals of precisely the same degree of intellectual and moral worth, and let the manners of the one be bland and attractive, and those of the other distant or awkward, and you will find that the former will pass through life with far more ease and comfort than the latter; for, though good manners will never effectually conceal a bad heart, and are, in no case, any atonement for it, yet, taken in connection with amiable and virtuous dispositions, they naturally and necessarily gain upon the respect and goodwill of mankind.

You will instantly perceive—if the preceding remarks be correct—that it is not only your interest to cultivate good manners, as you hereby recommend yourself to the favorable regards of others, but also your duty, as it increases, in no small degree, your means of usefulness. It will give you access to many persons, and give you an influence over those whom you could otherwise never approach; much less, whose feelings and purposes you could never hope, in any measure, to control.

"If I should point you to the finest model of female manners which it has ever been my privilege to observe," says a late writer, in a letter to his daughter, "and one which will compare with the most perfect models of this or any other age, I should repeat a venerated name—that of Mrs. Hannah More. It was my privilege, a few years ago, to make a visit to the residence of this distinguished female; a visit which I have ever since regarded as among the happiest incidents of my life. At that time, she numbered more than fourscore years, but the vigor of her intellect was scarcely impaired; and, from what she was, I could easily conceive what she had been when her sun was at its meridian. In her person, she was rather small, but was a specimen of admirable symmetry. In her manners, she united the dignity and refinement of the court, with the most exquisite urbanity and gentleness which the female character, in its loveliest forms, ever exhibited. She impressed me continually with a sense of the high intellectual and moral qualities by which she was distinguished, but still left me as unconstrained as if I had been conversing with a beloved child. There was an air of graceful and unaffected ease; an instinctive regard to the most delicate proprieties of social intercourse; a readiness to communicate, and yet a desire to listen; the dignity of conscious merit, united with the humility of the devoted Christian: in short, there was such an assemblage of intellectual and moral excellences beaming forth in every expression, and look, and attitude, that I could scarcely conceive of a more perfect exhibition of human character. I rejoice that it is the privilege of all to know Mrs. More through her works; and I can form no better wish for you than that you may imbibe her spirit, and walk in her footsteps."

SELF-POSSESSION.

Self-possession is the first requisite to good manners; and, where it is wanting, there is generally a reason for it, in some wrong feeling or appreciation of things. Vanity, a love of display, an overweening desire to be admired, are great obstacles to self-possession; whereas, a well-disciplined and well-balanced character will generally lead to composure and self-command. In a very elegant assemblage, in a large drawing-room in a Southern city, I saw a young lady walk quietly and easily across the apartment to speak to a friend, who said to her: "I wanted very much to get to you, but I had not the courage to cross the room. How could you do it?—all alone, too, and with so many persons looking at you!" "I did not think of any body's looking at me," was the reply; and in that lay the secret of her self-possession. Very modest people believe themselves to be of too little consequence to be observed; but conceited ones, think every body must be looking at them. Inexperienced girls, who are not wanting in modesty, are apt to dread going into a crowded room, from an idea that every eye will be turned upon them; but after a while they find that nobody cares to look at them, and that the greater the crowd, the less they are observed.

Your enjoyment of a party depends far less on what you find there, than on what you carry with you. The vain, the ambitious, the designing, will be full of anxiety when they go, and of disappointment when they return. A short triumph will be followed by a deep mortification, and the selfishness of their aims defeats itself. If you go to see and to hear, and to make the best of whatever occurs, with a disposition to admire all that is beautiful, and to sympathize in the pleasures of others, you can hardly fail to spend the time pleasantly. The less you think of yourself and your claims to attention, the better. If you are much attended to, receive it modestly, and consider it as a happy accident; if you are little noticed, use your leisure in observing others.

The popular belle, who is the envy of her own sex and the admiration of the other, has her secret griefs and trials, and thinks she pays very dearly for her popularity; while the girl who is least attended to in crowded assemblies, is apt to think her's the only hard lot, and that there is unmixed happiness in being a reigning belle. She, alone, whose steady aim is to grow better and wiser every day of her life, can look with an equal eye on both extremes. If your views are elevated, and your feelings are ennobled and purified by communion with gifted spirits, and with the Father of spirits, you will look calmly on the gayest scenes of life; you will attach very little importance to the transient popularity of a ball-room; your endeavor will be to bring home from every visit some new idea, some valuable piece of information, or some useful experience of life.

GOOD COMPANY.

"Good company," says Duclos, "resembles a dispersed republic: the members of it are found in all classes. Independent of rank and station, it exists only among those who think and feel; among those who possess correct ideas and honorable sentiments." The higher classes, constantly occupied with the absorbing interests of wealth and ambition, formerly introduced into their magnificent saloons a grave and almost diplomatic stiffness of manners, of which the solemnity banished nature and freedom. The amusements of the lower classes, which rather resembled a toil than a recreation, present to the spectator a procedure irreconcilable to good taste.

There are, moreover, too many points of resemblance between the manners and education of the higher and lower classes, to admit of our finding the elements of good society in either of them. The lower orders are ignorant, from want of means of instruction; the higher, from indolence and perpetually increasing incapacity. It is besides not a little curious that, even in the bygone days of ceremonious manners, the higher classes, by whom they were practiced, were uniformly taught by those illiterate persons of the lower classes who almost alone practice the art of dancing-masters.

It is therefore to the middle class, almost exclusively, that we must look for good society; to that class which has not its ideas contracted by laborious occupations, nor its mental powers annihilated by luxury. In this class, it is truly observed, society is often full of charm: every one seems, according to the precept of La Bruyère, "anxious, both by words and manners, to make others pleased with him and with themselves." There are slight differences of character, opinion, and interest; but there is no prevailing style, no singular or affected customs. An unperceived interchange of ideas and kind offices produces a delightful harmony of thoughts and sentiments; and the wish to please inspires those affectionate manners, those obliging expressions, and those unrestrained attentions, which alone render social unions pleasant and desirable.

FRIENDSHIP.

This subject was forcibly presented to my mind by a conversation I recently heard in a party of young ladies, and which I take as a pattern and semblance of twenty other conversations I have heard in twenty similar parties. Friendship was (as it very often is) the subject of the discussion; and, though the words have escaped my memory, I can well recall the substance of the remarks. One lady boldly asserted that there was no such thing as friendship in the world, where all was insincerity and selfishness. I looked, but saw not in her youthful eye and unfurrowed cheeks any traces of the sorrow and ill-usage that I thought should alone have wrung from gentle lips so harsh a sentence, and I wondered where in twenty brief years she could have learned so hard a lesson. Have known it, she could not! therefore I concluded she had taken it upon trust from the poets, who are fain to tell all the ill they can of human nature, because it makes better poetry than good.

The remark was taken up, as might have been expected, by a young champion, who thought, or said without thinking, that friendship was—I really cannot undertake to say what, but all the things that young ladies usually put into their themes at school: something interminable, illimitable, and immutable. From this the discussion grew; and how it was, and what it was, went on to be discussed. I cannot pursue the thread of the discourse; but the amount of it was this:—One thought friendship was the summer portion only of the blessed; a flower for the brow of the prosperous, that the child of misfortune must never gather. Another thought that all interest being destructive to its very essence, it could not be trusted, unless there was an utter destitution of every thing that might recommend us to favor, or requite affection. This lady must have been brought to the depth of wretchedness ere she ever could be sure she had a friend. Some, I found, thought it was made up of a great deal of sensibility, vulgarly called jealousy; that was, to take umbrage at every seeming slight, to the indescribable torment of either party. Some betrayed, if they did not exactly say it, that they thought friendship such an absolute unity, that it would be a less crime to worship two gods than to love two friends! Therefore, to bring it to its perfection, it was necessary that all beside should be despised and disregarded.

Others, very young, and of course soon to grow wiser, thought it consisted in the exact disclosure of your own concerns and those of every body else with which you might chance to become acquainted; others, that it required such exact conformity in opinion, thought, and feeling, as should make it impossible to differ; and others, that it implied such generous interference, even with the feelings as well as affairs of its object, that it should spend itself in disinterested reproaches and unasked advice. But, however differing else, all were sure that friendship but usurped the name, unless it were purely disinterested, endlessly durable, and beyond the reach of time and circumstances to change it; and all were going forth in the full certainty of finding friends, each one after the pattern of her own imagination, the first speaker only excepted, who was fully determined never to find any, or never to trust them, if she did.

I marked, with pained attention, the warm glow of expectation so soon to be blighted; and, reflected deeply on the many heart-aches with which they must unlearn their errors. I saw that each one was likely to pass over and reject the richest blessing of earth, even in the very pursuing of it, from having merely sketched, in imagination, an unresembling portrait of the object of pursuit. "When friendship meets them," I said, "they will not know her. Can no one draw for them a better likeness?"

It is the language of books, and the language of society, that friends are inconstant, and friendship but little to be depended on; and the belief, where it is really received, goes far to make a truth of that which else were false, by creating what it suspects. Few of us but have lived already long enough to know the bitterness of being disappointed in our affections, and deceived in our calculations by those with whom, in the various relationships of life, we are brought in contact. Perhaps the aggregate of pain from this cause is greater than from any other cause whatever. And yet, it is much to be doubted whether nearly the whole of this suffering does not arise from our own unreasonable and mistaken expectations. There are none so unfortunate but they meet with some kindness in the world; and none, I believe, so fortunate but that they meet with much less than they might do, were it not their own fault.

In the first place, we are mistaken in our expectations that friendship should be disinterested. It neither is, nor can be. It may be so in action, but never in the sentiment; there is always an equivalent to be returned. And if we examine the movements of our own hearts, we must be sure this is the case; and yet, we are so unreasonable as to expect our friends should be purely disinterested; and, after having secured their affections, we neglect to pay the price, and expect they should be continued to us for nothing. We grow careless of pleasing them; inconsiderate of their feelings, and heedless of the government of our own temper towards them; and then we complain of inconstancy, if they like us not so well as when dressed out in our best for the reception of their favor. Yet it is, in fact, we that are changed, not they.

Another fruitful source of disappointment in our attachments is, that while we are much more quick in detecting the faults of others than our own, we absurdly require that every one should be faultless but ourselves. We do not say that we expect this in our friends; but we do expect it, and our conduct proves that we expect it. We begin also with believing it. The obscurities of distance; the vail that the proprieties of society casts over nature's deformities; the dazzling glitter of exterior qualities baffle, for a time, our most penetrating glances, and the imperfect vision seems all that we should have it. Our inexperienced hearts, and some indeed that should be better taught, fondly believe it to be all it seems, and begin their attachment in full hope to find it so. What wonder then that the bitterest disappointment should ensue, when, on more close acquaintance, we find them full of imperfections, perhaps of most glaring faults;

and we begin to express disgust, sometimes even resentment, that they are not what we took them for.

But was this their fault, or ours? Did they not present themselves to us in the garb of mortal flesh?—and do we not know that mortals are imperfect?—that, however the outside be fair, the interior is corrupt, and sometimes vile? He who knows all, alone knows how corrupt it is! the heart itself, enlightened by His grace, is more deeply in the secret than any without can be; but if the thing we love be mortal, something of it we must perceive; and more and more of it we must perceive as we look closer. If this is to disappoint and revolt us, and draw harsh reproaches and bitter recriminations from our lips, there is but One on whom we can fix our hearts with safety; and He is one, alas! we show so little disposition to love, as proves that, with all our complainings and bewailings of each others' faultiness, our friends are as good as will, at present, suit us.

But are we, therefore, to say there is no such thing as friendship, or that it is not worth seeking? morosely repel it, or suspiciously distrust it? If we do, we shall pay our folly's price in the forfeiture of that, without which, however we may pretend, we never are or can be happy; preferring to go without the very greatest of all earthly good, because it is not what, perhaps, it may be in heaven. Rather than this, it would be wise so to moderate our expectation, and adapt our conduct, as to gain of it a greater measure, or, as far as may be possible, to gather of its flowers without exposing ourselves to be wounded by the thorns it bears. This is only to be done by setting out in life with juster feelings and fairer expectations.

It is not true, that friends are few and kindness rare. No one ever needed friends, and deserved them, and found them not; but we do not know them when we see them, or deal with them justly when we have them. We must allow others to be as variable, and imperfect, and faulty, as ourselves. We do not wish our readers to love their friends less, but to love them as what they are, rather than as what they wish them to be; and instead of the jealous pertinacity that is wounded by every appearance of change, and disgusted by every detection of a fault, and ready to distrust and cast away the kindest friends on every trifling difference of behavior and feeling, to cultivate a moderation in their demands; a patient allowance for the effect of time and circumstance; an indulgence towards peculiarities of temper and character; and, above all, such a close examination of what passes in their own hearts, as will teach them better to understand and excuse what they detect in the hearts of others; ever remembering that all things on earth are earthly; and therefore changeful, perishable, and uncertain.

KINDRED HEARTS.

Oh! ask not, hope thou not too much
    Of sympathy below;
Few are the hearts whence one same touch,
    Bids the same fountain flow;
Few, and by still conflicting powers
    Forbidden here to meet,
Such ties would make this life of ours
    Too fair for aught so fleet.

It may be that thy brother's eye
    Sees not as thine, which turns,
In such deep reverence, to the sky
    Where the rich sunset burns;
It may be that the breath of spring,
    Born amidst violets lone,
A rapture o'er thy soul can bring,
    A dream to his unknown.

The tune that speaks of other times—
    A sorrowful delight!
The melody of distant chimes;
    The sound of waves by night;
The wind that with so many a tone
    Some cord within can thrill;
These may have language all thine own,
    To *him* a mystery still.

Yet scorn thou not for this the true
    And steadfast love of years;

The kindly, that from childhood grew,
    The faithful to thy tears!
If there be one that o'er the dead
    Hath in thy grief borne part,
And watched through sickness by thy bed,
    Call *his* a kindred heart.

But for those bonds, all perfect made,
    Wherein bright spirits blend,
Like sister flowers of one sweet shade,
    With the same breeze that bend;
For that full bliss of thought allied,
    Never to mortals given,—
Oh! lay thy lovely dreams aside,
    Or lift them unto heaven.

CONVERSATION.

Good conversation is one of the highest attainments of civilized society. It is the readiest way in which gifted minds exert their influence, and, as such, is worthy of all consideration and cultivation. I remember hearing an English traveler say, many years ago, on being asked how the conversational powers of the Americans compared with those of the English—"Your fluency rather exceeds that of the old world, but conversation here is not cultivated as an art." The idea of its being so considered any where was new to the company; and much discussion followed the departure of the stranger, as to the desirableness of making conversation an art. Some thought the more natural and spontaneous it was, the better; some confounded art with artifice, and hoped their countrymen would never leave their own plain, honest way of talking, to become adepts in hypocrisy and affectation. At last one, a little wiser than the rest, explained the difference between art and artifice; asked the cavilers if they had never heard of the art of writing, or the art of thinking? and said he presumed the art of conversing was of the same nature. And so it is. By this art, persons are taught to arrange their ideas methodically, and to express them with clearness and force; thus saving much precious time, and avoiding those tedious narrations which interest no one but the speaker. It enforces the necessity of observing the effect of what is said, and leads a talker to stop when she finds that she has ceased to fix the attention of her audience.

Some persons seem to forget that mere talking is not conversing; that it requires two to make a conversation, and that each must be in turn a listener; but no one can be an agreeable companion who is not as willing to listen as to talk. Selfishness shows itself in this, as in a thousand other ways. One who is always full of herself, and who thinks nothing so important as what she thinks, and says, and does, will be apt to engross more than her share of the talk, even when in the company of those she loves.

There are situations, however, wherein it is a kindness to be the chief talker: as when a young lady is the eldest of the party, and has seen something, or been in some place, the description of which is desired by all around her. If your mind is alive to the wishes and claims of others, you will easily perceive when it is a virtue to talk and when to be silent. It is undue pre-occupation with self which blinds people, and prevents their seeing what the occasion requires.

Sometimes the most kind and sympathizing person will not do justice to her nature, but will appear to be cold and inattentive, because she does not know that it is necessary to give some sign that she is attending to what is addressed to her. She averts her eye from the speaker, and listens in such profound silence, and with a countenance so immovable, that no one could suppose her to be at all interested by what she is hearing. This is very discouraging to the speaker and very impolite. Good manners require that you should look at the person who speaks to you, and that you should put in a word, or a look, from time to time, that will indicate your interest in the narrative. A few interjections, happily thrown in by the hearer, are a great comfort and stimulus to the speaker; and one who has always been accustomed to this evidence of sympathy, or comprehension, in their friends, feels, when listened to without it, as if she were talking to a dead wall.

For the encouragement of those who feel themselves deficient in conversational powers, we will subjoin a notice of the lately-deceased wife of a clergyman in this state:

"I saw and felt, when with her, as few others have ever made me feel, the power and uses of conversation. With her it was always promotive of intellectual and moral life. And here let me inform you, for the encouragement of those who may be thinking they would gladly do as she did in society, if they were able, that when I first knew Mrs. B., her powers of conversation were very small. She was embarrassed whenever she attempted to convey her thoughts to others. She labored for expression so much, that it was sometimes painful to hear her. Still, her social, affectionate nature longed for communion with other minds and hearts, on all subjects of deepest import. Her persevering efforts at length prevailed, and her ardent love of truth gave her utterance: yes, an utterance that often delighted, and sometimes surprised, those who heard her; a readiness and fluency that are seldom equalled. Learn, then, from her, my friends, to exercise your faculties, whatever they may be. In this way only can you improve, or even retain them. If you have but one talent of any sort, it may not, with impunity to itself—it may not, without sin to you—be wrapped in a napkin. And sigh not for higher powers or opportunities, until you have fully and faithfully exercised and improved such as you have. Nor can you know what you possess until you have called them into action."

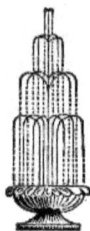

EXAGGERATION.

It is a great mistake to suppose that exaggeration makes a person more agreeable, or that it adds to the importance of her statements. The value of a person's words is determined by her habitual use of them. "I like it much," "It is well done," will mean as much in some mouths, as "I am infinitely delighted with it," "'Tis the most exquisite thing I ever saw," will in others. Such large abatements are necessarily made for the statements of these romancers, that they really gain nothing in the end, but find it difficult sometimes to gain credence for so much as is really true; whereas, a person who is habitually sober and discriminating in his use of language, will not only inspire confidence, but be able to produce a fine effect by the occasional use of a superlative.

Fidelity and exactness are indispensable in a narrative, and the habit of exaggerating destroys the power of accurate observation and recollection which would render the story truly interesting. If, instead of trying to embellish her account with the fruits of her imagination, a young lady possessed the power of seizing upon the points best worth describing, and could give an exact account of them, she would be far more entertaining than any exaggeration could make her; for there is no romance like that of real life, and no imaginings of an inexperienced girl can equal in piquancy the scenes and characters that are every day presented to our view. Extravagant expressions are sometimes resorted to in order to atone for deficiencies of memory and observation; but they will never hide such defects; and an habitual use of them lowers the tone of the mind, and leads to other deviations from the simplicity of truth and nature.

Another way of falsifying a narrative, is by taking for granted what you do not know, and speaking of it as if you did. This jumping at conclusions is a fruitful source of false reports, and does great mischief in the world. Let no one imagine that she is walking conscientiously, who is not in the habit of discriminating nicely between what she knows to be fact and what she only supposes to be such.

The frequent use of some favorite word, or phrase, is a common defect in conversation, and can only be guarded against by asking your friends to point it out to you, whenever they observe such a habit; for your own ear, having become accustomed to it, may not detect it. Some persons apply the epithets glorious or splendid to all sorts of objects indiscriminately, from a gorgeous sunset to a good dinner.

A young lady once tried to describe a pic-nic party to me in the following terms: "There were ten of us—four on horseback and the rest in carriages. We set off at a glorious rate, and had a splendid time in getting there; I rode the most elegant, perfect creature you ever beheld, and capered along gloriously. When we all got there, we walked about in the woods, and gathered the most splendid flowers, and dined under the shade of a glorious old elm-tree. We had our cold provisions spread out on the grass, and every thing was elegant. We had glorious appetites, too, and the ham and ale were splendid, and put us all in fine spirits. Some of the gentlemen sang funny songs; but one sang such a dreadfully sentimental one, and to such a horrid doleful tune, it made us all miserable. So then we broke up, and had a splendid time packing away the things; such fun! I had almost killed myself with laughing, and we broke half the things. But the ride home was the most splendid of all; we arrived at the top of the hill just in time to see the most glorious sunset I ever beheld!"

In this short account, the word "glorious" is used five times, and in all but the last, it is grossly misapplied. The same is the case with the word "splendid," except that it is not once used properly. "Elegant," too, is equally inapplicable to horses and cold provisions. Yet this style of conversing is so common, that it hardly arrests the attention of many, who nevertheless would condemn it at once, if they thought at all about it.

EGOTISM.

Has it ever happened to any but myself, to listen to I, I, I, in conversation, till, wearied with the monotony of the sound, I was fain to quarrel with the useful little word, and almost wish I could portray its hydra head, and present it in a mirror to my oracles, that they might turn away disgusted for ever with its hideous form.

I took up my abode for some time with a lady, whose habits of benevolence were extensive, and of whose true philanthropy of heart I had heard much. I expected to follow her to the alms-house, the hospital, and the garret, and I was not disappointed. Thither she went, and for purposes the kindest and most noble. She relieved their pressing wants; ministered consolation in the kindest tone; and gave religious instruction wherever needed. But, then, she kept a strict calendar of all these pious visitings; and that, too, for the entertainment of her company. All were called upon to hear the history of the appalling scenes she had witnessed; the tears of gratitude that had fallen on her hands; the prayers—half articulate—that had been offered for her by the dying; and to hear her attestations of disregard to the opposition she had to encounter in these her labors of love. Who, with such an appeal, could withhold their commendations? I, therefore, of course, as I listened again and again to the same tale to different auditors, heard many pretty complimentary speeches about magnanimity, &c.; and, getting somewhat weary, I drew nearer to the lady's guests, till I actually thought I heard from one—he was a clergyman, I believe—an inward whisper that he would like to refer his friend to the four first verses of the sixth chapter of Matthew, but that it would be impolite. If my listening powers were too acute when I heard this, let me turn monitor at once, and assure my young friends, if they would have their conversation listened to with pleasure, they must be economists with self as their subject.

On behalf of the very young, we certainly have it to plead, that they know very little of any thing but what is, in some sense, their own. If they talk of persons, it must be their parents, their brothers and sisters, because they are the only people they know; if they talk of any body's affairs, it must be their own, because they are acquainted with no other; if of events, it must be what happens to themselves, for they hear nothing of what happens to any body else. As soon, therefore, as children begin to converse, it is most likely to be about themselves, or something that belongs to them; and to the rapid growing of this unwatched habit, may probably be attributed the ridiculous and offensive egotism of many persons in conversation, who, in conduct, prove that their feelings and affections are by no means self-engrossed. But the more indigenous this unsightly weed, the more need is there to prevent its growth. It has many varieties; the leaf is not always of the same shape, nor the flower of the same color, but they are all of one genus; and our readers who are botanists will have no difficulty in detecting them, however much affected by the soil they grow in. The I's and my's a lady exhibits in conversation, will bear such analogy to her character, as the wares on the stall of the bazaar bear to the trade of the vender. Or, if she have a great deal of what is called tact, she will, perhaps, vary the article according to the demands of the market. In fashionable life, it will be my cousin Sir Ralph, my father the Earl, and my great uncle the Duke; the living relatives and the departed fathers; the halls of her family, their rent-rolls, or their graves, will afford abundant materials for any conversation she may have to furnish.

Among those who, having gotten into the world they know not how, are determined it shall, at least, be known that they are there, it is my houses, my s ervants, my park, my gardens; or, if the lady be too young to claim in her own behalf, my father's houses, &c., &c., will answer all the purpose. But, happily for the supply of this kind of talk, rank and wealth, though very useful, are not necessary to it. Without any ostentation whatever, but merely from the habit of occupying themselves with their own individuality, some will let the company choose the subject; but, be it what it may, all they have to say upon it is the I, or the my. Books, travel, sorrow, sickness, nature, art, no matter, it is I have seen, I have done, I have been, I have learned, I have suffered, I have known. Whatever it be to others, the I is the subject for them; for they tell you nothing of the matter but their own concern with it. For example, let the city of Naples be spoken of: one will tell you what is seen there—what is done there—what happens there—and making her reflections on all without naming herself; you will only perceive, by her knowledge and remarks, that she has been in Naples. Another will tell you how she came there, and why she went, and how long she staid, and what she did, and what she saw; and the things themselves will appear but as incidents to the idea of self.

Some ladies I have known, who, not content with the present display of their powers, are determined to re-sell their wares at second-hand. They tell you all the witty things they said to somebody yesterday, and the wise remarks they made to a certain company last night. I said—I remarked. The commodity should be valuable indeed to be thus brought to market a second time. Others there are, who, under pretext of confidence—little complimentary when shown alike to all—pester people with their own affairs. Before you have been two hours in their company, you are introduced to all their family, and to all their family›s concerns, pecuniary affairs, domestic secrets, and personal feelings—a sort of bird›s-eye view of every thing that belongs to them—past, present, and to come; and woe to the secrets of those who may chance to have been in connection with these egotists; in such a view, you must needs see ten miles around.

There is an egotism, of which we must speak more seriously. Faults, that in the world we laugh at, when they attain the dignity and purity of sacred things, become matter of serious regret. I speak nothing further of the ostentatious display of pious and benevolent exertion. We live at a time when religion, its deepest and dearest interests, have become a subject of general conversation. We would have it so; but we mark, with regret, that self has introduced itself here. The heartless loquacity—we must say heartless, for, in a matter of such deep interest, facility of speech bespeaks the feelings light—the unshrinking jabber with which people tell you their soul's history—their past impressions and present difficulties—their doctrines and their doubts—their manifestations and their experiences—not in the ear of confidence, to have those doubts removed and those doctrines verified; not in the ear of anxious inquiry, to communicate knowledge and give encouragement, but any where, in any company, and to any body who will listen, the I felt—I thought—I experienced. Sorrows that, if real, should blanch the cheek to think upon; mercies that enwrap all hearers in amazement, they will tell as unconcernedly as the adventures of the morning. The voice falters not; the color changes not; the eye moistens not. And to what purpose all this personality? To get good, or do good? By no means; but that, whatever subject they look upon, they always see themselves in the foreground of the picture, with every minute particular swelled into importance, while all besides is merged in indistinctness.

We may be assured there is nothing so ill-bred, so annoying, so little entertaining, so absolutely impertinent, as this habit of talking always with reference to ourselves; for every body has a self of their own, to which they attach as much importance as we to ours, and see all others' matters small in the comparison. The lady of rank has her castles and her ancestors—they are the foreground of her picture. There they stood when she came into being; and there they are still, in all the magnitude of near perspective; and, if her estimate of their real size be not corrected by experience and good sense, she expects that others will see them as large as she does. But that will not be so. The lady of wealth has gotten her houses and lands in the foreground. These are the larger features in her landscape; titles and the castles are seen at a smaller angle. Neither lady will admire the proportions of her neighbor's drawing, should they chance to discover themselves in each other's conversation. She, again—whether rich or poor—whose world is her own domesticity, sees nothing so prominent as the affairs of her nursery or her household; and perceives not that, in the eyes of others, her children are a set of diminutives, undistinguishable in the mass of humanity, in which that they ever existed, or that they cease to exist, is matter of equal indifference.

It is thus, that each one attributes to the objects around him, not their true and actual proportion, but a magnitude proportioned to their nearness to himself. We say not that he draws ill who does so: for, to each one, things are important, more or less, in proportion to his own interest in them. But hence is the mischief. We forget that every one has a self of his own; and that the constant setting forth of ours is, to others, preposterous, obtrusive, and ridiculous. The painter who draws a folio in the front of his picture, and a castle in the distance, properly draws the book the larger of the two: but he must be a fool, if he therefore thinks the folio is the larger, and expects every body else to think so too. Yet, nothing wiser are we, when we suffer ourselves to be perpetually pointing to ourselves, our affairs, and our possessions, as if they were as interesting to others as they are important to us.

GENTLENESS.

Nothing is so likely to conciliate the affections of the other sex, as a feeling that woman looks to them for support and guidance. In proportion as men are themselves superior, they are as accessible to this appeal. On the contrary, they never feel interested in one who seems disposed rather to offer than to ask assistance. There is, indeed, something unfeminine in independence. It is contrary to nature and, therefore, it offends. We do not like to see a woman affecting tremors, but still less do we like to see her acting the Amazon. A really sensible woman feels her dependence; she does what she can, but she is conscious of inferiority, and, therefore, grateful for support; she knows that she is the weaker vessel, and that, as such, she should receive honor.

In every thing, therefore, that women attempt, they should show their consciousness of dependence. If they are learners, let them evince a teachable spirit; if they give an opinion, let them do it in an unassuming manner. There is something so unpleasant in female self-sufficiency, that it not unfrequently deters, instead of persuading, and prevents the adoption of advice which the judgment even approves. Yet this is a fault into which women, of certain pretensions, are occasionally betrayed. Age, or experience, or superior endowment, entitles them, they imagine, to assume a higher place and a more independent tone. But their sex should ever teach them to be subordinate; and they should remember that influence is obtained, not by assumption, but by a delicate appeal to affection or principle. Women, in this respect, are something like children; the more they show their need of support, the more engaging they are.

The appropriate expression of dependence is gentleness. However endowed with superior talents a woman may be, without gentleness she cannot be agreeable. Gentleness ought to be the characteristic of the sex; and there is nothing that can compensate for the want of this feminine attraction.

Gentleness is, indeed, the talisman of woman. To interest the feelings is to her much easier than to convince the judgment; the heart is far more accessible to her influence than the head. She never gains so much as by concession; and is never so likely to overcome, as when she seems to yield.

Gentleness prepossesses at first sight; it insinuates itself into the vantage ground, and gains the best position by surprise. While a display of skill and strength calls forth a counter array, gentleness, at once, disarms opposition, and wins the day before it is contested.

SISTERLY VIRTUES.

Sisterly affection is as graceful in its developments to the eye of the beholder, as it is cheering to the heart where it resides. There are some who, though not deficient in its more important duties, are but too regardless of those lesser demonstrations of attachment, which are so soothing to the susceptible heart. Every delicate attention which tenderness prompts; every mark of politeness which refined society requires, ought to pervade the intercourse of brothers and sisters. It is a mistake that good manners are to be reserved for visitors, and that, in the family circle, negligence and coarseness may be indulged with impunity. Even nature's affections may be undermined or shaken by perseverance in an improper deportment, more than by lapses into error and folly. For the latter, repentance may atone, while the former check the flow of the heart's warm fountains, until they stagnate or become congealed.

I knew a father, himself a model of polished manners, who required of his large family to treat each other, at all times, with the same politeness that they felt was due to their most distinguished guest. Rudeness, neglect, or indifference were never tolerated in their circle. Respect to each other's opinion; a disposition to please and be pleased; care in dress, and courtesy of manner, were not considered thrown away, if bestowed on a brother or a sister. Every one of the group was instructed to bring amiable feelings and powers of entertainment to their own fire side. The result was happy. The brothers felt it an honor to wait upon their sisters, and the sisters a pleasure to do all in their power for the comfort and improvement of their brothers. This daily practice of every decorum, imparted to their manners an enduring grace, while the affections, which Heaven implanted, seemed to gather strength from the beauty of their interchange. I would not assert that fraternal or sisterly affection may not be deep and pervading without such an exterior, yet it is surely rendered more lovely by it; as the planets might pursue in darkness the order of their course, but it is their brilliance which reveals and embellishes it.

Every well-regulated family might be as a perpetual school. The younger members, witnessing the example of those whose excellence is more confirmed, will be led, by the principle of imitation, more effectually, than by the whole force of foreign precept. The custom of the older daughters, to assist in the education of their less advanced sisters, I rejoice to see, is becoming more common. It cannot be too highly applauded. What should prevent their assuming the systematic office of instructors, when circumstances are favorable to such an arrangement.

By what method can a daughter more fully evince her gratitude to her parents, than by aiding their children in the search of knowledge and of goodness. How amiable, how praiseworthy, is that disposition which prompts a young and beautiful creature to come forth as the ally of a mother, in that most overwhelming of all anxieties, so to train her little ones as to form at last an unbroken family in heaven. No better apprenticeship could be devised, and no firmer hostage given to God or man for its faithful performance.

HOME.

Where burns the lov'd hearth brightest,
    Cheering the social breast?
Where beats the fond heart lightest,
    Its humble hopes possess'd?
Where is the smile of sadness,
    Of meek-eyed patience born,
Worth more than those of gladness,
    Which mirth's bright cheek adorn?
Pleasure is marked by fleetness,
    To those who ever roam;
While grief itself has sweetness
    At home! dear home!

There blend the ties that strengthen
    Our hearts in hours of grief;
The silver links that lengthen
    Joy's visits when most brief;
There eyes, in all their splendor,
    Are vocal to the heart,
And glances, gay or tender,
    Fresh eloquence impart;
Then, dost thou sigh for pleasure?
    O! do not widely roam,
But seek that hidden treasure
    At home! dear home!

Does pure religion charm thee
    Far more than aught below?

Would'st thou that she should arm thee
Against the hour of woe?
Think not she dwelleth only
In temples built for prayer;
For home itself is lonely,
Unless her smiles be there;
The devotee may falter,
The bigot blindly roam,
If worshipless her altar
At home! dear home!

Love over it presideth,
With meek and watchful awe,
Its daily service guideth,
And shows its perfect law?
If there thy faith shall fail thee,
If there no shrine be found,
What can thy prayers avail thee
With kneeling crowds around?
Go! leave thy gift unoffered
Beneath religion's dome,
And be thy first fruits proffered
At home! dear home!

FIRESIDE INFLUENCE.

Is it not true that parents are the lawgivers of their children? Does not a mother's counsel—does not a father's example—cling to the memory, and haunt us through life? Do we not often find ourselves subject to habitual trains of thought? and, if we seek to discover the origin of these, are we not insensibly led back, by some beaten and familiar track, to the paternal threshold? Do we not often discover some home-chiseled grooves in our minds, into which the intellectual machinery seems to slide, as by a sort of necessity? Is it not, in short, a proverbial truth, that the controlling lessons of life are given beneath the parental roof? We know, indeed, that wayward passions spring up in early life, and, urging us to set authority at defiance, seek to obtain the mastery of the heart. But, though struggling for liberty and license, the child is shaped and molded by the parent. The stream that bursts from the fountain, and seems to rush forward headlong and self-willed, still turns hither and thither, according to the shape of its mother-earth over which it flows. If an obstacle is thrown across its path, it gathers strength, breaks away the barrier, and again bounds forward. It turns, and winds, and proceeds on its course, till it reaches its destiny in the sea. But, in all this, it has shaped its course and followed out its career, from babbling infancy at the fountain to its termination in the great reservoir of waters, according to the channel which its parent earth has provided. Such is the influence of a parent over his child. It has within itself a will, and at its bidding it goes forward, but the parent marks out its track. He may not stop its progress, but he may guide its course. He may not throw a dam across its path, and say to it, hitherto mayest thou go, and no farther; but he may turn it through safe, and gentle, and useful courses—or he may leave it to plunge over wild cataracts, or lose itself in some sandy desert, or collect its strength into a torrent, but to spread ruin and desolation along its borders.

The fireside, then, is a seminary of infinite importance: it is important, because it is universal, and because the education it bestows, being woven in with the woof of childhood, gives form and color to the whole texture of life. There are few who can receive the honors of a college, but all are graduates of the hearth. The learning of the university may fade from the recollection, its classic lore may molder in the halls of memory; but the simple lessons of home, enameled upon the heart of childhood, defy the rust of years, and outlive the more mature but less vivid pictures of after days. So deep, so lasting, indeed, are the impressions of early life, that we often see a man, in the imbecility of age, holding fresh in his recollection the events of childhood, while all the wide space between that and the present hour is a blasted and forgotten waste. You have perchance seen an old and half-obliterated portrait, and, in the attempt to have it cleaned and restored, may have seen it fade away, while a brighter and more perfect picture, painted beneath, is revealed to view. This portrait, first drawn upon the canvas, is no inapt illustration of youth; and, though it may be concealed by some after-design, still the original traits will shine through the outward picture, giving it tone while fresh, and surviving it in decay. Such is the fireside—the great institution furnished by Providence for the education of man.

PERSONAL APPEARANCE.
THE TEETH.

The prevalence of defective teeth in this country is the general subject of remark by foreigners; and whoever has traveled in Spain and Portugal is struck with the superior soundness and whiteness of teeth in those countries. Though not a cleanly people in other respects, they wash their teeth often, and, by means of toothpicks, carefully remove all substances from between them after meals. A little silver porcupine, with holes all over its back to insert toothpicks, is a common ornament on the dining tables of Spain and Portugal. The general use of them creates so large a demand, that students at Coimbra sometimes support themselves by whittling toothpicks, which are sold tied in small bunches like matches. They are made of willow, on account of its toughness and pliability. Toothpicks of metal are too hard, and are apt to injure the gums. There is the same objection, in a less degree, to quills. But willow toothpicks are preferable to all others; and they have the advantage of being the most cleanly, for they generally break in the using, and are thrown away. Few sights are more offensive to a person of any refinement than a toothpick that has been much used; it is, moreover, uncleanly, and therefore not healthy for the teeth. Food allowed to remain between the teeth, particularly animal food, is very destructive: it should be carefully removed after every meal, and the mouth thoroughly rinsed. This may seem to some like a great talk about a small matter; but these are simple precautions to take, and very slight trouble compared with the agony of aching teeth, or a breath so offensive that your best friend does not wish to sit near you. I can see no reason why a man's complexion should exclude him from the dining-table, but I do see a very good reason why he should be banished for not taking proper care of his teeth. A bad breath is such a detestable thing, that it might be a sufficient reason for not marrying a person of otherwise agreeable qualities. It is, moreover, perfectly inexcusable thus to transform oneself into a walking sepulchre. Nobody needs to have an offensive breath. A careful removal of substances from between the teeth, rinsing the mouth after meals, and a bit of charcoal held in the mouth, will always cure a bad breath. Charcoal, used as a dentifrice—that is, rubbed on in powder with a brush—is apt to injure the enamel; but a lump of it, held in the mouth, two or three times in a week, and slowly chewed, has a wonderful power to preserve the teeth and purify the breath. The action is purely chemical. It counteracts the acid arising from a disordered stomach, or food decaying about the gums; and it is the acid which destroys the teeth.

Every one knows that charcoal is an antiputrescent, and is used in boxing up animal or vegetable substances, to keep them from decay. Upon the same chemical principle, it tends to preserve the teeth and sweeten the breath. There is no danger from swallowing it; on the contrary, small quantities have a healthful effect on the inward system, particularly when the body is suffering from that class of complaints peculiarly incident to summer. It would not be wise to swallow that or any other gritty substance, in large quantities, or very frequently; but, once or twice a week, a little would be salutary, rather than otherwise. A bit of charcoal, as big as a cherry, merely held in the mouth a few hours, without chewing, has a good effect. At first, most persons dislike to chew it, but use soon renders it far from disagreeable. Those who are troubled with an offensive breath might chew it very often and swallow it but seldom. It is particularly important to clean and rinse the mouth thoroughly before going to bed; otherwise a great deal of the destructive acid will form during the night.

If these hints induce only one person to take better care of the teeth, I shall be more than rewarded for the trouble of writing. It is painful to see young persons losing their teeth merely for want of a few simple precautions; and one cannot enter stage or steam-car without finding the atmosphere polluted, and rendered absolutely unhealthy for the lungs to breathe, when a proper use of water and charcoal might render it as wholesome and pleasant as a breeze of Eden.

THE HAIR.

No part of the human frame offers a finer subject for the display of decorative taste and elegance than the hair:—the countenance, the contour of the head, and even the whole person, may be said to be greatly affected by its arrangement and dress. As the possession of fine hair is peculiarly prized, so is its loss proportionally felt.

Like every other portion of the human frame, the use of water to the hair is absolutely essential to its health, as it tends to relieve the secretions and open the pores of the skin. The frequency of the use of water, however, should be guided by circumstances. It may be set down as a regulating principle, that the stronger and more healthy the hair may be, the more water may be used with propriety; by the same rule, when the hair is weak and thin, it should not be washed more than once a-week. At such times, cold water alone should be used, when care should be taken to dry it well immediately after. Washing too often, dries up the requisite oily fluid that forms the nourishment of the hair.

Some judgment is necessary in the choice of brushes. Two are necessary: a penetrating and a polishing brush; the one composed of strong, and the other of fine hair. The penetrating brush (especially that used by ladies) should be made of elastic hairs, rather inclining to irregular lengths. The other should be made of firm, soft, silken hair, thickly studded. Unfortunately, however, we cannot but observe that penetrating brushes are often selected, so harsh and strong, that they fret the skin of the head, and injure the roots, instead of gently and gradually effecting the object for which they were intended.

Combs are merely used for the purpose of giving a form to the hair, and assisting in its decorative arrangement; to use them too often, is rather prejudicial than otherwise, as they injure the roots of the hair. Above all kinds, that of the small-toothed comb is the most injurious in this respect, as it not only inflames the tender skin, but, from the fineness of its teeth, splits and crushes the hairs in being passed through them. Persons must indeed be of very uncleanly habits, whose heads absolutely require the aid of this comb, as the brush alone sufficiently possesses the power of effectually cleaning the hair from scurf, dandriff, and dust, if constantly used.

To persons whose hair is in a declining state, the frequent and regular use of oil or bear's grease is often of much service, as it is calculated to assist in supplying that nourishment which is so necessary. No oil perhaps has ever acquired a greater celebrity than Rowland's Macassar; for this reason we cannot but recommend it to the notice of our readers.

One of the most pernicious methods of dressing the hair, at the expense of its health, is by curling. This not only dries up the moisture that circulates through the hairs, but the heat and compression thus used completely prevent proper circulation. When, however, the habit is persisted in, its ill effects may be much obviated by constantly brushing the hair well, and having it frequently cut, by which means the necessary circulation is kept up, and the roots invigorated.

THE HANDS.

"Why don't my hands look and feel as it would seem that the perfect Author of all things would have them?" How many a young man and woman have asked this question! and are troubled to know why it is that some persons have such bloodless hands, perfect nails, so free from hang-nails, as they are called, while their own hands look so much like duck's feet or bird's claws.

All sorts of cosmetics, the most penetrating oils, rubbing and scouring the hands, paring and scraping the nails, and cutting round the roots of the nails, are resorted to, in hopes of making their hands appear natural; but all avails nothing, and many a poor hand is made to perform all its manipulations incognito. About the piano, in the social party, in the house, and in the street, the hand—the most exquisite, or what should be the most beautiful and useful part of the human frame—is gloved. And why? Because it is not fit to be seen.

Now, reader, I am about to tell you of a positive cure. In the first place, never cut or scrape your finger-nails with a knife or scissors, except in paring them down to the end of the fingers. Secondly, use nothing but a good stiff nail-brush, fine soap, and water, and rub the nails and hands briskly with these every morning the year round. In the third place, I would have you know that surfeiting will invariably produce heavy, burning hands. An impure state of the blood will manifest itself in the hands sooner than in most other parts of the body. If you have bad hands, be assured that the quantity or quality, or both, of your diet is wrong.

If you try to profit by these suggestions, you will, before one year expires, be no longer ashamed of your hands.

DRESS.

There are some rules, which, being based on first principles, are of universal application. And one of these belongs to our present subject, viz: nothing can be truly beautiful which is not appropriate. Nature and the fine arts teach us this. All styles of dress, therefore, which impede the motions of the wearer—which do not sufficiently protect the person—which add unnecessarily to the heat of summer, or to the cold of winter—which do not suit the age or occupations of the wearer, or which indicate an expenditure unsuited to her means, are inappropriate, and, therefore, destitute of one of the essential elements of beauty. Propriety, or fitness, lies at the foundation of all good taste in dressing; and to this test should be brought a variety of particulars, too numerous to be mentioned, but which may be thus illustrated: The dress that would be very proper on occasion of a morning visit in a city, would be so out of place, if worn by the same person when making preserves or pastry, or when scrambling through the bushes in a country walk, that it would cease to look well. A simple calico gown and white apron would be so much more convenient and suitable, that the wearer would actually look better in them.

Some persons, also, toil early and late, and strain every nerve to procure an expensive garment, and think that once arrayed in it, they shall look as well as some richer neighbor, whose style of dress they wish to imitate. But they forget that, if it does not accord with their general style of living—if it is out of harmony with other things, it will so strike every body; and this want of fitness will prevent its looking well on them.

Let a true sense of propriety of the fitness of things regulate all your habits of living and dressing, and it will produce such a beautiful harmony and consistency of character, as to throw a charm around you that all may feel, though few may comprehend. Always consider well whether the articles of dress which you wish to purchase are suited to your age—your condition—your means—to the climate—to the particular use to which you mean to put them; and then let the principles of good taste keep you from the extremes of fashion; and regulate the form so as to combine utility and beauty, while the known rules of harmony in colors save you from shocking the eye of the artist by incongruous mixtures.

The character is much more shown in the style of dress that is worn every day, than in that which is designed for great occasions; and when I see a young girl come down to the family breakfast in an untidy wrapper, with her hair in papers, her feet slip-shod, and an old silk handkerchief round her neck, I know that she cannot be the neat, industrious, and refined person whom I should like for an inmate. I feel equally certain, too, that her chamber is not kept in neat order, and that she does not set a proper value upon time. However well a lady has appeared at a party, I would recommend to a young gentleman—before he makes up his mind as to her domestic qualities—to observe her appearance at the breakfast-table, when she expects to see only her own family; and, if it be such as I have just described, to beware how he prosecutes the acquaintance.

COMPRESSION OF THE LUNGS.

Few circumstances are more injurious to beauty than the constrained movement, suffused complexion, and labored respiration that betray tight-lacing. The play of intelligence, and varied emotion, which throw such a charm over the brow of youth, are impeded by whatever obstructs the flow of blood from the heart to its many organs. In Greece, where the elements of beauty and grace were earliest comprehended, and most happily illustrated, the fine symmetry of the form was left untortured.

But the influence of this habit on beauty is far less to be deprecated than its effects upon health. That pulmonary disease, affections of the heart, and insanity, are in its train, and that it leads some of our fairest and dearest to Fashion's shrine to die, is placed beyond a doubt by strong medical testimony.

Dr. Mussey, whose "Lectures on Intemperance" have so forcibly arrested the attention of the public, asserts that "greater numbers annually die among the female sex, in consequence of tight-lacing, than are destroyed among the other sex by the use of spirituous liquors in the same time." Is it possible that thousands of our own sex, in our own native land, lay, with their own hand, the foundation of diseases that destroy life!—and are willing, for fashion's sake, to commit suicide!

Dr. Todd, the late Principal of the Retreat for the Insane, in Connecticut, to whom science and philanthropy are indebted, adduces many instances of the fearful effects of obstructed circulation on the brain. Being requested by the instructress of a large female seminary to enforce on her pupils the evils of compression in dress, he said, with that eloquence of eye and soul, which none, who once felt their influence, can ever forget: "The whole course of your studies, my dear young ladies, conspires to impress you with reverence for antiquity. Especially do you turn to Greece for the purest models in the fine arts, and the loftiest precepts of philosophy. While sitting, as disciples, at the feet of her men of august minds, you may have sometimes doubted how to balance, or where to bestow your admiration. The acuteness of Aristotle—the purity of Plato—the calm, unrepented satisfaction of Socrates—the varied lore of Epicurus, and the lofty teachings of Zeno, have alternately attracted or absorbed your attention. Permit me to suppose, that the high-toned ethics of the Stoics

, and their elevation of mind, which could teach its frail companion, the body, the proud lesson of insensibility to pain, have won your peculiar complaisance. Yet, while meting out to them the full measure of your applause, have you ever recollected that modern times—that your own country came in competition for a share of fame? Has it occurred to you that your own sex—even the most delicate and tender part of it—exceeded the ancient Stoics in the voluntary infliction of pain, and extinction of pity? Yes; some of the timid and beautiful members of this seminary may enter the lists with Zeno, Cleanthus, and Chrysippus, and cherish no slight hope of victory. I trust to prove to you that the ancient and sublime Stoics were very tyros in comparison with many a lady of our own times. In degree of suffering, extent of endurance, and in perfection of concealment, they must yield the palm. I do assure you, that its most illustrious masters—fruitful as they were in tests to try the body—never invented, imagined, nor would have been able to sustain that torture of tight-lacing which the modern belle steadily inflicts without shrinking, and bears without repining sometimes to her very grave. True, they might sometimes have broken a bone, or plucked out an eye, and been silent; but they never grappled iron and whalebone into the very nerves and life-blood of their system. They might possibly have passed a dagger too deeply into the heart, and died; but they never drew a ligature of suffocation around it, and expected to live! They never tied up the mouths of the millions of air-vessels in the lungs, and then taxed them to the full measure of action and respiration. Even Pharaoh only demanded bricks without straw for a short time; but the fashionable lady asks to live without breathing for many years!

"The ancient Stoics taught that the nearest approach to apathy was the perfection of their doctrine. They prudently rested in utter indifference; they did not attempt to go beyond it; they did not claim absolute denial of all suffering; still less did they enjoin to persist and rejoice in it, even to the 'dividing asunder of soul and body.' In this, too, you will perceive the tight-laced lady taking a flight beyond the sublime philosopher. She will not admit that she feels the slightest inconvenience. Though she has fairly won laurels to which no Stoic dared aspire, yet she studiously disclaims the distinction which she faced death to earn—yea, denies that she has either part of lot in the matter; surpassing in modesty, as well as in desert, all that antiquity can boast or history record."

We quote the following from Miss Sedgwick: "One word as to these small waists: Symmetry is essential to beauty of form. A waist disproportionately small is a deformity to an instructed eye. Women must have received their notions of small waists from ignorant dress-makers. If young ladies could hear the remarks made on these small waists by men generally, and especially men of taste, they would never again show themselves till they had loosened their corset-laces and enlarged their belts."

<hr />

LETTER-WRITING.

It sometimes happens that, in fashionable penmanship, the circumstance that it is to be deciphered seems to have been forgotten. «To read so as not to be understood, and to write so as not to be read, are among the minor immoralities," says the excellent Mrs. Hannah More . Elegant chirography, and a clear epistolary style, are accomplishments which every educated female should possess. Their indispensable requisites are, neatness, the power of being easily perused, orthographical and grammatical correctness. Defects in either of these particulars, are scarcely pardonable. The hand-writing is considered by many, one of the talismans of character. Whether this test may be depended on or not, the fact that letters travel farther than the sound of the voice, or the sight of the countenance can follow, renders it desirable that they should convey no incorrect or unfavorable impression. The lesser niceties of folding, sealing, and superscription, are not beneath the notice of a lady.

Letter-writing is a subject of so varied and extensive a nature, that it can scarcely be reduced to rules or taught by precept; but some instructions respecting it may afford assistance in avoiding error, and obtaining a degree of excellence in this most important exercise.

When you write a letter to any person, express the same sentiments and use the same language as you would do if you were conversing with him. "Write eloquently," says Mr. Gray, "that is, from your heart, in such expressions as that will furnish."

Before you begin a letter, especially when it is on any occasion of importance, weigh well in your own mind the design and purport of it; and consider very attentively what sentiments are most proper for you to express, and your correspondent to read.

To assist invention and promote order, it may, as some writers on epistolary composition recommend, occasionally be of use to make, in the mind, a division of a letter into three parts, the beginning, middle, and end; or, in other words, the exordium or introduction, the narration or proposition, and the conclusion. The exordium, or introduction, should be employed, not indeed with the formality of rhetoric, but with the ease of genuine politeness and benevolence, in conciliating favor and attention; the narration or proposition, in stating the business with clearness and precision; the conclusion, in confirming what has been premised, in making apologies where any are necessary, and in cordial expressions of respect, esteem, or affection.

Scrupulously adhere to the rules of grammar. Select and apply all your words with a strict regard to their proper signification, and whenever you have any doubts respecting the correctness or propriety of them, consult a dictionary or some good living authority. Avoid, with particular care, all errors in orthography, in punctuation, and in the arrangement of words and phrases.

Dashes, underlinings, and interlineations, are much used by unskillful and careless writers, merely as substitutes for proper punctuation, and a correct, regular mode of expression. The frequent recurrence of them greatly defaces a letter, and is equally inconsistent with neatness of appearance and regularity of composition. All occasion for interlineations may usually be superseded by a little previous thought and attention. Dashes are proper only when the sense evidently requires a greater pause than the common stops designate. And, in a well-constructed sentence, to underline a word is wholly useless, except on some very particular occasion we wish to attract peculiar attention to it, or to give it an uncommon degree of importance or emphasis.

Postscripts have a very awkward appearance, and they generally indicate thoughtlessness and inattention. To make use of them in order to convey assurances of respect to the person to whom you write, or to those who are intimately connected with him, is particularly improper; it seems to imply that the sentiments you express are so slightly impressed upon your mind, that you had almost forgotten them or thought them scarcely worth mentioning.

MUSIC.

This accomplishment, so popular at the present time, is a source of surpassing delight to many minds. From its power to soothe the feelings and modify the passions, it seems desirable to understand it, if it does not involve too great expense of time. Vocal music is an accomplishment within the reach of most persons. "I have a piano within myself," said a little girl, "and I can play on that, if I have no other."

An excellent clergyman, possessing much knowledge of human nature, instructed his large family of daughters in the theory and practice of music. They were all observed to be exceedingly amiable and happy. A friend inquired if there was any secret in his mode of education. He replied, "When any thing disturbs their temper, I say to them sing; and, if I hear them speaking against any person, I call them to sing to me, and so they have sung away all causes of discontent, and every disposition to scandal." Such a use of this accomplishment might serve to fit a family for the company of angels and the clime of praise. Young voices around the domestic altar, breathing sacred music at the hour of morning and evening devotions, are a sweet and touching accompaniment.

Instrumental music, being more expensive in its attainment, both of money and time, and its indifferent performance giving pain to those of refined sensibility, seems scarcely desirable to be cultivated, unless the impulse of native taste prompts or justifies the labor. The spirited pen of Miss Martineau, in her "Five First Years of Youth," has sketched a pleasing description of a young lady, possessing a strong predilection for music. "She sang much and often, not that she had any particular aim at being very accomplished, but because she loved it, or, as she said, because she could not help it. She sang to Nurse Rickham's children; she sang as she went up and down stairs; she sang when she was glad, and when she was sorry; when her father was at home, because he liked it; and when he was out, because he could not be disturbed by it. In the woods, at noonday, she sang like a bird, that a bird might answer her; and, if she awoke in the dark night, the feeling of solemn music came over her, with which she dared not break the silence."

Where such a taste exists, there is no doubt that opportunities for its improvement should be gladly accepted. Where there is no taste, it seems cause of regret, when time, perhaps health, are sacrificed to the accomplishment. Even where a tolerable performance of instrumental music might probably be attained, without the prompting of decided taste, there may be danger of absorbing too much of time and attention from those employments which a female ought to understand and will be expected to discharge, and which are in reality of far greater importance.

FLOWERS.

"Who does not love a flower
 Its hues are taken from the light
Which summer's suns fling, pure and bright,
 In scatter'd and prismatic hues,
That smile and shine in drooping dews;
 Its fragrance from the sweetest air—
Its form from all that's light and fair—
 Who does not love a flower?"

In the two great floral kingdoms of nature, the botanical and the human, if we must yield the palm to that which is alike transcendent in the beauty of form and motion, and in the higher attributes of intelligence, innocence, and rural perfection, yet it can be no derogation to admire, with a rapture bordering upon enthusiasm, the splendid products of the garden; and especially when their beauties are combined and arranged with an exquisite and refined taste. What is the heart made of which can find no sentiment in flowers! In the dahlia, for example, we see what can be done by human skill and art, in educating and training a simple and despised plant, scarcely thought worthy of cultivation, to the highest rank of gayety and glory in the aristocracy of flowers. We may learn, from such success, a lesson of encouragement, in the education and training of flowers, of an infinitely higher value and perfection.

The vast creation of God—the centre and source of good—is every where radiant with beauty. From the shell that lies buried in the depths of the ocean, to the twinkling star that floats in the more profound depths of the firma-ment—through all the forms of material and animated existence, beauty, beau-ty, beauty prevails! In the floral kingdom, it appears in an infinite variety—in an unstinted and even a richer profusion than in other departments of nature. While these contributions are thrown out so lavishly at our feet, and a taste for flowers seems almost an instinct of nature, and is one of the most innocent and refined sentiments which we can cultivate, let us indulge and gratify it to the utmost extent, whenever leisure, opportunity, and fortune give us the means. There is no danger of an excess, under those reasonable restrictions which all our sentiments demand.

"But," says some cynical objector, "flowers are only to please the eye." And why should not the eye be pleased? What sense may be more innocently gratified? They are among the most simple and cheapest luxuries in which we ever indulge.

The taste for flowers—every where increasing among us—is an omen of good. Let us adorn our parlors, door-ways, yards, and road-sides with trees, and shrubs, and flowers. What a delight do they give to the passer-by! What favorable impressions do they, at once, excite towards those who cultivate them for their own gratification, and find, after all, their chief pleasure in the grat-ification which they afford to others! What an affecting charm—associated as it is with some of the best sentiments of our nature—do they give to the sad dwelling-places of the departed and beloved!

TIME.

"I saw the leaves gliding down a brook;
 Swift the brook ran, and bright the sun burned:
The sere and the verdant, the same course they took—
 And sped gayly and fast—but they never returned.
And I thought how the years of a man pass away—
 Threescore and ten—and then where are they?"

"Threescore years and ten," thought I to myself, as I walked, one rainy morning, as a sailor walks the quarter-deck, up and down a short alcove, extending before the windows of a modern house. It was one of those days in June, in which our summer-hopes take umbrage at what we call unseasonable weather, though no season was ever known to pass without them. Unlike the rapid and delightful showers of warmer days, suddenly succeeding to the sunshine, when the parched vegetables and arid earth seize with avidity, and imbibe the moisture ere it becomes unpleasant to our feelings, there had fallen a drizzling rain throughout the night; the saturated soil returned to the atmosphere the humidity it could no longer absorb; and there it hung, in chilling thickness, between rain and fog. The birds did not sing, and the flowers did not open, for the cold drop was on their cheek, and no sunbeam was there to expand them. Nature itself wore the garb of sadness, and man's too dependent spirits were ready to assume it—those, at least, that were not so happy as to find means of forgetting it. Such was the case with my unfortunate self.

I had descended to the breakfast-room, at the usual hour, but no one appeared; I looked for a book, but found none but an almanac. The books were kept in the library—beyond all dispute their proper place, had I not been in a humor to think otherwise. The house was too hot, and the external air was too cold; and I was fain to betake myself to that last resort of the absolutely idle—a mechanical movement of the body up and down a given space. And, from the alcove where I walked, I heard the ticking of the timepiece; and, as I passed the window, I saw the hands advance; every time I had returned, they had gone a little farther. "Threescore years and ten," said I to myself; "and a third or fourth of it is nature's claim for indispensable repose—and many a day consumed on the bed of sickness—and many a year by the infirmities of age—and some part of all necessarily sacrificed to the recruiting of the health by exercise. And what do we with the rest?" Nothing answered me but the ticking of the clock, of which the hands were traversing between eight and nine. They had nearly met, at the appointed hour, when the party began to assemble within; and each one commenced, for aught I could discover, the functions of the day, for neither their appearance nor their remarks gave any intimation that they had been previously employed. One, indeed, declared the weather made her so idle she had scarcely found strength to dress herself; another confessed he had passed an additional hour in bed, because the day promised him so little to do up. One by one, as they dropped in, the seats at the breakfast-table were filled; and, as a single newspaper was all the apparent means of mental occupation, I anticipated some interesting conversation.

I waited and I watched. One ran the point of his fork into the table-cloth; another balanced her spoon on the tea-cup; a third told backwards and forwards the rings on her fingers, as duly as a friar tells his beads. As such actions sometimes are the symptoms of mental occupation, I began to anticipate the brilliant results of so much thinking. I cried, hem! in hopes to rouse them to expression—and not quite unsuccessfully: for one remarked, it was a wretched day; another wished it was fine; and a third hoped it shortly would be so. Meantime, the index of the clock went round; it was gaining close upon ten before all had withdrawn from the table. My eye followed one to the window-place; where, with her back to the wall, and her eyes fixed without, she passed a full half hour in gazing at the prospect without, or wishing, perhaps, the mist did not prevent her seeing it. A very young lady was so busy in pulling the dead leaves from a geranium, and crumbling them in her fingers, I could not doubt but some important purpose was in the task. A third resumed the newspaper he had read for a whole hour before, and betook himself, at last, to the advertisements. A fourth repaired to the alcove, gathered some flowers, picked them to pieces, threw them away again, and returned. "Cease thy prating, thou never-resting time-piece!" said I to myself, "for no one heeds thy tale. What is it to us that each one of thy tickings cuts a link from our brief chain of life? Time is the gift of Heaven, but man has no use for it!"

I had scarcely thought out the melancholy reflection, when a young lady entered with an elegant work-box, red without and blue within, and filled with manifold conveniences for the pursuance of her art. Glad was I most truly at the sight. By the use of the needle, the naked may be clothed; ingenuity may economize her means, and have more to spare for those who need it; invention may multiply the ways of honest subsistence, and direct the ignorant to the use of them. Most glad was I, therefore, that the signal of industry drew more than one wanderer to the same pursuit, though not till much time had been consumed in going in and out, and up and down, in search of the materials. All were found at last; the party worked, and I, as usual, listened. "I think this trimming," said one, "will repay me for my trouble, though it has cost me three months' work already, and it will be three months more before it is finished." "Indeed!" rejoined her friend; "I wish I were half as industrious; but I have been working six weeks at this handkerchief, and have not had time to finish it: now the fashion is passed, and I shall not go on." "How beautifully you are weaving that necklace! Is it not very tedious?" "Yes, almost endless; but I delight in the work, otherwise I should not do it, for the beads cost almost as much as I could buy it for." "I should like to begin one this morning," interposed a fourth, "but the milliner has sent home my bonnet so ill-trimmed, it will take me all the day to alter it: the bow is on the wrong side, and the trimming on the edge is too broad. It is very tiresome to spend all one's life in altering things we pay so much for." "I wish," said a little girl at the end of the table, "that I might work some trimmings for my frock, but I am obliged to do this plain work first. The poor lame girl in the village, who is almost starving, would do it for me for a shilling, but I must save my allowance this week to buy a French trinket I have taken a fancy to." "Poor thing! she is much to be pitied," said the lady of the trimming; "if I had time, I would make her some clothes."

And so they worked, and so they talked, till I and the time-piece had counted many an hour which they took no account of, when one of them yawned, and said, "How tedious are these wet days; it is really impossible to spin out one's time without a walk." "I am surprised you find it so," rejoined the lady of the beads; "I can rarely take time for walking, though keeping the house makes me miserably languid."

And so the morning passed. It was nearly two o'clock, and the company dispersed to their apartments. I pretend not to know what they did there; but each one returned between three and four in an altered dress. And then half an hour elapsed, in which, as I understood from their impatience, they were waiting for dinner; each in turn complaining of the waste of time occasioned by its delay, and the little use it would be to go about any thing when it was so near. And as soon as dinner was over, they began to wait for tea with exactly the same complainings. And the tea came, and, cheered by the vivifying draught, one did repair to the instrument, and began a tune; one did take up a pencil, and prepare to draw; and one almost opened a book. But, alas! the shades of night were growing fast:—ten minutes had scarcely elapsed, before each one resigned her occupation, with a murmur at the darkness of the weather; and, though some persons suggested that there were such things as lamps and candles, it was agreed to be a pity to have lights so early in the midst of summer, and so another half hour escaped.

The lights, when they came, would have failed to relumine an expectation in my bosom, had not their beams disclosed the forms of various books, which one and another had brought in for the evening's amusement. Again I watched and again I listened. "I wish I had something to do, mamma," said the little girl. "Why do you not take a book, and read?" rejoined her mother. "My books are all up stairs," she replied; "and it is so near bedtime, it is not worth while to bring them down." "This is the best novel I ever read," said a lady, somewhat older, turning the leaves over so very fast, that those who are not used to this manner of reading, might suppose she found nothing in it worthy of attention. "I dare say it is," said another, whose eyes had been fixed for half an hour on the same page of Wordsworth's Poems; "but I have no time to read novels." "I wish I had time to read any thing," said a third, whom I had observed already to have been perusing attentively the title-page of every book on the table, publisher's name, date, and all; while a fourth was too intensely engaged in studying the blue cover of a magazine, to make any remark whatever.

And now I was much amused to perceive with what frequency eyes were turned upon the dial-plate, through all the day so little regarded. Watches were drawn out, compared, and pronounced too slow. With some difficulty, one was found that had outrun its fellows, and, determined to be right, gave permission to the company to disperse, little more than twelve hours from the time of their assembling, to recover, as I supposed, during the other twelve, dressing and undressing included, the effect of their mental and bodily exertions.

"So!" I exclaimed, as soon as I found myself alone, "twelve times round yonder dial-plate those little hands have stolen, and twelve times more they may now go round unheeded. They who are gone to rest, have a day less to live, and record has been made in heaven of that day's use. Will He who gave, ask no reckoning for his gifts? The time, the thoughts, the talents; the improvement we might have made, and made not; the good we might have done, and did not; the health, and strength, and intellect, that may not be our's to-morrow, and have not been used to-day; will not conscience whisper of it ere they sleep to-night? The days of man were shortened upon earth by reason of the wickedness the Creator saw. Threescore years and ten are now his portion, and often not half the number. They pause not; they loiter not: the hours strike on, and they may even go, for it seems they are all too much."

The young, with minds as yet unstored, full of error, full of ignorance in all that it behooves them most to know, unfit alike as yet for earth or heaven—the old, whose sum of life is almost told, and but a brief space remaining to repair their mistakes and redeem the time they have lost—the simple and ungift-ed, who, having from nature but little, need the more assiduity to fulfill their measure of usefulness, and make that little do the most it may—the clever and highly talented, who have an almost appalling account to render for the much received—they all have time to waste. But let them remember, time is not their own; not a moment of it; but is the grant of Heaven; and Heaven gives nothing without a purpose and an end. Every hour that is wasted, fails of that purpose; and in so far as it is wasted or ill-spent, the gift of Heaven is misused, and the misuse is to be answered for. Methinks I would be allowed to whisper nightly in the ears of my young friends as they lie down to rest, "How many minutes have you lost to-day, that might have been employed in your own improvement, in our Maker's service, or for your fellow-creature's good?"

NOVEL-READING.

Novel-reading produces a morbid appetite for excitement. The object of the novelist, generally, is to produce the highest possible degree of excitement, both of the mind and the passions. The object is very similar to that of intoxicating liquors on the body: hence, the confirmed novel-reader becomes a kind of literary inebriate, to whom the things of entity have no attractions, and whose thirst cannot be slaked, even with the water of life. And as intoxication enfeebles the body, and engenders indolent habits, so this unnatural stimulus enfeebles the intellectual powers, induces mental indolence, and unfits the mind for vigorous efforts. Nothing less stimulating than its accustomed aliment can rouse such a mind to action, or call forth its energies; and then, being under the influence of mental intoxication, which dethrones reason and destroys the power of self-control, they are always misdirected.

It also promotes a sickly sensibility. Dr. Brigham , speaking of the too powerful excitement of the female mind, says: "In them the nervous system naturally predominates. They are endowed with quicker sensibility and far more active imagination than men. Their emotions are more intense, and their senses alive to more delicate impressions. They therefore require great attention, lest this exquisite sensibility—which, when properly and naturally developed, constitutes the greatest excellence of woman—should either become excessive by too strong excitement, or suppressed by misdirected education." Novel-reading produces just the kind of excitement calculated to develop this excessive and diseased sensibility; and the effect is, to fill the mind with imaginary fears, and produce excessive alarm and agitation at the prospect of danger, the sight of distress, or the presence of unpleasant objects; while no place is found for the exercise of genuine sympathy for real objects of compassion. That sensibility which weeps over imaginary woes of imaginary beings, calls forth but imaginary sympathy. It is too refined to be excited by the vulgar objects of compassion presented in real life, or too excitable to be of any avail in the relief of real distress. It may faint at the sight of blood, but it will shrink back from binding up the wound. If you wish to become weak-headed, nervous, and good for nothing, read novels. I have seen an account of a young lady, who had become so nervous and excitable, in consequence of reading novels, that her head would be turned by the least appearance of danger, real or imaginary. As she was riding in a carriage over a bridge, in company with her mother and sister, she became frightened at some fancied danger, caught hold of the reins, and backed the carriage off the bridge, down a precipice, dashing them to pieces.

This excessive sensibility renders its possessor exquisitely alive to all those influences which are unfriendly to human happiness, while it diminishes the power of endurance. Extreme sensibility, especially in a female, is a great misfortune, rendering the ills of life insupportable. Great care should therefore be taken that, while genuine sensibility is cherished, its extremes should be avoided, and the mind fortified by strengthening the higher powers.

Novel-reading strengthens the passions, weakens the virtues, and diminishes the power of self-control. Multitudes may date their ruin from the commencement of this kind of reading; and many more, who have been rescued from the snare, will regret, to the end of their days, its influence in the early formation of their character.

It is, too, a great waste of time. Few will pretend that they read novels with any higher end in view than mere amusement; while, by the strong excitement they produce, they impose a heavier tax on both mind and body than any other species of mental effort. If any thing valuable is to be derived from them, it can be obtained with far less expense of time, and with safety to the morals, from other sources. No Christian, who feels the obligation of "redeeming the time, because the days are evil," will fail to feel the force of this remark. We have no more right to squander our time and waste our energies in frivolous pursuits, than we have to waste our money in extravagant expenditures. We are as much the stewards of God in respect to the one as the other.

FEMALE ROMANCE.

Most women are inclined to be romantic. This tendency is not confined to the young or to the beautiful, to the intellectual or to the refined. Every woman, capable of strong feeling, is susceptible of romance; and, though its degree may depend on external circumstances, or education, or station, or excitement, it generally exists, and requires only a stimulus for its development.

Romance indeed contributes much to the charm of the female character. Without some degree of it, no woman can be interesting; and, though its excess is a weakness, and one which receives but little indulgence, there is nothing truly generous and disinterested which does not imply its existence. It is that poetry of sentiment which imparts to character or incident something of the beautiful or the sublime; which elevates us to a higher sphere; which gives an ardor to affection, a life to thought, a glow to imagination; and which lends so warm and sunny a hue to the portraiture of life, that it ceases to appear the vulgar, and cold, and dull, and monotonous reality, which common sense alone would make it.

But it is this opposition, between romance and sobriety, that excites so strong a prejudice against the former: it is associated, in the minds of many, with folly alone. A romantic, silly girl, is the object of their contempt; and they so recoil from this personification of sentiment, that their chief object seems to be to divest themselves altogether of its delusion. Life is to them a mere calculation; expediency is their maxim; propriety their rule; profit, ease, or comfort their aim; and they have at least this advantage, that while minds of higher tone and hearts of superior sensibility are often harassed and wounded, and even withered, in their passage through life, they proceed in their less adventurous career, neither chilled by the coldness, nor sickened by the meanness, nor disappointed by the selfishness of the world. They virtually admit, though they often theoretically deny, the baseness of human nature; and, strangers to disinterestedness themselves, they do not expect to meet with it in others. They are content with a low degree of enjoyment, and are thus exempted from much poignant suffering; and it is only when the casualties of life interfere with their individual ease, that we can perceive that they are not altogether insensible.

A good deal of this phlegmatic disposition exists in many who are capable of higher feeling. Such persons are so afraid of sensibility, that they repress in themselves every thing that savors of it; and, though we may occasionally detect it in the mounting flush, or in the glistening tear, or in the half-stifled sigh, it is in vain that we endeavor to elicit any more explicit avowal. They are ashamed even of what they do betray; and one would imagine that the imputation of sensibility were almost a reflection on their character. They must not feel, or, at least, they must not allow that they feel; for feeling has led so many persons wrong, that decorum can be preserved, they think, only by indifference. And they end in being really as callous as they wish to appear, and stifle emotion so successfully, that at length it ceases to give them uneasiness.

Such is often the case with many who pass through life with great decorum; and though women have naturally more sensibility than the other sex, they, too, sometimes consider its indulgence altogether wrong. Yet, if its excess is foolish, it is surely a mistake to attempt to suppress it altogether; for such attempt will either produce a dangerous revulsion, or, if successful, will spoil the character. One would rather almost that a woman were ever so romantic, than that she always thought, and felt, and spoke by rule; and should deem it preferable that her sensibility brought upon her occasional distress, than that she always calculated the degree of her feeling.

Life has its romance, and to this it owes much of its charm. It is not that every woman is a heroine and every individual history a novel; but there are scenes and incidents in real life so peculiar, and so poetic, that we need not be indebted to fiction for the development of romance. Christians will trace such scenes and incidents immediately to Providence, and they do so with affectionate and confiding hearts; and the more affecting or remarkable these may be, the more clearly do they recognize the Divine interference. They regard them as remembrances of Heaven, to recall to them their connection with it, and remind them that whatever there may be to interest or excite their feelings here, there is infinitely more to affect and warm their hearts in the glorious prospects beyond.

It is natural that women should be very susceptible to such impressions; that they should view life with almost a poetic eye; and that they should be peculiarly sensitive to its vicissitudes. And though a Quixotic quest after adventures is as silly as it is vain, and to invest every trifle with importance, or to see something marvelous in every incident, is equally absurd; there is no reason why the imagination should not grasp whatever is picturesque, and the mind dwell upon whatever is impressive, and the heart warm with whatever is affecting, in the changes and the chances of our pilgrimage. There is indeed a great deal of what is mean and low in all that is connected with this world; quite enough to sully the most glowing picture; but let us sometimes view life with its golden tints; let us sometimes taste its ambrosial dews; let us sometimes breathe its more ethereal atmosphere; and let us do so, not as satisfied with any thing it can afford—not as entranced by any of its illusions—but as those who catch, even in this dull mirror, a shadowy delineation of a brighter world, and who pant for what is pure, celestial, and eternal. This is surely better than clipping the wings of imagination, or restraining the impulses of feeling, or reducing all our joys and sorrows to mere matters of calculation or of sense.

They are indeed to be pitied who are in the opposite extreme—whose happiness or misery is entirely ideal; but we have within us such a capacity for both, independent of all outward circumstances, and such a power of extracting either from every circumstance, that it is surely more wise to discipline such a faculty, than to disallow its influence.

Youth is of course the season for romance. Its buoyant spirit must soar till weighed down by earthly care. It is in youth that the feelings are warm and the fancy fresh, and that there has been no blight to chill the one or to wither the other. And it is in youth that hope lends its cheering ray, and love its genial influence; that our friends smile upon us, our companions do not cross us, and our parents are still at hand to cherish us in their bosoms, and sympathize in all our young and ardent feelings. It is then that the world seems so fair, and our fellow-beings so kind, that we charge with spleen any who would prepare us for disappointment, and accuse those of misanthropy who would warn our too-confiding hearts. And though, in maturer life, we may smile at the romance of youth, and lament, perhaps, its aberrations, yet we shall not regret the depth of our young emotions, the disinterestedness of our young affections, and that enthusiasm of purpose, which, alas! we soon grow too wise to cherish.

BEHAVIOR TO GENTLEMEN.

What a pity it is that the thousandth chance of a gentleman's becoming your lover should deprive you of the pleasure of a free, unembarrassed, intellectual intercourse with all the single men of your acquaintance! Yet, such is too commonly the case with young ladies who have read a great many novels and romances, and whose heads are always running on love and lovers.

Where, as in this country, there is a fair chance of every woman's being married who wishes it, the more things are left to their natural course the better. Where girls are brought up to be good daughters and sisters, to consider the development of their own intellectual and moral natures as the great business of life, and to view matrimony as a good, only when it comes unsought, and marked by such a fitness of things, inward and outward, as shows it to be one of the appointments of God, they will fully enjoy their years of single life, free from all anxiety about being established, and will generally be the first sought in marriage by the wise and good of the other sex; whereas those who are brought up to think the great business of life is to get married, and who spend their lives in plans and manoeuvres to bring it about, are the very ones who remain single, or, what is worse, make unhappy matches.

Very young girls are apt to suppose, from what they observe in older ones, that there is some peculiar manner to be put on in talking to gentlemen, and not knowing exactly what it is, they are embarrassed and reserved; others observe certain airs and looks, used by their elders in this intercourse, and try to imitate them as a necessary part of company behavior, and so become affected, and lose that first of charms—simplicity, naturalness. To such I would say, your companions are in error; it requires no peculiar manner, nothing to be put on, in order to converse with gentlemen any more than with ladies; and the more pure and elevated your sentiments are, and the better cultivated your intellect is, the easier will you find it to converse pleasantly with all. If, however, you happen to have no facility in expressing yourself, and you find it very difficult to converse with persons whom you do not know well, you can still be an intelligent and agreeable listener, and you can show by your ready smile of sympathy that you would be sociable if you could. There is no reason in the world why any one, who is not unhappy, should sit in the midst of gay companions with a face so solemn and unmoved, that she should seem not to belong to the company; that she should look so glum and forbidding that strangers should feel repulsed, and her best friends disappointed. If you cannot look entertained and pleasant, you had better stay away, for politeness requires some expression of sympathy in the countenance, as much as a civil answer on the tongue.

Never condescend to use any little arts or manœuvres to secure a pleasant beau at a party, or during an excursion; remember that a woman must always wait to be chosen, and "not unsought be won," even for an hour. When you are so fortunate as to be attended by the most agreeable gentleman present, do not make any effort to keep him entirely to yourself; that flatters him too much, and exposes you to be joked about.

How strange a thing it is, in the constitution of English and American society, that the subject, of all others the most important and the most delicate, should be that on which every body is most given to joke and banter their friends! Much mischief has been done by this coarse interference of the world, in what ought to be the most private and sacred of our earthly concerns; and every refined, delicate, and high-minded girl should set her face against it, and, by scrupulously refraining from such jokes herself, give no one a right to indulge in them at her expense.

As soon as young ladies go into general society, they are liable to receive attentions that indicate a particular regard, and, long before they are really old enough to form any such ties, they often receive matrimonial overtures; it is therefore highly necessary to know how to treat them. The offer of a man's heart and hand is the greatest compliment he can pay you, and, however undesirable to you those gifts may be, they should be courteously and kindly declined; and since a refusal is, to most men, not only a disappointment, but a mortification, it should always be prevented, if possible. Men have various ways of cherishing and declaring their attachment; those who indicate the bias of their feelings in many intelligible ways, before they make a direct offer, can generally be spared the pain of a refusal. If you do not mean to accept a gentleman who is paying you very marked attentions, you should avoid receiving him whenever you can; you should not allow him to escort you; you should show your displeasure when joked about him; and, if sounded by a mutual friend, let your want of reciprocal feelings be very apparent.

You may, however, be taken entirely by surprise, because there are men who are so secret in these matters that they do not let even the object of their affections suspect their preference, until they suddenly declare themselves lovers and suitors. In such a case as that, you will need all your presence of mind, or the hesitation produced by surprise may give rise to false hopes. If you have any doubt upon the matter, you may fairly ask time to consider of it, on the grounds of your never having thought of the gentleman in the light of a lover before; but, if you are resolved against the suit, endeavor to make your answer so decided as to finish the affair at once. Inexperienced girls sometimes feel so much the pain they are inflicting, that they use phrases which feed a lover's hopes; but this is mistaken tenderness; your answer should be as decided as it is courteous.

Whenever an offer is made in writing, you should reply to it as soon as possible; and, having in this case none of the embarrassment of a personal interview, you can make such a careful selection of words as will best convey your meaning. If the person is estimable, you should express your sense of his merit, and your gratitude for his preference, in strong terms; and put your refusal of his hand on the score of your not feeling for him that peculiar preference necessary to the union he seeks. This makes a refusal as little painful as possible, and soothes the feelings you are obliged to wound. The gentleman's letter should be returned in your reply, and your lips should be closed upon the subject for ever afterwards. It is his secret, and you have no right to tell it to any one; but, if your parents are your confidential friends on all other occasions, he will not blame you for telling them.

Never think the less of a man because he has been refused, even if it be by a lady whom you do not highly value. It is nothing to his disadvantage. In exercising their prerogative of making the first advances, the wisest will occasionally make great mistakes, and the best will often be drawn into an affair of this sort against their better judgment, and both are but too happy if they escape with only the pain of being refused. So far from its being any reason for not accepting a wise and good man when he offers himself to you, it should only increase your thankfulness to the overruling providence of God, which reserved him for you, through whose instrumentality he is still free to choose.

There is no sure remedy for disappointed affection but vital religion; that giving of the heart to God which enables a disciple to say, "Whom have I in heaven but Thee, and there is none on earth that I desire in comparison of Thee." The cure for a wounded heart, which piety affords, is so complete, that it makes it possible for the tenderest and most constant natures to love again. When a character is thus disciplined and matured, its sympathies will be called forth only by superior minds; and, if a kindred spirit presents itself as a partner for life, and is accepted, the union is likely to be such as to make the lady rejoice that her former predilection was overruled.

MARRIAGE.

Some young persons indulge a fastidiousness of feeling in relation to this subject, as though it were indelicate to speak of it. Others make it the principal subject of their thoughts and conversation; yet they seem to think it must never be mentioned but in jest. Both these extremes should be avoided. Marriage is an ordinance of God, and therefore a proper subject of thought and discussion, with reference to personal duty. It is a matter of great importance, having a direct bearing upon the glory of God and the happiness of individuals. It should, therefore, never be approached with levity. But, as it requires no more attention than what is necessary in order to understand present duty, it would be foolish to make it a subject of constant thought, and silly to make it a common topic of conversation. It is a matter which should be weighed deliberately and seriously by every young person. It was ordained by the Lord at the creation, as suited to the state of man as a social being, and necessary to the design for which he was created. There is a sweetness and comfort in the bosom of one's own family which can be enjoyed no where else. In early life this is supplied by our youthful companions, who feel in unison with us. But as a person who remains single, advances in life, the friends of his youth form new attachments, in which he is incapable of participating. Their feelings undergo a change, of which he knows nothing. He is gradually left alone. No heart beats in unison with his own. His social feelings wither for want of an object. As he feels not in unison with those around him, his habits also become peculiar, and perhaps repulsive, so that his company is not desired; hence arises the whimsical attachments of such persons to domestic animals, or to other objects that can be enjoyed in solitude. As the dreary winter of age advances, the solitude of this condition becomes still more chilling. Nothing but that sweet resignation to the will of God, which religion gives, under all circumstances, can render such a situation tolerable. But religion does not annihilate the social affections; it only regulates them. It is evident, then, by a lawful and proper exercise of these affections, both our happiness and usefulness may be greatly increased.

On the other hand, do not consider marriage as absolutely essential. Although it is an ordinance of God, yet he has not absolutely enjoined it upon all. You may, therefore, be in the way of duty while neglecting it. And the apostle Paul intimates that there may be, with those who enter this state, a greater tendency of heart toward earthly objects. There is also an increase of care. "The unmarried woman careth for the things of the Lord, that she may be holy, both in body and spirit; but she that is married, careth for the things of the world, how she may please her husband." But much more has been made of this than the apostle intended. It has been greatly perverted and abused by the church of Rome. It must be observed that, in the same chapter, he advises that "every man have his own wife and every woman her own husband." And, whatever may be our condition in life, if we seek it with earnestness and perseverance, God will give us grace sufficient for the day. But, he says, though it is no sin to marry, nevertheless, "such shall have trouble in the flesh." It is undoubtedly true that the enjoyments of conjugal life have their corresponding difficulties and trials; and if these are enhanced by an unhappy connection, the situation is insufferable. For this reason, I would have you avoid the conclusion that marriage is indispensable to happiness. Single life is certainly to be preferred to a connection with a person who will diminish instead of increase your happiness. However, the remark of the apostle, "such shall have trouble in the flesh," doubtless had reference chiefly to the peculiar troubles of the times, when Christians were exposed to persecutions, the loss of goods, and even of life itself, for Christ's sake; the trials of which would be much greater in married than in single life.

MARRIAGE HYMN.

Not for the summer hour alone,
 When skies resplendent shine,
And youth and pleasure fill the throne,
 Our hearts and hands we join;

But for those stern and wintry days
 Of sorrow, pain, and fear,
When Heaven's wise discipline doth make
 Our earthly journey drear.

Not for this span of life alone,
 Which like a blast doth fly,
And, as the transient flower of grass,
 Just blossom—droop, and die;

But for a being without end,
This vow of love we take;
Grant us, O God! one home at last,
For our Redeemer's sake.

FEMALE INFLUENCE.

Writers of fiction have not unfrequently selected this topic as the theme for poetry and romance; they have extolled woman as the being whose eloquence was to soften all the asperities of man, and polish the naturally rugged surface of his character; charming away his sternness by her grace; refining his coarseness by her elegance and purity; and offering in her smiles a reward sufficient to compensate for the hazards of any enterprise. But while the self-complacency and vanity of many of our sex have been nourished by such idle praise, how few have been awakened to a just sense of the deep responsibility which rests upon us, for the faithful improvement of this talent, and our consequent accountability for its neglect or perversion!

It were not a little amusing, if it were not so melancholy, to listen to the reasoning employed by many ladies, in evading any charges of non-improvement of this trust. She who perhaps but a moment before may have listened with the utmost self-complacency to the flattering strains of the poet, who had invested her sex with every charm calculated to render them ministering angels to ruder and sterner man, no sooner finds herself addressed as the possessor of a talent, implying responsibility, and imposing self-exertion and self-denial in its exercise, than she instantly disclaims, with capricious diffidence, all pretensions to influence over others. But we cannot avert accountability by disclaiming its existence; neither will the disavowal of the possession of a talent alter the constitution of our nature, which God has so formed and so fitted to produce impressions in, and receive them from, kindred minds, that it is impossible for us to exist without exerting a continual and daily influence over others; either of a pernicious or salutary character.

"Woman," to use the words of an accomplished living writer, "has been sent on a higher mission than man; it may be a more arduous, a more difficult one. It is to manifest and bring to a full development certain attributes which belong, it is true, to our common nature, but which, owing to man's peculiar relation to the external world, he could not so well bring to perfection. Man is sent forth to subdue the earth, to obtain command over the elements, to form political communities; and to him, therefore, belong the more hardy and austere virtues; and as they are made subservient to the relief of our physical wants, and as their results are more obvious to the senses, it is not surprising that they have acquired in his eyes an importance which does not in strictness belong to them. But humility, meekness, gentleness, love, are also important attributes of our nature, and it would present a sad and melancholy aspect without them. But let us ask, will man, with his present characteristic propensities, thrown much more than woman, by his immediate duties, upon material things; obliged to be conversant with objects of sense, and exposed to the rude conflicts which this leads to; will he bring out these virtues in their full beauty and strength? We think not—even with the assistance which religion promises. These principles, with many others linked with them, have been placed more particularly in the keeping of woman; her social condition being evidently more favorable to their full development."

Let us ever remember that every aggregate number, however great, is composed of units; and of course, were each American female but faithful to her God, to her family, and to her country, then would a mighty, sanctified influence go forth through the wide extent of our beloved land, diffusing moral health and vigor through every part, and strengthening it for the endurance of greater trials than have as yet menaced its existence. A spirit of insubordination and rebellion to lawful authority pervades our land; and where are these foes effectually to be checked, if not at their fountain head—in the nursery? Oh! if every American mother had but labored faithfully in that sacred inclosure, from the period of our revolutionary struggle, by teaching her children the great lesson of practical obedience to parental authority; then would submission to constituted authority, as well as to the will of God, have been far more prevalent in our land, and the whole aspect of her affairs would have been widely different.

How much more honorable to woman is such a position, than that in which some modern reformers have endeavored to place her, or rather force her. Instead of seeking hopelessly, and in direct opposition to the delicacy of her sex, to obtain for her political privileges; instead of bringing her forward as the competitor of man in the public arena; we would mark out for her a sphere of duty that is widely different. In the domestic circle, «her station should be at man›s side, to comfort, to encourage, to assist;" while, in the Christian temple, we would assign her an ennobling, but a feminine part,—to be the guardian of the sacred and spiritual fire, which is ever to be kept alive in its purity and brilliancy on the altar of God. She should be the vestal virgin in the Christian temple—the priestess, as it were, of a shrine more hallowed and honorable than that of Delphos.

A DIFFICULT QUESTION.

I remember, many years ago, to have occupied the corner of a window-seat, in a small but very elegant house in Montague-square, during a morning visit—more interesting than such visits usually are, because there was something to talk about. The ladies who met, had each a child, I believe an only girl, just of the age when mothers begin to ask every body, and tell every body, how their children are to be educated. The daughter of the house, the little Jemima, was sitting by my side; a delicate little creature, with something very remarkable in her expression. The broad projecting brow seemed too heavy for its underwork; and by its depression, gave a look of sadness to the countenance, till excited animation raised the eye, beaming vivacity and strength. The sallow paleness of the complexion was so entirely in unison with the features, and the stiff dark locks which surrounded them, it was difficult to say whether it was, or was not, improved by the color that came and went every time she was looked at or spoken of. I was, on this occasion, a very attentive listener: for, being not yet a woman, it was very essential to me to learn what sort of a one I had better be; and many, indeed, were my counter-resolutions, as the following debate proceeded:

"You are going to send your daughter to school I hear?" said Mrs. A., after some discourse of other matters.

Mrs. W. replied, "Really, I have not quite determined; I scarcely know what to do for the best. I am only anxious that she should grow up like other girls; for of all things in the world, I have the greatest horror of a woman of talent. I had never thought to part from her, and am still averse to sending her from home; but she is so excessively fond of books, I can get her to do nothing else but learn; she is as grave and sensible as a little woman. I think, if she were among other girls, she would perhaps get fond of play, and be more like a child. I wish her to grow up a quiet, domestic girl, and not too fond of learning. I mean her to be accomplished; but, at present, I cannot make her distinguish one tune from another."

Mrs. A. answered, "Indeed! we differ much in this respect. I am determined to make Fanny a superior woman, whatever it may cost me. Her father is of the same mind; he has a perfect horror of silly, empty-headed women; all our family are literary; Fanny will have little fortune, but we can afford to give her every advantage in her education, the best portion we can leave her. I would rather see her distinguished for talents, than for birth or riches. We have acted upon this intention from her birth. She already reads well, but I am sorry to say she hates it, and never will open a book unless she is obliged; she shows no taste for any thing but making doll's clothes and spinning a top."

At this moment a hearty laugh from little Fanny, who had set herself to play behind the curtain, drew my attention towards her. She was twice as big as my companion on the window-seat, though but a few months older; her broad, flat face, showed like the moon in its zenith, set in thin, silky hair: and with eyes as pretty as they could be, expressing neither thought nor feeling, but abundance of mirth and good-humor. The coloring of her cheek was beautiful; but one wished it gone sometimes, were it only for the pleasure of seeing it come again. The increasing seriousness of the conversation recalled my attention.

"I am surprised," Mrs. W. was saying, "at your wishes on the subject. I am persuaded a woman of great talent is neither so happy, so useful, nor so much beloved, as one or more ordinary powers."

"I should like to know why you think this," rejoined her friend; "it appears to me she should be much more so."

"My view of it is this," Mrs. W. replied: "a woman's sphere of usefulness, of happiness, and of affection, is a domestic circle; and even beyond it, all her task of life is to please and to be useful."

"In this we are quite agreed," said Mrs. A.; "but, since we are well set for an argument, let us have a little method in it. You would have your child useful, happy, and beloved, and so would I; but you think the means to this end, is to leave her mind uncultivated, narrow, and empty, and consequently weak."

"This is not my meaning," replied Mrs. W.; "there are many steps between stupidity and talent, ignorance and learning. I will suppose my child what I wish her to be, about as much taught as women in general, who are esteemed clever, well-mannered, and well-accomplished. I think it is all that can contribute to her happiness. If her mind is occupied, as you will say, with little things, those little things are sufficient to its enjoyment, and much more likely to be within her reach than the greater matters that fill greater minds. My less accomplished character will enjoy herself where your superior woman would go to sleep, or hopelessly wish she might. In short, she will find fellowship and reciprocation in every little mind she meets with, while yours is left to pine in the solitude of her own greatness."

At the close of this speech, I felt quite determined that I would not be such a woman.

Mrs. A. rejoined, "You have left my genius in a doleful condition, though I question whether you will persuade her to come down. I will admit, however, for I am afraid I must, that the woman of talent is less likely to find reciprocation, or to receive enjoyment from ordinary people and ordinary circumstances; but then she is like the camel that traverses the desert safely where others perish, because it carries its sustenance in its own bosom. I never remember to have heard a really sensible and cultivated woman complain of ennui, under any circumstances—no small balance on the side of enjoyment positive, is misery escaped. But, to leave jesting, admitting that the woman of more elevated mind derives less pleasure from the adventitious circumstances that surround her, from what money can purchase, and a tranquil mind enjoy, and activity gather, of the passing flowers of life—she has enjoyments, independent of them, in the treasures of her own intellect. Where she finds reciprocation, it is a delight of which the measure compensates the rareness; and where she finds nothing else to enjoy, she can herself. And when the peopled walks of life become a wilderness; and the assiduities of friendship rest unclaimed; and sensible gratifications are withered before the blight of poverty; and the foot is too weary, and the eye is too dim, to go after what no one remembers to bring; still are her resources untouched. Poverty cannot diminish her revenue, or friendlessness leave her unaccompanied, or privation of every external incitement consign her to the void of unoccupied powers. She will traverse the desert, for her store is with her; and if, as you have suggested, she be doomed to supply others what no one pays her back, there is One who has said, 'It is more blessed to give than to receive.'"

At this point of the discussion, I made up my mind to be a very sensible woman.

Mrs. W. resumed: "You will allow, of course, that selfish enjoyment is not the object of existence; and I think, on the score of usefulness, I shall carry my poor, dependent house-wife, far above yours. And for this very reason: The duties which Providence has assigned to woman, do not require extraordinary intellect. She can manage her husband's household, and economize his substance; and if she cannot entertain his friends with her talents, she can at least give them a welcome; and be his nurse in sickness, and his watchful companion in health, if not capable of sharing his more intellectual occupations. She can be the support and comfort of her parents in the decline of life, or of her children in their helplessness, according as her situation may be. And out of her house she may be the benefactress and example of a whole neighborhood; she may comfort the afflicted, and clothe and feed the poor, and visit the sick, and advise the ignorant; while, by the domestic industry, and peaceful, unaspiring habits, with which she plods, as you may please to call it, through the duties of her station, whether higher or lower, she is a perpetual example to those beneath her, to like sober assiduity in their own, and to her children's children to follow in the path in which she leads them. She may be superintending the household occupations, or actually performing them; giving employment by her wealth to others' ingenuity, or supplying the want of it by her own, according as her station is, but still she will make many happy.

"I am not so prejudiced as to say that your woman of talent will refuse these duties; of course, if she have principle, she will not. But literary pursuits must at least divide her attention, if not unfit her altogether for the tasks the order of Providence has assigned her; she will distaste such duties, if she does not refuse them; while the distance at which her attainments place her from ordinary minds, forbid all attempts to imitate or follow her."

"You have drawn a picture," answered Mrs. A., "which would convert half the world, if they were not of your mind already, as I believe they are. It is a picture so beautiful, I would not blot it with the shadow of my finger. I concede that talent is not necessary to usefulness, and a woman may fulfill every duty of her station without it. But our question is of comparative usefulness; and there I have something to say. It is an axiom that knowledge is power; and, if it is, the greater the knowledge, the greater should be the power of doing good. To men, superior intelligence gives power to dispose, control, and govern the fortunes of others. To women, it gives influence over their minds. The greater knowledge which she has acquired of the human heart, gives her access to it in all its subtleties; while her acknowledged superiority secures that deference to her counsels, which weakness ever pays to strength.

"If the circumstances of her condition require it, I believe the greater will suffice the less, and she will fulfill equally well the duties you have enumerated; shedding as bright a light upon her household, as if it bounded her horizon. Nay, more, there may be minds in her household that need the reciprocation of an equal mind, or the support of a superior one; there may be spirits in her family that will receive from the influence of intellect, what they would not from simple and good intention. There may be other wants in her neighborhood than hunger and nakedness, and other defaulters than the ignorant and the poor. Whether she writes, speaks, or acts, the effect is not bounded by time, nor limited by space. That is worth telling of her, and is repeated from mouth to mouth, which, in an ordinary person, none would notice. Her acknowledged superiority gives her a title, as well as a capacity to speak, where others must be silent, and carry counsel and consolation where commoner characters might not intrude.

"The mass of human misery, and human need, and human corruption, is not confined to the poor, the simple minded, and the child. The husband's and the parent's cares are not confined to their external commodities, nor the children's to the well-being of their physical estate. The mind that could illumine its own solitude, can cheer another's destitution; the strength that can support itself, can stay another's falling; the wealth may be unlocked, and supply another's poverty. Those who in prosperity seek amusement from superior talent, will seek it in difficulty or advice, and in adversity for support."

Here I made up my mind to have a great deal of intellect.

"If I granted your position on the subject of utility," said Mrs. W., "I am afraid I should prove the world very ungrateful by the remainder of my argument; which goes, you know, to prove the woman of distinguished talent less beloved than those who walk the ordinary paths of female duty. I must take the risk, however; for, of all women in the world, your women of genius are those I love the least; and I believe, just or unjust, it is a very common feeling. We are not disposed to love our superiors in any thing; but least of all, in intellect; one has always the feeling of playing an equal game, without being sure that no advantage will be taken of your simplicity. A woman who has the reputation of talent, is, in this respect, the most unfortunate being on earth. She stands in society, like a European before a horde of savages, vainly endeavoring to signify his good intentions. If he approaches them, they run away; if he recedes, they send their arrows after him. Every one is afraid to address her, lest they expose to her penetration their own deficiencies. If she talks, she is supposed to display her powers; if she holds her tongue, it is attributed to contempt for the company. I know that talent is often combined with every amiable quality, and renders the character really the more lovely; but not therefore the more beloved. It would, if known; but it seldom is known, because seldom approached near enough to be examined.

"The simple-minded fear what they do not understand; the double-minded envy what they cannot reach. For my good, simple housewife, every body loves her who knows her; and nobody, who does not know her, troubles themselves about her. But place a woman on an eminence, and every body thinks they are obliged to like or dislike her; and, being too tenacious to do the one without good reason, they do the other without any reason at all. Before we can love each other, there must be sympathy, assimilation, and, if not equality, at least such an approach to it as may enable us to understand each other. When any one is much superior to us, our humility shrinks from the proffers of her love, and our pride revolts from offering her our own. Real talent is always modest, and fears often to make advances towards affection, lest it should seem, in doing so, to presume upon itself; but, having rarely the credit of timidity, this caution is attributable to pride. Your superior woman, therefore, will not be generally known or beloved by her own sex, among whom she may have many admirers, but few equals.

"I say nothing of marriage, because I am not speculating upon it for my child, as upon the chances of a well-played game; but it is certain that the greater number of men are not highly intellectual, and therefore could not wisely choose a highly intellectual wife, lest they place themselves in the condition in which a husband should not be—of mental inferiority."

"Mrs. W.," answered her friend, "I am aware this is your strongest post; but I must not give ground without a battle. A great deal I shall yield you. I shall give up quantity, and stand upon the value of the remainder. Be it granted, then, that of any twenty people assembled in society, every one of whom will pronounce your common-place woman to be very amiable, very good, and very pleasing, ten shall pronounce my friend too intellectual for their taste, eight shall find her not so clever as they expected, and, of the other two, one at least shall not be sure whether they like her or not. Be it granted that, of every five ladies assembled to gossip freely, and tell out their small cares and feelings to the sympathizing kindness of your friend, four shall become silent as wax-work on the entrance of mine. And be it granted that, of any ten gentlemen to whom yours would be a very proper wife, not more than one could wisely propose himself to mine. But have I therefore lost the field? Perhaps she would tell you no; the two in twenty, the one in five or ten, are of more value, in her estimation, than all the number else.

"Things are not apt to be valued by their abundance. On the jeweler's stall, many a brilliant trinket will disappear, ere the high-priced gem be asked for; but is it, therefore, the less valued, or the less cared for? When beloved at all, she is loved permanently; for, in the lapse of time, that withers the charm of beauty, and blights the simplicity of youth, her ornaments grow but the brighter for wearing. In proportion to the depth of the intellect, I believe, is the depth of every thing; feelings, affections, pleasures, pains, or whatever else the enlarged capacity conceives. It is difficult perhaps for an inferior mind to estimate what a superior mind enjoys in the reciprocation of affection. Attachment, with ordinary persons, is enjoyed to-day, and regretted to-morrow, and the next day replaced and forgotten; but with these it never can be forgotten, because it can never be replaced."

As the argument, thus terminated, converted neither party, it is needless to say it left me in suspense. Mrs. W. was still determined her child should not be a superior woman. Mrs. A. was still resolved her child should be, at all ventures; and I was still undetermined whether I would endeavor to be a learned woman or not. The little Fanny laughed aloud, opened her large round eyes, and shouted, "So I will, mamma!" The little Jemima colored to the ends of her fingers, and lowered still farther the lashes that veiled her eyes.

EASILY DECIDED.

I was walking with some friends in a retired part of the country. It had rained for fourteen days before, and I believed it rained then; but there was a belief among the ladies of that country that it is better to walk in all weather. The lane was wide enough to pass in file, with chilly droppings from the boughs above, and rude re-action of the briers beneath. The clay upon our shoes showed a troublesome affinity to the clay upon the road. Umbrellas we could not hold up because of the wind. But it was better to walk than stay at home, so at least my companions assured me, for exercise and an appetite. After pursuing them, with hopeless assiduity, for more than a mile, without sight of egress or sign of termination, finding I had already enough of the one, and doubting how far the other might be off, I lagged behind, and began to think how I might amuse myself till their return.

By one of those fortunate incidents, which they tell me never happen to any body but a listener, I heard the sound of voices over the hedge. This was delightful. In this occupation I forgot both mud and rain, exercise and appetite. The hedge was too thick to see through, and all that appeared above it was a low chimney, from which I concluded it concealed a cottage garden.

"What in the name of wonder, James, can you be doing?" said a voice, significant of neither youth nor gentleness.

"I war'nt ye know what I am about," said another, more rudely than unkindly.

"I'm not sure of that," rejoined the first; "you've been hacking and hewing at them trees this four hours, and I do not see, for my part, as you're like to mend them."

"Why, mother," said the lad, "you see we have but two trees in all the garden, and I've been thinking they'd match better if they were alike; so I've tied up to a pole the boughs of the gooseberry-bush, that used to spread themselves about the ground, to make it look more like this thorn; and now I'm going to cut down the thorn to make it look more like the gooseberry-bush."

"And what's the good of that?" rejoined the mother; "has not the tree sheltered us many a stormy night, when the wind would have beaten the old casement about our ears? and many a scorching noon-tide, hasn't your father eaten his dinner in its shade? And now, to be sure, because you are the master, you think you can mend it!"

"We shall see," said the youth, renewing his strokes. "It's no use as it is; I dare say you'd like to see it bear gooseberries."

"No use!" exclaimed the mother; "don't the birds go to roost on the branches, and the poultry get shelter under it from the rain? and after all your cutting, I don't see as you're likely to turn a thorn-tree into a gooseberry-bush!"

"I don't see why I should not," replied the sage artificer, with a tone of reflectiveness; "the leaf is near about the same, and there are thorns on both; if I make that taller and this shorter, and they grow the same shape, I don't suppose you know why one should bear gooseberries any more than the other, as wise as you are."

"Why, to be sure, James," the old woman answered, in a moderate voice, "I can't say that I do; but I have lived almost through my threescore years and ten, and I have never heard of gooseberries growing on a thorn."

"Haven't you, though?" said James; "but then I have, or something pretty much like it; for I saw the gardener, over yonder, cutting off the head of a young pear-tree, and he told me he was going to make it bear apples."

"Well," said the mother, seemingly reconciled, "I know nothing of your new-fangled ways. I only know it was the finest thorn in the parish; but, to be sure, now they are more match-like and regular."

I left a story half told. This may seem to be another, but it is in fact the same. James, in the Sussex-lane, and my friends in Montague-square, were engaged in the same task, and the result of the one would pretty fairly measure the successes of the other; both were contravening the order of nature, and pursuing their own purpose, without consulting the appointments of Providence.

Fanny was a girl of common understanding; such indeed as suitable cultivation might have matured into simple good sense; but from which her parents' scheme of education could produce nothing but pretension that could not be supported, and an affectation of what could never be attained. Conscious of the want of all perceptible talent in her child, Mrs. A. from the first told the stories of talent opening late, and the untimely blighting of premature intellect; and, to the last, maintained the omnipotence of cultivation.

On every new proof of the smallness of her mind, another science was added to enlarge it. Languages, dead and living, were to be to her the keys of knowledge; but they unlocked nothing to Fanny but their own grammars and vocabularies, which she learned assiduously, without so much as wondering what they meant. The more dull she proved, the more earnestly she was plied. She was sent to school to try the spur of emulation; and brought home again for the advantage of more exclusive attention. And, as still the progress lagged, all feminine employ and childlike recreations were prohibited, to gain more time for study. It cannot be said that Fanny's health was injured by the over action of her mind; for, having none, it could not be easily acted upon; but, by perpetual dronish application, and sacrifice of all external things for the furtherance of this scheme of mental cultivation, her physical energies were suppressed, and she became heavy, awkward, and inactive.

Fanny had no pleasure in reading, but she had a pride in having read; and listened, with no small satisfaction, to her mother's detail of the authors she was conversant with; beyond her age, and, as some untalented ventured to suggest, not always suited to her years of innocence. The arcana of their pages were safe, however, and quite guiltless of her mind's corruption. Fanny never thought, whatever she might read; what was in the book, was nothing to her; all her business was to have read it. Meantime, while the powers she had not were solicited in vain, the talents she had were neglected and suppressed. Her good-humored enjoyment of ordinary things, her real taste for domestic arrangement, and open simplicity of heart, were derided as vulgar and unintellectual. Her talent for music was thought not worth cultivating; time could not be spared. Some little capacity she had for drawing, as an imitative art, was baffled by the determination to teach it her scientifically, thus rendering it as impossible as every thing else. In short—for why need I prolong my sketch?—Fanny was prepared by nature to be the beau ideal of Mrs. W.'s amiable woman.

Constitutionally active and benevolent, judicious culture might have made her sensible, and, in common life, intelligent, pleasing, useful, happy. Nay, I need only refer to the picture of my former paper, to say what Fanny, well educated, was calculated to become. But this was what her parents were determined she should not be; and they spent twenty years, and no small amount of cash, to make her a woman of superior mind and distinguished literary attainments.

I saw the result; for I saw Fanny at twenty, the most unlovely, useless, and unhappy being I ever met with. The very docility of a mind, not strong enough to choose its own part, and resist the influence of circumstances, hastened forward the catastrophe. She had learned to think herself what she could not be, and to despise what in reality she was; she could not otherwise than do so, for she had been imbued with it from her cradle.

She was accustomed from her infancy to intellectual society; kept up to listen, when she should have been in bed; she counted the spots on the carpet, heard nothing that was said, and prided herself on being one of such company. A little later, she was encouraged to talk to every body, and give her opinion upon every thing, in order to improve and exercise her mind. Her mind remained unexercised, because she talked without thinking; but she learned to chatter, to repeat other people's opinions, and fancy her own were of immense importance.

She was unlovely, because she sought only to please by means she had not, and to please those who were quite beyond her reach; others she had been accustomed to neglect as unfit for her companionship. She was useless, because what she might have done well, she was unaccustomed to do at all, and what she attempted, she was incapable of. And she was unhappy, because all her natural tastes had been thwarted, and her natural feelings suppressed; and of her acquired habits and high-sounding pursuits she had no capacity for enjoyment. Her love of classic and scientific lore, her delight in libraries, and museums, and choice intellects, and literary circles, was a fiction; they gratified nothing but her vanity. Her small, narrow, weak, and dependent mind, was a reality, and placed her within reach of mortification and disappointment, from the merest and meanest trifles.

Jemima—my little friend Jemima—I lived to see her a woman too. From her infancy she had never evinced the tastes and feelings of a child. Intense reflection, keen and impatient sensibility and an unlimited desire to know, marked her from the earliest years as a very extraordinary child; dislike to the plays and exercises of childhood made her unpleasing to her companions, and, to superficial observers, melancholy; but this was amply contradicted by the eager vivacity of her intellect and feeling, when called forth by things beyond the usual compass of her age. Every thing in Jemima gave promise of extraordinary talent and distinguished character. This her parents saw, and were determined to counteract. They had made up their minds what a woman should be, and were determined Jemima should be nothing else. Every thing calculated to call forth her powers was kept out of her way, and childish occupations forced on her in their stead. The favorite maxim was, to occupy her mind with common things; she was made to romp, and to dance, and to play; to read story books, and make dolls' clothes. Her physical powers were thus occupied; but where was her mind the while? Feeding itself with fancies, for want of truths; drawing false conclusions, forming wrong judgments, and brooding over its own mistakes, for want of a judicious occupation of its activities.

Another maxim was, to keep Jemima ignorant of her own capacity, lest she should set up for a genius, and be undomesticated. She was told she had none, and was left in ignorance of what she was capable, and for what she was responsible. Made to believe that her fine feelings were oddities, her expansive thoughts absurdities, and her love of knowledge unfeminine and ungraceful, she kept them to herself, and became reserved, timid, and artificial.

Nobody could prevent Jemima's acquiring knowledge; she saw every thing, reflected upon every thing, and learned from every thing; but without guide, and without discretion, she gathered the honey and the gall together, and knew not which was which. She was sent to school that she might learn to play, and fetched home that she might learn to be useful. In the former place she was shunned as an oddity, because she preferred to learn; and, finding herself disliked without deserving it, encouraged herself to independence by disliking every body. In the latter, she sewed her work awry, while she made a couplet to the moon, and unpicked it while she made another: and being told she did every thing ill, believed it, and became indolent and careless to do any thing. Consumed, meanwhile, by the restless workings of her mind, and tasked to exercise for which its delicate frame-work was unfit, her person became faded, worn, and feeble.

To be brief, her parents succeeded in baffling nature's promise, but failed of the fulfillment of their own. At twenty, Jemima was a puzzle to every body, and a weariness to herself. Conscious of her powers, but not knowing how to spend them, she gave in to every imaginable caprice. Having made the discovery of her superiority, she despised the opinions of others, while her own were too ill-formed to be her guide. Proud of possessing talent, and yet ashamed to show it; unaccustomed to explain herself; certain of being misunderstood, and least of all understanding herself; ignorant, in the midst of knowledge, and incapable with unlimited capacity; tasteless for every thing she did, and ignorant how to do what she had a taste for, her mind was a luxuriant wilderness, inaccessible to others, and utterly unproductive to its possessor. Unpleasing and unpleased in the sphere she was in, and yet unfitted by habit and timidity for any other, weariness and disgust were her daily portion; her fine sensibilities, her deep feelings, her expansive thoughts, remained; but only to be wounded, to irritate, to mislead her.

Where is the moral of my tale, and what the use of telling it? I have told it because I see that God has his purposes in every thing that he has done; and man has his own, and disregards them. And every day I hear it disputed, with acrimony and much unkindness, what faculties and characters it is better to have or not to have, without any consideration of what God has given or withheld; and standards are set up, by which all must be measured, though, alas! they cannot take from or add one cubit to their statures. "There is one glory of the sun, and another glory of the moon, and another glory of the stars; for one star differeth from another star in glory." Why do we not censure the sun for outshining the stars, and the pale moon for having no light but what she borrows?

Instead of settling for others what they ought to be, and choosing for ourselves what we will be, would it not be better to examine the condition in which we are actually placed, and the faculties actually committed to us? and consider what was the purpose of Heaven in the former, and what the demand of Heaven in the occupation of the latter? If we have much, we are not at liberty to put it aside, and say we should be better without it; if we have little, we are not at liberty to be dissatisfied, and aspiring after more. And surely we are not at liberty to say that another has too much, or too little, of what God has given! We may have our preferences, but we must not mistake them for standards of right.

Every character has beauties peculiar to itself, and dangers to which it is peculiarly exposed; and there are duties, pertaining to each, apart from the circumstances in which they may be placed. Nothing, therefore, can be more contrary to the manifest order and disposition of Providence, than to endeavor to be, or do, whatever we admire in another, or to force ourselves to be and do whatever we admire in ourselves. Which character, of the endless variety that surrounds us, is the most happy, the most useful, and most deserving to be beloved, it were impossible, I believe, to decide; and, if we could, we have gained little by the decision; for we could neither give it to our children, nor to ourselves. But of this we may be certain: that individual, of whatever intellectual character, is the happiest, the most useful, and the most beloved of God, if not of men, who has best subserved the purposes of Heaven in her creation and endowment; who has most carefully turned to good the faculties she has; most cautiously guarded against the evils to which her propensities incline; most justly estimated, and conscientiously fulfilled, the duties appropriate to her circumstance and character.

INFLUENCE OF CHRISTIANITY ON WOMAN.

The abject condition of the female sex, in all, out of Christian countries, is universally known and admitted. In all savage and pagan tribes, the severest burdens of physical toil are laid upon their shoulders; they are chiefly valued for the same reason that men value their most useful animals, or as objects of their sensual and selfish desires. Even in the learned and dignified forms of Eastern paganism, "the wife," says one who has spent seventeen years among them, "is the slave, rather than the companion of her husband. She is not allowed to walk with him, she must walk behind him; not to eat with him, she must eat after him, and eat of what he leaves. She must not sleep until he is asleep, nor remain asleep after he is awake. If she is sitting, and he comes in, she should rise up. She should, say their sacred books, have no other god on earth than her husband. Him she should worship while he lives, and, when he dies, she should be burnt with him. As the widow, in case she is not burnt, is not allowed to marry again, is often considered little better than an outcast, and not unfrequently sinks into gross vice, her life can scarcely be considered a blessing."

The same author remarks, that "there is little social intercourse between the sexes; little or no acquaintance of the parties before marriage, and consequently little mutual attachment; and as there is an absolute vacuity and darkness in the minds of the females, who are not allowed even to learn to read, there is no solid foundation laid for domestic happiness."

If we pass into the dominions of the crescent, we find the condition of females, in some respects, rather worse, it would seem, than better. For, in pagan India, debased and abused as woman is, she is still allowed some interest in religion, and some common expectations with the other sex, concerning the future state. But in Mohammedan countries, even this is nearly or quite denied her. "It is a popular tradition among the Mohammedans, which obtains to this day, that woman shall not enter Paradise;" and it requires some effort of the imagination to conceive how debased and wretched must be the condition of the female sex, to originate and sustain such a horrible and blasphemous tradition.

Even in the refined and shining ages of Egypt, Greece, and Rome, where the cultivation of letters, the graces of finished style, the charms of poetry and eloquence, the elegances of architecture, sculpture, painting, and embroidery, the glory of conquest, and the pride of national distinction, were unsurpassed by any people before or since—even then and there, what was the woman but the abject slave of man? the object of his ambition, or his avarice, or his lust, or his power? the alternate victim of his pleasures, his disgust, or his cruelty? the creature of his caprice? and, what is worse, the menial slave of her own mental darkness, moral debasement, and vicious indulgences? If history is not false, the answer is decisive. This, and only this, was she!

But how entirely has our religion reversed all this, and rendered her life a blessing to herself and to society. And as Christianity has done so much for woman, she ought in return to do much for Christianity. Every thing that can render life desirable, she owes to Christ. Think for one moment of the hole of the pit from which Christ has taken you! Think of what would be your present condition, had it not been for the Christian religion! You might have been with the debased and wretched victims of pagan oppression, cruelty, and lust; burning alive upon the funeral pile; or sacrificed by hands of violence or pollution; or cast out, and neglected, to pine in solitary and hopeless grief. Or, with the female followers of the false prophet, or, in more refined but unchristian nations, you might have been little else than the slave or the convenience of man, and left to doubt whether any inheritance awaits you beyond the grave.

From these depths of debasement and wretchedness, Christianity has taken you, and placed you on high, to move, and shine, and rejoice, in the sphere for which the Creator designed you. Not only has it made your condition as good as that of man, but, in a moral view, in some respects superior to it. How much, then, do you owe to Christ! To turn away from him with indifference or neglect, what ingratitude is this! How preposterous, how base, how unlovely, is female impiety! There was much sense in a remark made by an intelligent gentleman, who, although not pious himself, said: "I cannot look with any complacency upon a woman who does not manifest gratitude and love to Jesus Christ. Above all things, I hate to see so unnatural an object as an irreligious woman."

Such being the constitution and circumstances of woman, it is the manifest intention of God that she should be pre-eminent in moral excellence; and, through the influence of this, take a glorious lead in the renovation of the world. This she has to some extent ever done. Let all females of Christian lands consider well their high calling, their solemn responsibility, and their glorious privilege. While many of their sex have proved recreant to their trust, and wasted life in vanity and in vice, others—an illustrious constellation, the holy and the good of ancient time, the mothers and the sisters in Israel, "the chief women, not a few," of apostolic times, the bright throng that have since continued to come out from the world, and tread in the steps of Jesus, and lead on their fellow-beings to the kingdom of purity and joy—have proved to us that, as woman was first to fall, so she is first to rise.

Yes; though it is not hers to amass wealth; to aspire to secular office and power; to shine in camps and armies; to hurl the thunders of our navies, and gather laurels from the ocean, or to receive the vain incense offered to public and popular eloquence: yet, hers it is, to be robed with the beauty of Christ; to shine in the honors of goodness; to shed over the world the sweet and holy influences of peace, virtue, and religion; to be adorned with those essential and imperishable beauties, those unearthly stars and diadems, whose lustre will survive, with ever-increasing brightness, when all earthly glory will fade and be forgotten. Come, then; come to your high duty, your glorious privilege—come, and be blessed for ever!

IMPORTANCE OF RELIGION TO WOMAN.

There is nothing so adapted to the wants of woman as religion. She has many trials, and she therefore peculiarly needs support; religion is her asylum, not only in heavy afflictions, but in petty disquietudes. These, as they are more frequent, are perhaps almost as harassing; at least, they equally need a sedative influence, and religion is the anodyne. For it is religion which, by placing before her a better and more enduring happiness than this world can offer, reconciles her to temporary privations; and, by acquainting her with the love of God, leads her to rest securely upon his providence in present disappointment. It inspires her with that true content, which not only endures distress, but is cheerful under it.

Resignation is not, as we are too apt to portray her, beauty bowered in willows, and bending over a sepulchral urn; neither is she a tragic queen, pathetic only in her weeds. She is an active, as well as passive virtue; an habitual, not an occasional sentiment. She should be as familiar to woman as her daily cross; for acquiescence in the detail of Providence is as much a duty, as submission to its result; and equanimity amid domestic irritations equally implies religious principle, as fortitude under severer trials. It was the remark of one, who certainly was not disposed to care for trifles, that "it required as much grace to bear the breaking of a china cup, as any of the graver distresses of life."

Minor cares are indeed the province of woman; minor annoyances her burden. Dullness, bad temper, mal-adroitness, are to her the cause of a thousand petty rubs, which too often spoil the euphony of a silver voice, and discompose the symmetry of fair features. But the confidence which reposes on divine affection, and the charity which covers human frailty, are the only specifics for impatience.

And, if religion is such a blessing in the ordinary trials of life, what a soothing balm it is in graver sorrows! From these, woman is by no means exempt; on the contrary, as her susceptibility is great, afflictions press on her with peculiar heaviness. There is sometimes a stillness in her grief which argues only its intensity, and it is this rankling wound which piety alone can heal. Nothing, perhaps, is more affecting than woman's chastened sorrow. Her ties may be severed, her fond hopes withered, her young affections blighted, yet peace may be in her breast, and heaven in her eye. If the business and turmoil of life brush away the tears of manly sorrows, and scarcely leave time even for the indulgence of sympathy, woman gathers strength in her solitary chamber, to encounter and subdue her grief. There she learns to look her sorrow in the face; there she becomes familiar with its features; there she communes with it, as with a celestial messenger; till at length she can almost welcome its presence, and hail it as the harbinger of a brighter world.

Religion is her only elevating principle. It identifies itself with the movements of her heart and with the actions of her life, spiritualizing the one and ennobling the other. Duties, however subordinate, are to the religious woman never degrading; their principle is their apology. She does not live amidst the clouds, or abandon herself to mystic excitement; she is raised above the sordidness, but not above the concerns, of earth; above its disquietudes, but not above its cares.

Religion is just what woman needs. Without it, she is ever restless and unhappy; ever wishing to be relieved from duty or from time. She is either ambitious of display, or greedy of pleasure, or sinks into a listless apathy, useless to others and unworthy of herself. But when the light from heaven shines upon her path, it invests every object with a reflected radiance. Duties, occupations, nay, even trials, are seen through a bright medium; and the sunshine which gilds her course on earth, is but the dawning of a far clearer day.

Suggested Reading

Historical Works

Letters on the Improvement of the Mind, Hester Chapone (1773)

A Vindication of the Rights of Woman, Mary Wollstonecraft (1792)

A Room of One's Own, Virginia Woolf (1929)

Books

The History of Manners, Norbert Elias (1939)

Behavior in Public Places: Notes on the Social Organization of Gatherings, Erving Goffman (1963)

Troping the Body: Gender, Etiquette, and Performance, Gwendolyn Audrey Foster (2000)

The Sum of Small Things, Elizabeth Currid-Halkett (2017)

Articles

"Reform or Ruin: 'A Revolution in Female Manners,'" Mitzi Myers, Studies in Eighteenth-Century Culture, Vol. 11 (1982)

"A Question of Manners: Status and Gender in Etiquette and Courtesy," Michael Curtin, The Journal of Modern History, Vol. 57, No. 3 (1985)

"The Feminization of Etiquette Literature: Foucault, Mechanisms of Social Change, and the Paradoxes of Empowerment," Jorge Arditi, Sociological Perspectives, Vol. 39, No. 3 (1996)

www.ingramcontent.com/pod-product-compliance
Lightning Source LLC
Chambersburg PA
CBHW021350090426
42742CB00009B/801

9 781943 115525